The Ministers Manual for 1990

SIXTY-FIFTH ANNUAL ISSUE

MINISTERS
MANUAL
(Doran's)

1990 EDITION

Edited by

JAMES W. COX

1817

HARPER & ROW, PUBLISHERS, SAN FRANCISCO

New York, Grand Rapids, Philadelphia, St. Louis
London, Singapore, Sydney, Tokyo, Toronto

Editors of THE MINISTERS MANUAL

G. B. F. Hallock, D.D., 1926–1958
M. K. W. Heicher, Ph.D., 1943–1968
Charles L. Wallis, M.A., M.Div., 1969–1983
James W. Cox, M.Div., Ph.D.

Acknowledgments are on page 307.

THE MINISTERS MANUAL FOR 1990.
Copyright © 1989 by James W. Cox. All rights reserved.
Printed in the United States of America. For information
address Harper & Row, Publishers, Inc., 10 East 53rd Street,
New York, NY 10022.

FIRST EDITION

The Library of Congress has cataloged the first printing of
this serial as follows:

The ministers manual: a study and pulpit guide, 1926–. New
York, Harper.

V. 21–23 cm. annual.
Title varies: 1926–46, Doran's ministers manual (cover
title, 1947: The Doran's ministers manual)
Editor: 1926– G. B. F. Hallock (with M. K. W. Heicher,
1942–   )

1. Sermons—Outlines. 2. Homiletical illustrations. I. Hallock, Gerard Benjamin Fleet, 1856–, ed.
BV4223.M5   251.058   25–21658 rev*
                   [r48n2]

ISBN 0–06–061594–x

89 90 91 92 93 HC 10 9 8 7 6 5 4 3 2 1

CONTENTS

CONTENTS

PREFACE

Recently I received a letter from a pastor in England. This is what he had to say about *The Ministers Manual:* "I felt that I must write and say how useful I find the book. I have two parishes to look after and some Sundays have to produce three different sermons. Doran's is a mine of useful ideas. I use it every week for sermons, school assemblies, and magazine material. It is also interesting to browse through, and I have found some of the sermons personally very helpful. The sermons are thoroughly biblical and have useful applications together with apt illustrations. I find that my own ideas are generated by them, and as well as being a useful pastoral tool, it is helpful for my own faith."

Over the past several years, a number of features have been added to *The Ministers Manual* without omitting anything. As a result the book has been getting gradually larger and unwieldy for the user. The *Manual* this year has rearranged and combined some features, while omitting a few others. In place of the "Evening Service," you will find a "Lectionary Message," which follows the gospel readings in the Common Lectionary, as a significant part of the Sermon Outlines and Homiletic and Worship Aids for Fifty-two Weeks. This whole combined section is now Section Two of *The Ministers Manual,* and thus you will find in one convenient place a nonlectionary sermon and a lectionary sermon for every Sunday, together with helpful worship materials.

It is our belief that these changes will in some ways enhance the value of the *Manual.* We anticipate that you will continue to send us contributions of your own original high quality material, which it is a continuing joy to share with the thousands of readers of *The Ministers Manual.*

I am grateful to the many persons who have contributed directly or indirectly to the production of this book: to the trustees of The Southern Baptist Theological Seminary and to President Roy Honeycutt for their practical encouragement; to Alicia Gardner, office services supervisor; to Lisa Redden and Debbie Kyle, who typed the manuscript; and to Clara McCartt and Dr. Lee R. McGlone for valuable editorial assistance. I am also appreciative of the careful work of the editorial staff at Harper & Row, San Francisco.

James W. Cox
The Southern Baptist Theological Seminary
2825 Lexington Road
Louisville, Kentucky 40280

SECTION I.
General Aids and Resources
Civil Year Calendars

1990

JANUARY	FEBRUARY	MARCH	APRIL
S M T W T F S	S M T W T F S	S M T W T F S	S M T W T F S
1 2 3 4 5 6	1 2 3	1 2 3	1 2 3 4 5 6 7
7 8 9 10 11 12 13	4 5 6 7 8 9 10	4 5 6 7 8 9 10	8 9 10 11 12 13 14
14 15 16 17 18 19 20	11 12 13 14 15 16 17	11 12 13 14 15 16 17	15 16 17 18 19 20 21
21 22 23 24 25 26 27	18 19 20 21 22 23 24	18 19 20 21 22 23 24	22 23 24 25 26 27 28
28 29 30 31	25 26 27 28	25 26 27 28 29 30 31	29 30

MAY	JUNE	JULY	AUGUST
S M T W T F S	S M T W T F S	S M T W T F S	S M T W T F S
1 2 3 4 5	1 2	1 2 3 4 5 6 7	1 2 3 4
6 7 8 9 10 11 12	3 4 5 6 7 8 9	8 9 10 11 12 13 14	5 6 7 8 9 10 11
13 14 15 16 17 18 19	10 11 12 13 14 15 16	15 16 17 18 19 20 21	12 13 14 15 16 17 18
20 21 22 23 24 25 26	17 18 19 20 21 22 23	22 23 24 25 26 27 28	19 20 21 22 23 24 25
27 28 29 30 31	24 25 26 27 28 29 30	29 30 31	26 27 28 29 30 31

SEPTEMBER	OCTOBER	NOVEMBER	DECEMBER
S M T W T F S	S M T W T F S	S M T W T F S	S M T W T F S
1	1 2 3 4 5 6	1 2 3	1
2 3 4 5 6 7 8	7 8 9 10 11 12 13	4 5 6 7 8 9 10	2 3 4 5 6 7 8
9 10 11 12 13 14 15	14 15 16 17 18 19 20	11 12 13 14 15 16 17	9 10 11 12 13 14 15
16 17 18 19 20 21 22	21 22 23 24 25 26 27	18 19 20 21 22 23 24	16 17 18 19 20 21 22
23 24 25 26 27 28 29	28 29 30 31	25 26 27 28 29 30	23 24 25 26 27 28 29
30			30 31

1991

JANUARY	FEBRUARY	MARCH	APRIL
S M T W T F S	S M T W T F S	S M T W T F S	S M T W T F S
1 2 3 4 5	1 2	1 2	1 2 3 4 5 6
6 7 8 9 10 11 12	3 4 5 6 7 8 9	3 4 5 6 7 8 9	7 8 9 10 11 12 13
13 14 15 16 17 18 19	10 11 12 13 14 15 16	10 11 12 13 14 15 16	14 15 16 17 18 19 20
20 21 22 23 24 25 26	17 18 19 20 21 22 23	17 18 19 20 21 22 23	21 22 23 24 25 26 27
27 28 29 30 31	24 25 26 27 28	24 25 26 27 28 29 30	28 29 30
		31	

MAY	JUNE	JULY	AUGUST
S M T W T F S	S M T W T F S	S M T W T F S	S M T W T F S
1 2 3 4	1	1 2 3 4 5 6	1 2 3
5 6 7 8 9 10 11	2 3 4 5 6 7 8	7 8 9 10 11 12 13	4 5 6 7 8 9 10
12 13 14 15 16 17 18	9 10 11 12 13 14 15	14 15 16 17 18 19 20	11 12 13 14 15 16 17
19 20 21 22 23 24 25	16 17 18 19 20 21 22	21 22 23 24 25 26 27	18 19 20 21 22 23 24
26 27 28 29 30 31	23 24 25 26 27 28 29	28 29 30 31	25 26 27 28 29 30 31
	30		

SEPTEMBER	OCTOBER	NOVEMBER	DECEMBER
S M T W T F S	S M T W T F S	S M T W T F S	S M T W T F S
1 2 3 4 5 6 7	1 2 3 4 5	1 2	1 2 3 4 5 6 7
8 9 10 11 12 13 14	6 7 8 9 10 11 12	3 4 5 6 7 8 9	8 9 10 11 12 13 14
15 16 17 18 19 20 21	13 14 15 16 17 18 19	10 11 12 13 14 15 16	15 16 17 18 19 20 21
22 23 24 25 26 27 28	20 21 22 23 24 25 26	17 18 19 20 21 22 23	22 23 24 25 26 27 28
29 30	27 28 29 30 31	24 25 26 27 28 29 30	29 30 31

1

Church and Civic Calendar for 1990

JANUARY

1 New Year's Day Festival of the Christening
5 Twelfth Night
6 The Epiphany
14 Missionary Day
15 Martin Luther King, Jr.'s Birthday
15–21 Week of Prayer for Christian Unity
18 Confession of St. Peter
19 Robert E. Lee's Birthday
25 Conversion of St. Paul

FEBRUARY

1 National Freedom Day
2 Presentation of Jesus in the Temple
11 Race Relations Sunday
12 Lincoln's Birthday
14 St. Valentine's Day
18–25 Brotherhood Week
19 Presidents' Day
22 Washington's Birthday
24 St. Matthias, Apostle
25 The Transfiguration (alternate)
27 Shrove Tuesday
28 Ash Wednesday

MARCH

2 World Day of Prayer
4 First Sunday in Lent
11 Second Sunday in Lent
17 St. Patrick's Day
18 Third Sunday in Lent
25 Fourth Sunday in Lent
The Annunciation

APRIL

1 Fifth Sunday in Lent
Passion Sunday
8 Palm Sunday
Passion Sunday (alternate)
8–14 Holy Week
12 Maundy Thursday
13 Good Friday
15 Easter
22 Low Sunday
25 St. Mark, Evangelist

MAY

1 Law Day
Loyalty Day
May Day
St. Philip and St. James, Apostles
6–13 National Family Week
13 Mother's Day
19 Armed Forces Day
20 Rural Life Sunday
21 Victoria Day (Canada)
24 Ascension Day
28 Memorial Day
31 The Visitation

JUNE

3 Pentecost (Whitsunday)
10 Children's Sunday
Trinity Sunday
11 St. Barnabas, Apostle
14 Flag Day
17 Corpus Christi
Father's Day
24 Nativity of St. John the Baptist
29 St. Peter and St. Paul, Apostles

JULY

1 Dominion Day (Canada)
Independence Sunday
2 The Visitation (alternate)
4 Independence Day
22 St. Mary Magdalene
25 St. James the Elder, Apostle

AUGUST

6 The Transfiguration
15 Mary, Mother of Our Lord
24 St. Bartholomew, Apostle
26 Women's Equality Day

SEPTEMBER

2 Labor Sunday
3 Labor Day
17 Citizenship Day
21 St. Matthew, Evangelist and Apostle
29 St. Michael and All Angels

OCTOBER

1 Child Health Day
7 World Communion Sunday
8 Columbus Day
  Thanksgiving Day (Canada)
12 Columbus Day (alternate)
14 Laity Sunday
18 St. Luke, Evangelist
24 United Nations Day
28 Reformation Sunday
   St. Simon and St. Jude, Apostles
31 National UNICEF Day
   Reformation Day

NOVEMBER

1 All Saints' Day
2 All Souls' Day
  World Community Day
11 Stewardship Day
   Veterans' Day
18 Bible Sunday

Thanksgiving Sunday
22 Thanksgiving Day
25 Christ the King
30 St. Andrew, Apostle

DECEMBER

2 First Sunday of Advent
6 St. Nicholas Day (Orthodox)
9 Second Sunday of Advent
10 Human Rights Day
15 Bill of Rights Day
16 Third Sunday of Advent
21 Forefathers' Day
   St. Thomas, Apostle
23 Fourth Sunday of Advent
25 Christmas
26 St. Stephen, Deacon and Martyr
27 St. John, Evangelist and Apostle
28 The Holy Innocents, Martyrs
31 New Year's Eve
   Watch Night

Common Lectionary for 1990

The following Scripture lessons are commended for use in public worship, with some modifications, by various Protestant churches and the Roman Catholic church and include first, second, Gospel readings, and Psalms according to Cycle A from January 1 to November 25 and according to Cycle B from December 2 to December 31.

EPIPHANY SEASON

January 6 (Epiphany): Isa. 60:1–6; Ps. 72:1–14; Eph. 3:1–12; Matt. 2:1–12.

January 7: Isa. 42:1–9; Ps. 29; Acts 10:34–43; Matt. 3:13–17.

January 14: Isa. 49:1–7; Ps. 40:1–11; 1 Cor. 1:1–9; John 1:29–34.

January 21: Isa. 9:1–4; Ps. 27:1–6; 1 Cor. 1:10–17; Matt. 4:12–23.

January 28: Mic. 6:1–8; Ps. 37:1–11; 1 Cor. 1:18–31; Matt. 5:1–12.

February 4: Isa. 58:3–9a; Ps. 112:4–9; 1 Cor. 2:1–11; Matt. 5:13–16.

February 11: Deut. 30:15–20 or Eccles. 15:15–20; Ps. 119:1–8; 1 Cor. 3:1–9; Matt. 5:17–26.

February 18: Isa. 49:8–13; Ps. 62:5–12; 1 Cor. 3:10–11, 16–23; Matt. 5:27–37.

February 25: Lev. 19:1–2, 9–18; Ps. 119:33–40; 1 Cor. 4:1–5; Matt. 5:38–48.

Last Sunday after Epiphany (Transfiguration): Exod. 24:12–28; Ps. 2:6–11; 2 Pet. 1:16–21; Matt. 17:1–9.

LENT

February 28 (Ash Wednesday): Joel 2:1–2, 12–17a; Ps. 51:1–12; 2 Cor. 5:20b–6:2 (3–10); Matt. 6:1–6, 16–21.

March 4: Gen. 2:4b–9, 15–17, 25–3:7; Ps. 130; Rom. 5:12–19; Matt. 4:1–11.

March 11: Gen. 12:1–4a (4b–8); Ps. 33:18–22; Rom. 4:1–5 (6–12), 13–17; John 3:1–17 or Matt. 17:1–9.

March 18: Exod. 17:3–7; Ps. 95; Rom. 5:1–11; John 4:5–26 (27–42).

March 25: 1 Sam. 16:1–13; Ps. 23; Eph. 5:8–14; John 9:1–41.

April 1: Ezek. 37:1–14; Ps. 116:1–9; Rom. 8:6–11; John 11:(1–16), 17–45.

April 8 (Palm/Passion Sunday): Isa. 50:4–9a; Ps. 118:19–29; Phil. 2:5–11; Matt. 21:1–11; or Isa. 50:4–9a; Ps. 31:9–16;

Phil. 2:5–11; Matt 26:14–27:66 or Matt. 27:11–54.

April 9 (Monday): Isa. 42:1–9; Ps. 36:5–10; Heb. 9:11–15; John 12:1–11.

April 10 (Tuesday): Isa. 49:1–7; Ps. 71:1–12; 1 Cor. 1:18–31; John 12:20–36.

April 11 (Wednesday): Isa. 50:4–9a; Ps. 70; Heb. 12:1–3; John 13:21–30.

April 12 (Thursday): Exod. 12:1–14; Ps. 116:12–19; 1 Cor. 11:23–26; John 13: 21–30.

April 13 (Good Friday): Isa. 52:13–53:12; Ps. 22:1–18; Heb. 4:14–16; 5:7–9; John 18:1–19:42 or John 19:17–30.

April 14 (Easter Vigil): Gen. 1:1–2:2; Ps. 33: Gen. 7:1–15, 11–18; 8:6–18; 9:8–13; Ps. 46; Gen. 22:1–18; Ps. 16; Exod. 14: 10–15:1; Exod. 15:1–6, 11–13, 17–18; Isa. 54:5–14; Ps. 30; Isa. 55:1–11; Isa. 12:2–6; Bar. 3:9–15, 32–4:4; Ps. 19; Ezek. 36:24–28; Ps. 42; Ezek. 37:1–14; Ps. 143; Zeph. 3:14–20; Ps. 98; Rom. 6:3–11; Ps. 114; Mark 16:1–8.

SEASON OF EASTER

April 15 (Easter Sunday): Acts 10:34–43 or Jer. 31:1–6; Ps. 118:14–14; Col. 3:1–4 or Acts 10:34–43; John 20:1–18 or Matt. 28:1–10.

April 15 (Easter Evening): Acts 5:29–32 or Dan. 12:1–3; Ps. 150; 1 Cor. 5:6–8 or Acts 5:29–32; Luke 24:14–39.

April 22: Acts 2:14a, 22–32; Ps. 16:5–11; 1 Pet. 1:3–9; John 20:19–31.

April 29: Acts 2:14a, 36–41; Ps. 116:12–19; 1 Pet. 1:17–23; Luke 24:13–35.

May 6: Acts 2:42–47; Ps. 23: 1 Pet. 2:19–25; John 10:1–10.

May 13: Acts 7:55–60; Ps. 31:1–8; 1 Pet. 2:2–10; John 1:1–14.

May 20: Acts 17:22–31; Ps. 66:8–20; 1 Pet. 3:13–22; John 14:15–21.

May 24 (Ascension): Acts 1:1–11; Ps. 47; Eph. 1:15–23; Luke 24:46–53 or Mark 16:9–16, 19–20.

May 27: Acts 1:6–14; Ps. 68:1–10; 1 Pet. 4:12–14; 5:6–11; John 17:1–11.

SEASON OF PENTECOST

June 3 (Pentecost): Acts 2:1–21 or Isa. 44:1–8; Ps. 104:24–34; 1 Cor. 12:3b–13

or Acts 2:1–21; John 20:19–23 or John 7:37–39.

June 10 (Trinity Sunday): Deut. 4:32–40; Ps. 33:1–12; 2 Cor. 13:5–14; Matt. 28: 16–20.

June 17: Gen. 25:19–34; Ps. 46; Rom. 5:6–11; Matt. 9:35–10:8.

June 24: Gen. 28:1–10; Ps. 9:1–10; Rom. 5:12–19; Matt. 10:24–33.

July 1: Gen. 32:22–32; Ps. 17:1–7, 15; Rom. 6:3–11; Matt. 10:34–42.

July 8: Exod. 1:6–14, 22–2:10; Ps. 124; Rom. 7:14–25a; Matt. 11:25–30.

July 15: Exod. 2:11–22; Ps. 69:6–15; Rom. 8:9–17; Matt. 13:1–9, 18–23.

July 22: Exod. 3:1–12; Ps. 103:1–13; Rom. 8:18–25; Matt. 13:24–30, 36–43.

July 29: Exod. 3:13–20; Ps. 105:1–11; Rom. 8:26–30; Matt. 13:44–52.

August 5: Exod. 12:1–14; Ps. 143:1–10; Rom. 8:31–39; Matt. 14:13–21.

August 12: Exod. 14:19–31; Ps. 106:4–12; Rom. 9:1–5; Matt. 14:22–33.

August 19: Exod. 16:2–15; Ps. 78:1–3, 10–20; Rom. 11:13–16, 29–32; Matt. 15:21–28.

August 26: Exod. 17:1–7; Ps. 95; Rom. 11:33–36; Matt. 16:13–20.

September 2: Exod. 19:1–9; Ps. 114; Rom. 12:1–13; Matt. 16:21–28.

September 9: Exod. 19:16–24; Ps. 115:1–111; Rom. 13:1–10; Matt. 18:15–20.

September 16: Exod. 20:1–20; Ps. 19:7–14; Rom. 14:5–12; Matt. 18:21–35.

September 23: Exod. 32:1–14; Ps. 106:7–8, 19–23; Phil. 1:21–27; Matt. 20:1–16.

September 30: Exod. 33:12–23; Ps. 99; Phil. 2:1–13; Matt. 21:28–32.

October 7: Num. 27:12–23; Ps. 81:1–10; Phil. 3:12–21; Matt. 21:33–43.

October 14: Deut. 34:1–12; Ps. 135:1–14; Phil. 4:1–9; Matt. 22:1–14.

October 21: Ruth 1:1–19a; Ps. 146; 1 Thess. 1:1–10; Matt. 22:15–22.

October 28: Ruth 2:1–13; Ps. 128; 1 Thess. 2:1–8; Matt. 22:34–46.

November 1 (All Saints' Day): Rev. 7:9–17; Ps. 34:1–10; 1 John 3:1–3; Matt. 5:1–12.

November 4: Ruth 4:7–17; Ps. 127; 1 Thess. 2:9–13, 17–20; Matt. 23:1–12.

November 11: Amos 5:18–24; Ps. 50:7–15; 1 Thess. 4:13–18; Matt. 25:1–13.

November 18: Zeph. 1:7, 12–18; Ps. 76; 1 Thess. 5:1–11; Matt. 25:14–30.

November 22 (Thanksgiving Day): Deut. 8:7–18; Ps. 65; 2 Cor. 9:6–15; Luke 17:11–19.

November 25 (Christ the King): Ezek. 34:11–16, 20–24; Ps. 23; 1 Cor. 15:20–28; Matt. 25:31–46.

ADVENT

December 2: Isa. 63:16–64:8; Ps. 80:1–7; 1 Cor. 1:3–9; Mark 13:32–37.

December 9: Isa. 40:1–11; Ps. 85:8–13; 2 Pet. 3:8–15a; Mark 1:1–8.

December 16: Isa. 61:1–4, 8–11; Luke 1:46b–55; 1 Thess. 5:16–24; John 1:6–8, 19–28.

December 23: 2 Sam. 7:8–16; Ps. 89:1–4, 19–24; Rom. 16:25–27; Luke 1:26–38.

CHRISTMAS SEASON

December 24, 25 (Christmas Eve/Day): Isa. 9:2–7; Ps. 96; Titus 2:11–14; Luke 2:1–20; also, Isa. 62:6–7, 10–12; Ps. 97; Titus 3:4–7; Luke 2:8–20; Isa. 52:7–10; Ps. 98; Heb. 1:1–12; John 1:1–14.

December 30: Isa. 61:10–62:3; Ps. 111; Gal. 4:4–7; Luke 2:22–40.

December 31 (New Year's Eve): Eccles. 3:1–13; Ps. 8; Col. 2:1–7; Matt. 9:14–17.

Four-Year Church Calendar

	1990	1991	1992	1993
Ash Wednesday	February 28	February 13	March 4	February 24
Palm Sunday	April 8	March 24	April 12	April 4
Good Friday	April 13	March 29	April 17	April 9
Easter	April 15	March 31	April 19	April 11
Ascension Day	May 24	May 9	May 28	May 20
Pentecost	June 3	May 19	June 7	May 30
Trinity Sunday	June 10	May 26	June 14	June 6
Thanksgiving	November 22	November 28	November 23	November 25
Advent Sunday	December 2	December 1	December 2	November 28

Forty-Year Easter Calendar

1990 April 15	2000 April 23	2010 April 4	2020 April 12
1991 March 31	2001 April 15	2011 April 24	2021 April 4
1992 April 19	2002 March 31	2012 April 8	2022 April 17
1993 April 11	2003 April 20	2013 March 31	2023 April 9
1994 April 3	2004 April 11	2014 April 20	2024 March 31
1995 April 16	2005 March 27	2015 April 5	2025 April 20
1996 April 7	2006 April 16	2016 March 27	2026 April 5
1997 March 30	2007 April 8	2017 April 16	2027 March 28
1998 April 12	2008 March 23	2018 April 1	2028 April 16
1999 April 4	2009 April 12	2019 April 21	2029 April 1

Traditional Wedding Anniversary Identifications

1 Paper	7 Wool	13 Lace	35 Coral
2 Cotton	8 Bronze	14 Ivory	40 Ruby
3 Leather	9 Pottery	15 Crystal	45 Sapphire
4 Linen	10 Tin	20 China	50 Gold
5 Wood	11 Steel	25 Silver	55 Emerald
6 Iron	12 Silk	30 Pearl	60 Diamond

Colors Appropriate for Days and Seasons

White. Symbolizes purity, perfection, and joy and identifies festivals marking events, except Good Friday, in the life of Jesus: Christmas, Epiphany, Easter, Eastertide,

Ascension Day, Trinity Sunday, All Saints' Day; weddings, funerals. Gold may also be used.

Red.   Symbolizes the Holy Spirit, martyrdom, and the love of God: Good Friday, Pentecost and Sundays following.

Violet.   Symbolizes penitence: Advent, Lent.

Green.   Symbolizes mission to the world, hope, regeneration, nurture, and growth: Epiphany season, Kingdomtide, Rural Life Sunday, Labor Sunday, Thanksgiving Sunday.

Blue.   Advent, in some churches.

Flowers in Season Appropriate for Church Use

January.   Carnation or snowdrop.
February.   Violet or primrose.
March.   Jonquil or daffodil.
April.   Lily, sweet pea, or daisy.
May.   Lily of the valley or hawthorn.
June.   Rose or honeysuckle.
July.   Larkspur or water lily.

August.   Gladiolus or poppy.
September.   Aster or morning glory.
October.   Calendula or cosmos.
November.   Chrysanthemum.
December.   Narcissus, holly, or poinsettia.

Historical, Cultural, and Religious Anniversaries in 1990

Compiled by Kenneth M. Cox

10 Years (1980). *January 4:* President Carter announces an embargo on grain sales to the Soviet Union. *March 27:* Mount Saint Helens volcano erupts in Washington state, covering much of the Northwest with ashes and smoke. *April 25:* U.S. hostage rescue mission fails in the Iranian desert. *July 15:* The Games of the XXII Olympiad open in Moscow, without the U.S. and many other nations. *December 19:* Prime interest rate reaches 21.5 percent at many major U.S. banks.

25 Years (1965). *January 4:* President Johnson, in his State of the Union address, outlines his Great Society programs to fight poverty in the U.S. *February 1:* Rev. Martin Luther King, Jr., and 770 others are arrested at Selma, Alabama, during demonstrations against state voter-registration regulations. *February 21:* Malcolm X, leader of the Muslim organization of Afro-American Unity, is shot and killed at Harlem's Audubon Ballroom. *June 7:* Supreme Court strikes down a Connecticut law prohibiting the sale of birth-control devices. *August 12:* Violent riots begin in Los Angeles' Watts section. *Debuts:* International Society for Krishna Consciousness, in New York; the Grateful Dead; the miniskirt, in London.

40 Years (1950). *January 25:* Alger Hiss is convicted of perjury for concealing his membership in the Communist party. *August 17:* Pope Pius XII issues *Humanis generis,* condemning existentialism and other theories. *Debuts:* National Council of the Churches of Christ in the United States; FBI's "Ten Most Wanted" list; Otis self-service elevator; minute rice.

50 Years (1940). *May 7:* Winston Churchill succeeds Neville Chamberlain as Britain's prime minister. *May 10:* German *Blitzkrieg* begins in Holland. *June 14:* German army enters Paris, and France and Germany sign armistice (June 22). *November:* President Roosevelt defeats Wendell Willkie to win an unprecedented third term in the White House. *Debuts:* Penicillin as an antibiotic; nylon stockings in the U.S.

60 Years (1930). *March 12:* Mahatma Gandhi begins a civil disobedience movement in India. *September 29:* Lowell Thomas begins a nightly radio network news program that will run until 1976. *November 2:* Haile Selassie I is proclaimed King of Kings in Ethiopia. *Debuts:* Plexi-

glass; Grant Wood's *American Gothic;* comic strip "Blondie"; Hostess Twinkies; sliced bread.

75 Years (1915). *April 24:* Poison gas is first used by the Germans in World War I. *May 7:* German submarine sinks the *Lusitania,* killing 1,145 and rousing the U.S. to go to war with Germany.

100 Years (1890). *July 2:* Sherman Antitrust Act is passed by Congress, to curtail the power of U.S. business monopolies. *December 29:* Massacre of 350 Sioux by U.S. cavalry at Wounded Knee ends the last major Indian resistance to white settlement in America. *Debuts:* Yosemite National Park; Daughters of the American Revolution; EverReady dry cell battery.

125 Years (1865). *April 9:* General Robert E. Lee surrenders to General Ulysses S. Grant at Appomattox Court House, Virginia, ending the Civil War. *April 14:* President Lincoln is assassinated by John Wilkes Booth at Ford's Theater in Washington. *December 18:* Thirteenth Amendment to the Constitution takes effect, prohibiting slavery or any other denial of liberty without due process of law. *Debuts:* Salvation Army; Stetson hat; *The Nation.*

150 Years (1840). *June 2:* English novelist Thomas Hardy is born in Upper Bockhampton, Dorset, England (d. 1928). *November 14:* French artist Claude Oscar Monet is born in Paris (d. 1926). *November 15:* French sculptor François Auguste Rodin is born in Paris (d. 1917). *Debut:* Adhesive postage stamp.

175 Years (1815). *June 18:* The Battle of Waterloo is fought by armies of Napoleon and Wellington. *November 20:* Britain, Portugal, Prussia, and Russia guarantee the perpetual neutrality and inviolability of Switzerland.

200 Years (1790). *July 16:* Resident Act passed by Congress, calling for a new federal city to be designed and laid out on the banks of the Potomac River near Maryland's George Town. *Debut:* Dental drill.

300 Years (1690). *An Essay Concerning Human Understanding* and *Two Treatises of Civil Government* published by English philosopher John Locke, the latter presenting a theory of limited monarchy. *Debut:* Diving bell.

450 Years (1540). *July 28:* Thomas Cromwell, advisor to King Henry VIII, is executed. *September 27:* Pope Paul III recognizes the Society of Jesus, founded in 1534.

Anniversaries of Hymns, Hymn Writers, and Hymn-Tune Composers in 1990

Compiled by Hugh T. McElrath

25 Years (1965). *Death* of Eleanor Farjeon (b. 1881), author of "Morning has broken"; Homer Hammontree (b. 1884), composer of HAMMONTREE ("Fill all my vision, Savior, I pray"); Fred C. M. Hansen (b. 1888), revisor of "Built on the rock, the church doth stand"; Harry D. Loes (b. 1892), composer of REDEEMER ("Up Calvary's mountain") and other tunes.

50 Years (1940). *Death* of Carl Boberg (b. 1859), author of "How great Thou art"; Laura S. Copenhaver (b. 1868), author of "Heralds of Christ."

75 Years (1915). *Birth* of Sydney Carter, author of contemporary songs, including "Lord of the dance" and "Every star shall have a carol"; E. Margaret Clarkson, author of "So send I you," "We come, O Christ, to Thee," and numerous other texts; Robert L. Edwards, author of "De-

clare, O heavens, the Lord of space"; Su Yin-Lan (d. 1937), composer of SHENG EN ("The bread of life for all men broken"). *Death* of Fanny J. Crosby (b. 1820), author of many gospel songs, including "Blessed assurance," "Rescue the perishing," "I am Thine, O Lord," "Jesus, keep me near the cross," and "To God be the glory"; William Cummings (b. 1831), arranger of MENDELSSOHN ("Hark, the herald angels sing"); William Howard Doane (b. 1832), composer of tunes especially for Fanny Crosby texts, including RESCUE, I AM THINE, NEAR THE CROSS, TO GOD BE THE GLORY; John T. Grape (b. 1835), composer of ALL TO CHRIST ("Jesus paid it all"); John S. B. Hodges (b. 1830), composer of EUCHARISTIC HYMN ("Bread of the world in mercy broken"); Anna B. Warner (b. 1820), author of "Jesus loves me."

100 Years (1890). *Birth* of Ernest Bullock (d. 1979), composer of BERRY DOWN ("Not with a choir of angels without number"); Daniel Iverson, author and composer of "Spirit of the living God"; Hugh Martin (d. 1964), author of "O God in heaven, whose loving plan," "Lord Christ, in Thy footsteps," and other hymns. *Death* of Henry M. Dexter (b. 1821), translator of "Shepherd of eager youth"; Frederick H. Hedge (b. 1805), translator of "A mighty fortress is our God"; Thomas Helmore (b. 1811), composer/arranger of VENI EMMANUEL ("O come, O come Emmanuel"); Richard F. Littledale (b. 1833), translator of "Come down, O love divine."

125 Years (1865). *Birth* of Peter P. Bilhorn (d. 1936), composer of WONDROUS STORY ("I will sing the wondrous story"); C. Silvester Horne (d. 1914), author of "Sing we the king," "For the might of Thine arm we bless Thee," and others; Lawrence Housman (d. 1959), author of "Father eternal, ruler of creation," "When Christ was born in Bethlehem," and others; Lewis E. Jones (d. 1936), author of "Would you be free from the burden of sin" and its tune, POWER IN THE BLOOD; Rudyard Kipling (d. 1936), author of "God of our fathers, known of old," "Father in heaven who lovest all," and others; George Currie Martin (d. 1937), author of "Thy words to me are life and health"; James Rowe (d. 1933), author of "Love lifted me"; Jean Sibelius (d. 1957), composer of FINLANDIA ("Be still, my soul"); Ida R. Smith (d. 1951), author of "I belong to the King." *Birth* of Richard R. Terry (d. 1938), composer of NEWMAN ("Praise to the Holiest in the height"); Emily D. Wilson (d. 1942), composer of HEAVEN ("When we all get to heaven"). *Death* of Hugh Stowell (b. 1799), author of "From every stormy wind that blows"; William V. Wallace (b. 1814), composer of SERENITY ("Immortal love, forever full"); Isaac Williams (b. 1802), author of "Be Thou my guardian and my guide."

150 Years (1840). *Birth* of J. L. Macbeth Bain (d. 1925), composer of BROTHER JAMES AIR; Joel Blomquist (d. 1930), composer of DET AR ETT FAST ORD ("O breath of life, come sweeping through us"); John

White Chadwick (d. 1904), author of "Eternal ruler of the ceaseless round"; William C. Gannett (d. 1923), author of "Praise to God, your praises bring"; Ira D. Sankey (d. 1908), composer of gospel song tunes, including TRUSTING JESUS ("Simply trusting every day"), HIDING IN THEE ("O safe to the rock that is higher than I"); INTERCESSION ("I have a Savior, He's pleading in glory"), SANKEY ("Encamped along the hills of light"), and THE NINETY AND NINE ("There were ninety and nine that safely lay"); Frederick Lucian Hosmer (d. 1929), author of "Thy kingdom come, on bended knee" and other hymns; Robert Jackson (d. 1914), composer of TRENTHAM ("Breathe on me, breath of God"); John Stainer (d. 1901), composer of CROSS OF JESUS ("Cross of Jesus, cross of sorrow"), WYCLIFF ("All for Jesus, all for Jesus"), ST. BENEDICT ("Savior, teach me day by day"), and others; John A. Symonds (d. 1893), author of "These things shall be! a loftier race"; Daniel W. Whittle (d. 1901), author of "There shall be showers of blessing," "Moment by moment," "The banner of the cross," and other gospel songs. *Death* of Mary Duncan (b. 1814), author of "Jesus, tender shepherd, hear me."

175 Years (1815). *Birth* of Ithamar Conkey (d. 1867), composer of RATHBUN ("In the cross of Christ I glory"); John A. Lloyd (d. 1874), composer of tunes, including ABERGELE ("Spirit of God, attend our prayers") and GROESWEN ("All my hope on God is founded"); John Zundel (d. 1882), composer of BEECHER ("Love divine, all loves excelling"). *Death* of Matthias Claudius (b. 1740), author of "We plow the fields and scatter."

225 Years (1765). *Birth* of Oliver Holden (d. 1844), composer of CORONATION ("All hail the power of Jesus' name").

250 Years (1740). *Birth* of Matthias Claudius (d. 1815), author of "We plow the fields and scatter"; John Fawcett, (d. 1817), author of "Blest be the tie that binds" and "Lord, dismiss us with Thy blessing"; Augustus Toplady (d. 1778), author of "Rock of ages, cleft for me" and "How blest are they, O Lord"; Samuel Webbe (d. 1816), composer of WEBBE ("O

God of love, O king of peace") and MEL-COMBE ("New every morning is the love" and "O Spirit of the living God").

275 Years (1715). *Birth* of Christian F. Gellert (d. 1769), author of "Jesus lives and so shall I." *Death* of Nahum Tate (b. 1652), author of "While shepherds watched their flocks by night" and, with Nicholas Brady, compiler of the Tate and Brady Psalter ("The New Version," 1696).

300 Years (1690). *Birth* of Henry Carey (d. 1743), composer of SURREY ("Come, O thou traveler unknown" and "Creator Spirit, by whose aid"). *Death* of Johann J. Schutz (b. 1640), author of "Sing praise to God, who reigns above."

325 Years (1665). Publication of *Erneuerten Gesangbuch*, source of LOBE DEN HERREN ("Praise to the Lord, the almighty"). *Death* of Johann Schop (b. c.1600), composer of ERMUNTRE DICH ("Break forth, O beauteous heavenly light") and WERDE MUNTER ("Jesu, joy of man's desiring").

350 Years (1640). *Birth* of Johann J. Schutz (d. 1690), author of "Sing praise to God, who reigns above." Publication of *The Bay Psalm Book*, popular title of the first book printed in North America, containing metrical psalms sung to some tunes still in use (OLD HUNDREDTH, for example).

375 Years (1615). *Birth* of Richard Baxter (d. 1691), author of "Lord, it belongs not to my care" and "Ye holy angels bright." Publication of the Edinburgh Psalter of Andro Hart, important edition of the *Scottish Psalter,* the source of surviving psalm tunes DUNDEE ("O God of Bethel, by whose hand"), YORK ("God is our refuge and strength"), and MARTYRS ("O God of truth, whose loving word") among others.

500 Years (1490). *Birth* of Nikolaus Decius (d. 1541), author of "All glory be to God on high" and its tune, ALLEIN GOTT IN DER HOH.

1175 Years (815). *Death* of Stephen the Sabaite (b. ca. 725), probably source of "Art thou weary, art thou languid."

1650 Years (340). *Birth* of Ambrose, Bishop of Milan (d. 397), author of the original text of several hymns, including "O splendor of God's glory bright," "O God of truth, O Lord of might," and "O God, creation's secret force."

1775 Years (215). *Death* of Clement of Alexandria (b. ca. 170), author of the original text of "Shepherd of tender youth," "Jesus, our mighty Lord," and others.

Quotable Quotations

1. I'm not afraid to die. I just don't want to be there when it happens.—Woody Allen

2. The proper question to be asked about any creed is not, "Is it pleasant?" but, "Is it true?"—Dorothy L. Sayers

3. In a war of ideas it is people who get killed.—Stanislaus J. Lec

4. God is present even in and through his silence.—Charles E. Crain

5. Given the human situation as we know it today, hell will freeze over before the meek will inherit the earth! But God has ways of bringing it off that we know nothing about.—Steven P. Vitrano

6. We haven't really wrestled with the full implications of the Christian faith until we have wrestled with the "resurrection from the dead" in the context of growing old . . . and dying.—Edmund Steimle

7. Without God, we cannot. Without us, God will not.—St. Augustine

8. The burnt child shuns the fire until the next day.—Mark Twain

9. Love makes all the difference between an execution and a martyrdom.—Evelyn Underhill

10. If you turn up your nose at people, you will drown when the rains come.—Peter Kreeft

11. The most terrible systems of the human race are distortions of longing for peace, quiet, love.—Fred B. Craddock

12. The only limits that should be set in the search for truth are the limits of truth itself.—T. B. Maston

13. The first duty of love is to listen.—Paul Tillich

14. Blessed are the young, for they shall inherit the national debt.—Herbert Hoover

15. Where law ends tyranny begins.—William Pitt

16. The task of organized religion is not

to prove that God was in the first century but that he is in the twentieth.—Samuel H. Miller

17. Everybody's friend is nobody's.—Arthur Schopenhauer

18. Some Christians have a very small Savior, for they are not willing to receive him fully and let him do great and mighty things for them.—Dwight L. Moody

19. The big difference with Jesus is that, while he is master, he is a master with a servant's heart and a master with love as his motive, and he makes us his own!—C. Neil Strait

20. Judgment is the dark line in the face of God.—Billy Graham

21. We dare not trade in biblical metaphors for psychological ones: unconditional positive regard cannot replace the blood of the Lamb.—H. Stephen Shoemaker

22. A child who has not been loved and encouraged and praised and hugged is a child who can never love others.—Elizabeth Achtemeier

23. Character is what a man is in the dark.—Dwight L. Moody

24. All religions united with government are more or less inimical to liberty. All separated from government are compatible with liberty.—Henry Clay

25. Every submission to our fear enlarges its dominion.—Samuel Johnson

26. Mother is the name for God in the lips and hearts of little children.—William Makepeace Thackeray

27. The soul is dyed with the color of its leisure thoughts.—W. R. Inge

28. Our Lord said, "Feed my sheep"; he did not say, "Count them."—Dora Chaplin

29. A religion without the element of mystery would not be a religion at all.—Ralph L. Woods

30. The good life becomes ours, not by struggle and effort, but by surrender and discipleship.—John N. Gladstone

31. The life beyond the world is, in very deed, the inspiration of the life that now is.—Ernst Troeltsch

32. If God is, if you exist only because a loving God fashioned you out of nothing but love, then that God wants you to know him.—Walter J. Burghardt, SJ

33. In Hollywood all marriages are happy. It's trying to live together afterwards that causes the problems.—Shelley Winters

34. Do all the good you can,
By all the means you can,
In all the places you can,
At all the times you can,
To all the people you can,
As long as ever you can.—John Wesley

35. It is easy to be tolerant when you do not care.—Clement F. Rogers

36. Books are good enough in their way, but they are a mighty bloodless substitute for life.—Robert Louis Stevenson

37. We need to do more than to sponsor a *Christian subculture.* We need *Christian counterculture* that sets itself alongside the secular rivals and publishes openly the difference that belief in God and his Christ makes in the arenas of thought and action.—Carl F. H. Henry

38. The devil loves to fish in troubled waters.—John Trapp

39. If there is hope for America, it will come through our vigorous proclamation and application of the Christian message.—Carl F. H. Henry

40. The Lord has more truth yet to break forth out of his holy Word.—John Robinson

41. Only the educated are free.—Epictetus

42. Wish not so much to live long as to live well.—Benjamin Franklin

43. Conscience: the Inner voice which warns you that someone may be looking.—H. L. Mencken

44. Human salvation lies in the hands of the creatively maladjusted.—Martin Luther King, Jr.

45. Our labors for justice will always be corrupted by our nature—as Saul's temper corrupted him. Yet corruption is not depravity, and frail human beings may still honor the good by giving a life and perhaps a death for it.—Richard C. Marius

46. Life only demands from the strength you possess. Only one feat is possible—not to have run away.—Dag Hammarskjöld

47. If you think education is expensive, try ignorance.—Derek Bok

48. The best way to train up a child the way he should go is to travel that road occasionally yourself.—Josh Billings

49. The religion of the atheist has a God-shaped blank at its heart.—H. G. Wells

50. Money can cure hunger: it cannot cure unhappiness. Food can satisfy the appetite but not the soul.—George Bernard Shaw

51. There is in repentance this beautiful mystery—that we may fly fastest home on broken wing.—William L. Sullivan

52. You can make more friends in two months by becoming really interested in other people than you can in two years by trying to get other people interested in you.—Dale Carnegie

53. I could never believe in a God who did not know how to laugh.—James K. Feibelman

54. Legalism is simply law growing cancerously.—E. G. Selwyn

55. Ordinary vision would stand at the foot of the cross and say, "This is the end." Only the eyes of faith could take in that scene and say, "This is the beginning."—Kenneth Chafin

56. Happiness grows at our own firesides and is not to be picked in strangers' gardens.—Douglas Jerrold

57. We cannot go back and undo or redo any of the past, but the significance it has for us can be altered.—John R. Claypool

58. Despair is the fate of those who know something about sin and nothing about redemption.—Allan M. Parrent

59. Nobody can make you feel inferior without your consent.—Eleanor Roosevelt

60. To believe with certainty, we must begin with doubting.—Polish saying

61. God's word in all its impudent glory must be spoken to the powers that be, asking, Why?—David G. Buttrick

62. There is no prayer so blessed as the prayer which asks for nothing.—O. J. Simon

63. Don't throw away the old bucket until you know whether the new one holds water.—Swedish proverb

64. I cannot conceive how a man could look up into the heavens and say there is no God.—Abraham Lincoln

65. In taking revenge, a man is but even with his enemy; but in passing it over, he is superior.—Francis Bacon

66. To be angry is to revenge the fault of others upon ourselves.—Alexander Pope

67. Natural man has only two primary passions: to get and to beget.—Sir William Osler

68. What does not destroy me makes me stronger.—Friedrich Nietzsche

69. The risen Christ doesn't come in to change the lives of deserving people or pious people or religious people. He comes to change the lives of willing people.—Richard P. Hansen

70. Read the Scripture, not only as a history, but as a love-letter sent to you from God.—Thomas Watson

71. The secret of happiness is not in doing what one likes but in liking what one has to do.—James M. Barrie

72. I talk and talk and talk, but I haven't taught people in fifty years what my father taught by example in one week.—Mario Cuomo

73. I tremble for my country when I reflect that God is just.—Thomas Jefferson

74. One advantage of graduating from seminary is that you can manufacture a lot of excuses for doing wrong and be theological in your disobedience.—Haddon W. Robinson

75. To be like Christ is to be a Christian.—William Penn

76. What we ask of religion is to have our children launched, our youths married, and our old people buried. Otherwise, we say, "Don't call us, we'll call you."—James K. Feibleman

77. Inspiration without theology is like the grin of the cat without the cat.—Anonymous

78. Pure logic is the ruin of the spirit.—Antoine de Saint-Exupéry

79. Evangelism has nothing to do with finding people as much as possible as we are, convincing them they are already our kind of people, and providing for them a comfortable environment in which they

can feel better about themselves. Evangelism is the proclamation and the demonstration of the coming kingdom of God.—Charles H. Bayer

80. As scarce as truth is, the supply has always been in excess of the demand.—Josh Billings

81. Outside of Jesus Christ, God can be an unknown factor, or worse yet, a terrifying reality.—Neil Babcox

82. Every situation—no, every moment—is of infinite worth; for it is the representative of a whole eternity.—Goethe

83. Patriotism is the last refuge of a scoundrel.—Samuel Johnson

84. Music is a glorious gift of God and close to theology.—Martin Luther

85. One of the lessons of history is that nothing is often a good thing to do and always a clever thing to say.—Will Durant

86. Life is the art of drawing sufficient conclusions from insufficient premises.—Samuel Butler

87. Every man is in an omnibus in which all of his ancestors are seated.—Oliver Wendell Holmes

88. There is something in humility which strangely exalts the heart.—St. Augustine

89. Nature is the art of God.—Dante Alighieri

90. Propaganda is the art of persuading others of what one does not believe oneself.—Abba Eban

91. You may argue about the trustworthiness of the Bible if you wish; you may find some justifiable criticism of the church and its organization, but you can never deny the evidence of a godly life.—Robert A. Penny

92. If you tell the truth you don't have to remember anything.—Mark Twain

93. No man who is occupied in doing a very difficult thing, and doing it very well, ever loses his self-respect.—George Bernard Shaw

94. Never despair. But if you do, work on in despair.—Edmund Burke

95. "Gods" are among the chief devices used by nations, races, religions, and sexes to steal the promise of humanity for themselves alone and keep the rest of humanity less than human.—Hal M. Warheim

96. Those who know the least obey the best.—George Farquhar

97. Self-control is at the root of all virtues.—Samuel Smiles

98. Imagination is the eye of the soul.—Joseph Joubert

99. A prejudiced person will almost certainly claim that he has sufficient warrant for his views.—Gordon W. Allport

100. When an idea is wanting, a word can always be found to take its place.—Goethe

Questions of Life and Religion

These questions may be useful to prime homiletic pumps, as discussion starters, or for study and youth groups.

1. What was God's purpose in Creation?

2. How do Adam and Eve represent all of us?

3. Is God more than a person?

4. How can we know what God is like?

5. Is nature a reliable revealer of God to us?

6. Do miracles set aside natural law?

7. Why does the world need a messiah, a Christ?

8. Is the church necessary to Christianity?

9. In what sense is the Bible the Word of God?

10. How far does the Bible have authority over our lives today?

11. How can God be three and one at the same time?

12. What is the role of music and song in the worship of God?

13. What is the work of the Holy Spirit in the world today?

14. What are some basic guidelines for telling right from wrong?

15. How should church and government relate to each other?

16. What sort of people should church leaders be?

17. Is education a proper object of Christian missions?

18. Should the biblical doctrine of elec-

tion cut the nerve of evangelism and missions?

19. How can concerned Christians best do evangelism?

20. Is God to blame for evil in the world?

21. Is suffering always or ever a punishment for sin?

22. In what ways does God reveal himself?

23. What is "progressive revelation"?

24. What value do the books of the Apocrypha, "the deuterocanonical" books of the Bible, have for all Christians?

25. What do we mean by inspiration (of the Bible)?

26. What can children and young people do to improve home life?

27. What can an individual do to combat crime in residential areas?

28. How can Christians relate to people of other faiths?

29. How can our desire for acceptance affect our morals, positively and negatively?

30. Is the use of reparations a good way of achieving justice?

31. What are the positive uses of anger?

32. How can we bring anxiety and worry under control?

33. What should our attitude be toward ministers and other authority figures in the church?

34. Is there a conflict between faith and certainty?

35. Is there a conflict between compassion and sentimentality?

36. Does compulsion have a role in achieving moral behavior?

37. When is confrontation of an adversary a Christian duty?

38. What happens in Christian conversion?

39. Is fear an admission of unbelief?

40. How does covetousness affect one's life and behavior?

41. Can we square evolution with the biblical account of Creation?

42. What is the Christian teaching on death?

43. What resources are available to people struggling with moral failure?

44. What is the meaning behind the many names for God in the Bible?

45. Is it wrong to wish for riches?

46. What will it mean to be a true disciple of Jesus Christ in our own day?

47. Is doubt a normal part of Christian experience?

48. What is our religious duty concerning the environment?

49. How can we achieve equality for all people?

50. Who is responsible for the evil in the world?

51. In what way can family become an idol to us?

52. How free are we or can we be?

53. Is personal fulfillment the highest goal for an individual?

54. What is our responsibility for the use of our gifts or talents?

55. How can we determine what is good?

56. How does the grace of God enter our lives?

57. Is greed an illness, a sin, or both?

58. Is a feeling of guilt a normal experience?

59. What is the role of religion in mental health?

60. Is honest speaking of our mind always the best policy?

61. How does the biblical idea of "hope" differ from wishful thinking?

62. Is humility a virtue?

63. What is modern idolatry?

64. What is our duty when others are threatened or oppressed?

65. Is it possible to be perfect?

66. Is joy a possibility in a time of suffering or deprivation?

67. Must we ever judge others' motives?

68. Does grace eliminate the need for law?

69. How can we appropriately express gratitude?

70. What can we do to help our friends through an experience of grief?

71. What is love?

72. What makes a happy marriage?

73. Can meditation contribute to spiritual and physical health?

74. Do miracles happen today?

75. Why should we have foreign missions?

76. What can motivate us to obey God?

77. How can the elderly and infirm continue in Christian service?

78. Is there a better way than tolerance?

79. What are the essential ingredients of peace?

80. What political activities are or are not appropriate for churches?

81. Is Bible prophecy intended to be a blueprint for churches?

82. What is the providence of God?

83. How can offended and offending parties achieve reconciliation?

84. Does a feeling of rejection mean that God has actually rejected us?

85. Does the Bible favor "resurrection" or "immortality" in describing or defining "the life to come"?

86. Why was the Book of Revelation written?

87. According to our Scriptures, what are the rewards of a life pleasing to God?

88. What is the meaning of Baptism?

89. What is the meaning of the Lord's Supper or the Eucharist?

90. Are self-fulfillment and sacrifice mutually exclusive?

91. "What must I do to be saved?" (Acts 16:30).

92. How secure are we, once we have trusted ourselves to the Lord's care?

93. Is selfishness a legitimate factor in personal motivation?

94. What does the Bible teach us about sex?

95. Is "sin" an outmoded concept?

96. How can young people be brought more fully into the planning process in church?

97. How can we best order our duty of stewardship?

98. Can the Bible help us in our thinking and behavior about alcohol?

99. What can we do in times of temptation?

100. Does tradition have binding force on us today?

Biblical Benedictions and Blessings

The Lord watch between me and thee, when we are absent from one another.—Gen. 31:49.

The Lord bless thee, and keep thee; the Lord make his face to shine upon thee, and be gracious unto thee; the Lord lift up his countenance upon thee, and give thee peace.—Num. 6:24–26.

The Lord our God be with us, as he was with our fathers; let him not leave us, nor forsake us; that he may incline our hearts unto him, to walk in all his ways, and to keep his commandments, and his statutes, and his judgments, which he commanded our fathers.—1 Kings 8:57–58.

Let the words of my mouth, and the meditation of my heart, be acceptable in thy sight, O Lord, my strength, and my redeemer.—Ps. 19:14.

Now the God of patience and consolation grant you to be likeminded one toward another according to Christ Jesus; that ye may with one mind and one mouth glorify God, even the Father of our Lord Jesus Christ. Now the God of hope fill you with all joy and peace in believing, that ye may abound in hope, through the power of the Holy Ghost. Now the God of peace be with you all.—Rom. 15:5–6, 13, 33.

Now to him that is of power to establish you according to my gospel, and the preaching of Jesus Christ, according to the revelation of the mystery, which was kept secret since the world began, but now is manifest, and by the scriptures of the prophets, according to the commandment of the everlasting God, made known to all nations for the obedience of faith: to God only wise, be glory through Jesus Christ for ever.—Rom. 16:25–27.

Grace be unto you, and peace, from God our Father, and from the Lord Jesus Christ.—1 Cor. 1:3.

The grace of the Lord Jesus Christ and the love of God, and the communion of the Holy Ghost, be with you all.—2 Cor. 13:14.

Peace be to the brethren, and love with faith, from God the Father and the Lord Jesus Christ. Grace be with all them that love our Lord Jesus Christ in sincerity.—Eph. 6:23–24.

And the peace of God, which passeth all understanding, shall keep your hearts and minds through Christ Jesus. Finally, brethren, whatsoever things are true, whatsoever things are honest, whatsoever things are just, whatsoever things are pure, whatsoever things are lovely, whatsoever things are of good report; if there be any virtue, and if there be any praise, think on these things. Those things, which ye have both learned, and received, and heard, and seen in me, do; and the God of peace shall be with you.—Phil. 4:7–9.

Wherefore also we pray always for you, that our God would count you worthy of this calling, and fulfill all the good pleasure of his goodness, and the work of faith with power; that the name of our Lord Jesus Christ may be glorified in you, and ye in him, according to the grace of our God and the Lord Jesus Christ.—2 Thess. 1:11–12.

Now the Lord of peace himself give you peace always by all means. The Lord be with you all. The grace of our Lord Jesus Christ be with you all.—2 Thess. 3:16–18.

Grace, mercy, and peace, from God our Father and Jesus Christ our Lord.—1 Tim. 1:2.

Now the God of peace, that brought again from the dead our Lord Jesus, that great shepherd of the sheep, through the blood of the everlasting covenant, make you perfect in every good work to do his will, working in you that which is well-pleasing in his sight, through Jesus Christ, to whom be glory for ever and ever.—Heb. 13:20–21.

The God of all grace, who hath called us unto his eternal glory by Christ Jesus, after that ye have suffered a while, make you perfect, establish, strengthen, settle you. To him be glory and dominion for ever and ever. Greet ye one another with a kiss of charity. Peace be with you all that are in Christ Jesus.—1 Pet. 5:10–11, 14.

Grace be with you, mercy, and peace, from God the Father, and from the Lord Jesus Christ, the Son of the Father, in truth and love.—2 John 3.

Now unto him that is able to keep you from falling, and to present you faultless before the presence of his glory with exceeding joy, to the only wise God our Savior, be glory and majesty, dominion and power, both now and ever.—Jude 24–25.

Grace be unto you, and peace, from him which was, and which is to come; and from the seven Spirits which are before his throne; and from Jesus Christ, who is the faithful witness, and the first begotten of the dead, and the prince of the kings of the earth. Unto him that loved us, and washed us from our sins in his own blood, and hath made us kings and priests unto God and his Father; to him be glory and dominion for ever and ever.—Rev. 1:4–6.

SECTION II.

Sermons and Homiletic and Worship Aids for Fifty-two Sundays

SUNDAY: JANUARY SEVENTH

SERVICE OF WORSHIP

Sermon: The Rivals

TEXT: Matt. 2:3

Christmas may be for the angels and the shepherds; it may be for the children and the innocent among us. But the Epiphany is quite another story. And the reason that there are fewer of you here today than there would be on Christmas Eve is that you recognize the difference, and it troubles you like Herod. It has a different cast of characters, this feast of the Epiphany, a quite different edge to it. The manifestation of Christ to the Gentiles is God's most dangerous act of show-and-tell: it is no longer charming; it is now challenging.

I. Some of you have heard me say before that I think the only person who takes the challenge of the Epiphany seriously, the only one in the whole narrative who really seems to understand what is really at work on that Judean hillside, is Herod the king.

(a) Consider the circumstances: it is not in the nature of angels to understand anything; angels just sing and announce and interrupt dreams. Consider the shepherds: they are filled with both terror and wonder, but not one of those shepherds, no matter how devout, appears to understand what is going on. They go back marveling and praising God, but they have to get on with the busy business of minding sheep. Mary

and Joseph simply do as they are told, and that is very good indeed.

(b) Only Herod seems to understand just what is happening and just what its implications are. Not in our text does he evidence the slightest doubt for an instant that the wise men are telling the truth. He takes them and everything they have to say very seriously indeed. And when he hears what they have to say, he has the good sense, the native intelligence, to be disturbed. We should congratulate Herod on his paranoia: it is the sign of an alert, intelligent king; he at least knew that there was something more than melodrama going on in the outskirts of his kingdom, and he was determined to deal with it, to do something about it.

II. Now just what was it that Herod heard, what is "this" of our text, "when Herod the king heard this"?

(a) It was the question of the wise men he heard: "Where is he who has been born king of the Jews, for we have seen his star in the east and are come to worship him." Herod heard that, and he was disturbed. Herod was a Jew. He was familiar with Jewish prophecy and Jewish expectation. A spiritual messiah, such as could be idealized, worshiped, expected, but never seen beyond Temple and Scriptures was a perfectly agreeable hope that might keep people's minds off their troubles and out of mischief. But a king of the Jews born

16

under the sign of a star and sought out by gentile sages, this was something to be taken quite seriously. Herod had not gained or maintained his position by failing to take rivals seriously. He understood that there are many princes but only one king.

(b) This is what Herod heard. He was troubled because he recognized a threat to the status quo, that margin of reality he had carved out of experience and opportunity by lots of blood and a fair amount of sweat and plenty of tears on the part of everybody else. That is what the status quo is: carving out of experience and opportunity a slender moment for ourselves that we can call our own. And all Jerusalem was troubled with him.

III. And so, what does he do? He does what any good corporate, industrialist, megapolitical leader does. He did his research, or he got his research department, the wise men, to do his homework for him. "Then," it says, "Herod summoned the wise men secretly and ascertained from them what time the star appeared." And then he sent them on their way to find the child, with directions to get back to him as soon as possible so that he might come and worship also—one of the most disingenuous verses in the Bible.

(a) If that first response was shrewd and cunning, the second was desperate and ruthless: "Then Herod, when he saw that he had been tricked by the wise men, was in a furious rage, and he sent and killed all the male children in Bethlehem and in all that region who were two years old or under, according to the time which he had ascertained from the wise men." That is the most chilling verse in the Bible. The slaughter of the innocents, we call it, and we have seen it again and again and again, power born of fear, fear sustained by power.

(b) Herod saw who Jesus was—that was the great manifestation—not a little babe some few days old; not some idealized, spiritualized, sentimentalized symbol of nice and good things; not some platitude in diapers. He saw Jesus as the only rival worth taking seriously in a world of pretenders, usurpers, hustlers, and fakes. He saw God and recognized as the shrewd man that he was that it was either Herod or God: it could not be both. Make your choice, take your mark, now is the moment, Herod or God.

IV. The kings came and worshiped at the manger. They, our ancestors and our gentile representatives, saw the holy child in behalf of the whole world over which he will reign: this is no provincial king, no tribal deity. They saw and worshiped.

(a) But Herod, who did not worship and did not see, heard and understood, and his rivalry we all know as our own. What Herod would have destroyed with blood and intrigue, we too would attempt to destroy by trivia and sentiment and indifference. Death by good taste and warm feeling is still as deadly as death by the sword, make no mistake. This is why the reality of Christmas is in a Christ who cannot be known simply by the wisdom of this world, for the wise men did not really know what they saw. This is why the reality of Christmas is a Christ who cannot be overthrown by the ruthless exercise of power, for ruthless, ruthless Herod is dead, but Christ yet lives. This is why the reality of Christmas cannot be smothered even by the trivial and the sentimental, for at the heart of that story is truth made tangible, not symbolic but real. God made flesh for us that we might be made divine for God.

(b) The rivalry still goes on, does it not? The matter has not been settled; the world is not for an instant decided for Christ. Wise men still seek him out, still worship, and still do not know what it is that they see. The powerful still resist and oppress, the meek still hope for him, and all of us wonder how we can manage in this old dispensation. The circumstances have not and will not change. Christ will not come to conquer us. He will not invade and take us by force or by stealth. He will not say, "Enlist in my army, you are mine"; that would be far too easy and no real victory. When we will have won the battle, it will be the battle to see him as he is and to receive him as our own. Only then, only in that moment that is yet to be for all of us, only then shall the church militant, the fighting church, become the church triumphant, the church at peace, the church at rest in Christ.—Peter J. Gomes

Illustrations

THE INCONVENIENCE OF CHILDREN.   Our Gospel reading from Matthew recounts the flight of the holy family into Egypt. Herod wants to destroy the child. The rearing of children is never without consequences—at times, even life-threatening consequences. Children can be inconvenient and considered a drain on our personal and national resources ("another mouth to feed" mentality). However, faith counsels another way. In the words of Father James T. Burtchaell, C.S.C., children make us cut the bread thinner, but love is cut thicker. Children enrich, nurture, mature, and enlarge mutual love. Life would have been easier, on the natural level, for Mary and Joseph (all the rumors would have never even started) without Jesus. But without Jesus, we would never have sung their praises. Without Jesus, the holy family would have been neither holy nor family.—William F. Maestri

BORN IN THE GRAVE.   In the Nuremburg War-Crime Trials a witness appeared who had lived for a time in a graveyard in Wilna, Poland. It was the only place he—and many others—could live, when in hiding after they had escaped the gas chamber. During this time he wrote poetry, and one of the poems was a description of a birth. In a grave nearby a young woman gave birth to a boy. The eighty-year-old gravedigger, wrapped in a linen shroud, assisted. When the newborn child uttered his first cry, the old man prayed: "Great God, hast Thou finally sent the Messiah to us? For who else than the Messiah Himself can be born in a grave?" But after three days the poet saw the child sucking his mother's tears because she had no milk for him.—Paul Tillich

Sermon Suggestions

HOPE FULFILLED.   TEXT: Jer. 31:7–14. (1) It is preceded by prayer, verse 7. (2) It is accomplished in God's providence, verses 8–11. (3) It is the occasion of great rejoicing, verses 12–14.

THE BLESSINGS OF CHRIST.   TEXT: Eph. 1:3–6, 15–18. (1) The blessings given, verses 3–6. (2) The blessings received, verses 15–18.

Worship Aids

CALL TO WORSHIP   TEXT: Rev. 1:8. I am Alpha and Omega, the beginning and the ending, saith the Lord, which is, and which was, and which is to come, the Almighty.

INVOCATION.   Lord, open us to the freshness of this new year with all its potential. May we worship and serve faithfully, making of our lives a gift of thy love to others. In the name of Jesus, who was in the beginning and will be in the end.—E. Lee Phillips

OFFERTORY SENTENCE.   "No servant can be the slave of two masters; for either he will hate the first and love the second, or he will be devoted to the first and think nothing of the second. You cannot serve God and Money" (Matt. 6:24, NEB).

OFFERTORY PRAYER.   O Lord, thou who of old art the same and forever true, bless these gifts we bring in the newness of this year and use them to share that love that is timeless, through the Christ of the ages.—E. Lee Phillips

PRAYER.   Merciful and gracious God, you are the fountain of all mercy and blessing, and you have opened the hand of your mercy to fill us with blessings and the sweet effects of your loving-kindness. You feed us like a shepherd; you love us as a friend; you think of us without ceasing, as a careful mother of her helpless baby; and you are more than merciful to all who reverence you. As you have spread your hand upon us for a covering, so also enlarge our hearts with thankfulness. Let your gracious favors and loving-kindness endure forever and ever upon your servants, and grant that what you have sown in mercy may spring up in duty. Let your grace so strengthen our purposes that we may avoid sin and walk in the paths of your commandments, so that we, living here to the glory of your name, may at last enter into the glory of our

Lord, to spend a whole eternity in giving praise to your glorious name.—Adapted from Jeremy Taylor

LECTIONARY MESSAGE

The Dawn of a New Day
TEXT: Matt. 3:13–17

What a strange way to start a messianic ministry! Why would the sinless Son of God voluntarily undergo a Baptism of repentance for the remission of sins? The Scriptures had pictured the Messiah moving in regal splendor to his coronation in Jerusalem, not submitting to an obscure reformer in the waters of Jordan.

I. *The call to commitment (vv. 13–15).* In John, the voice of prophecy silent for centuries announced the long-awaited day of the Lord. By responding to John's call, Jesus affirmed his passionate conviction that the kingdom of God was about to come (v. 2). Through Baptism we dramatize the expectation that life itself can be transformed.

John viewed the impending change in terms of fiery catastrophe and thus wanted his messiah to be an apocalyptic storm trooper. In like manner, we often seek a savior who can solve all our problems by divine fiat rather than one who identifies with our deepest predicament.

In overcoming John's reluctance to baptize him, Jesus insisted that this broken world will be "made right" only as we show people how to change. Jesus' Baptism was a scandal by which he made our burdens his burdens and our shame his shame. For us, Baptism is not a "work" done to please God but is a "gift" from him who repents and confesses *with* us and *for* us as a sheer act of grace.

II. *The crossing over Jordan (v. 16).* In coming up out of the water, Jesus left the wilderness behind and entered the Promised Land of fulfillment. For us, Baptism is the boundary between two worlds, a decisive Rubicon to be crossed, a river of no return that provides passage into the new age of the Messiah.

In this act of obedience to his mission, Jesus experienced a direct revelation from God. This explains why his teaching ministry was based, not on ancient tradition or on scribal authority, but on his personal communion with the Father.

The descending of the Spirit like a dove does not mean that Jesus had never before experienced God's Spirit in his life. Rather, he was now equipped to use the power of the Spirit in his ministry to others.

III. *The consecration of the Servant-King (v. 17).* Although Jesus was in direct communication with God, the divine message that he heard came from two passages of Scripture. This suggests that we can be in personal contact with God when we meditate on passages that declare his will for our lives.

The first quotation, from Ps. 2:7, was the coronation formula of the Davidic King, authorizing Jesus to rule in human hearts as God's earthly viceroy. This regal status points to the total claim he has the right to assert in our lives.

The second quotation, from Isa. 42:1, was the ordination formula of the Suffering Servant, which commissions Jesus to reign by renouncing self. His only scepter was a selfless love; his only crown was cruel thorns; his only throne was a rugged cross. To accept such a sovereign is to reject every claim to human greatness (see Matt. 20:26).—William E. Hull

SUNDAY: JANUARY FOURTEENTH

SERVICE OF WORSHIP

Sermon: Our Christian Witness
TEXT: John 1:37–51

I. *Through a simple invitation.*

(a) Our first responsibility. Faith is a family affair. Religion and religious concern should not end with the members of one's own family. But they certainly ought to begin there. Those closest to us by blood ties are the ones to whom we should witness first. If a man's faith can help him to overcome his exaggerated and callous rebellion against his parents, his rivalry with brothers and sisters, his careless disregard of the needs of his mate, or his neglect of his children, then these members of his own family will take notice and most likely will want for themselves what has made him a better person.

Andrew took the most natural and reasonable course. When he found the Christ, he went to get his brother, Simon. "And he brought him to Jesus."

If our faith will not commend itself to the members of our own family, something serious may be wrong. Have we become more reasonable, more responsible, more considerate of others? Or have we become harder to live with, more argumentative, more intolerant? To be sure, the most devout Christian person cannot in some cases win to Christ some members of his own family. And often failure may not at all be his own fault. But if our religious experience makes us imagine ourselves superior and possessed of the right to lord it over others, we will fail—and should. We can hardly expect to win anyone to the Christ we say has made us what we are.

(b) The simplicity of our Christian witness. It seems that Christianity had its most rapid growth in the early days and years of the church. Why? Not because the first Christians were brilliant theologians; not because they were skilled debaters; not because they had impressive religious upbringing. Christianity spread like wildfire because plain people were willing to tell about what the Lord had done for them. It has always been so. The apostles, the prophets, the evangelists, and the teachers could not carry the load of proclaiming the gospel by themselves. Without the help of all sorts of ordinary people, the gospel would have foundered in Jerusalem.

Andrew simply said to his brother, Simon, "We have found the Messiah" (v. 41, RSV). Then he brought him to Jesus. What happened after that was the work of Jesus. This is what makes the real difference: Jesus Christ does what we cannot do. It is comparatively easy to bring someone to Jesus. But Jesus it is who does the "impossible" job of effecting the conver-

sion of that person. Yet a simple testimony, a faithful Christian life, and a sincere concern are in most cases all that is necessary to put someone in the very presence of Jesus. Our glibness, our formal faith, and our phony interest leave people cold when they see Jesus nowhere about.

(c) Far-reaching consequences of our witness. We never know what the end result of bringing someone to Jesus will be. Andrew had no idea of the future influence of his brother, Simon. But Jesus knew. " 'You are Simon, the son of John. Your name will be Cephas.' (This is the same as Peter, and means 'Rock')" (v. 42, TEV).

Simon Peter gave the Lord considerable trouble from time to time. He angrily argued when Jesus shared with the disciples the fact that he must be arrested and die. When Jesus left him to stand watch at the garden of Gethsemane, he went to sleep. He impatiently cut off the ear of the servant of the high priest when Jesus was arrested. He denied Jesus when asked if he was not one of his disciples. He gave up in disillusionment when Jesus was crucified. Quite a while later, he got into a sharp and hurtful dispute with the Apostle Paul.

Still, Jesus called him "Rock." Why? Because he knew this: that even though Simon Peter often said and did the wrong thing, in his inmost self he kept an unshakable loyalty to his Lord. During the trial of Jesus he hovered nearby; the terror of the moment did indeed put shameful words of frantic denial on his lips, but loyalty kept him from running away. He hung on, close enough to read an unspoken reproach in the eyes of Jesus, turned questioningly in his direction. His awkward mistakes were balanced by an eager devotion. When people turned away from Jesus in droves, Peter stayed. Jesus asked the twelve, " 'And you—would you like to leave also?' " Impulsively, but with wholehearted love, Peter answered for all, " 'Lord, to whom would we go? You have the words that give eternal life' " (John 6:67–68, TEV). Before the thousands who had come to Jerusalem to celebrate the Feast of Weeks (Pentecost) it was Peter who stood up to declare the crucified and risen Jesus as the Christ. In response to Peter's sermon, over three thousand souls came to faith and baptism.

Does not Andrew, who with simple brotherly concern brought Simon Peter to Jesus, deserve to share the honor accorded his brother?

II. *Through a difficult discussion.*

(a) The scope of our witness. We do not know where our discipleship will lead us or the kind of people to whom our Lord will lead us to witness. Jesus says, "Come with me." Following that command can take us anywhere and lead us to anybody. Discipleship is open-ended. Our witness belongs with Jesus, and we may expect to find him among the strangers, the poor, the physically and mentally ill. Among these people he worked during the "days of his flesh," and here he has been found ever since. But his interest encompassed others, too. He had a deep concern for all.

Among these was a class of people whom we might quickly write off today. They make us nervous. They tend to shake our simple faith. We do not know how to answer their questions or how to deal understandingly with them. We may even "curse" them by regarding them as blasphemous or hopeless. So we ignore them. Jesus did nothing of the kind. He made a special trip to deal with a man who had a skeptical turn of mind, and took Philip along. Nathanael was a skeptic, and Jesus was deeply interested in him. Philip would seek him and witness to him; then he would come to Jesus.

(b) A reasonable witness. Philip based his witness to Nathanael not only on his personal experience and belief. He also appealed to the Scriptures, to the prophetic testimonies in the Law and the Prophets. Some people need more than just our word and our assurance that what we say is true. They want our testimony backed up with facts and reasons. And that is not asking too much. Why should people be expected to make a decision as important as the decision to be a Christian if they have to make it in an intellectual vacuum? Peter, whose faith apparently came

so easily, said, "Be ready at all times to answer anyone who asks you to explain the hope you have in you. But do it with gentleness and respect" (1 Pet. 3:15–16, TEV).

(c) Dealing with doubt. We should not be surprised at anything that people might say when we bear our Christian witness. Experience could disillusion us, but it should make us shockproof. Nathanael sneered, "Can there any good thing come out of Nazareth?" The fact that this could have been a byword did not make it any easier to listen to. The question could have been the beginning of a long, bitter, and fruitless argument. Some people do seem more intent on winning a debate than on winning a person. Philip was willing to let Nathanael find the answer for himself. He said, "Come and see."

More and more, we will be required to witness to people who raise all sorts of questions about the Christian faith. Perhaps some of us will have to look to friends better equipped than we ourselves to deal with some of these questions. But there is always something helpful that each of us can do. In medicine, when general practitioners are not trained to treat a particular disease intensively they refer the patient to a specialist. Sometimes, this may be the best thing that we can do. However, we should not push off our own responsibility onto someone else. It should be clear to us that the help of another is needed.

(d) The witness of the Spirit. In all that happened among Jesus, Philip, and Nathanael, the Spirit of God was at work. Deep called unto deep; the depth of the divine resources answered the depth of human need. Jesus was aware of Nathanael and his need while Nathanael was still "under the fig tree," that is, while Nathanael was at home. Philip simply followed up something that God's Spirit had already begun. However easy or however difficult a conversion may be, results are, in the last analysis, the work of God. God is already at work when the first act or word of human concern takes place.

When the Apostle Paul looked at the far-flung Roman Empire, he saw a formidable giant. Rome was indeed powerful. Rome had crucified Jesus. Rome had put

Paul himself in prison. Not a moment of his life could he live outside the shadow of Rome. Still he could say, "I have complete confidence in the gospel: it is God's power to save all who believe, first the Jews and also the Gentiles" (Rom. 1:16, TEV). Rome might be powerful, but God was more powerful. Today, our problems are great, but God is greater. God's concern precedes our concern; God is at work even before we begin to witness. God has given us something important to do, but the real burden of our task is upon him whose Spirit cultivates the soil and nurtures the seed of our testimony.

(e) Finding certitude. We can never obtain enough Bible or theological knowledge to be able to answer all the questions of those to whom we witness, to say nothing of the questions that perplex us personally. God has not made it possible for us to surround him with our mind. But he can and will give us an inner assurance that is better than slick answers and foolproof systems. The man who had sneered, "Can there any good thing come out of Nazareth?" could later say, "Thou art the Son of God; thou art the king of Israel." When Philip said, "Come and see," he beckoned Nathanael along a path that led to the only saving knowledge.—James W. Cox

Illustrations

FIRSTHAND KNOWLEDGE.   Our weakness and incompetence in the church is often due to the secondhand character of our religious faith. Pastor and people live on a traditional or a hearsay religion. Like the Jewish exorcists in Ephesus, too many of us are saying, "We adjure you by Jesus whom Paul preacheth." There is an absence of firsthand knowledge, of personal fellowship, in our witness. The source of our hearsay faith may be excellent; our tradition, our heritage, our education and teachers may be of the best. One could scarcely improve upon St. Paul, but Christ's power is not transmissible to any unpossessed of direct union with him in whom we can do all things.—Henry Sloan Coffin

THE HERESY OF ORTHODOXY.   Orthodoxy will . . . become heresy if the orthodoxy test is applied to methodology. Some methods of Christian life and growth and the fact that those methods have been generally accepted and almost universally utilized by the churches help to explain the growth, vitality, and strength of some groups today. Unity of methods has been particularly evident in the area of evangelism, in educational organizations and programs, and, to a lesser degree, in financial policies.

While there is strength in uniformity, there is real danger if churches seek to maintain that uniformity by pressure or ostracism. How tragic it will be if there is developed an orthodoxy of methods and individuals and churches are considered heretical if they do not conform to the generally accepted pattern.—T. B. Maston

Sermon Suggestions

GOD'S TRUE SERVANT.   TEXT: Isa. 42: 1–9. (1) A champion of justice. (2) An example of patience. (3) An instrument of God. (4) A prototype of Jesus Christ.

CHRIST FOR ALL.   TEXT: Acts 10:34–43. (1) His program, verses 34–36. (2) His works, verses 37–38. (3) His witnesses, verses 39–41. (4) His purpose, verses 42–43.

Worship Aids

CALL TO WORSHIP.   "O send out thy light and thy truth: let them lead me; let them bring me unto thy holy hill, and to thy tabernacles" (Ps. 43:3).

INVOCATION.   Thou mighty One, whose power moves in the changing of the seasons and in the circuit of the stars, be no less a lord to us, and let thy gentle strength live in our souls, that all their times, their coming and going, shall be in the path of thy will and true to thy wisdom.—Samuel H. Miller

OFFERTORY SENTENCE.   "Take ye from among you an offering unto the Lord: whosoever is of a willing heart, let him bring it, an offering of the Lord" (Exod. 35:5).

OFFERTORY PRAYER. Loving Lord, let our gratitude for those who nurtured us in the faith be reflected in this offering, that it might nurture others in the daily walk with Jesus Christ.—E. Lee Phillips

PRAYER. Most merciful God, Power of our souls, Healer of our diseases, unto thee would we come. Amid the haste and hurry of common life thou seemest to pass away. Amid the cares and anxieties and all the turmoil of our inner mind we cannot hear thee knocking at the door, seeking to enter and to bless. But now would we quiet our souls before thee; now would we feel ourselves enwrapped with thy unspeakable presence and know thee as the joy and strength of life. Quicken thou our faith and hope and aspiration that we may be upborne above all unrest and irritation and be made sharers in thy perfect calm. Lengthen these moments of prayer, we beseech thee, until our whole life becomes a continual aspiration after thee.—Samuel McComb.

LECTIONARY MESSAGE

Witness in the Wilderness
TEXT: John 1:29–34

John the Baptist functioned like a Shakespearean herald who appeared to announce that the drama was about to begin, then disappeared as the main actor took center stage. His witness to Jesus was based, not on earthly kinship that he might have claimed, but on a divine revelation regarding the person and work of Christ (v. 31).

I. *The removal of sin (v. 29).* The image of Jesus as the Lamb of God was shaped by three great Old Testament tributaries: (a) the priestly use of the lamb in the daily sacrifice and at the Passover celebration (see 1 Cor. 5:7; 1 Pet. 1:19); (b) the prophetic use of the lamb as a symbol of the Suffering Servant (see Isa. 53; Acts 8:32–35); and (c) the kingly use of the apocalyptic ram as leader of the flock of God (see Rev. 5:6, 12; 7:14, 17; 17:14; 22:1, 3).

None of these Old Testament strands claimed that the lamb actually bore away the sin of the world. Jesus went far beyond inherited imagery in meeting our need to be free of the crushing burden of guilt. As we partake of the "blood of the lamb" in the Lord's Supper, we experience the forgiveness of sin (see Matt. 26:28).

II. *The ranking of superiority (v. 30).* John the Baptist was older than Jesus, he began his ministry before Jesus, and he baptized Jesus. In Jewish practice, this would make John the master and Jesus the disciple. But John realized that Jesus was the preexistent Son of God and so was "before" him in an eternal sense (see v. 15), although "after" him in a historical sense. Therefore, he ranked Jesus as his superior rather than as his inferior (see John 3:30).

We still tend to subordinate the pupil to the teacher, the follower to the leader, the younger to the older. Elaborate status systems determine prestige in the social "pecking order," e.g., who takes precedence in seating arrangements at a formal banquet. Where does Jesus stand in our hierarchy of rankings? Have we, like John, learned to put him ahead of all others?

III. *The remaining of the spirit (vv. 31–34).* The hidden Messiah was revealed at Jesus' baptism when the Holy Spirit came down from heaven as realistically as a bird descending out of the skies to light on Jesus' shoulder. Old Testament prophets had occasionally been seized by the Spirit, but this time the Spirit "remained" on Jesus. That enabled him to give the Spirit "without measure" to others (3:34) and to promise his disciples that the Spirit would be with them "for ever" (14:16).

This threefold witness of John defines a savior able to meet our deepest needs: (a) in relation to the past, we need to be free from the burden of our sins; (b) in relation to the present, we need a master who is preeminent over every competing claim; (c) in relation to the future, we need an indwelling spiritual presence that will not desert us no matter what may come.

Those who allow Jesus to function in this fashion as an all-sufficient savior join with John in declaring him to be the Son of God (v. 34).—William E. Hull

SUNDAY: JANUARY TWENTY-FIRST

SERVICE OF WORSHIP

Sermon: An Audience of One Man

TEXT: Dan. 3:16–28

By and large, our overall ministry to others may be reduced periodically to one person, and our ministries administered one at a time. This story out of the third chapter of Daniel hangs on this simple truth.

The story, simply stated, is this. It was reported to King Nebuchadnezzar that three Jews—Shadrach, Meshach, Abednego—had ignored a decree demanding that at a given time all men should fall down and worship a golden image that the king had set up. Nebuchadnezzar confronted the three men with the report, along with the threat of the fiery furnace for their disobedience. The men did not deny the report, neither did they yield to the decree. And the threat was carried out. The fact that they were later miraculously delivered may not be the most important part of the story. The climax, it seems to me, comes at the point where these men say, "Be it known unto thee, O king, that we will not serve thy gods, nor worship the golden image which thou hast set up." Let me tell you what this audience of one man witnessed.

I. *Nebuchadnezzar saw faith in action.*

(a) The account, first, speaks of a faith that commands positive action. Faith that is not acted upon is not really faith. There also comes a time when the most splendid declaration of faith is made not with the lips at all but with one's life. It is best that a man keep his mouth closed regarding his faith unless he is very sure that he will act upon what he says he believes.

(b) When the time came for these three men to declare themselves, they were not asked, What do you believe? They were being asked, rather, in a most concrete, realistic, though inaudible way, Does your faith command your loyalty? Does your faith elicit your absolute devotion? Does your faith have any real conviction behind it?

(c) The only positive thing these men actually said was something such as, "If it be, our God is able to deliver us." Their fate might be death; it might be deliverance. They would leave that with God. But in either case, their faith remained the same; they would not alter their stand. And at the center of their faith stood these words: "But if not." It is here that faith declares itself. They could not know precisely what God's will was regarding the king's threat. But they did know God's will regarding their action. "But if not, be it known unto thee, O king, that we will not serve thy gods, nor worship the golden image which thou hast set up."

II. *Nebuchadnezzar saw faith with conviction.*

(a) We will miss the point of this whole story if we see in it only an example of "life in scorn of consequences." Far deeper is this thought: There are times when I must act in accordance with a great inner conviction, not because I am courageously unafraid of facing the consequences to me personally (actually, I may be scared stiff!), but because I cannot bear the thought of what my insincerity will do to that one person before whom I stand!

(b) If they had had escape only in mind, they might well have reasoned among themselves that bowing before a golden image could easily be done with mental reservations. "We can do what the king says and still believe in our God . . . anything to satisfy his whims; it really does not matter that much." But they could not and would not underestimate the importance of that one man, that "congregation of one person."

(c) This is precisely where we stand. The most far-reaching influence of our daily routine may well lie in the framework of what we are and what we do as well as what we say in the presence of one person. Under such circumstances, how can we get across to an unbelieving mind the validity of our faith? And the answer is—by letting him see that we mean business!

III. *Nebuchadnezzar saw faith that made a difference.*

(a) What difference, really, can one person make? What does it really matter what we are to one single individual, when with or without that one person we are surrounded by an admiring host of others? How important is one man . . . or even three men? Well, listen: "O king, there are certain Jews that will not bow down and worship your gods." How many? Three in number, that's all. Only three? But these men were not playing church that day. They meant business with God.

(b) I am not convinced that the king was persuaded to change his infamous decree simply upon seeing these three men delivered from his fiery furnace. My faith in the integrity and faithfulness of God convinces me to believe that even if these three men had perished in the flames, the king would still have had invincible evidence of the reality of God by the convincing integrity of these men's undaunted faith. And because of them, the king proclaimed these memorable words that gloriously affected a host of others: "Blessed be the God of Shadrach, Meshach, and Abednego, who hath sent his angel and delivered his servants that trusted in him and have changed the king's word and yielded their bodies that they might not serve nor worship any god, except their own God." That's how important one man is and can be!

IV. *A waiting audience of one man.* I tell you, dear friends, there's somebody out there waiting just for you, someone who needs you very much. And you know, it may be that whenever that one person sees the depth of your faith and the sincerity of that faith manifesting itself under strange and adverse circumstances, he will be greatly moved by the Spirit of God acting through you. And as a result of that one person's life, who knows how many, many others will be touched!—Othar O. Smith

Illustrations

PERSONAL EVANGELISM.   Hand-picked fruit is often the best. Many have been "won by one." John Bunyan, author of *Pilgrim's Progress,* came to Christ by overhearing three women talking intimately with joy of the things of Christ. William Carey, the father of modern missions, was won to Christ by the importunity of a fellow apprentice shoe cobbler by the name of John Warr.—Benjamin P. Browne

WORTH OF THE INDIVIDUAL.   During the days of the blitz on London a delightful story went the rounds. After a particularly devastating raid, one of the poor, little East End streets was almost completely obliterated, but at one end several houses, almost miraculously, were spared. Next day a warden called to see how many were still living there. He knocked at the door, which hung on two pieces of carpet ingeniously arranged to form a hinge. A woman pushed it aside.

"Morning," said he.

"Morning," she replied.

"Tell me," he went on, "how many of you are living here now?"

"Well," she said, "there's Bill, and 'Arry, and Lizzie; there's George—that's me husband—then there's Joe and Jimmie, Sarah and. . . ."

" 'Ere, half-a-mo," said the warden, cutting her short, "I don't want names; I only want numbers."

There was an ominous silence. The woman looked him straight in the eyes; she put her hands on her hips, and when a woman does that one can look out for trouble. "They ain't got numbers," said she. "They've all got names!"—John Trevor Davies

Sermon Suggestions

PROMISE AND FULFILLMENT.   TEXT: Isa. 49:1–7. Like the Lord's "Servant," Christ and his church (1) are especially chosen by God, (2) are God's secret weapon in the world, (3) are at last recognized and honored because of God's faithfulness.

WHAT MAKES YOUR RELIGIOUS LEADERS THANKFUL.   TEXT: 1 Cor. 1:1–9. (1) Your experience of the grace of God in Christ Jesus. (2) Your expression of this grace—in a fullness of knowledge; in a completeness of ability to put this understanding into words; in the variety of spiritual gifts among Christ's people. (3) Your promise as believers, sustained to the end by God's faithfulness.

Worship Aids

CALL TO WORSHIP. "There were great voices in heaven, saying, The kingdoms of this world are become the kingdoms of our Lord, and of his Christ; and he shall reign forever and ever" (Rev. 11: 15).

INVOCATION. O God, who hast given us eyes to see and ears to hear and minds to understand, do so deal with us in this hour of worship, that what we see and hear and think might revert to the glory of God and the upbuilding of that kingdom that knows no end, whose Creator we worship and adore.—E. Lee Phillips

OFFERTORY SENTENCE. "And it is in God's power to provide you richly with every good gift; thus you will have ample means in yourselves to meet each and every situation, with enough to spare for every good cause" (1 Cor. 9:8, NEB).

OFFERTORY PRAYER. Gracious Lord, you have given us much, though it may seem little. Grant that we may give with love what we may consider little, praying that you will multiply it as the loaves and fishes for your glory and the blessing of others.

PRAYER. O most merciful Lord, grant to us your grace, that it may be with us and labor with us and persevere with us even to the end. Grant that we may always desire and will that which is most acceptable and dear to you. Let your will be ours and our wills follow yours in everything and agree perfectly with it. Grant to us, above all that can be desired, to rest in you and to have our hearts at peace in you. You are the true peace of the heart and its only rest; outside of you all things are hard and restless.—Adapted from Thomas à Kempis

LECTIONARY MESSAGE

A Gospel for the Forgotten
TEXT: Matt. 4:12–23

We like to ensure the success of a venture by attempting it at the best possible place. By contrast, Jesus launched his ministry at the worst possible time, when his forerunner, John the Baptist, had been arrested, and in the worst possible place, Galilee on the northern edge of Palestine (v. 12). In so doing, he demonstrated that his coming was a sheer act of grace for those who expected it least.

I. *Beginning in "the region of death" (vv. 12–17).* Galilee was the contraction of a Hebrew phrase meaning "circle of the Gentiles." It referred to the pagan periphery of the Holy Land, despised by the pious as a place of darkness since the days of Isaiah (9:1–2). In this shadowed region, rather than at Mount Zion in Jerusalem, Jesus began his work.

By announcing that the kingdom of heaven was "at hand" *there,* in lowly Galilee, Jesus was proclaiming the nearness of God in the most unpromising circumstances imaginable. We like to look for God at "holy places," but the good news is that he is willing to establish his throne in a secular wilderness bereft of hope.

II. *Unlikely people—unlimited possibilities (vv. 18–23).* Fishermen were not noted for their piety in ancient Galilee, which means that Jesus not only started in the wrong place but also with the wrong people. Yet the initiative was entirely his own. He interrupted their daily toil, laid total claim on their commonplace lives, then promised them a new future of incalculable influence on others.

Jesus dared to make himself the key to this unlikely venture. Instead of bidding them to follow the Torah of the rabbis or the ritual of the priests, he invited them to apprentice themselves to his unfolding ministry. They were to lash their lives to his life (J. H. Jowett) and henceforth become Christ-bound men (E. Kaesemann). To this day, Christianity "is neither a dogmatic system nor an ethical code, but a Person and a Life" (J. B. Lightfoot).

III. *A universal offer (v. 23)*. What boundless scope Jesus achieved in those narrow confines. The universality of the gospel is hinted in the word *all* (see 28:19–20): Jesus went to *all* kinds of people in *all* kinds of places to meet *all* kinds of needs. We usually think of missions in geographical terms, as if defined by the distance traveled. But one can go to the ends of the earth and still be provincial in attitude or selective in outreach. By contrast, Jesus stayed close to home and yet attempted to touch every life within his reach.

His method was threefold: (1) By teaching he anchored his message in the Scriptures, seeking to show how it fulfilled the greatest hopes of the past. (2) By preaching, he sought to generate a "revolution of rising expectations" that God's future kingdom could at last be established on earth. (3) By healing every disease he responded with compassion to the present plight of his hearers who were afflicted in body, mind, and heart (v. 24). No wonder great crowds came from every direction to follow him (v. 25). The world is still eagerly looking for someone who cares like that!—William E. Hull

SUNDAY: JANUARY TWENTY-EIGHTH

SERVICE OF WORSHIP

Sermon: Personality and Faith: Three Holy Women
TEXTS: 1 Sam. 1:1–8; Luke 2:36–40

The history of our faith is the history of those who are witnesses to the light, who have waited for, hoped for, worked for, and seen the light, and by whose vision our own is enlightened. Light itself is an abstraction: it only makes sense when we are enabled to see by it, and, when we see, we see others who, too, are witnesses to the light and become themselves sources of that light. Such are the "three holy women" of which we speak today, the three women of our two lessons who in their own and differing ways testify to the light of the world on this Feast of Lights.

I. The first of these you will recognize from the Old Testament lesson as Hannah, the mother of the great judge of Israel, Samuel. We hear of her in the First Book of Samuel, caught up in the fervent prayer for a child, annoying the priests in the temple by her incessant ceaseless, wordless prayer, an anticipation of the importunate widow in the New Testament story a few thousand years and a few hundred pages later.

(a) She prays and she prays and she prays, this Hannah, and then she is given the son for whom she prays, and, in a moment of consecration not unlike that of her descendant sister Mary, she offers the child up in these words to the high priest: "For this child I prayed; and the Lord has granted me my petition which I made to him. Therefore I have lent him to the Lord: as long as he lives he is lent to the Lord." Then in chapter 2, immediately after this, comes Hannah's song, again, not unlike that song of Mary, the Magnificat, in which she sings of the lovingkindness of the Lord and of the righteousness that is to come: Hannah celebrates the future by the birth of this child whom she has lent to the Lord.

(b) And we know that one child, that child Samuel, the greatest judge of Israel, the fierce and mighty prophet of God; God's gift to his mother, lent by his mother back to God, forever, a strange and mighty transaction. Hannah becomes the means whereby God chooses to shine a light into the darkened world: she is the bearer of that light; she gives witness to it.

II. The second holy woman is she, of course, around whom this feast day is celebrated and the purification is the first and oldest of the feast days associated with the Virgin Mary. Now most of us, if we tell the truth, have a hard time dealing with Mary, filled as we are either with Catholic piety or Protestant ignorance on this subject.

(a) If half of what the church teaches is so, and half of what feminism has taught us is helpful, then we have in the person spirit of her whom we call Ever Blessed and Virgin, in this Mary, the supreme and most available example of light shining in the world, God's ingenious use of his Creation for his creatures. Unlike Hannah, Mary did not pray for a son. And unlike Hannah's story, it is God who lends to Mary and not the other way around. We hear little from her throughout the Gospel: we do not know her feelings at the deepest moments of her joy and sadness, feelings at least conveyed in the vehicle of words. We know her magnificent song, we sense her sorrow at the cross, her grief at the tomb, but, for the most part, hers is a silent though eloquent witness across the pages of the Scripture, but is there anyone who speaks more whom we think we know better?

(b) Could it be that she is holy, not because she is so different from us all, but rather because she is so representative of us all, as we are fundamentally and could be ultimately? Is not the suffering Mary, the weeping Mary, the rejoicing Mary, the quiet and pondering Mary, the slightly confused Mary, and the willingly obedient Mary, that Mary who must carry on with incomplete information with imperfect understanding in an impure world, is not this what we are called upon to do, not by choice, but by the arbitrary demands of circumstances in which we frequently find ourselves?

(c) To recover the mystery of the Mother of our Lord is in some sense to recover her humanity, his, and our own: no abstraction, she, but rather the personality of faith made real in flesh and blood, as only the bonds of motherhood and childhood can.

III. The third holy woman of this day and our lessons is, of course, the prophetess Anna, the daughter of Phanuel of the tribe of Asher, she who was of a great age and spent all her days, according to the text, "worshiping and fasting in the Temple day and night."

(a) Anna did not pray for a child, nor was she given one: she prayed for the wellbeing of God and the well-being of the people of God, and when she saw the young child and his mother at the ritual of purification she was moved enough to believe that she had seen what she had been praying for. She had literally lived to see the light.

(b) She is hardly the stuff of which heroines are made, even then, not to mention now, simply a pious footnote in the New Testament text, and yet she too was there, a silent witness, a living testimony that there was something worth waiting for, that there was something worth praying for. "And coming up in that very hour," the text says, "she gave thanks to God and spoke of him to all who were looking for the redemption of Jerusalem." She saw the light, and she spread it, and she talked about it day in and day out. That for which she had been seeking, she now saw and shared.

IV. Hannah, Mary, Anna: none of these women cast for themselves in their time a large role in the affairs of the world. Ambition as we know it was unknown to them. And yet the church continues to tell the story, their story, and the older we get the more we begin to realize that the story of redemption, theirs and ours, cannot be told without them. In short, these holy women represent that range of qualities with which God has equipped us all that we, with them, might in some measure be living vessels of faith in our place and in our time responding to our needs and opportunities with the graces and gifts given to us. To be holy is not to be perfect, to be holy is to be a bearer of light in the darkness, not that we may be seen, but that we and others may see and that we may see him who is the light of the world, even Jesus Christ our Lord.—Peter J. Gomes

Illustrations

HANNAH'S SORROW.   She staggered with her sorrow; she fell against the altar; she did not know what she was saying or where she was going; she actually forgot her own name and did not answer when her name was spoken. Aaron himself would have been provoked to say to Hannah to put away her wine. Hannah was a saint; but she was a woman-saint, and hence her reeling heart. Hannah was able to command herself sometimes for weeks and months after she had been again at Shiloh. But something would happen in the household that would soon show that even Shiloh had made Hannah nothing better but rather worse; for her chastised and well-bridled tongue would all of a sudden break out again till, had it been in Greece or in Rome, she would have been called a fury rather than a woman and a saint. The milk of human kindness, not to say of womanhood, would suddenly turn to burning brimstone in Hannah's bosom. For days and weeks she would be able in the strength of the Shiloh meat to teach them their letters and to play with Peninnah's children better than if they had been Elkanah's and her own. She would toss them up in the air and make them light on their father's knee till he clean forgot his sin and his shame and his pain. But the very next moment Hannah was within an inch of dashing them against the stones. Elkanah's happiness through any other wife but herself, and his rapture over her adversary's child's delightful ways, made Hannah sometimes go away to her bed like a she-tiger to her den.—Alexander Whyte

A CALM AND TERRIBLE GLADNESS. The Magnificat is terrifying. If there are two things in the Bible which should make our blood run cold, it is one; the other is that phrase in Revelation, "the wrath of the Lamb." If there is not mildness in the Virgin Mother, if even the lamb, the helpless thing that bleats and has its throat cut, is not the symbol of the harmless, where shall we turn? There are no cursings here, no hatred, no self-righteousness. Instead there is mere statement. He has scattered the proud, cast down the mighty, sent the rich empty away. We have the treble voice, a girl's voice, announcing without sin that the sinful prayers of her ancestors do not remain entirely unheard, and doing this, not indeed with fierce exultation, yet a calm and terrible gladness.—C. S. Lewis

Sermon Suggestions

THREE GIFTS THE CHRIST BRINGS.   TEXT: Isa. 5:1–4 (1) Light. (2) Joy. (3) Victory.

DISSENTERS.   TEXT: 1 Cor. 1:10–17. (1) The real problem—competitive strife. (2) The potential solution—recognition of the power of self-denying unity given in Jesus Christ. (3) The urgency—"lest the cross of Christ be emptied of its power."

Worship Aids

CALL TO WORSHIP.   "They that wait upon the Lord shall renew their strength; they shall mount up with wings as eagles; they shall run and not be weary, and they shall walk and not faint" (Isa. 40:31).

INVOCATION.   Open our minds this day, O Lord, to thoughts of thee and thy purpose for us on this earth. Give us vision and courage to match our vision and humility to live by faith, our Maker and our All.

OFFERTORY SENTENCE.   "Now if you obey me fully and keep my covenant, then out of all nations you will be my treasured possession. Although the whole earth is mine, you will be for me a kingdom of priests and a holy nation" (Exod. 19:5–6a, NIV).

OFFERTORY PRAYER.   Lord, you have made us in Jesus Christ your special people, and there is work for us to do. Help us to be faithful in obedience and generous in love, so that your name may be honored among all people and all may be touched by your grace.

PRAYER.   Eternal God, we pray for those who love us and for those who, it may be, dislike us. Take from us any evil thing that hinders the flow of love from soul to soul. Pour upon us the spirit of brotherhood, in the strength of which we may bear each other's burdens, and cover with a mantle of charity our brother's weakness. If any are estranged from us, do thou pluck out of their hearts and ours any root of bitterness and unite us again in the bonds of mutual affection. If any are irritable or weak or nervous, give us a spirit of unwearied forbearance, that we may be to them a source of strength and poise and self-control. As we go among our fellows, may we ever manifest a patient temper, a kind and happy spirit, a love that beareth all things, endureth all things, believeth all things. These blessings we ask in the name of Jesus Christ thy Son our Lord.—Samuel McComb

LECTIONARY MESSAGE

The Keys of the Kingdom

TEXT: Matt. 5:1–12

The Beatitudes are not platitudes! Rather, they are a controversial guide to fulfillment that throws down the gauntlet to popular human values. Composed as a poetic hymn with two stanzas of four lines each, the first quatrain (vv. 3–6) describes the inward, personal relationship of kingdom disciples to God, while the second (vv. 7–10) describes their outward, social relationship to the world.

I. *Four paths to fulfillment (vv. 3–6).* Jesus first described the characteristics of those in whose lives God can reign as king:

(a) Absolute need (v. 3). Jesus embodied what it means to be "poor in spirit" (2 Cor. 8:9) in his utter dependence upon God to provide. Those who put their entire trust in God rather than in earthly treasure (see Matt. 6:19–21) are those who offer him empty hands and an open heart in which to reign (see 19:21–22).

(b) Ultimate concern (v. 4). This refers, not to the natural grief common to every person, but to that costly caring for God's cause that Jesus incarnated when he wept over Jerusalem (Luke 19:41). Those who are willing to "let their hearts be broken with the things that break the heart of God" are precisely those who will rejoice as he makes right the iniquities that others exploit.

(c) Complete submissions (v. 5). *Meek* does not mean "weak." Rather, the word was used of a "broken" horse or a "tame" pet, i.e., of strength harnessed and under control. Jesus was "meek" (11:29) in Gethsemane when he prayed "nevertheless, thy will be done" (26:39), Paul when he cried "this one thing I do" (Phil. 3:13).

God will entrust his earth to those who, unlike Adam, are willing to accept the disciplines and restrictions of so great a stewardship by putting him first (cf. 6:33).

(d) Urgent desire (v. 6). The truly hungry and thirsty will do anything to get food and drink. When we come to God with a passionate longing for salvation he will satisfy our deepest appetite. How much we miss simply because we do not desire it intensely enough (7:7–8)!

II. *The creativity of conflict (vv. 7–10).* The world says, Be rich, happy, self-confident, and satisfied. Jesus says, Be poor, grieving, submissive, and hungry! Here are two kingdoms in conflict, with the disciples caught in the middle!

(a) The merciful (v. 7) are those who show love to the loveless that they might lovely be. For Jesus, mercy was a daring determination to disregard human scruples by accepting those who can make no claim on us.

(b) The pure in heart (v. 8) are those who embrace sinners yet are not compromised by their sin. The word *pure* means "unmixed, unadulterated," a condition of the heart determined by inner intentions rather than by outward associations.

(c) The peacemakers (v. 9) are not "peacekeepers" but those who, like Jesus, mediate between hostile camps (Eph. 2:14). When we serve as agents of reconciliation (2 Cor. 5:18), we show our spiritual heredity as children of the "God of peace" (Heb. 13:20).

(d) The persecuted (v. 10) are not masochists or martyrs but those who provoke retaliation from evil because their lives challenge its dominance of the status quo. In a climactic conclusion (vv. 11–12), Jesus anticipates the paradox of the cross by asserting that true bliss belongs to those who live on that frontier where evil makes a final but futile stand against the triumphant kingdom of the Messiah.—William E. Hull

SUNDAY: FEBRUARY FOURTH

SERVICE OF WORSHIP

Sermon: The Higher Loyalty

TEXT: Acts 4:19

The torch of freedom in the hand of Lady Liberty is held high to all humankind. Here is strikingly symbolized America's high calling to be the friend of the weak, the downtrodden, the persecuted, the needy, the poor, the homeless, the "wretched refuse." Though founded on religious freedom, such idealism is the heritage of the Judeo-Christian faith that holds to such tenets as these: "The meek shall inherit the earth"—"Blessed are the poor in spirit"—"Blessed are the peacemakers. . . ."

I. With the renewing of our national pride may we realize that our high calling is not to police the world, for we, too, stand under the judgment of God, but to invest our great resources in life-giving ministries to the least of these our brothers and sisters.

(a) Part of what we are trying to say is that the call of freedom is always a call to responsibility. Freedom and responsibility are opposite sides of the same coin. As the Bible declares, "To whom much is given, of him is much required."

(b) We have a right to be proud as Americans—but we have a responsibility as Christians, as humans, to the rest of the world, and it is not to export violence, arms, but to care for the world—to love others to life and not condemn them to death—to love our neighbor as ourself—and the neighbor as Jesus taught so dramatically in the parable of the Good Samaritan can be anyone in need regardless of race, creed, color, or political persuasion.

II. The Scripture lesson illustrates the higher loyalty, which to forget and neglect is to miss our true destiny in the community of nations and in the history of the world.

(a) In the early church when Peter and John, two of its outstanding preachers, proclaimed the power of Christ even over disease and death, the religious leaders and other vested interests in the status quo became disturbed and had the two apostles arrested. They forbade them to speak any more in the name of Jesus. Peter and John were confronted with the conflict of loyalties. They did not want to be disobedient to the civil authorities who in the Jewish community were the same as the religious leaders, yet they believed: Christ is Lord. What should they do? Their decision lives on in those memorable words so courageously spoken by the Apostle Peter: "Whether it be right in the sight of God to heed men more than God, you judge. We can but speak the things which we have seen and heard."

(b) Where had they learned this higher loyalty? The answer is discovered in an interesting note as recorded in the account of this incident in the Book of Acts. The account reads in the thirteenth verse of the fourth chapter, "The members of the council were amazed to see how bold Peter and John were, and to learn that they were ordinary men of no education. They realized then that *they had been companions of Jesus.*" To be a companion of Jesus always points one to the higher loyalty.

III. Peter and John had been present, no doubt, when during Jesus' ministry the religious leaders had sought to entrap him by raising the question concerning conflicting loyalties: "Is it right that we should pay taxes unto Caesar?" How Jesus so masterfully answered, the human race has never been able to forget. "Show me a coin," he says. He asks, "Whose inscription is on this money?" They reply, "Caesar's." Jesus then says, "Render unto Caesar the things which are Caesar's and to God the things that are God's." In these days of fervent patriotism, do we need to be reminded of the higher loyalty lest *we* render to Caesar the things that are God's?—John Thompson

Illustrations

FRUIT OF FAITHFULNESS. From prison Martin Niemoeller addressed the following words to the members of his Berlin parish: "Let us thank God that he upholds me as he does and allows no spirit of despair to enter into Cell 448. Let the parish office know that in all ignorance of what is coming I am confident and that I hope to be ready when I am led along paths which I never would have sought for myself."—Charles L. Wallis

WORDS TO LIVE BY. One thing can never be forbidden: namely, what goes on in the depths of the heart. We may be forbidden to go to church, the Bible may be taken away from us, but the divine Word can never be torn out of our hearts. For this reason it is important to assimilate the word of Scripture so inwardly that we have a source of nourishment when outwardly the Bible is missing. Many of those who went through the suffering of concentration camp or imprisonment were deprived of their Bible but wrote out whole parts of it from memory for themselves or for others. Friends, how much would you be able to do under similar circumstances? How much could you repeat of the parables of the Lord, of the stories of the Gospel, of the Letters of the apostles, of the Psalms and the Prophets? The much criticized learning of the Bible by heart takes on at once quite another aspect and gains new importance in view of these times of trial.—Emil Brunner

Sermon Suggestions

GOD'S LAWSUIT. TEXT: Mic. 6:1–8, NEB. (1) The case for the prosecution: a wayward and ungrateful people. (2) Hypothetical reparations by the defense: bribery with good and costly deeds. (3) God's requirements: (a) to do his revealed will as prescribed, (b) to be faithful to him and to serve others from the heart, (c) to "live in humble fellowship" (TEV) with him.

PARADOXES OF THE CROSS. TEXT: 1 Cor. 1:18–31. (1) It is wisdom. (2) It is power. (3) It is glory for God.

Worship Aids

CALL TO WORSHIP. "Worthy is the Lamb that was slain to receive power and riches and wisdom and strength and honor and glory and blessing" (Rev. 5:12).

INVOCATION. O Lord, let our worship today rise to the heights of your glorious person, to which you have been lifted from the depths of the humiliation of your cross, so that we may glory in that cross that towers over "the wrecks of time."

OFFERTORY SENTENCE. "Now as you excel in everything—in faith, in utterance, in knowledge, in all earnestness, and in your love for us—see that you excel in this gracious work also" (1 Cor. 8:7, RSV).

OFFERTORY PRAYER. O Lord, who of old art the same and forever true, bless these gifts we bring and use them to share that love that is timeless, through the Christ of the ages.—E. Lee Phillips

PRAYER. How we long to see you, Father. Then the fears, the doubts, the questions would disappear. Long do we cry for just a glimpse of you, thinking that such would be sufficient. Yet, in our more rational moods we know that our sins blot out a clear view of your wonder and glory. Then our thinking clears, and we remember that grace has opened the way for us to see you in your glory as you reveal yourself to us in Jesus Christ. Challenge us to learn more of him that we may be cleansed of our offenses and delivered from our failures. In this sacred hour teach us to trust, to wait quietly, to pray fervently, to worship humbly, and to be patient as we seek to follow your spirit across the terrain of life. Pray, Father, meet us in power that we may experience your grace in Jesus' name.—W. Henry Fields

LECTIONARY MESSAGE

The Quiet Revolution
TEXT: Matt. 5:13–16

One problem with radical Christianity is that it is always so unpopular. How can disciples as controversial as those described in the Beatitudes (5:11–12) ever have any influence in this world? The startling answer of Jesus is that such ordinary folk do have an unnoticed but incalculable impact like that of salt and light. Both are crucial all out of proportion to their recognized worth.

I. *The salt of the earth (v. 13).* Although a simple substance, salt had a wide variety of valuable uses in ancient Palestine: as antiseptic for surface wounds, as preservative for meat, as seasoning for meals, as stimulant for soil, as catalyst for heating, and as seal of a covenant. Although inexpensive to purchase and inconspicuous in use, it nevertheless transformed whatever it touched. Just as salt is seldom given credit for the changes that it works, even so kingdom disciples are the best hope of a world that may ignore or despise them.

A critical problem arises, however, when salt loses its potency. This can happen only by adulteration, e.g., salt gathered in crusts from the marshes along the Dead Sea was sometimes contaminated by impurities that made it worthless, so that housewives would fling it out the window to mingle with the sand of the street. The disciple is warned not to become insipid by allowing alien values to compromise the purity needed for a potent witness.

II. *The light of the world (vv. 14–16).* Light was one of the richest symbols in the Old Testament, referring to the saving revelation of God that dispels the darkness of sin. In describing his followers as the light of the world, Jesus was making them responsible to reflect his saving truth (John 8:12). He did not say that they *ought* to be, or some day *would* be, or might *like* to be salt and light; rather, they already *are* these realities because of their relationship to him. Just as it is the nature of light to shine, so it is the nature of the Christian life to furnish guidance to others.

But light needs visibility in order to shine, e.g., from a lamp on a stand or a city on a hill (vv. 14b–15). Open oil lamps were often extinguished by suffocating the flame under a clay meal tub called a "bushel" measure (v. 15a). Jesus was frequently pressured to hide his light by retreating from danger, but he resisted the temptation to let controversy snuff out his witness (John 9:4–5). Here he calls upon his followers to "so shine" that God's saving presence in the world will be unmistakably clear (v. 16).

Two things are common to salt and light: (1) Both must be singular and separate in order to function properly. (2) Yet both must merge and mingle with their surroundings in order to fulfill their mission. This dialectic of pure-yet-spent points to the central Christian paradox of "in-but-not-of" the world. Our witness must be based on a balance of separation and penetration. There must be a "holiness" and a "worldliness" about everything we do. We cannot escape *from* one world *to* another but must be *in* one world yet *of* another.—William E. Hull

SUNDAY: FEBRUARY ELEVENTH

SERVICE OF WORSHIP

Sermon: The Light of the World
TEXT: John 8:12

I want to ask you to think with me what Jesus means when he declares himself to be the "Light of the World" or the "Light of Life." The words come down to us out of the old Hebrew Temple where he spoke them first. They pierce into the center of our modern life. Nay, they have done much to make our modern life and to make it different from the old Hebrew Temple where they were spoken first. It will be good indeed if we can feel something of the power that is in them and understand how clear is the conception of the Life which they include, how far our present Christianity is an embodiment of that conception, how far it fails of it, how certain it is in being ever truer and truer to that conception that the faith of Christ must come to be the Master of the soul and of the world.

I. We may begin, then, by considering what would be the idea of Christ and his relation to the world which we should get if this were all we knew of him—if he as yet had told us nothing of himself but what is wrapped up in these rich and simple words. "I am the Light of the World."

(a) They send us instantly abroad into the world of nature. They set us on the hilltop watching the sunrise as it fills the east with glory. They show us the great plain flooded and beaten and quivering with the noonday sun. The sun may be tumultuous with fiery splendor; the atmosphere may roll in billows of glory for its million miles; but light as related to earth has its significance in the earth's possibilities. The sun, as the world's sun, is nothing without the world, on which it shines, and whose essential character and glory it displays.

(b) That is the parable of the light. And now it seems to me to be of all importance to remember and assert all that to be distinctly a true parable of Christ. A thousand subtle, mystic miracles of deep and intricate relationship between Christ and humanity must be enfolded in those words; but over and behind and within all other meanings, it means this—the essential richness and possibility of humanity and its essential belonging to divinity.

(c) How clear Christ is! It is redemption and fulfillment which he comes to bring to man. Those are his words. There is a true humanity which is to be restored and all whose unattained possibilities are to be filled out. There is no human affection, of fatherhood, brotherhood, childhood, which is not capable of expressing divine relations. Man is a child of God, for whom his Father's house is waiting. The whole creation is groaning and travailing till man shall be complete. Christ comes not to destroy but to fulfill. What is the spirit of such words as those? Is it not all a claiming

of man through all his life for God? Is it not an assertion that just so far as he is not God's he is not truly man? Is it not a declaration that whatever he does in his true human nature, undistorted, unperverted, is divinely done and therefore that the divine perfection of his life will be in the direction which these efforts of his nature indicate and prophesy?

II. The Christian is nothing but the true man. Nothing but the true man, do I say? As if that were a little thing! We are still haunted by the false old distinction of the natural virtues and the Christian graces. The Christian graces are nothing but the natural virtues held up into the light of Christ. Manliness has not been changed into godliness; it has fulfilled itself in godliness.

(a) As soon as we understand all this, then what a great clear thing salvation becomes. Its one idea is health. Not rescue from suffering, not plucking out of fire, not deportation to some strange, beautiful region where the winds blow with other influences and the skies drop with other dews, not the enchaining of the spirit with some unreal celestial spell, but health— the cool, calm vigor of the normal human life; the making of the man to be himself; the calling up out of the depths of his being and the filling with vitality of that self which is truly he—this is salvation!

(b) Of course, it all assumes that in this mixture of good and evil which we call man, this motley and medley which we call human character, it is the good and not the evil which is the foundation color of the whole. Man is a son of God on whom the devil has laid his hand, not a child of the devil whom God is trying to steal. That is the first truth of all religion. That is what Christ is teaching everywhere and always. "We called the chessboard white, we call it black"; but it is, this chessboard of our human life, white not black—black spotted on white, not white spotted upon black.

(c) See also here what a true ground there is for the appeal which you desire to make to other souls. It must be from the naturalness of the new life that you call out to your brethren. You must claim your brother for the holiness to which his nature essentially belongs. "Come home!"

"Come home!" "I have found the homestead!" "I have found the Father!" "I have found the true manhood!" "I have found what you and I and all men were made to be!"

There are two sorts of attraction which draw, two sorts of fascination which hold human nature everywhere—the attraction of the natural and the attraction of the unnatural.

III. The mystery of man! How Christ believed in that! Oh, my dear friends, he who does not believe in that cannot enter into the full glory of the Incarnation, cannot really believe in Christ. Where the mysterious reach of manhood touches the divine, there Christ appears.

(a) Men talk about the Christhood and say, "How strange it is! Strange that Christ should have been—strange that Christ should have suffered for mankind." I cannot see that so we most magnify him or bring him nearest to us. Once feel the mystery of man and is it strange? Once think it possible that God should fill a humanity with himself, once see humanity capable of being filled with God and can you conceive of his not doing it? Must there not be an Incarnation? Do you not instantly begin to search earth for the holy steps? Once think it possible that Christ can and are you not sure that Christ must give himself for our Redemption? So only, when it seems inevitable and natural, does the Christhood become our pattern. Then only does it shine on the mountaintop up toward which we can feel the low lines of our low life aspiring. The Son of God is also the Son of man. Then in us, the sons of men, there is the key to the secret of his being and his work. Know Christ that you may know yourself. But, oh, also know yourself that you may know Christ!

(b) How every truth attains to its enlargement and reality in this great truth—that the soul of man carries the highest possibilities within itself and that what Christ does for it is to kindle and call forth these possibilities to actual existence. We do not understand the church until we understand this truth. Seen in its light the Christian church is nothing in the world except the promise and prophecy and picture of what the world in its idea is and

always has been and in its completion must visibly become. It is the primary crystalization of humanity. It is no favored, elect body caught from the ruin, given a salvation in which the rest can have no part. It is an attempt to realize the universal possibility. All men are its potential members. The strange thing for any man is not that he should be within it but that he should be without it. Every good movement of any most secular sort is a struggle toward it, a part of its activity. All the world's history is ecclesiastical history, is the story of the success and failure, the advance and hindrance of the ideal humanity, the church of the living God.

IV. Are there not very many of us to whom the worst that we have been seems ever possible of repetition; but the best that we have ever been shines a strange and splendid miracle which cannot be repeated? The gutter in which we lay one day is always claiming us. The mountaintop on which we stood one glorious morning seems to have vanished from the earth.

(a) The very opposite of all that is the belief of him who knows himself the child of God. For him, for him alone, sin has its true horror. "What! have I, who once have claimed God, whom once God has claimed, have I been down into the den of devils? Have I brutalized my brain with drink? Have I let my heart burn with lust? Have I, the child of God, cheated and lied and been cruel and trodden on my brethren to satisfy my base ambition?" Oh, believe me, believe me, my dear friends, you never will know the horror and misery of sin till you know the glory and mystery of man.

(b) Here, too, lies the sublime and beautiful variety of human life. It is as beings come to their reality that they assert their individuality. In the gutter all the poor wretches lie huddled together, one indistinguishable mass of woe; but on the mountaintop each figure stands out separate and clear against the blueness of the sky. The intense variety of Light! The awful monotony of Darkness! Men are various; Christians ought to be various a thousandfold. Strive for your best, that there you may find your most distinctive life. We cannot dream of what interest the world will have when every being in its human multitude shall shine with his own light and color and be the child of God which it is possible for him to be—which he has ever been in the true homeland of his Father's thought.

(c) What then? If Christ can make you know yourself; if as you walk with him day by day, he can reveal to you your sonship to the Father; if, keeping daily company with him, you can come more and more to know how native is goodness and how unnatural sin is to the soul of man; if, dwelling with him who is both God and man, you can come to believe both in God and in man through him, then you are saved—saved from contempt, saved from despair, saved into courage and hope and charity and the power to resist temptation and the passionate pursuit of perfectness.

(d) It is as simple and as clear as that. Our religion is not a system of ideas about Christ. It is Christ. To believe in him is what? To say a creed? To join a church? No, but to have a great, strong, divine Master whom we perfectly love, whom we perfectly trust, whom we will follow anywhere, and who, as we follow him or walk by his side, is always drawing out in us our true nature and making us determined to be true to it through everything, is always compelling us to see through falsehood and find the deepest truth, which is, in one great utterance of it, that we are the sons of God, who is thus always "leading us to the Father."—Phillips Brooks

Illustrations

OPPOSED BY DARKNESS.   We deceive ourselves if we think of primitive people in the "dark" remote areas of the world, still without digital watches and microwave ovens. We deceive ourselves if we think only of derelicts crawling along the "dark" alleyways of our cities. It is also darkness to refuse to hear the truth and to tolerate no teacher or preacher or politician who tells it. It is to avoid certain sections of town so as not to be disturbed by the conditions in which some have to live. It is to avoid any book or any speaker who shatters my illusions of innocence in this evil world. It is not to ask questions at work, at home, or at church because I prefer to let sleeping dogs lie. It is to persuade myself that problems in the church, in the schools, in the neighborhood, in society at large are really none of my business. No wonder, then, that sermons on God's love for the world come into such darkness as judging light. That Jesus' presentation of himself as light for the world should create opposition among those who held heavy investments in darkness comes really as no surprise at all.—Fred B. Craddock

WALKING IN THE LIGHT.   To be a follower of Christ is to give oneself body, soul, and spirit into the obedience of the Master. And to enter upon that following is to walk in the light. When we walk alone we are bound to stumble and grope, for so many of life's problems are beyond our solution, and, if we try to settle them ourselves, we are bound to go wrong. When we walk alone we are bound to take the wrong way, because we have no secure map of life. We need the heavenly wisdom to walk the earthly way. The man who has a sure guide and an accurate map is the man who is bound to come in safety to his journey's end. Jesus Christ is that guide; he alone possesses the map to life. To follow him is to walk in safety through life and afterward to enter into glory.—William Barclay

Sermon Suggestions

WHEN GOD IS NOT IMPRESSED.   TEXT: Isa. 58:3–9a. (1) *Situation:* Religious rites and ceremonies are a normal and proper expression of faith. (2) *Complication:* These practices, however, may become a convenient, inexpensive, and empty substitute for more significant expressions of faith. (3) *Resolution:* Redefine these rites and ceremonies in terms of their inner meaning and requirements, such as costly justice and demanding compassion.

WHO ARE THE WISE?   TEXT: 1 Cor. 2:1–11. (1) People taught by the Spirit, (2) who perceive the wisdom of the cross, (3) and who let that cross argue God's case.

Worship Aids

CALL TO WORSHIP. "Arise, shine; for thy light is come, and the glory of the Lord is risen upon thee" (Isa. 60:1).

INVOCATION. Lord of light and love, we come in anticipation; we come in hope; for you in Jesus Christ have broken through the darkness of our lives. Brighten our presence in worship today with the light of life.—Donald W. Musser

OFFERTORY SENTENCE. "The Lord is good to all: and his tender mercies are over all his works" (Ps. 145:9).

OFFERTORY PRAYER. You have been gracious to us, O Lord. You have reached out and touched us with your love. As we give today, we give out of thankfulness, and we ask that you will use our gifts so that others may come to know you and feel the touch of the Master's hand.—Donald W. Musser

PRAYER. Almighty God, we come before you with heads bowed. We are painfully aware of our sin. The number of the varieties of them is too great to mention even the smallest fraction of them. Indeed, we cannot be aware of them all. We know that we are sinful people. Father, forgive us.

We come before you with needs, too, Father. Some of us are sick and others are scared and others are tired and others are so beset by the brutality of the pace at which life is lived that they are simply unable to respond to the needs of your world. We need your healing and your courage and your rest and your peace. We need your presence with us now and in all of our days. Lord, indwell us, imparting, by your presence, the things that we need in order to deal redemptively with our world.

There are those of our number who have suffered loss. Someone they love has died. We can't be philosophical about a death that touches our own life. Father, accompany those who walk through the valley of the shadow. Be, for them, the light to show the way through the darkness and out into your bright day.

We give you thanks for the things that we have received of you. Material things are the easiest for us to recognize. For these gifts, make us truly thankful. For the others, make us sensitive to the giving of them, so that we don't forget to give you thanks and praise for them. Let no spiritual blessing escape our notice. We need them more than we can know. For all of these blessings we give you thanks. And we humbly ask for more. More blessings, more of your presence, more of your grace, more peace, more courage, more of whatever we need to face life. Help us face it not just so as to get by, but help us face life in such a way that we may conquer. We do not ask for personal success. Give us a faithful heart that we may be participants in your victories!—W. Barry Carter

LECTIONARY MESSAGE

The New Morality
TEXT: Matt. 5:17–26
Was Jesus a "conservative" or a "liberal"? These terms are very debated by many contemporary religious leaders who assume that one label is good and the other is bad, hence a person must choose between them. Notice how Jesus dealt with that issue in this passage.

I. *The old and the new (vv. 17–20).* Jesus' teaching was so revolutionary, e.g., in the Beatitudes, that it seemed to threaten the established religious order. "Think not" (v. 17) sought to correct those who saw him as replacing the religion of sacred Scripture. That accusation must still be faced, for Jesus *did* begin a movement that abolished Sabbath observance, circumcision, Temple sacrifice, and other central features of the Old Testament.

Instead of being a Bible-destroyer, Jesus insisted that his mission was to "fulfill" the deepest intention of God's Word (v. 17). Negatively, not a dotted *i* or a crossed *t* would be removed or compromised. His "conservatism" was complete! But, positively, a new age was coming when everything in the Law would be "accomplished," permitting the "jots and tittles" of the past to be superceded. His "liberalism" was just as complete (v. 18)!

How can both be true at the same time? Because "fulfillment" preserves that which it transforms. Marriage is very different from courtship yet includes all of its meaning. Oaks are nothing like acorns, yet nothing of the latter is lost in the former. God's new order is the crown and consummation of his old order. Jesus went *beyond* the Old Testament but not *against* it. Hence his followers are to honor the foundations of the past (v. 19) and yet "exceed" the results that they achieve (v. 20). The key test of our faith is, "What do we *more?*" (v. 47).

II. *An ethic of intention (vv. 21–26).* The Ten Commandments clearly outlawed murder (Exod. 21:12), but this prohibition was restricted in scope to certain types of killings, mainly involving fellow Israelites (v. 21). By contrast, Jesus tracked murder to its lair in the angry heart. Because thoughts and feelings are the father of overt actions, he sought to curb the deadly deed by rooting out the hidden grudge that lies behind it. In so doing, he "con-served" everything of value in the sixth commandment, yet "liberated" it so as to control motives as well as conduct (v. 22a).

This wider application forbade the use of demeaning epithets that cheapen the dignity of others by labeling them as "blockheads" or fools (v. 22b). Instead of a churlish contempt for others that destroys "reverence for life" (Albert Schweitzer), we are to go to any length to effect reconciliation, even if we are the innocent party (v. 23). Restored relationships are more important than high religious moments (v. 24). Therefore, never leave a quarrel unsettled but act urgently and decisively to resolve the most petty grievance (vv. 25–26).

What a transformation Jesus wrought by his hermeneutic of fulfillment! At first this commandment seems to have no relevance for us, since we never consider literally killing another person. As interpreted by Jesus, however, it becomes a guide to attitudes and actions about which we must decide every day. Truly, there is an ethic of "surpassing righteousness" (v. 20).— William E. Hull

SUNDAY: FEBRUARY EIGHTEENTH

SERVICE OF WORSHIP

Sermon: The New Commandment

TEXT: John 13:31–38

The "new" is a constantly recurring theme of the Bible.

In keeping with this exciting theme, Jesus gave a new ethical commandment: "A new commandment I give to you, that you love one another; even as I have loved you, that you also love one another" (John 13:34, RSV).

We want to keep this new commandment before us as we think about Christian morality.

I. *What is Christian morality?* The new commandment tells us. Christian morality at its heart is concerned with love. The Christian ethic is an ethic of love.

(a) The commandment to love, however, was not new. People who lived before Jesus came and people untouched by the Christian gospel knew it was better to love than to hate, just as they knew that it was better to tell the truth than to lie, better to protect human life than to kill.

(b) What then is new about the new commandment? The quality of love. We are to love one another as Jesus has loved us: "Love one another; as I have loved you, that you also love one another" (John 13:34). That is new, radically new.

(c) Early Christians knew that they were called to this kind of morality, to a lifestyle made possible by this kind of love. Paul wrote to the Ephesian Christians: "And walk in love, as Christ loved us and gave himself up for us, a fragrant offering and sacrifice to God" (Eph. 5:2, RSV).

II. *Three observations.* In pursuing our theme of Christian morality, let us make several observations.

(a) First, Christian morality and Christian faith must never be separated. The

Bible stresses that religion and morality must be held together, that religion nurtures and sustains morality while morality gives evidence that religion is authentic and real.

(1) This is one of the most obvious things about biblical faith, and supporting illustrations are numerous. Take, for example, the Ten Commandments. The first four are concerned with our relationship with God, while the remaining six are concerned with our relationship with people. The first four are religious; the last six, ethical. Jesus said great religion is fulfilled in love of God and love of neighbor. Love of God is theological; love of neighbor is ethical.

(2) One of our great tragedies is that we often try to separate faith and morality. But that is like trying to separate the back and palm of my hand. It can't be done, and if I should try I would succeed only in getting a mutilated hand. Just so, we get a mutilated gospel.

On the other hand, there are many who are greatly concerned about morality and social action but care little or nothing about the Christian faith. The tragedy here is that morality is cut off from its source, the soil that nurtures it, and the springs that renew it.

(3) Those who try hard to make our world a more human, just, loving, and compassionate place to live—and may their number increase—should remember that they can be like an army which gets too far from its base of supply. The army at last may be defeated, not by the enemy, but by hunger, fatigue, and low morale. When we get too far from the source and springs of renewal of Christian morality, we may at last be overcome by our own weariness and fatigue.

(b) Second, Christian morality is the result of our salvation, not the cause.

(1) We are saved by grace, not by our best and highest ethical striving. We don't win God's acceptance by being good. I bring empty hands to God, and I say to him, "I have nothing to bring to you. I wish I had full hands. I would like to bring you many moral virtues." God looks at me and says a most wonderful thing: "Your empty hands are enough. If you had all the moral wealth in the world, you couldn't buy my salvation. It is of grace. It is a gift."

(2) Salvation by grace and legalism are two different kinds of religion. Legalism is a do-it-yourself kit of salvation. In legalism we do not come to God with empty hands. We come with full hands bearing gifts of personal achievement. We put God under obligation to us. We earn our salvation. Legalism negates grace. That is why Jesus and Paul were so severe on legalism. Legalism claims to be the root of salvation. Christian morality and good works are its fruits.

(c) Third, our religious life is to be tested and judged by our moral quality of life. That may sound shocking. Yet that is exactly what the Bible says.

(1) Each of us sooner or later asks, How can I know that I am saved? The New Testament gives us two tests by which we can tell—one spiritual and one moral. "When we cry, 'Abba, Father!' it is the Spirit himself bearing witness with our spirit that we are children of God," said Paul (Rom. 8:16, RSV). That is the spiritual test. And there is the moral and social test: "We know that we have passed out of death into life, because we love the brethren" (1 John 3:14, RSV). How often the moral quality of life validates the spiritual experience.

(2) If we are not right with the brother, we cannot be right with God. The failure to love our brother is proof that we do not love God. John wrote, "If any one says, 'I love God,' and hates his brother, he is a liar; for he who does not love his brother whom he has seen, cannot love God whom he has not seen" (1 John 4:20, RSV).

III. *Who can obey it?* In seriously considering the new commandment, there is an inescapable question: Who can obey it? It seems to be an impossible commandment. We often find it hard to give ordinary love, to say nothing of a love like that of Jesus. Power from beyond ourselves is given so that the impossible commandment becomes possible, although never as perfectly as Jesus lived it. Let us make these observations.

(a) First, God has loved us first. "We love him," John told us, "because he first loved us" (1 John 4:19).

We learn to love by responding to love.

We cannot love unless somebody loves us first. Love cannot be returned unless it is first given.

(b) Second, the grace of Christ is available. The grace that first saved us is always with us. There can be new meetings with Christ and fresh experiences of his grace. When we fall on our faces, the grace of Christ picks us up, stands us on our feet, and helps us get started again.

(c) Third, the Holy Spirit gives us the power to love. How often we are no match for our unruly hearts. All day long my heart has been filled with bitterness, resentment, and hatred. I am being burned up on the inside and know that I am. I cannot manage my own heart. Is there help?

Yes, there is help. The Holy Spirit can give us power to love. "God's love," wrote Paul, "has been poured into our hearts through the Holy Spirit which has been given to us" (Rom. 5:5, RSV).

(d) Fourth, we find a loving, forgiving, affirming, and supportive fellowship in the church. Because of the nature of the Christian fellowship, Paul could admonish the church of Ephesus: "Be kind to one another, tenderhearted, forgiving one another, as God in Christ forgave you" (Eph. 4:32, RSV).

IV. Our world, so hostile, broken, and estranged, needs to see again the kind of love it first saw in Jesus, and in its best and most wistful moments wants to see again. But unless the world can see this love in Christians and the church, where will it see it? Are you willing to be the kind of person through whom Christ can love his world?—Chevis F. Horne

Illustrations

THE LOVE WE CELEBRATE.   Now this love God commands is not moonlight and roses, starry-eyed saints with lilies in hand. It's a tough love, and over the ages countless men and women have shrunk from it, found it impossible, unreasonable, absurd. It means that I can murmur: "Look, Lord, I don't pretend to understand you, but I still love you. Though you puzzle me day after day, I still love you. Though you tolerate wars, let a Hitler live and six million Jews die, I still love you. Though you do nothing about earthquakes in Guatemala, political prisons in the Gulag Peninsula, bloated bellies in flight from Cambodia, I still love you. Though you sit impassively in high heaven while innocents die in the womb and the nations brace for nuclear suicide, I still love you. Though one fourth of the people you claim to love go to sleep hungry each night, I still love you. Though my father and only brother died of cancer within three weeks of each other, and my mother turned senile, I still love you. Sometimes I'm not sure why I love you, but this I do know: that if you could give your own Son to a bloodsoaked death for me, you must care deeply—more deeply than my dull intellect can fathom."

Harsh though it seems, this is the type of love God demands of me. But even this is not enough. Jesus not only commanded: "You shall love the Lord your God with all your heart, and with all your soul, and with all your mind" (Matt. 22:37). He added; "You shall love your neighbor as yourself" (v. 39). In fact, "This is my commandment, that you love one another as I have loved you" (John 15:12).—Walter Burghardt

WHEN LOVE DISPLACES HATE.   We shall have accorded to love the preeminence which it deserves in our scale of values; we shall seek it and proclaim it as the highest virtue and the greatest boon. We shall not be ashamed to have "suffered much extremity for love," in the full realization that love is the medicine for the sickness of the world, a prescription often given, too rarely taken. We shall have realigned our faith in God to include more faith in human beings, and extended our identifications to include more brothers, more sisters, more sons and daughters in a vastly wider family concept. "For love is the desire of the whole, and the pursuit of the whole is called love." Plato said this, even before Jesus taught that "God is love," which means the same thing.—Karl Menninger

Sermon Suggestions

THE CHOICE.   TEXT: Deut. 30:15–20. (1) All decisions or postponements have consequences. (2) God confronts us with decisions of ultimate consequence. (3) If we choose life and commit ourselves to its requirements, blessing will follow.

JEALOUSY IN THE SERVICE OF CHRIST. TEXT: 1 Cor. 3:1–9. (1) Jealousy in Christian service is human, but immature. (2) The ultimate success of Christian service is the work of God, not of humans.

Worship Aids

CALL TO WORSHIP. "O love the Lord, all ye his saints: for the Lord preserveth the faithful, and plentifully rewardeth the proud doer. Be of good courage, and he shall strengthen your heart, all ye that hope in the Lord" (Ps. 31:23–24).

INVOCATION. Lord, let the light of faith shine in saddened hearts, reveal sinful hearts, heal broken hearts, encourage struggling hearts, challenge open hearts, and motivate all hearts to a meaningful worship and a holy praise. Through the light of the world: Christ Jesus.—E. Lee Phillips

OFFERTORY SENTENCE. "Why spend money on what does not satisfy? Why spend wages and still be hungry? Listen to me and do what I say, and you will enjoy the best food of all" (Isa. 55:2, TEV).

OFFERTORY PRAYER. It is all yours, O God, everything that we call our own, yet we often use it as if you were not involved. Deliver us from our unhappy and unproductive self-indulgences by helping us to bring our earthly possessions under your wisdom and guidance.

PRAYER. Gracious Lord, you cause rain to fall upon the earth, upon the just and the unjust, and you cause it not to rain. In a world thus fashioned we thank you for people who nonetheless take risks—farmers, entrepreneurs, investors—people who plant not knowing if there shall be harvest; develop products not knowing if any man shall buy; save and invest in others' dreams not knowing if they shall have aught to show for it; people who do not bury their talents or clutch them in faithless parsimony or throw them away on baubles but launch out upon the deep—to build a better mousetrap, open a better garage, grow a better grain—people who would rather fail than never have tried. Not alone for personal gain, not alone for the blandishments of power. But that others may eat, be warmed, have work, buy and sell products of quality and social worth. Teach us, employers and employed, white collar and blue collar, frayed collar and frayed hopes, how much we need each other and how much, precisely from each other, we have to learn: that hourly workers are not always dumb or management smart; that most of us know a thing or two about our work others need to know and do not; that she who would be the greatest of all must be the servant of all and a good listener; and that we all inhabit one earth and shall all one day die. When business is good, cause us to recall thee our maker and be modest, and when it is poor, to persevere and remain steadfastly kind and fair, even to a fault and especially to vulnerable people. For we remember our Lord's days upon earth. As the years pass, swifter than a weaver's shuttle, may we bury what must be buried, grieve and move on, with the alacrity of God who, when Christ had lain in the bonds of death for three days, said, Enough of that, and raised him from the dead.—Peter Fribley

LECTIONARY MESSAGE

The Fidelity of the Family
TEXT: Matt. 5:27–37
The stability of the home is being shaken to its foundations by assaults from three sources: (1) sexual promiscuousness that compromises the unique commitment on which marriage is based; (2) rampant divorce that shatters ties binding parents and children to each other; (3) poor communication that frustrates the trust level necessary to achieve genuine intimacy. Jesus deals directly with all of these problems in our text.

I. *The scarlet letter (vv. 27–30).* Moving from the sixth to the seventh commandment in the Decalogue, Jesus cited the familiar moral imperative that outlawed any extramarital sexual relationships with another man's wife (v. 27). This time he tracked adultery to its lair in the lustful look (v. 28). His words do not condemn the spontaneous awakening of a healthy sexual desire but warn against the covert glance that deliberately seeks to exploit another person's sexuality for one's own self-gratification. A woman should not be treated as an impersonal object to be selfishly manipulated, even in the privacy of the imagination.

So important is the responsibility of relating to others as a "thou" rather than an "it" (Martin Buber) that we must resort to radical surgery, if necessary, to excise the offending member (vv. 29–30). Having just made the point that inner attitudes can corrupt as much as outward acts, Jesus intended for these injunctions to be taken, not literally, but seriously. May his priorities give us the courage to amputate unworthy passions before they consume our souls!

II. *The ultimate union (vv. 31–32).* The Old Testament practice of providing "a certificate of divorce" (Deut. 24:1) sought to discourage the hasty dissolution of a marriage by providing an orderly procedure administered by a mature person who could offer helpful counsel before all ties were cut (v. 31). The people of Jesus' day debated legitimate grounds for divorce, but he transcended such discussion by teaching that nothing should be allowed to rupture the marital bond, whether it be a legal divorce proceeding or an illegal unchastity that destroys marriage prior to divorce (v. 32). God's original intention in creating us "male and female" was to make possible a union that would never be dissolved (cf. Matt. 19: 3–9).

III. *A trustworthy tongue (vv. 33–37).* The people of Jesus' day had developed an elaborate system of religious oaths designated to reinforce the integrity of the tongue by calling God to witness (v. 33). The only problem with such a practice was the implication that one must tell the truth only when on oath, leaving unsworn words to be careless and trivial. In response, Jesus swept away the whole system of swearing by pointing out that God is present everywhere, hence every word must be spoken as if "under oath" (vv. 34–36). Honesty is not guaranteed by impressive religious formulas but by a consistency of character that requires us to say what we mean and to mean what we say.

Our public life is full of corrupted language: the inflated claims of advertising, the "doublespeak" of politics, the "white lies" of flattery, the "reverse spin" of public relations. These distortions condition us to say what we think others want to hear rather than disclose who we really are. No wonder marriage counselors report that poor communication is the greatest single cause of domestic difficulty. Nothing helps resolve marital problems more than to discuss them openly and to reach conclusions that are honored in word and in deed.— William E. Hull

SUNDAY: FEBRUARY TWENTY-FIFTH

SERVICE OF WORSHIP

Sermon: The Christian and Perfection

TEXTS: Matt. 5:48; Phil. 3:12–21

Paul could speak in glowing absolutes about what it means to live in the spirit of Christ and to walk in his way. Yet he could often rebuke Christians, as in Corinth, because they so failed to embody what he taught Christians are like. The transformation of which he spoke was not yet a full, accomplished fact! And there is the problem! How do we reconcile the perfectionism we so often preach with the actual lives of Christians like ourselves?

I. *God demands perfection.*

(a) Let us clarify one thing at the outset. God does demand perfection, and the Christian will be made perfect. When you became a Christian, whether you realized it or not, you were taking dead aim on perfection. Sooner or later, God will perfect all his true disciples. He will not stop until he has purged sin from our lives. He is in the business of turning us into the children of God.

(b) Therefore goodness does matter. Although perfection is one of those impossible possibilities, it should be our aim in life—even when we always fall short. It makes a difference whether a Christian is moral or immoral, good or bad, loving or indifferent. And the conduct of church members is a proper concern to the church. We must all avoid the kind of conduct or character that gives non-Christians opportunities to criticize the church and through it the Christian faith. God expects Christian to be good, Christ-like people!

II. *The Christian is not yet perfect.*

(a) But having said that, we must confess that Christians and the church are not yet perfect. Even Paul said of himself, "Not that I have already obtained this or am already perfect. . . ." Not only are we not perfect, one could even say that in human terms not every Christian is necessarily nicer or better than every non-Christian.

(b) It is essential that we understand how God perfects his disciples. When we profess faith in Jesus Christ, God plants a seed of new life in us, and throughout a lifetime of development, we struggle cooperatively with his Spirit to produce the fruit of the new life. Conversion is only the first step in a long path of Christian discipleship that progressively moves redeemed sinners toward the goal of being perfect as God is perfect. So it should not be surprising that it takes a lifetime and beyond to perfect real sinners—people like us who make up the Christian church!

(c) The only authentic test of the perfecting power of Christianity is in comparing the individual Christian's new life with one's old life, not all Christians to all non-Christians. Here the Christian faith promises at least two things: that each Christian is better than he or she individually would be without being a Christian and that each healthy Christian will grow spiritually year by year. But we remain people on the way. None of us has yet arrived. We must always say with Paul, "Not that I have already obtained this or am already perfect." The Christian need not posture about perfection!

III. *The Christian is on the move toward perfection.*

(a) And that leads me to a third affirmation: The Christian is on the move toward perfection. Paul says, "I press on to make it my own, because Christ Jesus has made me his own. . . . I press on toward the goal."

(b) For that reason, C. S. Lewis has suggested that God is easy to please but hard to satisfy. We are that way with our own children. When my first child came home from school and could read Dick and Jane, I turned handsprings I was so happy. But I would have been foolish to have given him Plato and then been disappointed that he could not read philosophy. I was pleased that he could read, but I wasn't satisfied until he could read Plato and Aristotle, Shakespeare and Hemingway, not until the riches of human history and culture were open to him. When my children began to walk, the resemblance to young Frankenstein was rather remarkable. Nevertheless, I was pleased. But I wasn't satisfied until they could run as fast as the wind and as free as a deer. God is like that. He is pleased with the first infant, stumbling steps of Christian discipleship and with each stage of Christian growth. But he won't be satisfied until one day we are made perfect.

(c) Perhaps that is what Paul is getting at when he says, "I press on toward the goal for the prize of the upward call of God in Christ Jesus." We are all "on the road," found at different locations, driving different machines. But none of us has yet arrived! For some of us, discipleship is easy and natural; for others, it is difficult and unfamiliar. But as long as Christians are on the road and moving forward, we should be patient with ourselves and understanding of others. More than that, we need to link hands with and help our weaker brothers and sisters. The church is a redemptive fellowship of sinners who are in the slow, difficult process of being turned into saints.

IV. One day we will arrive at our goal. We will reach our Father and home. Then there will be no more weak bodies, battered psyches, and broken relationships. There will be no more unconquerable habits, frayed nerves, or uncontrollable tempers. We will be made whole, integrated, joyful, at peace, and all our sins finally will be washed away. There will no longer be a command to be perfect, but God will breathe upon us with his Holy Spirit and state an incredible fact: "You are perfect." And then we will truly be saints, in fact as well as in name, redeemed children of the living God, who by grace have become perfect even as God is perfect!—Richard D. Cunningham

Illustrations

UNSOCIAL BEGINNINGS. While the infant is a socially dependent being, he is not even to the slightest degree a socialized being. Even at the age of two the child is, when measured by standards applied to adults, an unsocialized horror. Picture, if you can, an adult who is extremely destructive of property, insistent and demanding that every desire be instantly gratified, helpless and almost totally dependent on others, unable to share his possessions, impatient, prone to tantrums, violent and uninhibited in the display of all his feelings. Such behavior, normal to a two-year-old, would be monstrous in a man. Unless these qualities are markedly altered in the process of becoming, we have on our hands an infantile and potentially evil personality. Hobbes well said that the wicked man is but a child grown strong.—Gordon W. Allport

UNTANGLING HUMAN RELATIONS. As Paul said in writing instructions to the Christians of Ephesus, "Be ye therefore imitators of God . . . and walk in love." That picture of perfection makes it possible to love even our enemies—not the personality we see today, but the ultimate and beautiful picture of the ideal. Here is the basis for straightening out all human relations that have gone awry. It establishes the husband, wife, children, friends in their own legitimate importance. But it does far more than that. Our mental image of the perfect man or woman or child is creative. We become creators with God and imitators of God. And the people we thus hold lovingly in our thought as we

imitate God are inspired to try to come up to the faith we have in them. Thus they give back to us their love—and, behold, the problem in personal relations is solved!

Jesus used this method on Peter. There was no more impulsive, vacillating, unpredictable disciple than Peter. He was the most unrocklike of the twelve. But Jesus saw him as he was to become—as he was in the pattern mind of God. So the very first thing Jesus did after meeting Peter was to look him hard in the eye and say, " 'You are Simon, son of John. You shall be called Cephas'—that is, Peter, which means Rock."—Lewis L. Dunnington

Sermon Suggestions

PROVIDENCE ALL THE WAY. TEXT: Isa. 39:8–13. Because God cares for his people, (1) he has a plan for them, verses 8–9; (2) he will meet their unfolding needs, verses 9–12; (3) they can join in a hymn of rejoicing, verse 13.

TRUE CHRISTIAN LEADERS. TEXT: 1 Cor. 3:10–11, 16–23. (1) Will build on the foundation of Jesus Christ. (2) Will treat God's people as his very temple. (3) Will serve on the basis that they belong to the people who belong to Christ and that the people do not belong to them.

Worship Aids

CALL TO WORSHIP. "I will instruct thee and teach thee in the way which thou shalt go: I will guide thee with mine eye" (Ps. 32:8).

INVOCATION. Lord, we have come to church today because we are looking for a word from you. We do not care very much how you speak it, whether through the songs or the prayers or the Scriptures: we just know that we must hear your voice today. Help us to hear what you would say to our hearts.—James M. King

OFFERTORY SENTENCE. "As God's dear children, try to be like him, and live in love as Christ loved you, and gave himself up on your behalf as an offering and sacrifice whose fragrance is pleasing to God" (Eph. 5:1–2, NEB).

OFFERTORY PRAYER. Everliving God, whose will it is that all should come to you through your Son Jesus Christ: Inspire our witness to him, that all may know the power of his forgiveness and the hope of his resurrection; who lives and reigns with you and the Holy Spirit, one God, now and forever.—*The Book of Common Prayer*

PRAYER. O Lord our God, in all the earth there is no name like thy name. In all the earth there is no heart like thine. There is no love and no welcome such as thou dost grant. Not the earth itself is so open to our footsteps, to go every whither, as thou art to our hearts' desire; for we are invited to come back, to enter in, and to dwell in thee. Or, if we be weak and unable to find thee, thou dost seek and save us. Nor, if we be humble, though we be cast into the extremity of life, wilt thou disdain us. With the humble and the contrite thou dost delight to dwell. We rejoice that thou art thus welcoming to thee those that can rise and find thee, helping their infirmity. And we rejoice that thou dost not alone accept those who come, but that thou art abroad by thy Word and by thy Spirit, awaking those that sleep, giving life to those that are dead, healing those that are sick, and by all influences drawing souls back to God, their Source and their Head.

We give thanks to thee for all thy mercies to us in days gone by. How many there are we cannot tell. More than the leaves in summer, more than the stars at night, shining in our darkness they have illumined our way, they have filled us with comfort and with blessedness, and thy thoughts are yet unfulfilled.

All the purposes of thy soul are fruitful of good to us. What time we are able to accept it, thou art waiting for us to be loved. Thou art waiting for us to be able to appreciate and to enter into the fellowship and fruition of thy nature. As we wait for our children, taking care of them until they come up to us, so art thou waiting for us, longing to bless in overmeasure, while doing exceeding abundantly more than we ask or think. And when at last, in the other and better land, our eyes are cleansed, and we have come to the measure of the stature of perfect men in Christ Jesus, we shall see how, on every side, unappreciated good, unappropriated mercies lie strewn thick as blossoms in the summer. We rejoice in this fullness of thy nature, in this royal generosity, in this outflowing, overpouring abundance of thy thoughts and thy deeds of goodness. What are we, that we should withstand thy nature? What are our fears, that they should fend off these precious promises? What is guilt, what is remorse, and what are all our humiliations and self-renunciations, that they should take us away from thee, when it is because we are weak that thou dost desire us to come and because we are wicked that thou dost desire to forgive us and to establish us again in righteousness? Why should we keep away from thee by reason of sickness, when it is thine office to be Physician to our souls? Why, because we are selfish and empty of love, should we not come to the summer of love?

O our Father! We beseech of thee that we may cease to look upon ourselves for reasons either of dissuasion or of persuasion. May we look upon our God. May we be won by thy goodness, by thy gentleness, by thy loving mercy to us. And, we pray thee, as thou dost accept most generously and abundantly the feeblest endeavor, the smallest advances, in the fewest things even; as thou art he that will not break the bruised reed nor quench the smoking flax until thou dost bring forth judgment unto victory, we pray thee that they who are consciously environed on every side, and who are yet striving for some things good, may have enough courage given them, and hope, not as good, but because God is merciful and gracious. And may thy goodness in forgiving and bearing with them make them ashamed of their ingratitude. May it make them ashamed of the evidences which they heap up before thee of their indifference and disobedience, of their godless lives and conversation. May we all be ashamed. Grant us not that shame which takes us from thee, but that shame which brings us to thee.

We beseech of thee that thou wilt grant us from day to day, out of our experience of thee, more and more to grow in grace; and growing in grace, may we grow in the knowledge of our Lord and Savior Jesus Christ.—Henry Ward Beecher

LECTIONARY MESSAGE

Indiscriminate Love

TEXT: Matt. 5:38–48

I. "You have heard it said of old . . . an eye for an eye." *Lex talionis,* they called it. It was old; old as Hammurabi, and its practice was Roman and Greek worldwide. Justice was another name for it; retributive justice. "An eye for an eye." A practical concession was *lex talionis,* to keep people from the overkill, the ego-satisfying revenge to which we are all predisposed. Here is no liberation for the oppressor, but the oppressor gets his/her just desserts. Here is no reconciliation for malefactor and victim, but separation and alienation. It is the love practiced by first-century tax collectors and Gentiles; it is, the justice that we hear twentieth-century political candidates rave about in the context of "law and order." Old stuff, this *lex talionis,* this resistant kind of justice.

II. "But I say to you. . . ." Jesus takes back the concession and puts the law in its proper context. Jesus prohibits resistance and retribution and demands of his followers the kind of justice that God loves, the justice that the prophets Amos, Micah, and Isaiah sang about: the justice that rolls down like waters, the righteousness like an ever-flowing stream; the justice that the Lord requires of us, the justice that loves kindness; the clean justice that ceases to do evil, learns to do good, corrects oppression, defends the parentless, and pleads for the widow. The old justice makes for a blind and toothless world. But Jesus' justice, the justice of the prophets and the justice that God's love makes for a new world, a world of right relationships. Jesus will not be satisfied with dead-letter tradition nor with softened accommodations. He has got a new hermeneutic for a new way of living.

III. "Love your enemies." This is what Jesus says. This is the content of Jesus' novel interpretation, the focal point of his greatest sermon, the keystone of his ethic. This is the justice we call love. Glen Stassen calls enemy love the "surprising, transforming initiative" we can take in relationships, both personal and international. This is the kind of love, wrote Dietrich Bonhoeffer, that "asks nothing in return, but seeks those who need it. And who needs our love more than those who are consumed with hatred and utterly devoid of love? Who in other words deserves our love more than our enemy?" In his great sermon on "Loving Your Enemies," Martin Luther King, Jr., said that "when Jesus said, 'love your enemies,' he is setting forth a profound and ultimately inescapable admonition. . . . The chain of evil—hate begetting hate, wars producing wars—must be broken, or we shall be plunged into the dark abyss of annihilation." "Love indiscriminately as God does," is how John Howard Yoder summarizes the politics of Jesus: "Love your enemies."

IV. But Lord, how? He gives us the answer in the text. Indiscriminate love begins with understanding oneself as a sibling with all other children of God. Enemy love begins with realizing that the sun sets and rises in Teheran and Toledo, in Leningrad and in Los Angeles. Lavish, extravagant love begins with the awareness that there is drought and famine in every land. When we are able to "reframe" the one whom we perceive as enemy; when we, says pastoral theologian Charles Gerkin, awaken to the realization that we are more like the one who wrongs us than different from them, then we acquire the capacity to love indiscriminately, to love our enemies, to forgive them, as Christ has forgiven us.—Jeffrey Allan Kisner

SUNDAY: MARCH FOURTH

SERVICE OF WORSHIP

Sermon: Christ of the Upward Way: Which Way Is Up?

TEXTS: Luke 22:14–30; Phil. 3:7–14

Are these two texts in the Gospel and in the Epistle at odds? Jesus says the greatest is the youngest and the leader is the one who serves. Yet does Paul's upward call in Christ Jesus mean pressing downward?

I. *Paul's "upward call" and "pressing on."* Which way is up? To answer this question we need to look closely at Paul's understanding of knowledge in Christ and the purpose of knowledge in the community.

(a) Paul begins by telling us that pressing upward really means pressing downward. Paul says he counts all his gains as losses for the sake of Christ. The way upward is not a knowledge of things, his position, or the law. Knowledge, for Paul, was grounded in participation in the sufferings of Christ and in being conformed to his death.

(b) What does this upward way of knowledge then mean for us? First, the upward way teaches us that knowledge is not measured by the success ladder or a vertical scale of accomplishments and achievements. In fact, the way of knowledge is the very opposite of the model whereby knowledge is private gain. Why? Paul says the purpose of knowledge is for understanding, for forming and cultivating the self in community, and for forming character. The way of the cross is a confession of our identity, which is also formulated within community.

(c) Which way is up? The upward call is really a movement upward, though redefined. The upward call is not a plea for a false humility or a low self-esteem. Neither is it a condemnation of ambition. The upward call is not a disregard of his human dignity or of the dignity Christ Jesus gives to all people. Rather Paul is emphasizing that the upward call is founded on God's righteousness through faith in Christ. The

cross of Christ surpasses all human achievement and all human striving.

(d) In the context of the church community, pressing on demands the formation of character. This process draws us outside of ourselves to receive the gift and the strangeness of knowledge. We know this from Paul's own life story. Knowledge of Christ led him out of his own world and cultural biases and transformed him into receiving the foreign. For example, his affirmation that "there is neither Jew nor Greek, male nor female, slave nor free" took him outside of a narrow vision (Gal. 3:28). The church today must be drawn out of its narrowness to receive the foreign.

II. *The object of our knowing.* When then is the object of our knowing? What is it we ought to know? In Luke we read that Jesus told his disciples to be servants. We would expect the disciples to know the directions Jesus' ministry would take since they were around him the most. Yet during the Last Supper at the end of Jesus' public ministry, he was needing to teach them about the object of knowledge, servanthood. To make matters worse, they were sitting around having a dispute about who would be the greatest! Jesus was telling them, What I am doing is becoming a servant.

(a) Jesus then pointed out to them that ignorance or failure to be a servant for the kingdom leads to betrayal. "One of you at this table will betray me" (22:21). They began to question one another. Who would betray him?

(b) Jesus was trying to tell his disciples that knowledge as participation in his sufferings and as becoming a servant of the kingdom is not a neutral position. We either become a servant or we betray Christ. Ignorance is not knowing. Jesus said on the cross, "Father, forgive them, for they know not what they do."

III. *The challenge of the upward call.* God requires us to become a Christ for others as God has become incarnate in the suffering and Passion of the cross. Whoever would be the greatest needs to become as the youngest, says Luke. The leader must be a servant. The upward call, says Paul, is a movement downward, if we think of it in terms of the vertical success ladder. Paul redefines the way upward. He says he has not attained this perfection or this knowledge. It is a lifelong process of being open to the gift of knowledge in Christ Jesus.

(a) "But I press on to make it my own because Christ Jesus has made me his own" (3:12). Through God's grace Paul found that the ultimate reality lies in living faithfully to the way of the cross. This is the upward way. As we live and form our character so that all people will be able to sit at the Lord's banquet and feast on the Lord's Supper, we press onward and upward.

(b) Paul says, "I seek to know only Christ and him crucified." To ask God for knowledge means to be a student of what may seem foolish or strange to society. It means to open ourselves to a world beyond our immediacy, to a life that is formed by God's righteousness.

(c) This is the paradoxical nature of the upward way. Which way is up? Like the disciples, we misunderstand greatness. Servanthood is not a call to be a doormat or the instrument of injustice. The upward call, redefined as servanthood in sharing the sufferings and being conformed to Christ's death for the sake of the kingdom, is our striving.—Karen L. Carter

Illustrations

THE HOMESICKNESS OF THE SOUL. There is an old legend of the Western Isles concerning a sea king who desired the company of a human being. One day he heard in his cavern under the sea a cry, a little human cry, and rose to the surface of the water to discover a child in a derelict boat. Just as he was about to make for the little vessel and take the child, a rescue party intervened, and he missed his prize. But, so the legend says, as they drew away with the one so nearly lost, the sea king cupped his hand and threw into the heart of the child a little sea-salt wave and said, as he submerged, "The child is mine. When it grows, the salt sea will call him

and he will come home to me at the last."

It is only a Gaelic legend, but it enshrines the timeless truth. God has put in the heart of every one of us a longing for himself.—W. E. Sangster

CROSS BEARING.　　If thou bear the cross cheerfully, it will bear thee and lead thee to the desired end—namely, where there shall be an end of suffering, though here there shall not be.

If thou bear it unwillingly, thou makest for thyself a burden and increasest thy load, which yet notwithstanding thou must bear.

If thou cast away one cross, without doubt thou shalt find another, and that perhaps more heavy.—Thomas à Kempis

Sermon Suggestions

ADAM AND YOU.　　(First Sunday of Lent) TEXT: Gen. 2:4b–9, 15–17. (1) Our origin—from God. (2) Our obligation—to manage God's world. (3) Our options—to obey and know God's life; to disobey and taste of death.

THE HARBINGER OF DEATH AND THE PIONEER OF LIFE.　　TEXT: Rom. 5:12–19, RSV. (1) Adam's disobedience led to death for all. (2) Christ's obedience led to "acquittal and life for all."

Worship Aids

CALL TO WORSHIP.　　"Commit thy way unto the Lord; trust also in him; and he shall bring it to pass" (Ps. 37:5).

INVOCATION.　　O Lord, who in the Word dost speak to us and in the community of the redeemed dost keep coming to us; break in upon our souls and lift us up to new levels of praise, aligning our hearts with thy purposes and our praise with thy will, to the glory of thy name.—E. Lee Phillips

OFFERTORY SENTENCE.　　"Keep your life free from love of money, and be content with what you have; for he has said, 'I will never leave you nor forsake you' " (Heb. 13:5, RSV).

OFFERTORY PRAYER. We put our trust in you, O Lord, for our daily bread; and we render our stewardship to you to the end that others may have their daily bread and your word, the bread of life.

PRAYER. Always and forever God, from whom we come, in whom we live, to whom we go, who has no beginning and knows no end, we join hearts and spirits and voices to praise and worship you. Bidding Father, Lord and Master of us all, as we seek your presence, free us from the distractions of our lives and let us in these holy moments be lost in wonder, love, and praise.

Gracious God, Father of our Lord, Jesus Christ, our worship is hindered because we come as children with dirty hands and soiled hearts. We have fractured our relationship with you and with other people, and we have not been true to who we are. We confess our sin: we seek cleansing for being at peace with sin in our lives, for having no sense of shame, for exploiting the wants of others, for lacking moral passion, for hoarding the gospel and being immune to its demands, for forgetting the high cost of forgiveness. Pardon us for gloating privately over the misfortune of another, for our obsession with status and success, for standing on the sidelines of life, for living in the fast lane toward regret. Forgiving Father, whose gift to us is new beginning and real life in Jesus Christ, hear our confession and repentance and wash us clean again.

O faithful God, whose Son has shown us the true way, we enter this season of repentance and examination and renewal with longing to follow that true way. We want to be done with lesser things. Guide us now in this time of pondering deeply our lives and our future in Christ. Grant us strength for the sojourn in the wilderness. Make us bold to resist temptation. Let us hear again the call to the examined life. Lord Jesus, we pray for a life disciplined in obedience to you, for fasting that moves beyond the stomach to the will and to the heart. Grant us the desire to hunger and thirst for you. Quicken us with the courage to wait for you, with wisdom to see you, with purity to follow and serve you. In the

posture of Christ and by the gift of your Spirit, let us know again the blessedness of love, peace, joy, patience, kindness, goodness, humility, self-control, and faithfulness. As we live this journey these holy days, O God, give us to know as we have never fully known before Jesus Christ in the fellowship of his suffering and in the power of his Resurrection.—William M. Johnson

LECTIONARY MESSAGE

How Are You Answering?

TEXT: Matt. 4:1–11, RSV

I. *Tempted by the devil.* The New Testament writings teach that we humans are "up against" the devil as we live out our lives. A popular magazine carried a report some time ago about the complaint made to some bishops by a group that did not want the words in their church catechism about the devil to be changed. A revision committee had proposed to delete all mention of the devil in an effort to be more modern in thought. But as complaints mounted against the proposed change, the committee submitted a modified version to the bishops, admitting that the word about a devil gives people a clearer idea of what they're "up against."

There is much we do not know about the devil, or about evil. We still speculate about how he became what he is and why he does what he does; we seek always to grasp a knot of ignorance in order to unravel it or to take some dangling string of revelation and tie it down for the sake of logic. Meanwhile, the story about how Jesus also had to face and handle satanic suggestions teaches us about how we can answer them with wisdom and strength.

II. *Temptation—the ordeal.* This story is instructive on at least three levels: Jesus was tested on how he would use his powers, what he would give priority, and whether he would strictly follow principles in his life and work. The struggles of our souls are also in those three arenas of concern.

(a) Making stone into bread—the use of our powers to serve our own bodies, has to do with how we will answer our real, felt needs. Jesus answered the devil by a clear and forthright trust in God's prior planning for life's basics. Influenced by Scripture-wisdom, Jesus refused to honor his body in a way that would jeopardize his spirit. The right answer to the devil is always one that grows out of Scripture-wisdom.

(b) Disregarding the laws of life—viewing oneself as an exception to the law of "sowing and reaping"—is the focused suggestion in the devil's concern to have Jesus resort to dramatics to win friends and influence a wow-crazed populace. We, too, face that crafty suggestion, lured to consider how to arouse the admiration of crowds by daring the spectacular—and with expectation that we cannot lose with the risk because of God.

Jesus answered that life makes no exceptions; all who cross the lines God has set are in danger of relentless law for such violation. The laws of time, nature, and the rightful order of things allow no exemptions. We risk foolheartedness to end in sure ruin.

Life makes no exceptions where sin is concerned. No angels attend the foolish; no safety is guaranteed for the silly. We must not test God by risking our silly and selfish planning, but trustingly obey his sometimes slower but surer demands. The right answer to any suggestion to display self is to submit to the law of humility. How are you answering?

(c) Like Jesus, we too have heard the devil's suggestion about how best to achieve power: that "fall down and worship me" spells *compromise* with history in order to control it. But compromise always works against rightful commitment to principle. Furthermore, Jesus knew that the last word about history is not the devil's but God's. Our service must be to God and to God alone. No compromise with evil—no cheating or scheming to "get control" in human affairs. There is no progress apart from principles. How are you relating to the world around you? Can you be bought?

III. *Then the devil left him.* There are times of respite from the moral struggle. We are not *always* under assault; there are times of rest and renewal, but whether those are times of renewal indeed depend upon how we answer during the struggle that precedes. We are not *always* under assault, but we must always be ready to answer aright when we confront our spiritual foe. We need not become his victim if we answer him as we should.—James Earl Massey

SUNDAY: MARCH ELEVENTH

SERVICE OF WORSHIP

Sermon: Only Not through Me!
TEXT: Matt. 5:16

In the loving intention of God, the Temple was to have been a place of prayer for all nations. Instead, it had become sordid, commercial, unworthy, so that the very name of God was diminished by it. What is the Son to do, the true Son, the Father's true Son? There is only one thing he can do. The Father's name is being dishonored—"Out with you!" He cries and overturns the tables and ejects the moneylenders.

This brings me very nicely to Solzhenitsyn. He points out to us that all the great proverbs of Russia have to do with truth; for example, "One word of truth shall outweigh the whole world." Then Solzhenitsyn asks, "What is the ordinary brave man or woman to do in the face of the lie?" His answer is, "The ordinary brave man will not participate in the lie. He will not participate in wicked actions. He will say, 'Let that come into the world. Let it even reign supreme. Only not through me!'" And there is the message of our Lord cleansing the Temple. Let the lie come. Let it even reign supreme, "only not through me!" Have you ever said it? What are the implications of it? Let me draw them out in four exhortations.

I. Here is the first one. Recognize the

lie! "Ah!" you say, "You are the preacher. You tell us what it is." But I am not going to. I know what the lie is in the Christian church. I know some of the lies that distort society. I talked to a man during the week who is a very gifted artist, and he knows the lie in his art. Do you know it in your school system, in your profession, in your business? Do you know it in politics?

Have you seen the lie? Do you discern it? Are you aware of what's going on? If you don't know what it is, how can you take your stand against it? And sometimes the lie is so great that it is hard to see it at all. It is by the lie that we see everything else. Let it come into the world. Let it even reign supreme, only not through me. What is it where you work, where you play? Can you recognize the lie?

II. Here is the second exhortation. Believe in the value of the individual, in the usefulness of the solitary voice.

(a) "One word of truth," says Solzhenitsyn, "shall outweigh the whole world"— your word of truth in the face of the lie you discern and recognize. We live by these words of truth. By Paul's words, for example. The issue was whether the good news of Christ was a gospel of grace or a gospel of works, and Paul spoke the redeeming word. Or think of Luther. "It is neither safe nor right to go against conscience. Here I stand, I can do no other, God helping me." There is a single word of truth that outweighs the whole world, and thank God for it.

(b) Have you any sense of what it means to speak the one word of truth that outweighs the world and of the places it comes from? Isn't it an irony, isn't it a kind of fearful symmetry that the best words of freedom in our time have issued, not from Ottawa or Washington or from London or Moscow, but from a prison camp in the Gulag, written on little scraps of toilet paper and smuggled out to help save our world? If you do not speak it, the one word of truth may not be spoken, and the world will be darker because of it.

III. Here is the third thing. Know your dimensions!

(a) Some of us know our physical di-

mensions. We not only know them, we are worried about them, and so we ought to be, some of us. But we don't know our spiritual dimensions. We don't know how much space we occupy. We measure ourselves and we measure our children by their possessions, by what they've got, by how many people work for them, by how big their house is or by other trivia. We do not judge them by what they are, by the quality of substance that's in them. Have you any sense of your own self?

(b) Do you remember Sir Thomas declared of the king's action, "I oppose it," he said. "I do. Not my pride, not my spleen, not any other of my appetites, I do." And some of us hardly have an "I" by which to oppose anything. Did you know that Nathaniel Hawthorne wrote notes for a novel in which the chief character never appears? Some of us feel like that about life, about ourselves. We keep waiting for the chief character to appear because we don't know who we are or what we stand for or what matters to us. Then Sir Thomas, having examined himself, examines Norfolk, feeling his shoulders, his waist, and his thighs, and demands of him, "Tell me, is there anywhere here any single sinew that does not merely serve Norfolk's appetites, but is just Norfolk?" Where do you locate yourself?

IV. Here is the last thing. Count the cost.

(a) There is a cost. If you speak the one word of truth that outweighs the world of lies, then you had better not want anything that the lie can give you. Perhaps the Stoics are right: to want anything very much is to be vulnerable because if you want it badly enough you might just sell yourself to get it, the only self you have! "Ah!" says our Lord. "Part with that true self and whatever else you possess or win, you have made the worst of all possible bargains." That is the cost if you speak the true word.

(b) What is it I have said to you? Listen! Don't let anybody or anything make you what you are not. All your battles are struggles for yourself, and in every moment you hold yourself in your hand, and sometimes the only way to keep yourself is to say, "Only not through me!" Do you want a text? Here it is at the end: "Let your light so shine before men that they may see your good works and glorify your Father who is in heaven."—R. Maurice Boyd

Illustrations

THE LIGHT IS EVERYTHING. George Stephenson was fond of expounding the theory that his famous engine was driven by fuel and steam indeed but only because these derived their light and power from the sun. The lamp is not important; the light is everything. The light, coming from God, belongs to God and should shine for his glory. If it should shine only for man it might be a pride-filled exhibitionism; shining for God it is true piety.—George A. Buttrick

THEATRICAL GOODNESS. This saying of Jesus is a total prohibition of what someone has called "theatrical goodness." At a conference at which D. L. Moody was present there were also present some young people who took their Christian faith very seriously. One night they held an all-night prayer meeting. As they were leaving it in the morning they met Moody, and he asked them what they had been doing. They told him; and then they went on, "Mr. Moody, see how our faces shine." Moody answered very gently, "Moses wist not that his face shone." The goodness that is conscious, that draws attention to itself, is not the Christian goodness.—William Barclay

Sermon Suggestions

THE ANATOMY OF FAITH. TEXT: Gen. 12:1–4a (4b–8). (1) A demanding command. (2) An inspiring promise. (3) Decisive obedience.

WHAT PUTS US RIGHT WITH GOD? TEXT: Rom. 4:1–5 (6–12), 13–17. (1) Not our good works and religious rituals. (2) But the grace of God who regards our faith as acceptable righteousness.

Worship Aids

CALL TO WORSHIP. "Thus speaks the high and exalted one, whose name is holy, who lives forever: I dwell in a high and holy place with him who is broken and humble in spirit, to revive the spirit of the humble, to revive the courage of the broken" (Isa. 57:15, NEB).

INVOCATION. Be pleased, O Lord, to come to us and dwell with us. We confess our sinfulness and unworthiness, but we also trust your mercy. We need you: we need your encouragement and your strengthening help, so that we can become what you would have us to be in the world in which you have placed us.

OFFERTORY SENTENCE. "Let your light so shine before men, that they may see your good works, and glorify your Father which is in heaven" (Matt. 5:16).

OFFERTORY PRAYER. These tithes and offerings, Lord, are some of the light that we set to shining in the world. May the beams of blessing radiate to the ends of the earth.

PRAYER. Almighty God, in whose goodness we have been created; in whose love we have been redeemed; in whose presence we worship; and in whose name we pray, as with all Creation and believers around the world, we praise your holy name.

God of Creation, whose first bidding was light; God of Redemption, whose best gift was the Light of the World, Jesus Christ our Lord, we pray today for the removal of darkness from our lives. For the darkness of our eyes, in that we seek not your face and see not the needs of others, we pray for healing and light. For the darkness of our minds, in that we wander and stumble in fear and despair, we pray for healing and light. For the darkness of our hearts, in that we become cold and hard and harbor evil, we pray for healing and light. For the darkness of our spirits, in that we sense not your coming and receive not your presence, we pray for healing and light.

O God in Christ, who has created and redeemed us to be the light of the world, make us noble and true to shine forth in a world captured by darkness. May we offer the good news of Jesus Christ who is the Light and Life for all.

God of goodness, God of love, God of presence and holy name, we worship you and pray in the name of Christ.—William M. Johnson

LECTIONARY MESSAGE

The Higher Moments
TEXT: Matt. 17:1–9, RSV

I. *He was transfigured.* Following Jesus obediently has always meant being introduced to higher moments and a higher life for believers. This passage provides a distinct instance. Going with Jesus to this place of his choice put Peter, James, and John in candidacy for an entirely new experience—seeing the glory of God.

It all happened while Jesus was praying (Luke 9:29). Prayer was a major experience with Jesus, the time with his Father when he could report, listen, and be renewed. This time of prayer was a high moment when Jesus was "transfigured," his face illuminated and his garments glowing under the glorious light. The happening was by divine direction and with immediate impact upon the three startled viewers. Experiencing the glory of God is always a high moment for a human.

II. *The deeper drama.* Like Moses before him, Jesus was reflecting in his face the divine glory of God from their time together. But there was more that happened: he was allowed to converse with Moses and Elijah. And why? The experience with these two former leaders was crucial for Jesus at that time. According to Luke's account, Moses and Elijah talked with Jesus about his coming death, his imminent ordeal in Jerusalem; Matthew does not mention this, content to report their appearance, which itself meant more than meets the eye.

Was Jesus being reassured by Moses that, like him, his death would be from other than physical causes (see Deut. 34:7; John 10:18)? Was Elijah conversing with Jesus to reassure him of a promised ascension, as he himself experienced at the hands of God (see 2 Kings 2:11)? The account has details about a deeper drama, a drama called *involvement* in God's plan of salvation. Thus the appearance of Moses and Elijah—all within the context of that high moment of spiritual realization through experienced glory!

III. *The human reactions.* The higher moments cannot be preserved—despite all efforts to enshrine them in buildings, monuments, or reports. They happen, and they have meanings that must be understood and regarded. As for this moment, it meant reassurance for Jesus as he faced his coming Passion at Jerusalem. And for the three disciples it was to mean that Jesus was God's supreme agent, the beloved Son whose word must be heard as final: "Listen to him" (17:5b).

The wisest action that follows a high experience is, not building something to enshrine the meaning, but bowing the knee and humbling the self to live out the meaning. More booths and buildings? Enough of these! Our need is more ordered lives, ardent worship, and obedient listening to the radiant Lord.

IV. *About sharing the high moments.* The word of caution was necessary—both then and now. We can experience far more than we should try to explain. Reporting glorious moments can be ill-timed and ill-advised. A necessary reticence must attend the footsteps after an experience of the holy. The effects are best lived out, not shouted forth. Years later, Peter would recall the vision on that mountain and reassure his readers that he was an eyewitness to the meaning of who Jesus really is (see 2 Pet. 1:16–19). By then, time had sifted his pride, and life had readied him for relevant sharing. He then knew what we must learn: that meanings are best shared when we can witness about them in *character* and not just talk about them in proud *chatter.*—James Earl Massey

SUNDAY: MARCH EIGHTEENTH

SERVICE OF WORSHIP

Sermon: Just Say No!
TEXT: Mark 10:17–22

Greed almost always kills—if not physically, then certainly emotionally, relationally, or spiritually. Oscar Wilde once wrote, "In this world there are only two tragedies. One is not getting what one wants, and the other is getting it." He was trying to warn us that no matter how hard we work at being successful, success will not satisfy us.

Mark tells about a man who had all anyone could ever want, and yet it wasn't enough. He had fame, comfort, wealth, and power. Yet his soul was still hungry . . . for meaning, for the sense that he had figured out how to live so that his life really mattered.

Essentially, Jesus told him that he had to learn how to do without the things to which he had become addicted. He had to learn how to say no to himself! The man walked away sorrowful for, as Mark wrote, "he had great possessions" (10:22).

I. Several years ago, *Fortune* magazine made a study of yuppies—the name ascribed to the generation of young adults who are taking their places in the business world of the 1980s. *Yuppies* is an acrostic for "young urban professionals." The study revealed some disturbing things about this group of contemporary Americans.

(a) These young adults are intensely committed to living what they consider to be "the good life." They define the good life as a life-style in which a person can enjoy good things. Their goals include making enough money to buy gourmet foods, own expensive foreign cars, live in pleasant surroundings, and vacation in exotic places.

(b) In order to reach their goals, yuppies are willing to make some necessary trade-offs in their personal lives. They will forego marriage until they can be sure it will not interfere with their money-making careers. None of those interviewed intend to have children because they see children as an inconvenience and an interference with their career goals.

They see their employers as a means to an end, their jobs as stepping-stones to better positions, and the families into which they were born as people who "act like something is owed to them." For these young adults, self-serving is the total way of life. Saying no to self is the one absolutely forbidden rule.

II. Not all of us are motivated by greed, however. Many of us subscribe to what has been called "the new morality of need." It seems that the language of need is taking over contemporary life.

(a) For example, rarely do you hear anyone say, "I wanted a new set of golf clubs, so I bought a new set." Instead, you will hear an avid golfer say—rather defensively, "I really needed a new set of golf clubs." You are not apt to hear a middle-aged man confess that he bought the new sports car for "the fun of it." He will more than likely explain his need for a change of self-image in order to stay competitive in business. Even in saying it, he feels good about his purchase. The need justified the purchase. The need made everything all right.

(b) Unfortunately, "I need" often means no more than "I want." In other words, sometimes it's just a way of talking to camouflage selfishness and self-serving. It sounds so much better to talk about need than greed, or need than desire.

All of this has an impact upon the Christian life-style. When it comes to making a choice between giving to the anonymous poor, supporting congregational ministries, financing a church building project, or spending on our own loved ones, the moral priority is not arguable. The father who says, "Sorry, preacher, but charity begins at home," and puts nothing in the offering plate is not making a feeble excuse. He has, in fact, put his finger precisely on what motivates most household spending.

(c) Allow me to make just one more interesting point about need. Those of us who talk about needing a new car or a new coat are usually those who already have a car or a coat. Those who have no car or coat may talk about wanting one, but rarely do they talk about needing one.

Those who talk about the mountains and the beach as places they need to get away to are usually those who get to experience the great outdoors quite regularly. The mother of six who raises her family in the squalor of a fifty-dollar-a-month shack rarely talks about needing to get away to the beach or the mountains.

III. But there is at least one other way to live in relationship to things and wealth. It is defined in the call of Jesus to a simpler, sacrificial life-style.

(a) Typically, when the affluent life-style of Americans is held up for comparison to the light of the New Testament, there is an immediate defensive reaction. Even Christians interpret the challenge to a simpler life-style as a call for people to live in impoverishment.

However, Jesus challenged only one man to total divestiture of personal wealth. Even the closest disciples apparently maintained their ownership of fishing boats. Zaccheus was commended for restoring, with generous interest, that which he had defrauded from others (Luke 19:1–10). There is no suggestion that he gave away everything he owned. In the early church, Barnabas gave away much of his wealth, but there is no indication that he lived in poverty after his donations (Acts 4:36–37).

(b) The New Testament principle is not poverty. Nor is the Christian solution to greed to simply give. There are temptations even in our giving, especially if we use our money and resources as ways to meet our own needs. Even in the service of Christ and his church, we sometimes use money to satisfy our need to control, to manage, to influence.

(c) The Christian life-style is one of self-denial. It is the life that responds to the call to say no to your self and your personal desires and needs. It is life dedicated to voluntarily doing without, to voluntarily going without, to voluntarily depending upon God for your total welfare and well-being.

Jesus sounded the theme of self-denial again and again. Immediately after he had been revealed as the Son of God, Jesus said to his followers: "If any man would come after me, let him deny himself (i.e., say no to himself) and take up his cross and follow me."

It is the language of sacrifice, a language not entirely foreign to our culture.

(d) Every one of us makes trade-offs of one kind or another. In order to have one thing, we forego something else.

Here's the Christian's trade-off. It means giving beyond the point where it hurts. Sacrifice means loss. It means that I intentionally deny myself something I want . . . something I may be convinced that I need . . . in order to be of service to my Lord.—Gary C. Redding

Illustrations

LIFE WITH MEANING. Mike Milliton demonstrates the point. After a brilliant military career, Mike entered Harvard Law School. His *cum laude* graduation set him immediately into a successful practice. He was on the way to a big home and a well-earned reputation as a trial lawyer.

Still, law left him feeling as though he was only a well-paid referee at courthouse contests over penny-ante issues where the stakes were much higher than the issues. Ultimately, Mike decided to leave his practice and enter an Episcopal seminary. Earning a second *cum laude* degree, this time in theology, he moved his family to Central America where he even now serves as a missionary.

The torrid and sometimes monsoon climate near the equator has brought him much sickness. He has, from time to time, been put to bed for weeks to deal with chronic hepatitis. The Indians he chose to serve spoke a language for which he could find no adult teacher. The housing in the jungle village is barely adequate.

Have all these circumstances led him to second guess his decision? Hardly. "This is really living!" he said. "At last, my life has meaning!"—Gary C. Redding

A DOUBLE MEMORIAL. After reading the inscription on the monument to the memory of Lord Shaftesbury, I thought of all that this great man had done for the social life of Britain—of his battles fought on behalf of little children whose tender lives were blighted by the twelve- and sometimes sixteen-hour day down in the coal mines; of the prison reforms he accomplished; of his labors on behalf of the Ragged Schools for Boys; of the laws enacted on behalf of the chimney sweeps and other exploited classes.

On the day his funeral service was held in Westminster Abbey, it seemed as if the whole of England had emptied itself into London. Tens of thousands of people—working men rubbing shoulders with nobility—stood in the rain, and thousands of them wept.

"There was a ten-talent man," you say. "How he inspires us!" But Lord Shaftesbury would never have become "the Great Emancipator" if his heart had not been fired with the love of God. And who was responsible for that? Not his mother, not his father—because they thought of nothing but empty, vain, social activities. It was a servant in the home by the name of Mari Millis who taught him how to read the Bible and how to pray and who stamped the character of Christ upon the mind and heart of a little lad. Lord Shaftesbury carried to the day of his death a gold watch she gave him with her blessing.—John Sutherland Bonnell

Sermon Suggestions

IS THE LORD AMONG US OR NOT? TEXT: Exod. 17:3–7. (1) *Situation:* Like the people of Israel, God has led and blessed us. (2) *Complication:* Like Israel, we tend to forget past blessings when present difficulties arise. (3) *Resolution:* Nevertheless, God is patient with us, accommodates to our lack of faith, and awaits our maturity.

YOUR STANDING WITH GOD. TEXT: Rom. 5:1–11. (1) What is the subject? Peace with God. (2) Whom is it for? Those justified by faith. (3) Where is it found? At the cross of Christ. (4) How does it happen? Through being saved by Christ's life. (5) When does it happen? Now! (6) Why does it happen? Because of God's love for us.

Worship Aids

CALL TO WORSHIP. "Be strong and of a good courage, fear not, nor be afraid of them: for the Lord thy God, he it is that doth go with thee; he will not fail thee, nor forsake thee" (Deut. 31:6).

INVOCATION. Give us to know, holy God, in the worship of this hour, that we are creatures of purpose and there is a divine meaning for our existence. Sober us with the reality of thy constant watch-care and generous strength, through the Holy Spirit and the savior Son.—E. Lee Phillips

OFFERTORY SENTENCE. "And walk in love, as Christ loved us and gave himself up for us, a fragrant offering and sacrifice to God" (Eph. 5:2, RSV).

OFFERTORY PRAYER. Bless our offerings of love, O God, as we remember Christ's sacrifice for us, but bless our offerings in any case, O God, that others may discover and rejoice in your salvation.

PRAYER. Take us all into thine embrace. Be with the children that come up from the gates of the morning. Let them not by wrong training, evil example, or disastrous circumstance be turned away from thy purpose for them. Steady our boys and girls in their tumultuous years amid the waywardness of this generation. Keep their self-respect unsullied. Save them from the contagion of this unclean world, and may they be strong to offer thee valiant service in the years ahead. Be with the mature in the floodtide of their power. Let no prosperity spoil them, no disappointment crush them, no faithlessness overtake them. Keep them true to the knightly vows they took in their chivalrous years, and let their strength be glorified in thy service. Support the aged, now drawing near the river across whose flood they see in vision the shining battlements of the heavenly city. Establish them in their going and give them a triumphant welcome on the other side.

So encompass us in all our varied needs, we pray thee, and in thine everlasting arms enfold us, every one.—Harry Emerson Fosdick

LECTIONARY MESSAGE

A Universal Need

TEXT: John 4:5–26, RSV

I. *The wearying labors of life.* The woman Jesus met and addressed at the well in Sychar had a monotonous, wearisome, but necessary task of drawing water if she was to live. The bright touch in the story is not that she was kind enough to please Jesus as a man, letting him use her vessel (it being the only one available since she brought both bucket and rope of her own); no, the bright touch in the story is that she was open to draw water for Jesus as a Jew, she being a Samaritan—"for," as the narrator commented, "the Jews have no dealings with Samaritans." Tired as she might have been, and despite any previous preoccupation, the woman granted this Jew's request for a drink. Jesus then opened to her a new line of thought, which opened to her a new lane in life. And she needed one!

That woman was like us: She was entrapped by the wearying labors of life, drawing water every day in the quest to keep living. Her natural thirst was perennial, and it was a pointer to a deeper need that demanded attention. Jesus understood her plight; thus his conversation as recorded after her kind deed of giving him a drink from her vessel.

After her first words, uttered in rash prejudice, Jesus spoke a promise and offered a hope. It was a word that went beyond the wearying work assigned to her

hands and even beyond the vain religion to which she clung. His word was about her deepest need for life at its best. This is the need of Everyman.

II. *The worth-bestowing power of true worship.* The word Jesus gave the woman about worshiping God "in spirit and in truth" was a promise that God can be approached and experienced—and that this experience of relating to God as he intended fits us for life at its best.

God is still in the business of bestowing worth. He still specializes in changing lives and meeting the deepest human needs. God still wants to be known—and experienced in truth.

This story lifts our view beyond human centers and racial differences and religious customs. It tells us that life at its best is more than a matter of *living on,* just "making it" by whatever means possible. There is a new lane we humans can follow and a new life we can have. Defective views leave us defective, while truth corrects our faultiness and sin. Jesus spoke to help that woman at both points. Thus the story. That woman's response of openness, honesty, and full regard for Jesus made all the difference in her needy life. He can make any needed difference in our lives today when we are honest, open, and accepting of his word to us.

That well in Sychar is still used today. A church has been built around it. It is possible to look up from the churchyard and see the top of Gerizim, the ruined tower on its rocky knoll, the relic of a once-proud Samaritan temple that stood as a rival to the worship center at Jerusalem. But this story has long eclipsed that *site.* It is always so when we let truth carry us beyond sterile tradition. It is with this that Jesus is still concerned.—James Earl Massey

SUNDAY: MARCH TWENTY-FIFTH

SERVICE OF WORSHIP

Sermon: Grieving for Our Sins

TEXTS: 2 Sam. 12:15b–24; Eph. 4:1–6; John 6:24–35

The last couple of years in our nation have found us with scandals of various and sundried kinds. Hundreds have resigned from public office. Iran-Contra is still unresolved and now "Pentagate" has uncovered terrible "goings-on" in the Pentagon.

Scarcely a week goes by that some scandal related to public officials is not exposed.

And those of us who may tend to say that all this scandal means the world is going to hell in a handbasket may need to remember that scandal has been around for a long time. Like in King David's time. He had a bad scandal in his reign. You remember it, don't you? Let me refresh the details for you.

I. King David had just gotten up from his nap. He was walking out on the balcony surveying his kingdom when, lo, he saw a beautiful woman taking a bath.

(a) Bathsheba was very beautiful. Later that evening he sent for her. They had a few drinks in the palace, one thing led to another, and before long she sent word to David that she was very much with child. Now that was a problem, but not for the reasons it might be today. The problem was that she was another man's property—Uriah, the Hittite. He had defiled another man's chattel, his property.

(b) So, the husband became the problem. David invited Uriah home from battle.

Then, the serious scheming started.

"I'll tell you, Uriah, I know you've been fighting hard. We've started a new program of R and R. Go home and take your rest a few days, spend some time with your beautiful wife, Bathsheba." Instead of going home, he spent the night with the king's palace guard.

II. The next day David invited him back and got him drunk, hoping he would then go home, sleep with Bathsheba, and the baby she was carrying would be blamed on him. No deal. Uriah wrapped himself up in the blanket and went to sleep in the palace guard room.

(a) The next day, David wrote a note to General Joab, "Make this dummy an officer and put him in the front lines where the fighting is the heaviest. I want him brought home in a sack." A few days later the message came. Uriah's dead! Eventually, after a period of mourning, Bathsheba came to live with David and bore his son.

(b) Nathan the prophet knew what was happening. He went to David and told him that someone in the kingdom, a rich man with many sheep, had taken a poor man's ewe for his own and left the poor man with nothing. David was royally ticked and said, "Tell me who this scoundrel is, and I'll kill him myself."

"You, your majesty. You are the one who has done this. Uriah was the poor man and Bathsheba the ewe."

David confessed, repented, and Nathan forgave him, but that wasn't the end of it. He told David that someone in David's family would suffer for David's sins. So, when the child was born he was sick and, after a week of lingering, died. While the child lived David fasted and mourned, grieved and prayed. But when the child died, he bathed, went to worship, ate, and resumed life much to the surprise of the courtiers.

(c) Some months later David and Bathsheba had another son, and Nathan called him *Jedidiah,* which in Hebrew means "beloved of the Lord." It was a way of saying to David and the kingdom that God had forgiven him. David and Bathsheba named him Solomon.

III. How many of us right now in this congregation are carrying extra baggage from the grief and guilt of a moment of indiscretion done years back? The sin has long since played out, been gone, done, finished. But unlike David, who set his face to the future, you are still glancing over your shoulder to see if that past is gaining on you. With guilt and grief, looking for them keeps them there.

(a) God is in the business of forgiving and blessing. Even the old covenant is full of that.

The rainbow curls itself around earth's shoulders: "I won't ever do this again. It's over. I will relate to my human creatures differently."

Nathan appears at the door, "I've seen the boy, David."

"What did you call him, Nathan? Ichabod? 'The glory of the Lord has departed'?"

"No, David. I called him, Jedidiah—'the beloved of the Lord.' "

(b) God takes our sin seriously. But

what is closest to God's heart is not our sin but his grace.

There may be some guilts and griefs that you and I need to leave right on the pew where we are today and let the custodial staff sweep them up and throw them away with the rest of the trash in the first part of this new week.

(c) Whatever needs touching today with the oil of the Spirit of God—sight, hearing, touching, walking, tasting, feeling, sensing—let it be touched in the name of Jesus the Christ. All of our names are Jedidiah, "beloved of the Lord." In the name of the Father and of the Son and of the Holy Spirit.—Thomas H. Conley

Illustrations

A MISSPENT LIFE. One morning a chambermaid in a New York hotel found the body of a young man lying on the bed. He was dead with a bullet hole through his head. On the dresser, she found his last will and testament, written on a sheet of hotel paper. It read like this, as it was printed in a daily paper.

"I leave to society a bad example. I leave to my friends the memory of a misspent life. I leave to my father and mother all the sorrow they can bear in their old age. I leave to my wife a broken heart and to my children the name of a drunkard and a suicide. I leave to God a lost soul, who has insulted his mercy." He wrote it all out and signed it and then shot himself.

It came out later at the coroner's inquest that he had been a very likable young fellow. He had been known as "a good spender." He was one who never cared a rap for what it might cost. His appetites had gotten away with him—he no longer had them; they had him. He had forgotten the rules of the game.—Charles R. Brown

ACCUSER AND DEFENDER. Luther once said that "at first" God is my accuser and my heart, my defender. What he meant was that when God addresses to me the whole, unconditional law that makes its absolute claim upon me, as is done in the Sermon on the Mount, my heart immediately moves over to a defensive position and says to me, "How can God demand this of me? You really cannot help it if evil thoughts spring up in your heart and all kinds of things bubble up in your unconscious mind. You are responsible only for that sector of your ego which you can control as an acting, willing, conscious person. You can say," whispers my conscience, arguing as my attorney, "that any demand that goes beyond this sector is not your responsibility."

But then comes the second act, says Luther, and the tables are turned. Here my heart is the accuser, and God is my defender. What Luther means is that in the second act, when God has overcome me, my conscience can only say to me in all candor, "You did not come from the hands of God in the state you are in now, with all your ulterior motives and all the evil impulses above and below the threshold of your consciousness. Therefore everything that is in you is charged to your account." But then God makes the ultimate reply to this self-accusation; he tells me that he will take over my defense and that he will not allow these terrible things that are in and behind my thoughts and words and deeds to separate me from him.—Helmut Thielicke

Sermon Suggestions

WHO—ME? TEXT: 1 Sam. 16:1–13. (1) *The Story:* The choice of David to be king. (2) *The Meaning:* When God has work to be done, he may choose unlikely people of little promise to do it (see 1 Cor. 1:26–31).

WHEN LIGHT BEGINS TO SHINE. TEXT: Eph. 5:8–14, NEB. Christians are compared to light. Therefore (1) we have a new and different character, verse 8; (2) we produce wholesome fruits of this character, verse 9; and (3) our lives then stand in a kind of inevitable judgment on "deeds of darkness," verses 10–13.

Worship Aids

CALL TO WORSHIP. "Lord, who shall abide in thy tabernacle? Who shall dwell in thy holy hill? He that walketh uprightly, and worketh righteousness, and speaketh the truth in his heart" (Ps. 15:1-2).

INVOCATION.   O God of light, shine upon every dark corner and shadowy place of our lives with the light of judgment and justice, chastening and compassion, healing and renewal, that we may worship thee in the purity and holiness of Christ, our Savior.—E. Lee Phillips

OFFERTORY SENTENCE.   "And he said unto them, 'Take heed, and beware of covetousness: for a man's life consisteth not in the abundance of the things which he possesseth' " (Luke 12:15).

OFFERTORY PRAYER.   Lord, help us through the act of giving and through what we give to participate truly in what life is meant to be.

PRAYER.   Almighty God, in your son, Jesus, you heal your people paralyzed with fear and bound to be our own worst enemy. You forgive us our sins and free us to a new lease on life, unbound and unburdened.

Yet we are often quick to distrust change for the better in others and in ourselves and, like the demons of Jesus' day, call Christ enemy, not Lord.

Make this community a house of healing. Forgiven by you and by one another, may we offer each other the prayers of the faithful and help that helps, to the end that we may live lives of hope and grace.—Peter Fribley

LECTIONARY MESSAGE

The Light by Which We See

TEXT: John 9:1-41, RSV

The theme of light working against darkness is a near-constant in the Gospel of John. The instances are too plentiful to need elaboration (chaps. 1, 3, 5, 8, 9, 11, 12). The highest use of the image is seen when Jesus is explained as the light-sharer, pushing back the darkness of the human condition, granting us deliverance and insight. This story is about Jesus as the light by which we see.

I. *I am the Light of the World.* One sun illuminates this planet, and one Savior alone serves as our given deliverer. It is he who was sent, and he alone makes manifest the works of God. Whether our experience of life has been afflicted by problems of parental failure (see v. 2) or personal failure, the corrective is found in the one who alone works God's delivering will. The giving of sight to the man born blind illustrates how one can be made whole in a setting where brokenness prevails and be made to see in the midst of conditions of darkness.

Born blind: an endemic condition was overcome by the help of Jesus, whose work is to restore, to renew, to enable. His work shows itself in the results others can verify as real, observable changes. "Is not this the man who used to . . ." (v. 8).

II. *The witness of the newly sighted.* The word of a witness is always crucial when a defense is needed. The man who had now received his sight gladly confessed this blessing. When questioned about how it happened, he merely told how it came about. He was "of age," and he spoke clearly for himself. He had received what he needed, he witnessed about how it happened, and he gave honor to the Lord who had done the deed. His personal word of witness was strong, clear, and pointed. His was the theology of experience—which went beyond mere theorizing. His sight had come, but he had also received insight about who Jesus is. Thus that line: "and he worshiped him" (v. 38).

III. *Why some do not see.* There is a deeper blindness than physical eyes that lack sight. Some see not because they cannot, while others see not because they will not. As the saying has it, "There are none so blind as those who refuse to see."

Some facts are plain and can be viewed by anyone who looks openly at them. The insights of faith become plain whenever the divine facts are acknowledged. Jesus called attention to his works as observable deeds that pointed beyond him to God. He called his deeds "works of God" because they were plainly done by the power of God. Those who refused to acknowledge what was so plainly before them acted as if blind—which became their judgment (v. 39). Had they been without sight, and sought it, Jesus could have helped them; but refusing to see meant that they blocked themselves off within dark walls of selfishness.

IV. *Are we blind or do we see?* This is the question posed by the account. Beginning with a case of actual physical blindness— which Jesus corrects by granting physical sight to the afflicted man—the story finally highlights the need for spiritual sight regarding Jesus in his saving role. How we react to Jesus shows either acceptance or rejection, regard or resistance, faith or folly. Are we blind or do we really see and honorably believe on Jesus?—James Earl Massey

SUNDAY: APRIL FIRST

SERVICE OF WORSHIP

Sermon: When a Man Turns Over a New Leaf

TEXT: Acts 9:27

We are all familiar with the story of the man who goes from bad to worse. We are not so familiar, however, with the story of a man who turns over a new leaf. Such a man was Paul the apostle. We turn, therefore, to an unfamiliar chapter in the story of Paul to see what happens when a man turns over a new leaf in life.

I. For one thing, Paul soon found out that the general public held his past against him. Everywhere he turned, instead of finding hospitality, he found hostility.

(a) He went first of all, of course, to the synagogue to preach to the Jews who were living in Damascus. The burden of his sermon was that Jesus is the Son of God. And these Jews, what did they say? They said, "Isn't this the man who just last week was here to put to death the followers of this Christ? How can we believe what he says when we remember what he has been doing?" He went from there to Jerusalem and went straightway, of course, to the disciples of Jesus. There, if anywhere, he would find hospitality. He did not! He found the same hostility.

He turned next to the Hellenists who were Gentiles in Jerusalem, sympathizers with Jewish religion but not Jews by race. They, at least, because of their broader and more cosmopolitan sympathies and background might have understood him and might have given him hospitality. But not at all! They felt so violently about him that some of his friends came and warned him of their intention to kill him and got him out of Jerusalem and on a boat that took him back to Tarsus, his home, where he came from.

As we try to make a right judgment upon them and upon Paul, we recognize, of course, that common sense was on the side of the public. As they tried to see their position and make their judgment, they probably reasoned it out something like this: People do not often change overnight. People may improve slightly one way or the other or the emphases of a man's life may shift from one place to another, but by and large a man's character usually persists along the lines in which it began.

(b) So we as a part of the general public are likely to reason in our own minds. Once a warlike nation, for instance, always a warlike nation. Once a troublemaker, always a troublemaker. It takes more than gracious promises to change the nature of a people. The general public would hold their past against them. Or, if a man came along who had had a bad record, the record perhaps of a loafer or a drifter or a waster, the general public would say, Once a loafer, always a loafer; once a drifter, always a drifter; once a waster, always a waster. Don't forget, a man does not change the whole color and temper of his life overnight. So, common sense is on the side of the public, and nine times out of ten the public would be right. And yet the whole company of twice-born men and women are aligned against the common sense of the public. And before we join the great band of the general public and hold a man's past against him, we had better remember the twice-born men like Paul who rerouted their lives and turned over a new leaf.

II. So far the story, as we find it in this chapter of Paul's life, is a dark one. There was, however, one bright spot in it. It comes at the point where Paul arrived in Jerusalem and is refused hospitality by the disciples.

(a) And at that very moment comes this line: "Barnabas, however, got hold of him and brought him to the apostles." Barnabas got hold of him. Sometimes I think that is the brightest line in the gospel. Why, the thing that drew him to Christ and to the gospel of Christ was the fact that a man could have a second chance in life, that God did not hold a man's past against him, that if a man had sincere and earnest intentions to live a better life, God would accept those intentions.

(b) You may remember something about Barnabas, for he was the man who sold a farm in order to give the money that the farm brought to the Christian disciples for the work they wanted to do. He was a generous personality, outgoing, a person who saw something that he recognized to be good, was willing to take a chance, and was glad to risk something. He had the discernment in this case to see in Paul a real, honest, and sincere desire to be a different kind of person and to live a different kind of life than he had lived hitherto. And he was willing to risk his place in society and his reputation and everything else that he had to sponsor this man against every other group that was opposed to him. He believed in the God who could make all things new. He believed in Paul.

(c) The story of Christianity is just about that. It is the story of a God who took a chance on men with a bad past. It is the story of a God who came among human beings in the shape of a human personality and one after another got hold of men, not just their minds or their manners, but got hold of their whole being and made them new men. It is the story of a God who takes a chance with you and me, with all the bad past of our inheritance and all the record

of our failures, and says to us, I put my trust in you and in your growth.

III. The proof of Paul, of course, is to be found in the manner in which he met the hostility. It might have been his undoing. Yet the fiercer the hostility, the more vigorous Paul became. One of the lines of the story makes that quite clear. "Paul became more and more vigorous." He knew that what he believed was true, that what he was doing was right, and it did not make any difference to him if the whole world was against him. That is the secret of his growth, in spite of all the closed doors and all the opposition to every step that he took.

(a) The way from bad to better is a hard way. The general public will not understand; it will hold the past against you. It is important to remember, however, that it not only takes character to go from bad to better but also it makes character. A person who has the internal resources to face that hostility without a grudge and without resentment and moves steadily step by step along the way he has chosen because he knows it to be right is a person who will grow in moral strength and vigor from day to day.

(b) So much then for this unfamiliar chapter in the story of Paul. It brings to our mind this very significant fact in a day when our outlook perhaps is unduly dark and our confidence is waning: There are men and women who turn over a new leaf. And there are, God be praised, other people, like Barnabas, who see the best in them and get hold of them and bring them right up to scratch. Those are the people who, like Jesus, show forth the glory of a God who reaches down and gets hold of people who are trying to turn over a new leaf.—Theodore Parker Ferris

Illustrations

NO PLACE TO HIDE.   Man's conscience is his intuition of right and wrong; his feeling of the praiseworthiness or blameworthiness of what he has done; his sense of inner integrity, either maintained or outraged. There is no place to hide from conscience, for he carries it within himself. In the endeavor to improve the safety of airplane travel, one means that was employed was to place in commercial aircraft a sealed set of instruments with graphs to record flight data. The altitude at which the plane was flown, its speed, its changes of course—all were recorded. After the flight was over, the records were taken out and studied. No matter what the pilot might say, the testimony of the instruments could not be expunged or denied. This was a mechanical conscience, as E. Stanley Jones has called it, traveling with the plane constantly and recording constantly everything about it. The conscience that man carries within himself is like that. It also goes with him everywhere, and it is terrifyingly accurate. There is no place to hide from what it records.—Jack Finegan

ENERGY FOR RIGHT LIVING.   One of our American educators, frail in body but powerful in influence, said, "When I'm tired I just plug into the universe!" That is prayer. I hardly know a better practical description of it—plugging in on the universe.—Harry Emerson Fosdick

Sermon Suggestions

OF BONES AND BLESSING.   TEXT: Ezek. 37:1–14, especially verse 5. (1) God sometimes faces in his people—individually or collectively—a difficult situation, like the skeleton of a once-thriving life. (2) What is worse, it may be a condition of long standing—"very dry" and entirely unpromising. (3) However, God is resourceful and as almighty Creator can give new life and promise.

WHAT THE CHRISTIAN LIFE IS LIKE. TEXT: Rom. 8:6–11. (1) Its outlook is spiritual. (2) Its power is the Spirit of Christ. (3) Its promise is resurrection.

Worship Aids

CALL TO WORSHIP.   "Know therefore that the Lord thy God, he is God, the faithful God, which keepeth covenant and mercy with them that love him and keep his commandments to a thousand generations" (Deut. 7:9).

INVOCATION.   O Lord, almighty and everlasting God, who hast brought us to the beginning of another week in safety and mercy; wash over our spirits as we sing and pray and listen, and so deal with us as to cleanse us from sin and revive us in service and cause us to show forth the Christ, in whose name we pray. Amen.—E. Lee Phillips

OFFERTORY SENTENCE.   "This is the thing which the Lord commanded, saying, Take ye from among you an offering unto the Lord; whosoever is of a willing heart, let him bring it, an offering of the Lord" (Exod. 35:4b–5a).

OFFERTORY PRAYER.   Lord, we know that there are many causes of yours that need our support even when we do not feel like giving, and so we give. Grant unto us such generosity of spirit that we may give with a truly willing heart, realizing that we are your agents for good.

PRAYER.   O Lord, our Lord, how excellent is your name in all the earth. From beginning to forever, you are God. Creator and Sustainer of all, we enter your sanctuary with gladness and assurance. We worship you with praise and adoration. Blessed be the name of the Lord.

Eternal God, Lord of all season, winter time is a reflective season; hard weather keeps us close. Creation lies fallow, absorbing the snow and rain, preparing for the coming of spring again. Bulbs planted in the final warmth of fall lie in wait beneath the ground. Brittle, dull grass covers the dormant cold ground. Trees bare of leaves bend in the gusty wind yet display a solemn beauty in their starkness. But winter turns inward, preparing and waiting for the flourish of spring. And so it is with our lives, too, O God. In this Lenten season of repentance and examination, we look toward the renewal of Holy Week and the new life from the cross and Resurrection. As we walk that hard journey with Christ through his Passion and destiny to the cross, we pray for your Spirit to warm and guide us.

Forgive us, loving Father, for all that hinders our companionship with Christ, that betrays our discipleship, that mocks our obedience to the call. We yearn for a sincere longing after Christ; for a will to set our vision and allegiance solely on him; for a singleness of purpose to love and serve him with unwearied steadfastness and unmeasured humility. So may it be with our lives, dear Lord. Let this time of inward journey and self-examination prepare and ready us for that which is sure and certain to come in Christ. And may our worship today encourage and ennoble us in that resolve. We pray in Christ who shows us the way to life and walks alongside us.—William M. Johnson

LECTIONARY MESSAGE

Jesus, Illness, and Death

TEXT: John 11:(1–16), 17–45

I. *Jesus and illness.* The compassion of Jesus for people who were ill, and his evident mastery in dealing with both the people and their problems, are ably highlighted in the Gospel accounts. The range of illnesses was wide, and the miseries they caused were sometimes prolonged and intense. The Gospels tell us that Jesus was a master in treating miseries, and the stories abound that describe his ministry of healing.

Martha's word to Jesus is thus understood: "Lord, if you had been here, my brother would not have died." Was this part confession of faith and part rebuke? The rebuke, however mild, might suggest itself in that Jesus had been expected to come and see Lazarus after illness beset him; but although notified, Jesus had not come right away. Now he was on the scene, in the street approaching the family house, but Lazarus was now dead. Part rebuke or lament of an unfulfilled concern? The statement of Martha to Jesus reflected her trust that he could have helped her now-dead brother to have been spared that fate. Like so many, many others in the territories that Jesus traversed as he ministered, Martha knew him as a man of compassion for people in need, and she knew his competence in meeting those needs— even when it took some miracle to do so.

II. *Jesus and death.* The sickness Lazarus suffered led to his death, as some sicknesses do; but his death was not final for him. Jesus also had a ministry that often overcame the onslaught of the death experience. It happened again in the raising of Lazarus.

Martha's conversation with Jesus was more than mild rebuke and the lament of bereavement. Did she anticipate that out of his love for them Jesus would give Lazarus back his life? Was this her hope and prayer when she said, "Even now I know that, whatever you ask from God, God will give you"?

Fully aware of what he intended to the glory of God, Jesus gave Martha a word about the future: "Your brother will rise again." She returned a soft answer that she believed he would, "in the resurrection at the last day." Then Jesus spoke with authority—accenting the *how* over the *what,* the *means* over the *result:* "I am the resurrection and the life." The basis of the resurrection is not faith in it but the promise of God that it will be. The means of resurrection is the sovereignty of Jesus over death. God has invested rulership in Jesus, and that lordship includes victory over death. Thus the response of Jesus to the family grief and his delivering deed of calling Lazarus to return to this life. So summoned, Lazarus returned, raised from death to the glory of God.

III. *Our faith in the resurrection.* Scripture tells us that all who have died will rise from death "in the resurrection at the last day." All die—even those who experienced healing finally died, and those who were raised by Jesus from the state of death died again. His raising of Lazarus was for a time, but it was not the final time. The final time will include us all. It will happen at that point in *post*-history when the sovereignty of Jesus is fully exercised to fulfill history. On that "last day," Jesus will call every name. One perceptive preacher commented that if Jesus had not specifically limited his concern to Lazarus when he called for *him* to "come forth," *all the dead* might have gotten up at his call! But the time of all will come. So it has been planned; so it shall take place. Meanwhile, we go on as the believing ones, experiencing the eternal in this sphere of the temporal—and looking beyond this life with its limits and experiences of longing and lament.—James Earl Massey

SUNDAY: APRIL EIGHTH

SERVICE OF WORSHIP

Sermon: The Palm Sunday Demonstration

Texts: Mark 11:1–10; Matt. 21:1–9; Luke 19:28–38

What Jesus and his friends did on Palm Sunday we would now call a "demonstration."

When Jesus rode into the city, his friends from Galilee, and presumably others who were attracted by the excitement, began to shout, "Blessed is he that cometh in the name of the Lord. Hosanna in the highest!" Jesus himself didn't say one single word; he gives us not one clue to what he was thinking or to what he meant. We have the one, single, bare fact: He entered the city in such a way as to demonstrate his claim and to make indubitably clear what his claim was.

I. At first, this seems to many of us completely out of character. We do not normally think of Jesus as the kind of person who makes claims, let alone leads a demonstration. We think of him as a kind, gentle person, long-suffering, who never made any excessive demands upon anyone. We think of him that way because we like to think of him that way. But he was not like that. He made enormous demands.

(a) This is no mildly mannered man who never made any claims on anyone; this is a man whose claims were so great that only a few were prepared to accept them. To be sure, this is only one side of him. There is the other side, his compassion for the weary and the weak. "Come unto me all ye that labor and are heavy laden, and I will rest you." There is his infinite tenderness for the widow who had already lost her husband and now had lost her son and for the woman about to be stoned.

(b) Our temptation is to wash out the stern side of the picture because we do not like it, and it is perfectly natural to see why we don't like it. When he rode into Jerusalem he was demonstrating his claim upon the people. He did not slip into the city anonymously by night. He might be rejected by the people, but he could not be neglected by them. They all knew that he was there, and they all knew that he was neither a tourist nor a pilgrim nor an observer. He was there as one who made a claim on his people.

II. He not only demonstrated his claim, but he did it in such a way as to make the nature of it absolutely clear. Riding on an ass—that simple, Anglo-Saxon word which means "donkey"—he made it plain that he was not making a political claim. That little beast of burden was the poor man's animal. No royal pretender would have deigned to ride on such an animal.

(a) He knew that people could not live without a political structure, without a government. He was not trying to destroy the government or undermine its authority. He had something quite different in mind.

He does not want to take over the government of any country. All he asks is that the government of every country recognize the higher government of God. And what he means by that we must translate into our own language, for now we are told by one of our neighboring theologians that we cannot use the word *God* in church. I do not know what other word we can put in its place, but in case some of you do not know what it means, this is what it seems to me that he is talking about.

(b) There are laws written into the constitution of the universe that take precedence over any man-made laws, in the sense that they are prior to any man-made laws, and the basis upon which all the laws men make must rest. For example, it is written into the constitution of the universe that if you treat any human being as something less than human—not only on the race issue but in any relationship—if you treat him as something less than human, you will become less than a human being yourself. If you behave like a brute, you will eventually become a brute.'

III. His claim surely was not a political one, else he would not have ridden into the city on that little lowly beast of burden, the poor man's beast. It is becoming increasingly clear what his claim was. It certainly was not for anything personal. He was not asking anything for himself—position, power, or prestige—nothing. It was the claim of God making itself known and felt in him upon every human being, the claim of God on you and me.

(a) To bring this to our contemporary scene, the claim of God upon you and me and every other human being is to be himself; to be himself—in his religion; to say and do what he really believes, not what he thinks he ought to say and do or what he has been taught to say and do; to be himself—in his business; to be on the level with his partners as well as with his competitors; to be himself—in his personal life; to be what he is, not what he thinks others want him to be. This is the claim of God on every human being. He wants every one of us to be our real self—to strip off the shame, to quit the pose, to forget the pretense, to be the person we really are.

(b) Palm Sunday was a demonstration made by one man alone; a demonstration of the simple, single claim of God upon the life of every human being. Most of the people who took part in the demonstration missed the point of it. They loved the shouting, the glory, and all the excitement of it; but they did not see the cross at the end of the road, and they did not like the price that they had to pay. And those for whom it was intended, the leaders, crushed it.

(c) People have not changed very much, even people like you and me; after all these centuries we have not changed very much. There are always a few who see more than the glory and are willing to pay the price, and sometimes it is the very person you would least expect to see it.—Theodore Parker Ferris

Illustrations

THE APPEAL OF THE CROSS.   In April 1848, three young Englishmen, all subsequently distinguished, found themselves on a holiday trip in Paris in the midst of the revolution which overthrew King Louis Philippe. The men were Jowett, a future Master of Balliol; Stanley, later Dean of Westminster; and Palgrave, a poet and later the editor of the *Golden Treasury.* Palgrave kept a diary of their trip, in which there is an entry describing the sack of the Palace of the Tuileries by the mob. Everything was being smashed, when suddenly the mob reached the chapel, broke in the doors, and found themselves confronting the huge painting of Christ crucified behind the altar. Someone called out, "Hats off." Heads were bared, most of the crowd knelt down, and the picture was carried out to a neighboring church in "the most utter silence—'you might have heard a fly buzz.' "—Henry Sloane Coffin

NOT FAR FROM THE KINGDOM.   In 1946, when Albert Camus, an unbeliever, was writing an editorial for *Combat,* the magazine of the French Resistance, this is what he wrote, and I believe that if Jesus had known it, he would have said, "Praise God! He is not far from the kingdom." With that incomparable clarity of language and conscience, he wrote, "Let us suppose that certain individuals resolve that they will consistently oppose to power the force of example; to authority, exhortation; to insult, friendly reasoning; to trickery, simple honor. They would be preparing for the future. Who can fail to see the positively dazzling realism of such behavior?"—Theodore P. Ferris

Sermon Suggestions

THE VOICE OF EXPERIENCE OF GOD. TEXT: Isa. 50:4–9a. (1) It is encouraging. (2) It is grounded in obedient suffering. (3) It is self-authenticating.

A REDEEMING PATTERN FOR PRIDEFUL PEOPLE.   TEXT: Phil. 2:5–11. (1) Pride is listed as first of "the seven deadly sins." (2) Pride works all kinds of mischief, even in the Christian community. (3) Jesus Christ, who had the highest credentials and rights, set the example of "self-emptying" for the sake of others. (4) God will reward self-humbling with satisfactions that self-seeking could never achieve. (5) Therefore, work toward the attitude of Christ, verses 1–5.

Worship Aids

CALL TO WORSHIP. "And when he was come nigh, even now at the descent of the Mount of Olives, the whole multitude of the disciples began to rejoice and praise God with a loud voice for all the mighty works that they had seen; saying, Blessed be the King that cometh in the name of the Lord: peace in heaven, and glory in the highest" (Luke 19:37–38).

INVOCATION. Lord, come riding into our hearts this day as we recall the triumphal entry of Jesus Christ, into Jerusalem. Allow us to join with those who so long ago laid down their cloaks and waved palm branches as we dedicate our lives in obedience and serve the King of Kings with rejoicing.—E. Lee Phillips

OFFERTORY SENTENCE. "Set your mind on God's kingdom and his justice before everything else, and all the rest will come to you as well" (Matt. 6:33, NEB).

OFFERTORY PRAYER. Our Father, as you have graciously given to us, so may we gratefully give to you, so that we may hasten the progress of your kingdom in this world.—James W. Cox

PRAYER. O Father, as we begin this Holy Week commemorating the coming of the Lord with power to establish his kingdom among us, keep us from a casualness that would cause us to think that we can pass through these days as innocent bystanders. Make us as sensitive to the fickleness of our own lives as we are to the vacillating ways of a Pontius Pilate, a betraying Judas, or the denying ways of a Simon Peter.

Grant us courage to follow Jesus, so that in his Passion we may discover the truth that we can have eternal life. In these days before us, keep us at the cross until its deep mysteries unfold, at least in part, for our own life. Teach us through that horrible event that we really are only sinners, but sinners who are loved by God in Christ Jesus and who can be saved by his grace and sacrifice made on our behalf.

During the week before us teach us anew that the agonies of this world are the agonies that you feel and that you are dying a thousand deaths that people may be reconciled to you and to one another. Inspire us through all the meaning of Eastertide to be faithful to our high calling of being instruments of your love and reconciliation. Unite us in a fellowship that rejoices with those who rejoice and weeps with those who weep. Grant to those who are sick in mind, body, or spirit the mercy of your healing. Grant to those who are lonely, bereft of loved ones or friends, a sensitivity to the companionship of your abiding presence. Grant to the stranger within our gates a sense of oneness with your people. Grant to the lost the light of your searching that they may be found.

In the days ahead may your highest aspiration for your church be confirmed in and through us; and on every front, may the kingdoms of this world become the kingdoms of our God and of his Christ.—W. Henry Fields

LECTIONARY MESSAGE

Why Jesus Died
TEXT: Matt. 26:14–27:66, RSV
I. *He sought to betray Jesus.* The death of Jesus is understood initially as due to human contrivance.

(a) There was the traitorous deed of Judas, who had bargained with the religious leaders so that Jesus could be apprehended (26:14–16, 47–50).

(b) There was the crafty work of Joseph Caiaphas, the high priest, who instigated the plot to have Jesus killed (26:59–68; 27:1–2). Caiaphas and other members of the Sanhedrin helped Judas map the plan they rigorously followed. Caiaphas headed the court proceeding that judged Jesus and condemned him to death. That high priest schemed with full intent, eager to rid the people of this popular leader.

(c) There was also the civil agreement of Pilate, who inflicted the death sentence upon Jesus. The Jews were under Roman rule, which limited their self-government at several strategic points, the death penalty being one of them. Had Jewish freedom not been curbed, Jesus might have died at the hands of a stoning mob, but he was crucified due to Roman control. We remind ourselves of this when we recite that awesome sentence in the Apostles' Creed, "suffered under Pontius Pilate." Falsely accused of being an agitator, a threat to the authority of Rome, Jesus was crucified as a political criminal. The crafty Jewish leaders had so contrived the case against Jesus that Pilate felt trapped and obliged to go along with them. The very stating of the case made it appear political, which stirred Pilate to act politically. His washing of his hands after the decision (27:24) shows that he viewed the whole matter as a dirty business.

(d) There was, yet again, the bloodthirst of the misguided mob, whose members showed that Jesus should be crucified (27:22–23, 25). The problems of the crowd-mind are too familiar to need elaboration here.

Why was Jesus killed? He died as the result of a calculated scheme, the treachery of a onetime follower, political pressure tactics, and the hotheadedness of a mob. Jesus was the victim of human contrivance: a secret plot, a scared politician, a "sorry" follower, and a silly populace.

But the New Testament declares that there was more involved in his death than mere human circumstance or clever plotting.

II. *The curtain of the Temple was torn in two.* With this happening just after Jesus "yielded up his spirit" (27:50–51), the fact of the tearing led to a theology of his death.

(a) The tearing of the curtain meant that the barrier that blocked man from God was no longer in effect.

(b) The tearing of the Temple curtain meant that God had passed full sentence upon sin when Jesus died.

(c) The torn curtain meant that Jesus fully satisfied God as the needed offering for sin and that repeated sacrifices could now end. Thus that earlier word from Jesus during the Passover meal: "This [cup holds] my blood of the covenant, which is poured out for many for the forgiveness of sins" (26:28). Paul later added his interpretive word with the declaration, "Christ died for our sins" (1 Cor. 15:3).

III. *God was acting in Christ.* Jesus did not die as a mere victim; he died as a volunteering Savior. He died in our place and for our peace. He died in the will of God, according to the plan of God. "God was in Christ reconciling the world to himself" (2 Cor. 5:19). Thus his death, which uncovers our human guiltiness while at the same time it shows the aggressive goodwill and grace of God. The death of Jesus was no isolated fact listed on the daily ledger of Pilate; it remains a feature within the gracious planning and purpose of almighty God. We see our sin in what happened to Jesus, and we can see beyond that sin in what Jesus has made to happen for us.— James Earl Massey

SUNDAY: APRIL FIFTEENTH

SERVICE OF WORSHIP

Sermon: The Morningside View of Life
TEXT: John 20:1–18

There is something magical about mornings, isn't there? Especially bright, clear mornings when the "beasties and things that go bump in the night" have all disappeared and the sun shines on us warmly and beneficently.

I. The disciples must have discovered this.

(a) Think about that awful evening they had: an argument at dinner about which of them was the greatest disciple; one of them going out and betraying the Master;

that scuffle in the Garden of Gethsemane, and Jesus taken away by the soldiers; the long night of waiting and shifting back and forth from court to court, finally ending at Pilate's place; Peter's vehement denials of relationships and his brokenheartedness afterward; the news that Jesus was being beaten and would be crucified like a common criminal. It was a night that didn't end with the coming of daylight, a night that brought darkness at midday and an earthquake in the city of Jerusalem. And the next day, too, was dark as night for them, a time of fear and confusion, doubt and apprehension.

(b) But then came the morning, the morning after.

They could hardly wait for it. They began running toward it before it was dawn. First the women, coming to the tomb. Then Peter and John, when they heard the tomb was empty. And then Mary was there, gentle Mary, when the sun finally rose, casting soft shadows across the rocks. Mary, who had been a prostitute, a soldier's plaything, one of life's castaways. It is one of the most memorable scenes in history. Jesus standing quietly behind her as she knelt at the mouth of the tomb, weeping because his body was not there. Her pathetic plea when she thought he was the gardener: "Oh, tell me where they have taken him, so that I can go to him and anoint his body." The soft, personal word spoken by Jesus: "Mary." The sudden recognition. The tears of joy. The worship!

II. Did you notice this: There is no more night in the Gospel after this. That's right. John's Gospel has had a lot of night scenes.

(a) But then it was over, and there was no more night. Jesus appeared to his disciples in Galilee as the day was dawning, and their bad luck at fishing turned to stupendous good fortune, and they had breakfast together on the seashore. The night had been banished!

(b) Those accustomed to studying the symbolism in the Gospel of John say this is part of the message of the writer, and the true nature of the Christian faith, that now it is morning forever! The darkness is past, however things may appear, and God is in charge of the world. For those who

have eyes to see and hearts to believe, there will never be darkness again. Not real darkness, not blinding, suffocating, never-ending darkness. For the light has overcome the darkness, as the Gospel promised, and overcome it for all eternity.

III. We tend to forget the message, don't we?

(a) I think of a dear, beautiful woman who worships with this congregation and of something she told me that happened many years ago. She was married very young and had a little baby. Then one day her husband deserted her. She was all alone in the world, a long way from home, with her child. All the light had gone out of her life. Finally, in desperation, she took the little money she had and went to Yosemite National Park, where she had once known great happiness. For six days she walked and climbed and sat and thought. The heaviness was almost more than she could bear. And then, on the sixth day, she was sitting on a great boulder and noticed that she was staring at a tuft of grass growing out of the rock. It was a miracle, she thought, the way the grass grew out of the rock. For years, the weather had worked on the rock, heating and freezing it, until finally some erosion had occurred and some of the rock had become powder, and eventually some grass seed had caught in the eroded section and had found enough nourishment to spring into life.

"It was the message I needed," she said. "I knew it had taken ages for that rock to break down and for life to grow on it. And I realized that, however long it took, my own barren existence would be fruitful and productive again, that God would make something grow in me the way he had made the grass grow on that rock. It was a turning point in my life. I was able to go home again and live, because I knew that God would bring life out of death."

What she had found was the morningside view of life. In fact, God had already done it!

(b) Knowing this doesn't mean that life is always easy for us. It isn't Life is still filled with strife and pressure and overwork and betrayal and death. It was for the disciples. It has been so for the saints of every age. But the message of Easter is that God is with us and will bring all our nighttimes to glorious, eternal morning. We only have to remember what he has done in Christ and know that, as Paul says, this is the "first fruit," the promise of what is to come. When we remember this, we can turn any dark situation into a lighter one.

IV. Earlier, I said that the Gospel doesn't show us any more night scenes after the Resurrection, that after that stupendous event it became interested only in morning scenes. After saying this, I realized there is one exception, not in the Gospel of John but in the Gospel of Luke. Yet the exception is very special. It is the account of the two disciples from Emmaus returning home after the Crucifixion, dejected and unhappy because the One in whom they had placed their hope for a better tomorrow had been killed. Jesus appears to them on the road, but they do not realize who he is. He listens to the story of their despondency and then interprets the prophecies to them about the Messiah's death and Resurrection. By the time they get to Emmaus, the evening is upon them. They invite their mysterious companion to spend the night with them. While they are eating, there is something about his prayer over the bread, or the way he breaks it, that provides the sudden recognition of who he is, and then he vanishes. And what do they do? They jump up from the table and rush back to Jerusalem to tell the others! It is night, but they act as if it is day. They forget all about the hazards of traveling at night on a lonely road where robbers prowl. They ignore the dangers of the city where their Lord was crucified. They behave as if it were high noon and they were going out for a turn around the park! The darkness is still there, but it is aglow with possibility, for they have just discovered the morningside view of life.

This is what Easter is all about, isn't it? Not even death itself is able to quench the light and hope and joy that God gives.

What a difference it makes in the life of any individual to have this morningside view of things.

V. It will all be different in the morning. That's the word of the Resurrection.

That's the promise of Easter.

It will all be different in the morning! That's what faith is all about, isn't it? The morning after, the new view of things, the recognition that sets the darkness aglow with possibility, the knowledge that nothing, not even death itself, can separate us from the love of God.

"Mary," he says.

"Rabboni!" she exclaims.

And the night has vanished forever.—John Killinger

Illustrations

RESURRECTION EMPHASIS.   This, then, was the first immediate consequence of Paul's conversion experience. Jesus, he now knew, was alive, by the power of God. From this point right on to the end of his life, the Resurrection was central in the apostle's thinking. It could not be otherwise. Protestant theology, concentrating on the atoning sacrifice of the cross, has not always done justice to this apostolic emphasis on the risen life. We can certainly agree with Denney when he says that "nothing could be more curiously unlike the New Testament than to use the resurrection to belittle or disparage the death." But it is not a case of belittling or disparaging the death. It is a case of recognizing with Paul that without the Resurrection the death would have been powerless to save; and that without a risen, living, present Christ, with whom through faith the believer can come into union, all the benefits of the death would have had to stand unappropriated forever. It was on the resurrection fact that the church was built. It was the resurrection gospel that the apostles preached. It was the experience of union with the risen Christ that made them the might men of God they were. The fact of the matter is that, so far from belittling the death by laying all the emphasis we can upon the Resurrection, we are doing what is most likely to interpret that death in its full redeeming value; and we are in far graver danger of belittling it when the resurrection emphasis is lacking.—James S. Stewart

VICTORY. For my part, I feel certain that among the stories circulated about the Resurrection of Jesus Christ, one in particular has a legendary touch, but such a right touch. Hear Matthew: "And . . . the tombs also were opened, and many bodies of the saints who had fallen asleep were raised, and coming out of the tombs after his resurrection they went into the holy city and appeared to many" (27:52–53, RSV). The meaning is unmistakable. The Resurrection of Jesus Christ is the living proof that God "brings with him"—beautiful phrase!—"those who have fallen asleep." All through life's day we shall walk with the Christ, often as the Stranger, because he never obtrudes or overrides. Before the journey's end we shall ask many questions, experience many heartaches, be molded by many of life's disciplining disappointments. And then, suddenly, whether we shall be young, middle-aged, or old, we shall find that the day is far spent, that the shadows are gathering, and at last the night descends. In that moment our eyes shall be opened, and we shall know him, but now no longer as One who will vanish from our sight. He will be the living, traveling Companion along the unknown valley's way to the highroad of God's eternity. Then shall come to pass the saying, "Death is swallowed up in victory" (1 Cor. 15:54, RSV).—Elam Davies

Sermon Suggestions

THIS IS THE GOSPEL TRUTH! TEXT: Acts 10:34–43. (1) The good news is for all Jew and Gentile alike. (2) The good news centers in Jesus Christ—what he was and what he did. (3) The good news is the subject of our preaching and witness, and forgiveness of sins is its object.

THE GREAT ESCAPE. TEXT: Col. 3:1–4. Escaping the gravitational pull of earthly desires (1) is based on the Easter victory of Christ; (2) requires "the expulsive power of a new affection" (see Gal. 5:16, 22); (3) enjoys a security the world does not know and cannot appreciate; and (4) anticipates a glorious future with Christ.

Worship Aids

CALL TO WORSHIP. "Blessed are they that have not seen, and yet have believed" (John 20-29b).

INVOCATION. Omnipotent Lord, before whom graves must open, the dead must rise, and the wicked are confounded; break the glow of Easter across our brows and shine the resurrection light into our hearts, that in all rejoicing we may praise and magnify thy holy name.— E. Lee Phillips

OFFERTORY SENTENCE. "He that taketh not his cross, and followeth after me, is not worthy of me" (Matt. 10:38).

OFFERTORY PRAYER. O God, we have hardly begun to take up the cross of him who had no place to lay his head. Grant that the offering we bring may be a token of our growth toward true discipleship.

PRAYER. Almighty God, in Creation you called forth light out of the darkness; as the night has passed and dawn's light has birthed this holy day, you have given our earthly lives back to us again. We praise you for the gift of today and the sparkling aliveness of spring. Redeeming God, in resurrection you have called forth forever light out of sinful darkness; as the night of death has been defeated and resurrection's light has made today Easter Sunday, you have given us the salvation gift of eternal life. We worship you as King of Kings and Lord of Lords.

God of miracles, only you can create emptiness to proclaim fullness, for now by an empty cross you have granted us full pardon and forgiveness. By an empty tomb you have made manifest full salvation and eternal life for all who will believe and receive. Only you can take our empty lives and make them whole and complete in Christ. Thanks be to God. Holy God, Father of our risen Lord, like the followers of Jesus who encountered the Resurrection first, we come today with longings much like theirs. With all of them, we, too, gather behind the locked doors of our fears. Let us hear and experience again your blessing of *Peace be with you.*

Like Peter, we wait in the anguish of betrayal, seeking forgiveness and another chance. As with him, seek us out and bid us back to the family and home, and favor us with the invitation to feed your sheep. Like Mary, we come not knowing and wondering where you are. As with her, call us tenderly by our names so that we, too, shall surely know it is you. Like Thomas, we wrestle with doubts. Gently touch us and allow us to touch your presence. And in glad response, we shall proclaim, "My Lord and my God."

And as we walk our roads to Emmaus, share the journey with us and instruct us in your truths, so that we may be able to look back and remember with joy and understanding burning within us like a holy fire. God of resurrection: we believe he is alive, and we give thanks. Blessed be the name of our Lord. Alleluia, Alleluia.—William M. Johnson.

LECTIONARY MESSAGE

His Resurrection

TEXT: Matt. 28:1–10, RSV

This narrative is one of the most significant about the basis of the Christian faith; it is short, succinct, and begins without apparent drama. But dramatic it is, and its message is indispensable to all that went before, concerning Jesus of Nazareth. The drama? His rise out of death.

I. *The first witnesses.* There were those who saw the Lord alive after he had been crucified and entombed. This story is based upon their reported experience.

The Resurrection happened! Bona fide witnesses attested that Jesus returned from death. His tomb was empty on the morning of the third day after his body had been placed there; the great stone blocking the entrance had been rolled back, and the soldiers stationed outside to guard the place were all paralyzed with fright when the numinous happening of his Resurrection occurred. The two Marys who first felt the impact of the happening also felt fear, but it was a fear more like awe, mingled with the joy of expecting to see him alive again. Small wonder these first witnesses "ran to tell his [other] disciples" (28:8).

II. *The report confirmed.* The joy of an expected reunion heightened when those who had *heard* the report actually *saw* Jesus alive again. "Jesus met them and said, 'Hail!' " Never a greeting so deeply felt! Never a person so warmly welcomed! Never an intensity of intimacy so grippingly experienced! So the two Marys "came up and took hold of his feet and worshiped him" (v. 9). Sensitive to this shock from his presence, Jesus reassured them, quieting their frightened emotions, "Do not be afraid." The Resurrection happened! That happening stands as confirmed fact reported by witnesses of worth.

III. *No isolated event.* The Resurrection of Jesus from death was never preached and reported as an isolated event, nor even as a historical surprise. The church rightly recalls that the Old Testament foretold the happening, that Jesus himself repeatedly announced that it would occur within three days after his death, and that his true followers would indeed see him alive again after that.

This was no isolated event. It was connected with Old Testament hopes. It was connected with the needs of his people. It was connected with the plan of God to "save the people from their sins." As Paul later explained, "For as in Adam all die, so also in Christ shall all be made alive" (1 Cor. 15:22). The Resurrection was his vindication and a forecast of our future. What happened to Jesus will happen to those who look to him as Savior.

IV. *The promised experience.* The first witnesses were instructed to "go and tell." A part of their report was to include his promise that he would show himself: "They will see me" (v. 10b). He did show himself, and those who saw were fully satisfied. That is the promised experience for all the people of God. We will see him! Because of his Resurrection, there is this hope for our future. His Resurrection was in the plan of God; so is our own. Death does not spell *finis*—it leads to fulfillment, fullness, through his Resurrection. We will see him and share his exalted life and likeness.

V. *Conclusion.* The truth about his Resurrection is meant to influence our beliefs, our behavior, and our expectation. This truth puts believers at new frontiers of faith and experience. And where this truth is known and aptly regarded, its power remains an evident force to give meaning in every crisis—even that final crisis called death!—James Earl Massey

SUNDAY: APRIL TWENTY-SECOND

SERVICE OF WORSHIP

Sermon: Then What Happened?

TEXTS: Acts 4:32–35; John 20:19–31

It's the first Sunday after Easter. You can get your old pew back now. It's nice to see smiling faces in familiar places again.

We're here this morning to pick up the story, see what happened next. The story goes on, you know. Some think it ended at Easter. Easter sounds like the perfect climax to a story; a happy ending, a whopper of a miracle, lots of good visuals for the movie version. If a good story is supposed to have a strong ending, they don't get much better than a resurrection. How do you top that?

I. But the story doesn't stop there. This morning we look at what happens next. The two passages selected for the readings this morning from the lectionary are passages that focus on what happened next: first, John's record of the appearance of Jesus to the disciples in the upper room.

(a) They're all there, all there except Thomas. Jesus appears in the room; actually, he materializes right before them. Then he breathes on them, which is the way God put life into the first humans, Adam and Eve in the Garden of Eden. What is happening here is that something new is being created. Jesus breathes on them the breath of life and says, "Receive the Holy Spirit." Then he gives them the power to forgive sins.

(b) Pentecost comes fifty days after Easter. This scene in John is on the night of Easter. So there is a difference in chronology between the two records but an agreement on what happened after Easter, what came next. And what came next, they both say, was the church. And the Spirit, they say, is the Spirit of Jesus. It's Jesus who breathed his breath into them.

II. Now return to Thomas. He's featured prominently in this story. Because of this story Thomas is called "the doubter," and "Doubting Thomas" is a phrase that has become a part of our vocabulary. But in order to understand this story, Thomas should be called "Thomas the Tardy," because Thomas represents all of those who didn't get there in time for a resurrection appearance. Only a few had that privilege. Only a few saw the resurrected Jesus. But John is saying that's not what makes you a Christian anyway.

(a) Seeing the resurrected Christ is not what makes you a Christian. Being empowered by the Spirit of Christ is what makes you a Christian. In other words, it's not something that you experienced in the past, but it's the way that you are living in the present that makes you a Christian.

(b) And that's why when Jesus appeared to Thomas in a special appearance, kind of a command performance, eight days later, Thomas is reprimanded by Jesus for wanting to see before he believes, as if it were a sign of weak faith, as if real Christians don't need to have signs, don't need to have evidence before they believe.

Then Jesus says this, and this is addressed to all the rest of us. This is addressed to all of those who come after Thomas. He says, "Blessed are those who have not seen and yet believe." And that's the point of this whole story. Blessed are those who have not seen the resurrected Christ and yet believe and give evidence of having his Spirit in their lives.

III. It's a marvelous scene. It's really the birthday of the church. That's what's being described here. It's John's version of Pentecost. It says that the church is the church when it has the Spirit of Christ. "Where the Spirit of the Lord is, there is the one true church. . . ."

(a) That's what the church is supposed to look like if it is empowered by the Spirit of Jesus. It's called *koinonia,* which we translate as "fellowship," and you can see it means a kind of radical caring for one another. The story tells us this fellowship, this *koinonia,* happens when persons are more important than possessions. This fellowship happens when I can see that what I have is given to me in trust so that I will use it for the growth of Christ's kingdom.

(b) And that's contrary to the self-serving, popular interpretation of Christianity, that sees Christ's blessing as giving us personal prosperity. But wealth is not the sign of being a Christian. Generosity is the sign of being a Christian. Because, "where the Spirit of the Lord is . . ." Luke makes this abundantly clear, not only in the Acts of the Apostles, but also in the first book he wrote called the Gospel according to Luke. In both books he makes it abundantly clear, "where the Spirit of the Lord is . . ." there will be concern for the poor. And that's why, when he describes the ideal church, the church that is empowered by the Spirit of Jesus, he said, "There was not a needy person among them."

(c) And we know that they were not all of "one heart and one soul." They didn't all agree. They didn't all get along. Not only Paul, in his letters, who talks about it all the time, but even Luke, in the Acts of the Apostles, talks about the divisions among them. So, this is an idealized picture of the church.

But do you know where they got it? This is important. Do you know where they got this? They got it from Deuteronomy. They got it from God's command to Israel, given to Israel as it entered into the Promised Land. God said, "You're going into the Promised Land. It's like starting all over, right? So let's get it right. Let's do it right this time. Every seven years I want to forgive all debts *so there will be no poor among you.*"

That's the way God wants it. And Luke is saying that just as God expected Israel to be a special kind of community because of the grace given to them in the Exodus, so God expects us to be a special kind of community in the church because of the grace given to us in the Resurrection. The church is where people ought to be able to see what kind of community God wants in this world. The church is where there ought to be fellowship in this world, real fellowship, community, and love. "There will be no poor among you," because you are not a community if some eat and others don't.

IV. That's the standard that is held up in the Bible, the standard of hospitality. So in the church, Luke says, there are to be no strangers, no foreigners. In the church everyone is welcome because the church is the community God created. This is where people ought to be able to see the way things are supposed to be. From the very beginning God wanted it this way. He wanted a community among all people. But it's never been that way, until now. Now it's here in the church.

Listen to the description: "They were all of one mind and one soul, and there was no one in need among them." Later in his letters, Paul will say, "Now there is no longer Jew nor Greek, slave nor free, male or female." In other words, no longer will the differences between people make any difference, but "we are all one in Christ Jesus." No more foreigners, no more strangers. That's what the church should be—a community where none is allowed to be poor and where strangers are welcome.—Mark Trotter

Illustrations

WHAT HAS CHRISTIANITY TO OFFER?   A cynical observer once remarked that so far as he could see there were three attitudes commonly adopted toward religion: (1) Religion is true, and I've got it; (2) religion is false, and I've seen through it; and (3) it really doesn't matter whether it is true or false because it is entirely irrelevant anyway.

There is sufficient truth in the gibe to give it a sting.—F. A. Cockin

BETWEEN EASTER AND PENTECOST. If the whole demand for experience heads us straight toward Pentecost, candor compels me to say that the church is not living in Pentecost.

It is living between Easter and Pentecost. Easter stands for life wrought out, offered; Pentecost stands for life appropriated, lived to its full, unafraid and clearly and powerfully witnessing to an adequate way of human living.

The church stands hesitant between the two. Hesitant, hence comparatively impotent. Something big has dawned on its thinking—Christ has lived, taught, died and risen again and has commissioned the church with the amazing good news. But something big has yet to dawn in the very structure, makeup, and temper of the life of the church—Pentecost. Easter has dawned; Pentecost has not. If the church would move up from that between-state to Pentecost, nothing could stop it—nothing!!—E. Stanley Jones

Sermon Suggestions

THE DRAMA OF THE AGES. TEXT: Acts 2:14a, 22–32. (1) Act I: The eternal plan of God. (2) Act II: The revelatory life of Christ. (3) Act III: The hostile response of the lawless. (4) Act IV: God's last word (see v. 36).

ALL OF THIS IS OURS. TEXT: 1 Pet. 1:3–9. (1) Our hope. (2) Our inheritance. (3) Our security. (4) Our testing. (5) Our sustaining motivation.

Worship Aids

CALL TO WORSHIP. "Lift up your heads, O ye gates; even lift them up, ye everlasting doors; and the King of glory shall come in. Who is this King of glory? The Lord of hosts, he is the King of glory" (Ps. 24:9–10).

INVOCATION. Open us, Lord, to fresh winds of the Spirit, moving, prodding, convincing, convicting, enabling, and challenging. Cause us to catch a vision of thy directives and to hear the voice of thine entreaties, through Jesus, the Resurrected One.—E. Lee Phillips

OFFERTORY SENTENCE. "And God is able to make all grace abound toward you; that ye, always having all sufficiency in all things, may abound to every good work" (2 Cor. 9:8).

OFFERTORY PRAYER. Lord, all that we have we owe to you. For you are the source of our beings. We have received much by your grace. In gratitude, then, we open our hearts and pockets and checkbooks to say simply, "Thank you, Lord." So bless our offering.—Donald W. Musser

PRAYER. How do we worship you, God? Is it worship when we stand awestruck before a sunrise and feel an inspiration we cannot explain? Is it worship when we marvel at the beauty of a violet growing wild in the woods, yet so intricately made that we know it is the work of a master artist?

Is it worship when we see the fleeting smile of a baby, catch something of the wonder of innocence, and remember that such was our gift once, too? Is it worship when the sparkling day shimmers in newness, with fresh green growth and cascading blooms on trees waving in the gentle breeze to bring refreshment and joy to weary life? Is it worship when a few moments of conversation by the way of busy life gives hope to another and courage to the fainthearted? Is it worship when the words of a saint of faith clutch the mind and heart and reinvigorate determination? Is it worship when an age-old truth finds its home in a young heart and lights up an uncreased face with understanding? Is it worship to walk in the shoes of sorrow, feel the pain of loss, experience the agony of separation, and know that behind it all there is the sunrise of eternal hope? Is it worship to struggle to make ends meet, pinch pennies and cut corners and still contribute to the needy, the hungry, and the mighty work of the church? Is it worship to open the gates of laughter and spread hearty mirth, like rays of sunshine across the drab landscape of demanding life? Is it worship to vent anger at hatred, to feel frustration with hostage-takers, to deplore war and senseless killing of innocent people? Is it worship to fight substance abuse and crippling disease and selfish enterprises? Is it worship to bring to bear upon the cries of men and women everywhere the gift of love that lifts and strengthens and encourages and saves?

What is worship, Father? Is it still abiding in your presence long enough to find direction for life, listening to your word revealed and then moving out from the sanctuary to let you do your thing among people through us? Or is it simply bringing all that we are, all that we have done, all that we know, and all that we can become, and laying it before you, offering it as a sacrifice to you? You see, we don't have much to bring, we haven't always done the best with what we have. Maybe that is why we try to make other avenues our mode of worship. Maybe that is why we can't always understand how to meet you. Maybe worship isn't all feeling. Maybe it is a matter of committing and giving out of commitment so that you are made better known in the world. Whatever worship is, Father, this morning we want it, we really do. So we pray that you will let it happen. Then we will know what it means to worship you with all our heart, mind, soul, and strength.—Henry Fields

LECTIONARY MESSAGE

The Confirming Presence

TEXT: John 20:19–31, RSV

The Lord is always eager to deal with us and to confirm his presence in the midst of our crises. But he does more: He orients us to service as we build on the experiences we gain through interacting with him.

I. *The textual scene.* Hidden away in protective seclusion, the disciples were cowering in fear. They could envision no good future for themselves because their Leader was no longer with them. Fearful of those Jewish leaders who had had Jesus killed, the disciples now sulked in dire foreboding about themselves. What a shocking weekend! What a disappoint-

ment to their previously high hopes for him—and themselves with him!

What could the future now hold?

Then, "Jesus came and stood among them and said to them, 'Peace be with you.'" (20:19). The Presence was a welcomed one! The greeting was a familiar one! The surprise was a heartening one! The result was life-renewing! Fears subsided as he walked among them, showing his hands and side. "Then his disciples were glad when they saw the Lord" (20:20b).

II. *The Lord still confirms his presence, acting in his unique and unmistakable way.*

(a) He enters into our experience by his own initiative, breaking through all barriers. Despite "the doors being shut . . . for fear" (20:19). His familiar greeting of *shalom!*—spoken declaratively with his upraised hands spread in the familiar gesture of conferred blessing—this was the needed word, and their fear subsided. There is nothing quite like the word of Jesus to deal with our fears and nothing quite like a sense of his presence to deal with our aloneness.

(b) He enters into our setting to assist us at our points of need, helping us to deal with the present that pulls upon us. In the case of those disciples, the problem was fear that reduced them to cowards hiding in fright. Jesus dealt with them at that point of their need. He still deals with his followers at their points of need, whatever those needs might be.

III. *The Lord still confirms his presence, readying for mission those who receive his help.*

(a) The second uttering of *shalom* was with the future in view: he was helping them to anticipate going beyond the hour then upon them. "As the Father has sent me, even so I send you" (v. 21). The "breathing" upon them was emblematic of freshness that would attend their lives and work, and it was symbolic of their reception of his very Spirit as they remained open to further enablement to serve his interests.

IV. *Conclusion.* We must remember, all of us, that true believers are heirs to the companioning Presence of our Lord. We do not now see him as did those who knew him in the flesh; but as Jesus told Thomas,

"Blessed are those who have not seen and yet believe" (20:29).

There is that familiar story about the little boy flying his kite on a rather cloudy day. One of the adult neighbors passed by, and deciding to chat for a moment, he asked the boy what he was doing. Told that he was flying his kite, the neighbor teasingly remarked, "But I don't see it. How do you know it's still up there?" The little boy smiled as he returned reply, "Because I can feel a strong tug on my string!" The confirming Presence of the Lord is like that for us. Now and again he strengthens us in his unique and unmistakable way, sharing himself in our crises, aiding us at our points of need, and girding us for continuing his work. This is the heritage of every believer.—James Earl Massey

SUNDAY: APRIL TWENTY-NINTH

SERVICE OF WORSHIP

Sermon: The "Other" Great Commission

Text: Luke 24:36–49

The Great Commission. What is the first thing that comes to mind? For most of us, Matt. 28:19–20 wells up in our thoughts and leaps to our tongues. We've heard countless sermons and Sunday school lessons on it; we can say it from memory: "Go and make disciples of all nations, baptizing them in the name of the Father and of the Son and of the Holy Spirit, teaching them to observe all that I have commanded you; and lo, I am with you always, to the close of the ages." But Luke records a Great Commission, too. We often neglect or overlook it. I suppose it tends to be obscured by the long shadow cast by the more famous one in Matthew. That's a great loss because Luke's version is so rich and deep in its message and meaning. It should not be ignored. Let's look at this "other" Great Commission. [Read Scripture.]

In these few verses, describing Jesus' encounter with the disciples after Easter, Luke lays out four major crossbeams of the Christian faith, which support and define our commission to go and tell.

I. First, the Resurrection.

(a) Luke drives home the point that the same Jesus who was nailed to a cross and died on Friday was the Christ who arose on Easter Sunday morning. He was no phantom. It was no hallucination.[1] Luke builds suspense for this revelation earlier in chapter 24. Mary and the other women took spices to the tomb to complete the burial process, only to find that it was empty! The two disciples on the road to Emmaus recognized Jesus at the supper table, when he broke and blessed the bread, and Luke suggests that he had appeared to Simon Peter as well.

But, our text contains the clearest picture: Jesus appears to all of the disciples. Now, there must have been something different about Jesus. The disciples did not recognize him. They thought it was a spirit. They were startled and frightened. Isn't that strange? I mean, they had virtually lived with Jesus for three years. No doubt they had had little trouble recognizing Lazarus when Jesus raised him from the dead. Why didn't they recognize Jesus? The answer may be that Jesus' Resurrection was no simple return to his worn out earthly body. It was a glorified body, the same but somehow different—a glorified body in which he would presently be exalted and ascend to the Father. As one theologian has put it, it was a "borderline event."[2] Luke goes to great lengths,

1. William Barclay, "The Gospel of Luke," in *The Daily Bible Study Series* (Philadelphia: Westminster Press, 1975), 297.

2. Hendrikus Berkhof, *Christian Faith* (Grand Rapids, MI: Eerdmans, 1986), 316.

though, to affirm the reality of a physical Resurrection. Jesus shows them his hands and feet and lets them touch him. Even while they still disbelieve in joy and wonder, Luke delivers the clincher: Jesus asks for something to eat! Now, Jesus might well have been hungry. But to record that simple historical fact is not why Luke includes it here. Luke reports it again to affirm the "fleshiness" of the Resurrection. Spirits don't get hungry, because they have no bodies to nourish. So whatever the precise bodily form he took, Jesus—the man—had come out of the grave.

(b) Why is the Resurrection so important to Luke? Well, it validates Jesus' life and teachings—he was who he said he was. It was a divine "well done" that confirmed Jesus' obedient ministry.[3] It is how we know God was in Jesus. It brought the disciples to faith and explains the rapid growth of the Christian movement. Christianity was not founded on the made-up story of confused and desperate disciples but on the historical fact of the risen Lord. And for us today it is a promise of hope. Even for us finite, sinful, undeserving people, life—not death—is the ultimate reality.[4] We *are* a resurrection people.

But there is more.

II. (a) Luke next tells us that Jesus opened the disciples' minds to Scripture and placed himself squarely as the fulfillment of scriptural prophecy: " '. . . everything written about me in the Law of Moses and the prophets and the Psalms must be fulfilled!' Then he opened their minds to understand the Scriptures and said to them, 'Thus it is written, that the Christ should suffer and on the third day rise from the dead' " (vv. 44b–46). Here, too, Luke gives a hint of this early in the chapter. At the tomb the men in dazzling apparel tell the women, "Remember how he told you . . . that the Son of man must . . . be crucified, and on the third day rise" (vv. 6–7). And on the road to Emmaus, Jesus "interpreted all the Scriptures and

the things concerning himself" (v. 27) and "opened the Scriptures" for them (v. 32).

(b) The disciples surely had read and studied the Scriptures. They had lived with Jesus for three years, heard his preaching, and even received private tutoring. But it was only on the far side of Easter—after they encountered the living Christ—that they fully appreciated the significance of Scripture. Only with the eyes of Christ did the complete picture of prophecy crash through their nearsightedness and penetrate their numb skulls to the point of recognition.

(c) We should not be too hard on the disciples because this is so for us, too. We normally think of Scripture revealing Jesus: testimony to the event; the story of the character; a means to an end. Luke, however, does something unexpected. He turns this thinking around—back on itself. To be sure, Scripture is how we come to know Jesus, but Jesus—the risen Christ—also reveals Scripture! And like the first disciples, it is really only after we have experienced the risen Christ that Scripture becomes integrated and sensible and full of meaning.

Without Christ, Scripture for us is antiquated literature or a list of legalistic precepts, at best. With Christ, it is a living word—brought into the present with grace-filled instruction. Yes, Scripture reveals Christ, yet the reverse is also true: Christ reveals Scripture.

But there is more. What do we do with the risen Christ and the Scripture he illuminates?

III. (a) Luke tells us that Jesus gave his disciples, and gives us, an urgent task. In verses 47ff., he says, ". . . repentance and forgiveness of sin should be preached in his name to all nations, beginning from Jerusalem. You are witnesses of these things." Here, also, there is an earlier foretaste. After the women learned of the empty tomb, they went and told the disciples (which the disciples dismissed as an idle tale). And the two disciples from Emmaus got up in the middle of the night—tired and worn out after a day's travel—to trek seven miles to Jerusalem to tell the others what they had seen (v. 33).

---

3. Fisher Humphreys, *Thinking about God* (New Orleans, LA: Insight Press, 1974), 204.
4. Ibid.

So, Jesus charges the disciples to be witnesses—proclaimers of the good news of repentance and the forgiveness of sins to everyone—not just to Jews but to all nations, including the Gentiles. Fortunately for us, the disciples faithfully discharged the task. But for their obedience, we would have no New Testament, no church, and no good news of salvation.

(b) Jesus gives us that same charge—to all Christians, not just to ordained ministers. When Jesus commissioned the disciples, they knew nothing of ordination. The practice of ordination didn't come until sometime later. They were simply believers who, like us, had experienced something wonderful and were driven to tell others. Just as the disciples' preaching and writing was crucial to our meeting Jesus, so too is our witness crucial to our children and grandchildren's knowing Christ. It has been often said, and it is true, "the church at any given point in time is only one generation away from extinction."

IV. But is there more? Indeed, so. In proclaiming the risen Christ as revealed in Scripture, and who reveals Scripture, the disciples were given a helper—the Holy Spirit.

(a) In verse 49, Luke quotes Jesus as saying, "I send the promise of my Father upon you; but stay in the city, until you are clothed with power from on high." Even before Pentecost, the Holy Spirit was present and active. The whole story of Jesus is stamped indelibly by the Holy Spirit—from birth, to baptism, to temptation, to ministry in power, to Resurrection. This is a vital theme throughout all of Luke's Gospel. But in a short while that same Spirit would come in its fullness—with special, unique power—to energize and transform that forlorn band of disciples. Only then would they be able to proclaim the good news with a fervor and intensity that belies any charge of a concocted story.

(b) At Pentecost, the Spirit came, not only to help those disciples, but to abide and stay with the Christian community. We, too, therefore, have the help of that same Spirit to point back to the risen Christ, helping us interpret Scripture and

energizing us for the task of proclaiming the good news of Christ.

(c) If this is true, why are we sometimes so reluctant to do it? If there is good news to tell—news able to transform people and families and cultures, why are we not beating a path to the world to share it? The answers are many, but Luke suggests several.

(1) For all of our pious "God-talk," maybe deep down inside at the gut level we aren't sure about the *Resurrection.* Maybe we doubt no less than the disciples did at first. And even if we believe it, perhaps we haven't really made it a part of our daily lives. The risen Christ can't just be a vague notion of belief or even a distant object of worship: He must be a "friend" that we walk and walk with every day.

(2) And how about *Scripture,* which we've said both reveals Christ and is illuminated by Christ? What a treasure of inspiration we can find there! But how many of us spend more than a few minutes a day (if that) ingesting its teaching? For all the lip service some of us pay to believing the Bible, we spend precious little time reading it and making *it* a part of our lives.

(3) We've said God has also sent the *Holy Spirit* to comfort, encourage, and empower us. But the Holy Spirit won't use us and work in us against our will. We have to open the door to the Spirit. How do we do it? Well, for starters, through the disciplines of silence, meditation, and prayer. Not just prayer when there is a crisis, but planned, routine, continual, sustained prayer in which we stand open to the indwelling of the Holy Spirit of God to transform and empower us for the tasks of the kingdom.

(4) I think Luke is saying that each of us must settle the basic question once and for all, Is Jesus Christ really Lord of my life? If so, we will do what he commands us to do. Not on our own power—but through the instruction of Holy Scripture and the inspiration of the Holy Spirit! That was how the disciples two thousand years ago were able to turn the ancient world upside down for Christ, and that's the only way we'll be able to do it, too!—Brent Walker.

Illustrations

EVANGELIZING THE WORLD.   The quickest way to evangelize the world is to deepen in the church as a whole the spirit of evangelism, because we can make up our minds that the world is never going to be won for God by apostles, however gifted or however diligent. Apostles are few in number, and their contacts are limited. What is wanted is a great multitude of faithful witnesses, men and women who make no pretense to special gifts but who nonetheless have the love of Christ in their hearts and seek by life and lip to commend him to their kinsfolk and neighbors as he gives them guidance and opportunity. The kingdom of heaven, said Jesus, does its work like leaven, where innumerable tiny particles seek by association with other tiny particles to communicate a divine potency that will energize and transform the particles they touch. Every life has contacts with other lives, and if these contacts can be Christianized and harnessed to the evangelistic purpose, we shall inevitably reach a far wider circle and reach it far more effectively than we ever could if we depended solely on a few gifted men.—Henry Cook

THE WORLD AT OUR DOOR.   At the mayor's prayer breakfast in our city, the presiding officer said that all creeds were welcome. As one looked over the crowd it became apparent that he meant creeds like Baptists, Methodists, and Presbyterians. He did not include the Jews, Muslims, and Buddhists. But those people are present in great numbers in our country now. There are more religions in the United States than variations of the Christian religion. We will have to cross the barriers and refuse to stereotype the people so that we can minister and witness to them as Jesus did to the woman by the well on that hot day.—James W. Carter

Sermon Suggestions

MASS EVANGELISM.   TEXT: Acts 2:14a, 36–41. (1) A convincing message, verses 36–37. (2) A drastic challenge, verses 38–40. (3) A clear-cut response, verse 41.

GUIDELINES FOR A RESURRECTED LIFE. TEXT: 1 Pet. 1:17–23 (1) Take Christian living seriously, verse 17. (2) Consider the cost of your salvation, verses 18–21. (3) Let genuine love determine your behavior, verse 22. (4) Thank God for the regeneration that is the source and sustenance of what God wants you to be, verse 23.

Worship Aids

CALL TO WORSHIP.   "Blessed be the God and Father of our Lord Jesus Christ, which according to his abundant mercy hath begotten us again unto a lively hope by the Resurrection of Jesus Christ from the dead . . . to an inheritance incorruptible, and undefiled, and that fadeth not away, reserved in heaven for you" (1 Pet. 1:3–4).

INVOCATION.   God of purpose, seal in our hearts this day the reality of our Savior, who accomplished all things thou didst plan and returned to glory in triumph. Let the sunshine of our faith break through any cloudiness in our hearts, that we might, at last, behold the vision of the glory of our risen and ascended Lord.—E. Lee Phillips

OFFERTORY SENTENCE.   "The voice of him that crieth in the wilderness, Prepare ye the way of the Lord, make straight in the desert a highway for our God" (Isa. 40:3).

OFFERTORY PRAYER.   O Lord, give us the love, the wisdom, the will, and the means to open paths for the progress of the gospel in our community and in the wide world, and use our tithes and offerings to further that goal.

PRAYER.   Thank you for this day. Thank you for the life you have given us, for the sacred opportunity we have now to travel as pilgrims on this earth. Thank you for those people who by your grace have enriched and enlightened us so that we embrace and celebrate life, including our own. Cause us to live in such a way that, insofar as it depends on us, others will rejoice and be glad that they are, wonder of wonders, alive!

How has it come to pass, Lord, that there are multitudes of people who in heart and word curse the day they were born, who resent the challenge of being alive, who reject the privilege of living life to the fullest and best? How has it come to pass that for individuals and for nations, life is cheap, including human life, to be lived out, or ended, any way a person sees fit? Why do so many people settle for a new day by trying to have it be at best just a rerun of yesterday, a repeat of what has already happened, an acceptance of the notion that all things work together to signify nothing, nothing at all.

Give to us, Lord, the sense of community, of neighborliness, of ties that bind us together in love that should be ours—and can be ours—because we are a church. Help us to care for and minister to one another as brothers and sisters in Christ. Help us to recognize well the uniqueness that each of us possesses; may we discover just as well that we are knit together in one body, members of the body of Christ, where all the parts are joined and working and related together to be a living, dynamic, empowering church. Shame those of us who excuse ourselves, letting others attempt to do not only their work but our work as well. Shame those of us who decide we are unnecessary and unimportant, not because such a decision is true, but because it provides us with nice-sounding reasons to stop being responsible Christian disciples.

Shame those among us who have a puffed up sense of our own worth, matched by a poor sense of the worth of other people—their skills, their talents, their overall contribution to a going, glowing, growing church. Shame those among us who are sure of what others can learn from us but dismiss all too quickly what we can learn from others.

Do more than shame us, Lord. Don't permit us just to wallow in embarrassment and shrivel up in sin. Give us a vision of ourselves and others that is true, according to your will. Help us to have such a loving and personal relationship with each other that we fulfill well the mystery of

Christ's way for us, bearing our own burdens and also helping each other to bear the burdens that are carried. As we pick up and carry our cross of Christian discipleship, in the Master's service, may we not be above receiving or giving help as we try to be faithful to you by loving one another. Prompt and prod us to see that when we try to do everything, we are as sure to fail as when we try to do nothing.

Lord, God, equip us with the deep enthusiasm and excitement and energy that should be ours as we accept from you the gift of a new day. May all that is boring or dull be accepted by us as part of what must be done in order to achieve what is worthwhile to you. By your Spirit open our eyes to things past and things to come, and enable us to behold the privileges and opportunities, the responsibilities and challenges, of this present time. By your Spirit enable us to go far beyond chronically cursing all things great and small to become compassionate crusaders of your kingdom of righteousness, justice, peace, and love. May the soft complacency that defeats us be replaced by the sure persuasion that makes us more than conquerors through the living Christ who loves us, now and forever.—Gordon H. Reif

LECTIONARY MESSAGE

And Their Eyes Were Opened

TEXT: Luke 24:13–35, RSV

A Revealing Expression. One of the most revealing expressions in Scripture speaks about our eyes being opened, about seeing in a deeper sense than with our physical sight. Another, higher level is involved by which we become spiritually aware, gain understanding of something otherwise unknown, and experience realities ordinarily beyond our grasp. There is really more to life "than meets the eyes." Our text is about this new and higher seeing.

I. *On seeing one's sinful condition.* There is an experience of seeing that disturbs the self and brings guilt. This was the situation of Adam and Eve after they selfishly clutched after knowledge, trying to be like God in the wrong way. After their failure to obey God, both the man and his wife felt suddenly vulnerable, guilty, unhappy, embarrassed, ashamed—"the eyes of both were opened, and they knew that they were naked" (Gen. 3:7). Theirs was a new knowledge but of a darksome kind; it was about themselves as failures, as sinners in the sight of an offended God.

Sinning always generates a sad knowledge of one's own self. It is a knowledge that weakens and exhausts, distracts and dulls, pains and punishes. Sin splits us inside. It makes us radically aware of our sorry preferences and our painful predicament. The opening of the eyes through sinning is an experience that disturbs the self and brings guilt to the soul.

II. *On seeing one's spiritual resources.* In 2 Kings 6 we have another story of eyes being opened—this time the eyes of the servant of a prophet who was blessed to see beyond the problem of the danger they faced when surrounded by enemy forces on the search for them. The young servant had risen early to do his morning chores and was overcome with fear when he saw horses and chariot surrounding his master's dwelling. But the prophet Elisha refused to panic; he rather prayed—"O Lord, I pray thee, open his eyes that he may see." And God did it! The Lord opened the eyes of the young man, and he saw more than the enemy forces; he saw also other horses and chariots from God, ready to overcome those enemy forces.

The true believer knows when in crisis that it is never a question of fate but a time for ready faith. There are always spiritual means available from God to meet our human needs. There are spiritual resources to match any and all of life's demands. Paul was calling attention to this when he wrote about the "riches" in Christ Jesus, by which God will supply our every need (Phil. 4:19).

III. *On seeing the living Lord.* The textual story tells about those two disciples who were surprised by joy when they met their now-risen Lord after his disturbing ordeal with death by Crucifixion.

Sad and dejected in feeling, the two had been on their way to Emmaus, almost beside themselves in disappointment after all that had happened across the previous weekend.

But "while they were talking and discussing together," Jesus himself drew near and walked with them (24:15), unrecognized and certainly unanticipated. By the time the three reached Emmaus they had explored many passages and details of Scripture under his tutelage. Once in the town, they sat to share the evening meal—at which time Jesus revealed himself by the way he presided at the table. "And their eyes were opened and they recognized him; and he vanished out of their sight" (24:31).

IV. *Living by inner sight.* One of the greatest gifts from God is the gift of insight, seeing with eyes of faith. It happens again and again as we open ourselves to the Word of God, follow the will of God, and involve ourselves in the work of God. There is more to life than "meets the eye." While "seeing is believing" with so many, there is also a believing that brings sight.—James Earl Massey

SUNDAY: MAY SIXTH

SERVICE OF WORSHIP

Sermon: Celebrate All of It!
Texts: Zech. 14:20–21; Phil. 4:4–7

A word or two about Zechariah—because he's not the best known of the Old Testament prophets. His ministry—spanning only a couple of years—came about five hundred years B.C. We don't have much data on him, except that he and Haggai are linked together in that era when some of the exiles return from Babylon to rebuild the wall and the temple in Jerusalem. An older Haggai urges the returnees to work and rebuild—but it's a hard time. An awful lot of Jews are still in captivity, the Jerusalem community is small and weak, and the mood is one of discouragement and even despair.

So Zechariah summons all the optimism and the exuberance of his youth to change the attitude of gloom and doom in the streets of Jerusalem. His visions and oracles are the preaching of a man who has a great dream.

The eagerly awaited "day of the Lord" is his theme in this last chapter. Every third verse contains the phrase *on that day*. And Zechariah describes God's vindication of his promises and his rescue of his people.

But the "day of the Lord" wasn't exactly as the prophets said, or at least as they were interpreted, and after two thousand years, the reappearing of our Lord is yet delayed. But the theme of such writings—the specialness of life, all of it, is still valid. Granted, it's easier to hold that life-view if you believe that God's about to break into history and straighten things out. But for those of us on the pilgrimage of discipleship, those who've dug in for the duration, who will follow Christ if he returns tomorrow, next year, or twenty centuries from now, there's a great theme here—it is, "All of life is special . . . celebrate it!"

There are three bases, I think, on which we may celebrate life, and they all have to do with our identity as Christians. Who are we, after all—we Christians?

I. First, we are people who've looked backstage . . . and have found the key.

(a) Now Christians are a "holy" people (holy meaning special) not because we are better or stronger than anyone else—but because through Jesus Christ we've been let in on the purposes of God. We've been backstage of history—and we believe that God's intention is to reshape and renew life . . . because that reshaping and renewing has begun in our own lives. Despite our weaknesses and failures, we've been overtaken by the forgiveness of God. And life—all of it—becomes special.

History is going somewhere . . . life has purpose . . . the plan of God for all the ages is redemption and renewal. We know it because we've been behind the scenes with Jesus Christ and have the key!

(b) So, earning a living, for example, becomes not just a job but a way of serving God.

And sexuality becomes—not merely a biological function—but a way of intensifying and reinforcing a committed marital relationship . . . and a celebration of our physicalness.

Family becomes more than just the people we live with; it becomes the crucible where lives and attitudes are molded.

Politics . . . money . . . use of time—one after another of the "on stage" activities of life are lived with an awareness of this deeper meaning: that God is in the business of bringing wholeness to his Creation—including us—and that makes life special.

It makes church special . . . for when the world asks, "Where is wholeness? Where is understanding? Where is a perspective on reality that makes sense?" we can say, "Over here! We're finding out how and why."

II. Second, we can celebrate all of life because we're people who've looked into the tomb . . . and found it empty.

(a) We are resurrection people, but what does that mean? Hope, yes . . . life after death, yes . . . power, yes . . . but mostly for our here-and-now lives it means what happened in the upper room after the Crucifixion. He was there. It's hard to know all that happened, but he was just there. And Thomas was regaining his balance and his faith . . . and what they learned that day was that they'd never be alone again. And that fact—that every situation in life is shot through with his presence—is good reason to celebrate!

(b) Now that doesn't draw the sting of life's dark moment. Pain, drabness, darkness, evil, and trouble are part of life, and God's not happy with them—but he's with us as we encounter them and seek to change them.

Celebrate all of life . . . because the grave is empty. He's not there and then . . . he's here and now!

III. Finally, we celebrate all of life because we're people who've looked at the world . . . and found our ministry.

(a) More than once, the church has retreated from life—has celebrated its own life with God and tried to shut out the sound and fury of the marketplace . . . but it won't do. It won't do because he who walks through life with us was conversant with plowed fields, scattered grain, crooked landlords and lustful people, wheat and fish, wine and bread, hunger and tears, laughter and hurt. You can't follow Jesus Christ and shut all that out . . . any more than you can shut out the cries of the hungry and homeless . . . the injustice suffered by the poor . . . the bleakness of those lives who've lost their way following the secular savior of our time and are in desperate need of the gospel.

(b) Looking at our world, we have found what our lives are about . . . ministry! Little or great, Christ makes our service special.

Maybe it's helpful to remember that our word *enthusiasm* comes from the Greek *en Theos*, literally, "in God." So there is reason to celebrate the specialness of life. We live it in faith, in hope, and in the daily presence of God!—William L. Turner

Illustrations

IN THE END.   That love shall in the end, as it is now in the eternal verities, be all in all, must remain for the Christian a postulate not of knowledge but of faith. And that, too, is well, since faith is possible for all men, and knowledge is not.—L. W. Grensted

PRAYING WITHOUT GIVING UP.   I remember an overworked missionary nurse in a hospital in Angola who told a group of us how she had complained to her superior that, after her twelve hours on duty with many extra calls beyond her routine tasks, she was simply too exhausted to pray, and that her interior life had ebbed away. She had gone on to explain with special bitterness the situation with which she was faced at that moment. At the close of the day, she still had twelve more African patients to wash before going off duty. After that all she would be able to do would be to throw herself on her bed in exhaustion when she came to her room. Her older colleague heard the outburst, in love, and suggested that it was not really necessary to wait until she got home to pray. If she washed each of these next twelve Africans as though each were the body of Christ,

her praying could begin at once.—Douglas V. Steere

Sermon Suggestions

WHEN THE SPIRIT PREVAILS.   TEXT: Acts 2:42–47. (1) Structured disciplines will follow. (2) Spontaneous expressions will follow. (3) Evangelistic outreach will follow.

THE PROBLEM OF PAIN.   TEXT: 1 Pet. 2:19–25. (1) Pain is inevitable—all suffer sooner or later. (2) Some pain is deserved—we may foolishly invite it. (3) Some pain is unjust—we may suffer willingly for the sake of Christ our example. (4) Suffering may advance the cause of God and bless the lives of others.

Worship Aids

CALL TO WORSHIP.   "Oh that men would praise the Lord for his goodness, and for his wonderful works to the children of men! For he satisfieth the longing soul, and filleth the hungry soul with goodness" (Ps. 107:8–9).

INVOCATION.   Bless us in this time of worship, Lord, as we gather our thoughts, shape our prayers, and sing the songs that give glory to thy name.—E. Lee Phillips

OFFERTORY SENTENCE.   "As we have therefore opportunity, let us do good unto all men, especially unto them who are of the household of faith" (Gal. 6:10).

OFFERTORY PRAYER.   Lord, may our efforts to do good on behalf of the great mass of humankind not blind us to the needs of those close to us; and may our attention to our Christian neighbors not hinder our concern for all people everywhere.

PRAYER.   Holy God, Lord and Master of heaven and earth, of sky and sea, O thou in whom all things live and abide; O inviting One, who dost bid us to seek thee and who art ever ready to be found, to know thee is true life forever, to praise thee is our soul's deepest desire, to worship thee is our heart's highest delight.

Grant us thy blessing and presence, O God, as we come before thee with praise and thanksgiving. May we worship thee with gladness. May we praise thee with spirit. May we know thee best in our risen Lord. Endearing and understanding Father, who dost abhor our sins but dost adore ourselves, cleanse us from our sins; set us right.

Lord Jesus, Light shining in our darkness, make us children of light, too; make whole our brokenness, burn away the scattered debris, cleanse our secret faults.

O Father and God of our risen Lord, like the would-be followers then, we now tend to follow Christ at a distance. It just seems safer that way: no threat of being called fanatic or faint-hearted. O God, empower us to walk close with him, to learn of him, to be like him, to serve with him. From him may we know how to forget self but never forget thee. May we learn of him the power of gentleness, the grace of humility, the greatness of servanthood, the freedom found in service to thee. O Master, let us walk with thee and like thee.— William M. Johnson

LECTIONARY MESSAGE

The Good Shepherd and His Sheep

TEXT: John 10:1–10, RSV

The substance of this passage—which the writer explained as figurative speech, or a parable—moves our thought past the point of story to real life: not everyone who deals with sheep is a bona fide shepherd, and not everyone who deals with people does so for their good. This discourse is a statement about the contrasts between good shepherds and bad, between selfish religious leaders and the loving Shepherd, whose manner, concern, and voice bespeak that love. The passage is a word about Jesus. It is a personal statement from Jesus about his position and open intention as God's Son.

I. *Religious thieves and robbers.* Clandestine activities can be found in every sphere of human life; hidden motives are all too common in human relations. But when hypocrisy, subterfuge, and stealth motivate religious leaders, then what was bad has become worse. Spiritual banditry is in view here, the picture being a rebuke against any motivation that does not move a leader to seek the interests of the people. Chapter-and-verse instances of such selfishness abound in our time.

II. *The voice of the Good Shepherd.* The true shepherd acts with openness—and love. The marks that identify that shepherd are many: a familiar voice, a trusted accent, and a caring presence. Jesus is such a Shepherd for his people. In truth, "he calls his own sheep by name and leads them out." Jesus specializes in intimacy, he deals with his people as individuals, so trust in him rightly develops, and love for him steadily grows. Following *this* Shepherd is a matter of "life and death."

III. *Life with the Good Shepherd.* This Shepherd grants guidance and access to rich "pasture" for the sheep. "I am the door," Jesus declares, meaning that he grants access to the richer life that God makes available by his grace. Life with him is the open gate to God.

This Shepherd is motivated by interest to see that his sheep are both safe and full. This is the intent of that now-classic expression about having *life in abundance.*

Please note the accent: not abundance of *things* but abundance of *life.* The focus here is on salvation, which is life in its fullest sense, which leads finally to life beyond death. But the abundance is already being experienced in that life with the Shepherd had an eternal quality in it.

IV. *"I am the door."* The claim of Jesus here is distinctive and exclusive. He is the Savior by "divine right." He alone grants access to God. He alone could effect our salvation and security by "laying down his life for the sheep." So there is more here than a mere claim. There is declared intention: "I came that they may have life." There is appealing promise: "If any one enters by me, he will be saved." There is exclusive legitimacy: "All who came before me are thieves and robbers." And so are all who have come after him, despite their promises, pledges, and claims.

The note of exclusive legitimacy has always been a strong one in the Christian message about Jesus. Thus his granted title of honor—*Christ.* The Christian church makes no apology for this declared truth; its members rather boldly make their declaration of it—in love, which exemplifies *his* spirit and makes his saving presence felt.—James Earl Massey

SUNDAY: MAY THIRTEENTH

SERVICE OF WORSHIP

Sermon: Parent Power
TEXT: Eph. 6:1–4

Every parent I know is concerned about their children. They are faced with so many dangerous decisions: drugs, sex, alcohol, rebellion, deviant life-styles.

In the face of it all, parents seem to be more and more tentative about raising their children.

There is a crisis of confidence among parents—especially among those who understand what their children face in the modern world.

The result of all this is obvious. For the first time in history, the filiocentric—or child-centered—family has become the norm. Children seem to rule most families. Children have assumed positions of power.

The order of the day for any parent who wants to be a successful father or mother . . . who wants to achieve some measure of sanity . . . is to get and maintain control.

A parent must be able to control a child before he can really support and love the child. If a child is to feel secure, he needs parents who are effective and who cannot be manipulated. Children will look down on adults they can manipulate and control.

I want to suggest five principles of parental power. I do not mean to imply that these principles will miraculously solve all your problems. However, I do believe that if you will evaluate your parenting style in the light of these principles, you will become a better, more effective, more powerful parent.

I. The first is purpose. What is it that you are aiming for in this parenting responsibility?

(a) Do you know your purpose, your intention in raising the child God has given to you? What are you about? Are you raising an athlete . . . a Rhodes scholar . . . a beauty queen . . . a future president . . . a son (or daughter) to carry on the family name . . . or business?

(b) Purpose is the picture you have of yourself as a parent—the kind of parent you want to be. It is the picture you have of your child—the kind of person you want him or her to be. It is your own personal mission. It is a statement of the kind of business you are in as a parent.

(c) In the text the parenting purpose is stated clearly: ". . . bring them up in the training and instruction of the Lord" (6:4). That is the overriding concern of God for Christian parents.

Christian parents have an obligation to teach their children the Word and the will of God. Christian parents have a responsibility to instill within their child a desire for a personal relationship with God through Jesus Christ.

II. What's the second principle for achieving parental power with your children? It is the principle of pride.

(a) We work hard to be the best in our vocation. We exercise faithfully and guard our diet in order to maintain the best possible health. We service our automobile at regular, suggested intervals to maintain it in the best working condition. We toil and sweat in our yards and on our houses in order to attain the best manicured lawn and loveliest house on our block.

Unfortunately, when it comes to our children, we are not always so diligent. We are so busy achieving a reputation for having the best of everything else, we have only the leftovers of time, energy, and even affection to give to our children for our children.

(b) To hold to your commitment, you must believe that what you are committed to is the right thing to be committed to. People who have pride—or confidence, in this sense—tend to have the strength to follow-through on their commitment to do the right thing, even when there are strong pressures to do otherwise.

(c) When parents have this unwavering confidence, then they are able to instill it within their children. Confidence is a learned response to the circumstances of life.

III. The third principle is patience. The text reads: "Fathers, do not exasperate your children . . ." (6:4a).

(a) Adult pressures are overwhelming our children. We are forcing the children to become miniature adults before they are finished growing up. The first-century word from Ephesians may have more relevance today than when it was first penned.

(b) Another aspect of this appeal to patience, however, relates to parental anger. Children sense the weakness of adults. Children are especially sensitive to the weakness betrayed in an uncontrollable temper. Angry adults sometimes think their loud voice, snarled lips, red faces, protruding veins, and pounding fist speak to children of strength, power, and force.

It doesn't take the child long, however, to learn that when father or mother are like that, they are, in fact, out of control. Then, that which we had counted on to help us win the battle with the kids, actually becomes the weapon with which we fatally wound ourselves.

IV. The fourth principle is persistence.

(a) When you talk about persistence, you're not talking about trying to do something. You're talking about actually doing it. People who say, "Well, I tried," usually are offering an excuse for not having accomplished something. Many people make all kinds of noise about doing something with hardly any follow-up. The text reads, ". . . bring them up in the training and instruction of the Lord" (6:4b).

(b) Parents, beware! If your devotion to the Lord is on again, off again . . . if you run hot and cold in your personal Christian life . . . if your worship habits are unpredictable from week to week . . . if you do not pray and study God's Word as you seek to make important decisions, how will you ever have positive power in your children's spiritual life?

V. The final principle for having power with your children is the principle of perspective.

(a) Perspective is the capacity to see what really is important in any given situation. For the Christian, it means seeking God's perspective in all matters pertaining to this family.

(b) Getting God's perspective on the problems we face in our families is crucial to having a Christian home! Having God's perspective will guard us against trivializing the significant and weighty issues our children face. It will help us take more seriously the things we tend to dismiss too lightly.

(c) Achieving God's perspective of our life means that fathers and mothers must spend time together with God . . . and time alone with God! Parents who regularly spend time with the heavenly Father will consistently reflect his disposition and power in the hardest place on earth to be a Christian—the home!

Well?—Gary C. Redding

Illustrations

MOTHER POWER.   Monica prayed faithfully for her son. When he was converted, this son, later known as St. Augustine, said, "If I am thy child, O God, it is because thou didst give me such a mother."

OUR HEREDITY FROM GOD.   A boy twelve years old, lost in a crowd ages ago, said to his amazed mother, "Wist ye not that I must be about divine business?" What a grab bag? No wonder Emerson peeped into every cradle, looking for a new seer.

No one can tell what may turn up. A child may skip parents and grandparents, go far back and pick up some lost trait, or gift, and remake an age. Who can explain Plato or Dante or Lincoln or Darwin?

There is our heredity from God—the chief fact about us—which dignified our dust and makes us a little lower than the angels.—Joseph Fort Newton

Sermon Suggestions

UP—TOWARD HOME.   TEXT: Acts 7:55–60. (1) Our true home is where Jesus is—in the presence of God and with God's authority. (2) Our true vocation is that of Jesus when this earth was his temporary home—to live and die in the spirit of Jesus (v. 60).

A SPIRITUAL ODYSSEY.   TEXT: 1 Pet. 2:2–10. (1) What we were—nobodies, rejected. (2) What we are—God's own people, precious. (3) What we can be—witnesses to God's marvelous grace.

Worship Aids

CALL TO WORSHIP.   "Wherefore he saith, When he ascended up on high, he led captivity captive, and gave gifts unto men" (Eph. 4:8).

INVOCATION.   Together as a small part of the great family of faith, we come before you this morning in faith and expectation, Father. We believe that you love and care for us in all circumstances of life. Our faith holds us steady when at times we cannot see where the road we are traveling will take us. In trust we bring the struggles and joys, the tears and laughter to you, knowing that only in your presence will we find help and have life underscored with rejoicing. On this special day as we focus on family, we gather in expectation of the invasion of your understanding, guiding, loving Spirit. To deal with life adequately, we need that abiding presence as Counselor and Friend. Pray, Father, let us not be disappointed in our expectations as in faith we come to abide in your love for yet a little while.—W. Henry Fields

OFFERTORY SENTENCE.   "Give unto the Lord, O ye kindreds of the people, give unto the Lord glory and strength. Give unto the Lord the glory due unto his name: bring an offering, and come into his courts" (Ps. 96:7–8).

OFFERTORY PRAYER.   Blessed be your name, O God. You have brought us to this hallowed place, and you have enriched us with many tokens of your love for us. Receive now this material expression of our gratitude and praise.

PRAYER.   On tiptoe we come, Father, lest we disturb sacredness and tarnish holiness. We do not know how to pray. We so many times are forced to admit that we do not even know how to act when we enter into the powerful wonder of your presence. But we long for you with an ache in our souls at times, even as we dread the meeting on other occasions. The little bit we know about you whets our appetite for more understanding of you even as it calls us to caution lest we misunderstand you. Acting on the little bit we know and trusting the much that Jesus revealed concerning your nature, we quietly pause in your presence and reverently speak our heart's longing.

The glory of the created order, the intricate designs of loveliness, the master artistry of your handiwork call forth our praise to you, the Creator. How marvelous indeed are your works, O Lord. How thankful we are for all that you have made. Especially this morning are we grateful for the creation of the family and all that means to ordered life in this world. Thank you for the gift of mothers and grandmothers who in so many creative ways have made and are yet making your love real to us. Thank you for caring brothers and sisters who lighten life's load. Thank you for providing fathers whose efforts help sustain the home. Enable us all in the family we share to be those whose love is patient and kind, whose spirits are forgiving and uplifting, whose attitudes are turned to doing good rather than gloating over empty victories. Grant us a love that is not easily discouraged, but that will persevere through the ups and downs of life; through days of sunshine and days of shadow; through days of high health and days of devastating illness; through life at its best and death with its finality.

Grant that we may recognize and accept the humanity of parents and the inabilities of children; the weakness of the flesh and the failings of the human spirit. Help us to understand something of all our need for reliance on you in every encounter we have with one another across the days and years of our lives.

And let us learn how to care for the family of humanity in your Spirit, Father. May we be disturbed and uneasy as long as there are homeless folks among us, hungry folks about us, lonely folks everywhere. May we be disturbed and uneasy as long as war is waged, as long as racism is rampant, as long as hatred is harbored among us. Oh, this morning, King Jesus, let your presence awaken us to the needs of the family of humanity that we will be inspired to do something to meet the need and help the family.

Now as we continue for a while to abide in your presence, lead us to the cross and give us your blessing, we pray.—W. Henry Fields

LECTIONARY MESSAGE

A Dialogue about Destiny

TEXT: John 14:1–14, RSV

I. *I go to prepare a place for you.* The disciples had followed Jesus in his coming and going, which had been considerable during his rather brief ministry. But now he spoke about a going on his part that would leave them behind—at least for a time (13:33, 36).

The news was unsettling, and the reason rather ambiguous, at least at first. Thus that calming word of Jesus to them: "Let not your hearts be troubled." He was concerned that the terror of the turmoil his death would occasion should not undermine their faith in what he had promised them. Their agitation is understandable: they still had no proper comprehension about the death Jesus was about to undergo. The word of calm was soon followed by a needed imperative: "keep on trusting in me" (v. 1).

The trust would be rewarded: faith in Jesus would mean a place for each one "in my Father's house," a place into which they would be ushered after his return to receive them as his faithful own.

II. *I will come again.* This promise of Jesus is usually understood to refer to the Second Coming of the Lord in the end time, but was it not also inclusive of his

reappearance in the circle of disciples after his Resurrection? The return from death was initial, while the coming back to receive the disciples into full glory with himself "in the Father's house" would be final.

Throughout this passage there is an emphasis upon a promised presence: "I will come again"; "I will take you to myself, that where I am you may be also." It will be a great happening. It will be a unique event. It will be an unprecedented occurrence. It will be an involving result. Jesus has promised to "come again."

III. *I am the Way, and the Truth, and the Life.* This statement, given by Jesus to clarify an answer he had already given, is one of the great "I ams" in John's Gospel account. Since the life of God resides in him, and since the truth about God is revealed through him, Jesus declared that he is "the Way" to God. That this is the intended focus of the saying seems clear from the next line in the couplet, "no one comes to the Father, but by me" (v. 6b).

It is the faith and message of the Christian church that in Jesus the world has access to God as he is best known. In the person of Jesus there is the basic reality by which we meet with God as he wills to be known. Thus to know Jesus is to know the Father. There are depths here that only our experience with Jesus can help us to discern, and there are heights here that forever beckon us to explore as our faith seeks further understanding. The significance of Jesus is not essentially in his teaching, nor his miracles, but in the revelation he makes of God in his person. Thus his numinous statement: "I am in the Father and the Father in me" (v. 10).

IV. *Our privileges through his name.* Faith in Jesus, and continuing discipleship in the will of God, links us by grace within a fellowship of privilege.

(a) There is the privilege of experiencing Jesus.

(b) There is the privilege of knowing the Father through him.

(c) There is the privilege of praying in his name—which means to make our appeal to God with Jesus as our authorizing benefactor: "If you ask anything in my name, I will do it" (v. 14). In *his* name means, then, to ask in keeping with his character and concerns. These are distinctive and practical privileges to which every person stands invited as part of the world God loves and desires to save (John 3:16–18).—James Earl Massey

SUNDAY: MAY TWENTIETH

SERVICE OF WORSHIP

Sermon: The Great Assurance

TEXT: Matt. 28:16–20

The passage from which I am preaching this morning is normally referred to as the Great Commission. However, I want to focus on the last part of verse 20, "Lo, I am with you always, to the close of the age." This, I will refer to as the "great assurance." The reason I want to focus on this verse is because I believe we will never fulfill the Great Commission, until we realize the great assurance. The only thing that can truly convince us to share the good news is the joy of the presence of Jesus in our lives and the realization that he goes with us every step of the way.

I. The great assurance of Jesus includes a who, a when, and a where.

(a) The who is Jesus. Jesus, himself, promises to be with us. We are all to be aware, as the disciples were beginning to realize, that Jesus did not mean he would be present in bodily form, as he had been. Rather Jesus is with us in Spirit, the Holy Spirit of God. Jesus could promise that it was indeed he who would be with the disciples and us, though he is present through the form of the Spirit.

(b) Verse 20 also explains when Jesus will be with us. He promised simply to be with the disciples and us always, to the close of the age. The close of the age is the time when Jesus would return visibly, and life and the world as we know it would come to an end. Therefore, he assured them that his presence began again at his Resurrection and would continue until the "close of the age," and then beyond that into eternity as they had expected.

(c) And, because he was promising his presence until the "close of the age" or "the end of the world," it is something that is to continue to take place here on earth. The ones who follow Jesus can be assured that it is *he* who is with us *always* and *every*where.

II. The great assurance is directly related to the Great Commission in this way. The assurance of the presence of Christ gives us the motivation, the strength, and the guidance to share the gospel in all places to all people.

(a) When Jesus came to the disciples, in verse 17, "they worshiped him, but some doubted." Some were not able to realize that Jesus was actually present with them. And isn't that true of many of us today? Those who doubted his presence were not prepared to accept his commission. However, most of the disciples did realize his presence. And when they did they were overwhelmed with joy and could do nothing else but worship him.

(b) The presence of Jesus is also the source of strength that is needed to fulfill the Great Commission. In Jesus rested the authority or the power of heaven and earth. Therefore, as his followers went out to share the gospel they could expect that same strength because Jesus would be with them. The presence of Jesus gives us the strength to fulfill the Great Commission.

(c) And also the presence of Jesus gives us the guidance needed to fulfill the Great Commission. The disciples were to teach people the things that Jesus had taught them. They would be able to do this because Jesus himself would be with them to point the way and to remind them.

III. I have said so far that Jesus has promised to be with us, and because he is with us, we have the motivation, strength, and guidance to fulfill the Great Commission. However, you already realize it is not quite that simple. We do have some responsibility. That responsibility is to make ourselves aware of the presence of Christ.

(a) Prayer is one practice that will help us to realize the presence of Christ. We can not help but be aware of Christ's presence as we converse with him. Prayer does help to make us aware of the presence of God.

(b) So does the Bible. Because the Bible is the word of God we can encounter him through Bible reading and meditation. His presence with us will help the Bible to become the living Word.

(c) We can also become aware of the presence of God through commonplace things and events. The budding of trees and blooming of flowers can make us aware of his presence. The smile of a child, or the loneliness of an elderly person may be the faces of Christ among us. The majesty of the mountains or the despair of the ghetto also may remind us of the presence of Christ.

Using these tools, or many others, we can become more aware of the presence of Christ with us. As we realize his presence we will be able to fulfill the commission he has given us.

IV. Jesus has not given us the great assurance because we fulfill the Great Commission. We fulfill the Great Commission because he has given us the great assurance.

Jesus does not live with us because we live for him. We live for him because he lives with us.

Let us leave today rejoicing, remembering that as we go, wherever we go, Jesus will go with us.—Bruce Day

Illustrations

A WORKING FAITH. MacDonald wrote to Keith Falconer, a young missionary: "This is a practical working faith: first, it is man's business to do the will of God; second, God takes on himself the special care of that man; third, that man should be afraid of nothing."—E. Stanley Jones

GOD AND THE DESERT. A journey is described in the story of the Bedouin guide who led a traveler over a mountain pass after a night spent in an oasis in the valley now far below them. As he stopped his mount at the top of the track, he contemplated for a long moment and then looked out at the new vista of sand wastes that had just opened ahead of them. Inhaling deeply the pure, dry, clean, empty, and odorless wind of the desert, he said, "Can you still smell the exquisite fragrance of the orchards behind us? Its headiness is that of wine and its warmth a woman's. But do you now smell the wind of the wilderness? It is the breath of God." We can move from security in our beliefs to trust in God.—Robert A. Raines

Sermon Suggestions

GOD IS ACCESSIBLE. TEXT: Acts 17: 22–31. (1) The quest for God (or a god) is universal, verse 22. (2) Such a quest can lead to frustration and desperation, verses 23a, 24–25. (3) Yet God has made himself accessible, verses 23b, 26–31 (see also Heb. 1:1–4).

YOUR DEFENSE AS A CHRISTIAN. TEXT: 1 Pet. 3:13–22, especially verse 15b. (1) Expect to give account of your Christian convictions. (2) Live what you profess. (3) Make your point with consideration of the feelings of others.

Worship Aids

CALL TO WORSHIP. "Trust in him at all times; ye people, pour out your heart before him: God is a refuge for us. Selah" (Ps. 62:8).

INVOCATION. Gracious Lord, let our minds be saturated with the profundities of the faith this day. Align our wills with those purposes that risk for others, live to give, and radiate the presence of the Savior, whom today we worship and adore, with thee and the Spirit.—E. Lee Phillips

OFFERTORY SENTENCE. "The earth is the Lord's, and the fullness thereof; the world, and they that dwell therein" (Ps. 24:1).

OFFERTORY PRAYER. O God, knowing who the owner of the earth really is, knowing who is truly Lord of all things and all who live on this earth, we can only render unto you what is yours already. Yet you have given us the power and privilege of doing this act of worship, and we thank you now and offer to you what is yours in faith and with joy.

PRAYER.   Thou whose light is about me and within me and to whom all things are present, help me this day to keep my life pure in thy sight. Suffer me not by any lawless act of mine to befoul any innocent life or add to the shame and hopelessness of any erring one that struggles faintly against sin. Grant me a steadfast scorn for pleasure bought by human degradation. May no reckless word or wanton look from me kindle the slow fires of wayward passion that will char and consume the divine beauties of any soul. Give me grace to watch over the imaginations of my heart, lest in the unknown hour of my weakness my secret thoughts leap into action and my honor be turned into shame. If my friends trust me with their loved ones, save me from betraying their trust and from slaying the peace of a home. If any dear heart has staked its life and hopes on my love and loyalty, I beseech thee that its joy and strength may never wither through my forgetfulness or guilt. O God, make me pure and a helper to the weak. Grant that even the sins of my past may yield me added wisdom and tenderness to help those who are tempted.

Save our nation from the corruption that breeds corruption. Save our innocent sons and daughters from the secret curse that requites the touch of love with lingering death. O Jesus, thou master of all who are both strong and pure, take our weak and passionate hearts under thy control, that when the dusk settles upon our life, we may go to our long rest with no pang of shame and may enter into the blessedness of seeing God, which thou hast promised only to the pure in heart.—Walter Rauschenbusch

LECTIONARY MESSAGE

The Mandate Before Us
TEXT: Luke 24:46–53, RSV

I. *Thus it is written.* Throughout so much of the New Testament our attention is called to some quotation from an Old Tes-

tament writing, preceded by the stated pointer, "It is written." This constant appeal to the prophetic literature and other portions of Scripture had worthy precedent in Jesus' own teaching and preaching ministry. In all the Gospels, Jesus is reported as making a regular and precise use of Old Testament writings as he taught, debated, and even faced the events in his life (the temptation experience is an instance). The present textual passage shows Jesus referring again to the known Scriptures, pointing out in them those promises and criteria by which his own person and ministry were to be recognized and understood.

Here the teaching reference from Jesus pointed to two crucial events in his life as the Christ: (a) his Passion/death, and (b) his Resurrection from death. No precise passages are cited by the evangelist, but it is to be assumed that known references were a part of early church tradition—as reflected in other writings in the New Testament.

The gospel of salvation is rooted in a sacrificial death and a dramatic, vindicating Resurrection of Jesus from that necessary death. At the heart of the gospel is a suffering love, a love exemplified by a suffering Christ. The main concern in the Scriptures is to inform us about this and to help us appreciate and appropriate the meaning and effects of this message.

II. *Repentance/forgiveness of sins should be preached.* The call to repentance is a perennial concern in human life—the terms of God's will are steadily assaulted in selfish waywardness and stubborn resistance. It is a necessary message, an imperative word that immediately clarifies our human duty before God. The mind needs to open itself to God's claims, and the life needs to undergo God's converting action. The necessity for change is matched by the promise that brings it into human reach.

The call to repentance alerts all to *need,* on the one hand, and to *newness,* on the other. Acting upon the call results in the forgiveness of sins, salvation, by means of "his name." And this result is for all—for all have this need.

III. *The mandate before us.* This passage is Luke's short version of the Great Commission statement, his record about the Lord's authorizing word for his followers to go forth in the world, spreading the message about the promise of salvation. The passage reports that Jesus not only authorized our going forth but that he also mandated that we do so.

We Christians have a *given work*. And we have a *given word* about his work. Our work is sharing the news of salvation, stating this possible result to all nations, and doing so as "witnesses of these things" (24:48). We are to speak our given word from the vantage point of those who have experienced what we now invite others to receive. The message must be distinct, our understanding must be clear, and our attitude must be accepting in order to meet people in *his* Spirit as we mention his name. Meanwhile, he would have us know that this authorized work is attended and enabled by his Spirit. Thus that word of promise from Jesus that the church would have more than mere human means by which to do the commanded task. Effective witnessing always demands an enabling "power from on high" (v. 49).—James Earl Massey

SUNDAY: MAY TWENTY-SEVENTH

SERVICE OF WORSHIP

Sermon: Hobbled and Hopeful

Text: Gen. 32:13–32

I. (a) Jacob is running scared. It's twenty years since his dirty tricks against a blind father and an easygoing brother sent him running for cover. For those twenty years, he's been bobbing and weaving, ducking and dodging the trickery of his uncle Laban. He's finally free of that . . . and he's going back home. Word comes that Esau is on his way to meet him, and he just happens to be bringing four hundred men along. After twenty years to brood over his stolen blessing and the vow he made about it—"When my father dies, I'll kill Jacob" (see 28:41)—after twenty years, is Esau coming to meet Jacob in friendship or in hostility?

Jacob guesses hostility, so he divides up everything—goats and ewes and rams and cows and bulls and menservants and maidservants—to soften the blows of Esau's wrath. As it turns out, he doesn't need to worry. Esau forgives him and is reconciled to him. But before he knows that, and while he feels like his hours are numbered, Jacob has this dark night of the soul where God is the adversary, the enemy, the antagonist who wrestles against him on the banks of the river.

(b) As I read this story, I realize that there are times when my name is Jacob . . . and so is yours.

The dark night of the soul comes when . . . the lab report comes back positive . . . the heart attack says "retire" long before you are ready to say it . . . the accident or the stroke paralyzes . . . the children deeply disappoint . . . the marriage dies . . . the job disappears . . . the prejudices and injustices deepen against you. When dreams lie crushed in the dust of living, we are Jacob—down in that dirt and darkness, wrestling with God.

What can you expect when you wrestle with God? Some of the same things Jacob found, I think.

II. You can expect a new name, for instance. Just before the end of this wrestling match, Jacob says to his adversary, "Tell me your name" (v. 29).

(a) Sometimes the great need in the life of faith is to name God correctly and not reduce him to false notions and superstitions . . . most of the time, however, the great need is not to name God but to name ourselves, i.e., to decide who we will be in relation to God. And in the struggle of our souls, there are many names available to us. One of these may be the new name by which you choose to be identified—cynic . . . skeptic . . . loner . . . fatalist . . . strict humanist. A lot of people come out of the clinches with God and the darkness with just such names.

(b) Jacob came out with the better new name, Israel. This name has various meanings in the Old Testament, but here it's "the one who strives with God." I'd translate that, "a faithful struggler." Jacob's whole life was a series of conversions and backslidings, of being close to God and being distant. But the important thing is that Jacob kept his grip on God after that dark night—he asked questions, he wept, he knew anger and discouragement, he was still cowardly and self-serving from time to time . . . but he kept his grip on God. That was the blessing! To live on as a pilgrim in trust, in learning, and in growing. When you struggle with God, you might get a new name. I hope it is the same one—faithful struggler . . . because that's who Christ calls you to be as his follower this morning.

III. You also might get a limp or a scar. In the course of his struggle with God, Jacob's thigh was wrenched, and he limped away from the battle.

(a) Sometimes you do lose something in the struggle with God.

It may be those easy certainties about God and faith that bite the dust. It may be the innocence of a childish perception of reality. Or it could be those quick answers about a truth far too profound for a cliché or a bumper sticker. Indeed, the hour of struggle may rattle your whole concept of God right down to the foundation. And you may have to limp for a while, but remember this about a limp or a scar. It's a mark of meaning. It reminds you of something that happened . . . and of something you learned.

(b) How much we learn when we recall our scars and our lameness! They are marks of meaning that remind us of the shaping, strengthening power of God. Jacob's thigh got wrenched, but his soul got stretched. He limped for a while . . . but the old schemer became fit for the greatest spiritual and moral responsibilities of his lifetime.

(c) And if you yearn to serve God with your gifts, remember this. I doubt that there's a scar or a limp or a wound or a sin back there that God cannot use to make you more aware of and sensitive to those around you who need your gospel of love. When you struggle with God in the dark

nights of life, you'll probably lose some things and walk away with a limp or a scar. But with his help, the wounds can be marks of rich meaning as you move on.

IV. What can you expect when you wrestle with God? A solid hope. After he was wounded in the struggle, the text says that Jacob would not turn loose. He wouldn't turn loose this experience until he had wrung a blessing out of it.

(a) There was a later day—much later— when One stood in the midst of friends and said, "Touch my scars, Thomas." Touch and see that the scars and the limp are not the last words on spiritual pilgrimage. The final words are resurrection and hope! Whatever may die in the struggle— cherished ideas, naive perspective, immature faith, flawed understanding . . . God not only waves to us from our yesterdays, he beckons to us from tomorrow.

(b) The Hebrew word for "wrestled" is very close to the word *Jabbok*—the name of the river in this story. It's probably an intentional play on words. What's interesting is that Jacob renamed it *Peniel*—"the face of God." The very place of his struggle became his salvation setting. The "sun rose upon him" as he moved on with his limp . . . and he "lifted up his eyes" to deal with the old struggles of life in a new way. Out of his pain came new understanding of who he was, of something lost, and of solid hope gained!—William L. Turner

Illustrations

PREPARED IN THE WILDERNESS.   God is in life's lovely things, but sooner or later all of us come to the place where, if we are to find God at all, we must find him in a wilderness. How we admire people who do that! When Helen Keller says about her blindness and deafness, "I thank God for my handicaps, for through them I have found myself, my work, and my God," that is something! I can find the divine in the Ninth Symphony or in sunsets when the sun, supine, lies "rocking on the ocean like a god," but to find God where Helen Keller found him, or Moses, that calls for insight.—Harry Emerson Fosdick

MADE BY A CROSS.   E. Stanley Jones, the missionary, said that for many years of his life he had borne a cross and had prayed that it be removed. At last it was removed and, he said, he found himself praying for another cross, for that one had been the making of him.

Sermon Suggestions

GETTING ON WITH GOD'S BUSINESS. TEXT: Acts 1:6–14. (1) A troublesome question—times and seasons. (2) The substantive issue—worldwide witness. (3) Essential preparation—concerted prayer.

EXPECTATION AND ADMONITION.   TEXT: 1 Pet. 4:12–14; 5:6–11. As faithful Christians (1) we expect in some ways to suffer for our commitment, (2) we must follow proven tactics for handling the threats to our obedience, and (3) we may depend on God for strength to fulfill our calling.

Worship Aids

CALL TO WORSHIP.   "Behold I stand at the door, and knock: if any man hear my voice, and open the door, I will come in to him, and will sup with him, and he with me" (Rev. 3:20).

INVOCATION.   Thou art knocking at the door of our church, O Lord, and will we let thee in? Thou dost come with blessings for us, and will we receive them? Thou desirest to work in the world through us, and will we permit thee? Enter, Lord, that we may know the joy of fellowship with thee.

OFFERTORY SENTENCE.   "Therefore, as ye abound in every thing, in faith, and utterance, and knowledge, and in all diligence, and in your love to us, see that ye abound in this grace also" (2 Cor. 8:7).

OFFERTORY PRAYER.   Lord, our God, pervade this offering that it might be Spirit-led and live to bless the needy, heal the sick, save the lost, and build the church, to which end we pray that many souls will be added because it is prayerfully dedicated in Jesus' name.—E. Lee Phillips

PRAYER.   God of all our yesterdays, we are a people called to remember. Gifted with memory, looking back, we know who you are, what you have done for us in Jesus Christ, and by your grace, whose we are. God of our today, we come before your presence with singing and in silence, with praise and adoration. Your Spirit is among us and within us, and we are made glad. God of all our tomorrows, Time is in your hand, and if granted a future, may we accept it with gratitude and serve you obediently and joyfully. Eternal God, Alpha and Omega, we rest our past and hope our future in you. Thanks be to God.

Embracing God, Father of the Holy Spirit, at Pentecost, the descending Spirit created unity out of chaos, harmony out of discord, understanding out of confusion. We as a people desperately need a fresh indwelling and understanding of your Spirit among us. "Holy Spirit, Light Divine, shine within this heart of mine." May this be our prayer of heart and will.

Abiding and understanding Father, again we find ourselves suffering from abundance and come praying for our needy souls. We pray for those too busy, having too many things to do, and who have lost the rhythm of life and forsaken sabbath rest; for those with so much learning and knowledge that we are above and ignorant of those isolated and ashamed because of not being able to read or write and are stuck on zero. We pray for those with too many things in our lives and hearts, so that there is no opening or room for you; for those too familiar with the good news, jaded by banquets of sermons and music and worship, but who have lost that quivering of the Spirit at really hearing and being captured by the call and demand of the gospel.

Lord, forgive us and let us find our abundance in thee. Save us from ourselves and guide us to thee.—William M. Johnson

LECTIONARY MESSAGE

Jesus' Prayer List

TEXT: John 17:1–11

You can tell much about a person from his or her prayer list. Some people have on their prayer lists the hungry and starving of the world, while other people pray only over their own full plates. Some people put at the top of their list "freedom and justice for the poor and downtrodden"; other people place "a raise and a new car" at the top of theirs. Some prayer lists are full of names—Jane, who is fighting cancer; Bob, who needs to find work; the Smiths, who have a new baby—while other prayer lists are only blank sheets. Some people put themselves on their prayer lists under "confession" ("God be merciful to me a sinner"). But others enter their own names under "adoration" ("God, I thank thee that I am not like other people"). You can tell a great deal about people from their prayer lists.

Taken in this light, Jesus' own prayer list is something of a shock, perhaps even a scandal. In the passage for today, Jesus, nearing the end of his life, prays a long and beautiful prayer of intercession. In this prayer he gives thanks, praises his Father, and pleads for his followers, but he also—and this is the shock—refuses to pray for the world. "I am not praying for the world," Jesus says, "but for those whom thou hast given me" (John 17:9, RSV).

We have always been taught that it is the duty of Christians to to care for and to pray for the world. What are we to make of the fact that our Lord himself, in his high priestly prayer, refused to put the world on his prayer list?

I. Some would suggest that Jesus refused to pray for the world because the world is evil and has been rejected by God. There is plenty of evidence for this idea, of course. A glance at the newspaper head-lines would seem to reveal a world beyond even the power of prayer: government by bribery, business by greed, and public life by violence. Given the kind of world we live in, it seems a small wonder that Jesus said, "I do not pray for the world."

But this suggestion is simply not true. The world has not been rejected by God. Indeed, John himself has told us that God loved the world so much that he gave his only son (John 3:16). There must be some other reason why Jesus refused to pray for the world.

II. Another possibility is that Jesus wanted his followers to make a clean break from the world, wanted them to be "church people" uncontaminated by involvement in the world. But this suggestion is wrong, too. Later in the very same prayer, Jesus says that he is sending his disciples "into the world," just as the Father has sent him into the world.

III. In the final analysis, the ironic truth is that Jesus refused to pray at that moment for the world not because he hated the world or rejected the world but because he deeply loved the world and finally saves the world. What Jesus was doing in this prayer was offering gifts to the Father. He offered the gift of himself, because his earthly ministry was complete. He also gave his disciples to the Father, for "they are thine." But the world was not yet ready to give as a gift. One day the world will cease to be in rebellion, cease its hating and its violence against God. Until that day, though, Jesus sends us—his disciples—into the world he loves, just as the Father sent him, so that "the world may believe." The promise is that, by God's mercy to the world through our service and love, one day the world will come to the light of Christ, and Jesus' prayer will finally be finished: "I pray now for the world, offering it at last to thee, for it is thine."—Thomas G. Long

SUNDAY: JUNE THIRD

SERVICE OF WORSHIP

Sermon: The Purpose of the Church
TEXT: Acts 2

The subject of this sermon is the purpose of the church. Whenever an institution is in a state of confusion, one of the most clarifying things it can do is to investigate its original purpose. When that purpose is clearly perceived, then assessments can be made and new directions taken.

Surely, no day could be more appropriate on which to consider this theme than the day of Pentecost, for it is the day on which the individual followers of Jesus became acutely conscious of their collectivity. They were no longer individuals, they were a group, a church, a congregation, with a purpose and a function to fulfill in the world. That is the theme, and there is the occasion for it: Pentecost; the purpose of the church.

I. We must begin by acknowledging the fact that the purpose of the church is twofold.

(a) The purpose of the church is to save us from sin. Or, if you withdraw from the word *sin*, there is another word which you can put in its place that means more or less the same thing, *selfishness*. The purpose of the church is to save us from selfishness, that instinctive and impulsive tendency in ourselves to turn inwardly upon ourselves, to think first of ourselves, to live life in terms of our own advantage and so to lose our life by trying to find it. The church exists for the purpose of saving us from that catastrophe, and it does so by various means.

Of course, above all else the church rescues us from these forces which hurt us by holding before us constantly the figure of the one supremely healthy person, Jesus. Week after week, day after day, the church tries, often ineffectively to be sure, inadequately, but nevertheless tries to hold up before us the figure of man as he is meant to be, adjusted to life, sacrificially dedicated to life, making the most of his own life, able to handle his own difficulties magnificently well, and the church says to its people, here is what life is meant to be. Put out of your mind the negative aspects of a morality that is based on "don'ts" and look at this figure. Let his Spirit dwell in you and you in him. Remember that is what you are meant to be, for there is a Christ in you. Be the Christ that is in you. That, therefore, is a part of the purpose of the church: to be a hospital for sinners.

(b) So, the purpose of the church is to glorify God. The church is here, in one sense, regardless of what people are doing or thinking or being. It is our human response to the Creator of our lives and of the universe. It is our attempt to say, Here is what God is, and in contrast to all the ugliness and falsehood and impurity and all the other forces which corrupt life, this is divine, and we stand here to pay our tribute, to make our response, to show forth that which is eternally good, to glorify God.

Therefore, the services of the church are intended not primarily to please you but to please God. Therefore, the church, if it is true to its mission, cannot cater always to you or to any other congregation, nor can it accommodate itself to the ways of men and women. To be sure, it must never lose its sympathy with suffering humanity, but when the church begins to preach an ethic which is cut to fit the easygoing ways of humanity, then it has failed to glorify God.

II. There are three pertinent observations to be made about this twofold purpose of the church.

(a) The first one is the most important. It is that the church succeeds in saving men only so long as it continues to glorify God. I do not know whether you are aware of how strongly that cuts across every popular notion that thrives in this country at the present time or not. The church fulfills its function on a human level only so long as it continues to keep its eye on something far beyond. We are sorry to say that the church is always tempted to use its resources for human therapy, a very real temptation and one for which we have deep sympathy.

When you come to church you ought to get something. It always interests me to ask people why they come to church, why they come to this particular church. They often answer that they come here because they get something, and that is valid, that is natural, that is human. But there is a sense—and I think if we could see it we would enlarge our whole concept of life and of the church—there is a sense in which if you come to church primarily to get something, you will go away empty; only when you come to give something, do something, will you get the real thing. If you come here to get a lift to carry you through the week, you may get it, but you only get a lift when you come here to let yourself be humble in the presence of the mighty God of the universe and let his demands upon you be made known, no matter how hard they may be.

(b) Now there is another observation that ought to be made on this twofold purpose of the church, and it is this: unless the church fulfills this twofold purpose, all the other activities of the church are meaningless. The church engages in innumerable activities. We run a school, we run a business office, we run countless organizations, we run recreation centers, we run a music department. But if we no longer have the power to save people from their inner deterioration, then those activities have no meaning whatsoever, and one of the things that distresses some of us sometimes as we look at the church critically is that we cannot help but feel that the activities of the church have usurped the purpose of the church. We see people frantically engaged in ceaseless activity without any apparent sign that they have firmly in their minds what the original purpose was: namely, to make sick people well and to glorify God.

(c) One final observation, briefly mentioned. The only time the church ever comes anywhere near fulfilling this twofold purpose is when it is filled with the Spirit of Jesus. Do not forget that. For Jesus in himself combines and unites the two things that the church is trying to do. Christ Jesus came into the world to save sinners. That is what he was for. And in him all the fullness of the Godhead dwelt bodily, so that in Christ we have the upward look toward God, to glorify him, and also the outward look toward distressed humanity, to serve them. And it is only when that Spirit dwells in a church that it has any chance of fulfilling its real purpose. Some people are always bewildered theologically as to what the Spirit is, the Holy Spirit, which came to the individuals who followed Jesus on this day of Pentecost. The simplest way to say it is that the spirit that took hold of the people was the Spirit of Jesus.

III. So what we pray for in this church and in every other is that Jesus, his Spirit, will fill this church. That his Spirit of goodwill and outgoingness will be in every usher and in every pew and in every person who sits in that pew; in every minister who conducts a service and every corporate act of worship here, that his Spirit may dwell in it; in every organization that the church promotes and in every family; that Christ's Spirit of willingness to go and to give and to spend and be spent may dwell in this place.—Theodore Parker Ferris

Illustrations

THE IMAGE OF CHRIST. This is what we mean when we speak of Christ dwelling in our hearts. His life on earth is not finished yet, for he continues to live in the lives of his followers. Indeed it is wrong to speak of the Christian life: we should speak rather of Christ living in us. "I live, and yet no longer I, but Christ liveth in me" (Gal. 2:20). Jesus Christ, incarnate, crucified and glorified, has entered my life and taken charge. "To me to live is Christ" (Phil. 1:21). And where Christ lives, there the Father also lives, and both Father and Son through the Holy Ghost. The Holy Trinity himself has made the dwelling in the Christian heart, filling his whole being and transforming him into the divine image. Christ, incarnate, crucified and glorified, is formed in every Christian soul, for all are members of his Body, the

Church. The Church bears the human form, the form of Christ in his death and Resurrection. The Church in the first place is his image, and through the Church all her members have been refashioned in his image, too. In the Body of Christ we are become "like Christ."—Dietrich Bonhoeffer

WHO IS THE CHURCH? The company of them that hear and heed this call constitute the "army" of God. The army he has won, "bought with a price," is the church. Everyone who heeds the call of Christ belongs to it, be he Catholic, Quaker, Methodist, or Reformed. One thing only is decisive: Have you really heard, and really heeded the call, or have you made but an exterior gesture of joining this or that? And because this decisive matter can never be seen, judged, or evaluated from the outside; because unlike any military forces of a great king, no one can see or enumerate those who have become part of the "church army" of God; because this hearing and heeding of God's call is a hidden matter, known only to God himself, we speak also of the invisible church.—Emil Brunner

Sermon Suggestions

WHEN THE HOLY SPIRIT IS AT WORK. TEXT: Acts 2:1–21. (1) The gospel is fitted to each individual's need. (2) Witnesses come from every quarter.

UNITY AND DIVERSITY IN COMMUNITY. TEXT: 1 Cor. 12:3b–13. (1) The unifying confession, verse 3b. (2) The diversifying service, verses 4–11. (3) The confirming explanation, verses 12–13.

Worship Aids

CALL TO WORSHIP. "But now in Christ Jesus ye who sometimes were far off are made nigh by the blood of Christ. For he is our peace, who hath made both one, and hath broken down the middle wall of partition between us. . . . Now therefore ye are no more strangers and foreigners, but fellow-citizens with the saints, and of the household of God" (Eph. 2:13–14, 19).

INVOCATION. Blessed Lord, let this be the time when all we are is so committed to all thou dost reveal that we will be obedient to all thou dost will, through our crucified and risen Savior, Jesus Christ.—E. Lee Phillips

OFFERTORY SENTENCE. "As every man hath received the gift, even so minister the same one to another, as good stewards of the manifold grace of God" (1 Pet. 4:10).

OFFERTORY PRAYER. God, our name is Christian. In some ways we've been given that name; in some ways we've claimed that name: in all ways particular persons in this world come to understand what the name means as they observe us and relate to us. It is not a small thing; rather, it is a very sacred thing, to be called a Christian disciple. Lord, Jesus, you are depending upon the likes of us—sinners, each and every one—to do the Christlike thing, to be the Christlike people. We with one accord forbid the thought that you should depend upon us in vain.

By ourselves we know we would be found wanting in our goal to be a Christian people, a Christian church. Yet that is the abiding wonder and glory of our faith: we are not alone, you are present with us as you promised you would be. So we turn to you and ask that you equip us with the qualities and characteristics and attitudes we need to serve you wisely and well. We want the world to stand up and take notice of our lives so that by what we do and say, by what we are, someone, someplace, perhaps when we least expect it, will be persuaded for sure that the Lord is risen: The Lord is risen indeed!—Gordon H. Reif

PRAYER. Spirit of the living God, come fresh and abundantly on us this hour. Let the peace and beauty of your eternal kingdom, so vastly different from the fighting madness and ugliness of our world, enable us to experience a deep sense of worship. In the silence and in the waiting, we seek your presence, O God. Speak to our flirting hearts and our false allegiances to the Savior who truly saves: Jesus Christ our Lord. Holy Spirit of Pentecost, who came to unite a long-divided people and bring the vision and very presence of God, come upon us and make of us one body. Burn from our tongues divisive and defeating words. Strip from our hearts malice and ill will. Join to our spirit the joy and goodwill, the humility and kindness of your divine Spirit.

O Holy One, who is in our midst, by your constant and forever love, touch us with gladness of heart and willingness of spirit to worship thee only and to serve others always. So let it be, Lord of all.

Forgiving Father, who brooded over the world as it was created and who broods over us until we are shaped in the full image of Christ, we confess our sin. We have tarnished and twisted that holy image. We have abused your good Creation, neglected and hurt your children, failed ourselves, and ignored and forgotten you. Lord God, who wills for us wholeness and completeness in you, accept our confessions and let your costly grace, which is greater than all our sins, cleanse us aright.

Generous God, Lord of all blessing, our prayers turn to thanksgiving. We give thanks for the smell of rain bouncing on hot thirsty pavement; for sounds and delights of small children at camp; for the grace of healing that comes with the gentle flow of time; for unexpected holy moments when we fully see and truly know; for the gift of the Spirit that groans our deepest sighs; for lazy, pink clouds playing in the sunset; for treasured memories that warm the heart; for the cross and Jesus Christ who gives us hope in our suffering, grace on our journey, salvation in our forever. Thanks be to God and our Lord, Jesus Christ, in whom we pray.—William M. Johnson

LECTIONARY MESSAGE

Getting Ready to Be the Church

TEXT: John 20:19–23

Beginnings are important, which is one reason why we remember birthdays and anniversaries. When was the church born? Just as human gestation involves several stages over many months, so the church was being formed from the moment when Jesus first called his disciples until they were ready to proclaim him as Lord at Pentecost. In this text, we view the church in the womb, as it were, already alive and growing but not yet able to survive on its own. Notice how Jesus helped it to become a viable organism.

I. *Presence.* The disciples had already seen the empty tomb (vv. 6–8) and heard an eyewitness report of Jesus' Resurrection (v. 18), but that was not sufficient to banish fear and provide courage (v. 19a). The missing element was the presence of Jesus himself. So with us, there is no substitute for an experience of the risen Lord in our lives.

Jesus came, not when they were seeking him, but when they expected him least. Recognizing their shattered morale, he comforted them with his peace (v. 19b) despite their recent abandonment of him (16:32). No wonder they responded to his gracious acceptance with joy (v. 20). How often does Jesus penetrate the locked doors of our hearts, where we are defensively barricaded against forces we are too weak to conquer, and gladdens life with the promise of his peace.

II. *Purpose.* The primary concern of Jesus was not to coddle his followers into a passive "peace of mind" but rather to infuse them with an incredible sense of purpose. He dared to challenge a dispirited, defeated band to perpetuate his own ministry, which had so recently ended on a cross. Their mission was to become the visible continuation of his earthly work as he prepared to return to the Father (see 17:18).

The heart of their assignment is described in verse 23. They are to anticipate the divine judgment of eternity by offering here on earth the forgiveness of sins that others may accept or reject (see Matt. 16: 19). But why would anyone spurn such an offer? Because it comes from one who was despised, discredited, and apparently destroyed by the religious leaders of his day! We seek forgiveness at a great white throne, not at an old rugged cross!

III. *Power.* If the disciples were to be sent by Jesus as he had first been sent by God, they would need the Holy Spirit in whose power he had worked (see

1:32–33). Receiving the Holy Spirit here (v. 22) seems to conflict with Acts 2:4 where the Holy Spirit was said to come at Pentecost. But the difference is that here the Spirit came as a gentle "breath," whereas there the Spirit came "like the rush of a mighty wind." Here the disciples remained in secret, but, seven weeks later, they were so filled with the Spirit that they spoke boldly in public.

This suggests that all Christians receive the Holy Spirit as soon as they are risen with Christ in Baptism. But we must cultivate that indwelling Spirit until impelled to give a fearless witness to the world. Such a process of intensification requires a great deal of fellowship and prayer (Acts 1:14a). Many a church has developed to the point described in John 20. May we not stop until we become the kind of church described in Acts 2!—William E. Hull

SUNDAY: JUNE TENTH

SERVICE OF WORSHIP

Sermon: The Thrill of the Trinity
TEXT: Matt. 28:19

Matthew's Gospel begins with a genealogy of Jesus tracing his Jewish ancestry right back to Abraham and then describes his birth. Matthew's Gospel ends with this same Jesus, who has been crucified and raised from the dead, sending his little group of disciples on a worldwide mission with these astonishing words: "Go therefore and make disciples of all nations, baptizing them in the name of the Father and of the Son and of the Holy Spirit. . . ."

That's quite a story to be compressed into one little book. From an episode in the life of one little nation to the vision of a mission to all nations; from the tale of a man who acted and spoke very much like one of his people's prophets, from whom he continually quoted, to this supernatural figure who founded a community committed to plunge the whole human family into a new and holy way of life, symbolized by the waters of Baptism in the name of the triune God—this is what these Gospels proclaim, and it is only our familiarity with the story that blinds our eyes to its splendor and leaves our hearts untouched by its excitement.

I. It all has to do with what is either the most important question to which we can seek an answer or one that is totally meaningless—the reality, the name and nature of the one true God, and the possibility of both knowing him and loving him. I say

"the *name*" not because we have a choice of gods offered by different religions, just as we have a choice of friends, but because in our culture nearly all who believe in God think of one sovereign, transcendent Being, the source of all that is, from whom we come, to whom we go.

(a) Thus it comes about that most believers today are Jahwists. With different degrees of fervor they tell the pollsters, "Yes, I believe in God." It's all so simple and practical. There can't be more than one Boss of the universe. He tells us how to live, and anything that helps us draw on his support is a bonus. Not to believe in God could be dangerous to your health. It's all reasonable, logical enough, if you don't ask too many questions, and, to be honest, rather boring. "The Lord our God is one Lord," yes; monotheism, the belief that there is one good and merciful Lord, not many good gods and bad gods, merciful gods and cruel gods, reliable gods and capricious gods, is a glorious revelation we owe to the Old Testament, but sheer oneness is not a very exciting quality. It can be like worshiping a zero. To arouse a living faith we need a God who reflects the diversity as well as the unity of our own nature and our own experience.

(b) When Jesus came, this vision of God was enormously enriched. Not only did he tell of a God who was "Lord of heaven and earth," but he told his followers they could call him *Abba* which, in the language of the day, is to be translated "Daddy." This was God who expected the best from his human family but welcomed all who were humble enough to confess their need. There was nothing stuffy about the prayers of Jesus. Ordinary people were thrilled to overhear a prayer like this: "I thank thee, Father, Lord of heaven and earth, for hiding these things from the learned and wise, and revealing them to the simple." The disciples' excitement mounted as they came closer to him, until one day when he asked them directly, "Who do you say that I am?" Peter gave the answer: "The Christ of God." Then, one by one, those closest to him realized that this was not just a messenger telling them about God, but God himself among them, and after he had risen from the dead, even the skeptical among them were driven to fall at his feet with the words, "My Lord and my God."

(c) So it was that, when he passed from their sight, the words that rang in their ears were of our text: "Go therefore and make disciples of all nations, baptizing them in the name of the Father and of the Son and of the Holy Spirit. . . ." That's how the church was born. They did receive power—that mysterious spiritual power, which they knew to be the Spirit of God, fell on them, and on the day of Pentecost they had an even more thrilling experience than that of the prophet Isaiah, and they knew that their mission was to bring the news of this amazing God into all the world, baptizing all "in the name of the Father, the Son, and the Holy Ghost."

II. At regular intervals someone points out in a book or a sermon or a private argument that the word *Trinity* does not occur in the Bible. It doesn't. Neither does the word *sacrament* or *Christmas* or the expressions *Ground of all Being* or *personal Savior.* Those who make this point usually go on to declare that the doctrine of the Trinity was dreamed up centuries after the time of the apostles and elaborated by medieval theologians in incense-filled rooms. But those who would scrap the doctrine of the Trinity on the grounds of obscurity usually end up with a conception of God that is cold and impersonal—even more obscure.

(a) The point is that this doctrine was not a late invention of scholars who had

not enough to keep their minds busy, nor was it ever a purely intellectual construct to be imposed on the Christian mind. From the beginning it was a vital expression of the Christian experience of God. The first disciples were all Jewish and therefore profoundly monotheist. They were the last people to dream up three Gods. But they had to find some way of telling what had happened to them when they came to know Jesus and found in him the saving presence of God. They pondered the words, "He who has seen me has seen the Father." "I and my Father are one." They had to find some way of celebrating the thrill of Pentecost when they were swept into a new community by what could be nothing less than God the Holy Spirit opening their eyes to the living presence of Jesus.

(b) From that day to this when the church is truly alive, it thrills to the tune of, "Glory be to the Father and to the Son and to the Holy Spirit." The Trinity is more of a song than a statement, an inspiration rather than a creed. To rob the church of this vision of God in which our spirit responds to his in adoration and praise is to reduce Christianity to nothing more than ethics with a halo. Gone is the mystery, the wonder, and the power.

(c) We musn't downplay the theology and think of it as an attempt to reduce a vivid religious experience to a series of propositions. There is a thrill of the mind as well as of the heart. When the infant churches turned to confront the philosophies of the Greeks and the rhetoric of the Romans, as well as those within their own ranks who wanted to abandon the doctrine of the Trinity, they produced an array of scholars who met every challenge to the orthodox faith. To this day you will find that scholars, writers, and artists who become Christian believers are nearly always converted to the church that still baptizes in the name of the Father and of the Son and of the Holy Ghost.

III. This is the power and thrill that lies behind the call of Christ to make disciples. To evangelize is not to proselytize for our particular versions of the gospel. It is to invite a spiritually hungry generation to the banquet of a God who is forever alive and active as a Trinity of love into which we are called. For love is personal; therefore, we find our true selves in the eternal love that exists in the divinity who is one God in three persons.—David H. C. Read

Illustrations

GOD AS FATHER. If God is "the Father," in nature and character and operation, then we derive (if we are parents) our characteristics from him. We are reproducing, no doubt on a microscopic scale and in a thoroughly faulty manner, something of the character of God. If once we accept it as true that the whole power behind this astonishing universe is of that kind of character that Christ could only describe as "Father," the whole of life is transfigured. If we are really seeing in human relationships fragmentary and faulty but real reflections of the nature of God, a flood of light is immediately released upon all the life that we can see.—J. B. Phillips

THE PERSONAL CHRIST. We must have the historic Christ and more. We must have the living Christ. But a living Christ who only ruled his kingdom in the unseen by general laws would be no sufficient Savior. He must be personal to us. He must be our Savior, in our situation, our needs, loves, shames, sins. He must not only live but also mingle with our lives. He must charge himself with our souls. We believe in the Holy Ghost. We have in Christ as the Spirit, the Sanctifier of our single lives, the Reader of our hearts, the Helper of our most private straits, the Inspirer of our most deep and sacred confessions. We must have one to wring from us, "My Lord and my God." We need not only the risen Christ but also the returned Christ; not only the historic Christ, nor the heavenly, but the spiritual, the intimate, the Husband of the soul in its daily vigor, its daily conflict, its daily fear, its daily joy, its daily sorrow, its daily faith, hope, love.—P. T. Forsyth

Sermon Suggestions

MIGHTY DEEDS . . . GREAT EXPECTATIONS. TEXT: Deut. 4:32–40. (1) God

has done great things for his people. (2) God expects great things from his people.

ROUND ABOUT TO THE TRIUNE GOD. TEXT: 2 Cor. 13:5–14. (1) God touches our lives with grace through Jesus Christ his Son. (2) That acquaintance leads us to experience of the love of God as Father. (3) Consequently, we have fellowship with God and one another at the deepest level through God's Holy Spirit.

Worship Aids

CALL TO WORSHIP. "Make a joyful noise unto the Lord, all ye lands. Serve the Lord with gladness: come before his presence with singing. . . . Enter into his gates with thanksgiving, and into his courts with praise: be thankful unto him, and bless his name" (Ps. 100:1–2, 4).

INVOCATION. We come to you, O Eternal Lord, recognizing that you have created us to seek you, to love you, and to find our identity within the community of your faithful people. Help us so to participate in this worship experience that we may be opened to receive your gifts of grace, new glimpses of truth, and a deeper experience of the bountiful life you have given us.—Donald W. Musser

OFFERTORY SENTENCE. "Every man shall give as he is able, according to the blessing of the Lord thy God which he hath given thee" (Deut. 16:17).

OFFERTORY PRAYER. Lord, show us the way of life through this exercise of worship. Magnify the central, deemphasize the peripheral, and crown the redemptive with thy power and peace.—E. Lee Phillips

PRAYER. Lord, God, when we look out at this world, do we behold anything worth seeing? Do we ever see your power and glory? Do we see evidence of your presence in our midst?

If we do see something of you, some evidence that you are real and you are here, does that make our lives any different? Does the vision that our earth has been designed and visited by you enrich our lives, give purpose to our day-to-day living, affect the decisions and goals we make for ourselves, help us in our relationships with one another and our attitudes toward each other? If we say we believe in you, how different does that make us from those who say they do not believe in you?

Does believing in you lead us to take your commandments seriously? Does believing in you cause us to lean upon you in time of need and to thank you in time of prosperity? Does believing in you prompt us to know that we belong to you, that we are accountable to you for the kind of lives we live, the work we do, the words we say, the games we play?

When we see you in this world, does our vision center around a person named Jesus, a cross on a hill, an empty tomb with a stone rolled away? When we see you in this world, does that give us hope, does that give us power, does that make us more loving, more resolved to pursue the things that make for peace?

Can we look at you, believe in you, and still be a carbon copy of the world and the world's values; or do we live according to the beat of a distant drummer: does life—our own and others'—have an added dimension of sacredness and precious worth? Can we see you in this world, believe in you, and still be all wrapped up in ourselves, live for our own self-interests alone; or do we know that our reason for being on this earth is to accomplish, led and nourished by your Spirit, something that contributes to your eternal kingdom of love and righteousness?

Such thoughts to consider, Lord! How they jolt us out of complacency and indifference! So many times we believe in you without really asking what that means. So many times we believe in you without struggling or even considering the effect our faith in you can have, should have, must have, on our day-to-day living and our basic attitudes and our relationships with one another. So many times we are so busy responding to or imitating the ways of the world, we become too exhausted to do what is far more important: proclaiming, promoting, practicing on earth the ways of the Lord. Our earnest prayer is that you will become so involved in our lives, your Spirit so much at home in us and in our midst, we will proceed to live on this earth, never forgetting or denying who we are, adopted children of the One God, thanks to what you have accomplished in Jesus Christ. We do not want to be just another reflection of the world. We do not want to be just frail creatures of dust. We do want to be imitators of Christ, Christian disciples who feel themselves to be joined with others in turning this world and its values right-side up—because to us has been entrusted the message of reconciliation, the gospel of hope and love and peace.

Give to us all resurrection power, so that through us, in us, beyond us your holy will may indeed be done, on earth as it is in heaven. And then we will have the matchless pleasure and privilege of living lives worth living.—Gordon H. Reif

LECTIONARY MESSAGE

The Great Commission

TEXT: Matt. 28:16–20

We have become too familiar with the Great Commission! It has lost its power to surprise, to shock, even to scandalize us. Imagine a defeated leader, brutally rejected and crucified, asking only eleven of his followers—the twelfth having proved a traitor—to win the whole world! "Impossible nonsense," we might respond, except for an awareness that this incredible mandate has already been fulfilled a thousandfold more than its first hearers could have ever imagined. Indeed, have any marching orders ever had greater impact in human history? Why is this possible?

I. *The promise.* It was not anything about the disciples that encouraged success but three things about Jesus:

(a) He elicits worship even from doubters. Traditional translations say that "*some* doubted" (v. 17), but the Greek says simply that all of them worshiped yet also doubted. They were compelled to acknowledge his greatness even though they did not fully understand it. Like the epileptic father, they cried, "We believe, help our unbelief!" (see Mark 9:24). Better to bring our doubts to Christ than to put off worshiping him until we have them all resolved.

(b) He exercises a cosmic sway. Since all authority is from God (Rom. 13:1), to delegate that authority to Christ is to make him God's viceroy for the human race. Since Christ's sovereignty extends to "heaven and earth" (v. 18), there is nowhere we can go in this world that has not already been claimed by Christ. We sometimes speak of "foreign" missions as if the farther we go from home the more remote we are from Christ, but this verse tells us that every person we meet is subject to his lordship.

(c) He goes with us to the edges of time and space. Neither duration nor distance dilutes the sense of Christ's nearness that the eleven felt with him on the mountaintop (v. 20). If his authority is universal, then there are no barriers to his presence. We do not follow footprints in the sands of time but footfalls as he walks beside us as our eternal contemporary.

II. *The pattern.* No blueprint is given for this stupendous undertaking, only a simple guideline with three parts for ministering wherever we may "go" (v. 19):

(a) "Make disciples." Jesus had done that for them; now he bids them do the same for others. The picture is one of enlisting apprentices who learn to become craftsmen in the fine art of living by first watching and then practicing under the tutelage of those who are more advanced in the needed skills.

(b) "Baptize in the name." Baptism is a drama that reenacts the central events of Christ's saving ministry. By entering into these experiences, we literally take the name of the heavenly family and live forevermore out of that adopted relationship. Just as crossing over Jordan was the passage from wilderness to Promised Land for the Israelites, for us baptismal waters are the boundary between an old age and a new.

(c) "Teaching them to observe." Mature religion strives to maintain a healthy balance between inwardness and outwardness. The presence of Christ is with every disciple baptized in the name of the Holy Spirit, but this subjective guidance is supplemented by the objective teachings commanded by the historical Jesus. Christianity is not just emotional feelings; it is also concrete observances that show others the power of Christ to control our conduct.—William E. Hull

SUNDAY: JUNE SEVENTEENTH

SERVICE OF WORSHIP

Sermon: Fathers Count
TEXT: Prov. 17:6

In our contemporary society nothing is more important than the parent-child relationship. In this sermon we shall be dealing essentially with the relationship of the father and the child. The discussion of this can be an embarrassing one for us fathers when we think of our role and responsibilities. No doubt there are times when all parents feel inadequate.

I. Increasingly, I have come to feel that nothing is more important in our society than a renewed understanding of the biblical role of the father.

(a) To identify with a son or a daughter, to be the father that all of us would like to be is no easy thing in our culture. There is the matter of sheer physical presence. Some fathers are away, as I have said, all of the week and cannot be present because of their work. It is very difficult for them to share the authority and the responsibility because of the necessity of their daily living. Too often the father has become mainly a provider and a partner, a breadwinner, and one who is called upon when his children are in difficulty; yet nothing is more important than this matter of learning to build this relationship as it ought to be built.

(b) There are many kinds of daddies, you know. There is the "nervous wreck daddy"—the fellow who comes home from the office, and his wife has been trained to sing the song to the children, "Daddy's tired. Don't bother him; don't ask him any questions. Your father has had a hard day today. Be quiet."

And then there is the "bronze-statue" type. He is hard and cold and unresponsive, and while he loves his children, he is remote, and they cannot really communicate with him.

Then there is the "run-along daddy" type. To every question his response is, "Run along; I'm busy now."

II. Let us notice two or three biblical instances that I think speak to us in this matter.

(a) One is found in a very strange book, the Book of Judges, chapter 11, verses 30 through 35. Here in capsule is the strange story of an Old Testament judge by the name of Jephthah. He made a vow that if he had victory over the children of Ammon he would sacrifice unto the Lord the first thing that came forth from the door of his house upon his return. When he returned in victory the first thing he saw was his lovely daughter, and he took her life. It is a sordid and sub-Christian story, but I think in some sense it may suggest to us, as modern fathers, certain things that are of tremendous importance. Sometimes we, too, unconsciously sacrifice our children for lesser values.

(b) Over in Genesis, chapters 24 through 34, there is another interesting story and a tragic one. It is the story of the home of Isaac and Rebekah. As you know, it was a home of domestic rivalry, competition, partiality, jealousy, duplicity, dishonesty. A scheming mother taught Jacob all the tricks of the trade, and he used them again and again. The name *Jacob* means "deceiver." Sometime if you want to make an interesting study, take your Bible and study the life of Jacob under the title, "How Chickens Come Home to Roost." He lived to eat the bitter fruit of his own cultivation. There was the clever trick in connection with his marriage to Leah and Rachel. There was the father-in-law who robbed him of his flocks; there was the shame of Dinah, his daughter, who was defiled by her own brethren; there was the sale of Joseph into slavery and the pa-

thos and anguish of all the years of paying for the actions he had taken. You see, domestic tranquility and joy cannot be built on dishonesty, immorality, and self-centered indulgence. The word *Isaac* means "laughter," and in many ways he was a joke as a father, a tragic weakness that branded generations to come.

(c) But perhaps the most attractive of all the pictures of a home in the Old Testament is described in one verse in Joshua, chapter 24, verse 15. Joshua was Moses' great successor, as you recall. He said, "I know not what others may do, but as for me and my house, we will serve the Lord." The interesting thing is that Joshua begins with himself. A parent cannot share a faith that he, himself, does not possess. This is the great tragedy of so many parents. They want their children to possess what they are not willing to possess themselves. Christian discipleship demands a price they are not willing to pay, and they somehow imagine they can teach their children to honor values they do not honor. Joshua had courage and commitment and conviction. He made no apology for his faith and his children rose up to call him blessed.

(d) Perhaps the loveliest of all relationships, however, as an example for us fathers, is found in the story in Luke 15 of the two lost sons and the forgiving and loving father. There were two boys at home, you remember—one a boy who was lost as a prodigal, the other who was lost because of self-righteousness. It is the story of our loving and forgiving Father. It is our model and our standard, the standard of God himself.

III. How can I be a better father, you ask? Let me suggest four simple things. You can share yourself with your children. This is what they want most. You can let them know that you love them. One thing that comforts me is that, regardless of the mistakes we make, if our children know we care for them, they can endure almost any mistake. In the third place, you can enjoy them. Someone has said, "One way to be a bad parent is not to get any fun out of it." Finally, you can practice your own faith. When the ancient Jew said, "Train up your child in the way he should go, and when he is old he will not depart from it," he was speaking both from an act of faith and a deep conviction.

Indeed, children are the bearers of the continuity of life. They evince man's faith in tomorrow. In the Christian context, children are the glory of parents and the parents the glory of children and all subservient to the heavenly Father.—Luther Joe Thompson

Illustrations

A FITTING WORD.   As a lad about ten years of age, I entered the May Day track meet presided over by my schoolteacher father. (He later entered the ministry.) I wanted to win that fifty-yard dash, and my family was pulling for me. But a tall fellow I'd never seen before came up and, as I expected, won it. I was bitterly disappointed, fell down at the end of the race. My father picked me up and said a thing I'll never forget: "Son, you won't believe it now but you won that race, because you did the best you could."—Gaston Foote

IDENTITY.   I grew up in a small, friendly world. My father and mother loved each other, and they loved me. I didn't stop to ask what the meaning of my life was, what the purpose of it was. I simply did each thing as it came and tried to make the best decision I could. I never asked myself, Who am I? I knew. I was Theodore Ferris, Walter Ferris's son, of Port Chester, New York.—Theodore Parker Ferris

Sermon Suggestions

DESPISING OUR BIRTHRIGHT.   TEXT: Gen. 25:19–34. (1) The story: Esau, in a moment of weakness, forswore his most precious possession—his birthright, "with all rights and privileges thereunto appertaining." (2) The meaning: A stupid decision made in a time of temptation can begin an entire sequence of dreadful consequences. (3) The application: God offers to us a way of escape from the forces that, at worst, threaten to destroy us; or that, at least, tend to rob us of peace and joy (see 1 Cor. 10:13).

THE ULTIMATE REMEDY.   TEXT: Rom. 5:6–11. (1) We, the human race, were weak—sinners all. (2) God nevertheless showed his love for us by the gift of his Son, who died for us. (3) Therefore, we can here and now enjoy our reconciliation to God by participating in the life of the risen Christ.

Worship Aids

CALL TO WORSHIP.   "Sin unto him, sing psalms unto him: talk ye of all his wondrous works. Glory ye in his holy name: let the heart of them rejoice that seek the Lord" (Ps. 105:2–3).

INVOCATION.   Lord, your mercies fill our hearts with joy. Let our mouths be filled with praise, and let this place of worship echo with psalms and hymns and spiritual songs.

OFFERTORY SENTENCE.   "Give unto the Lord the glory due unto his name: bring an offering, and come before him: worship the Lord in the beauty of holiness" (1 Chron. 16:29).

OFFERTORY PRAYER.   Lord God, as we lay by in store a portion of all our worldly goods, do so bless this portion as to use it for much good, because the Holy Spirit pervades it, our prayers dedicate it, and the world needs the Savior it proclaims.—E. Lee Phillips

PRAYER.   Almighty God, owner of forever, keeper of the universe, God of eternal goodness, author of this beautiful Lord's day, in the stillness of this holy place and in the silence of our pulsing hearts, hear our many voices of praise and worship. O Holy One, though our steps come from various paths and our needs and concerns are many, in oneness, we seek your presence and worship you as Lord of all. Gracious and sustaining Father, whose love and goodness comes to us, as silently and generously enter every trembling and waiting heart and grant us your glad assurance and peaceful resting place.

Understanding Father, God of kind

mercy and gentle forgiveness, hear now our confession of sin and desire for recovery and cleansing. We call you light but walk too often in darkness; we call you peace but do violence to others, to your Creation, and even to ourselves; we call you joy yet live our days in sadness and even bitterness; we call you hope but spend our days stumbling in despair; we call you love yet despise others, crouch in fear, and harbor distrust in our hearts. Lord Jesus, who has borne our pain and carried our sorrows away, who has suffered and died for our sins, forgive us again and restore us to rightness and oneness with you, with others, and with ourselves.

Heavenly Father, Lord and Master of us all, who has shown us your face in Jesus Christ and in him given us salvation and good news of redemption, bless the work and ministry of our mission endeavors here. Strengthen all who labor to deepen our mission education, to touch the lives of girls and boys, women and men, to nurture the movement of your Spirit in their lives. Widen our understanding of missions and convict us of our privilege and call to share the gospel with all persons.

Healing and comforting God, O great physician, God of tender heart and abiding comfort, who in Christ has suffered for all who suffer, we pray today for all who are suffering in body, in mind, in spirit, whose hearts are broken. May your healing and reclaiming presence encircle them with hope and wholeness. Grant us the humility and courage to suffer with you and the blessing to be comforters with you. In Jesus who suffered that we may know life and be comforted, we pray.— William M. Johnson

LECTIONARY MESSAGE

Harvesting—An Urgent Ministry

TEXT: Matt. 9:35–10:8

The thirty-eighth verse of chapter 9 is the key verse of this passage—"Pray ye therefore the Lord of the harvest, that he will send forth laborers into his harvest." The verses in the rest of the passage define and limit the intended harvest for that time, but we may take Jesus' concern for the multitudes (9:36) to be of universal import for those who would be his followers.

I. *The condition of the people.* Surely the message of Jesus is most necessary and most appreciated where it is most lacking. We know people who are "fainting," becoming distressed to exhaustion as sheep that have wandered long and are wounded to the point of hopelessness by the conditions of their lives. And what about the numbers—the "multitudes"? We cannot have any realistic concept of the millions who dwell in even one of our great cities, much less of the countless numbers in smaller cities and towns and in isolated regions in every land and corner of the earth. The harvest to be gathered for our Lord—or else to be left to perish for eternity—is, indeed, in Jesus' word, "plenteous."

Then Jesus moves on rapidly from being passive sympathizer to being the eager provider for their rescue—"the harvest truly is plenteous, but the laborers are few." Workers are needed to bring into the "storehouse" of the Lord this plentiful harvest.

The kind of worker needed is the kind who will devote arduous, body-draining work, long hours of mental application, deep longing and labor of heart and soul, to the speedy, timely, life-saving harvest of God's people.

Jesus begins with those who have been his closest learners thus far. Verses 1 and 8 of chapter 10 tell of the great powers that will be theirs as they begin and carry on their tasks. They also tell what will be the evidence of their claim—the establishment of conditions characteristic of the kingdom of heaven.

II. *The ministry of harvest laborers.*

(a) We may think that Jesus was unnecessarily harsh in his restriction of their ministry to Israelites only. But the true test of our witness, as well as the most necessary, is among those of our own household, our own neighborhood, our own community. He is not really excluding the rest of the world's people. He is calling upon the strongest natural allegiance in expressing, not condemnation, but sympathy for those he terms "lost sheep of the house of Israel." He is showing the logic of starting with those nearby who share similar spiritual teaching and expectations.

(b) Their message is to be that the kingdom of heaven is near at hand. We cannot begin to say what it means in all its implications. But we can say that the real thing will be beyond our fondest dreams and hopes.

(c) Their evidence that their message is true is to be found in the conditions they are able to bring about. They are to heal sickness of all kinds, both of body and of soul. No greater or more blessed work can be undertaken than this of laboring in God's harvest.

III. *Motives for harvest laborers.* As if the natural abhorrence of such waste as Jesus sees in the waiting harvest, if it is not garnered, is not sufficient motive, he also appeals to the sense of fairness of those he calls.

Our sense of justice is within us like a conscience. We could cry endlessly over the injustice of what people do to each other. Our homes, schools, and offices are often scenes of the kind of injustice that we think is terrible in the crimes we read and hear of. The source of injustice is in the loss of love and respect for people's tender hearts.

The sense of justice that urges on a truly laboring disciple is that of fairness, that what is so needed by others has been so freely received by him that he should feel the obligation to give as freely.—John R. Rodman

SUNDAY: JUNE TWENTY-FOURTH

SERVICE OF WORSHIP

Sermon: What Was Wrong with the Older Brother?

TEXT: Luke 15

"A certain man had two sons." Two sons, raised in the same home. Yet how different they were. The younger son rebelled against his father. The older son remained faithful. The younger son ran away. The older son stayed home. The younger son was undisciplined. The older son had his life closely ordered and rigidly regulated. The younger son was a playboy. The older son was a plowboy. How different these two sons were.

Yet they have this much in common. As the story develops, we discover that both of the boys come under Jesus' judgment. Why? It is obvious to all why the younger son would be labeled a sinner, for he openly rebelled against his father, wasted his father's money, ran with a fast crowd, fell into every conceivable kind of immorality, and ended up a physical and spiritual wreck. But why does the older brother come under Jesus' condemnation?

I. First of all, the older brother had the wrong attitude.

(a) Picture the scene. For months, the younger brother had been gone. No word had come from the far country about the wayward son. Perhaps he was in desperate need. Maybe he was dead. Every morning when the father got up, he would go out on the porch and scan the horizon for any sign of his son coming back home. In the evening just before the sun set, the father would follow the same ritual. Each day the lines of despair deepened in his face.

Then one day as the older brother returned home from work, the good news was given to him. "Your brother has come home. He is safe. He's back with us now."

How did the older brother respond? Did he say, "Fantastic. Where is he? I've really missed seeing him." No, verse 28 tells us, "But he became angry and was not willing to go in." That's what was wrong with the older brother. He had the wrong attitude.

(b) The message of this parable is that the measure of your Christian maturity is not the actions of your life but your attitude toward sinners who have found their way back into the Father's house. Are you critical or compassionate? That is the key.

II. Notice this second thing in the story.

The older brother not only had the wrong attitude. He also had the wrong focus.

(a) Listen again to verse 29: "For so many years I have been serving you, and I have never neglected a command of yours; and yet you have never given me a kid, that I might be merry with my friends." Five times in that one short verse, the older brother uses the words *I, me,* or *my.* He was so occupied with casting glances at his own righteousness, that he never had time to be concerned about anyone other than himself.

(b) In times past we would say that the older brother was self-centered or selfish. Now we would diagnose him as being narcissistic. This term, *narcissistic,* comes from the Greek legend of a man named Narcissus who fell in love with his reflection in a pool and pined away in rapture over it.

(c) The older brother was in love with himself. He was so busy patting himself on the back for his own righteousness that he was unable to feel anything for his wandering brother who had come back home. Underneath the outer facade, his only concern was for himself.

III. Look at the story again and notice this third thing about the older brother— he had the wrong motive.

(a) When he complained that after having kept the commandments of his father, the father had never given him a kid, that he might be merry with his friends, he was revealing the motive behind his actions. The older brother did not stay home because he loved his father. He did not follow his commandments because he wanted to please his father. He stayed home and obeyed his father's commandments for what he could get out of it.

(b) We've often heard the question, "If you were put on trial for being a Christian, would there be enough evidence to convict you?" But take the question a step further and ask, "What if they had to establish motive?" Why do you do the things that you do? Why do you go to church? Why do you read your Bible? Why do you pray? Why do you give your money? Why? What is your motive?

(c) Why do you do the things you do? Are you pushed by a desire for attention or by fear or by outside pressure? Or do you do the things you do because the "love of Christ constrains you"?

IV. In verse 30 we see something else. The older brother had the wrong understanding.

Speaking of this prodigal brother who had just returned home, the older brother called him "this son of yours." Not my brother, but your son. The father caught that and tried to correct it in verse 32 when he called the prodigal "this brother of yours." What the older son failed to understand is the meaning of brotherhood. The men and women around us are not just God's children. They are also our brothers and sisters.

V. Ultimately, the problem with the older brother was that he had the wrong relationship with his father.

(a) He was devoted to his father's law; but he was not in sympathy with his father's heart. He stayed in his father's house; but he was not at home with his father.

(b) Jesus' parable of the older brother is a reminder that the heart of the Christian faith is not a matter of rules or rituals but of a relationship. When your relationship is right, when you really love the Father, then your understanding will be right, for you will recognize others as your brothers; and your motive will be right, for you will want to please God; and your focus will be right, for you will be more concerned about others than about yourself; and your attitude will be right, for you will rejoice with those who come back to the fellowship of the father. The key is your relationship with the father.

(c) Hear this final thought. Verse 28 says that just as the father went out to welcome the prodigal home, he also went out to the older brother to exhort him and encourage him to come back home. That is the word that comes to you this morning. Whether you are like the prodigal who is lost in the far country, or like the older brother who is lost at home, you can come back to your Father's house. He loves you now as much as he ever did. His arms are outstretched to you. If you will acknowledge him again as your Father, then you too can come home.—Brian L. Harbour

Illustrations

GENUINE BROTHERHOOD. A little boy was told by his doctor that he could save his sister's life by giving her some blood. The six-year-old girl was near death—a victim of a disease from which the boy had made a marvelous recovery two years earlier. Her only chance for restoration was a blood transfusion from someone who had previously conquered the illness. Since the two children had the same rare blood type, the boy was the ideal donor.

"Johnny, would you like to give your blood for Mary?" the doctor asked.

The boy hesitated, his lower lip started to tremble. Then he smiled and said, "Sure, Doc. I'll give my blood for my sister."

Soon the two children were wheeled into a room where the transfusion was done. As the blood was siphoned into Mary's veins, one could almost see new life come into her tired body. The ordeal was almost over when Johnny's brave voice broke the silence. "Doc, when do I die?"

It was only then that the doctor realized what the moment of hesitation, what the trembling of his lip, had meant. Little Johnny actually thought that in giving his blood, he was giving up his life. Yet he did it because she was his sister.—Brian L. Harbour

VANITY AND EGOISM. What shall we do with vanity and egoism then, if these universal, unsocial traits are ubiquitously present in the personality scheme of every human being? The art of attaining happiness consists in taking egoism and vanity and diverting them into socially useful channels. If you are vain because you have a pretty face, a fur coat, an eight-cylinder automobile, ten thousand dollars in the bank, or a genealogical chart dating to the Puritan fathers, your pride and vanity are childish. One little streptococcus may easily kill you and deprive you of your basis for self-esteem. A playful hurricane may rob you of all your possessions. It is unwise to be vain about any possession, because possessions are notorious for their perverse tendency to vanish. Just as happiness consists in doing something, never in being something or having something, so the cure of vanity and pride, two egregiously disruptive character traits, consists not in putting your possessions aside and courting Our Lady of Poverty but in diverting all your life's efforts to their useful elaboration in the larger cooperation of human life.—W. Beran Wolfe

Sermon Suggestions

THE FUGITIVE. TEXT: Gen. 28:10–17. (1) The problem: Circumstances may cause one to find oneself in a lonely, apparently God-forsaken path. (2) The solution: In the crisis time, God may manifest himself to us in some unusual way or comfort us through faith in his promise and presence.

THE GREAT DIFFERENCE. TEXT: Rom. 5:12–19. (1) Because of Adam, we are pronounced, Guilty! (2) Because of Christ, we are pronounced, Not guilty!

Worship Aids

CALL TO WORSHIP. "Let us search and try our ways, and turn again to the Lord. Let us lift up our heart with our hands unto God in the heavens" (Lam. 3:40–41).

INVOCATION. God of hope and God of glory, we recognize that you have created us to seek you, to love you, and to find our identity within the fellowship of your faithful people. We thank you for seeking us when we were lost, for bearing our griefs and carrying our sorrows, and for making us whole by the healing of the cross. Draw us close to the cross and the wounded healer. Draw us close to you. Draw us close to one another.—Donald W. Musser

OFFERTORY SENTENCE. "And he said unto them, Take heed what ye hear: with what measure ye mete, it shall be measured to you: and unto you that hear shall more be given" (Mark 4:24).

OFFERTORY PRAYER. Lord, give us to understand the way to the true riches. Grant to us the grace to be giving and forgiving, and let us enjoy the inner fruits of blessing others.

PRAYER.   Lord, God, so many people seem to live for nothing. They fill their lives with all the activities and attitudes that signify nothing at all. They are busy, busy, busy, and they really never discover why. They have calendars that are cluttered with commitments, but full calendars don't always mean full lives. They struggle and scramble to meet their deadlines, but doing that does not give them the satisfaction of being really alive. And in the spaces, the intervals, where all the frantic activity ceases, they look at themselves and see lives that are hollow and barren and empty. They have so much to do, they don't know how they can do any more, but even so, there are those ever-disturbing moments when reluctantly but honestly they find themselves asking, perhaps crying, "Is this all there is?"

Many people, no small number of them being church people, go through the motions of being alive, of doing today what they did yesterday, of getting ready for tomorrow by planning to repeat today. No God-given purpose organizes their lives; no living God takes them by the hand; no Shepherd leads them in paths that are safe and sure. They can't make any real, acceptable, worthwhile sense out of their days all by themselves; but, even worse, their relationship with you is so poorly cultivated, so distant and impersonal and vague, they don't receive or even recognize the help and guidance you provide either. So many people "believe" in you, but as a stranger believes in a stranger or as an enemy believes in an enemy or as a student believes in a statistic.

Many people believe what you have done for other people, how you have turned the world of other people upside down, how active you have been in other days and places. And it all seems good, interesting, appropriate—except the wall is firmly built, so that what you have done for others is not something you can or will do for *us*. You have not told us that, we tell ourselves that, and we live accordingly.

God of our fathers, God of other people, God of just about everyone except us,

be our God, too. God of other sinners, be our God, too. God of other prodigals, be our God, too. God of other people neither too good nor too bad to be wonderfully upheld by your tender, loving care, be our God, too. God of other people now busy doing the work of your kingdom of love and righteousness, be our God, too.

We do wait upon you as you have asked us to do. We do hear your knocking at the door of our particular lives, and we open ourselves to you. Come into our lives, Lord Jesus. Find a welcome from us full and complete. We want to be where our true home is: with you. Be in our midst in such a way that we can, each one, feel your presence, learn your will for us, be given the equipment of the Spirit we need to be faithful. You have promised to be with us always: be with us NOW.—Gordon H. Reif

LECTIONARY MESSAGE

Amid Warnings, Some Assurances

TEXT: Matt. 10:24–33

It hardly seems necessary for the Lord to warn his disciples that a servant is not above his master or that a disciple is not above his teacher. But the revelation comes when he says that it should be sufficient that the servant is *as* his master and the disciple is *as* his teacher (v. 25).

I. That assures us all that, conversely, the master and the teacher are not, by reason of either their fortunate positions or their superior knowledge, *above* the servant and the disciple. It is not, as men commonly practice, that some people, because of wealth, birth, office, or favor, are in that respect better people, higher in the scale of human value. We have it written, "all men are created equal," all are of equal worth in the sight of God and the Lord Jesus Christ.

II. The great hidden secret, of which Jesus speaks in the twenty-sixth and twenty-seventh verses as inevitably to be revealed, taken from hiding and spoken abroad in daylight, is that the value of every human being is absolute. The Lord feels the necessity of emphasizing this great truth with a parable about sparrows.

Although they are insignificant in value to men, they are not insignificant in the eyes of God—he is with them, even whenever or wherever they fall. The next treatment is reminiscent of the passage in the Sermon on the Mount in which Jesus compares us to the flowers of the field in value, assuring us of never having to worry about clothing, which is itself of a value hardly worth mentioning compared to the life given in faith to God (Matt. 6:28–34).

Here Jesus, by assuring the disciples that what man never bothers to measure— something as insignificant as a bird of the field—is not only significant to God but also attended by him. This is just the point. The Father's attendance in the death or life of a sparrow heightens our understanding of the degree of his caring for every last one of us. The minuteness of his concern for what may to many seem the least item of human concern—a single hair of one's head—is a measure of the immeasurable love of which each of us is the recipient.

III. It seems that the last lesson many of us ever truly understand or appreciate is that revealed in verse 28—of the human being, it is the soul, not the body, that is of intrinsic worth. Consistently through all the known centuries, those who have thought deeply about life and its meaning have derogated the pleasures and comforts of the body as not worth considering in the same thought with the soul and its welfare. Most of us place the values of life in the same order in which Abraham Maslow enumerates the priorities of his "hierarchy of human needs"—the physiological, having to do with keeping life going, come first; the next are those having to do with protecting and maintaining the life; then those of relationship with others, society, and self; and last, in whatever time and with whatever resources are not expended in providing the others, we attend to our complete "self-actualization." That is the picture of the human priorities that Jesus was warning us against.

IV. The kind of life we must live is the life in Christ. He tells us he will confess us if we confess him before men. Here the emphasis of the original is valuable. The Greek puts it, "Whoever confesses *in* me, him will I confess; and whoever denies *in* me, him will I deny." The confession *in* Christ is a possibility only when the soul of a person has fellowship with Christ and is alive by his grace. Destitute of grace, we can only deny; we lose if we lack his fellowship.

So the warnings—to grant equality; to concern oneself with the soul, not the body; and to live in close fellowship with Christ—derive their meanings from the absolute truth of the worth of the human being.—John R. Rodman

SUNDAY: JULY FIRST

SERVICE OF WORSHIP

Sermon: Start Walking

TEXT: Eph. 5:1–16

"Ask for the ancient paths" (Jer. 6:16). That almost sounds subversive! Who thinks like that nowadays, anyway? "Put yourselves on the ways of long ago," another translation reads. There you will find "the good way." The prophet's message was not one of saying that old is automatically better. But experience tested by time has something to teach us: that is what was being said. There is a way, a right way to follow. "Walk in it," we are admon-ished—or as the simpler title of today's sermon has it, "Start Walking."

For us, far removed from Jeremiah, there exists a second covenant revealed through the life and witness of Jesus Christ. Several facets of that covenant describe the Way and the ways in which we are to walk. There are directives such as these: "Walk in the light"; "Walk in love"; "Walk in newness of life"; and finally, "Walk by the Spirit." These are the lofty places on which we are to set our feet as people of the covenant made real in Jesus Christ. Let us fix these things in our minds.

I. "Walk as children of light," wrote the Apostle Paul. The alternative journey obviously has to do with darkness, with groping and stumbling and no clear direction.

(a) Even when we think we know what we are doing, crossing a darkened room in our own homes at night, the chances are good that we will trip over something or bump into the furniture; not easily do we move through the dark. Step from the shadows, our faith bids us, and walk in the light.

(b) It is the light of Jesus Christ about which we speak, the light of his teachings and example. He himself said, "I am the Light of the World; whoever follows me will not walk in darkness but will have the Light of Life." This statement apparently came from Jesus' lips during a Jewish festival time, the Feast of Tabernacles. Tradition had it that on the first day of that feast four golden candelabra, each having four golden bowls, were lighted in a certain courtyard area of the Hebrew Temple. These flames sent their brightness out over the entire city of Jerusalem. It is not known if these great lights were lit on successive evenings. It does seem to be evident, however, that there was no illumination whatsoever on the very last evening of the feast. Perhaps it was then, on the last evening when light was so notably absent that Jesus declared, "I am the Light of the World." No festival flames burned at that moment; the declaration by Jesus that he was Light in which no darkness existed at all could not help but leave a profound impression upon his listeners. How quickly people might have said, Let us walk in this light forevermore.

II. We who have such propensities to find and do a new thing really cannot improve upon that ancient prescription to walk in the light—the light of Christ our Lord. Recognize that, if once we start walking in this particular way, soon we also shall learn about walking in love.

(a) This is not a walk of sentimentality or subjectivity. Love—as Christ loved us—is described by service and unselfishness. It is full of compassion: bearing all things, believing all things, hoping all things, enduring all things. Love is unfailing—persevering, patient, and lasting. It possesses

renewing power for both giver and receiver. It is a balm of healing, a gift of the highest order.

(b) The full meanings of love are not exhausted, even by this description. As a pathway to pursue, love is not all that unusual or unknown: it is mostly untried. The reminders cannot be repeated often enough, to start walking—walking in love. "This is my commandment," said Jesus, "that you love one another as I have loved you."

III. Walk in light. Walk in love. And then our covenant understanding as people of faith has us walk also in newness of life.

(a) Paul's symbolism is graphic; we and other congregations practice it often as candidates are immersed in the baptismal pool. Their entire bodies are lowered into the water, signifying a release and burial of their former lives, which existed without relationship to God. They then are raised up, to stand erect as persons committed to the Way and truth and life of their Lord. The baptized individual confesses, "I no longer am what I once was. I stand henceforth in the light and love and newness of life offered through Jesus Christ." Buried with Christ, renewed by him: that is the testimony we share.

(b) Our walk in newness of life expresses the exhilarating wonder of "living by dying." Jesus constantly emphasized this point, calling his followers to save life by giving it away. Here is high adventure; here is a pursuit for life with purpose and goal.

IV. And lest we presume that in all our endeavor we walk alone, this final counsel is given, also from the New Testament Scriptures: "Walk by the Spirit."

(a) Being Spirit-led and Spirit-filled means that Christ dwells within, enabling us to demonstrate what elsewhere are called the "fruits of the Spirit." These are love, joy, peace, patience, kindness, goodness, faithfulness, gentleness, and self-control. We are not the instigators of these behaviors but are capable of expressing them because of our walk by the Spirit, the Spirit of Christ.

(b) Has anything radically new or different been said today? Has a message like this never been heard before? Hardly!

The instruction to walk in light, to walk in love, to walk in newness of life, and to walk by the Spirit undoubtedly sounds very familiar to many among us. But still it is true, as Jeremiah said, that every person comes to a crossroads. When that happens the prophet advised that we "look and ask for the ancient paths, where the good way is, and walk in it." He was not talking about the latest fad or the impulse of the moment. He was addressing the deepest needs of our lives, in effect, telling us to start walking. That walk is to be marked by light, love, newness, and spiritual power.—John H. Townsend

Illustrations

WHO AM I?   I am the secret of health and happiness. I am the inspiration of youth and solace of old age. I am always available. I am invincible and eternal. I am the antidote for crime, poverty, cruelty, and fear. I am the conqueror of disease, despotism, and despair. I am the healer of hatred, sin, and injustice. I am the copartner of truth and righteousness. I am the remedy for the world's wants, wars, and woes. I am the builder of churches, chapels, and cathedrals. I am the guide of preachers, prophets, and poets. I am the creator of lofty music, pictures, and architecture. I am the handservant of faith, mercy, and charity. I am the fulfilling of the Law. I am the greatest thing in the world. I am Love.—Grenville Kleiser

OUR GUIDANCE SYSTEM.   The main thing for us in this world is, not being sure about what God's will is, but seeking it sincerely and following what we do understand of it. Many people have expressed to me convictions, that I have considered to be erroneous, about what God wanted of them. I have refrained from arguing with them. In the first place, who am I that I should claim to know better than they what God's will is, or to judge his secret purposes, when he is leading a soul along paths that seem to me to be unexpected? And then if I argued with them I should shake their faith, and it is their faith that matters, even if they make mistakes. Their faith will bring them closer to God. And

"from obedience to obedience," as Frommel said, they can be corrected by God, brought to a clearer vision of what his will is. A few years later we shall see them admitting their mistake. But it is clear that they would never have found it out if they had not first begun to obey in what they thought was right.—Paul Tournier

Sermon Suggestions

IN COMBAT WITH GOD.   TEXT: Gen. 32: 22–32. (1) Jacob's need: a sense of identity and purpose. (2) God's provision: a new name and purpose revealed in spiritual struggle.

WHAT YOUR BAPTISM MEANS.   TEXT: Rom. 6:9–11. (1) That you have died to sin and buried the old life. Has the old life lessened its grip on you? (2) That you have been raised with the living Christ and now "walk in newness of life." Have new desires, loves, and aims awakened in your life, which clearly come from God?

Worship Aids

CALL TO WORSHIP.   "We have thought of thy lovingkindness, O God, in the midst of thy Temple. According to thy name, O God, so is thy praise unto the ends of the earth: thy right hand is full of righteousness" (Ps. 48:9–10).

INVOCATION.   As we meet in worship, O Lord, help us to see that the mercies by which we live are for all people everywhere, and we pray that your name be praised and your will be done everywhere.

OFFERTORY SENTENCE.   "Offer unto God thanksgiving; and pay thy vows unto the most High" (Ps. 50:14).

OFFERTORY PRAYER.   Holy God, we are grateful for the freedom of worship we enjoy and the liberty of soul we can express in Christ Jesus. Let this offering serve as a catalyst of liberation for every soul within its reach that longs for God.—E. Lee Phillips

PRAYER. Eternal God, Lord of Creation and Father of Jesus Christ our Lord, in Creation you called forth light and in Jesus Christ, you gave us the Light of Life. Thanks be to God, Father and Master of us all. There is much darkness in our lives, O God, so we seek Christ. Jesus is the Light of the World, so forgive us for preferring darkness and stumbling in our blindness. May we come to the Light and see again. Jesus is the Living Water and the Bread of Life. Forgive us for hungering and thirsting after that which does not satisfy but only addicts and jades our tastes. Guide us to find and fill our appetite in thee alone. Jesus is the Way and the Truth. Forgive us for wandering away and for flirting with falsehoods. Set our feet on the right way beside you. Open our hearts and heads to the truth that sets us free and gives us meaning. Jesus is the Resurrection and the Life. Forgive us for living as if this were not true or did not matter. May our words and ways show forth the hope and victory of his Resurrection, and let our lives be found in his life. May Jesus Christ who has come to reveal you, O God, be revealed in our lives as we follow and learn of him.

Receive now our prayers for others and ourselves, dear Lord. We pray for those whose lives have fallen apart and who feel overwhelmed by defeat; for those coming to terms with the limits now set in their lives; for those weary of faking it but afraid of what being honest may mean; for those paralyzed in loneliness and who long for the sound of another heartbeat; for those committed to the unhindered search for truth and who are finding it costly; for those who have taken a leap of faith and are enjoying new beginnings; for all who are seeking your will and call in their lives; O God, hear these and all the whispers of our hearts, even now as we worship and praise you.—William M. Johnson

LECTIONARY MESSAGE

A Declaration of War on Loyalties

TEXT: Matt. 10:34–42

In this passage, Jesus' instructions to his disciples are put into his most personal terms so far.

He first tells them, "Think not that I am come to send peace on earth; I come not to send peace but a sword." In amazement we ask, Is this not he of whom the angel declared, "Behold, I bring you good tidings of great joy, which shall be to all people . . ." and of whose coming the multitude with the angel proclaimed, "Glory to God in the highest, and on earth peace, goodwill toward men"?

In the next verses, Jesus goes on to carry forward to fuller understanding the declarations of verse 21, of brother delivering brother; a father, the child; children, their parents. Here he sets a son against his father, daughter against mother, daughter-in-law against mother-in-law. The crucial test of love for Christ comes in relation to those of one's own family. Loyalty here is relative (pardon the pun). Whether we can surrender family members to Christ ultimately determines whether we can relate to them. We must "lose" that part of "life" in order to "find it." This is indeed a crucial test—it may be the "cross" that Jesus says (in verse 38) is the crux of worthiness.

But a more difficult statement follows these hard ones—"He that findeth his life shall lose it: and he that loseth his life for my sake shall find it." Jesus calls for divisions (to which call we respond, "Enough already!") instead of unification between a man and the people he holds most dear, his family—mother, father, brother, sister. He also commands his own followers to completely disregard that for which men give their all—their own lives!

How we humans deify our lives! Our bodies must be made "fit," not for what they are expected to do, but for comparison with others. Our homes must have, not simply enough to support the necessities of sustenance, but they must be show-places of more convenience, comfort, and entertainment than anyone could use—really use—in many lifetimes. And our reputations, our positions, our respect are so much evaluated and checked up on that they never really become what they should be—the marks of self-sacrificing, dedicated achievement—and are truly "lost" in all the concentrated self-seeking.

In this selfish "finding" of our own lives, families become embellishments—to be flaunted if complimentary and suitably reflecting our "success"—or to be cast aside if inconvenient, burdensome, or shameful.

Is he not attempting to teach his disciples, before they could go and preach a revolutionary gospel, some vital truths? The temporal is not the real; it is the spirit that is eternal, not the body; the inner is to be the master of the outer, the noble of the ignoble. They must first really submit themselves to these transformations.

If "he that findeth his life shall lose it: and he that loseth his life for [Christ's] sake shall find it," then we are bound to ask, Where *is* my life? The only possible answer must be that word in Col. 3:3: "Ye are dead, and your life is hid with Christ in God." As verse 4 says, "When Christ, our life, shall appear, then shall ye also appear with him in glory." Is this the identity he is declaring when he says (Matt. 10:40), "He that receiveth you, receiveth me, and he that receiveth me, receiveth him that sent me"?

A transformation must take place in the disciple just as complete as that of the recovered addict or alcoholic, who indeed must know the deadliness of his addiction to the extent that he must "die" completely to it in order to be free to live for anything else. A disciple of Christ must come at once to the end of the rope of self-centered, self-aggrandizing, self-apotheosizing life. He must lose it for eternity.

Jesus knew that the instruction of apostles may not omit the hardships before the rewards, the work before the rest, the degradation before the glorification, the loss of family before the gaining of the world.—John R. Rodman

SUNDAY: JULY EIGHTH

SERVICE OF WORSHIP

Sermon: The Gospel Confronts Us with a Challenge to Discipleship

TEXT: Mark 8:27–38

Mark assembled the material in his Gospel forty years after Jesus died, twenty years after Paul's first letter. Mark does not write biography; he writes theology. He believes the long-hoped-for, divinely ordained messianic age breaks into world history—your history and mine—with the birth, ministry, death, and conquering of death by the power of God in Jesus of Nazareth, whom we therefore dare call Christ.

Mark writes, not as a historian, but as a poet; not an archivist, but an image-maker. He does not ask, What do we know about Jesus of Nazareth? He asks, What makes Jesus of Nazareth, crucified, dead, and buried, the living Christ; and what difference does it make for us and our world right now?

I. We look first of all to the passage we read a few moments ago. Remember? Jesus and his friends there at Caesarea Philippi? "Who do people say that I am?" asks Jesus. He receives replies emerging from the promises of the Hebrew Scriptures depicting the breaking in of the messianic age of justice, harmony, peace. "You are Elijah . . . You are one of the prophets."

(a) "OK," replies Jesus, "So who do you say that I am?" Peter rises to the occasion: "You are the Messiah." "Correct," says Jesus. And then he adds an absolutely dumbfounding, incredible, monumentally perverse image to his messiahship: "I must go to Jerusalem, suffer, and die."

(b) Mark believes that human life can be salvaged only by those who risk its glory and its wreckage. He believes that the Savior of our world is not one who muscles it around but one who grieves for it. Healing comes, he writes, not from the conqueror but from the victim, and the only necessary credential for those who would mend a broken humanity lies in identification with the wounded, the crippled, the injured, the outsider. We cannot understand Mark unless we share his conviction that the Christian life is at least participation with those who themselves suffer and are rejected by the world at large.

II. But more. Not only do we share the suffering of this world; Mark tells us that to follow Jesus runs the serious risk—indeed, the inevitability—of running afoul of those in charge of our world. And who appears to be in charge?

(a) How do the Prince of Peace and those who seek to follow him make out in a world where the juggernaut of national security justifies any deception, any alliance, any weapon that not only intimidates and threatens to annihilate our antagonist but, even more subtly, is so extraordinarily good for business? Allegiance to the servant Christ, friends, who identifies with justice, a fair share, a Creation where resources are given to all humankind without privilege or favor and where our diversity as peoples is divinely designed to elicit a grand harmony—such allegiance to Christ in the face of cynicism, self-interest, and imperial appetites will be exercised only at some significant cost.

(b) Do you recall how Peter, that Christian "everyperson," responds to that lethal prophecy of Jesus? He chokes on it. "Hey, Lord, not you!" Peter cries. "The one who comes to save our world doesn't end up getting trashed. We expect success, not failure; a celebrity, not a reject. Enough talk about a Jerusalem slaughter!"

III. Mark has got a handle on us, I think. Throughout his Gospel the disciples distort, misapprehend, resist, mistake, avoid, repudiate the implications of Christ's ministry in our world. You see, just as Mark confronts us with the inevitability of the cross amid faithful discipleship, so he confronts us with our resistance to it.

(a) Sound familiar? Feel familiar? Don't most of us live day by day riddled with Peter-like resistance to the cost of discipleship? In contemporary America we can find it difficult to glimpse the dimensions of Christ's invitation to the risks of love. We find ourselves bombarded from every side not with challenges to courage or with invitations to self-abandonment; we seldom encounter an urgent summons to risk ourselves, our incomes, our ambitions, our prestige, our credentials for some noble and humane cause.

(b) On the contrary, we find ourselves inundated by blandishments to pamper ourselves. As a physician said not long ago, "It's a sin to feel bad anymore." If it feels OK, it is OK. I'll never forget a magazine advertisement showing a model, in resplendent ski togs, sprawled on an oriental rug amid the splendor of her Upper East Side Manhattan apartment, her ultrafashionable gear nearby. "I love me," read the caption. "I'm not conceited. I'm just a good friend to myself. And I like to do whatever makes me feel good." I suppose that's one way to go through life. It surely sustains a consumer economy.

IV. But there's an alternative life-style. You all know the name of Dietrich Bonhoeffer. He left Union Seminary in 1939 to return to Germany because, as he wrote to Reinhold Niebuhr, "I shall have no right to participate in the reconstruction of Christian life in Germany after the war if I do not participate in the trials of this time with my people. . . ." Bonhoeffer ended up on the gallows for joining a church refusing to bend its knee to the Third Reich and finally joining in a conspiracy to assassinate Hitler. He did it for Christ's sake.

V. So, friends, what say you? How do you respond to One who says that to bring about the healing of our broken world we must go to the most wounded of settings, there to risk suffering, rejection, and death? Do you, do I, does this church respond as Peter? "Rejection? Suffering? No way. We want a winner's religion. We covet popularity and success for our faith and our church."

Or, as we encounter that suffering, rejected Christ, and the mandate for our discipleship, can we pray, as we sang not an hour ago, and truly mean it: We bring our hearts before thy cross, To finish thy salvation. God grant it may be so.—James W. Crawford

Illustrations

THREAT TO PEACE.   The threat to American security today is represented not so much by an outside enemy as by the fact that decision making with respect to national security and the programs connected to it is being carried out by people who have no financial stake in peace.—Norman Cousins

GRASPING OUR HOUR. Our capacity to sympathize with others in their sufferings is strictly limited. We are not Christs, but if we want to be Christians we must show something of Christ's breadth of sympathy by acting responsibly, by grasping our "hour," by facing danger like free men, by displaying a real sympathy which springs not from fear but from the liberating and redeeming love of Christ for all who suffer. To look on without lifting a helping hand is most un-Christian. The Christian does not have to wait until he suffers himself; the sufferings of his brethren for whom Christ died are enough to awaken his active sympathy.—Dietrich Bonhoeffer

Sermon Suggestions

FACTORS IN PREPARATION FOR LEADERSHIP. TEXT: Exod. 1:6–14, 22–2:10. (1) Unpromising beginnings. (2) The discipline of hardship. (3) The mysterious providence of God.

OUR PERSONAL INNER BATTLE. TEXT: Rom. 7:14–25a. (1) Situation: As a believer, I want to do right. (2) Complication: As a human being, sin in my nature works against what I want to do. (3) Resolution: I find victory over the guilt and power of sin through our Lord Jesus Christ.

Worship Aids

CALL TO WORSHIP. "How beautiful upon the mountains are the feet of him that bringeth good tidings, that publisheth peace; that bringeth good tidings of good, that publisheth salvation; that saith unto Zion, Thy God reigneth" (Isa. 52:7).

INVOCATION. O Lord, we thank you for bringing us to the sunshine of another day; we thank you for bringing us to each other; we thank you for bringing us to your house. We bring ourselves to you because we need you. Come to us by your Spirit and permeate our presence.—Donald W. Musser

OFFERTORY SENTENCE. "For unto whomsoever much is given, of him shall be much required: and to whom men have committed much, of him they will ask the more" (Luke 12:48).

OFFERTORY PRAYER. O thou, who lovest to the end, we consecrate this offering to the cause of the gospel and ask that it might lift and enlighten and bring to thee all who are blessed by its sharing.—E. Lee Phillips

PRAYER. O God our Father, whose Son forgave his enemies while he was suffering shame and death: Strengthen those who suffer for the sake of conscience; when they are accused, save them from speaking in hate; when they are rejected, save them from bitterness; when they are imprisoned, save them from despair; and to us your servants, give grace to respect their witness and to discern the truth, that our society may be cleansed and strengthened. This we ask for the sake of Jesus Christ, our merciful and righteous Judge.—*The Book of Common Prayer.*

LECTIONARY MESSAGE

Blessed Rest for the Burdened

TEXT: Matt. 11:25–30

The Gospel of Matthew in this passage condenses all the necessary truth of Jesus' ministry in a fashion that includes a statement so much like the words of the Gospel of John that it has been called "the Johannine passage."

I. The futility of sophistry and science in satisfying the needs of the human spirit has a fresh statement in the first verses of this section. Not only do the learned men of his time fail to discern the scriptural truth in what he says, but they also are unable to offer anything approaching satisfaction for men's spiritual needs.

(a) Mythology is the human search for an intellectually satisfying theory of worldly phenomena, replacing the sense of sheer mystery and awe with convictions formed after conscious consideration. Enough has been revealed to the conscious mind of mankind in the natural phenomena represented in the myth to form a background for true religious development, resulting in the genuine thought structures of knowledge and philosophy. But there is something missing—the gods of the great mythologies, Greek and Roman, have no concept of universal obligation devolving upon either themselves or human beings, although they do evolve a somewhat whimsical system of ethics.

(b) The universality of sacrifice among primitive religions attests to a universal sense of obligations unfulfilled and of prohibitive mores violated. The Law is established because of a need to express and accommodate this universal debt.

(c) Science—rational analysis of phenomena, forms, and substances and their actions and effects—is still not in possession of "all things," as they are revealed to Jesus directly and to believers by him. The nature of science is not such that it can reach to the spirit or reveal a person's hopeless helplessness before God; much less can it supply deliverance.

II. The completeness of Jesus' unique revelation is apparent from his next words.

(a) Jesus is the only one who knows God. What entire generations of the wise and learned have failed to find, Jesus has been given from eternity. Jesus utters a unique claim to a power and a wisdom that supersedes all the books of the Law. He is the translator of the language of God for human understanding. Revelation—direct information from and about God—comes only to those wise enough to be simple and direct and to trust in him. He has knowledge to explain the mysteries that plague natural man, such that even those whose minds are filled with natural, rational, and empirical learning must come to depend upon him for their ultimate answers.

The wisdom of the simple lies in being aware that they cannot know God or his kingdom unless he reveals it to them.

The great Greek philosopher Socrates was said by the Oracle at Delphi to be the wisest man on earth. When asked why, Socrates gave the explanation that he was the only one, differing from all the teachers and orators and governors he had talked with, who knew that he knew nothing. "Let him that thinketh he standeth take heed lest he fall" (1 Cor. 10:12, kjv). Any reference to the word *fall* in a concordance will reveal the many kinds of people who will not stand, even in the things of earth, much less before God.

III. Christ's invitation is to take a yoke that is restful.

(a) It is an open invitation for all who are loaded down with both personal and religious duties that seem to get them nothing. Jesus is aware of all that the scribes and Pharisees have laid on the Jews, the onerous requirements of gifts, temple taxes, and special occasions. Their yoke is hard and their burdens heavy and fruitless.

(b) It is an invitation not merely to exchange yokes, but it offers an easy yoke, easily borne, whose duties are within the believers themselves.

(c) It is itself a rest from spiritual deprivation and it consists of new loyalty to One for whom work is not tiring. It brings only the labors of love. Unlike that of the law, it places emphasis on the justice, mercy, and love of God. Its labors are "such burdens as wings are to a bird or sails to a ship." All our needs are met in him. His yoke binds us to peace and power as well as pardon.—John R. Rodman

SUNDAY: JULY FIFTEENTH

SERVICE OF WORSHIP

Sermon: The Power that Enables Us to Cope

Text: Psalm 139

Someone has called the 139th Psalm a paean of praise to the "Divine Psychiatrist"; a little dramatic and anthropomorphic perhaps but interesting in light of our recurring need for soul therapy. This is not only a psalm about God's transcendence, that he is "Wholly Other," as Karl Barth would say. It is also a song about the gracious closeness of God to us as frail and puzzled humans.

I. "How precious to me are thy thoughts, O God. How vast is the sum of them. . . . If I could count them they are more than the sand."

(a) More than the sand? God's thoughts directed toward us? The theology of the seashore! Take a handful of sand and let it trickle through your fingers. Can you count the grains? And the astrophysicists tell us that planet earth where we sojourn is but a grain of sand on the infinite "beaches" of the cosmos. We don't talk about single galaxies anymore but of clusters and superclusters with their celestial seashores.

(b) When you can't count the grains anymore, when you are through trying to comprehend the cosmic dust of the universe, remember the psalmist says, in effect, that the boggling of your minds is the encounter of God's grace reminding us that you and I count and that his "precious thoughts," which we can't number, are directed our way to enable us to cope.

II. I have often discovered that the reason we can't cope with the raw material of today's experience is due to the subtle subliminal ties we have to the past—your past and mine. The past has a way of intruding into this moment. We are reminded of our inadequacies, our failures and of the disastrous debacles that have occurred. We feel guilty and threatened. The psalmist knows it! Listen: "Thou does beset me behind and before. . . ."

(a) G. K. Chesterton was once asked why he became Roman Catholic. His terse answer was, "In order to get rid of my sins." And, said John S. Whale, "if you dismiss that as morbid eccentricity, you don't know your own heart."

(b) We cannot cope until we can accept ourselves, and we cannot accept ourselves until we sense that we are forgiven . . . radically forgiven. Men and women, God has covered the past with his limitless grace. He has already wiped out our transgressions as he dawns with the sun of a new day. No, the past is not forgiven because we repent. We repent because the past is forgiven.

III. Again, I have discovered that the reason we cannot cope with much of the pressure of today is because of our dread of tomorrow. Not only has the past a way of curling into our present moment, but our thoughts run on, and we are overwhelmed by the possibilities of the future.

(a) It is little good at such times to be given bits of chirpy advice . . . such as, "Cheer up, today is the first day of the rest of your life." It doesn't work. Perhaps in our darkest moments that's the very thing that intimidates us. In any case, we know ourselves better than others know us. They see the persona, which is a combination of what they want to see and what we want to project if we can. They don't try to come to terms with the person, and we often are daunted in our effort to do it. "Who am I?" asks the young person, and if we off-handedly dismiss this question as a piece of narcissistic preoccupation, we will be guilty of misreading not only a cry for help but of misinterpreting our own longing as we try to come to terms with the future. The psalmist would never have analyzed it at all in that way. His idiom of thinking was religious, not psychological, but what he had to say combined them both. Listen again! "Thou has beset me behind and before. . . ." Before it all takes place. Before the tomorrows crowd into the present.

(b) The whole of the poem is a protest against this mechanistic interpretation of life . . . this boxed-in picture. God is before you, the author proclaims. The very One who was there when you were intricately and wonderfully made in your mother's womb. The one who is in heaven and (believe it or not) in hell, shattering its very power to hold you captive.

That's what God gives us as we realize that he has "beset us before." We are not going to be there on our own. We are not locked into inevitability. New possibilities exist when he is there because preeminently he is the God of the now.

IV. So, lastly, I am slowly coming to understand what the psalmist means when he says, "Thou has beset me behind and before, and layest thy hand upon me." Present tense. This special moment. This above all.

(a) God wants us to come just as we are because he "lays his hand upon us," even when we are put out and rebellious. That's what grace is . . . the power that enables us to cope because we can be confident in him even when we have little confidence in much else.

(b) Not that he gives us answers to the deepest questions concerning our existence. He never does. The Bible isn't a book of answers, it is not a compendium of proof texts we can offer (or sometimes, as we do, hurl) at one another.

(c) Anyone acquainted with Frederick Beuchner's life story knows how from the age of eight he was forced to stare into the nightmare of much of existence. He and his brother, early one morning, heard the self-inflicted gunshot that took his beloved father's life. Things would never be quite the same for him, though he ended up being a novelist, poet, and theologian. Always the "unanswerables" will be there. How does he face them? Listen to his words! "God doesn't give us answers. . . . He gives us himself."

(d) That's what the psalmist discovered. That's what Jesus discovered. This is what God's grace means . . . the power that enables us to cope, as quietly and tenderly he takes your hand and mine and bids us go the next step with him.—Elam Davies

Illustrations

CONSIDERING THE HEAVENS. It is said that when President Theodore Roosevelt entertained naturalist William Beebe at Sagamore Hill, they would play a game on a bright starry night. Going out into the pitch darkness they would look up with naked eye to the skies and begin to name the planets and the constellations: Pleiades, Orion, Pegasus, etc. After a while there would be silence and Roosevelt would say, "Now, I think we're small enough. Let's go to bed!"—Elam Davies

WHY ME? The story of Dawn, "a testimony" as she likes to call it: She is a doctor's assistant in a very busy office in Chicago. One day, shown into the room where I expected the doctor to appear in minutes (only to discover that this was the first step in long travail!), Dawn put her head around the door. "You're from the Fourth Church?" "Yes," I confessed, wondering what was to come next. "My husband and I have gone to hear you . . . sometimes." The last word with a hint of homiletical examination! "I'm a member of the Assemblies of God church. I want to tell you about my experience."

In short sentences the story came out. "God saved me. . . . I gave my life to him . . . and guess what? . . . It tumbled in! I developed a heart problem. My husband lost his executive job . . . and recently he died of cancer. 'WHY ME, Lord?' I cried again and again. What do you think he said?" I mumbled something about God's mysterious ways. "So what?" she cut in, "What's new?" At that moment all my theological training was reduced to impotence by two-word logic! "What do you think he said? . . . Why not?" Expecting this divine provocation to be followed by an outburst of blatant religious skepticism, I was overwhelmed when after a moment's silence she continued. "But I found his grace is sufficient, for today and every day. One day I said to him, 'Lord, you've forgiven me. Now I forgive you!' "—Elam Davies

Sermon Suggestions

SURVIVING UNPOPULARITY. TEXT: Ps. 69:6–15. (1) Unpopularity may be for God's sake. (2) Surviving unpopularity is possible through self-denying love for God's sometimes undeserving people and through trust in God's help and justice.

WHEN GOD'S SPIRIT DWELLS IN YOU. TEXT: Rom. 8:9–17. (1) You will recognize God as your own Father. (2) You will be a fellow heir of God with Christ.

Worship Aids

CALL TO WORSHIP. "It is a good thing to give thanks unto the Lord, and to sing praises unto thy name, O most High: To shew forth thy lovingkindness in the morning, and thy faithfulness every night" (Ps. 92:1–2).

INVOCATION. This morning we have much to thank you for, O Lord. We have life, and we have survived all hindrances to be able to be present among the company of your worshiping people. We know that we have survived, and we pray that you will now help us to believe that we are more than conquerors through him who loved us and gave himself for us.

OFFERTORY SENTENCE. "Verily, verily, I say unto you, He that believeth on me, the works that I do shall he do also; and greater works than these shall he do; because I go unto my Father. And whatsoever ye shall ask in my name, that will I do, that the Father may be glorified in the Son" (John 14:12–13).

OFFERTORY PRAYER. Holy God, let us divest ourselves of all that stands between us and thee, and in the process teach us such generosity in giving as to enlarge our vision and bring many to the foot of the cross, whence cometh our help and hope.—E. Lee Phillips

PRAYER. Almighty God, who has kept us safe through the night in the folds of your everlasting arms; inviting Father, who bids us seek your presence and rejoice in holy communion with you; abiding Spirit, who joins our lives and hearts together in glad adoration and songs of praise; may we rightly worship you and worthily magnify your name.

O Lord, our Lord, how excellent is your name in all the world. Redeeming Master, Lord of cleansing forgiveness, we confess our sins.

We are rich in things and poor in soul; we overlook the gifts we have and envy the gifts of others. We walk about with stones in our hands ready to hurt and unprepared to forgive. We are loud and abrasive in our impatience, ignoring how to wait upon you quietly. Thinking first of ourselves, we overlook the needs of others. Lord, who knows us best, there are other sins in our lives, too. Wash us fresh and clean and restore purity to our hearts and spirits.

With new vision and freedom that comes with your forgiveness, O God, we turn our thoughts to the cries of others. We pray for those who have no respite from the oppressive heat, who are captured in hopelessness, who are defeated and beaten by the fate of the weather, who have forgotten how it feels to be a person; for those who, in their own way, are longing and thirsting for thee.

Strong Father of us all, you of tender mercy and generous grace, sustain your weary and wandering children.

Our God, we pray for ourselves. Help us be a church that truly loves you first and most of all. Help us be a people that shares the good news with gladness, integrity, and goodwill. As the Body of Christ, lift us to dream new dreams and approach fresh avenues in being church in a troubled and fearful world. Empower us to love one another in unconditional love and witness to your indwelling presence and Spirit. Help us to live openly and expectantly in the abiding hope of the Resurrection and the life of our Lord, Jesus Christ . . . in whom we pray.—William M. Johnson

LECTIONARY MESSAGE

The Seed and the Soils

TEXT: Matt. 13:1–9, 18–23 (A companion Old Testament reading might be Isa. 55:1–13.)

The application of this parable is to those who hear the Word of God and may become immediately interested in it. What responses beyond this does the parable describe for us? It predicts four possibilities: some will soon have succumbed to the wisdom of the world; some will have passed beyond this interest for some other; for some the skepticism around them will have overtaken their interest with doubt; for still others, a depth of spiritual wisdom will fill their lives.

I. We first must recognize the goodness, the purity, the potency of the "seed," the Word of God.

(a) Certainly one might expect no good results from the spreading abroad of a mixed, contaminated, dried, or dead seed. But we know God will not give us a harmful or impotent Word. We are positively informed that "God will have all men to be saved and come to a knowledge of the truth." The Word itself—the same Word we now hear—has too often brought the desired fruit for us to look for fault in it.

(b) Then what of the power of life in that Word? The life is put into it by God. It is *for* all people. We cannot look to God for the fault if some who receive his Word react negatively or grow poorly from it. Many might say, God could cause all who hear his Word to respond positively and fruitfully to it, growing lives of strength and blessing. God could not and would not do that. Even though he has all power, there are some things he cannot do. He cannot make a lie true; he cannot make a fire cold; he cannot make evil good. His creatures try to do these things by perversion and willfulness. God cannot fulfill a conclusion based on contradictory premises, and it would be a contradiction for him to create man free to make choices (possessing freedom we all cherish), free to be individually different from every other human being, and then command us to behave in all the same ways. We are free. The response to the Word, then, is the response of the soil into which it is cast and is not due to the "seed" itself nor to the "Sower."

II. This has often been called "the parable of the soils," for it clearly describes the conditions that lead to the forthcoming effects.

(a) "Wayside soils" represent hearers of shallow preparation, lacking understanding of religious principles. They may not object to Christianity—they just take it as one of life's peculiar interests, appealing to some but not to them. They may take part in its observances to please a friend or a loved one but have no part in its spiritual riches; they are still, deep down, "without hope and without God in the world." The lightly received Word is soon forgotten in the press of other fleeting interests, of which the world is so full.

(b) "Stony ground" represents hearers who have a quick and enthusiastic response to the Word because of a facile personality but who lack the depth of character to respond maturely and with lasting conviction. They simply sway whichever direction the wind blows. They react enthusiastically but only briefly. They cannot be counted on when the hardships come because their inner beings—their hearts—are too hard for any tender roots of reformation to penetrate. They do not change in any responsible way to the implications of the Word. Therefore, when examination by hardships comes to test them, they have no resources and no lasting strength. They question and even blame God. Can it be that their efforts at self-recognition are too close to the surface to make way for the strong growth resulting from self-examination? The Word *does*, by its very nature, sooner or later force a self-examination. These shallow-soiled personalities cannot go through with it.

(c) "Thorny ground" represents hearers in whose lives other, preexisting interests already have a good start. The seed springs up, but it is choked by the competition for nutrients. The Word competes in the otherwise good soil of this person's heart for time and attention, for consciousness and consideration. The hearer is too busy; he has too many people dependent on him; he is too important to an organization; he has too many responsibilities of social or business connections to give the necessary portion of himself to God's Word. If such a one only knew the fruitfulness of the Word of God, how it would add enrichment to every other legitimate interest, how it would add its own strength and ability to every other honorable commitment, his life would be first examined, then purified, then comforted, and finally made victorious. But no—he has to care for his investments, his business customers, his club, or even his family concerns before he can spare his vitality to nourish the Word to its own fruitfulness.

III. There is a fourth kind of soil, a fourth variety of response to the Word of God, which gladdens the heart of the "sower" and promises all of us the possibility of eternal life. There is good soil, and it nurtures seed in every way. There is a profitable kind of hearer, and he responds to the Word in the ways Jesus describes. He *hears* the Word; he *understands* it; and he bears fruit and brings it forth.

This good kind of "hearing" is different

from the less profitable kind. It *takes in* the truth it receives. There is in this hearer's mind a background knowledge of human nature and a perception of reality not shared by the others. There are standards of truthfulness waiting to be fulfilled by the truth. This hearer disciplines himself to examine, analyze, and devote a portion of time and effort to knowing what he is hearing. The profitable hearer not only truly receives and accepts the Word, but he also *understands* it. How many are not willing to undergo the arduous mental exercise necessary to arrive at the meaning of God's Word? We say it must be simple, that no one needs to be a mental giant to apprehend the significance of God's Word for his life. True enough. That emphasizes the essential nature of the "understanding" with which the profitable hearer re- ceives the Word. This "understanding is essentially a matter of the *will* rather than of the mind. The hearer must not substitute any degree of sincerity alone for the needed set of will that pushes him to *accept* the truth he understands. As with the farmer who told the county extension agent, "I already know *how* to farm twice as well as I am farming," so it is true of most sincere hearers of God's Word that they readily understand more than they have yet applied of its truth.

Then the Word bears its fruit in the life and work of the profitable hearer. He receives the God of the Word, he applies God's truth to his life, and he has then to add light of hope, water of tears, perhaps, and patience of faith, till time is right, to see his glorious reward—a hundredfold or sixtyfold or thirtyfold.—John R. Rodman

SUNDAY: JULY TWENTY-SECOND

SERVICE OF WORSHIP

Sermon: Put Your Shoes Back On!
Texts: Exod. 3:1–8, 10–12; Rom. 8: 18–24

There are times and places in life to which we turn aside. Times that allow us to clear our minds. Places that offer us rest. We wonder in those places why the world cannot be more of a place of rest; why the rush of our days cannot yield more time for careful thought. We wish for a world where we can run safely, barefoot. But reality demands shoes for protection, a job for security, and for survival. We are grateful for the respite of barefooted days, yet the time always comes to put our shoes back on.

I. Scripture describes Moses as a Hebrew boy and young man growing up in Pharaoh's court, then exiled as a fugitive after killing an Egyptian. We find him in our lesson this morning a political outcast, tending sheep far from home. The vicissitudes of time and chance have brought the urbane Israelite to the wilderness, a desolate wasteland. The story goes that he spies a burning bush some distance off. He doesn't run to smother the flames or herd the sheep to safer ground, but he turns aside to get a closer look. Here is something new, something totally other than his experience. He moves in awe of this bush that burns yet is not consumed. He hears his name called twice. This is definitely out of the ordinary. He doesn't run. He is curious. He wants to know what is happening to him. "Here I am!" he cries.

(a) It is God who answers: "Do not come near; put off your shoes from your feet, for this is holy ground." I guess this is what many pop spiritualists would call a "mountaintop" experience. With life uprooted and family left behind, Moses meets God alone. Traveling in the wilderness with a flock of sheep, Moses reaches holy ground.

(b) In this story Moses doesn't anticipate his encounter with God. He is not a religious pilgrim seeking enlightenment. One would think, if Moses knew the sacredness of the place, he would have shown more reverence from the outset. No, the place is not the important aspect of the story. Moses grazes his sheep there. When he spies the burning bush he approaches it, brimming with unabashed curiosity. Only when God chooses to speak does Moses know he stands on holy ground. God's presence makes this place holy. Without God it holds no power. Moses builds no shrine, commemorating this place forever. He hasn't got time. After much resistance, Moses is turned around and on his way to do what God calls him to do: to confront Pharaoh and rescue the people of Israel.

(c) God establishes with Moses that any ground can be holy ground if God so chooses. God establishes that any time can be holy time when God enters history. History suddenly has become the realm where God works; this earth, this planet, is declared the place where God acts. Where we stand in our place and time we also, like Moses, stand before God on holy ground.

II. Well, so what? What real difference can that make in our lives? It's the same difference between Moses who approaches the burning bush in curiosity and Moses who leaves in awe and wonder, with a purpose to his life.

(a) The difference in our lives is our discovery that God can transform any experience into holy experience. We can be aware of God's presence anywhere. God is not limited to our shrines, our beautiful sanctuaries. God is an active God, alive and at work in the world. And God is concerned about the enslaved and oppressed of our world. Wherever we find ourselves, on mountaintops or in combat zones, God can find us. When we are found by God, no matter what time or what place, we stand on holy ground.

(b) But from all these places, like Moses, we have to put our shoes back on and walk back down the mountain. God calls us to a sacred time and place for a reason. There is much work to be done. In this holy place we experience something of God's love and acceptance; yet we also experience something of God's terrible wrath and sorrow that people are suffering out there.

III. In Romans, Paul writes that all Creation eagerly longs to be proclaimed holy, yet groans still in the pain and travail of this real life. Our stand on holy ground is but a taste, the firstfruits of the Spirit, of what God has in store for all people. It is God's promise. It is our hope. In this hope

we are saved, and it is this hope that gives us the courage to put our shoes back on and face our groaning world.

(a) This means walking the earth with the eyes of faith, seeing people as being made holy, in the image of God. It means rejecting those institutions that demean and destroy others. It means condemning torture as a valid tool of interrogation here or anywhere else in the world. It means refusing to live a life-style that consumes without thought, while a majority of the world goes without food or fuel. This revelation calls us to a radical participation in this body, this family, this people, this community, this church, this tradition, this history, this planet, even this cosmos.

(b) The interconnection of all Creation is central to Paul's conviction that through our human response to God's contact, we rescue not ourselves but the cosmos itself. We wait with all Creation for the time when holiness will be apparent throughout all time and in all places. We return from our mountaintop, with our shoes back on, ready to tackle the tasks of righteousness that are the business of the children of God.

(c) We stand, as no other people have stood throughout history, facing the task of building a world community. This building must be done on the basis that all the planet is holy ground. This is our greatest task; this is our greatest hope. From our viewpoint such a task seems a human impossibility. From the side of Mount Horeb, in the shadow of a burning bush, such a task is God's possibility. For it is God who transforms us into beings who can recognize God's presence. It is God who tells us to remove our sandals, who transforms our hearts and minds; and it is God who sends us out with shoes securely tied to proclaim the holy in all times, in all places, and in all life.—Marcus S. Walker

Illustrations

THE BURNING BUSH.   The burning bush is our confrontation in middle life by some fact or condition or situation which does not fit our view of life. In the moment of that confrontation, one of the gravest temptations of middle life is upon us: whether to protect such peace of mind as our view of life yields us and hurry past the unanticipated burning bush or else to cling to an inadequate view of life, trying to curtain off from sight and mind whatever will not fit it, counting the safety of even a poor harbor better than the perils of the open sea.

What is the burning bush? It may be any one of many things that will not fit the view of life which one has worked out by middle age. It is, for example, monotony when one had reckoned on a life filled with interesting experience. Or it is catastrophe, sharp, crushing, terrifying, which befalls the beloved or oneself or falls across the wider landscape. Or it is adversity when one had counted on comfort. Or it is discovering to one's dismay that the self does not fit the role into which it has been drawn. Or it is discovering that God as he is does not fit the neat theology we had constructed.

In any and all such times the basic question which confronts us in the burning bush is this: Is one ready as yet to know God as he is?—Lewis J. Sherrill

GOD'S TOTAL SUPPORT. This need for total protection is none other than the need for God. The psalmist, who has found it, exclaims, "Thou dost beset me behind and before, and layest thy hand upon me" (Ps. 139:5). The words admirably express the experience of the believer, his sense of being enfolded in God's protective care. Faith is a double support—in front and behind. In front are God's promises on which faith is founded. But the believer is not limited, like the revolutionary, to counting on the future. He also gets support from behind, from a solid historical reality, from what God has done in the past, in which we see the manifestation of his love and the pledge of what he will do in the future.—Paul Tournier

Sermon Suggestions

THE CALL OF GOD. TEXT: Exod. 3:1–12. (1) It comes to the undeserving. (2) It may come in a strange way. (3) It comes in the context of genuine need. (4) The implica-

tions and responsibilities may seem overwhelming. (5) The God who calls promises his presence.

WHY SUFFERING CAN BE DISCOUNTED. TEXT: Rom. 8:18–25. (1) Because an incomparable destiny awaits us. (2) Because God is at work even now to bring all things into harmony with his glorious purpose.

Worship Aids

CALL TO WORSHIP. "Both young men, and maidens; old men, and children: Let them praise the name of the Lord: for his name alone is excellent; his glory is above the earth and heaven" (Ps. 148:12–13).

INVOCATION. O Lord, there are no limits to your worthiness. You are for us—for us all, young and old. Let the mouths of babies praise you; let the dying gasps of those worn with the years praise you. Beyond all that we can ask or think, see or feel, is the glory of the mystery that is you, yet revealed to us in your Son, our Lord Jesus Christ. So put your praise in our hearts and mouths and lives.

OFFERTORY SENTENCE. "And if thou draw out thy soul to the hungry, and satisfy the afflicted soul; then shall thy light rise in obscurity, and thy darkness be as the noon day" (Isa. 58:10).

OFFERTORY PRAYER. Lord, as we open our pocketbooks, open our hearts and instruct us in the ways of stewardship that include time and service in the name of Jesus.—E. Lee Phillips

PRAYER. God, you are busy, very busy. You have to be far busier than we can imagine, even when our imaginations run wild. It seems embarrassing to ask you to take time out for us. We talk, sometimes scream, about our crowded schedules; we want other people to be aware that, as busy as they are, until they've seen *our* schedule, they haven't seen anything!

Still, we do become almost silent when we ponder the humanly impossible perplexities of being the Manager of this vast, mysterious, seemingly limitless universe.

And it's all yours!—every particle, every atom—split and unsplit—every speck of it. And that includes us! So we pray that you will not pass us by, as you proceed to take care of all the things and events and people crying for your divine ministry. We don't want you to ignore anyone, to put anyone on hold, but we don't want you to ignore us either, to pay attention to us at a time that is more convenient for you. We don't want our words and thoughts to be placed on some heavenly recording system that you will play back when you are through working, ready to rest. This is our time of church worship: this is the time when we as a congregation pour out our praises, confess our sins, plead for mercy, ask for help, seek you guidance. We don't want to be talking to empty air; we're not engaged in a game of play-acting: we want to sense and be supported by your Presence, your Power, your Spirit. We can only be one place at a time and, for the most part, do one thing at a time, think one thought at a time, make one commitment at a time. We are counting on your being the one God who is not so limited, not so confined.

Yet, to be regarded by you at all, to think that you have a deep, personal interest in us, at this time, or any other time, is to know something of your matchless goodness and also to discover that we must be very special to you—not one bit better than anyone else, but very special. And that makes us feel very good, very good indeed. It makes us feel so good, we don't even want to do all the talking in this privileged—sacred—relationship we have with you. We want you to do some talking—maybe even a lot of talking—revealing to us why we are so special in your sight and what you want us to be like, what you want us to do, because we are numbered among your special people.

Do you want us to do a better job than we're doing of seeing this world through your eyes? Do you want us to reflect your Spirit more, and the world's spirit less, as we live from day to day, decision to decision, relationship to relationship? Do you want us to grow in maturity, not so much

by being tough and rigid and unteachable as by being sensitive and caring and compassionate to those round about us and beyond us who have needs we can help satisfy, hurts we can help heal, questions we can help answer, problems we can help solve, burdens we can help carry? Do you want us to be the salt of the earth as much as you ever have, so that we will be good for this world, a seasoning for Christ, that people will not throw out and tread upon but that will help others to go beyond existing to living lives abundant, rich, and full? Do you want us as your special people to do special things, even if those special things seem so small in a universe so vast? Things like being kind to those not necessarily kind to us; being friendly to those who think they have no friends; giving food to those who have no idea where their next meal is coming from; dropping the complaining spirit and picking up the attitude of gratitude; being trustworthy to those convinced nobody can be trusted? Do you want us to do little things like that now, so we can be ready for life's bigger things tomorrow? Do you want us to be so filled with your Spirit we have both the desire and the resolve to go about on this earth, as our Master did, doing good, being good, feeling good?

Well, you tell us, Lord. We surely cannot discover your will for our lives all by ourselves. That's why we're here today; that's why we're concerned that you honor us with your presence, that you participate actively in our worship. We want light in the midst of our darkness, courage to get up one more time and keep going, cleansing so that we hate neither ourselves nor other people, direction so that we travel and keep traveling on the road that leads to our true home, patience and compassion so that we don't just put up with each other but enrich each other. These, we know, are some wants that you alone make possible. We do want for ourselves all those qualities you desire us to have.

So, honor us with your presence, bless us with your love, strengthen us with your Spirit. And busy as you are, you will know we are also busy giving you the praise, being your disciples, carrying our cross, sharing in love the good news of Jesus Christ.—Gordon H. Reif

LECTIONARY MESSAGE

The Troublesome Parable

Text: Matt. 13:24–30, 36–43

From the very first, the parables of Jesus have been considered to be allegories, and various interpreters have given various assignments to the identities of all the elements of the parables, depending upon the point in history in which they were working. Certainly, Jesus meant to use the features of life he mentioned in the parables as representations of our spiritual condition(s), but we must exercise caution in attributing some exact representation to each feature of every parable. We may apply them as far as applicable, perhaps, but the central message of each of the parables is the one that must stand out.

I. *The mystery of the presence of good and evil in God's world.* The husbandman had a good field. He planted good seed in it. While he was asleep, his enemy sowed evil imitation seed in the same field, oversowing the good seed originally planted. How did it happen? Who is to blame? What can be done about it?

When the early plants arose from the ground, helpers could see that some different plants were mixed in with the good and could not understand why good seed planted in good soil by a good husbandman should produce alien weeds side by side with the good grain. The problem has been with mankind from the very beginning, and we all are forced to deal with it. We may choose one of several explanations, some of which are unpleasant and misleading.

(a) Atheism is the resultant answer given by one attempt to solve the problem. The argument goes that a good and benevolent God must want to eliminate evil; an omnipotent God could eliminate evil; but, since evil does exist, God either is too weak or he is unwilling to do away with it. Hence, the God we all believe in must not exist.

(b) Some would have us believe that evil does not exist, that it is a figment of

human imagination and can be eliminated by right thinking.

(c) Another theory holds that evil is a necessary element of life, that God created evil as well as good, and that both are constituent elements of the universe. To this way of thinking, evil is just "the other side of the coin," since anything with a top must have a bottom and anything good must have a bad side.

II. *A better understanding of the truth.* We cannot present all the arguments of theodicy, but we can see some of them briefly.

(a) First, to create human beings, God could do nothing but create us free to be godly or to be ungodly. To be human, a person must be a free moral agent, responsible for one's own decisions. Inherent in our freedom is the freedom to decide wrongly as well as rightly. God could not choose for us in advance. If we say he should have, we say he should not have created human beings. To say that God *could* have made us morally free and still have made us so we would *always,* rather than just sometimes, fulfill the possibility of choosing rightly is simply to change terms and beg the question.

Mankind would, in that case, become completely what the books and motion pictures have horribly depicted as *The Stepford Wives* and *The Stepford Children.* No act, the outcome of which can possibly be predicted or determined, however "good," could possibly be a free act. The consequent pain of people ensuing on their own mental or willful perverseness, or the pain others feel because of it, must be attributed to the moral nature of free human beings whose real choices result in real consequences.

(b) But moral evil is only half the story. There are difficulties, pain, sorrow, and death not traceable to human choices, coming in the form of floods, earthquakes, blight, drought, and fires from lightning. It is true that in many instances the border between evil resulting from human choice and evil completely independent of man's moral failure is difficult to establish. David Hume uses this nonmoral evil to assail God. He argues that a truly benevolent, omnipotent God would not have created a world in which his creatures would constantly be subject to natural catastrophe. He could have created a world in which every person would be protected by instant changes in all the laws of nature he has discovered, which now cause hurt.

If he had made such a world, it would have been unnecessary for people to be wise or good, loving or protecting toward others, or to adopt moral or spiritual natures. In other words, again, if God had created such a world, he need not have made us people who have souls to win. A nonthreatening world would have been followed necessarily by an un-won heaven for nonsinners for whom Christ need not have died.

III. *A strategy for the growing period.* In the meantime, we must grasp the central idea of this parable. No matter how we see the wheat and tares, they must be allowed to grow together until the harvest. They may represent the good and evil in every human being; they may be the evil and good people in the world; they may be the church and its problems or the law-abiding citizens and the criminals.

(a) As one grows, so does the other. We have long ago disapproved the fallacy that the world is getting progressively better. Discord, greed, injustice, and indifference are still very much with us. The darnel (*Lolium temulentem*) looks very much like wheat. The possibility of weeding out the tares from the good field without damaging the wheat is exceedingly remote. The pulling up suggested by the workers is not a practicable solution.

(b) The strategy for the time being is to allow both to grow together until the harvest. The Judgment *is* coming. We must prepare for it. Hence, the urgency of our mission and evangelism becomes more pronounced. Tares do not change into wheat, but no one can safely say which is which in the growing period. The work of God can be done in lives that are human, and we must be dedicated to doing it.—John R. Rodman

SUNDAY: JULY TWENTY-NINTH

SERVICE OF WORSHIP

Sermon: Let Pharaoh Go

TEXTS: Exod. 1:8–22; Heb. 11:32–34, 12:1–2

Shiphrah and Puah were ordinary women who did extraordinary things. They had no power. They were considered weak. But they showed enormous courage—playing a large role in the redemptive history of Israel. Let me remind you of their story.

I. Once upon a time there was a Pharaoh in Egypt who started having trouble sleeping at night, worrying that he didn't have enough to worry about. He started playing the "What If" game:

"What if these Hebrews were to start birthing babies like rabbits?"

"What if these Hebrews were to join our enemies and start a war against us?"

"What if these Hebrews escaped from our country and our control over them?"

(a) Boy Scout Pharaoh wanted to be prepared. Nothing wrong with that. Interests had to be protected, you know. National security depended on it. He showed skill as a politician by naming the possible risks and dangers to his people and enlisting their help in the plan of action. "Let us . . ," said Pharaoh. "Let us together build a safe future for our children." The Egyptians couldn't say no to such a worthy call to action.

(b) Plan number one was instituted with slave labor inflicted on the Hebrews. Pretty soon whips were cracked and commands were barked to keep Hebrews bending over bricks for buildings and bending over fields for planting. Bent backs were intended to decrease the expanding numbers of Hebrews. But bent backs only served to increase the bitterness.

II. With plan number one failing, Pharaoh decided to try plan number two. He called in the Hebrew midwives for this one: Shiphrah and Puah.

(a) Now Pharaoh explained to the two midwives that for the good of the nation and for the security of the children of Egypt, he wanted them to be part of a secret and daring mission to kill all the boy Hebrew babies. And the midwives were asked to do this at the moment the boy babies were born.

Pharaoh had no idea what he was asking. How does a midwife to childbearing women, whose very vocation is grounded on the hope of assisting in bringing life, drop the vocation with a stab wound of death in the birthing room?

Pharaoh had no idea what he was asking. All he could see was his precious and imagined threat to Egyptian national security. All he could see were two ordinary women, who had no power, whom he considered weak, and who would certainly obey him.

(b) But Shiphrah and Puah knew who they were. They knew their vocation meant assisting in life, not death. They knew they had no power before Pharaoh. So they let Pharaoh go—to think his own thoughts, to go his own way—while they followed their way assisting in life.

It didn't take long for Pharaoh to get news of their defiance. Hebrew mommas were strolling boy babies up and down the streets showing them off, proud to have a son. The midwives were called in for the scolding. "Can't practice civil disobedience in this country," said Pharaoh.

The midwives looked Pharaoh straight in the eye and told him a cockamamy story about the Hebrew women delivering their babies so much more vigorously than Egyptian women that the babies were already being burped from their first feeding by the time the midwives arrived. Shiphrah and Puah surely must have thought that such a noble lie could easily pass by Pharaoh. After all, what did he know about birthing babies?

(c) We all learn the patterns of the weak defying the strong at an early age: children refusing to eat split-pea soup for dinner; teenagers cutting their hair in special geometric designs. And we keep up our training in defiance as adults by taking ten items into the eight-item checkout line at the grocery.

But the stakes are higher now than haircuts and grocery baskets. Shiphrah and Puah remind us that the powers of Pharaoh to institute suffering and injustice in our land are strong.

III. Who are our Pharaohs? They are slave masters who want to convince us that there are no hungry in this land, only the lazy and irresponsible. Have you ever tried to hand that word of comfort from Pharaoh to the mother working two jobs at minimum wage to support her three children?

(a) Who are our Pharaohs? They are national Pharaohs who want to convince us that being held hostage in the greatest terrorist act in human history, with the whole human family targeted for destruction, is for our security. Have you ever tried to explain the billions for bombs to our children?

(b) Who are our Pharaohs? They are church growth specialists who want to persuade us that our churches need a pastor who is a benevolent dictator. How do we explain this, with all of us equal before God in our call to be disciples?

(c) Who are our Pharaohs? Any institution or any person who rules or controls our lives. Anyone or anything that stands in our way of claiming our high calling from God.

Our Pharaohs expect us to slave away in brickyards without asking value questions or caring questions or authority questions. Slave masters don't expect, want, or permit their slaves to grow or change. Pharaohs want to keep things in their control.

IV. How do we let these Pharaohs go so that we can follow our God of life? We are surrounded by a cloud of witnesses, like Hebrews 11 talks about, like Shiphrah and Puah, who down through the ages have boldly and defiantly resisted the injustice of the powerful.

(a) Our defiant cloud of witnesses includes people like Harriet Tubman who let Pharaoh go to lead black slaves to freedom on the underground railway. People like Rosa Parks who let Pharaoh go to refuse to move to the back of the bus.

The Anabaptists wrote the handbook on defiance. They let Pharaoh go to defy the injustice of the state in the face of enormous resistance and persecution.

(b) There are churches around our country today who let Pharaoh go to care for the forgotten and broken in our land regardless of the current government policies, giving up the seduction of giant church buildings and big business, success-model number gains.

V. Surrounded by a cloud of witnesses like Shiphrah and Puah and Harriet and Rosa, we are invited, expected, and urged to move away from Pharaoh and his oppressive ways—to enter another door with the sign "Birthing Room" in bold letters across it. And in that birthing room are the neglected, the broken, the wounded, groaning in travail with the whole of Creation. The God who holds that door open for us does not look at our degrees or ask for our resume. This God bends down and whispers in our ears "a secret and hidden wisdom, one decreed before the ages for our glorification"—as Paul says in 1 Corinthians: "None of the [Pharaohs] or rulers of the age understood this, for if they had they would not have crucified the Lord" (1 Cor. 2:8).

But we know to step into that room alive with hope. "What no eye has seen, nor ear heard, nor the heart of people conceived, what God has prepared for those who love God" (1 Cor. 2:9).

We know the grandeur and courage of people who follow our God. We know the remarkable resources available to us when we let Pharaoh go.—Nancy Sehested

Illustrations

COMBATIVE COMPETITION.   There's an ancient Greek legend that illustrates beautifully the plight of combative competition. In one of the important races, a certain athlete ran well, but he still placed second. The crowd applauded the winner noisily, and after a time a statue was erected in his honor. But the one who had placed second came to think of himself as a loser. Corrosive envy ate away at him physically and emotionally, filling his body with stress. He could think of nothing else but his defeat and his lust to be number one, and he decided he had to destroy the statue that was a daily reminder of his lost glory.

A plan took shape in his mind, which he began cautiously to implement. Late each night, when everyone else was sleeping, he went to the statue and chiseled at the base hoping so to weaken the foundation that eventually it would topple. One night, as he was chiseling away the sculpture in violent and envious anger, he went too far. The heavy marble statue teetered on its fragile base and crashed down on the disgruntled athlete. He died beneath the crushing weight of the marble replica of the one he had grown to hate. But in reality he had been dying long before, inch by inch, chisel blow by chisel blow. He was the victim of his own stressful, competitive envy.—Lloyd J. Ogilvie

THE MESSAGE OF DANIEL.   What then is this book saying to us? I think it says four things. First, that human institutions, whether they be political, ecclesiastical, or otherwise, are capable of gross error. The error is usually in proportion to the power and pride of the institution, whether it be ecclesiastical or political. Second, this book is saying that extreme attempts are made to produce total conformity to the error. We see this in the Roman Empire. When it was about to fall apart at the seams, the emperor deified himself and set up emperor worship and commanded that there be no dissent. Third, it is saying that God's call to obedience can be heard above the tumult, above the bands, and above the flag-waving. This means that his call may be costly and extremely dangerous. Anyone who embarks on a course of obedience to God when his government is on collision course with God must be prepared for the fiery furnace. And fourth, it says that God alone is ultimately the Lord of history, that he is greater than kings and their furnaces, as well as their gas chambers.—Clarence Jordan

Sermon Suggestions

THE GOD WHO ACTS.   TEXT: Exod. 3:13–20. (1) He is characterized by his name, verses 13–14. (2) He is characterized in his relationships, verse 15. (3) He is characterized by his promises, verses 16–20.

GOD AT WORK FOR US. TEXT: Rom. 8:26–30. (1) To help us in particular in our weaknesses as we pray, verses 26–27. (2) To help us in general in everything as we stage by stage fulfill his purpose, verses 28–30.

Worship Aids

CALL TO WORSHIP. "Come unto me, all ye that labour and are heavy laden, and I will give you rest. Take my yoke upon you and learn of me; for I am meek and lowly in heart: and ye shall find rest unto your souls" (Matt. 11:28–29).

INVOCATION. Gracious Lord, take our hand and lead us by your Spirit into your overwhelming Presence. Caring Father, look down upon our tears of sorrow and comfort us. Righteous Judge, jar our complacency and self-righteousness into heart-felt repentance. Lover of our souls, knit together our lives, mend our brokenness, and lead us to tears of joy.—Donald W. Musser

OFFERTORY SENTENCE. "For all the law is fulfilled in one word, even in this: Thou shalt love thy neighbor as thyself" (Gal. 5:14).

OFFERTORY PRAYER. Generous Lord, who hast graced us beyond our deserving and blessed us beyond our imagining, accept now this portion of our earnings and bring both giver and recipient into a closer walk with thee.—E. Lee Phillips

PRAYER.
Leader: O God of truth and fact, forgive us for the myths we generate: about our heritage, to falsify the past;
People: about ourselves, to hide our present faults;
L: about those strange to us, to justify our lack of charity;
P: about others, to inflate our egos;
L: about you, to avoid your blinding clarity.

P: Give us courage to seek and to face all truth;
L: give us humility to see with less distortion;
All: and give us grace to act upon the truth your Spirit leads us to perceive.—Donald W. Musser

LECTIONARY MESSAGE

More Understanding of the Kingdom
TEXT: Matt. 13:44–52
These parables of the kingdom of heaven help us see more clearly things that pertain to our soul's welfare.

Verses 44 and 45–46 apply to the fulfillment of Jesus' command in Matt. 6:33. The treasure and the pearl are the equivalents of the "kingdom of God and his righteousness," which are worth giving up everything—even life itself—to possess, but which are in turn the givers of life and all its good things.

I. The discovery of treasure in a field would be a stroke of most exceptional luck, like a Texan bothered by the black goo in his feed yard or a prospector stumbling on white rock with little yellow specks in it. In this case, the treasure discovered represents the kingdom of heaven, the home and source of all joy. The finder at once experiences great joy and recognizes great opportunity, which he takes measure to secure and perpetuate. But like any such treasure, it is useless unless it has utility to others who are willing to trade other values for it. It must eventually be disclosed and shared, or its value becomes stale. The kingdom of heaven—not like the kingdoms of earth—is worth every commitment and sacrifice it calls for.

II. The parable of the pearl is slightly different from that of the treasure. The finding of the pearl is the result of a seeking that is favored by the odds, whereas the treasure is discovered by an unlikely accident. The joy over the treasure is sudden and surprising; that of the pearl-finder is a deep and stirring satisfaction over such great success in an arduous and painstaking endeavor. The merchant knows there must be exceptionally large, unusually lustrous, and therefore highly valuable pearls. But to maintain his business, he must buy and sell pearls of all sizes and value ("goodly pearls"). He must be startled and amazed over the value of the one pearl he "finds" that is "of great price." For any dealer, such a once-in-a-lifetime prize must be cherished at all costs. The two parables are alike in this, that what is found is of more worth than all the rest of a person's gifts or possessions. Will he sell the pearl? He probably will; his proceeds would guarantee he could not want for anything for the rest of his life.

Again, this is parallel to Matt. 6:33— success in life, as in the kingdom, is worth all the seeking, searching, and sacrifice one expends for it.

III. Seeing the kingdom of heaven as a net that gathers together all kinds, which must be sorted at the end of time, reminds us once more of the coming Judgment. "This is the way it will be at the end of the age," that the good will be fathered into safekeeping and the bad will be cast out. In the meantime, the net collects all kinds.

In the meantime, the gathering of the kingdom will include every race and nationality on earth. But the time will end. Then there will be a new classification into only two kinds—"good" and "bad." Verses 41 and 42, although not a part of this passage, shed some light on this separation. The offenders will be cast into a furnace of fire. And, as is done with the wise and foolish virgins in the parable about them, only one kind of people will be admitted to the glory, and the other kind will be excluded.

We are so accustomed to repeated opportunities to change for the better that we cannot imagine the end of opportunity. "Now is the accepted time" falls on deaf ears. As the bumper sticker says, "Cancer cures smoking."

IV. Perhaps we must tell these stories and ask Jesus' question more often—the question he here (v. 51) asks those disciples in the house with him, "Have you *understood* all these things?" The understanding, however, requires *both* interpretation of Jesus' symbols *and* spiritual submission, an open heart, to receive the enlightenment they may convey.

The question is of utmost importance to every soul's welfare. Without understanding, all men are lost. With it, these similitudes of the kingdom may help enlighten us all to salvation, to personal spiritual growth, to a holy life, and even to a teaching life.—John R. Rodman

SUNDAY: AUGUST FIFTH

SERVICE OF WORSHIP

Sermon: The Personal Dimension of Faith

Text: 2 Sam. 18:1, 5, 9–15

God save the contemporary church or the contemporary Christian from ever falling back again to that sometimes demonic kind of personal piety that forgot the world existed. God also save the contemporary church and the individual Christian from a kind of social activism that forgets that God cares about real, live, breathing human beings with names and sorrows and sadnesses and hopes and dreams. The life of faith is not a matter of choosing which way to go—this way or that way— the life of faith is a matter of learning how to live at the crossroads creatively, how to stay in that intersection where the public and the private come together—where life and faith meet, live under the yellow light, if you will. That is where the Bible lives. The Bible lives under the yellow light. Page after page speaks of God's concern with the good of the whole. But also, page after page tells the particular stories of particular people and particular ways in which the love of God touched their lives, what happened to them when their lives were touched by the love of God, and how it affected the whole, and thus it comes full circle.

I. This Sunday I want us to look at the story of David and Absalom. There seems to be in Scripture no story in which the public and private dimensions of faith meet in a more poignant way. It is a story set at the intersection. First, there is the public side of the story—civil war is raging in the Hebrew kingdom. The country is torn asunder. The heir to the throne has rebelled against the king, but there is also the private side of the story. Tears flow down the king's cheek. A father is heartbroken. It was even more poignant because David did love Absalom so, and he was so lovable, they say.

(a) Well, there he is, King David. Caught in the ambiguities that are an inevitable part of any human life. Caught no less than we, caught no less than Absalom, hanging there between heaven and earth—between what he should do and what he wants to do, between his public obligations and his personal pain. Between his head and his heart, he is caught. What the Bible is doing here is opening that door that says "private" on the outside and ushering us into the heart of where David lives—David, the human being. When we get there, we see what we had not expected to see. This turns out to be our story.

(b) It must be said that it is not everybody's story, because everybody who lives is not caught on the horns of moral dilemmas and between and among the ambiguities of life. For some, their lives are reflected in Joab's story. Joab doesn't struggle with internal conflicts; he is one of those bottom-line fellows. What's right is what is in your own best interest. What's wrong is what doesn't serve you. The idea is to win, to get on top of the heap and if you are there already, you do whatever you need to do to stay there.

(c) What you get with Joab is what you see all the time—the public and the private are exactly the same. It is not the same with David and, I would suspect, with you and with me. David knows already what life is teaching us everyday: that human existence is ambiguous and often confusing and there is a certain amount of anguish that is inevitable in human existence and there is not a thing we can do about it except weep.

II. The Scriptures know our anguish. We are helpless before it. We cannot, for example, die for our children—though there is not a parent here who wouldn't have taken his or her child's place when we saw them suffering if we could. It is our story, this mirror. David makes us look at the ironic truth about ourselves full in the face: that just as soon as we realize the value of something, it is taken away from us, and the hardest of all human griefs to bear is the grief for what has never been. Look in the mirror. Just as David begins to love his son or realize that he loves his son, he loses his son. Just as he realizes that winning is not everything, he wins what he doesn't want, and he loses the very thing he wanted more than anything in the world.

(a) It is an amazing story, and if you turn it, this story, this mirror, this way and that way, you get to see all sorts of other stories reflected in it, as a mirror in the living room seen from the hall can enable you to see what is going on in still another room. It's that kind of miraculous mirror story. If you turn it this way and that, you see all sorts of things, all sorts of other stories that are essentially the same story.

(b) Look at the broken relationships and moral compromises in your own life. The way your kids have let you down or the way you have let your kids down. The irreparable losses, the forever-unfinished business that you had with someone you loved and who is now gone. It is all there in David's story.

III. Look at one other story with me before we're done. There is another story about father and son. There is a story of the God whose son died. This time the son died in our place and for our sake. You know it well. The essential elements of the story are sitting right there on the table—bread and wine, sacrifice and salvation, all undeserved gifts, and they do not take our loss away, but they do make possible new life after the loss. They do not take our loss away, but these gifts let us know that God knows what we are going through and have gone through and, if we are human beings, will go through again.

To all the broken-hearted and all the grief-stricken and all the conflict-torn, an invitation comes, "Take and eat." To all the Davids in this world, to all the sons and all the daughters and all the fashion designers, even to old Joab himself, the invitation comes. "Eat, this is my body broken for you. Eat up, eat all you want. There's all the grace in the world here." Thanks be to God.—Joanna Adams

Illustrations

FOR GOD. Sometime in his senior year of college, in 1949, Jim Elliot wrote these words in his diary: "God, I pray Thee, light these idle sticks of my life and may I burn for Thee. Consume my life, my God, for it is Thine. I seek not a long life but a full one, like You, Lord Jesus."—Jack Mayhall

THE CALVARY ROAD. A saintly African Christian told a congregation once that, as he was climbing the hill to the meeting, he heard steps behind him. He turned and saw a man carrying a very heavy load up the hill on his back. He was full of sympathy for him and spoke to him. Then he noticed that his hands were scarred, and he realized that it was Jesus. He said to him, "Lord are you carrying the world's sins up the hill?" "No," said the Lord Jesus, "not the world's sins, just yours!" As that African simply told the vision God had just given him, the people's hearts and his heart were broken as they saw their sins at the cross. Our hearts need to be broken, too, and only when they are, shall we be willing for the confessions, the apologies, the reconciliations, and the restitutions that are involved in a true repentance of sin.—Roy and Revel Hession

Sermon Suggestions

A DAY OF REMEMBRANCE. TEXT: Exod. 12:1–14, especially verse 14. (1) Then: In the history of redemption, God has invested certain days with special meaning. (2) Always: Regular observance of special memorial events has continued to keep alive the sources of spirituality. (3) Now: The call is to recovery of former vitality through rededication to the most meaningful devotional habits.

MORE THAN CONQUERORS. TEXT: Rom. 8:37–39. (1) The powers that threaten us. (2) The love that gives us victory.

Worship Aids

CALL TO WORSHIP. "Bless the Lord, O my soul: and all that is within me, bless his holy name" (Ps. 103:1).

INVOCATION. Lord, we feel that "through many dangers, toils, and snares" we have come to this place. Grant that we may receive such blessings today as will help us to help others find their way through the same problems and difficulties and join us in blessing your holy name.

OFFERTORY SENTENCE. "Give unto the Lord the glory due unto his name: bring an offering, and come before him: worship the Lord in the beauty of holiness" (1 Chron. 16:29).

OFFERTORY PRAYER. Lord, the offerings we bring to this place are only a faint gesture of our love, but you give importance to them. You receive them and use them to spread the good news of your love and the salvation that is in Jesus Christ. Thank you for allowing us to have a share in your work in the world.

PRAYER. Burdened is how some of us feel as we come into your presence this morning, Father. There is a burden for the world and the situations across land after land where people are battling and dying and threatening freedom. There is the burden that comes because of the pains of loved ones who are suffering from diseases that cannot be cured and emotional traumas that drain the energy from them. There are the burdens of loss that weigh heavily upon some of us, loss of jobs, loss of wealth, loss of health and the ultimate loss of a life dear to us. Added to these are the burdens we carry for our children as they face the world with all its pressures and demands that are not in keeping with the highest that we hold. And there are the burdens of our personal sins that so often shut out the light we need to guide us aright in the world where we live and move and have our being. You understand these burdens, Father. You have carried them time after time and have shown us how to deal with so much that we face. This morning give us the assurance we need once again to handle the fears that such burdens always bring. By the presence and power of your Spirit, make us brave that we may move forward into the future armed with trust and faith such as will give us the strength to bear the burden even as we are given the light to illumine the pathway we are called to walk.

Lift our eyes to the broader horizons of life, we pray. Enable us to catch a glimpse of beauty, to see some grand sunrise, to behold some fragile flower, to glimpse the wonder of a soft smile, and to experience the warmth of some human love that will declare your presence with us. Open our eyes and hearts and lives to the transforming power of your presence in so much that we miss because we are too engrossed in our problems to see the potentials you are trying to show us all about us.

Now in these quiet moments, call us to you. Still the anxious beating of our hearts. Quiet the roaring tumble of our thoughts. Calm the fretting cares of our concerns, and for a little while, here in this sacred place, let us be together with you as if we were each alone in your presence.—W. Henry Fields

LECTIONARY MESSAGE

The Wonderful Means of Supply

TEXT: Matt. 14:13–21

Time for talking, for teaching, even for healing, had been exhausted. The time of hunger, of need for food, had come.

But Jesus was not willing to leave the multitudes to shift for themselves, so far from the city and the villages. He told his disciples, "They do not need to leave; *you* give them something to eat."

I. *Their small supply.*

(a) Like us, the disciples knew the demand was too great for their meager supply. We also face great demands for the physical needs of people. Beggars besiege

our church offices. The number who would share is insignificant compared to the number in need. Anyone who sends a few dollars to a food fund, to an orphans' home, to a home for the aged, or anywhere else soon receives requests from dozens of other agencies asking for help of all kinds.

(b) Our resources are too limited, as theirs were. The disciples had just enough for their own needs—adding up to five loaves and two fishes. It would surely not suffice if divided. Many would still be in need if any were subtracted. But did they react negatively? Did they outright refuse? Did they complain and offer excuses? No—they only *stated* what they *had*. They were, at heart, generous, and, in fact, also needy.

II. *Jesus' request for surrender.* Jesus says, regarding the small supplies of the disciples, "Bring them to me." He must begin with what we have.

(a) It is a principle of life in this world that what is to be must come out of what is. Even though he had all power, he must start with our stock. He must depend on us today to bring to him the admittedly inadequate resources at our command. There must be something for him to start with. Like the disciples, we must take a positive step by bringing it to Jesus.

(b) If we surrender our supply, he will multiply it. We share the sad misgivings of the sower described in Psalm 126, "He that goeth forth and weepeth, bearing precious seed." We take the last stores from the cupboard, the last precious grains from the last crop—the margin between us and starvation—and must throw them into the ground, give them the earth. But even though we sow in tears, we shall reap in joy.

(c) Jesus' work is different from a government project. These disciples cared nothing for their cut or percentage, their graft, or their special territory. Corruption was not known to these suppliers. They were honest. They knew their resources. They surrendered them to Jesus, and he multiplied them enough for a little more than the need.

III. *Jesus' multiplication of the offering.* The disciples gave their food to Jesus, who blessed it and broke it, giving it back to the disciples, who in turn gave it to the multitude.

(a) Jesus made the difference. He lifted the loaves up to heaven before returning them. He called on the power of God. As the Spirit of God multiplied those few loaves, he will generously return to any person all that he gives. The regeneration of salvation is a miracle of God. A man gives him a poor, dying spirit and receives in return eternal life, with its resultant grace, love, and power. Whoever used to be a taker and a keeper is now a supplier to others. Whoever once was fearful of life and the future, now has courage and stamina unknown. Whoever was sad and lonely and miserly now is a joyful seeker of fellowship and of opportunities for generosity.

(b) The restoration of righteousness is even more wonderful when we have experienced the guilt of our own self-centered sinfulness and cruelty, our inconsiderate lawlessness of body and spirit. When Jesus asks, "How many loaves have you?" we are freshly appalled to have to reveal what we have made out of all he has already done for us. We need to tell him plainly, and surrender to him such as we are, to know the miracle of what he returns for use in his ministry. Righteousness comes only from him. Tenderness, sympathy, sensitivity, and love grow anew in our hearts, ministering the touch of God to all around us.—John R. Rodman

SUNDAY: AUGUST TWELFTH

SERVICE OF WORSHIP

Sermon: Jumping the Waves with Jesus
TEXTS: Psalms 121; Rom. 9:1–5; Matt. 14:22–33

I. I think we all have a basic picture of what happened when the Hebrews crossed the Red Sea. The king of Egypt had told them they could leave the country. But after they had left, the Pharaoh changed his mind. Perhaps he realized the financial implications of losing all these people. Quickly Pharaoh summoned his chief officers and arranged for the entire cavalry of Egypt to go after the Hebrews and bring them back.

(a) The commander could see that this would be an easy campaign. No need to rush. The cloud cover would pass by morning, and then they'd simply surround these slaves and return them to their proper homes. The ring leaders like Moses and Aaron would probably be terminated, and life would get back to normal—as it should be.

But what was causing the cloud that stood between the Egyptian army and the Hebrew camp? It says in the passage we read that God, who had been visible in the form of a cloud, leading the people forward, moved around behind them so as to provide a protective cloud cover.

(b) The next morning, as you know, Moses raised his arm, the waters separated, the Hebrews walked across on more or less dry earth, the Egyptians went in to follow, their chariots got clogged with the soft ground, and the waters then closed in over the armored soldiers so that they all drowned.

There are different ways of understanding exactly how and where this event took place, as well as what it all means. But what interests me at this point is the way we see God in this story, and the way we see life.

II. This could have been a nice little story without slaves being whipped and soldiers being drowned, without firstborn children being slain in the dark of night. The Egyptians could have been a kind and progressive people. They could have given every Hebrew a pat on the back, could have given them their independence and sufficient provisions for a great journey, and then sent them off into the wilderness with every blessing and good wishes.

(a) Yet in the real world, life as it really is, only refugees are sent on their way, while slaves are held in an iron grip. So God didn't make this a fairy tale. God led these people out of the harsh misery of their Egyptian toil, took them forward to face the dangers of the life that lay ahead, and even went so far as to destroy the forces that would have thwarted their escape.

(b) We live—and God deals with us—in the real world, a world of life and death, blood and tears. And God didn't spare the Hebrews from their fears, but he spared them from their worst fears coming true. The army came after them, sure enough, but he stood between them to provide an escape. Not a nice story, but a true story, and a meaningful story.

III. This gives us some connection to our Gospel reading this morning. Not just the fact that both stories have something to do with water. But the fact that God deals with real life, real people, with their warts and fears and imperfections.

(a) What this story comes to mean is not that Peter's faith should have been able to keep him afloat, waves bouncing off his knees . . . but that Jesus could hold Peter's hand in the storm, could allow him to have his crisis of faith, allow him even to sink as you or I would sink, and yet keep him from going under and drowning.

(b) To me, that gives me some confidence, that I don't have to be a superhuman person, free from every worry and safe from every harm, free from the circumstances that befall other people. I can be a real person living in a real world, as you and I do. I can wonder and worry and work and make mistakes, and live my life the best I know how, and God who is there at my side will hold my hand and keep me from sinking under the waves.

(c) What waves? Being without a job? Experiencing family difficulties? Discovering that life looks different than it did ten years ago? Wondering whether to change jobs midstream, or wondering whether to let go and retire? Waves of sickness, misfortune, stress, and wishful thinking . . .

IV. Look at Psalm 121. It says the Lord is your keeper. The Lord is the protective shade that keeps the intense heat of the sun, or the eerie dangers of the night, from smiting you. He will keep you from all evil; he will keep your life.

(a) It doesn't say that the sun will never shine unbearably hot upon you. It says the Lord will give you shade. It doesn't say that you will never wonder at the dangers of the night, but that they will not fall upon you. It doesn't say that life will always be a pleasant story, but that God will always stand between us and the evil that threatens us.

(b) I want to leave you with the memory of something that probably we have all done, sometime or another. Remember as a child at the beach, jumping over the waves that were rolling in over the sand? If water and waves symbolize the chaos that rolls in upon us from time to time throughout life, then consider that, holding the hand of our Lord and Savior, we can jump the waves with confidence, or after we take a splash we can get back up and go at it with renewed vigor and determination. In the end of it all, you can be sure, we'll be on solid ground.—Brian Weatherdon

Illustrations

WHAT IS FAITH? Any sort of definitive statement about faith presents a paradox, a fact which places it immediately in the category of spiritual reality. True faith lets God, and yet it volunteers to help. It says, "I am poor and weak and blind," and yet shouts, "I can, I will, I do." It says, "Thy will be done," and yet it resolves. It waits, yet it runs. It has not seen God, yet it endures as having seen him who is invisible.

Faith has a strange capacity for certainty, even beyond the sphere of physical proofs. With it, seeing is not believing, but believing is seeing. When the lazy legs of logic and reason limp in the upward climb toward knowledge, faith has a way of mounting up on wings like eagles to view the landscape o'er. When understanding fails and falls by the wayside in its weary upward climb, faith perches itself on the highest pinnacle and sees farther than human eye can see.—Ellis A. Fuller

THE IMPERATIVE OF RESPONSIBILITY. With no difficulty, I can picture myself lying on the pallet, the center of the crowd's attention. I can imagine myself enjoying the ability to use my distress to manipulate my friends. I can certainly imagine the comfort I would draw from the words, "My son, your sins are forgiven." But when, following the indicative of forgiveness, I heard the imperative of responsibility—"Rise, take up your pallet, and walk"—I think my inclination would have been to murmur, "No thanks; I think I'll just stay here on the stretcher."—William Sloan Coffin

Sermon Suggestions

A MIRACLE OF DELIVERANCE.   TEXT: Exod. 14:19–31. (1) The story: God saved his people Israel by dramatic acts of his providence, and Israel's oppressors perished. (2) The meaning: (a) God uses natural means to accomplish his purposes. (b) Yet such acts must be seen as works of the care of God. (c) These phenomena are rightly regarded with reverent awe by those who benefit and with fear by those who oppress.

A HEART AFLAME.   TEXT: Rom. 9:1–5. (1) Because of a great heritage and great promise. (2) Because of a great God and a great salvation.

Worship Aids

CALL TO WORSHIP.   "Blessed is the man that trusteth in the Lord, and whose hope the Lord is" (Jer. 17:7).

INVOCATION.   We thank you, O Lord, that you are God. You have proven your trustworthiness to your people again and again, though fear and doubt have often shattered their faith for a season. Renew our faith: we believe; help our unbelief, and so will we find that blessing that awaits us.

OFFERTORY SENTENCE.   "Every man shall give as he is able, according to the blessing of the Lord thy God which he hath given thee" (Deut. 16:17).

OFFERTORY PRAYER.   Lord, we give because we have reason to give and something to give and high purposes to fulfill. We ask that the love of the Savior might saturate our gifts, lift others to within sight of thy glory, and, at last, bring the angels to sing over the salvation of the lost.—E. Lee Phillips

PRAYER.   "O Thou fount of every blessing, tune our hearts to sing thy grace." We praise you for your Word of grace spoken so decisively and conclusively in Jesus, the Messiah. May this Word read, spoken, sung through the experience of worship grant *us* such insight into ourselves to know that with all of our trying and striving, we are still unprofitable servants.

From this confrontation may our minds and hearts reverberate with that Word that is our only hope: "the *grace* of our Lord Jesus Christ." Except for your abounding grace, we could not experience another breath. We praise thee, O God, for the grace by which we live, the grace of this new day, for the grace by which we are saved.

We have been called into the church to become citizens of the *world*. May this sanctuary never become a retreat from our worldly responsibility, but may it always be as a launching pad from which we are catapulted by your love to go into all the world and all the worlds of men and women, young people, boys and girls. We pray for the world in all of its brokenness—for deliverance for peoples where governments oppress—for salvation from fears that would squander the world's largess on nuclear arsenals.

Experiencing the *fullness* of your grace in Christ, may our lives be as a paean of praise and thanksgiving and may the most difficult task be not a burden but a delight, through him who for the joy that was set before him endured the cross, despising the shame.—John Thompson

LECTIONARY MESSAGE

A Lesson in Faith
TEXT: Matt. 14:22–23

A president of a men's college often advised the graduating class, "Gentlemen, be careful what you go after in life; the chances are you will get it." Yes—human determination, orientation, and organization are so strong a combination that a high degree of success is almost a certainty. Then what? Can we live with our attained objectives? Suppose we achieve our goal early in our career. Are we able to fabricate a motive for the rest of our life, or will we flounder and fritter, half alive as long as we live?

Peter had to learn the lesson about faith, that enough to begin is not enough to continue, that immediate goals, when realized, can leave one without a means of support for the rest of the way.

I. *Disciples in a storm-tossed boat.* All the disciples had to learn about the power of the storm and to take it as nothing exceptional even while following Jesus' instructions. Perhaps he needed to have them get into the ship, and thus into the storm, as much for their good as to provide him with solitude for his prayer time.

We may accept their experience as an example of our own. Many times modern disciples following Jesus' instructions find themselves in storms and in danger. We may, as they had just done, see Jesus perform the impossible and unexpected and in great confidence go about our Christ-directed lives. Do we experience hard going? Do we face natural powers in opposition? Would we recognize the storm-tossing as the very experience that will bring the Master of Life to save us with his control over our trouble? We can expect the world to continue being the world in all its dark ways, as well as in its beautiful ways, when we follow Christ. We shall not escape the trials and ordinary blinding blasts of life merely because we are about his work. Indeed, it almost seems that to do his work we must go into places of known danger in the most dangerous of times.

II. *Jesus joining his disciples in their trouble.* After a night of praying, Jesus was conscious of the need of his disciples, to whom he would now and henceforth devote his most loving attention. This is one more incident in which it is apparent that he is *always* aware of his disciples' concerns and needs. "And in the fourth watch of the night Jesus went unto them, walking on the sea."

But—strangest of all—they were afraid to see him come. We can understand. What *could* they think? Surely a human body could not be supported by the surface of so thin a fluid as water! It had to be a spirit. But they learned differently. Not only was he coming, but he was coming on the water without a boat.

Faith is the power in us that believes the unbelievable even when we do *not* see it. For most of us, a certain amount of seeing is necessary to establish our faith. We strive to believe in what we have not seen, but it is possible only when we see something that helps us realize how strong God can make a person. This is one of the reasons why a truly consistent Christian life on our part is so important—to young and learning watchers, a transformed life or a mature life in Christ can be the evidence necessary in their growth to a faith that doubts not. We do grow in Christ. "It is I; be not afraid" (v. 27). "Because thou hast seen me, thou hast believed: Blessed are they that have not seen, and yet have believed" (John 20:29).

III. *Peter's insufficient faith perfected.*

(a) Jesus often remarked on the slowness of people to believe the Law and the Prophets and on the resistance that he found to the evidence of his Sonship. He responded to Peter's request, "Bid me come unto thee on the water," by the simple word, "Come."

And in the power of that command, Peter walked on the water toward Jesus. *He walked on the water!* Great and simple faith is evidenced by those steps. We must not let his beginning to sink blind us to the great power of his instant faith and its accomplishment. True, he did start without thinking; but when he thought and sank, it was not the starting that was wrong. Again, however, faith to begin is not enough. We wonder why it was not. However many steps he took, each one should have provided evidence enough for the following one, continuously, to his goal.

(b) We may speculate on the reasons for his beginning to sink, but to whatever we attribute it, it is of even greater importance to attribute his rescue to Christ. The added weight of the sinking Peter did not cause Jesus to make the slightest depression in the water—his strength and his willingness to save are strong enough for all who will take the first steps of faith. Perhaps our motives are mixed, as Peter's may have been, and, like him, we can never expect to be able to say, "Look, God, no hands!" We can't do it ourselves. It is sufficient for us that Jesus is still ready to stretch forth his hand and catch us, as he caught Peter. Then echoing Jesus we must ask, "Why did you ever doubt?" Perhaps so that Jesus could perfect a faith in you that becomes evidence for the ones watching you, as Peter became a strengthener of his brethren.—John R. Rodman

SUNDAY: AUGUST NINETEENTH

SERVICE OF WORSHIP

Sermon: People Who Suppose They Have No Personal Relationships with God

TEXT: Isa. 45:5

Every counselor meets people unaware that they have any personal relationship with God. Now, from the Christian point of view that is impossible. A man can no more avoid dealing with him than a man can live in a physical universe made up of protons and electrons and not deal with them. He may be ignorant about them and unaware of them, but he certainly deals with them all the time.

I quoted a verse of Isaiah's where the prophet pictures God saying to Cyrus the Persian, "I girded thee, though thou hast not known me." Cyrus was king of Babylon; he was a polytheist. He knew little or nothing about Israel's God, acknowledged not relationships with him or obligations to him. Nonetheless, Israel's God said to him, "I girded thee, though thou hast not known me."

I. How familiar an experience it is to be ministered to by forces we do not recognize! That experience began in the womb. Every mother can say to her newborn babe, I girded thee, though thou hast not known me.

(a) During long ages man did not understand the physical universe, but still the sun warmed him, the rain refreshed him, the returning seasons fed him, and the stars guided his wandering boats. A young child does not see that he is undergirded by his country's institutions, unaware even that there is a Constitution of the United States or a Bill of Rights; but later the national life that has long given him security begins saying to him, I girded thee, though thou hast not known me.

(b) Surely this truth applies to our relationships with God. Some people seem to think that God does not enter into a man's life, liberate him, guide him, employ him to noble ends, unless God is consciously recognized and received. But the God of the Bible does not so behave. Rather like the sun he comes in through every crack and crevice where he can find a way. With many a fine man, therefore, who says he disbelieves in God, God has been dealing, even using him, it may be, as he did Cyrus, for great ends saying, "I girded thee, though thou hast not known me." Someone here today should feel that true about himself.

II. Consider the explanation this provides for some fine characters we know. Cyrus played a creative part in his time. In his release of captive nations in Babylon, he ended one of his generation's most grievous wrongs and, helping to reestablish the exiled Jewish community on Mount Zion, he made a contribution to history to which we are all indebted. Yet he did not know God. Cyrus is a symbol of some people who often perplex us—high-minded, useful lives who do not recognize God.

(a) Some of our great scientists belong in this group. While today we comfortably worship here, in many an obscure laboratory they seek cures for ancient lamentable ills and, finding them, will make it a point of honor, without profit to themselves, to share their knowledge with the world. Let the preachers stop to share their knowledge with the world. Let the preachers stop quarreling with such scientists and emulate a little, if they can, their

disinterested love of truth and their un-
selfish service. But some of them do not
recognize God.

(b) So it is with some philanthropists.
While too many so-called Christians make
of their religion an emotional retreat into
a make-believe world of personal comfort
for themselves, these philanthropic soldiers of the common good are out in the
real world, fighting real foes—poverty,
unemployment, the inhumanities of our
economic life, and the insanities of war.
They are great spirits; our children will
rise up to call them blessed. But some of
them do not recognize God.

(c) What shall we say about such folk?
Some people use such scientists and philanthropists as arguments against religion.
See, they say, these splendid men and
women living without God! But they are
not living without God. They are supreme
examples of the unrecognized God. Listen
to the New Testament: "He that doeth
good is of God." And again, says the New
Testament, "He that abideth in love
abideth in God, and God abideth in him."
There in the service he renders, in the love
that motivates him, in the mission that has
mastered him, is God, girding him, even
though unknown.

III. Turn now to ourselves, and see
where this truth comes home to us. When
any man tells me that he has no personal
dealings with God, I feel sure he is mistaken.

(a) Oh, for example, in the moral realm!
Someone here has come so close to going
to pieces in moral dishonor—financial,
sexual, what you will—that you do not yet
understand why you did not go to pieces.
There, on the verge of the precipice you
stood, and something held you back—a
face rose before you, a hand held you, so
that you did not fall, and here you are
today with some disgraceful things un-
done. Something at the heart of your life
has presented to temptation's appeal a resistance that surprised you. You do not
believe in God? Where do you think God
is? Just among the stars? There at the center of your life, the patient guardian of
your honor, is the real God. Many a year
he has been trying to make some of us
hear his voice and recognize it: "I girded

thee, though thou hast not known me."

(b) Or, again, many of us have tried to
give up God and have never quite succeeded. We say there is no God, and then
we go out under the stars at night and
wonder. A vast, law-abiding universe this,
to have come by accident, as though a man
should throw a font of type upon the floor
and by chance it should arrange itself into
a play of Shakespeare. Strange universe,
without God! Or we try to say there is no
God, and then we are married, and the
first baby comes, and there wells up in us
the purest love that human beings know,
the love of parents for a little child. Queer
business, for a man to walk about the
streets with a love like that in his heart,
trying to think that there is nothing corre-
sponding with it in the reality from which
the man's heart and the man's home came.
Strange universe, without God!

(c) We have never succeeded in getting
rid of God. There is a flame in our heart
that will not go out. Friends, if there were
no God it would be easier to disbelieve in
him than it is! We cannot get rid of God,
because all that is best in us is God in us.
The flame is he, and there in the center of
our life for many a year he has been trying
to make us hear, "I girded thee, though
thou hast not known me."

IV. Indeed, our thought carries us farther. Not individuals alone but mankind as
a whole neglects and forgets God. Yet because of that does God lose his hold upon
the reins of human destiny? Rather, there
is a power greater than ourselves that, recognized or not, goes on its everlasting
way. Sometimes I come alone into the
church just to see the cross over the alter.
It is strange that it should be there. That
cross stands for one of the darkest deeds
in history. What worse thing can be said
about this world than that it is the kind of
place where that could happen—so glorious a person done to so cruel and shameful a death. So, long ago, Pilate sat in
judgment upon Jesus, but not now! Now
Jesus sits in judgment on Pilate. Long ago,
his judges condemned Socrates, but not
now! Now Socrates condemns his judges.
Long ago, the inquisitors tried Galileo,
but not now! Now Galileo tries his inquisitors. There is an everlasting fact beneath

the aphorisms of the race: "No lie can last forever"; "Truth will out"; "Truth crushed to earth will rise again"; "He laughs best who laughs last." Say our worst about this world, it is indeed a place where many a violent dictator has laughed, but where no dictator ever laughs last. Within the shadow, recognized or not, often neglected, forgotten, betrayed, the Power not ourselves that makes for righteousness has said to man, "I girded thee, though thou hast not known me."

V. What, then, is the conclusion of the matter? That we ought to be contented to go through a long life ministered to by an unrecognized God? Upon the contrary, this sermon has been preached in vain if all the way through you have not felt the pity of being served by the Eternal Spirit of all grace and still not knowing him.

(a) The central experience in man's personal relationship with God is prayer. Now, I contend that everybody prays. Call it by what different names they may, all men pray. For a man to say he never prays is as if a man should say that he never responds to nature's beauty.

(b) Well, praying is as universal as that. Not by aggressive activity alone does any one of us achieve all that he inwardly possesses or lives by. In receptive hours rather, when we are hospitable to something higher than ourselves, we are enriched. Every soul knows that. Of course we pray—sometimes, to be sure, unwittingly, as though a man by accident left the door of his spirit open and some God-like idea or feeling strayed in—but sometimes consciously, experiencing a divine invasion that is unmistakable.—Harry Emerson Fosdick

Illustrations

AS ONE UNKNOWN.   He comes to us as One unknown, without a name, as of old, by the lakeside; He came to those men who knew Him not. He speaks to us the same word: "Follow thou me!" and sets us to the tasks which He has to fulfil for our time. He commands. And to those who obey Him, whether they be wise or simple, He will reveal Himself in the toils, the conflicts, the sufferings which they shall pass through in His fellowship, and as an ineffable mystery, they shall learn in their own experience who He is.—Albert Schweitzer

RECOGNIZING THE TRUTH.   One of the most charming stories of the last generation was Jean Webster's *Daddy Long Legs.* Many of you will recall the gist of the tale, how a young girl in an orphanage was befriended by a person whom she did not know. He took a fancy to her when she was a very little child and befriended her, keeping himself unknown. Year after year the favors flowed in upon her from her unknown friend. She grew up through girlhood and young college womanhood, her opportunities provided by this friend she did not know. Once she saw him, but she did not recognize him. She had imagined him looking other than he did look, and so even when she saw him she did not know him. What if the story ended there? Why, what a way to end a story—served through long years by a friend and then not knowing him! No! She found him out at last and loved him, her long unrecognized benefactor. I beg of you, do not let your life story end without that consummation!—Harry Emerson Fosdick

Sermon Suggestions

OUR DAILY BREAD.   TEXT: Exod. 16: 2–15. (1) Need and disenchantment. (2) Grace and provision.

ARGUING FOR GOD.   TEXT: Rom. 11: 13–16, 29–32. (1) God desires the salvation of all people—Jews and non-Jews alike. (2) God's strange ways are designed to achieve the salvation of both Jews and non-Jews with utter faithfulness to his purpose.

Worship Aids

CALL TO WORSHIP.   "And ye shall know the truth, and the truth shall make you free. . . . God is a spirit: and they that worship him must worship him in spirit and in truth" (John 8:32; 4:24).

INVOCATION. O God, within us there are prayers that know no words; joys that seem to have come from some high heaven above the earth, bringing new life to our wearied souls and lifting them beyond their strength to things eternal; sorrows that stand forever in silence before thy face, humbled by a mystery in which light and darkness are mingled deeper than our sight; exaltations that brighten the brow like flames of Holy Spirit, burning the dross away until the truth shines through flesh and blood; remembrances that lay their hallowing hands on all hours with a benediction sweeter than peace. Hear us, O God, though we do not speak.—Samuel H. Miller

OFFERTORY SENTENCE. "And they came, every one whose heart stirred him up, and every one whom his spirit made willing, and they brought the Lord's offering to the work of the tabernacle of the congregation, and for all his service, and for the holy garments" (Exod. 35:21).

OFFERTORY PRAYER. Gracious Lord, accept now this portion of all we have been given that it may be blessed of thee and may do more than we ever thought or dreamed, because we bless it in the name of the Father, the Son, and the Holy Ghost.—E. Lee Phillips

PRAYER. Almighty God, Lord of all power, by divine will and decisive word you spoke Creation and all its richness into being. O Master Creator, your handiwork flows with assured precision and thoughtful rhythm. And, in the fullness of time, you sent your Son in the holy power of unconditional love to serve and save all people.

O mighty One, who still is in control and commands all powers that be, in awe and gratitude we worship and praise you, God of power.

Surrounding God, Lord of all presence, as in the words of old, wherever we may go, you are there: in the restless wind, in the cry of absence, in the outer edge of space, in the secret pocket of our soul, in the dark of death, in the face of Christ, in these and all, you are there. In awe and gratitude, we worship you, God of all presence.

Infinite God, Lord of all knowing, in the overwhelming vastness of knowledge and thought, who are to seek and know thee? O understanding One, unto whom all hearts are open and every thought is known, you who know and love us best; who from the beginning felt our deepest need and yearning and in Jesus Christ came humbly, in awe and gratitude, we worship and praise you, God of all knowing.

Holy Designer, Maker of us all, continue to make us more like you. Restore us anew in forgiving our sins as we confess our hearts to you. Today we seek pardon for our sin of thinking we know it all and that we are all powerful. Forgive our arrogance and pride.

O God in Christ, remove our bent to turning away and against you. Soften our hearts and gladden our spirits to turn toward you. And in Christ, empower us to turn with you to others. Grant us wisdom and courage to receive and use the towel of service. God of all power, knowledge, and presence, God of Jesus Christ our Light and Lord, in you we pray.—William M. Johnson

LECTIONARY MESSAGE

Successful Faith—Hoping Against Hope

TEXT: Matt. 15:21–28

What a person does when confronted by a tragic circumstance reveals much about that person. What a certain mother did when facing an ineradicable destructive illness that had bested her daughter was a lesson in faithful persistence, or persistent faith, for all who have heard about Jesus Christ.

I. *The silent Jesus.*

(a) Jesus had just finished a frustrating interview with the Pharisees over the true source of human defilement and had had to explain it even to his disciples. Seeking a change and, perhaps, a less oppressive atmosphere, he crossed the border into a gentile territory, whose people were despised by the Jews.

(b) He was known, even in this country of Tyre and Sidon, for his remarkable expression of truth and for his love and willingness to heal those whom life had maimed or sickened. He may even have left the land of Gennesaret to seek some rest from the crowds brought to him there for healing.

(c) Jesus was looking for the refreshing experience of finding someone who believed, who saw God through all the deeds, who could draw close enough to perceive who Jesus really was. No wonder that when the Canaanite mother came to him crying, "Have mercy on me, Lord," he saw in her "Lord" a seed of what he sought and gave himself pause in silence rather than refusing outright to grant her wish.

She was pleading for the great loving charity of a renowned teacher and miracle worker. She interceded for her daughter knowing her status before Jesus, showing hope born of desperate courage. And Jesus answered her not a word. How disappointing! And yet she continued to hope.

If we occasionally feel that our earnest petitions in prayer are not being answered, think how she felt. If we seem to ask and ask and hear nothing, we all too easily interpret the silence as a rejection. We expect instant results, but there are times when we cannot receive them. This question of the meaning of Jesus' silence is a difficult one for us. We ought to search more deeply in ourselves. He cannot do for us what we should be doing for ourselves. He cannot remake the laws of the world and of human relations for us without first remaking us. His silence may be a message in itself, if we are open to listen to him.

II. *An example of persistent faith.*

(a) The disciples around Jesus in this instance are somewhat a disappointment to us. They seemed to be more self-centered than Christ-centered. They interpreted the woman's petitioning as aimed at them, "She crieth after us," failing to see their opportunity as gentlemen to be kind and considerate, missing the opening for them as disciples to introduce a seeker favorably to their master.

We must ask ourselves whether we are too much bothered by the needy—spiritually, socially, or financially—to help them see the Lord, to break our circle around him and clear the way for them to see him as the glory of their lives. We must question whether we want him too much for ourselves to hear the true seeking of the cries around us.

But the woman's response to Jesus' silence was to reassure herself that he was the one she sought, the one with power and compassion. Her course was to persevere because he was the one who could meet her great need.

(b) This mother was pleading for her daughter. She was not asking for herself, but for another. She may have had more courage because of the pitiful condition of the girl, seeing herself with a tinge of guilt for failing to prevent or cure the illness herself. We all ought to be more sensitive to others' needs than to our own, having the courage of faith to intercede on their behalf as this mother did.

(c) She never contradicted Jesus when he told her his mission was to the ones he affectionately called "lost sheep of the house of Israel." She was aware she was a pagan and an outcast and from an accursed land. She could only answer his refusal to "take the children's bread" and cast it to the "little puppies" under the table by saying, "Truth, Lord." But she pursued his metaphor for her own blessing. She argued convincingly that the crumbs that fell—not the children's bread, but the discard—were still there for the pets. She convinced him that although they were dogs, they were still there in the household, a household not of land and race but of the spirit. God had made them all, and there was sufficient for all.

(d) The mother drew close to Jesus. It was he that she needed, and he saw her logic and no doubt her wit along with the faith that made her hope against hope. What a glorious result! "Her daughter was made whole from that very hour." He could only say with respectful address, "O woman, great is thy faith."

Let us never be discouraged by apparent rejection. It may be that Jesus has come into our country to see the proving and the maturation of our faith.—John R. Rodman

SUNDAY: AUGUST TWENTY-SIXTH

SERVICE OF WORSHIP

Sermon: Disciples in Difficult Places
TEXT: Phil. 4:22

While it is always difficult to be a disciple, it is never impossible. Regardless of your age, your geographical location, or your vocation, you can live for Jesus. Even in the hardest of places and in the most unlikely surroundings, people have—and still do—live for him.

One verse that assures us of this was written by the Apostle Paul to the Philippian Christians. He wrote, "All the saints salute you, chiefly they that are of Caesar's household" (4:22).

I. (a) These saints were living in an unusual place. They were saints in "Caesar's household." The word *household* refers to either a family or a home. In all probability they were members of his civil service or a part of his guard or they were slaves who served in his palace.

Can you imagine a harder place to be a saint than in Caesar's household? To live for Christ under the nose of this cruel and despicable man who hated Christianity must have been extremely difficult. Yet the Apostle Paul sends this greeting from some Christians who were doing just that.

(b) There is a message in this for you and for me. It is this: If a person could be a disciple in Caesar's household, then one can be a disciple anywhere. If it was possible to be a Christian in that place, then it is possible to be a Christian any place.

There are at least three places where it is especially difficult to be a disciple today. I want us to look at those places with the understanding that if a person could be a disciple in Caesar's household, then we can be a disciple in these places also. The three places where it is hard to live for Christ today are schools we attend; social circles we move in; and the businesses where we work.

II. It is hard for young people to live for Christ today. We are living in a time of unprecedented moral confusion. The prevailing moral philosophy in today's America is, "If it feels good, do it."

(a) People have always violated moral standards. But for the first time in the history of the world, many people are not even sure that there is such a thing as an absolute moral standard. Add to the moral confusion of our age excessive freedom, and the problem is volatile.

(b) I am persuaded that it is harder to live for Jesus in the schools and universities today than it has ever been in the history of the world. But as difficult as it is, it is not impossible. If there could be saints in Caesar's household, there can be saints in our schools.

Yet there is a price to be paid. It requires a deep commitment to Jesus Christ and his Word. We cannot survive the pressures of today without being anchored to him.

Absolute freedom is absolute nonsense. It leads to complete frustration and emptiness. It is only as we attach our lives to Jesus that we can ever fulfill our intended purpose. It is only through commitment to him that our lives can produce the beautiful melody that God wants to come from them.

III. The social circles we move in are also hard places to be a disciple. Young people are not the only ones who face social pressures. Adults also know what it is to be tempted to conform and compromise—to go along in order to get along.

(a) Someone has said that every person is born an original and dies a copy. Life is often a gradual process of whittling away our distinctiveness until we are all just alike.

Many Christians today are like the chameleon. The chameleon's ability to change its color to match its environment is part of its defense mechanism.

There are a lot of chameleon Christians today. They are so busy trying to conform to the world around them that they live in nervous exhaustion. They have forgotten the admonition of the Apostle Paul that we are not to be conformed to this world (see Rom. 12:1–2).

(b) While it is hard to live for Jesus in the social swirls of our communities, it is not impossible. Listen! If there could be saints in Caesar's household, there can be saints at the country club. In fact, if you cannot live for Jesus at the country club, then you need to get out. Your first calling is to be a saint. It is to live for Jesus Christ.

IV. Another place where it is hard to be a disciple today is in the business world. It is hard to live for Christ there because many people check their Christianity at the door when they go to work.

(a) Many people believe that Christianity should be confined to the sanctuary and practiced most consistently by those in clerical collars or choir robes. The truth of the matter, however, is that it was meant for the smoke-filled office, the mechanic's shop, the construction site, the cab of an eighteen-wheeler, and the executive suite. In fact, Christianity looks best when it is dressed in blue denims, a mechanic's overalls, a housewife's apron, or the executive's business suit.

(b) If there could be saints in Caesar's household, then a person can be a Christian where you work. If these saints could live for Jesus Christ in the hardest of all places, surely you can live for Jesus Christ at your place of employment. It is simply a matter of commitment. If you want to live for Jesus, then you can.

There is no higher calling than to devote your life to the spread of God's Word. If you will see your work in that light, it will transform both you and your work. Your work will no longer be a drudgery. You will suddenly become concerned about both the quality and the quantity of your work. For even the way you do your work will be a means of preaching God's Word to those who do not believe it or practice it.

V. We can live for Christ in those hard places. The hard places, in fact, have always been the places where the most effective witness for Jesus Christ has been carried out.

With which Gospel do you think your friends at school, in the social circles you move in, and at your place of business are most familiar?

Are they closer to the kingdom of God—or farther from it—because of the Gospel According to You?—Gary C. Redding

Illustrations

BOLD CONFESSION.   There is an old story concerning the time when a certain monarch commanded one of the early Christians to recant and give up his devotion to Christ. The king threatened to banish him if he refused. But the man replied with a smile, "You cannot banish me from Christ, for he said, 'I will never leave thee nor forsake thee.'" The ruler angrily threatened, "I will confiscate your property." The Christian replied, "My treasures are laid up on high, you cannot get them." The monarch flew into a rage and exclaimed, "I will kill you!" The Christian answered, "I have been dead with Christ for fifty years, and my life is hid with Christ in God." No wonder the ruler angrily confessed, "What can you do with such a fanatic?"—G. Ray Jordan

FAMILY INFLUENCE.   A lady was brought into court for a crime. A sociologist had been assigned to interview her, for she had frequent brushes with the law. The sociologist asked her, "Can you think of anything in your childhood that might have turned your life?"

After a moment's reflection, she related this childhood incident. Her parents divorced, and her mother had to take a job, which required her to work nights. After school she would go out and play with the children. As darkness fell, the other parents would call to their children, "Come home, now, it's getting dark." But, said she, no one ever called me home. I have wondered if things would be different had someone called me by name and said, "It's time to come home now."—C. Neil Strait

Sermon Suggestions

WHEN FAITH BREAKS DOWN. TEXT: Exod. 17:1–7. (1) Situation: Things go well and faith in God is bright and obedient, verse 1a. (2) Complication: Difficulty comes, and questions and doubts arise, verses 1b–3. (3) Resolution: Because God cares for his people he blesses them despite their unworthiness, verses 4–7.

WHY PRAISE GOD? TEXT: Rom. 11: 33–36, NEB. (1) He is the Source of all that is. (2) He is the Guide of all that is. (3) He is the Goal of all that is.

Worship Aids

CALL TO WORSHIP. "Lift up your hands in the sanctuary, and bless the Lord. The Lord that made heaven and earth bless thee out of Zion" (Ps. 134:2–3).

INVOCATION. Today let our praise to you rise like the sun at dawn, growing brighter with gratitude and joy until our lives break forth in a paean of dedication and service.

OFFERTORY SENTENCE. "Therefore, my beloved brethren, be ye steadfast, unmoveable, always abounding in the work of the Lord, forasmuch as ye know that your labour is not in vain in the Lord" (1 Cor. 15:58).

OFFERTORY PRAYER. Searching Lord, let us behold thee in the mirror of thy Word and see thee reflected in the faces of need about us, as we give to make a difference and live to go about doing good in Jesus' name.—E. Lee Phillips

PRAYER. Creator God, whose breath is like the dawn of a new day and whose arms cradle us through the dark of night, whose hands hold the paths of our steps, and whose call gives direction to our lives; O Holy One, whose grace comes in the shadows as well as in the sunlight, we worship you as Lord and Master of all Creation and all providence. We praise you as genesis of life and salvation. Blessed by the name of our Lord!

Understanding Father, Giver of forgiveness, grant us wisdom to see our foolishness and humility to seek your gracious pardon. We confess our hardness of heart; we lack any sorrow for our sin; we ignore the cost of your free grace to us and place sin at the door of others. Father, forgive us and bring cleansing refreshment to our spirits.

Eternal God, Lord of all time and place, morning's cool gives hint that the seasons are changing. As autumn makes way, we are reminded it is a time of transition, and so we pray for all who are beginning a new journey. We pray for young children making their way to school for the first time; for parents who watch them leave with a tear in their eye and a longing in their heart. We pray for youth headed to middle school and high school; for teachers who offer shape and guidance to their learning. We pray for those going to college and graduate school; for all who are beginning seminary and giving answer to your call in their lives.

Lord Jesus, you who abide us to come and follow you: we pray for ourselves, and for our discipleship in you. Lead us to know the power and freedom of full surrender to you. As expression of our gratitude for you, may we offer our gift of total obedience to you. Lord, we have been confused by all the other voices in our lives and have been led astray by them. Help us to turn our ears and our eyes and our hearts toward you and come home. May we find our delight in you.

Remove the debris from our eyes that we may see you more clearly. Strike the distractions from our hearts that we may love you more dearly. Make way, make way in our lives, that we may follow you more nearly.—William M. Johnson

LECTIONARY MESSAGE

The Crucial Question
TEXT: Matt. 16:13–20

The personal nature of the relationship with Christ is emphasized in the Gospels. The questions at Caesarea Philippi marked the necessity of individual response. Jesus' question can legitimately be interpreted that he asked, "But who do *you* say that I am?" (Matt. 16:15). The crucial question is whether the disciples, and particularly Peter, recognized him as the Messiah.

I. *This rock.* Several systems of Christian belief have developed from the interpretations of "this rock." All acknowledge that Peter's confession is essential to each interpretation.

Peter gave a very personal answer of who he knew Jesus to be. Jesus himself identified the significant elements in the answer.

(a) The correct answer about the identity of the Messiah is based on divine revelation. Self-revelation is the basis of knowledge of God. Paul wrote the Romans that God had "announced" the gospel himself (Rom. 1:2, NEB).

(b) The blessing upon Peter was because of personal acceptance of the revelation. The importance of personal response is emphasized. God's revelation could be given to all, everywhere, but individual acceptance is essential for the correct answer to the crucial question.

(c) Peter was blessed because of his public confession. There is no way to know if others of the Twelve would have made the same response. Peter was the one who did and was the recipient of the messianic benediction. Jesus on another occasion stated that those who made a confession would be acknowledged as believers (Luke 12:8). Paul also emphasized the importance of public acknowledgment (Rom. 10:9).

II. *My church.* Centuries of identifying the church has resulted in variations at establishing the most approved form.

Jesus almost certainly used some derivation of the word for the Old Testament congregation. His concern was for establishing those who would be recognized as belonging to him and with whom he would be willing to be identified.

Need for identification with a group does not seem to be as important in today's society as in earlier times. Yet, even in a time of individualism, identity and "belonging" still have great value. To be a part of the people of God, the fellowship of those who have acknowledged the Messiah, still has great significance.

III. *The gates of Hades.* The ancient city gates had several important functions. The application to only one of these would limit the possible significance of the reference.

(a) Gates were a part of the city's defense. The victory of Christ and his church is assured by the announcement that the gates of Hades will not be able to withstand their efforts. For those who frequently ask, "Why is evil present in the world?" this should not be interpreted as being accomplished either immediately or easily.

(b) Gates, as walls, are used to contain or restrain. If Hades is interpreted to mean death or the grave, the people of Christ are given assurance that they will experience ultimate victory. Even the "last enemy" will not be able to contain or overcome them.

(c) The city gate for ancient society was the place of counsel and government, the embodiment of secular society. The congregation of God is reminded that there is a responsibility for this element of society and that ultimately this too will be subject to the Lord of Life.—Arthur L. Walker, Jr.

SUNDAY: SEPTEMBER SECOND

SERVICE OF WORSHIP

Sermon: Why We Work

TEXT: Col. 3:23

In this message I want to consider a little, but worthwhile, question about work: Why? Why do we work? I believe that if we all clearly understood why we work and if we were all working for a good reason, there would be a genuine improvement in the quality of life in North America.

I. Have you ever asked yourself why you work? Maybe you work just to get a paycheck along with other benefits, such as a pension, vacations, and hospitalization insurance. If it were not for these, would you walk away from your job tomorrow? And when you are old enough to retire, are you going to quit your job with great joy and relief?

(a) I have a feeling you would agree with me that one of the reasons we're in trouble these days is that many people are working only for money—nothing more. As a result, some medical doctors are doing a marginal job, some teachers are doing a lot of damage to our children, some preachers are dishonoring the name of Christ, and some assembly-line workers are turning out products that have to be taken back for repair the day after you buy them.

(b) But the problem is not just that some of the results of work are shoddy and not up to par. What's worse, and even tragic, is that when people don't know why they are working, they lose one of the major joys that human beings can have. Doing work that one feels is significant and important is one of the greatest privileges a human being can have. When a majority of a nation's work force works only for money and for little else, life in that nation turns dismal.

(c) In dealing with issues like these, we are actually entering the area of religion. Often we do not realize that religion is concerned with mundane, workaday matters. Some religion, of course, has nothing at all to do with ordinary work because it is totally otherworldly, encouraging people to separate themselves from the world of work. But as soon as anyone becomes familiar with the Bible, he or she discovers that the Christian faith has a great deal to do with work.

II. One of the most attractive elements of the Christian faith is that it turns the workplace into a place of worship. In this regard I want to read some sentences from Colossians 3 which were originally addressed to workers in the first century.

(a) These workers, I must say, were actually slaves. Now, before we wonder how something written long ago to slaves could possibly be useful for us today, we must remember that slaves then carried out many of the same tasks that our work force today performs. The Bible, in addressing slaves, is not condoning slavery as such but is simply taking that existing social situation and speaking directly to people who were involved in it.

(b) What the Bible says here in Colossians 3 to the slaves of the first century is also very appropriate for working people today. If slaves were instructed to think of their work as serving Christ, people who are free workers should most certainly consider their work a service to the Lord.

What Colossians 3 says to us is liberating and revolutionary. Viewing ourselves in our work as serving Christ, who is our Master in heaven—this idea jars us. Does this include ordinary work like driving a truck, building a house, or working at a computer terminal for hours on end? Yes, it does; this principle applies to ordinary, everyday work. But is Christ really interested in our ordinary work? Yes, he most certainly is.

The Bible says that the God who exists has revealed himself fully in the person of Jesus Christ, and this Jesus is so interested in me that he wants me to think of all the work I do as something I do for him.

(c) When this message first came to those first-century slaves, it changed everything for them. Their bosses remained important, but they could now look past their bosses to Jesus Christ the Lord. When they had a job that was not particularly pleasant, they could do it well because they knew that in so doing, they were pleasing the Lord Jesus Christ. You see, Christianity is a force that always frees slaves. These slaves were invited to free themselves from the narrow service they had been giving their masters. They were encouraged to work hard and to view their work as done for God himself.

III. The Bible's message about work, which freed slaves in the first century, can still bring freedom to workers who believe the Bible and who want to serve Jesus Christ today.

(a) People who believe in Jesus Christ and who are part of the work force would have an unusual answer if someone were to ask them, "Why are you working?" They would say, "I am doing this because Jesus wants me to do it. I am doing it for him. I am doing it as well as I can because I don't want to present inferior work to Jesus. Christ has saved me, and he wants me to do everything, even my work, for his glory."

(b) I realize this sounds very different from what we usually hear. But, believe me, when you take the entire Bible's message, this is where you come out. Work is one of the greatest goods in the world. The God who is at the center of Christianity is a working God. On the sixth day of his creating work in the beginning, God made our first parents and put them in charge of the rest of his Creation; he gave to people the responsibility of working and taking care of the earth.

(c) The Bible proclaims a gospel for the workers of the world. Working people, unite around the Bible and discover that your work is as holy as the sacrament of Baptism. Your work is significant as the very plan of the almighty God. Work is good and beautiful. Our work is the best gift we can offer to God our Creator.

IV. Take a look at your life, and ask yourself if you are involved in work that you can offer to Christ. Of course, before you can do that, you have to take a look at Jesus Christ himself. Maybe you have never believed in him. If so, what I have been talking about has probably sounded pretty ridiculous to you.

(a) Do you understand that Jesus Christ is the Son of the living God and that he has died on the cross to pay for human sin? Do you realize that if you believed in Jesus Christ and threw yourself on him fully, he would save you and bring you to glory when you die? Do you know that when you believe in Jesus Christ, he will send his Holy Spirit into your life and change you through and through? He will make your life beautiful and meaningful as never before.

(b) God is interested in your work. He wants you to ask why you do what you do. God wants you to turn to his Son, Jesus Christ, surrendering to him completely so that your life will be changed for the good. This change will surely involve your work, too.—Joel Nederhood

Illustrations

STILL WORKING.　　Think of Moses, who at eighty years of age led three and a half million people out of captivity. Or Caleb, who at eighty-five . . . said, "Give me that mountain." Or Colonel Sanders, who at seventy . . . discovered "finger lickin' " good chicken. Or Ray Krock, who after seventy introduced a Big Mac to the world. Then there's Casey Stengel, who at seventy-five became the manager of the Yankees. . . . And there's Picasso, still painting at eighty-eight, and George Washington Carver, who at eighty-one became head of the Agriculture Department. There's Thomas Edison, who at eighty-five invented the mimeograph machine, and John Wesley, who was still traveling on horseback and preaching at age eighty-eight.—John C. Maxwell

KEEP ON GROWING.　　One could go on and on describing the avenues of growth. Suffice it to say here that this process should never end. The growing Christian never graduates or retires. He will grow while growing older. Some persons grow bitter and sour with advancing age. The difference in them and the sainted Christian who seems to grow sweeter with every passing year might be summarized by saying that whereas the former is only "growing old" the latter is continuing to "grow."

And such will be kin to the alpine climber whose tombstone contains the simple but pregnant inscription, "He died climbing!" Or like the youthful university student who passed away shortly before graduation. Commenting on his premature passing, his college president noted that although he died before his furrow was finished, he left it with his plow pointed in the right direction.—Robert Hastings

Sermon Suggestions

ON EAGLE'S WINGS.　　TEXT: Exod. 19: 1–19, RSV. (1) God chooses a people. (2) God delivers these people. (3) God works through his elect for the blessing of all people.

BEHAVING AS A CHRISTIAN SHOULD.
TEXT: Rom. 12:1–13, especially verses 1
and 2. (1) What we must do: (a) offer ourselves to God; (b) let ourselves be transformed. (2) How we can do it: by the
mercies of God. (3) To what end will we
do it: to know and do the will of God.

Worship Aids

CALL TO WORSHIP. "For we are laborers together with God: ye are God's hus-
bandry, ye are God's building. According
to the grace of God which is given unto
me, as a wine master-builder, I have laid
the foundation, and another buildeth
thereon. But let every man take heed how
he buildeth thereupon" (1 Cor. 3:9–11).

INVOCATION. Lord, as we gather, give
to us that oneness of spirit and resolve of
will that has characterized the church
down through the ages. Allow us to be
agents of reconciliation and disciples of
love because we have taken the time to
worship and call thy name in prayer.—E.
Lee Phillips

OFFERTORY SENTENCE. "As every man
hath received the gift, even so minister the
same one to another, as good stewards of
the manifold grace of God" (1 Pet. 4:10).

OFFERTORY PRAYER. Lord, we who are
grateful for the opportunity to earn our
way, now give for those who in body and
soul are needier than we are. Through thy
Spirit do what we cannot do, but what we
know in thee is possible.—E. Lee Phillips

PRAYER. We cry to thee for justice, O
Lord, for our soul is weary with the iniquity of greed. Behold the servants of Mammon, who defy thee and drain their
fellow-men for gain; who grind down the
strength of the workers by merciless toil
and fling them aside when they are mangled and worn; who rack-rent the poor
and make dear the space and air which
thou hast made free; who paralyze the
hand of justice by corruption and blind the
eyes of the people by lies; who nullify by
their craft the merciful laws which nobler
men have devised for the protection of the

weak; who have made us ashamed of our
dear country by their defilements and have
turned our holy freedom into a hollow
name; who have brought upon thy Church
the contempt of men and have cloaked
their extortion with the Gospel of thy
Christ.

For the oppression of the poor and the
sighing of the needy now do thou arise, O
Lord; for because thou art love, and tender as a mother to the weak, therefore
thou art the great hater of iniquity and thy
doom is upon those who grow rich on the
poverty of the people.

O God, we are afraid, for the thunder-
cloud of thy wrath is even now black above
us. In the ruins of dead empires we have
read how thou hast trodden the wine-
press of thine anger when the measure of
their sin was full. We are sick at heart when
we remember that by the greed of those
who remember a weaker race that curse
was fastened upon us which still lies black
and hopeless across our land, though the
blood of a nation was spilled to atone.
Save our people from being dragged
down into guilt and woe by men who have
no vision and know no law except their
lust. Shake their souls with awe of thee
that they may cease. Help us with clean
hands to tear the web which they have
woven about us and to turn our people
back to thy law, lest the mark of the beast
stand out on the right hand and forehead
of our nation and our feet be set on the
downward path of darkness from which
there is no return forever.—Walter
Rauschenbusch

LECTIONARY MESSAGE

Cost of Discipleship
TEXT: Matt. 16:21–28
The Twelve were called upon to acknowledge the Messiah before they were
asked to accept the terms of discipleship.
Jesus' concern for the masses and for the
disciples was both what was required to
understand messiahship and discipleship.
Understanding was essential for a willingness to accept the cost of discipleship.

I. Death is essential to redemption, but

it is the prelude to resurrection. The teaching of Jesus concerning the nature of his ministry was summed up in verse 21. His ministry was certainly very different from that which was expected both in the Old Testament concept of Messiah and in the concept of lordship held by the Twelve. Messiahship involved outcomes more than had been previously understood.

(a) Suffering and death added a dimension to the role of the Messiah in salvation that had not been understood previously.

(b) Resurrection would reveal an aspect of both God's power and salvation that would go beyond earlier understanding.

II. Peter could accept lordship, but he could not accept the price of lordship. Just as Jesus' teaching continued for some time, Peter had opportunity to consider some of the teachings and as a consequence attempted to turn Jesus from his purpose. Peter renewed the temptations that had been offered in the wilderness experience. The renewed temptation was "to take the short and easy route to the Messiah's throne."

(a) Many today want the ultimate values of relationship with Christ without accepting the price of this relationship.

(b) Jesus taught that the disciple also must take up a cross in order to follow him. The denial of self and selfish concerns is the price required of the one who would become what God intended for his follower.

(c) The acquisition of wealth and the accomplishment of all the goals of success are not worth the cost of one's life-soul! Possessions and success are temporal values that lose value and will ultimately cost more than life.

III. The choice between safety (security) or one's life reflects the warning of inevitable judgment. Throughout this passage Jesus reflects a choice.

(a) He made the choice to do the will of his Father, and this choice will result in his rejection by the religious leaders.

(b) Jesus called upon Peter to make a choice between following him or being the stumbling block for Satan.

(c) His call to all disciples to follow him is a choice between discipleship, which gives life, and the choice of personal security, which means ultimate death.

Jesus' promise that some of his followers would see him coming in his power reflects again that his suffering in Jerusalem and the death on the cross were not to be the ultimate end. Whatever the explanation for seeing "the Son of man coming in his kingdom" the promise to his disciples is that the events to take place will be the releasing of a divine power in the lives of individuals and of the world.—Arthur L. Walker, Jr.

SUNDAY: SEPTEMBER NINTH

SERVICE OF WORSHIP

Sermon: Believe That Life Is Worth Living, and Your Belief Will Create the Fact
TEXT: Mark 7:1

I. Have you participated in some aspect or ritual of life that arrested your growth, your maturation, your "becomingness" under God?

(a) None of us would consciously seek arrested development in our lives; neither did the Jews. Those who came to Jesus were devout men and women; they honored the traditions of the fathers, but in so doing, they neglected the life of the Spirit.

(b) We might ask ourselves, why would men and women in any religious tradition in any century or time deny the privilege of participating in the unfolding of God's Creation, to hear, to receive, to live the new commandments of God?

(c) Well, for many reasons, as many reasons as there are attributes to our blessed human nature. Not the least among them is the possibility that in our youth we had been successful. I can think of no greater burden in our society than for a young man or woman to do well in school and to live in the very understandable assumption that life is like school. It most assuredly is not. So one develops a spectrum of expectations about life that, for this reason or that, can never be fulfilled.

(d) When one goes out into life, having succeeded early on as a student or perhaps in one's early professional life and one is relatively untroubled by failure or grave personal disappointment, that success brings with it a great fright of that which is new. Such success encourages one to honor the traditions of the fathers, or, as we say in the colloquial idiom, "to play the game," to be part of the institutional life of our world, not challenging any aspect of the world—not the political life, not the mores of the culture, not the religious life of the church. It encourages one to honor the traditions of the fathers and to fear when God does whisper in our souls, fearing that we might break step with those around us. So Jesus tutors us about arrested existence, however generated.

II. Jesus calls us to the inward journey, to the inner life of your soul and mine. We reflect upon our society and our generation, and we think of men and women through the ages who have wrestled with the problem of freedom and determinism.

(a) Are we determined? Or is it possible that there can be some listening, some listening in your soul and mine that surmounts all of these environmental factors? Is there a listening in your soul and mine that surmounts our heritage? How easy it is for any one of us to say, "I would have been this or that had I been born into another family, a wealthy family, a prominent family, a well-educated family." How easy it is for us to fall back into the outward journey and the assumption that in some fateful fashion we have been determined by the world around us.

(b) Not so says the Christ. "Come with me," says this Jesus. "Live with me in the unfolding of God's commandment. Participate with me in the growth of his Creation in your soul." And Jesus said to those who would hear him, "Man's ultimate giving to life is what comes out of him." Not what goes into man, not the environment that impinges upon him, nor the heredity that is the structure of his genetic train. No, it is what comes out of a man that counts. Yet, in our depression, frustration, or fear

that we are determined, evil thoughts, murderous thoughts, deceitful thoughts, pride—how many things do come out of us in our frustration, in our fear that we are determined?

III. We read in Holy Scripture, from one end to the other, that man is created in the image of God. Man was called of God in the beginning of time to join with him in the unfolding and direction of his Creation. Did not Jesus turn to his disciples when they were confounded by his miracles and say to them, "Greater things than this shall you do in my name"?

(a) Jesus calls us to honor the truth of the past. He calls us to be good students, to succeed in our learning, yet not be trapped by our success. God calls us to be successful in any discipline we undertake, but he also calls us to open ourselves to yet more and more and more truth.

(b) Jesus calls us to think of his commandments as a precious whispering of the Spirit in our prayers as we come together at his holy table to be fed this morning and to hear again in a new way the promises of God.

(c) Go to the God room of your life. Go to your soul, pull in the traditions and truth of the fathers; honor it, and move beyond it. You and I, on this day, are called of God to receive the whispering of his angels, to receive in our souls the new commandments of our heavenly Father.— Spencer M. Rice

Illustrations

CHERISH YOUR VISION. He who cherishes a beautiful vision, a lofty ideal in his heart, will one day realize it. Columbus cherished a vision of another world, and he discovered it; Copernicus fostered the vision of a multiplicity of worlds and a wider universe, and he revealed it; Buddha beheld the vision of a spiritual world of stainless beauty and perfect peace, and he entered into it.

Cherish your visions; cherish your ideals; cherish the music that stirs in your heart, the beauty that forms in your mind, the loveliness that drapes your purest thoughts, for out of them will grow all delightful conditions, all heavenly environment; of these, if you but remain true to them, your world will at last be built.—James Allen

WHAT WE CALL EVIL. Much of what we call evil is due entirely to the way men take the phenomenon. It can so often be converted into a bracing and tonic good by a simple change of the sufferer's inner attitude from one of fear to one of fight; its sting can so often depart and turn into a relish when, after vainly seeking to shun it, we agree to face about and bear it cheerfully; that a man is simply bound in honor, with reverence to many of the facts that seem at first to disconcern his peace, to adopt this way of escape. Refuse to admit their badness; despise their power; ignore their presence; turn your attention the other way; and so far as you yourself are concerned at any rate, though the facts may still exist, their evil character exists no longer. Since you make them evil or good by your own thoughts about them, it is the ruling of your thoughts which proves to be your principal concern.—William James

Sermon Suggestions

WHEN A PEOPLE IS SPECIAL TO GOD. TEXT: Exod. 19:1–9. (1) God delivers them. (2) God gives them a holy task. (3) God stays in touch with them.

THE GOOD OF GOVERNMENT. TEXT: Rom. 13:1–10. (1) It is authorized by God. (2) It is for our good. (3) Its aims can be better achieved through love than through law.

Worship Aids

CALL TO WORSHIP. "Thou wilt keep him in perfect peace, whose mind is stayed on thee: because he trusteth in thee. Trust ye the Lord for ever: for in the Lord Jehovah is everlasting strength" (Isa. 26:3–4).

INVOCATION. You never change, O Lord, but we are always changing, sometimes for the better, sometimes for the worse. Grant us steadier progress in our life of faith as we contemplate what you are and seek after what we may become through your grace.

OFFERTORY SENTENCE. "What shall I render unto the Lord for all his benefits toward me? I will take the cup of salvation, and call upon the name of the Lord. I will pay my vows unto the Lord now in the presence of all his people" (Ps. 116:12–14).

OFFERTORY PRAYER. For some of us it is easy and painless to give; for others, a strain and sacrifice. But it is a source of joy for all who consider all your benefits, O Lord, whether rich or poor. Some would give more, who can only give less; some give less, who could give more. Yet you are able to use and multiply all that we bring to you. So we bring our offerings and ask you to bless them.

PRAYER. O heavenly Father, who hast filled the world with beauty: Open our eyes to behold thy gracious hand in all thy words; that, rejoicing in thy whole creation, we may learn to serve thee with gladness; for the sake of him through whom all things were made, thy Son Jesus Christ our Lord.—*The Book of Common Prayer*

LECTIONARY MESSAGE

Restoring Those Who Sin

TEXT: Matt. 18:15–20

The way that God, who is pictured as a shepherd in the earlier verses of chapter 18, deals with his erring sheep seems to lead naturally to the way one should deal with an erring brother. Jesus said, Spare no effort in making things right with your brother.

God's love for the lost sheep is only an indication of the effort expected of the Christian in winning one who has sinned. Jesus gave specific ways to mend broken fellowship.

I. *Go to the brother.* The admonition to be reconciled could be expected from One later described by the words, "While we were yet sinners, Christ died for us." On another occasion (Matt. 5:23–24) Jesus placed the responsibility for initiating reconciliation with the wrongdoer. He suggested here the one wronged should initiate reconciliation. More than who should take the lead is the emphasis upon the importance of reconciliation.

II. *Tell him the problem.* Jesus emphasized discussing the problem, for it assures that both the one wronged and the one who has done the wrong understand the problem. There is the possibility that the one who wronged another did not understand the nature of the hurt. There is also the implication that the one harmed may be reading more into the incident than is actually there. The discussion could well assist each in understanding the true nature of the problem.

III. *Seek further help.* The call for additional help emphasizes that new concern must be given the search for reconciliation. The witnesses are to give evidence that attempts are being made for reconciliation and that the responses are the proper ones. The witnesses are to observe the attitudes and motives on both sides. Christian fellowship provides opportunity for relationships to develop. Christian fellowship also seeks to deal with every circumstance in love. The purpose of enlarging the fellowship is to move beyond selfish personal reactions that may hamper reconciliation. The atmosphere of fellowship created by witnesses is to demonstrate that there is a yearning for reconciliation and a sincere effort at establishing it.

IV. *Win him.* Jesus' admonition concerning one who has refused to hear the Christian assembly is difficult to interpret. The climate of the discussion would seem to indicate that Jesus was talking about the opposite of abandonment. He was saying to let the one who refuses to be reconciled become the object of even greater love.

Jesus says that to assume that the one who had done the wrong was a brother was an error. Since he is not already a brother then the responsibility is to make him one.

V. *Conclusion.* The emphasis upon a common Lord and a common purpose moves to agreement concerning truth. The purpose of reconciliation is common commitment to God's purpose. When two seek that purpose, each is lifted to a level beyond himself. Selfishness is no longer the basic motivation, and their search could well be God's purpose. Their petition will likely be for that which God wishes to happen. Though they may be limited in their understanding of that for which they should ask, the answer will be that which God knows to be best. Perhaps far more significant, Jesus seems to be saying that the action of believers has eternal significance. He calls upon the believers to be careful about those things in which they are involved.—Arthur L. Walker, Jr.

SUNDAY: SEPTEMBER SIXTEENTH

SERVICE OF WORSHIP

Sermon: Doubt and Faith

TEXT: Ps. 77:7–9, 14

These words reveal to us a man in what is a not uncommon state of mind, and it is of that state of mind I want to speak. The state of mind is this: that a man finds his thoughts about God in conflict with one another. There is one side of him which, when it is active, finds it an easy thing to affirm God. There is another side of him which finds it just as easy to doubt and deny the goodness of God and even to question whether there is, in any sense that really matters to anybody, a God at all.

It is hardly necessary, I think, to give other illustrations of this state of conflict in the soul, of doubt confronting faith and faith doubt: of something within us that instantly says, "Yes! A thousand times yes!" to all that the New Testament bids us to believe about God, wrestling with something else within us which whispers, and indeed sometimes even bawls down the corridors of the mind, "No! It cannot be; it is a dream."

That being the state of affairs, what are we to do about it? I want to put to you this: That there is an extremely important question in regard to this conflict which we ought to ask and to answer, which we ought to settle with ourselves, once and for all, and perhaps the sooner we do it, the better. It is this: To which of these two voices in the soul concerning God are we going to make up our minds deliberately and consciously always to give the greater weight? Are we going to adopt the policy of always putting our belief in God in the dock and making it justify itself before the magistrate of our doubts, and if it cannot do so, cast it out? Or are we going to adopt the policy of always putting our doubt, our unbelief, in the dock and making it justify itself fully before the magistrate of our belief, and if it cannot do so, cast it out?

For my part I have settled it with myself that without running away from doubts and questionings I am always going to put the greater emphasis on faith. I am always going to put my doubts in the dock first. I am going to doubt doubt before I doubt faith. When it comes to an issue, I am going to trust deliberately and consciously to trust my belief, my faith, that deep something within me which affirms God, which says yes to the God revealed in the New Testament, and to seek to direct my life accordingly. I have come to that conclusion for four main reasons, which I want to state to you very briefly.

I. The first reason is this: I have noticed this quite unmistakable fact about myself, and I can only ask you to observe whether it is not true of you also, that my doubts and skepticisms about God tend to grow in frequency and force when my personal life for one reason or another has dropped to what can only be called a lower level.

(a) When in an even greater degree than is usual the spirit of slackness has crept in, when personal attitudes to others have not been what they ought to be, when, in the presence of the high requirements of righteousness and truth, I have prevaricated and compromised and indulged myself, then the positive affirmation of faith in God has seemed to grow more difficult and the negative attitude of doubt and unbelief and fear more easy. The vision of God seems, in short, to vary with the order or disorder of my personal and moral life.

(b) Perhaps this is what Jesus had in mind when he said, Blessed are the pure in heart, for they shall see God. Seeing God, on the one hand, and a certain sincerity of mind, a certain singleness of purpose in relation to what we know to be good and evil or right and wrong, on the other hand, do undoubtedly go together. What, then, follows from this? Does it not plainly follow that the sensible thing to do, when it comes to a choice, is to trust, and to continue to trust, those things which I see most clearly when my life is at its best and to distrust the doubts which arise, or at least gain strength, when it is not at its best?

II. The second reason is this. I have noticed that as people live in the light of belief in God, so many of those very things in life which help to create and nourish doubt and unbelief tend either to disappear or, if not to disappear, to lose their power to defeat and overwhelm the soul. Let me say a word on both these points.

(a) First, then, belief in God tends to eliminate many of the evil things in life which suggest unbelief. Is there any question that a great many of such evil things are themselves, in the first instance, created by unbelief, by men's refusal to live as though there really is a divine purpose of righteousness and love at work in the world with which they have in the end to settle all accounts? They may cause unbelief, but they are themselves caused by unbelief and would disappear with the unbelief itself. I can stand here now and think of a half dozen evil situations I have personally observed, which are spreading a blight all around them, and which there is not the least hope of ever being put right until one or two persons involved can be brought to live a life of faith instead of a life of unbelief.

(b) Second, it has been found again and again that if a man, when he is confronted with some evil which suggests unbelief and skepticism and doubt to his soul, ignores the suggestion and tackles the evil on the basis of faith in God, then, it begins to lose all its power even to make precisely that suggestion. The evidence is that some of life's richest gifts come, like registered parcels, in coverings which are tough and ugly and heavily sealed and tied with a multitude of entangling knots. Tackle the knots, remove the coverings, in the faith that the gift is there, and, behold, you find the gift and the wonder of an overshadowing presence.

III. The third reason why I have decided always to trust my belief against my doubt is that I can see clearly why the God who speaks to my heart through all that is beautiful and good and true in human life and, above all, through Christ and the pages of the New Testament should have left me to make precisely this choice, should have left room for doubts and questionings. If his aim is, as the New Testament says it is, to bring me to a mature personal life, in which I am a son to him and not merely a slave or a puppet or a child, then he must leave room in my life for sheer adventurous faith and trust, for a readiness to affirm and commit myself to his goodness, even when I cannot for the life of me understand what he is at and evil things happen which I would have preferred otherwise. The point is, given the truth of my belief in God, I can see a reason why I am allowed to have doubts. But if I start from the supposition that my doubts are true and there is no God, I cannot see why something within me should speak so plainly and compellingly of him.

IV. The fourth reason is Jesus Christ. I look at Jesus and I see—well, what do I see? Not the somewhat meek and placid figure that looks down upon us from a stained-glass window or from the pictures in a book of Bible stories for children. God forbid. I see a being of, literally, tremendous intellectual power. The more I study the Gospels, the more I am impressed with the sheer mental force of Jesus.

(a) The beauty of the world deeply stirred his soul. His sayings and parables are those of a poet. I see, above all, a being of intense moral purity and strength, one so utterly released from himself that at one and the same time he has walked to the middle of the stage of history like a God and yet has been forever afterwards the very pattern of humility. As I stand alongside him I know, without any affectation, that I am infinitely small and poor, and he infinitely great and rich, in personal life. And further, I find this: Even as he is greater than I in every way, so he is the more certain than I am of God. The fog of unbelief and doubt which drifts at times across my spirit is absent from his.

(b) And if you say as you might well say, But was there not a time when Christ also doubted? did he not also in the weakness and agony of the cross cry, "My God, my God, why hast thou forsaken me"? the reply is that, when I come, as I must often come in this tragic world, to stake my life on Christ and on his vision of God rather than on my feeble thoughts and feelings, then I am more thankful than I can say that the cry of the Master is there recorded for us in the Gospels. For it shows that Christ himself at least once knew the fullest weight and pressure of those things which in our human life seem to hide the face of God, knew it as none of us can ever know it. Yes, and it shows too that even then he won the victory. For this is not a cry of defeat, not a cry of loss of faith: it is rather faith thrusting through to its final victory. It is faith asking a question, not unbelief asking it, for the question is addressed to my God, my God. And the answer was given to his cry, for shortly afterwards he said, "Into thy hands I commend my spirit." God succors our faith, not less, but more because of that cry upon the cross.

V. Will you think about these things? Will you, especially those who are younger, make this decision that, if and when it comes to a conflict of two voices in your soul, you will always trust that voice that speaks of God rather than that one that is minded to deny him? You will doubt your doubts before you doubt that to which all that is best within you really points, namely, that Christ is the Way and the Truth and the Life and to him and to his vision of God you may, you must, come what may, commit your whole being and your whole life.—Herbert H. Farmer

Illustrations

EASY ANSWERS.   A cartoon in a *New Yorker* magazine showed a middle-aged couple, at least I judged them to be middle-aged, . . . standing in the square of what appeared to be a small town. Across from them was a restaurant that offered FREE LUNCH, a library that proclaimed EASY ANSWERS, a pharmacy selling CURE-ALLS, and a repair shop that was advertising a QUICK FIX. And he said to his wife, "Hey, I like this town."—Bob Benson

GOD INCOGNITO. Dr. Jacks of England described a friend of his, a shoemaker, in words that apply to some people I know: "He spent his breath in proving that God did not exist, but spent his life in proving that He did." Friend, you do have dealings with God. Stop calling that experience by another name, and recognize it for what it is.—Harry Emerson Fosdick.

Sermon Suggestions

THE LEAST GOD EXPECTS. TEXT: Exod. 20:1–20. (1) The motivation, verses 1–2. (2) The mandate, verses 3–17. (3) The mystery of the mountain, verses 18–20.

THE BASICS OF CHRISTIAN TOLERANCE. TEXT: Rom. 14:5–12, especially verse 12. (1) Each of us is accountable to God. (2) Yet we are inclined to judge each other's way of serving God. (3) However, we have an obligation to be helpful and supportive, verse 13.

Worship Aids

CALL TO WORSHIP. "We have thought of thy loving kindness, O God, in the midst of thy temple. According to thy name, O God, so is thy praise unto the ends of the earth: thy right hand is full of righteousness" (Ps. 48:9–10).

INVOCATION. Lord God of the universe, the world that you have created is so vast that we cannot begin to comprehend its reach. It almost causes us to despair that a God who created something so big, so wonderful could have anything to do with us. But the fact is that on one tiny speck of dust some even tinier beings have gathered to worship their creator, and that

creator will hear them. Thank you, Lord, for caring as much for being with us while we worship you as you care about keeping our planet spinning in space. We don't know what we would do if you weren't that kind of God.—James M. King.

OFFERTORY SENTENCE. "Greater love hath no man than this, that a may lay down his life for his friends" (John 15:13).

OFFERTORY PRAYER. Through this offering, Lord, save the lost, comfort the grieving, feed the hungry, nurture the saints, and shed abroad the light of Christ Jesus in every corner of need.—E. Lee Phillips

PRAYER. She said it for so many of us, Father. "I am beginning to feel like I am losing the battle." We all get there sometimes. Strength goes and seems not to come back again. Body and mind grow tired of the wrestling matches we have to enter so often. And we know that we are not alone. Loved ones care and pray for us. Above all we have been taught that you never leave us and are an ever-present help. But this morning we just need to rest in you for a while, to cease the struggling and let go of all we are handling. Some here need to be assured that you will get them through the breaking point without breaking. We do not ask that we be blessed with either sunshine or shadow, only that we be aware of your presence with us. Then we will have courage in this place at this time to bear stress without grumbling and weariness without complaint. Then we will not face uncertainty without hope and goals long delayed without patience. Then we can keep on trusting when we cannot understand the "whys" of life. Father, remind us with constant repetition that is is the one who sticks gallantly to right, as you give the right, who in the end will be saved.

Yet sometimes we cannot help feeling that we are the ones Jesus meant when he was talking about people of little faith. We hear your truth, but doubts crowd into our minds and hearts, and sometimes we really do wonder if you care about us. Sometimes we even wonder if you hear our prayers. But in our more rational moments we know that we could not even live and face life without your caring and presence. So this morning, Father, give us the perfect and serene confidence that can lean back and say, "Into your hands I commit my spirit, for life, for death, and for life to come."—W. Henry Fields

LECTIONARY MESSAGE

No Limit to Forgiveness
TEXT: Matt. 18:21–35

Peter is frequently pictured as "everyman." His reaction is so typical that he could be any one of us. His question concerning the number of times one must forgive reflects the implied question, Do I have no rights for justice? The answer simply says, Imitate God.

I. Do not keep a count of the times of forgiveness. Jewish tradition set the limit of three times for forgiveness. No human should be expected to be more generous than God, and the interpreters limited his forgiveness according to Amos 1:3; 2:1. One was very gracious if he forgave four times. Peter thought he had been unusual by forgiving the sinning brother seven times. The unlimited forgiveness of God is reflected in that seventy times seven means "without limit."

To be able to forgive without limit also means that the number of times previously that forgiveness has been given is not remembered. If forgiveness has been exercised properly one even forgets that he has been sinned against, so there is nothing to be counted.

II. Human forgiveness can never compare with the forgiveness shown by God. In the parable of the forgiving king, the debt was so great that, in fact, it could never be repaid. In addition, Jesus very pointedly emphasized that the man did not have the means to pay (18:25a). Both conditions emphasize the generosity of the forgiven debt. Each also emphasizes the nature of God in his willingness to forgive those who seek his mercy. The same conditions prevail: The debt we owe God is far beyond reckoning, and we have no way to repay any amount owed to God. How great is his mercy in that he does forgive even though this is true.

When these truths are applied in human relations the believer is made aware that the offense of any person against us is shown to be trivial compared with our sins against God.

III. An unforgiving spirit is incapable of receiving God's forgiveness. Jesus' final word on this parable says much about both human and divine nature. His emphasis on being forgiving as a condition for being forgiven (Matt. 6:12, 14–15) seems to indicate that one must understand forgiveness in order to accept it. The sad truth is that the same applies to love. One must know how to love in order to be able to accept love.

Jesus' picture of the reaction of the king to his unforgiving servant also reflects God's expectation of his people. The king is described as "angry" (18:34) because his forgiving attitude is not imitated by his servant. Jesus clearly taught that the standard of God is to be practiced by his followers. This led Alfred Plummer to write, "The love that forgives is as necessary as the faith that prays."

The Christian attitude in human relations is clearly that which mediates to others the love and forgiveness one has received from God. To be able to exercise the most difficult social experience of forgiveness indicates that one appreciates the nature of God's attitude in forgiving those who sin against him.—Arthur L. Walker, Jr.

SUNDAY: SEPTEMBER TWENTY-THIRD

SERVICE OF WORSHIP

Sermon: On Being Self-Made and Falling in Love with Our Creator!
TEXTS: Job 42:1–6; James 4:13–17; 5:7–11; Mark 9:38–50.

Yes, the title of the sermon is mine, but the idea belonged to another. His name was Joseph Parker, and he was a splendid British preacher of another generation. I can't recall his exact words, but they said, in effect, that the main problem with self-made men was that they frequently fell in love with their creator. Lose the sexist language, make it inclusive, and we have an accurate statement.

I. Or to put it in the words of the Epistle of James, "But now you are proud, and you boast; all such boasting is wrong." So, if you will allow me a trip from a long sermon title to a short sermon theme, I suppose it will deliver us to the concept of humility.

(a) I must confess that this characteristic has been rather far down the totem pole of Christian virtues for me.

I think that is so because my models of humility in my younger life were dishonest. They didn't mean to be, but my models appeared to want to look humble, and that led to a denigrating self-effacement that had all the subtlety of a slight-of-hand magician's rope trick. I was so turned off by this false self-castigation that I made the statement in my thirties that most of the folks I had seen in my life who were overly modest had every reason to be. But that was brash youthfulness. I've moderated that some; but I'm still leery of assumed humility that soft sells one's gifts in order to be thought humble. Much of it is like the preacher who said that he had "a magnificent sermon on humility, but I've not yet had a crowd big enough to preach it to."

(b) I can't speak from much experience, but I suspect that genuine humility, like most of the other Christian virtues, comes to us on our way to somewhere else. I'm

enchanted with the monarch butterfly. One afternoon I was busy pulling weeds, and suddenly one lit on my arm, and I was able for a few glorious moments to study its beauty. I think that's the way it is with Christian virtues like humility: We are busy here and there with other things, and suddenly something shows up in our lives. I'm fairly certain that if we try to catch it, grasp it, it will elude us.

(c) Drama and literature have always known about those mixed messages, so they employed a ready-to-walk-on character in those classic art forms. He was known as the *miles gloriosus*, the bragging soldier who reminded us at his appearance that we do have that tendency in us to be the kind of creatures that falls in love with his self-made image.

To move us from the *miles gloriosus* image, James reminds us of the limitations we all have. Hear him again,

Now listen to me, you that say, "Today or tomorrow we will travel to a certain city, where we will stay a year and go into business and make a lot of money." You don't even know what your life tomorrow will be! You are like a puff of smoke, which appears for a moment and then disappears. What you should say is this: "If the Lord is willing, we will live and do this or that" (James 5:13–15, TEV).

II. It was the struggle without corporate limitations that gave rise to the drama Job. Now, I do not take Job to be a literal man. This is not a historical documentary. Job is a sixth-century B.C. drama formed out of the struggle with our human suffering and how we ought to respond to a God who is, Job suspected, intimately related to it yet lets it go on. What was happening in Israel was that the old answers about suffering—that it is God's punishment for sin or is given to teach us something or always has some purpose to it or helps us to grow—are being questioned. The old theodicy—God's relationship to human suffering—was not holding up. It was leaking like a sieve.

(a) Job as a drama didn't have an answer yet. But the search was on. God as a "first cause," an "only cause," for the running miscellany of evil was fading fast. Job is a dramatic mold into which was poured the ingredients of the question.

(b) This is not a sermon on theodicy, but the question does arise out of our limitations and make humble beings of us all. The only way I have been able to make sense of it is to say that God has limited himself to give us and his universe freedom to be who and what we are. That includes the dark side in humans and the wild side in nature, and our suffering ultimately comes from one of those realms. And if there is a purpose it is not from God manipulating circumstances to teach us or punish us, but the purpose comes from us. Jesus has come to model for us how to take Calvarys and turn them into Easter mornings, how to take Golgothas and transform them into empty tombs. And just knowing that it can be done by us with his help is a tremendous power for our personal struggles. It gives birth to hope as well as to humility.

III. But there is more to this. If we truly understand our limitations, if we don't fool ourselves into thinking we are self-made and then fall in love with our creator, something happens. It makes us more inclusive.

(a) There is in us human beings a syndrome waiting to be activated. I have called it the "nation of the elect" syndrome. We want to feel special, closest to God, closest to the truth; we want to feel that we have been chosen, we are on the inside track, we have special knowledge of God and God's will and God's way. It is born out of our desire to be ever so close to God, but the end result is that it makes us so difficult to live with. We become the "nation of the elect" with the truth, nothing but the truth, the whole truth. And then we exclude those who aren't the "elect" like we are.

(b) It happened to the disciples in the Gospel read this morning.

They see and hear a man casting out demons in Jesus' name, but he's not a member of their clan. He's not certified. He doesn't have the proper shingle hung out, and he's not using the proper liturgy and language.

"There's a fellow over there casting out demons in your name, and he's not one of us. He's not using the right language, and he's not even saying it right, and he doesn't forgive them. I mean, Jesus, we've got to straighten him out right now."

"Well, James, is the healing working?"

"Yeah. Uh-huh! He's had two withered hands, a deaf mute, and a blind man so far, and yeah, he's done good."

"Well, go over and congratulate him and wish him well and get acquainted."

"But Jesus, he's not one of us!"

"Yes, he is, James. If he's not against me, he's for me. Let's include him in."

"But, Jesus. We don't know what all he believes. He might be one of those liberals from . . ."

"James! I've got other sheep not of this fold. One who does my will and way is a member of my greater family. Include him in."

"But we don't know what kind of works he does and . . ."

"James. If he so much as gives you a cup of water because you belong to me, then he'll have his reward."

"You mean he'll have the kingdom for a cup of water, and we've been busting our . . . sandal straps to follow you and . . ."

"In my kingdom everything counts," said Jesus. "Everything counts. Include him in."

(c) It is a humbling reality to lose our "nation of the elect" superiority, and "include in" those we thought "out" of the kingdom.

When we've really understood our corporate, human limitations we "include in" instead of "including out." It makes a difference when we remember who created us and fall in love with that creator. All the difference in everybody's world!—Thomas H. Conley

Illustrations

CHARACTER CHARACTERIZED. It is difficult to define character. Dr. W. H. Davis has contrasted it with reputation in somewhat the following way: Reputation is what people think you are; character is what God knows you are. Circumstances determine your reputation; what you believe and what you love determine your character. Reputation is your photograph; character is your face. Reputation is what you have when you come; character is what you have when you go. Reputation grows like the mushroom; character grows like the oak. Reputation goes like the mushroom; character is as lasting as eternity. Newspapers can make one's reputation; toil and consecration can make one's character. If you want to get a position, have a reputation; if you want to keep it, have a character. Reputation makes one rich or poor; character makes one happy or unhappy. Reputation is preserved on tombstones; character is preserved in the books of heaven.—Roland Q. Leavell

THE MAKING OF A SAINT.   A martyr, a saint, is always made by the design of God, for his love of men, to warn them and to lead them, to bring them back to his ways. A martyrdom is never the design of man; for the true martyr is he who has become the instrument of God, who has lost his will in the will of God, not lost it but found it, for he has found freedom in submission to God. The martyr no longer desires anything for himself, not even the glory of martyrdom.—T. S. Eliot.

Sermon Suggestions

GOD'S AMAZING PATIENCE.   TEXT: Exod. 32:1–14. (1) *Then:* The story of the making of the golden calf. (2) *Always:* It is a recurring theme of the Scriptures that God forgives and restores his erring and unworthy people. (3) *Now:* We get turned aside to many modern idols—money, fame, power, etc.—despite God's goodness and will for us, and yet he awaits our return with amazing patience.

TO BE IN HEAVEN OR TO BE HERE?   TEXT: Phil. 1:21–27. (1) A dual destiny, verses 21–22. (2) A dubious desire, verse 23. (3) A divine decision, verses 24–26. (4) A disciple's duty, verse 27.

Worship Aids

CALL TO WORSHIP.   "Hereby perceive we the love of God, because he laid down his life for us: and we ought to lay down our lives for the brethren. . . . My little children, let us not love in word, neither in tongue; but in deed and in truth" (1 John 3:16, 18).

INVOCATION.   O God of love: Our lives are isolated by our pretensions and cluttered with the debris of our own mistakes. We acknowledge our need for your judgment and your mercy. O Living Christ, deliver us from our bondage to sin and death and bring new life and hope to us all.—E. Paul Hovey

OFFERTORY SENTENCE.   "So then every one of us shall give account of himself to God" (Rom. 14:12).

OFFERTORY PRAYER.   Our Father, you have given us responsibilities, and we pray for your help in carrying them out. Forgive our failures and give us such a vision of our duty and the joy of performing it that we can be truly cheerful givers.

PRAYER.   O God, the creator and preserver of all mankind, we humbly beseech thee for all sorts and conditions of men; that thou wouldest be pleased to make thy ways known unto them, thy saving health unto all nations. More especially we pray for thy holy Church universal; that it may be so guided and governed by thy good Spirit, that all who profess and call themselves Christians may be led into the way of truth, and hold the faith in unity of spirit, in the bond of peace, and in righteousness of life. Finally, we commend to thy fatherly goodness all those who are in any ways afflicted or distressed, in mind, body, or estate; [especially those for whom our prayers are desired]; that it may please thee to comfort and relieve them according to their several necessities, giving them patience under their sufferings, and a happy issue out of all their afflictions. And this we beg for Jesus Christ's sake.—*The Book of Common Prayer*

LECTIONARY MESSAGE

Equality Before God
TEXT: Matt. 20:1–16

Difficult parables teach the importance of care in interpretation. This parable also emphasizes the concern Jesus frequently showed to those outside the mainstream of life. The unemployed workers were simply waiting for a chance. Application can be made to those in several modern-day conditions. The workers waiting for employment were the hourly laborers, the migrant workers, the dislocated employees, even the street people of their day. They also were the untrained who had little hope of changing their condition.

These laborers were the general populace. They worked for a daily wage that would provide only the necessities of life. They had not savings, and there were no discretionary funds. When there was no work, they went without. What they earned provided only the bare necessities for living.

I. *God's acceptance of all.* Every one of us would like to maintain that something about us gives us a preferential status. This parable clearly emphasizes the willingness of God to accept all who respond to his call. The householder seemingly offered employment to all who were available each time workers were identified.

Those familiar with the circumstances of the grape harvest claim that the imperative nature of using as many harvesters as were available seems to be the condition reflected.

Everyone available, including those who might not be acceptable if religious or social requirements were applied, was to be given an opportunity.

The very fact that Jesus ministered to such people and included them in his teaching method further acknowledges that God's concern is demonstrated toward all. No one can claim acceptance of God due to circumstances or affiliations.

II. *All were of equal importance.* At the end of the day's labor each was paid the same. Payment was based on the attitude of the employer. Each received what was promised, and some received more than was promised. The implication seems to be that if this seems unfair, it is because of the limited understanding of those who find it so.

III. *No group had a favored status.* There is the implication that each worker entered the employ as soon as there was an opportunity. Care must be exercised not to overemphasize this case. Above all else, it is stressed that no one receives less than was promised, but neither is favor shown for seniority or other circumstances unrelated to commitment. This parable does not give attention to the manner of work after the opportunity of service has been provided.

IV. *Generosity of God.* The involvement and opportunity of all is the consequence of the graciousness of the employer. That each is included is the result of the concern shown. The spiritual truth to be drawn is that our relationship with God is solely the result of his grace. It is always "the gift of God."

Significantly the workers are reminded also that they should not be concerned with the reward. The conclusion of the parable reminds that both the reward and a lack of penalty for not understanding or murmuring result from God's graciousness.—Arthur L. Walker, Jr.

SUNDAY: SEPTEMBER THIRTIETH

SERVICE OF WORSHIP

Sermon: What Have We Missed?
TEXTS: Hos. 5:15–6:6; Luke 15:1–10

"What woman, having ten silver coins, if she loses one coin, does not light a lamp

and sweep the house and seek diligently until she finds it?"

This parable is the second of three recorded in Luke 15 that are among the most familiar and cherished stories told by Jesus. In these three parables we see the reflection of One who loves unconditionally, seeks diligently, and rejoices unrestrainedly. When we hear these parables again there is something in us that wants to be loved, to be found, to rejoice.

I. We can see that woman who has lost something very precious as she overturns the house and sweeps every corner. There are no windows in the house in which she lives, only a low door. So there is very little light. She lights a candle or a lamp and looks . . . and looks . . . and looks. We can identify. Do you know what that feeling of panic is like? Sure you do. We don't have to explain this parable. You can feel the tightening of your stomach, your palms beginning to sweat. You will do anything to find that which is lost.

(a) Jesus says to them, and to us, "Here is God." God is one, first of all, who searches and seeks because you are valuable to him, more valuable than you and I will ever fully understand. Each coin was unique. In those days, there was not uniform mintage. This coin was different from all of the others and probably was a part of the woman's dowry. Traditionally she wore this coin in a veil or in a necklace. That one coin was as important as anything in the world. The Bible says it in different ways over and over again: "The hairs of your head (be they many or few) are counted. If God observes with care and concern the falling of a sparrow, how much more he cares for you." You are not just a cog in a wheel, a part of an impersonal company or community. You are to be part of the kingdom of God, and God loves you and seeks you out.

(b) Coins are also made to be used. It says the coin was still in the house. Sometimes we are in the kingdom. We have affirmed that Jesus Christ is Lord and Savior, but we're not in circulation. We have said, "I have other things on my mind. I can't be open to being used in this way by God." When the "coin" is out of circulation God continues to seek and to search and to call us home. Is that happening with you this morning? We get things all mixed up. We talk about net worth in terms of dollars when our real net worth is that we are a part of this net of God's care and concern. So that none will slip through it, we are a part of casting that net.

II. God is not only one who seeks and seeks and seeks, but he is one who seeks because he loves us.

(a) God continues to seek and to search, and all along he is near at hand when we turn to him. He is a God who is diligent and whose searching is pervasive. Even when you are going through difficult times, remember this: all of your experience is God's searching for you. Even when we are a part of his family, members of a redeemed people, he is seeking that we might come closer. All of the events of your life are a part of his seeking you always to come closer. And yes, we are reminded that this God who seeks us diligently and pervasively seeks us always with love.

(b) Dr. William Nelson was a professor of psychiatry at Duke University. He was convinced that in this age of education and science, we cannot believe in a personal God. While doing research he wrote a paper on the "Alexander the Great Complex." Alexander the Great, legend has it, when he had conquered the world, sat down and cried because there were no more worlds to conquer. This intrigued Dr. Wilson, and he wrote about those who have achieved and yet still feel empty. In the writing of it, he discovered that he was one of those people. God comes seeking the lost, not only in the down-and-out but the up-and-away as well.

III. Finally, we know that the God who loves us and seeks us is the one who wants to rejoice with us. Our relationship with him is not long faces and protracted sighs. Remember again those moments when anguish turns to discovery and separation to reunion: when the ring was found, when those important papers were found, when your child was found. How you wanted to tell everybody and have them rejoice with you. So God's kingdom is a kingdom of rejoicing. The main activity of the kingdom is not clucking over those who have been lost—"Why didn't they come sooner?" "Well, it's about time!"— but to rejoice with God that the lost have been found. It is at that moment we discover, not only the point the Pharisees missed, but the God they missed. The God of our Lord Jesus Christ is more than we can ever capture in words, but he is always the one who seeks us, loves us, and desires to rejoice with us forever.—Gary D. Stratman

Illustrations

OUR TRUE SITUATION. I heard recently of a yacht that was sinking off the coast of California, and the Coast Guard was radioed. The man who was the captain was a very famous financier, and he was desperate. The Coast Guard radioed back and said, "We'll come. What's your position?" And he said, "I'm the chairman of the board of First National Trust." That's not our position. Our position is that we are lost and may be found, that having been found we are to be a part of God's plan and purpose in the world.—Gary D. Stratman

FAITH IN CHRIST. Alfred Tennyson, walking in the garden with a friend, was asked what he thought of Jesus Christ. Pointing to some flowers Tennyson said, "What the sun is to these flowers, Christ is to my soul. He is the sun of my soul."—Charles L. Wallis

Sermon Suggestions

ON SEEING AND NOT SEEING GOD. TEXT: Exod. 33:12–23. (1) Moses intercedes with the Lord. (2) Moses seeks the guidance and blessing of God for himself and God's people. (3) Moses receives the promise of the Lord's presence. (4) The promise is realized when Moses and the people go forth on pilgrimage. (5) God gives this favor on his own initiative. (6) God grants to Moses only a glimpse of himself but enough to confirm his promise.

A SYMPHONY OF THE SPIRIT. TEXT: Phil. 2:1–13. (1) The aim: humility. (2) The example: Christ Jesus. (3) The energizing: God at work.

Worship Aids

CALL TO WORSHIP. "Having therefore, brethren, boldness to enter into the holiest by the blood of Jesus, by a new and living way, which he hath consecrated for us, through the veil, that is to say, his flesh; . . . Let us draw near with a true heart in full assurance of faith, having our hearts sprinkled from an evil conscience, and our bodies washed with pure water" (Heb. 10:19–20, 22).

INVOCATION. O God of Love who settest the solitary in families, grant that we, who have felt the chill loneliness of guilt and estrangement, may rejoice in thy gracious mercy and in the warm encouragement of the community of faith and concern in which we have been placed; to the end that thy will may be done in us and that this world's wanderers may find their way home. Through him in whose face we see thee.

OFFERTORY SENTENCE. "And whatsoever ye do in word or deed, do all in the name of the Lord Jesus, giving thanks to God and the Father by him" (Col. 3:17).

OFFERTORY PRAYER. Almighty God, from whom all good gifts come, accept our offerings today, meager or generous, and multiply their good for thy use and the work of the church for which Christ died.—E. Lee Phillips

PRAYER. O God, whose Spirit searches all things and whose Love bears all things, come with truth and mercy to us today. We are often blind to the ways that lead to the hearts and needs of others and to thy throne. Give thy light, O God, and take away our darkness. But when we see ourselves as we are, leave us not to stand confused and helpless in our guilt. Give us thy grace, O God, to take away our fears and to strengthen our laggard hearts. Grant, O Lord, that thy Word may give us increased understanding of the scope of our task as servants of Jesus Christ. May we be encouraged to seek new depths of dedication. May we be inspired to take more seriously our opportunities for preparation for the task of witnessing to thy truth to the ends of the earth.

LECTIONARY MESSAGE

Profession and Practice
TEXT: Matt. 21:28–32
The larger context includes the account of the entry of Jesus into Jerusalem as a royal personage and the cleansing of the Temple. This raised a question concerning claimed religious rights. Matthew tells of a challenge to Jesus and his authority by four religious groups (chapters 21 and 22). The first of these, the chief priests and elders (21:23), felt justified in rejecting all Jesus had claimed because they felt that their position gave them the greatest relationship with God. These same religious authorities were also outraged that Jesus permitted the masses to acknowledge him. Out of this background Jesus told the parable of two sons, neither of which wished to be obedient. He seems to be indicating that neither the religious leaders nor the masses yet had made the ideal response.

I. *Promises are inadequate.*

(a) Even well-meaning but empty promises are without results. Foxhole and deathbed promises can have dire religious consequences.

(b) Sincere promises to God require commitment that motivates the believer to follow through with religious responses.

(c) An empty promise may create the circumstance in which obedience is impossible. The person without sincere religious commitment may lose the capacity for obedience.

II. *Practice is the better response.*

(a) Neither son made an ideal response. The churlish son, who at first refused to obey, left much to be desired. He reflected a rebellious spirit even though he later acceded to his father's wishes.

(b) The second son displayed greater disobedience because he added untruthfulness to his refusal in practice. The harsher charge was leveled at the "religious" people who made claims that were not supported by practice.

(c) Some may respond affirmatively to God without an original intention to do so. There were obviously those of Jesus' day who were called the irreligious, the toll collectors and harlots (v. 31), who denied many of the claims of religion but practiced its more practical parts. These were even acknowledged by the religious as better than those who made religious claims that were not kept.

III. Application of the parable should not be limited to those of Jesus' day.

(a) The parable was a warning to those who claimed to be religious.

(1) The claim to possess all the truth needed can lead to false security and unfounded assurance.

(2) Religious feelings without expression of religious concern can produce a form of religion without the power of real religion (2 Tim. 2:5).

(3) Regular self-examination is needed to protect from falling into the habit of promises without practice.

(b) The parable holds hope for another chance for those who have failed in religious commitments.

(1) Prior disobedience does not lock one into an eternal separation from the will of the Father.

(2) God is willing to forgive past disobedience and to accept those who later repent of earlier insolence.

(3) God is not limited by ignorance nor shortsighted response to his invitation to service.—Arthur L. Walker, Jr.

SUNDAY: OCTOBER SEVENTH

SERVICE OF WORSHIP

Sermon: A Table in the Wilderness
TEXT: Ps. 78:9–25
I. "They spoke against God, saying,

'Can God spread a table in the wilderness?' "

Sounds very modern, doesn't it—speaking against God, saying, "What has he done for us lately?"

(a) There isn't anything new under the sun, is there? The more things change, as somebody says, the more they stay the same. We are still complaining about the state of the world.

Talk about a wilderness, we live in a wilderness, a chaos of crime and lies and injustice and pain and hurt and starvation and ignorance and hopelessness, and we join our voices to those of the Ephraimites of old, "Can God spread a table in the wilderness? Can God do anything to offset these terrible conditions? Can God really produce a sense of hope and promise in the midst of such a depressing, mind-boggling situation?"

(b) The point of the psalmist is that God does spread a table in the wilderness. He did for the Ephraimites traveling through the desert. "He commanded the skies above," says the psalm,

and opened the doors of heaven;
and he rained down upon them manna
  to eat,
and gave them the grain of heaven.
Man ate of the bread of the angels;
he sent them food in abundance.
(Ps. 78:23–25)

II. Manna is today believed to be the whitish secretions that fall from the tamarisk bush, which grew abundantly in the deserts of the Middle East. When the secretions fell, they became dry and flaky, and they were actually quite nourishing. It was these dried secretions that fed the Israelites in their wilderness wanderings. But it does seem a bit exaggerated to call them "the grain of heaven" and "the bread of the angels."

(a) Still, the psalmist was a man of faith, and to him the fact that God had provided anything to sustain his people in the desert was enough to call forth paeans of praise. To his mind, God had indeed "spread a table in the wilderness"—had provided a feast for the hungry wayfarers.

I suppose what one sees in a situation like that always depends on one's inner nature or disposition. The cynic or agnostic says it was only some sugary secretions from desert plants. The true believer says

it was "the bread of the angels" and "a table in the wilderness."

(b) Don't you suppose the person's life is richer who is able to see the religious significance in such events? Doesn't it make the world more personal? And, if we really believe that God exists and cares for us as individuals, doesn't it give more of a sense of reality to what we experience? In other words, wasn't there some real justification for the psalmist's describing the flakes of manna as "the grain of heaven" or "the bread of the angels"?

What faith has to deal with is the tension between the small, common gifts of everyday life and the presence of a transcendent God that is able to make those gifts seem special. It is easy enough, in the secular world most of us know so well, to relax the tension and treat the small things nonchalantly, as if they deserved no particular attention. So we found some white, flaky substance in the desert, and it happened to sustain life—so what?! But faith—being related to the God who created the world and continues to create life today—insists on something more. It insists that we spot the relationship between the small things and the hand of the Creator and that we live with heartfelt gratitude for the small things.

Do you see what I mean?

III. (a) Here is a wealthy businessman who drives to work every morning in his Porsche and zooms into the parking garage of a skyscraper in downtown Los Angeles. He rises to the fortieth floor on the express elevator, strides into a paneled office, and sits behind a rosewood desk while cutting deals involving hundreds of thousands of dollars. He has no time for religion, only for money, deals, clubs, and personal pleasures. He would sneer at you if you suggested that God has ever blessed his life with anything.

(b) On the street corner beneath this man's office window, there is a simple woman in an inexpensive, dark outfit. She jingles a tambourine and sings a plaintive hymn. When she goes into her apartment in the evening, she feeds the cat and heats some soup for her own supper. Before she eats the soup, she bows her head and says a prayer of thanksgiving for what she is about to receive.

Which of the two is richer? Which is closer to reality?

(c) That is particularly damning to the businessman I described. It suggests that the simple woman on the street corner is much more in touch with reality than he is. It also suggests, doesn't it, that the psalmist was no robot—he was able to see the hand of God in the miracle that sustained his ancestors in the wilderness and wished to celebrate in his own day the power of the deity to "spread a table in the wilderness."

IV. Let me ask again if God can perform such a feat in our day. Is it possible, in a world where there are wars and terrorism and starvation and unhappiness—a world "red in tooth and claw," as Tennyson put it—to see God's hand at work, continually sustaining his people? Is God mysteriously but satisfyingly here in the meager offerings of this table, feeding us on divine memories and on the rich hopes we need to enable us to walk and not faint in the modern world? Faith says he is; doubt says not. So coming here sifts us. It makes us declare ourselves again. Do we or don't we believe? Will we or won't we follow?

(a) Perhaps this is why we call the Lord's table a sacrament. The Latin word *sacramentum* originally meant an oath one swore, probably of a military nature. When we take the bread and cup, we swear an oath again to God and to Christ. We bind ourselves once more to serving in the divine army. We say, "I believe God can spread a table in the wilderness of life, and this table is the evidence of it."

(b) It is a permanent reminder that God is able to "spread a table in the wilderness." Maybe it isn't a lavish table. But it is faith's table—and that may just make it the richest table in the world.—John Killinger

Illustrations

IS LIFE FAIR? On Dec. 20, 1986, Sir Harry Platt, 100, died at his home in Manchester, England. Platt was unusual, not just because he lived to be 100, nor because he was considered to be a founder of modern orthopedic surgery, nor that he was a president of the Royal College of Surgeons and the International Federation of Surgical Colleges. Platt was a chronic invalid as a child. He suffered from the sort of bone and joint disabilities that became his life's work to cure. Imagine how easily Platt might have become embittered and felt sorry only for himself. Instead he, knowing the pain, decided to help others. "If at first you feel life has not been fair, . . ."—Davis W. Richardson

TAUGHT BY SUFFERING. I knew a woman who lost her only son in a plane crash. Rather than making her cynical, it made her extremely sensitive to the suffering of others. I have never known a person who could minister to others the way she could. Without being self-conscious she could walk through the doorway of another's pain and be at home there because she had been a great sufferer herself. There were so many ways she could say, "I know. I understand. I am with you."—Chevis F. Horne

Sermon Suggestions

TRANSFER OF POWER. TEXT: Num. 27: 12–23. (1) Moses saw the future but was not to lead in it, verses 12–14. (2) Moses cared for the people he had led and sought for them a suitable leader, verses 15–17. (3) Yahweh, the Lord, chose Joshua, upon whom Moses conferred some of his own authority, and Joshua stood ready to lead at the proper time.

ON TOWARD THE GOAL. TEXT: Phil. 3:12–21. (1) By humility, verses 12–13a. (2) By forgetting the crippling past, verse 13b. (3) By reaching toward the future, verse 14. (4) By trusting in the Lord Jesus Christ for our ultimate transformation, verses 20–21.

Worship Aids

CALL TO WORSHIP. "Sing unto him, sing psalms unto him: talk ye of all his wondrous works. Glory ye in his holy name: let the heart of them rejoice that seek the Lord" (Ps. 105:2–3).

INVOCATION. Lord, let our worship be uplifting, inspiring, and challenging, a pure and holy thing acceptable in thy sight, O Lord, our strength and our redeemer.—E. Lee Phillips

OFFERTORY SENTENCE. "I have shewed you all things, how that so laboring ye ought to support the weak, and to remember the words of the Lord Jesus, how he said, It is more blessed to give than to receive" (Acts 20:35).

OFFERTORY PRAYER. Gracious Lord, may the gifts of this local church be combined in harmony with the gifts of other churches for the glory of Jesus Christ, whom we remember today especially in sacrament and song.—E. Lee Phillips

PRAYER. Sustaining God: Amid the ugliness we have made of your Creation, you continue to surround us with beauty. Generous God of bright colors, rainbows and peacocks, orange pumpkins and pure blue sky, blazing autumn leaves and wordless sunsets all sing praises to your name.

Mighty God of our Creation and image, as we come into your presence and worship you, may our voices and our lives bring honor and glory to your name, too. Allow the gift of your Spirit to move among us graciously.

Abiding God, Lord beyond the Fall and in the cross, your love and Spirit will not let us go but point us to our sin. We turn uncomfortable. We tiptoe around confession and question its necessity in our lives, and in this we are judged!

Lord Jesus, as we stutter in voice and stumble in words, hear our clumsy attempts at confession and asking for forgiveness. Cleanse us first from the sin of being too good for our own good; for having little remorse or shame, for associating sin primarily with others and too infrequently with our own self.

Understanding Father, Lord of grace and redemption, in a world of suffering, forgive our ease; in a world distorted by inequity, forgive our excess; in a world short on servants, forgive our obsession with being number one. In a world of desperate need, forgive our addictive greed;

in a world waiting for humility, forgive our polished arrogance. In a world seeking encouragement, forgive our defeating cynicism. In a world twisted by pain and scars, forgive our unmarked bodies and our untouched hearts.

O God, in a dark world longing for the good news, forgive our indifference and embarrassed silence. Holy God, Father of the Holy Spirit, move among our confessions with tears of cleansing. Free us from the heaviness of our sin and let us now partake of your redeeming grace. For in our need, your grace becomes more than enough.

By your Spirit, take from us all that keeps us from you. Give to us will and obedience to follow you unashamedly. Save us from ourselves and give us wholly to your service for others. In him who has died that we might rise to new and eternal life, whose grace is sufficient for all our needs, whose Spirit lifts us up and surrounds us with beauty, in him we worship and pray.—William M. Johnson

LECTIONARY MESSAGE

Responding to God

TEXT: Matt. 21:33–43

Those who heard Jesus tell this parable could identify with much of its message. The imagery was well known. The Old Testament frequently referred to Israel as a vineyard. The practices of sharecroppers and absentee landlords were prevalent.

There is little doubt that the claim that Jesus is the "Son" was recognized. This means that those hearing Jesus knew that he was answering the question previously posed regarding his authority. Out of his claims of identity and authority he spoke truths they needed to understand.

I. *God's trust.* The Bible repeatedly pictures God as entrusting to his servants his world, his mission, his purpose. This parable identifies those to whom the trust is given and the result of the trust given.

(a) *The sharecroppers.* These are Israel. All God's possession and work had been left to his chosen people. Their history was the story of this trust.

(b) *The servants.* These were the spokespersons for God, the prophets.

(c) *His Son.* Earlier sharecroppers knew of the messianic Messenger only by prophecy. Jesus revealed himself as the fulfillment of that expectation. The conflict with the representatives of Israel made the identification obvious.

(d) *Hoped-for response.* Only by implication is God's hoped-for response described. He trusted the sharecroppers and hoped they would be faithful. He trusted the servants and hoped they would be effective. He turned to his Son to accomplish that which had previously failed. He turned to new sharecroppers to reestablish the care of his possession.

II. *Man's response.*

(a) *Response to privilege.* Even with the awareness of the ultimate judgment to be faced by the vinedressers, one must be impressed by the privilege given to them. They could care for and use the vineyard as their own. The vineyard is equipped with all that is needed. To permit men the privilege of caring for God's vineyard should be a challenge as well as a privilege.

(b) *Response to freedom.* The liberty given the vineyard keepers is impressive. There is the implication that they had total freedom of action. They were allowed to express their ultimate potential. Freedom of action is limited only by acknowledgment of responsibility.

(c) *Opportunity for rebellion.* Rebellion was an option because of the freedom allowed and the element of trust on which it was based. The interpretation, that the parable describes the response of humankind to God, allows for the same kind of break in relationship with God.

III. *God's response.* The response of God emphasized the accountability of the workers. They were free to act but must be willing to bear responsibility for those actions.

(a) *Response to rebellion.* When rebellion took place the workers were answerable directly to the owner. No other messengers were sent. He came himself. The workers lost their place. Their failure caused them to forfeit their relationship.

(b) *Response to renewal.* Others were given the place and opportunity. The parable clearly indicates that in God's work there are renewed opportunities.

(c) *Response to Israel.* The wicked workers were rejected because they had rejected the owner's way. Even Israel will be replaced because they have rejected God's way. Those who accept God's way will prevail.—Arthur L. Walker, Jr.

SUNDAY: OCTOBER FOURTEENTH

SERVICE OF WORSHIP

Sermon: The Bigot and the True Believer

Text: Gal. 5:6

That's the motto of the true believer—and Paul was surely one, although some have tried to lodge him with the bigots. A bigot, according to a dictionary I consulted, is "a person who is utterly intolerant of any creed, belief, or opinion that differs from one's own."

I am not for a moment denying that there is a lot of bigoted, intolerant, and narrow-minded religion around. Not one of us escapes the danger of letting our religious beliefs congeal like some of my Scottish Presbyterian ancestors to whom Oliver Cromwell addressed his familiar appeal: "I beseech you, gentlemen, in the bowels of Christ, to conceive it possible you may be mistaken." It is not often noted, however, that there is such a thing as a bigoted atheist or an intolerant agnostic. I would, therefore, plead for a new understanding of the phrase *true believer* and maintain that it is perfectly possible to hold firm religious beliefs without any intolerance or disrespect for the sincere convictions of those of other religions—or none at all.

I. Let me briefly sketch the background of this debate and then indicate how this flare-up in a first-century church in what we now call Turkey has something to say to Christians today.

(a) As you know, the first Christians were Jewish, and it was about the middle of the first century that Gentiles in large numbers began to be baptized and admitted to membership in the church. The question at issue was how a Gentile man or woman from a pagan background should be received into the church. Some, led by Paul, whose Jewish credentials were impeccable, held that all that was required was a declaration of faith in Christ as Lord and Savior and Baptism in his name. The opposition party protested that they had first to accept the Law of Moses, one of whose requirements was the rite of circumcision of all males.

(b) For a while the debate raged across the expanding church, and it was mostly thanks to Paul that it was finally settled. If Paul seems obsessed about the question of circumcision, it was because that rite was for him a symbol of the legalism from which he believed the gospel had set us free. So here he says that the demand that a Gentile convert should be circumcised undermines the freedom of the Christian believer. It might seem a minor matter, but he argues that one who receives circumcision is under obligation to observe "the whole Law."

II. Well, where do we come into this ancient argument? Simply as the beneficiaries of Paul's success in eliminating the requirement that a true Christian believer must first accept the requirements of the Jewish Law.

(a) If the other side had won, the Christian advance would probably have ground to a halt, and you and I would not be worshiping here today. Paul tells us in this letter that he squared off with none other than the Apostle Peter, who had visited the Galatian church and at first had mixed with the Gentiles but later withdrew from them because some ardent Judaizers had arrived from Jerusalem. "I opposed him to his face," said Paul, "because he was clearly in the wrong." We don't get Peter's side of the argument. But there is nothing obscure in the words he later uses in this Epistle in his attack on the Judaizers:

"They had better go the whole way and make eunuchs of themselves."

(b) I think when he wrote that he had forgotten his own reminder to the true believer that "the only thing that counts is faith active in love." He had the faith. But, like us, he was at times somewhat lacking in the love that should animate the true believer.

III. Are you a true believer? Your answer to that question—and mine—will depend on the kind of picture this phrase conjures up.

(a) If we are inclined to see quotes around the words *true believer* and start thinking about people you know who wear their religion like a cloak, hugging it tightly so that you never seem to reach the real person inside a cloak covered with conventional pieties and so thick that no new idea seems ever to have penetrated, a cloak that seems to shield them from sharing activities of normal human beings— the kind of person who makes you uncomfortable in case you offend and cautious in your conversation—then you may want to say, "Thank God I'm not a true believer: I don't want to be a bigot."

(b) On the other hand, your answer would, I am sure, be totally different if the phrase *true believer* evokes for you the picture of one who is, as we say, "a real Christian." That is what a true believer really is. Sometimes that faith is expressed in enthusiastic church activity; sometimes it is shyly concealed; but always it is expressed in deeds rather than words.

IV. There are two points that have come home to me with special force as I try to answer the question, Am I a true believer?

(a) One is that our chosen way of life must rest on a quite specific set of beliefs. Everyone acts on some basic convictions, whether they are specifically religious or not. The true believer is one who is not reluctant to say, "Credo: I believe." "I have made my choice." And the true Christian believer is one who can say with Paul, "To me to live is Christ and to die is gain." "I am persuaded that neither death nor life . . . nor things present nor things to come . . . shall be able to separate me from the love of God, which is in Christ Jesus our Lord."

(b) That leads me to the next truth that we miss. To be a true Christian believer does not involve dismissing or despising all other religions. On the contrary, a total yielding of ourselves to the call of Christ from the heart of God will mean an expansion of the mind beyond the narrow limits of this material world and expansion of the heart into the mysteries of a love that breaks all barriers and dissolves the bigotries. The true believer can never claim to possess here and now all truth about God and human destiny but expects and welcomes new truth from whatever direction it comes.

V. The true believer knows that the closer we come to Christ, the less intolerant and the more loving, the less arrogant and the more humble, the less bigoted and the more truly human, we must become. For when we say, "Credo: I believe," we are turning to the Light "that lighteth everyone who comes into the world" and "shines more and more unto the perfect day."—David H. C. Read

Illustrations

POWER OF HUMBLE SPIRITUALITY. A man who had visited Bernard at Clairvaux said, "I tarried a few days with him, and whichever way I turned my eyes I marveled, and thought I saw a new heaven and a new earth. As soon as you entered Clairvaux you could feel that God was in the place."

Coming away from Horace Bushnell's home, where the great seer was "passing into the unseen holy," Joseph Twitchell declared, "I felt as I left the house a mighty conviction of spiritual realities and a desire to live in them." There is power in a life like that.

Who can forget the story of Sir Galahad—or wants to forget it? One looked into his rapt face and thus described the experience:

While he thus spake, his eye, dwelling on mine,
Drew me, with power beyond me, till I grew
One with him, to believe as he believed.—G. Ray Jordan

COURAGEOUS OBEDIENCE.   Before World War II, writer Nora Waln wrote a book manuscript, *Reading for the Stars,* in which she exposed Hitler and his Nazi conspirators. The manuscript was intercepted in the German mails en route to an American publishing house. Fleeing to London, Nora Waln rewrote the book from memory and sent copies to Nazi hangman Heinrich Himmler. By way of reprisal, Himmler imprisoned seven of the author's anti-Nazi friends.

Miss Waln returned to Germany and offered her life for the freedom of her friends. Himmler promised to empty an entire prison if the writer would write her book to make Hitler look good. Refusing, Nora Waln said, "I am willing to forfeit my life, not my beliefs." She was not killed, but her willingness to die for her convictions can inspire all who must choose between obedience to God and adherence to human values.—Bessie L. Kennedy

Sermon Suggestions

THE INCOMPLETENESS OF LIFE.   TEXT: Deut. 34:1–12, especially verse 4. (1) Not only Moses' life, but every life is flawed and incomplete. (2) Despite our sin and limitations, God intends for us abundant and eternal life in Christ both here and hereafter (see John 10:10; 17:3).

THE LORD IS NEAR.   TEXT: Phil. 4:1–9, TEV. Therefore, (1) be joyful in your union with the Lord; (2) show a gentle attitude toward everyone; (3) do not worry about anything, but . . . ask God for what you need, . . . with a thankful heart; and (4) God's peace . . . will keep your hearts and minds safe. . . .

Worship Aids

CALL TO WORSHIP.   "The Lord is exalted; for he dwelleth on high: he hath filled Zion with judgment and righteousness. And wisdom and knowledge shall be the stability of thy times, and strength of salvation: the fear of the Lord is his treasure" (Isa. 33:5–6).

INVOCATION. God of grace and God of glory, come today to our benighted minds and illumine our thoughts. Come today to our vagrant wills and correct our ways. Come today to our laggard hearts and help us to love thee. For thou hast redeemed us, and we belong to thee.

OFFERTORY SENTENCE. "And let the beauty of the Lord our God be upon us: and establish thou the work of our hands upon us; yea, the work of our hands establish thou it" (Ps. 90:17).

OFFERTORY PRAYER. Yours, O Lord, is the greatness and the power and the glory and the majesty; for all that is in the heavens and the earth is yours. Yours is the kingdom, O Lord, and yours it is to be exalted as head over all. Both riches and honor come from you, and you reign over all. In your hand are power and might; in your hand it is to make great and to give strength to all.

Now therefore, our God, we thank you and praise your glorious name. We thank you for the goodness of all the gifts you have given us, and we bring gifts to you in return. We bring not only your tithe; we bring also our time. We bring our talents. We bring our very lives to you, in whom we live and move and have our being. And we pray that our gifts may be acceptable in your sight and may be useable for the furtherance of your kingdom.—Cindy Johnson

PRAYER. O God, we come before you this morning for you alone are worthy of our ultimate loyalty, our devotion, and our praise. We have gone lusting after other gods, and none seem able to fill this vacuum within us. Jobs, education, even family do not seem to be able to stand as ends in themselves. We desire in these quiet moments to be reminded of a purpose shrouded in mystery, to see again an everlasting mercy beyond the harsh judgments of time, performance, and accountability. Comfort us, heal us, for we are wounded.

Hear our prayers for those who need your strength as they face yet another round of treatments and therapies, for those who feel the pangs of grief and loss, for those who fear the loss of job and income. We pray for _____ and others whom we name in silence.

O God, we can understand why Jonah fled. The evil people outside our circle seem to be shown mercy, and those who are good appear to be struck down or ignored. We get angry, too, at the world, at ourselves, at you. Where can we go with our anger and our fear if it is not to you, O Lord. For in a fallen and unfair world, do you not move to us in love that judges us and frees us to serve? Hear our thoughts and words as we pray in the name of the Christ who taught us to pray saying . . . [the Lord's Prayer].—Gary D. Stratman

LECTIONARY MESSAGE

The Demands of Religion
TEXT: Matt. 22:1–14

Much is made of plurality in today's society. The major concern about plurality for many seems to be its implied permission to participate in every kind of belief and practice. The parable of the wedding feast with the emphasis on the failure of the guest to dress properly points up that relationship with Christ is more than a casual experience in which any type of behavior is permitted.

The relationship of the believer with God can be demanding. The requirements of God must be met.

I. *Response to grace.*

(a) The rejection of God's action of forgiveness and grace is not simply mildly discourteous. It is a rebellious insult. The parable reflects that people who reject God's grace are so perverted in spirit that they abuse and even kill the king's messengers. The action of the king in judgment stresses that the rejection is more than a mildly censurable reaction that really does not matter.

(b) How one responds to God's requirement is the very basis for acceptability. That which attracts one's attention and receives one's loyalty clearly indicates whether one is worthy (v. 8).

(c) The guilt of those who are punished resulted from giving too much attention to the ordinary affairs of life. The farm and business referred to (v. 5) were obviously illustrative of other distracting values that might claim the attention of any individual when the affairs of the day become more important than the invitation of God. Attention to such other attractions causes one to lose the opportunity to experience grace.

II. *Wrath and grace.* In no other place in Scripture is the relationship of wrath and grace more specifically pictured. The wrath of God and the loss of grace are intricately related.

(a) The invitation to the wedding feast was freely given. The invitation reflected that all the expected preparations had been completed. The extent of the number of those to whom the invitation was originally given is indicated by the number who are included as substitutes.

(b) The open-ended invitation to the "many as you find" reflects God's willingness to receive all who respond.

(c) The punishment of those who rejected the invitation and the treatment of the man who came to the feast without a wedding garment clearly reflect God's reaction to those who abuse his grace. Judgment and wrath are to be expected if grace is refused or abused.

III. *The requirement of grace.*

(a) Even though those who were expected to accept God's grace refused it, this did not permit any of the other guests to come with a wanton lack of preparation. This warning both must be given and heeded in our age of plurality. Laxity in relationship is not permitted. Seeking the will of God is both a requirement and an expectation even in receiving the grace of God.

(b) The many who are called (v. 14) may include all mankind, but the number of those who know the joy of fellowship is restricted to the few who properly respond. The "calling" that is given is not to eliminate but rather to establish the boundaries of acceptability.—Arthur L. Walker, Jr.

SUNDAY: OCTOBER TWENTY-FIRST

SERVICE OF WORSHIP

Sermon: Membership Has Its Privileges

TEXT: 1 Cor. 5:1–13

I. Our passage is the first of three cases where Paul gets quite upset with the Corinthian church on account of their questionable behavior. One of the cases has to do with church members taking each other to court. The last concerns their visiting prostitutes. The first, our passage, pertains to a man in the church who is living with his father's wife.

We can figure a few things about this situation. First of all, it's not incest. Paul says nothing about the woman being the man's mother. Instead, he calls her "his father's wife." So we doubt it's incest. Also, arguing by silence, it's also probably not adultery. That is, we may assume the father is either dead or has divorced the woman.

What's happening is that a member of the Corinthian church is living openly with his stepmother. We're not talking about a one-time incident or even a brief fling. He didn't have an affair. He didn't get drunk and make a mistake. Rather he has been and willfully continues to choose to sleep with this stepmother.

Two things bother Paul about this. One, such behavior is so grossly immoral that (as Paul says) "it is not even found among pagans." Now when the pagans think it's bad, then you know it's really bad. Not even a profane and promiscuous heathen would stoop to sleeping with his stepmother. Yet here is a Christian doing it. Must be giving the church quite a reputation.

The second thing that bothers Paul is the reaction of the church (or lack of reaction) to the whole affair. It's not only that there's obviously a moral problem going on. It's also that the church seems unfazed by the whole affair. They are "arrogant." It doesn't bother them.

When Paul said the church was "arrogant," he meant one of two things. He either meant that they were arrogant because of the situation or arrogant in spite of the situation. Either way, they apparently thought of themselves as such a broad-minded group of believers that something like this didn't hurt the church. In fact, in the eyes of the Corinthians, that such behavior was going on publicly, and yet they continued to accept this man as one of their own—this gave testimony to their tolerance. It proved they were an open-minded church.

II. Now where I come from, being open-minded is a virtue. It is a good thing for people to be understanding and accepting. Well-integrated and educated people develop the capacity to be open-minded. From my perspective, it is a mark of maturity and growth when I can accept as legitimate ideas and behavior and beliefs that differ from my own.

But only to a point. There is a problem with being overly open-minded.

The point being that when it comes to some things, we Christians are close-minded. I'm sorry, but we're not all-inclusive. Some things are not acceptable. At some point we say no. We are close-minded.

Or at least we ought to be. The Corinthians remind me of one of those churches that is so afraid of being thought of as fundamentalist that they'll accept any belief as legitimate. I mean, anything close. And in the name of branching out, they lose their roots as Christians. In accepting everything, they, in fact, lose their roots; they believe nothing.

The church at Corinth should've had a problem with this man and his behavior, but they didn't. Their rationale to Paul was, "Well, if we're not supposed to associate with our people . . . if we're not supposed to get contaminated by the outside world . . . well, the only way that's going to happen is if we never go out to the outside world."

Their idea was that if you had any interaction at all with the world, you were going to be exposed to a certain amount of immoral behavior. And you might as well get used to it. Unless you were a complete hermit, you were going to be around

this kind of thing. Christians have to expect and make allowance for less-than-ideal behavior in the world.

III. But Paul came right back and told the Corinthians they had completely distorted what he meant. He never meant that Christians were to separate themselves from the outside world. "You'd have to die for that to happen. And besides," says Paul, "I want you in the world. How else is the world ever going to find out about our faith unless we interact with them?"

"No, what I meant," he says, "is that you are not to accept a person who calls himself Christian and then grossly violates the faith. God'll judge those outside the church; don't worry about them. What you are to worry about is sweeping your own doorstep. I don't want the church out of the world; I want the world out of the church. Do not associate with one who calls himself 'brother' and yet repeatedly and openly sins. Don't even let him have the Lord's Supper with you."

See, Paul is real easy on pagans and real tough on Christians. He sweet-talks non-Christians. Promises that God can forgive all their mistakes. Offers the hope of salvation to the vilest offender. But if you're a Christian—you'd better straighten up and fly right. You are on a tight ship now. To whom much is given, much is expected. Case in point: Paul never says a word about the sin of the stepmother, who we assume is not Christian. But he judges with severity the Christian participant.

IV. Paul's punishment for the willfully immoral member was excommunication. He tells the Corinthians to drive this wicked Christian out of the church. Four times in one passage: "Let the one who has done this be removed from among you. . . . Deliver this man to Satan for the destruction of the flesh. . . . Cleanse out the old leaven that you may be a new lump. . . . Drive the wicked person from among you."

Paul gives his reasons for kicking the guy out by using the image of getting rid of the leaven before Passover. Leaven here is clearly an image for corruption and evil. "Get rid of the leaven before it ruins the whole lump."

Whatever Paul meant, it is quite clear that the harshest punishment that could possibly be meted out for this serious offender is that he be kicked out of the church. The worst thing they could do to him was to remove him from the body of believers. The only penalty horrible enough to be proportionate to his serious and repeated crime is that he be expelled from the membership of the Corinthian Christian church. Has it ever occurred to you what a precious thing membership in the Body of Christ really is? The most awful nightmare you could ever give me would be that somehow, for some reason, I would be kicked out of the church and left on my own in the world. My loving Christian family no longer my brothers and sisters. The Lord's table—gone. The restoring Word—gone. The tie that binds—gone. Sick or in the hospital, and no one to pray for me or care for me. Everything that has ever sustained me or given me a reason to live suddenly gone. I don't know what on earth I would do if someone took my membership away.

To me, membership here means that I belong to somebody. I belong to you, due to all of your support and care and friendship and help. I belong to the Church universal, participating in the divine scheme set from the beginning. And I belong to God, due to all his protection and guidance and mercy and love.

To paraphrase Paul: Membership has its privileges. Take my membership away, and what do I have? Nothing. Nothing at all.—John P. Chandler

Illustrations

THE TYRANNY OF THINGS.   A wealthy man was moving into a new house, and his next-door neighbor happened to be a Quaker. The Quakers, as you know, believe in simplicity and plainness of life. The Quaker neighbor watched as the movers carted in numerous pieces of furniture, a great deal of clothing, and many decorative pieces. Then he walked over to his wealthy new neighbor and said in his quaint Quaker way, "Neighbor, if thee hath need of anything, please come to see

me—and I will tell thee how to get along without it."—Warren W. Wiersbe

WATCHING OURSELVES.   I have to watch myself against the constant danger of a lowered standard in connection with my own life. There was a time when I believed in making a clean cut. There were certain things which I said were not legitimate to me because I was a Christian. I recognized certain standards in the matter of honesty and chastity. I had a certain standard of morality. Am I as sensitive to sin as I once was? Or is there on my part a tendency to compromise in regard to my sins? Have I become an expert in explaining away what I do? Have I become an expert in the work of self-justification? We must watch constantly against a lowering of the standard.—D. Martyn Lloyd-Jones

Sermon Suggestions

EXPERIENCES THAT TURN ONE TO GOD. TEXT: Ruth 1:1–19a. (1) Loss. (2) Loyalty. (3) Longing.

THE KIND OF CHRISTIANITY TO BE THANKFUL FOR.   TEXT: 1 Thess. 1:1–10, NEB. (1) Faith in action. (2) Love in labor. (3) Hope in fortitude.

Worship Aids

CALL TO WORSHIP.   "The Lord is great in Zion; and he is high above all the people. . . . Exalt the Lord our God, and worship at his holy hill; for the Lord our God is holy" (Ps. 99:2, 9).

INVOCATION.   Almighty and everlasting God, in Christ you have revealed your glory among the nations: Preserve the works of your mercy, that your Church throughout the world may persevere with steadfast faith in the confession of your Name; through Jesus Christ our Lord, who lives and reigns with you and the Holy Spirit, one God, for ever and ever.—*The Book of Common Prayer*

OFFERTORY SENTENCE.   "Therefore, as ye abound in everything, in faith, and utterance, and knowledge, and in all diligence, and in your love to us, see that ye abound in this grace also" (2 Cor. 8:7).

OFFERTORY PRAYER. Gracious God, bless this offering that what our hearts affirm in its giving and what our hands accomplish through its work might bring salvation to many and glory to God.—E. Lee Phillips

PRAYER. O God, we would escape from ourselves this hour, from our little and partial selves, from our mean and selfish selves. We would escape from our fragmentary and broken selves into thy greatness. Teach us once again the everlasting mystery that only as we lose ourselves in something higher than ourselves can we find ourselves.

To this end give us a great faith to live by. From doubt and disillusionment, from cynicism and rebellion, deliver us, good Lord. For uncertainty, give us confidence. Though we may not see all things clearly, let us see some great things plainly that we may live by them. O God, give us light enough to walk by.

Give us wisdom to live by, we beseech thee. We who walk so often blindly through the tortuous labyrinth of life, give us a clue this day. Let us have vision to see the way we ought to take through some perplexing circumstance. Let high decisions be made on the right side of great questions in thy sanctuary.

Give us love to live by, we pray thee. Enlarge our sympathies; deepen our understandings and compassions. Save us from resentfulness. Cast down within us pettiness and meanness, and lift us up to largeness of mind and heart that we may have the grace to take within the compass of our care those whom by prejudice we have shut out or through dislike have hurt.

Give us great causes to live for. O God, we thank thee for this difficult and serious time, this generation of many dangers and many open doors. Save us from living on a small scale in a great age. Open the eyes of some youths here to causes worth giving life to, that they may be glorified, not alone by what they are, but by what they identify themselves with. Lift us up into better days in the nation. Build justice into our economic order. Grant vision and courage to our statesmen. Make us equal to our international responsibilities and opportunities. And grant that we all may play a part in the things that matter most in our time, so that we may leave this world a fairer home for thy family.—Harry Emerson Fosdick

LECTIONARY MESSAGE

Making Civil Affairs Religious

TEXT: Matt. 22:15–22

One's relationship with governmental authority has always been troublesome to Christian believers. As even in the very days of Christ, how one might respond to government could result in reaction or even rejection by those with a different opinion. The mention of various religio-political parties in the scripture passage emphasizes the divisiveness of both the intent and circumstances of the events as recorded. Feelings ran high and diverse reactions were demonstrated. Jesus dealt with these by enunciating principles which superseded loyalties.

I. *Life cannot be divided between that which is secular and that called sacred.*

(a) Above all else Jesus taught the sovereignty of God over all life. God as Creator and Lord of life was to be worshiped and served (Deut. 10:20). His very nature gave him these prerogatives.

(b) Other authorities could be recognized in order that believers may live a peaceful life (1 Tim. 2:2) only if this does not conflict with loyalty to God.

(c) Even the attempt to divide life may allow a believer to disregard responsibility for actions or accountability for a portion of life and its duties. The principle of separation of church and state requires loyalty to each sphere of life but does not allow either to deny the claims of the other.

II. *Jesus clearly acknowledged the civil role of believers both individually and as churches.*

(a) Believers must accept their role to influence public life and policy. Religious commitment even requires that one exert civil influence both as an attempt to foster the morality of civil authority and to hold that authority accountable.

(b) The ends sought by civil authority never justify means that are unacceptable morally or religiously. Citizens have a responsibility to assist in the effort to establish acceptable principles of civil action.

(c) Christians can never deny their responsibility to be involved both in the service and in the administration required to establish order in society. In his answer, Jesus implies that such service is a debt owed by each citizen to the government that one should expect to be paid.

III. *Loyalty to God must take preeminence.*

(a) Accepting civil responsibility does not set one free from the requirements of discerning the will of God.

(b) The "rights" of God implied in this passage are not spelled out so completely as the obligation to the state. It may be assumed that Jesus concluded that the religious responsibilities of the godly were more clearly known from other biblical teaching.

(c) Clearly Jesus felt that properly acknowledging God would result in accepting responsibility for society and the state. That early believers seem to have understood this responsibility is demonstrated in 1 Pet. 2:13–17.

(d) The image of God in each human requires a respect for and a response to each person by virtue of "the likeness" that is inscribed there. This is the basis for the practice of ultimate "democracy."— Arthur L. Walker, Jr.

SUNDAY: OCTOBER TWENTY-EIGHTH

SERVICE OF WORSHIP

Sermon: The Riches of Renewed Reform
TEXT: 2 Cor. 5: 11–21

Occasionally we benefit from a fresh acquaintance with the richest treasures of our Christian heritage. Today we are compelled to look again at the mine of truth in our Reformation.

I. *Realism as a principle is encouraged by the Scriptures.* Everyone's ideas of religion need to be in tune with eternal verities. Our ideas are colored by many modern misconceptions of practical life; many of our common suppositions are pagan, as were those of Luther's time.

(a) For example, we have emerged from a period of blissful self-confidence into a new understanding of the slavery of human beings under sin.

Up until the Second World War it was very fashionable to be self-confident and optimistic about the human race, in spite of the statements in the Bible and the evidences of history. It was very unpopular to disclose or draw attention to the persistent social blights. Those were everywhere looked upon as anachronistic remnants of a truly bygone age and an outmoded religious viewpoint.

There were a few warning voices from the nineteenth century, but all in all they were held to be expressions of diseased minds.

(b) Realism is found in two forms, both described by Paul in his Second Epistle to the Corinthians, in the seventh chapter, verse 10—"For godly sorrow worketh repentance to salvation not to be repented of; but the sorrow of the world worketh death."

Are the "indulgences" of the world a true cover for the ills the world faces? We are covering our souls' despair with all kinds of indulgences these days. Where do we look for release from despair? To culture? To entertainment or sports? To speed? To gadgets, electronic and other?

What indulgences are men purchasing for their souls in this day? The older Distant Early Warning radar line and the newer Strategic Defense Initiative are seen as necessary precautions in a world of imminent threat of destruction. But what of the soul? Remote programming and tuning? More emphasis on education for a secular society?

It was time, in Luther's day, for people to face reality. And it is time in ours. The reality newly rediscovered in the Reformation was one of the riches we may claim today.

II. *A personal Savior.* Reality forced the pioneers of biblical truth to find a way of making known to the world the power of Jesus Christ. It is time to let the Creator and Master of human instincts remove the scales of illusion from the cultural chaos and ruthless destructiveness of our collective lives by leading us to personal salvation.

(a) Luther's own exhaustive search for satisfaction of his spiritual ordeal is an example of the lengths to which conviction drives men. How far has it driven us today? Has the Epistle to the Romans spoken its healing truth to you again?

We must examine the methods we are using to spread the essential news. In his evangelistic campaigns, Billy Sunday was severely criticized by one gentleman for his unorthodox methods. He is reported to have stated his willingness to use other methods and asked the gentleman to describe the most successful methods he used. After a lengthy pause with no response, Sunday declared, "I like mine better."

(b) And the answer we seek is Jesus Christ. He does satisfy and renew. We do not know all who followed him, but he lifted them by the hands, set them upon their feet, and gave them new life. And he provided them a home in eternity with him.

Without him, it is an unknown wilderness, where hate still prevails. With him, by faith, a new grace is ours.—John R. Rodman

Illustrations

ILLUSION OR POSSIBILITY. There are those who tell us that Christ is a spent force in humanity; that Carlyle was right when he stood before the Italian wayside crucifix and slowly shook his head and said, "Poor fellow, you have had your day"; that his day is over because he spoke to a simple age, but now we face a complicated, scientific age; that he was good, but not good enough—for us.

On the other hand, there are those who feel, with the Carlyle of later years, that his day is just beginning; that what has failed has been a miserable caricature and not the real thing; that even the partial application of his teaching and spirit has been one thing which has kept the soul of humanity alive; that he has been and is the depository and Creator of the finest and best in humanity; that when we have hold of him we have the key to God, to the meaning of the universe and to our own lives; that when we expose ourselves to him in simplicity and obedience, life is changed, lifted, renewed; that he is the one really unspent force in religion—he faces this age as the Great Contemporary and its Judge. One says that dependence upon Jesus is a bubble, an illusion; the other says it is an egg with untold redemptive possibilities.—E. Stanley Jones

OUR FIRST AND LAST FRIEND. There comes a time, said Eugene O'Neill, when we must make friends with God or we shall have no friend at all, not even ourselves. It is a word to be remembered as we grow older and our friends leave us to walk alone.

At last, when the lights of life go out and we enter the valley of the shadow, if we know our best Friend, we need not be afraid. He will be with us, and his rod and his staff will comfort us—our first and last Friend.—Joseph Fort Newton

Sermon Suggestions

A WORTHY PRAYER. TEXT: Ruth 2:1–13, especially verse 12. (1) Concerning a good deed. (2) Concerning a deserved reward. (3) Concerning a just and loving God.

IN DEFENSE OF A MINISTRY. TEXT: 1 Thess. 2:1–8. (1) Courage in face of opposition. (2) Desire to please God. (3) Self-giving affection.

Worship Aids

CALL TO WORSHIP. "Stand fast therefore in the liberty wherewith Christ hath made us free" (Gal. 5:1).

INVOCATION. God of grace and mercy, let the fresh, bracing, healing breezes of your liberating Spirit blow through our guilt, our fear, and our crippling legalisms and create within us clean and joyful and obedient hearts.

OFFERTORY SENTENCE. Unto whomsoever much is given, of him shall be much required: and to whom men have committed much, of him they will ask the more" (Luke 12:48).

OFFERTORY PRAYER. God of all wisdom, thou knowest our hearts, our resources, and our opportunities. Open our eyes that we may see what we are, what we have, and what we can do, to the end that the measure of our gifts may be acceptable in thy sight.

PRAYER. Almighty God, who hast given us this good land for our heritage: We humbly beseech thee that we may always prove ourselves a people mindful of thy favor and glad to do thy will. Bless our land with honorable industry, sound learning, and pure manners. Save us from violence, discord, and confusion; from pride and arrogance, and from every evil way. Defend our liberties, and fashion into one united people the multitudes brought hither out of many kindreds and tongues. Endue with the spirit of wisdom those to whom in thy Name we entrust the authority of government, that there may be justice and peace at home, and that, through obedience to thy law, we may show forth thy praise among the nations of the earth. In the time of prosperity, fill our hearts with thankfulness, and in the day of trouble, suffer not our trust in thee to fail; all which we ask through Jesus Christ our Lord.—*The Book of Common Prayer*

LECTIONARY MESSAGE

The Great Commandment

TEXT: Matt. 22:34–36

Many of the most profound statements of Jesus were given as answers to questions raised by those with whom he dealt. The question of the scribe could be seen as reflecting further confrontation. The response of Jesus, however, provides an in-depth definition of religion. He was concerned for more than current religious commandments. He had no interest in evaluating legalistic requirements.

I. *The question.* The scribe, in simpler language, might well have been asking Jesus, What is your religion? or, What values are most important to you?

(a) *Testing him.* Out of his own background the scribe knew of the 613 laws that the rabbis required to be kept by the faithful. Only 248 of these had a positive connotation. The others were prohibitions. This scribe would naturally ask his question from his own background. He was testing the religious emphasis of Jesus. His interest would have been shaped by his own commitment as to vital commandments.

(b) *A new emphasis.*

(1) Jesus was unconcerned about the emphases of the contemporary schools of theological thought. His emphasis was not related to the simplistic, legalistic commandments to which the scribe obviously referred.

(2) The answer of Jesus avoided religious activities and emphasized relationship with God. He was unconcerned with the characteristics of a religion that placed its major emphasis on understanding actions or rituals. Keeping the great commandment in Jesus' thought would be possible only in God's love.

II. *Love God.*

(a) Love of God demands more than a keeping of laws. It requires total submission of one's life to God. Loving God and acknowledging his lordship both are required in the life of the Christian.

(b) The whole self must be involved in loving God. All the powers God bestowed on human beings through Creation must respond to him.

(1) The heart requires the commitment of emotions.

(2) The soul involves the dynamics of actions.

(3) Thoughts, reasons, and abilities (skills) are bound up in the commitment of the mind.

(c) Love for God results in love for others. Love for others will be possible only when it grows from the love one has for God.

III. *Another question.*

(a) When Jesus asked the question about his own identity he seemed to imply that the religious leaders had been asking the wrong questions. This may even be the basis for the Gospel writer placing the two experiences of questioning together.

(b) Right religion requires the true Lord. Doing the right things is possible only when one has acknowledged the right Lord. Jesus could well have been emphasizing the need for correctly acknowledging the Lord who is to be loved with all one's being.

IV. *No other questions.*

(a) Once the truth was grasped that the importance lay not in the right activities or commandments but in the acknowledgment of the right Lord, no other questions were asked.

(b) Great religious commitment requires not just a great commandment but a great Lord.

(c) Once allegiance has been given to the proper Lord, nothing further is left to explore.—Arthur L. Walker, Jr.

SUNDAY: NOVEMBER FOURTH

SERVICE OF WORSHIP

Sermon: Living the Life to Come—Now!

TEXT: Rev. 7:1-12

Most of us have a facility for viewing heaven as the life to come. Yet, if we have learned anything about heaven, it is that heaven doesn't all lie in the future. It is somehow interconnected with life now. People who are prepared for heaven do not experience a severe disjuncedness when they die; they merely move into a new level of existence, as if the music of life were transposed and played in a different key. While we are in this life, we are constantly preparing for the next one. Almost every time Jesus referred to the afterlife, he did so in terms of how people live and the way this determines their happiness or unhappiness in the world beyond.

What are the marks of a good life? What ways of life should a person cultivate now with the expectancy of a smooth transition to the heavenly existence?

I. It is important to live simply.

(a) The heavenly life, we know, will be uncluttered and unencumbered, like a Shaker household where all the chairs and clothes are hung on pegs at night to facilitate the sweeping of the rooms. It will be like the unburdened way of a Zen monk, who carries all his personal belongings in a small box hanging from a string around his neck.

Living simply means taking time to smell the roses and generally being aware of the life and beauty around us.

(b) Jesus seemed always to be in touch with life around him. His vocabulary was filled with solid, functional language about birds, trees, flowers, fields, animals, and houses, and with these simple terms he helped people to understand eternal realities. As busy as he was in the years of his public ministry, he never allowed his vision to become cluttered and obscured. When he died, his only property was a seamless robe. He was the Son of God, yet lived as a peasant.

II. Living lovingly is also part of it.

(a) The Scriptures teach that "God is love" (1 John 4:8). And if heaven is defined more by the presence of God than by any other factor, which it surely is, then heaven must be the locus of the purest love imaginable.

(b) How different from other people are the people we know who deeply and genuinely love. It would be unthinkable, we say when one of them dies, for so-and-so not to be in heaven. It doesn't matter, at such times, whether the person is Catholic or Jewish or Protestant, Christian or Buddhist or Muslim. It is love, not some doctrinal or ideological construction, that identifies the person with God.

(c) Jesus said it is the lovers who will have first place in heaven, not the famous and powerful people. It is the lovers, and not even the people with a reputation for being religious, who will be honored by God. They will be called out and esteemed because they have welcomed strangers and clothed the naked and visited the sick and imprisoned; and others, who expected to be acknowledged for their importance in the world, will be disappointed and cast out.

III. Finally, living the life to come means living worshipfully.

(a) When we live simply and lovingly, we are living like the saints in heaven, and it is only a short step—so short we almost do not need to take it—to the realization that everything our eyes behold, including ourselves, belongs to God. And when this realization strikes us, there is nothing to do but to fall down and worship.

(b) There is a beautiful picture of it in the seventh chapter of the Book of Revelation. The writer, John, is caught up in a vision of heaven. He looks around and sees "a great multitude which no man could number, from every nation, from all tribes and peoples and tongues, standing before the throne and before the Lamb, clothed in white robes, with palm branches in their hands, and crying out with a loud voice, 'Salvation belongs to our God who sits upon the throne, and to the Lamb!' " (Rev. 7:9–10).

The angels too are worshiping, falling on their faces before the throne and saying, "Amen! Blessing and glory and wisdom and thanksgiving and honor and power and might be to our God for ever and ever! Amen!" (Rev. 7:12). Their words carry a sevenfold ascription, signifying the most complete and ultimate adoration possible.

One of the heavenly elders near the throne addresses John, asking, "Who are these, clothed in white robes, and whence have they come?" John, recognizing the question as rhetorical, says, "Sir, you know." The elder continues, saying that these were the people who came through "the great tribulation"—the period of intense suffering on earth. Their robes have been washed and made white through the blood of the Lamb.

(c) Whoever knows this, and lives with this vision, will live worshipfully in this life, expecting God to triumph over death and evil.—John Killinger

Illustrations

THE DOERS. C. S. Lewis has reminded us in a rather dramatic fashion that those persons who have convictions about the next world make the largest contributions in this world.—W. H. Hinson

ABUNDANT LIVING. "I have had such a good life, said one dear parishioner in her nineties, "that I do not see how heaven could be much better." I am sure that when she slipped away from this life she experienced no radical derailment of the soul but merely noticed that the train on which she was riding had entered a more serene and beautiful landscape.—John Killinger

Sermon Suggestions

A MARRIAGE MADE IN HEAVEN. TEXT: Ruth 4:4–17. (1) According to human custom. (2) According to divine providence (see Matt. 1:3–16).

THE WORD YOU HEAR. TEXT: 1 Thess. 2:9–13, 17–20. (1) It is the word of a human being—a fatherly word lived as well as spoken. (2) It is the Word of God—a demanding word at work in believers. (3) It is a word that brings ultimate joy to the messenger.

Worship Aids

CALL TO WORSHIP. "Wherefore God also hath highly exalted him, and given him a name which is above every name: That at the name of Jesus every knee should bow, of things in heaven, and things in earth, and things under the earth" (Phil. 2:9–10).

INVOCATION. It is our confession, our heavenly Father, and it is our joy to remember that while we are praising thee here below there is an anthem above, and when we think of what is above us and those who have been dear to us who have passed on, we join with the heavenly host and say, "Praise God from whom all blessings flow."

How they have been flowing for these many years into all our lives! How many times we have mistaken the meaning of these blessings; how often we have not called them blessings at all—but "praise God from whom all blessings flow" that the blessings still are flowing; that it has made no difference with our heavenly Father's bounty that we have counted it a little thing. O forgive us, gracious God, that we have ever underestimated, that we have missed in appreciation the divine Gift. And give us one more gift this morning: thy perpetual blessings, and especially as we worship here bring our lives into the great repair shop of thy love as we bring our foolishness and our sin and our needs, along with the better things.

O give us thyself, the presence of thyself, and all will be well, in Jesus' name. Amen.—Frank W. Gunsaulus

OFFERTORY SENTENCE. "Now the end of the commandment is charity out of a pure heart, and of a good conscience, and of faith unfeigned" (1 Tim. 1:5).

OFFERTORY PRAYER. Lord, align our priorities with thy will and fill this offering with thy purposes, so that how we live and what we give might resound to thine everlasting glory.—E. Lee Phillips

PRAYER. Abiding God, in whose providence and care we have been kept the night through; in whose goodness and mercy we have been birthed to a new Lord's day; and by whose gracious invitation we have come to this glad place and hour, receive our presence, mighty God, as expression of our gratitude and accept our worship as pure thanksgiving of our hearts.

Eternal and forever God, whom all the saints adore, we pause to remember the saints who have gone before us and in whose unseen presence we live and offer our best to you. In remembering them, O God, our hearts are quickened and warmed, for through and in them we came to know you. In their ordinary, unpublished lives, by their love and witness, we

have seen your face. In their joyful service and quiet sacrifices we have caught a glimpse of your sure call to faithful discipleship. From them and to you, dear God, may we live nobler lives, answer the higher call, see the long view and walk the narrow path. For all the saints, from beginning to this day, we rise up and call them blessed.

Loving God, whose eyes are teared with compassion and whose everlasting arms are opened with healing embrace, whose tender heart is always broken first, we pray now for our torn and hurting family. Lord, sometimes it seems our whole world is in dark travail. We pray for families shadowed by anger and pain and deep agony; for children wounded by the scattered debris of broken relationships and selfish choices; for youth struggling with self-esteem and wanting desperately just to be accepted and loved; for adults wandering in the wilderness of despair and defeat; for people slapped down by discouraging medical reports.

God of all time and all people, God who knows and loves us best, we worship and pray, we remember and we hope in the strong, saving name of Jesus Christ our Lord.—William M. Johnson

LECTIONARY MESSAGE

Setting a Bad Example
TEXT: Matt. 23:1–12

"No person is ever so devoid of value," goes the old joke, "that he cannot at least serve as a bad example." Indeed sometimes we learn best what we want to do or ought to do by coming into contact with someone doing the opposite. Watching loud parents at a youth baseball game yelling abuse at the umpire and shouting embarrassing rebukes to their own children when they strike out is a marvelous incentive to adopt a spirit of quiet forbearance. Observing an ambitious glad-hander working a crowd of people, slapping everyone on the back but really knowing none of them, makes one content and glad to have a few, cherished friends.

In this passage from Matthew, Jesus is teaching his followers about leadership and life-style, and he begins not by saying what they should do but by pointing to examples so extravagantly foolish and bad that one would want to avoid them like the chicken pox. Jesus' bad examples, in this case, are familiar ones: the scribes and the Pharisees. What made them worthy of avoidance? They preached eloquent sermons about the spiritual laws, but they failed to keep any of them themselves. They viewed worship as a fashion show, a chance to show off their new robes and fancy prayer stoles. Moreover, they always went to the head of the line at feasts and reserved highly visible pews for themselves in the synagogue.

Now we should remember that, historically, not every scribe and not every Pharisee fit into this hypocritical portrait. As F. W. Beare has said, for "most of the scribes and Pharisees . . . the Law was not a burden but a joy . . ." But evidently there were enough religious leaders who did flaunt their status and power, that Jesus' puncturing of their vanity no doubt struck a chord of recognition, and perhaps even laughter, among his hearers.

Jesus' goal, though, was not to make fun, but to make better disciples. "Do not do what they do," said Jesus, "for the greatest among you should live like a servant." Jesus replaced the bad example with a very threatening good one—a servant—and, thus, sent his disciples on a search mission through their own lives. "Are there places in my own life," he wanted them to ask, "where I am captive to the same vain, pompous, prestige-hungry religion?"

So, looking at ourselves, what do we see? We see some churches that count members and money rather than deeds of mercy and service. We see ministers who put *B.A.*, *Th.M.*, *D.D.* after their names, but little humility into their ministries. The story is told of Carlyle Marney that he was once given a tour of a new church building. Pointing to the cross atop the steeple, Marney's guide said, "That cross alone cost $25,000."

"That's strange," replied Marney. "Christians used to be able to get those for nothing."

So Jesus gives us two examples: a pompous bad example and a humble good one. It may seem, then, that the crucial question is, which one shall we imitate, the bad one or the good one? But Jesus finally poses an even deeper question than that: Whom will we serve? "You have one master," he said, "the Christ." If our master is self, then get out the fancy vestments, the expensive pew cushions, the empty words, and let's play church. If our master is Christ, however, then let us pick up our crosses of service and follow.—Thomas G. Long

SUNDAY: NOVEMBER ELEVENTH

SERVICE OF WORSHIP

Sermon: Abundant Giving

TEXT: Exod. 36:3b–7

"I need to ask the people of this church to do something. Your giving has exceeded the needs of the church for its work for the year. Would you please refrain from giving any more until you are notified of further need."

Does that sound incredible? It happened one time!

Let us recall the story of Moses, struggling to lead the people of Israel through the wilderness, as they complained about conditions and learned to follow him.

God summoned Moses up to the mountain where he revealed himself to Moses and entrusted the Law to him. At the same time, God instructed Moses to build a tabernacle as the center of worship for the people of Israel.

Moses came down from the mountain, gave the people the Law, and instructed them on building the tabernacle. He selected highly skilled craftsmen, Bezalel and Oholiab, to design and create the tabernacle according to the plan given. Moses encouraged the people to give generously of their possessions to support the building of the place of worship. The response was overwhelming (Exod. 36:3b–7).

All of a sudden Moses and the builders had a problem of abundance. There was more than enough to do the work the Lord had given his people to do. How does a generous outpouring like this occur? Is it possible for the people of a church to give this generously? Under what conditions will Christians give as the people did in building the tabernacle? Two conditions must be met if generosity is to overflow from God's people in supporting the work he has given us.

I. Abundant giving results from an encounter with God.

Moses had just been up on the mountain with God and had received a fresh revelation of his presence. In the presence of the living God, faith grows. When we have genuinely experienced God, our trust in him increases. Out of this trust, God's people are able and willing to do many things that would otherwise seem impossible. As we see Christ active among his people, we are challenged to greater faith and greater giving.

A leader's encounter with God often determines the people's awareness of God's presence. The people of Israel had learned, through many trials and errors, to trust God and their leaders. They had grown in faith. In addition to trusting Moses, the people knew they could trust Bezalel and Oholiab to direct the building of the tabernacle. Confidence in the leaders God calls makes it easier to share in his work. When leaders earn credibility and are trustworthy, God's people respond readily and generously to the needs presented and the work to be done. Such a combination results in great achievements for God.

When Christians see the church as Christ's Body and see him as the head of the Body, this understanding provides them a reason to give generously. The church is the channel through which Christ does his work. Our support of the church and its ministries reflects the depth of our belief in what Christ desires to accomplish through his church. A clear demonstration of what we believe is reflected in our investments of money and energies. Great faith produces generous giving.

II. Abundant giving results from commitment to God.

High commitment inspires unusual sacrifices.

Joe Delaney was a star running back for the Kansas City Chiefs. In the summer of 1983, while he was home in Louisiana, two boys were drowning in a pond near his home. Although he was not a good swimmer, he jumped in to try to save them. He was unable to do so and lost his life in the effort. Those who knew Joe said that it was typical of the life he lived and the way he played football. He was always ready to do his best and give himself to the needs of others.

The people of Israel committed themselves to build a place of worship. "And everyone whose heart stirred him and everyone whose spirit moved him came and brought the Lord's contribution for the work of the tent of meeting and for all its service and for the holy garments" (Exod. 35:21, NASB). What a beautiful picture for a church to see when it is considering the needs of its ministries!

To accomplish its mission, a church and its people must be committed to the ministries it has been given—winning the lost, making disciples of the saved, comforting those who hurt, feeding the hungry. To spread the gospel and to share God's love must be a passion, not a platitude. No greater evidence of a church's commitment to its ministries could be written than that "the people bring much more than enough for doing the work which the Lord commanded us to do."

A church's ministries cannot always be measured in dollars, but they must be deeply rooted in the lives of its members. How do you place a dollar value on mending a broken home or a life redeemed by Christ? How do you cost account a hospital in Nigeria? How do you financially audit a child's response to the love of Christ? In light of Christ's work, Christians should ask, "What are the needs?" and "What shall I give?" Commitment generates generosity. An old English proverb says, "He that gives his heart will not deny his money."

What a wonderful problem for God's people to face—abundance of resources to do God's work. God has been generous with us. He has lavished grace in abundance on all of us. He has allowed many of us in the United States to have much more than we need. Our country struggles economically as much with its surpluses as with its shortages.

What is the Christian's response to the abundance God has given? Should it not be said of Christians in America as Paul wrote of the Macedonian Christians: "Their abundance of joy . . . overflowed in the wealth of their liberality" (2 Cor. 8:2, NASB). Because, Paul further explains, "they first gave themselves to the Lord and to us by the will of God" (2 Cor. 8:5, NASB).

The work of Christ in any church will be well supported when the conditions are met as they were when the tabernacle was being built. Undergirding the ministries reflected in a church's budget is not a problem when God's people find the joy of generosity. Let it be said of this church, "The stuff they had was sufficient to do all the work and more."—Ernest White

Illustrations

PINNACLE OF HAPPINESS.   Albert Schweitzer, scholar, lecturer, Europe's master organist, in middle life threw everything away the successful years had brought. At last, when he had performed his first operation and had brought a black bundle of suffering humanity from the gates of death back to life, he exclaimed, "I wish my friends everywhere but knew the exquisite joy of an hour like this!" He reached that pinnacle of happiness as all must who find it, not by getting, but by giving.—Frederick Brown Harris

THE SACRAMENT OF SERVICE.   An old and wise story tells of two men cutting stone. The work was hard and the sun was hot. A passerby asked one man what he was doing. "Look and see for yourself; I am cutting a stone," was the rather curt reply.

Not far away he asked the other man the same question, and he said, with a gleam in his eye, "Sir, I am building a cathedral." One saw his work as merely a job all by itself, a thing to get done and have done with it. The other man saw the same work as it was related to a vast design, as having a place in a pattern, the working out of which would make a house of God. He felt it an honor to have a part in such a dream.

To know that our work, whatever it may be, has a place and part in the vast network of human service not only makes our labor lighter, but lifts it up and gives it meaning—we see its value in a larger context.—Joseph Fort Newton

Sermon Suggestions

WHAT IS REAL RELIGION?   TEXT: Amos 5:18–24. (1) Not mere waiting for God to set things right. (2) Not mere rites, ceremonies, and festivals of worship. (3) Rather, a worship of God embodied in genuine efforts to set things right in the world now.

DEAD OR ALIVE—IN GOD'S GOOD HANDS. TEXT: 1 Thess. 4:13–18. (1) The Lord will come for all who are united with him. (2) Then we shall always be with the Lord. (3) But now we can comfort one another with this blessed hope.

Worship Aids

CALL TO WORSHIP.   "We have thought of thy loving-kindness, O God, in the midst of thy temple. According to thy name, O God, so is thy praise unto the ends of the earth: thy right hand is full of righteousness" (Ps. 48:9–10).

INVOCATION.   Today, O God, help us to rejoice in the greatest of all gifts, the gift of your Son, Jesus Christ our Lord, who in turn has given himself for us an offering and a sacrifice to God for a sweet-smelling savour.

OFFERTORY SENTENCE.   "Jesus said unto him, If thou wilt be perfect, go and sell that thou hast, and give to the poor, and thou shalt have treasure in heaven: and come and follow me" (Matt. 19:21).

OFFERTORY PRAYER.   Almighty God, you proclaim your truth in every age by many voices: Direct, in our time, we pray, those who speak where many listen and write what many read; that they may do their part in making the heart of this people wise, its mind sound, and its will righteous; to the honor of Jesus Christ our Lord.—*The Book of Common Prayer*

PRAYER.   O Lord, in whose hands are life and death, by whose power we are sustained, and by whose mercy we are spared, look down upon us with pity. Forgive us that we have until now so much neglected the duty thou hast assigned to us and suffered the days and hours of which we give account to pass away without any endeavor to accomplish thy will. Make us to remember, O God, that every day is thy gift and ought to be used according to thy command. Grant us, therefore, so to repent of our negligence that we may obtain mercy from thee and pass the time thou shalt yet allow us in diligent performance of thy commands, through Jesus Christ.—Adapted from Samuel Johnson

LECTIONARY MESSAGE

Fuel for the Lamps
TEXT: Matt. 25:1–13

One day Jesus told his disciples a story about a wedding, and a number of years later, when Matthew wrote his Gospel, he understood that story to be a parable about the church. In Jesus' story, there were ten maidens on the wedding guest list. Five of them, Jesus said, were wise, and five of them were foolish. Old Matthew heard that story, thought about his congregation, and said to himself, "Yes, that's the way it is in the church. Some are wise and some are foolish."

Matthew knew that the church was never pure. It might be nice to dream of a church where everybody was good, faithful, full of grace, and wise, but Matthew knew that the real church was very much a mixed reality. There were weeds growing alongside wheat in the pews; the gospel net drew in bad fish as well as good ones; there were wise and foolish together in the church, Matthew knew.

What made some of the maidens wise,

said Jesus, was that they had brought along some extra jars of oil for their lamps. The other maidens had only the little bit of oil already in their lamps, nothing more, and this was definitely foolish because one never knows how long the wait may be for a wedding to begin. Sure enough, the bridegroom was delayed, and the flames in the foolish maidens' lamps began to go out.

Matthew heard that part of the story, too, thought again about his congregation, and said to himself once more, "Yes, that's the way it is in the church." Matthew's congregation was set out there in society and given the job of making disciples and baptizing and teaching and serving and waiting for that great day when the trumpet would sound and the great victory of God would break through and the marriage feast of the Lamb would begin. But it was proving to be a long wait. The days between Easter Day and Wedding Day were many and long and hard, and already many lamps were flickering because the oil of hope had run low.

If Matthew could see the church today, he would not be surprised. He would find a church in which some are still wise and some are still foolish. He would find a church in which some are prepared to wait and watch while others cannot make it through the long night. Some, even in the darkness, can pray, "Thy kingdom come," and then hold their lamps high as they work and worship and wait. Others, however, pray, "If the kingdom does not come today, I cannot go on." There are too many needs, too many hurting people, too few signs of progress, too little hope, and their lamps are going out.

The issue, Matthew would tell us, is oil. No one's lamp can remain lit without oil, and the time to secure it is now, not at the end when our own resources are burnt out. It will be too late then. But where do we get this oil? Matthew would tell us that our lamps can be supplied only when we repent of our own self-sufficiency and turn in trust and obedience to the One whose strength can become our strength, whose victory can become our constant hope, whose light can burn in our lives without ever being extinguished—the One who promised, even in the darkness, "I am with you always to the close of the age" (Matt. 29:20).—Thomas G. Long

SUNDAY: NOVEMBER EIGHTEENTH

SERVICE OF WORSHIP

Sermon: You Can Have It All

TEXT: Mark 8:34

I. The men and women of Madison Avenue really know where we live, don't they? The commercials are often the most upbeat, positive minutes you'll come across in watching television. Take that commercial for a product that hails from my home town. "You can have it all!" From clothes to cars, health to sexual attractiveness, it's all there for you. Don't settle for a slice of the pie, you can have the whole pie. Don't let anybody tell you that you can't have it all. And it seems so effortless in the commercial: perfect bodies that exercise but don't sweat, hammock and shade trees, easy conviviality, romance. You can have it all!

Christopher Lasch, in his book *The Culture of Narcissism*, observed, "Having no hope of improving their lives in any way that matters people have convinced themselves that what matters is psychic self-improvement: getting in touch with their feelings, eating health food, taking lessons in ballet or belly-dancing, immersing themselves in the wisdom of the East, jogging, learning how to 'relate,' overcoming the fear of pleasure." "You can have it all." The Christian church seems to follow along and offers a smorgasbord of activities aimed at "psychic self-improvement." Of course, much of this is good, even needed, but have we missed something essential?

II. The scene recorded in the Gospel of Mark just before our scripture lesson shows Peter making the great confession that Jesus is the Christ, the Messiah. He seems to have it all together. The Messiah! Think of what that will mean for his followers (for Peter); he can have it all! But then Jesus talks of his death, of going to the cross. Oh no, this can't be? Peter tries to hold him back from freely sacrificing his life. Jesus, his voice full of emotion, says, "Get behind me, Satan." Peter has missed something very essential, even though he has confessed that Jesus is the Christ.

Did Peter miss it all, end up on the wrong side when he sought to hold Jesus back from sacrificing his life for others? Even those who believe in the Christ can echo the thoughts of the Evil One. It was not for Peter, or for us, some intentional Faustian compact with the devil. We settle for what is expedient instead of what is essential. Remember this futile craving to have it all comes when we miss that which alone is worth having. We are told to seek first the rule and reign of God in our lives and all those things that matter will follow, but how do we do that? Jesus says if you want what really lasts you must first deny yourself. That does not mean giving up something for Lent. It means believing that there is something more important than your own comfort, power, prestige, or security. It means denying that self's claims to be king and following Jesus in making the will of God and the service of others the goal of life.

III. Yet to be his disciples, to experience all of life, we must take up our cross and follow him. I didn't say that, Jesus did! How easily we misunderstand that phrase. "What a cross he has to bear, what a mother-in-law he has." "She is bearing a tremendous cross with that man for a boss." We use the phrase for any sickness, inconvenience, annoyance. Yet as Jesus used the phrase it was not something thrust upon you but something you chose for Christ's sake. Here is the most dramatic way of saying, "This is what being a disciple of Jesus Christ will cost." To even mention the despised symbol of Roman execution must have shocked, even angered his listeners. It was not something made of gold to be worn around the neck.

The vertical portion of the cross was placed permanently at the sight of execution. The condemned person had to carry the heavy crossbar. Arriving at the place of crucifixion the criminal was thrown onto the crossbar, hands stretched out and nailed into place. The bar and condemned man were lifted to the top of the vertical position and jammed into place. The feet were nailed in such a way that there was just enough leverage for the one being crucified to lift himself up and breathe until the pain in the feet became so painful he slumped down again. This agonizing process lasted hours, often days. When finally the pain in the whole body became too great, suffocation took place and the one being crucified (with an awful gasp) died.

IV. We must see Jesus' cross as he did before we can accept and take up our cross and follow him. Jesus knew who he was because he continually gave himself up to the will of his heavenly Father. He discovered his true self. He was the Lamb of God who was slain for the sins of the world past, present, future. Can you be captured by that mind-boggling thought? In his perfect obedience of the cross is perfect love. This love is the only power that can save you and me our own destructive selfishness. So great a love, so great a sacrifice . . . let it happen to you again. That sacrificial love is the heart of our faith, not *trying* to be good or lovable or respectable. We can only be loved, accepted, forgiven into a new life. Let it happen again to you, for from it comes all that really matters and the wisdom to know what matters.

Then we begin to discover what it means to take up our cross and follow him. Jesus used the strongest image he could to portray what it means to follow him; not take up your options, nor your comfortable distance, but take up your cross. We give up all claims on ourselves to receive our true self. Jesus' "cross" was not so much the ghastly pain as being able to forgive those who rejected him. Why do you have to forgive? Whose sorrow and suffering are you running from? What part of your life needs to be made whole, what memory healed? In the answer to these questions you may find your cross; in taking it up and following him you will find life.

What better time than now to begin or begin anew the pilgrimage of taking up your cross and following him?—Gary D. Stratman

Illustrations

A SERIOUS SIN. In the traditional list of of the seven deadly sins, pride usually comes first. In a modern list, that position could be occupied by ingratitude.

God does not need our gratitude. God's ego does not have to be pumped up with praise and thanks from us mortals or from anything else in Creation. God is not so vain as to need constant flattery and is not so petulant as to turn against those who ignore him.

But we need to be thankful. When we ignore God, we act as if our lives were in our hands and do what seems best to us. When we do that, we destroy the order which God has made; we get crossed up in relationships with the people with whom we live and work and whom we love; we even reach the point where we destroy ourselves by catering to our own whims.

In grace, God has placed us where we are and has made himself known to us. In grace, God sustains us and directs us. In proper gratitude, we give thanks to him in worship and glorify him in daily service.— Roger H. Crook

PUTTING OUT THE FLEECE. In western North Carolina there is a large plant with the name *Stonecutter* displayed in tall, brightly lighted letters over the top of the plant. A young man was struggling with the growing awareness that God was calling him to preach. As he rode along the highway, he put out a fleece prayer. He said, "God, if I really am supposed to preach, let that *S* over there on *Stonecutter* go dark." As he returned home from work that night indeed the *S* was dark except for a tip of light at the bottom.

You would think that would settle the matter for him; but when he told me about it, he was still uncommitted. He majored on the tip of light at the bottom of the *S*. That is the trouble with fleece prayers— we do not believe the answer even after we make up the rules. God speaks to us many times. He leads us through the advice of Christian friends. He guides us through the Scriptures. But we do not listen. We want more proof, so we make up a fleece prayer. Instead of using our energy like that, should not we simply rejoice in God's leading and get to work doing his will?—T. Keith Edwards

Sermon Suggestions

THE DAY OF THE LORD—BAD NEWS, GOOD NEWS. TEXT: Zeph. 1:7, 12–18. (1) The bad news—the proud and the oppressors will receive the consequences of their evil ways. (2) The good news—the field will be cleared for God to do a new thing.

IF WE BELONG TO THE DAY. TEXT: 1 Thess. 5:1–11, NEB. (1) The "day of the Lord" will not take us by surprise. (2) We will be prepared for whatever comes, by faith and love and by our hope of salvation. (3) We will hearten and fortify one another.

Worship Aids

CALL TO WORSHIP. "Jesus answered and said unto him, if a man love me he will keep my words: and my Father will love him, and we will come unto him, and make our abode with him" (John 14:23).

INVOCATION. Lord of all bounty, expand our soul in the depths of appreciation as today we are reminded that every good and perfect gift is from above. In the name of him who keeps on giving, Christ Jesus, our Savior.—E. Lee Phillips

OFFERTORY SENTENCE. "For God is not unrighteous to forget your work and labour of love, which ye have shewed toward his name, in that ye have ministered to the saints, and do minister" (Heb. 6:10).

OFFERTORY PRAYER. Lord, make us so grateful for all we have been given that we will joyously share of our bounty that others may be blessed as we have been blessed, through Jesus Christ our Lord.—E. Lee Phillips

PRAYER. Eternal Spirit, thou dwellest in light unapproachable, beyond the power of our thought to comprehend or our imagination to portray. Yet thou art revealed to us in the order of the world we live in, in the truth our minds discover, in the inward presence of thy Spirit, and above all in Christ, thy Son. With reverent hearts we worship thee.

We would bring our fragmentary lives into the presence of thy wholeness. We would bring our transient thoughts into the light of thine eternity. We would bring our restless spirits into the calm strength of thine everlasting purpose.

See what complaints we have brought into thy sanctuary against the circumstances that have fretted us, against the human friends who have failed us, against the enemies who have wronged us, and even against the justice of thine order that has hurt us. Teach us, nevertheless, we beseech thee, to search our own lives, to see that each man is his own destiny, that each soul is its own heaven and its own hell. Send us back into our own souls to find there, by thy grace, peace and power and adequacy to conquer life. May we be victors and not victims.—Harry Emerson Fosdick

LECTIONARY MESSAGE

The Haves and the Have-Nots

TEXT: Matt. 25:14–30

Sometimes we read stories that are full of surprises and keep us in suspense all the way to the end. We rapidly turn the pages of a mystery novel, for example, wondering who the culprit will finally turn out to be. Other stories, however, reveal their secrets in the beginning, and as we read these stories we look, not for a surprise, but for the gradual unfolding of what we already know. We discover almost from the outset, for instance, that Hamlet is a flawed figure, and we follow the unraveling of his life to its inevitable tragic conclusion.

Jesus' parable of the talents is *not* a suspense story. It is one of those stories where we know in advance how the story will evolve. A wealthy man, the story begins, is on his way out the door on a journey, and he entrusts various sums of money—five talents, two talents, and one talent—to three of his servants. Then the story goes on to tell us what these servants did with their shares, but there are really no surprises here. Jesus has told us from the start that the servants received money "according to their ability." In other words, the one-talent servant is a man of little ability—we are told that up front—and so we watch to see the ongoing tragedy of his life unfold.

Sure enough, while the master is gone, the five-talent servant doubles his money, and the two-talent servant does the same. They are people of ability, and they live up to their billing. They are rewarded handsomely for their efforts. But the one-talent servant, short on competence and long on cowardice, predictably messes things up yet again and is punished for it.

This parable, then, marches inexorably toward its moral: "For to every one who has will more be given, and he will have abundance; but from him who has not, even what he has will be taken away" (Matt. 25:29, RSV). Or, to put it in common language, "The haves will get richer, and the have-nots will get poorer."

Now that is an unusual word to come from Jesus—a dangerous and easily misunderstood truth, really—and Christians must be careful where we speak that truth.

I. One place where we should not speak that truth is in the maternity ward of the hospital. We peer through the glass at all the bassinets, pink and blue blankets wrapped around the newborns. We already know, don't we, that some of those babies have parents who love them and will care for them and some of them have been born into homes where there is no love or nurture. Some of those babies are haves, and some are have-nots. "The haves will get richer, and the have-nots will get poorer." That is the truth, but in the maternity ward it is not the gospel truth, and Christians must not speak it about those born to privilege.

II. Another place where we should not speak the parable's truth is among the homeless. These people live in a world where the rich get richer, while what little they have is gradually stripped away from them. "The haves will get richer, and the have-nots will get poorer." That is the truth, but in the soup kitchen it is not the gospel truth, and Christians must not speak it about material wealth.

III. Christians must speak the truth of this parable only in the way that Jesus spoke it: It is a truth about the kingdom of God, not the riches of this life. What it really means to "have" is to possess the treasure of God's grace that does not perish. Those who are rich in grace and mercy will have their wealth increase. Those who are poor in forgiveness and compassion will find that even their souls shrivel away.

The world may not honor the treasure of the kingdom—righteousness, peace, meekness, love, mercy—but for those who invest their live sin these graces, there are finally no surprises. In the end the promised benediction comes, "Well done, good and faithful servant. You have been faithful over a little. I will set you over much" (Matt. 25:21, RSV).—Thomas G. Long

SUNDAY: NOVEMBER TWENTY-FIFTH

SERVICE OF WORSHIP

Sermon: The Highway to God
TEXT: Jer. 29:13

I am deeply impressed with the conviction that there are those listening today who need religion's basic message—that upon which all others depend. Therefore, I am speaking primarily to that man or woman who needs to turn his or her footsteps down the highway that leads to God.

No person on the face of the earth today is more than four steps away from God.

I. The first of these steps is what I would call a sense of need.

(a) No one can be helped until he realizes that he needs help. The person who has determined to go forward in his own strength has alienated himself from those streams of assistance that flow out from the throne of God.

Self-satisfaction, self-complacency is the key that effectively bars the door of the human heart. You may remember that it was the Pharisee who stood outside the gates of God's joy because he felt no need. It was the publican who was overwhelmed with a sense of sin, who prayed "God, be merciful to me a sinner," and who received the grace of God.

(b) There are certain things we can do to help God create this sense of need within us. In the first place, we can *look at ourselves.* "Know thyself," said the wise philosopher. We need to examine our lives—not just the living rooms and the libraries, but the attics, the cellars, and the hidden closets about which only we know. We need to see the darkened corners, checkered with cobwebs and littered with trash. We need to be open, frank, and devastatingly brutal in our self-analysis. But we dare not stop here: we must move on to *look at Jesus,* for he is God to us, the revelation of the Divine Spirit at the center of the Creation. And he is perfect, he who said, "Be ye therefore perfect, even as your Father which is in heaven is perfect." Measured by that standard, every one of us must acknowledge his or her sinfulness and nothingness.

II. The second step on the highway to God is the step of repentance.

(a) Now, repentance presupposes sin, and the blasé pride of our fickle generation has been too sophisticated to acknowledge that sin is real—particularly the sin in our own lives. No man, no woman can get to God while sin is in the way. There must be repentance, and repentance is first of all *confession,* taking the skeleton out of the closet. I like this illustration: When some impurity gets into drinking water or milk, the careful, cautious housewife sets in on the stove and *boils the poison out.* Confessing one's sins is "boiling the poison out," releasing the disease that holds one's mind in its awful bondage. The burden of a sin unconfessed is a brace that shackles the soul. It throws life off center and leads to disaster.

(b) But repentance is more than mere confession. There must also be a *moral disavowal of sin.* A person must hate sin enough to abandon it, not for a season, but forever. The trouble with so many well-intentioned people who are trying to live Christian lives today is that there has never been a final decree of divorcement between them and their sins but only a temporary separation that has led at last to a fatal reunion. There must be a moral disavowal that says NO to sin FOREVER.

III. The third step on the highway that leads to God is the step of consecration.

(a) This follows repentance logically as well as chronologically. Repentance is the laying of the bad things of life at the foot of the cross; consecration is the laying of all things there. The wise men brought to the infant Savior their gifts of gold and frankincense and myrrh. The gold represented their material possessions; the frankincense represented their deepest longings and aspirations, the dreams of their souls; the myrrh represented their lives, their sufferings, and if need be, their deaths. They brought everything they had and placed it at the feet of Christ.

(b) Many a person is missing the blessings of Christian joy because there is some area of his life or her life that has not been yielded to the Lord. It may be an individual's wrong attitudes toward people of other races; it may be a person's insensitive acceptance of the privileges of affluence in a world poverty-stricken and famine-ridden. If there is *any* area of life that has not been totally surrendered to God, then an individual has not yet taken the third step that leads down the highway to God.

IV. The last, best step on the highway to God is the step of faith.

(a) This is trusting God to do his part when we are perfectly sure that we have done ours. To the person who has felt a need, who has repented, who has made a full consecration of life, our God brings his priceless gift of salvation and life abundant and eternal. "This is a faithful saying, worthy of all acceptation, that Christ Jesus came into the world to save sinners."

(b) It is not enough to repent or to consecrate oneself—these acts alone may be ethical acts and religion is vastly more than ethics. There must be that final act when we accept what Jesus Christ has done for us and receive the life of God, his nature and his love, into our hearts by faith—it is this that transforms ethics into love and sets the heart of the universe aquiver with the throb of redemption. The Christian life in the end is a *love relationship*, a personal tryst between a human being and God, begun when we receive his cleansing power and love into our lives by faith. You can do that today, wherever you are, whoever you are. You can take this last step on the highway that leads to God.—Earl G. Hunt, Jr.

Illustrations

A FATHER'S EFFORT.   One of the happiest men I ever saw was a father who came forward in a commitment service with his son. That father was a quiet man. He was not involved in many church activities. In fact, he did not attend all of the church services. He had two sons. The older son had left home and was having a difficult life. The father came forward during the invitation with his younger son. He said something like this: "Pastor, my son is the most precious thing I have. I have fed him, clothed him, educated him, and cared for him. I almost failed, however, to give him the best thing I have. Today I prayed with him, and he received Christ. Now I stand here with him. This is our finest hour."—Robert L. Hamblin

GOD COMMITTED TO US.   You can depend upon God in a world of broken principles and shattered ideals. Years ago the late Dr. Roy L. Smith told a lovely story about a dear old couple who lived alone in a modest cottage on a tiny island in the Great Lakes area. They had no neighbors. They were friends of the Smith family, and the Smiths agonized over the peril that threatened this couple as their years advanced. One day they had a council of love and decided to invite the old man and his wife to spend the rest of their days as guests in the Smith household. The next morning Dr. Smith and his daughter went by boat to the island where the old couple lived by themselves. After the amenities

had been observed, as tactfully as he could Dr. Smith broached the purpose of their visit and extended the invitation. The old couple heard him through, and then the old man turned to his sweetheart of the lengthening years and said, "Of course, we can't accept the invitation, can we dear?" Dr. Smith began to remonstrate and restate his case, but the old man held up his hand for silence. "Roy," he said, "you simply don't understand; come and we'll show you." Then the old couple, arm in arm, led the Smiths out of the house and through the yard and along a winding pathway that led into the island wilderness until at last they came to a small clearing with a carpet of green grass and a border of beautiful flowers. In the center of this little clearing was a tiny mound with a snow-white cross at its head. The old man put his arm around his wife and then very quietly said, "We can't leave our island home, for, you see, we lost a son here." And so, my dear friends, no matter what happens, God can never leave this floating island in his skies because, you see, he lost a son here! *You can depend upon God.* When everything else collapses and fails, you can depend upon him.—Earl G. Hunt, Jr.

Sermon Suggestions

WHEN THE LORD GOD IS SHEPHERD. TEXT: Ezek. 34:11–16, 20–24. (1) He seeks his scattered sheep. (2) He provides for his gathered sheep. (3) He judges the oppressive sheep.

THE REIGN OF CHRIST.   TEXT: 1 Cor. 15:20–28, RSV. (1) The fact—in his Resurrection. (2) Its nature—the subjection of all things under him. (3) Its limits—until Christ is "subjected to him who put all things under him."

Worship Aids

CALL TO WORSHIP.   "Ho, every one that thirsteth, come ye to the waters, and he that hath no money; come ye, buy, and eat; yea, come buy wine and milk without money and without price. Wherefore do you spend money for that which is not bread? and your labour for that which satisfieth not? hearken diligently unto me, and eat ye that which is good, and let your soul delight itself in fatness. Incline your ear, and come unto me: hear, and your soul shall live; and I make an everlasting covenant with you, even the sure mercies of David" (Isa. 55:1–3).

INVOCATION. God of holiness, whose greatness covers the earth, whose mercy is ever about us, whose power is ever before us, whose love abides within us; open and move us to sing thy praise that we may leave this time of worship greater in spirit and soul than when we entered and ready to tell the world of the love that will not let us go.—E. Lee Phillips

OFFERTORY SENTENCE. "Every man according as he purposeth in his heart, so let him give; not grudgingly, or of necessity: for God loveth a cheerful giver" (2 Cor. 9:7).

OFFERTORY PRAYER. Lord, God, lands are being laid waste. Nations are rising up against nations. Cities are being destroyed. Lives are being lost. Being loved for many is only a forgotten dream. Security for many means somehow getting through another day. Many of the things we in this place and service call absolute necessities, for multitudes, are incredible luxuries.

We have times such as this time to render an offering unto the Lord, an expression of deep thanksgiving for blessings too many to count and not a single one deserved. We have times such as this time to proclaim the love of the Lord in the land of the living.

Use our offering this day, Lord, to accomplish a portion of your will in us and beyond us. May what we give promote the things that make for peace and brotherhood and goodwill. May what we give bring hope to the despairing, comfort to the suffering, wisdom to the ignorant, truth to the prejudiced, justice to the abused, the Word of Life to those who are ready to give up and die.—Gordon H. Reif

PRAYER. Lord, we usually find what we're looking for; we usually see what is truly important to us. If we search and strive and struggle to discover the things that are pleasing to us and concern ourselves very little with things that matter to you, could we ever be as those who see but do not see? Could we ever have our eyes wide open and still be blind? Could the things that catch our attention and fancy give ample evidence that our faith in you, our allegiance to you, is small and immature, urgently in need of growing up before it withers and dies?

So much of life is in the eye of the beholder. What are the things we see and behold, as individuals, as a church?

Many good things could be happening to us, many blessings showered upon us, but if we are looking only for things to find fault with or grumble about—if the complaining spirit has captured even a small part of our heart's affection—we could be living in an environment of great joy and not even know it. Many opportunities to serve you by helping others and righting wrongs and promoting good could be staring us in the face, but if we are looking for ways you and others can serve and help and comfort us, we could miss all the occasions of our serving you, because, not looking for them—indeed, concentrating on other things—what may seem obvious to others is hidden from our eyes. How true it often is that, seeing, we do not see—except what we're looking for.

Invitations to sacrifice and calls to cross-bearing can be everywhere round about us, but if we are consumed by the passion for comfort and ease, we may be blind to all that would ask us to inconvenience ourselves and more. If all we seek or desire is our personal pleasure, if the pursuit of our private happiness is our primary goal, we are not likely to be open to, or even aware of, doing those things that promote the common good, the general well-being of people, especially those who suffer and are in need.

It is possible to be insensitive in a world that cries out for compassionate caring. It is possible to build barns of false security in a world where there is far too much war, far too little peace; where some are overfed and many are poorly fed; where some are comfortable and many know only varying degrees of misery. It is possible to say, "Lord, Lord," and neither hear nor do what the Lord desires and requires.

Lord, God, forbid that our world, our vision, our scope of concern, our horizon of interest, should ever be shriveled up into such shallow possibilities. Forbid that we ever decide what is excellent and good and worthwhile by human standards alone. Forbid that the vision by which we live on this earth be man-made and not God-given. We are a people, Father, who do not want to be small of stature, spiritually speaking. We don't want to struggle so much with the molehills of life that we miss the mountains. We earnestly desire your spirit to dwell in our hearts, minds, and wills, so that we see and do things from your point of view. Enable us to wear well the spectacles of faith so that we can think some of your thoughts, promote some of your ways, obey your commandments, accept and share your forgiveness, be of good cheer, and discover the real possibilities that come to human beings, including this church, who live and move by faith alone.—Gordon H. Reif

LECTIONARY MESSAGE

The Hidden Christ

TEXT: Matt. 25:31–46

A church in a large city once became concerned about the large number of homeless people on the streets. These people rummaged through garbage cans for food, gathered what little money they had by begging, and slept in abandoned buildings. When winter came, the newspapers would frequently report that some of these people had died, either by freezing to death or by being burned in fires that were started to keep warm.

The officers of this church knew that they could not solve the problem of homelessness, but they could do *something*, so they decided to open the church building during the winter as an overnight shelter. The church invited street people in as guests, gave them a hot meal, and provided a safe place to sleep. Each night the church was full of people from the street.

Not everyone thought that this was a good program for the church to undertake. Many questions were raised. Was the church properly insured? What if there was a fire? What about sanitation? Could the volunteers from the church contract diseases? These were important questions, but the most important question was raised by a minister from another church. He did not like the fact that the homeless people were not being preached to. "Bodily care is not enough," he said. "Where is Jesus Christ in all this?"

That is surely the most important question a Christian can ask about any area of life: Where is Jesus Christ in all this? Sometimes, of course, we know the answer to that question.

I. *Jesus Christ is present in the Scripture.* The Bible is not merely a book of information or a historical record. It is a meeting place, a place of encounter. When we go to the Scripture in openness and trust, we hear there the living Word, who is Jesus Christ. Where is Jesus Christ? He is in the Bible.

II. *Jesus Christ is present in preaching.* Sermons are not the private opinions of ministers. In and through the words of the sermon, Jesus Christ himself speaks. Where is Jesus Christ? In preaching.

III. *Jesus Christ is present in the church.* The church is not just a human organization; it is also the Body of Christ. The life of the church is energized by the presence of the risen Christ. Where is Jesus Christ? In the church.

Jesus Christ is present in Bible, preaching, and church, but his presence is not confined to these places. Jesus Christ is Lord of all, and his presence fills the universe with grace. We cannot predict, nor can we control, the places of our meeting him.

In the passage for today, the parable of the sheep and the goats, there is a vision of the end of time. The kingly Christ divides all nations into the righteous and the unrighteous, but there is one experience that unites the two groups: They are both surprised to discover where Jesus Christ was present in life. He was present in the hungry, the poor, the prisoner, the sick, and the stranger. The righteous have been feeding and visiting and serving, because that is what God's people are called to do, unaware that they were ministering to Jesus Christ himself. The unrighteous have neglected service and thus missed encountering their Lord.

"Where is Jesus Christ in all this?" said the minister to one of the volunteers in the night shelter. "You just have to be there," replied the volunteer. "Then you would know."—Thomas G. Long

SUNDAY: DECEMBER SECOND

SERVICE OF WORSHIP

Sermon: The Terror and the Glory

Texts: Isa. 2:6; John 1:14

Glory is the beauty of power in action. Terror is the fear of destruction that sometimes the power leaves in its wake. Sometimes you see them separately. If you ever see the sun rise on a clear day, you see the glory of a new day; there is no terror about it, no terror of any kind; nothing but pure, sheer glory. At other times you may have the misfortune to see or be involved in a riot. That's terror, sheer terror, with no glory about it at all.

But there are times when you may have seen them together. If you have ever been through a hurricane at sea, especially through the tail of the hurricane when the sun is shining brilliantly and the wind whips the sea into fury, you may have seen the terror—that is, the possibility of destruction to the ship, and even to you, if your physical being isn't too steady or too strong and if your nervous system isn't too dependable—but you also see the beauty of the sea under those particular conditions, and the very fury of the wind and the sea is the glory of the storm. Thus, in the natural world terror and glory can go together; an event can be frightening and glorious at the same time. The glory and the terror are strangely inseparable.

I. What about God? Do they ever go together in him? Isaiah said that they do.

Isaiah lived in Palestine. He was familiar with earthquakes and storms in which both the terror and the glory were often seen. He knew from personal experience how a natural event could be frightening and at the same time thrillingly beautiful. But he was not talking about a storm in the natural world; he was talking about a storm in the moral world.

(a) He brought two charges against his nation, and it must have been difficult for him to do it because unlike all the other prophets, Isaiah was an aristocrat. He was not a farmer, he was a member of the court, on intimate terms with the king. He belonged to the establishment. He brought two charges against his nation at this particular time, and in general terms these were the two: materialism and magic. The materialism that he charged them with was the result of wealth. They were more prosperous at that particular time than they had ever been before and than they were likely ever to be again. The consequence of their wealth was a preoccupation with their own pleasures and comforts and, consequently, a decline in their sense of social responsibility—what was happening to other people; how they treated the poor, and the fatherless, and the widow, and the ones who were the victims of injustice.

(b) The other item of his charge was magic. Magic was the result of a spiritual vacuum, an empty place, into which practitioners of the occult rushed, and idols were set up. They were soothsayers, fortune-tellers, readers of the stars. They made their decisions, not after consulting the will of God, but after a visit to a man who read the stars or saw the future in a pack of cards. They worshiped idols who could be maneuvered to make things go their way and seldom if ever demanded of them anything that they would not gladly part with.

(c) This kind of materialism and magic, Isaiah said, God will not tolerate; it goes against the very grain of his being. Sooner or later, he warned, he will wipe out the wealth and wash away the idols. When he does, it will be terrible and glorious at the same time. The sight of the Lord God asserting himself will be frightening and glorious to behold.

II. The question for us, of course, is not what Isaiah thought, but what we think. Does this strange combination of terror and glory make any sense to you when you think about God?

(a) The glory of God, what is it? When anyone stops and asks you what you mean by a phrase that you have used all your life, it is not easy to answer him, to say exactly what you mean. I had to stop and think for a long time, and I'm not sure even now that I can say clearly what I mean by the glory of God. But the glory of God is essentially the radiance of his presence, which can be felt and seen.

(b) We don't hear much now about the terror of God, and for two reasons. First, we don't very much want to hear it, do we? There is enough terror in the world without bringing in the terror of God and making life more frightening than it is already. And the second reason is that there was a time when we heard too much about it. There was a time in the churches, and it was a long time (and not so long ago), when people heard more about the tortures of the damned than they did about the blessings of the saved. They got tired of it, and I don't blame them.

(c) The result of this emphasis is that we are inclined to leave it out altogether. If we think about God at all—and, of course, a great many people don't now—but if we do, we try to think about his glory, not his terror.

III. The time has come to put the two together again. Perhaps we can start with this very simple statement of fact. The terror of the Lord is a way of saying that there are some things that the moral universe will not tolerate.

(a) A church that goes the way of the world is on its way to oblivion. The society that cannot live without complete police protection at all times will not live long; and the society that is so preoccupied with its own comforts and pleasures that it is insensitive to and unaware of the needs of the people who are within its reach will not survive. And the person who thinks that he can get what he wants by violence alone will in the end have nothing.

(b) In a picture like this, you may say, Where is the glory? The glory of the Lord is a way of saying that the moral universe is a universe in which there is something too grand to be brushed aside by the foolish ways of man, something that rises above all our folly, above our mistakes, survives it, goes on in spite of it, and refuses to be ultimately ignored. There is something grand about that. Don't you think so?

IV. It is almost impossible for me to think of these things except in personal terms. Some people can, but I cannot.

(a) Jesus had both. Toward the end of his life, on his way to Jerusalem, Mark records how the disciples were following him at some distance and then adds, "As they followed, they were afraid." (Mark 10:32). You might think that they were afraid of what might happen to them when they got to Jerusalem. But in the preceding chapter you read that after Jesus had talked to them "they understood not the saying and were afraid to ask him" (Mark 9:32). There was something forbidding about him. There always is about true greatness.

(b) Let me speak my own mind. It may not be in tune with yours at all, but when I think about God, I have to think about him in terms of a Person. I cannot think of God as Mind with a capital *M*, or as Love with a capital *L*. I can think of God only as a thinking Person, whose thinking is completely surrounded by his love and is often expressed by his justice. I don't have a picture of him, but I have to think of him as a Person, not like any of us, not just another person, one person among others, but as a Person. And in him I can see both the terror and the glory.—Theodore Parker Ferris

Illustrations

THE POWER OF GOD. I heard William Temple only once, and that was at a five-day conference. . . . He told us then about a man who was in Ireland; there was a fierce thunderstorm. Everybody was frightened, and everyone went inside, closed the doors, windows, and blinds. When he saw an old lady standing in her open doorway, he was appalled. He looked at her and said, "Aren't you afraid?" She looked him straight in the eye and said, "I'm proud to have a God who can shake the world like that!"—Theodore Parker Ferris

THE LOVE OF GOD. Bethlehem and Calvary and all the dusty miles in between simply will not add up to power: they add up to an anguish in God's heart, with its marks still in his hands and feet. He will if he can. It's the offense of the cross. Captain Ahab, in Herman Melville's *Moby Dick,* caught a fleeting glimpse of it. "I know thee, thou clear spirit," he cried, looking up at the yardarms that seemed tipped with flame in the storm, "I know thee, and I know that thy right worship is defiance. I own thy speechless power; but to the last gasp of my earthquake life, I will dispute its mastery. Come in thy lowest form of love, and I will kneel and kiss thee; but come as power, and though thou launchest whole navies of full-freighted worlds, there's that in here that will defy Thee."—Paul Scherer

Sermon Suggestions

A BAFFLING QUESTION AND A PROMISING ANSWER. TEXT: Isa. 63:16–64:8. (1) The question, Isa. 63:15ff. (2) The answer, Isa. 64:8.

BASIC BLESSINGS. TEXT: 1 Cor. 1:3–9. (1) Knowledge of the gospel. (2) The ability to bring this knowledge to appropriate expression. (3) The manifold gifts to match the many-splendored grace of God.

Worship Aids

CALL TO WORSHIP. "O Zion, that bringest good tidings, get thee up into the high mountain; O Jerusalem, that bringest good tidings, lift up thy voice with strength; lift it up, be not afraid; say unto the cities of Judah, Behold your God" (Isa. 40:9).

INVOCATION. O thou Beginner of our yesterdays, Mystery of our today, and Hope of our tomorrows, we acknowledge in humility and gratitude our dependence on thee. Help us this morning to prepare our lives for the birth of thy love in us. We pray in the name of him who came to us in love, even Jesus Christ our Lord.—Donald W. Musser

OFFERTORY SENTENCE. "But to do good and to communicate forget not; for with such sacrifices God is well pleased" (Heb. 13:16).

OFFERTORY PRAYER. God of grace, we feel that we hardly make any sacrifice, so great are the compensations when thou hast opened our hearts in love and generosity. We know that thou lovest a cheerful giver and that we are loved. May others find the joy of thy boundless love because of our giving.

PRAYER. Eternal God, Lord of all seasons, this time of thanksgiving has turned our hands and hearts upward to you in gratitude. We have remembered your generous call and blessing upon us, and we give thanks. Forever God, Lord of all time, with grateful and open spirits we embrace now this holy moment in time: Advent. It is a season for silence, for preparing, for waiting, for expecting and receiving the wondrous gift of the Christ. O come, O come Immanuel, and in our hearts, do dwell.

Gracious God, Master of kind forgiveness, we confess that our lives are not ready to receive this best gift. Our hearts are in the wilderness, so cleanse us from our rebellious wandering. The rough spots of our lives plead for the smoothness of your tender healing. Our crooked ways yield to your mending, in making straight our paths. Bring low our mountains of pride and prejudice and lift up our valleys of despair and defeat. Merciful God, cleanse our wounds of sorrow with your pure joy and clothe us in your certain and abiding hope, Jesus Christ our Lord.

All-knowing and loving God, as we ready our spirits to offer acceptable gifts to you and to other people this holy season, may we first ask for some gifts that only you can provide. Gentle Father of quiet presence, we pray for the gift of silence. Like Mary and Joseph, we have much to ponder deep in our souls. Liberate us from our addiction to noise, and in the silence surround us with your redeeming presence and Word.

Patient Father, we pray for the gift of waiting. With the psalmist, let us wait for you and hope in your Word; to wait and discover enduring strength and clear direction; to wait and find our harmony in being in step with you.

Abiding Father, we pray for the gift of kneeling; to find again that sacred posture of the bent knee and the bowed heart. For on our knees we see your world differently and find the Christ again in unexpected places and faces. God of all faithfulness, grant us the gift of hopeful expectancy that we may lean forward and onward in our lives and with gladness and delight make way, make way for his joyful arrival and stay. Blessed is he who comes in the name of the Lord, for in him we hope and worship.—William M. Johnson

LECTIONARY MESSAGE

Learning to Be Watchful

TEXT: Mark 13:32–37

On the first Sunday in Advent, the church casts its gaze toward the end of time. Christmas is but a few weeks away, yet today we do not focus upon that well-remembered night in Bethlehem when our Savior first came but upon that future day "no one knows, not even the angels in heaven, nor the Son, but only the Father" (Mark 13:32, RSV), when Christ will come again "with great power and glory" (Mark 13:26, RSV).

Theologians call this day the *parousia,* and ordinary Christians call it the "Second Coming," but regardless of how we speak of that time, it embodies the Christian hope and conviction that God will not leave the world to its own devices. When people watching the six o'clock news, viewing the reports of yet another day of cruelty and violence, shake their heads sadly and mutter, "What's this world coming to?" the church dares to affirm that, in ways we do not understand and can hardly imagine, this world is coming to Christ because Christ is coming again to the world.

In the thirteenth chapter of Mark, Jesus speaks to his disciples about this day, promising them that history does not finally belong to the power-brokers and the war-makers who grab the daily headlines but only to Christ. The curtains of time would one day be drawn back, he told them, and all humanity would see the glory of God face-to-face. Take heed and watch, he warned them, for no one knows when that time will come.

But *how* should we watch? There are several possibilities.

I. Some people have grown weary of watching or never believed there was anything to watch for in the first place. For them, life is like an ironically sad merry-go-round, circling the same tired terrain day after weary day. The rich get richer; the poor get poorer; and history is "one damned thing after another." Since life is moving nowhere, all there is left to do is to somehow relieve the boredom: Make a killing in the stock market; gather power; watch out for number one; or numb the tedium with alcohol or drugs.

II. Others, however, have made a vocation out of watching for Christ. They are not on a merry-go-round but on a mountaintop. They have left behind responsibilities and obligations, have prematurely put on white robes, and have gathered on the hill to watch and wait. What about poverty, warfare, and human need? "Not our problem," they say. "When the Messiah comes, that will all be taken care of," they chirp, as they turn in their hymnals to "Lo! He Comes, with Clouds Descending."

III. In our text for today, Jesus teaches us a better way of watching. We do not wait like revelers on a merry-go-round or like otherworldly visionaries on a mountaintop but like servants taking care of a house during the Master's absence. We have been given work to do—"Feed my sheep. Tend my lambs. Take care of my house." If we who follow Christ are truly watchful, when Christ returns he will find us, not asleep nor in the midst of a reckless party, but rather speaking his gospel, loving his children, welcoming the lonely into his house, and keeping a light in the win-

dow joyfully expecting his return.—Thomas G. Long

SUNDAY: DECEMBER NINTH

SERVICE OF WORSHIP

Sermon: God Helps Those Who Cannot Help Themselves

TEXT: Matt. 1:21

"God helps them that help themselves" is one of the aphorisms of Benjamin Franklin. Its truth is obvious: we cannot sit around and wait for God to do something for us that he expects us to do for ourselves. But with the approach of Christmas we become aware of an opposite truth of far greater consequence, namely: God helps those who cannot help themselves. This truth lies very close to the heart of what Christmas and the Incarnation are all about: that God has come to help us most where we can help ourselves least—in dealing with the fact of sin.

I. The name *Jesus* means, literally, "the Lord is salvation." Matthew explains its meaning further by reporting that the angel of the Annunciation instructed Joseph to call his child Jesus—because he will save his people from their sins.

(a) I wonder if there is any way to suggest what good news this is? We are not accustomed to worrying much about our sins, as long as they don't get us into trouble with the law. This news may not seem quite as good to us as it did to the angel who first announced it over Bethlehem fields, largely because it has come to seem almost irrelevant. But it is nothing less than the good news of new life.

(b) No less than the good news of healing from mortal disease, or rescue from drowning, is the good news that God will save you from your sin. The doctor who makes the healing for your disease possible and the captain who sails his ship to your life raft are your saviors. They come to save you from a peril from which you cannot save yourself. So Christian faith believes that Jesus comes to save men and women in the peril of sin, which biblical faith has always diagnosed as the greatest

peril of all, from which men cannot save themselves.

So here we are, back again at the ugly word about which the Bible has so much to say and which we all find so difficult, and sometimes infuriating, to understand: sin! What is it?

II. Biblical faith, and particularly the faith of the New Testament, has always looked upon sin as something far more serious than a catalog of immoralities.

(a) This is sin: that man, made in the image of God, makes himself into the kind of person who can do all these things. When we look at Jesus Christ we see the measure by which we have spoiled the image, the distance that we have fallen from being the creatures God intended us to be. Looking at Jesus is like looking into a perfect mirror; he reflects by his goodness every flaw and imperfection in ourselves. Jesus is the representative man by whom we can measure ourselves before the face of God. No matter how good or how righteous or how respectable we imagine ourselves to be, when we compare even our best, to say nothing of our worst, with Christ, we see how marred and broken a thing we have made out of life. And this is what Christian faith takes most seriously!

(b) These are the two great commandments of biblical faith: You shall love the Lord your God with all your heart and mind and strength, and you shall love your neighbor as yourself. But when we hold ourselves up to this measuring rod, we see how we fail. Who of us loves God with all his heart? Much of the time we love other things more than God: our way of life, our comforts and securities. Who of us loves his neighbor as he loves himself? Much of the time we love our privileges and our advantages more than we love our neighbor. Now, if you protest that this is human nature, that these are the counsels of perfection, Christian faith answers, Precisely!

We are human, and they are counsels of perfection, and this is exactly what we are talking about. But once in a while a man does give himself in heroic love for a neighbor. Once in a while a man does show his love for God far beyond the ordinary limits of devotion. He loves God with every ounce of devotion in his soul. Then we see what life ought to be all the time, not just once in a while. When we look at Christ, we are brought to shame by what he shows us in ourselves.

III. But the closer we come to Christ, the more we realize the precious worth of a human soul with its wonderful capacity to respond to the love which is at the heart of Creation. And the more precious we discover life to be, the more terrible does the fact of human sin become.

(a) Jesus Christ, born in Bethlehem, crucified under Pontius Pilate, and raised from the dead by the power of God, can save us from the power of sin by showing us that we do sin, that we do break the image of God in which we are created, and that our love falls short of the glory of God. This is the first step in salvation: knowing that we need a Savior, a Savior to heal our souls that are as broken as that piece of china is broken from the perfect image in which it was made.

(b) Jesus Christ can also save us from the power of sin by turning the hardness of our hearts to love. Seeing Jesus forgive the woman taken in adultery, Jesus in the home of Mary and Martha, Jesus gathering the children in his arms, Jesus lifting Peter up out of sin and remorse, Jesus telling of the good Samaritan and the prodigal son, Jesus forgiving his tormentors—these all move us to turn away from sin, for they show us what life ought to be, and move us with love for such a life. In such love we feel a glory and a power to check the power of sin.

(c) Jesus Christ does come to bring God's love. His coming, when we face it with vigorous and unflinching imagination, turns us back from sin. We call this turning back *repentance*. It is the one thing God commands us to do. He will do the rest. For everyone who turns from his sin, truly seeking to be saved, God can do what

none of us could ever do: put the broken pieces of life together again.

IV. Sin is a serious matter, so serious that God suffered this much on account of it. How can we but do the same? But when we do, we find that God has done for us what we could not do for ourselves—taken away our sin and made all things new. The power of his name, Jesus—the Lord is salvation.—Robert E. Luccock

Illustrations

EMPTY HANDED.   The story is told of an old sailor who had been converted and found joy in his salvation. One day a comrade said to him, "I believe the Bible to be true and every word of it to be from God. I know that I am a sinner and that I can be saved only through the redemption that is in Christ, but I do not know how I am to be saved." The old sailor replied, "I do not know that I can tell you what it is or how to get it. But I can tell you some things it is not. It is not knocking off swearing and drinking and such like. It is not reading the Bible and praying and being good. It is not anything you have done or can do; it is believing and trusting to what Christ has done. It is forsaking your sins and looking for their pardon and the salvation of your soul through trusting in Jesus who died and shed his blood for sin."—J. Clyde Turner

GOD'S HELP.   We will see more and more that we are chosen, not because of our ability, but because of his power that will be demonstrated in our not being able.—Corrie ten Boom

Sermon Suggestions

WHEN GOD COMES.   TEXT: Isa. 40:1–11. (1) He brings a message of comfort, verses 1–5. (2) He asserts the trustworthiness of his Word, verses 6–8. (3) He demonstrates both strength and tenderness, verses 9–11.

WHY THE DELAY?   TEXT: 2 Pet. 3:8–15a. The Lord delays his coming because (1) he does not reckon time as we do; (2) he is gracious and forbearing; and (3) he is preparing to re-create the universe.

Worship Aids

CALL TO WORSHIP. "Oh, Lord, rebuke me not in thy wrath: neither chasten me in thy hot displeasure. For thine arrows stick fast in me, and thy hand presseth me sore" (Ps. 38:1–2).

INVOCATION. God of the promise, on whom we rely for life and its meaning: We confess that we have sinned against you by abandoning hope, by failing to accept your promises, by relying on ourselves to be both the sources and the object of our own faith. Forgive us, we pray, and once more open our hearts to your mercy, our minds to your promise, our hands to our neighbor in need. In this season of hope, restore us to faith in your providing care and your guiding love.—E. Paul Hovey

OFFERTORY SENTENCE. "And when he looked on him, he was afraid, and said, What is it, Lord? And he said unto him, Thy prayers and thine alms are come up for a memorial before God" (Acts 10:4).

OFFERTORY PRAYER. Generous Lord, through what we give today may others be introduced to the good news of Jesus Christ and the joy of doing thy holy will.—E. Lee Phillips

PRAYER. Surrounding God, Lord and Father of all nations, gathered with believers around the world, we raise our prayers of adoration and praise. Eternal God of everywhere, because beautiful feet have stepped upon mountains all over your world, your kingdom is greater than we know or understand. Author of all glad tidings, we give thanks today for those who have and are giving themselves to spreading the good news of Jesus Christ. May we in all our steps to share glad tidings—in service, in praying, in giving—be found generous and faithful.

Our Father of the Prince of Peace, allow us not to overlook the tie between tidings of good news and tidings of peace. Jesus Christ is our salvation and our peace, and in him, we find love that conquers fear, trust that overcomes falsehood, joy that fades our sorrow, hope that endures our despair, and peace that passes all understanding. In grateful response, free us to be people of light and redemption to a dark and lost world. O God of eternal presence, this Advent Sunday of peace, may our feet be beautiful, too.—William M. Johnson

LECTIONARY MESSAGE

In the Beginning
TEXT: Mark 1:1–8

The hardest paragraph to write, authors tell us, is the first one. Novelists, playwrights, essayists, and preachers spend a great deal of brooding time looking at a blank sheet of paper marked, "Page one." Once the first paragraph is in place, the rest of the composing seems to flow more gracefully and with less effort.

The reason for this difficulty in producing an initial paragraph undoubtedly has something to do with inertia, but it also points to the crucial nature of beginnings. Opening words set the direction and tone for all else that follows. Charles Dickens's "It was the best of times; it was the worst of times . . ." is one of the most celebrated and intriguing beginnings in literary history, while the clumsy cliché "It was a dark and stormy night . . ." has taken its share of kidding.

Our biblical text for today forms the opening words of the Gospel of Mark, or, as the writer phrases it, "The beginning of the gospel of Jesus Christ, the Son of God" (Mark 1:1, RSV). We do not know how long Mark pondered how to open his Gospel, but it was surely a momentous decision. How does one begin telling the greatest story ever told? What direction and tone are suitable for the narrative of God's saving love in Jesus Christ?

Mark's answer to these questions is surprising. He begins in the wilderness, the desert, the lonely place. He does not open with a drum roll, a brass band, or a choir singing the "Hallelujah Chorus" but with a lonely violin and the solitary "voice of one crying in the wilderness: Prepare the way of the Lord . . ." (Mark 1:3).

It is no accident that Mark begins his Gospel this way. He wants his readers to know that the gospel is a word, not just for easy times and softly lit sanctuaries, but for the wilderness of life where the winds blow hard and the dangers are many. Mark wrote to people who were wandering through their own wilderness. We are not certain what sort of stress Mark's church was experiencing. Perhaps they were being persecuted by the Roman government, but, whatever the cause, they were a people in crisis, cast into some kind of desert. Mark wanted them to know that the wilderness is not where God's salvation *ends* but where it *begins*.

I. The wilderness is a place where human hope perishes. It can be a surgical waiting room, a divorce court, or a welfare office, but the wilderness is always a place where our strength fades and our re-

sources are exhausted. It was precisely at the moment when the Hebrews' hope was dimmest, Mark reminds us, that Isaiah said, "In the wilderness prepare the way of the Lord. . . . Every valley shall be lifted up . . ." (Isa. 40:3,4, RSV).

II. The wilderness is a place where we must choose between sin and forgiveness, between death and the life God offers us. John the Baptist appeared in the wilderness, Mark tells us, calling for repentance. Just when the struggle seems too strong, when we are no match for the temptations around us, One "mightier than I" comes to save and forgive.

Whenever we are wandering in the wilderness and have lost our way, whenever the desert has burned away our hope and drained our strength, whenever we are prepared to write "the end" to our lives, Mark lifts us up and tells us, "It is here, in this place, that we see the beginning of the gospel of Jesus Christ."—Thomas G. Long

SUNDAY: DECEMBER SIXTEENTH

SERVICE OF WORSHIP

Sermon: Glory

TEXT: Isa. 35:1–10

The Spanish philosopher Unamuno said, "May God deny you peace but give you glory." I think he was speaking to people who want more out of life than being careful or just getting through it. For there are those who have a zest for life, who seek the glory of being fully alive NOW. In addition to experiencing all of life's exciting sights, sounds, smells, there is a need to do or produce something that goes beyond life. "Will I be remembered by something I did, achieved, contributed? Will it be by something that lives on in my children?" This is a quest for glory, though we may not call it that, which launches into the hurly burly, grabbing for all the "gusto" we can.

I. What we seem to grab is air. The glory we long for is real, but it cannot be wrested from the gods as Prometheus's

fire. For the first thing we must know is that glory comes from God. Glory does not come from piling up our accomplishments and then standing astride those achievements so all can see us. It comes from seeing the glory of God . . . once you have seen, you are never really the same again.

(a) That was Isaiah's vision of hope; looking past exile and estrangement he could say, "They shall see the glory of the Lord, the majesty of our God." Whatever that glory is, it seems to have the power to startle those who see it, from exiles to shepherds.

Ezekiel had such a vision that could only be described as light unapproachable. "Glory" for him was the light the Holy gives off. Glory is a lure, a beacon that calls us to a higher reality.

(b) In the Old Testament, *glory* literally meant "weighty," something of substance. To have a vision of even the light that surrounds the Holy is to see, not the ethereal, but that which is solid. This glory is enduring and effects change in all that see and believe. It was Handel who said, after writing the "Hallelujah Chorus," "I did think, I did see all Heaven before me and the great God Himself." It was in this writing of a masterpiece, which is still a wonder to us as we are swept away by its reflected glory, that he mellowed and came to see that he was not the creator but an instrument of the Creator. The changes became clear to many for, before that time, he was known for his ability to swear in five languages. Now the one who had seen the glory of God was considerably more kind and gentle in tongue and temper.

II. This great work of Handel brings to mind the second mark of God's glory; it shines brightest in the darkness of human need and longing.

(a) That is the story of Bethlehem: "In thy dark streets shineth the everlasting light." God's greatest glory came in a time of darkness and despair. The prophetic voice had been silent, the light had gone out in Israel just as it had in the Exile. Yet God broke through in human flesh; the star led to a stable, the magnificent light to a manger. Those who could see God in human form were no longer wandering in darkness. That was the hope of Isaiah fulfilled. He says in verse 5, and it is sung in Handel's "Messiah," "Then shall the eyes of the blind be opened."

(b) The eye opening of God's glory comes often when darkness surrounds us, as it did for George Frederick Handel. At age fifty-six, he was in the depths of mental depression; his career and his finances were bankrupt; he had made enemies in high places. Once the toast of London society, he was now called, in his adopted country of England, "that German nincompoop." By 1741, he had used up the last of his friends and resources. Yet it was in this very dark year that the light of the Messiah broke in upon him.

(c) Isn't this when Christ (the Messiah) comes in power? Isn't it when the voice of God seems muted, the light of his presence dim: after the death of a loved one, a painful divorce, a crushing defeat? Christ, the glory of God, comes to save us, to bring hope into a climate of despair. When we come to the end of ourselves and the limits of our own power to experience glory, then comes the salvation Isaiah promised long ago. Now is God's glory, our salvation, seen when the hands weak from grief are strengthened, the knees ready to buckle from the load of a feared medical diagnosis are steadied, made firm.

III. Glory, then, is from God alone. It is made known to us through Christ who was faithful even in the darkness of the cross and our sin. But that's not the end. That's the beginning, for in Christ we beheld his glory full of grace and truth. That glory now holds us and shapes us. It is that grace and truth that is now to be seen in us. Christ, in us, the hope of glory.—Gary D. Stratman

Illustrations

CHRIST THE FOUNDATION. Harvard University declared in that school's charter that Christ is to be "laid in the bottom." He is the foundation of all learning and living.—W. H. Hinson

SOLIDARITY WITH THE POOR AND OPPRESSED. I've gradually come to see that these people have learned to know Jesus as the God who suffers with them. For them, the suffering and dying Jesus is the most convincing sign that God really loves them very much and does not leave them uncared for. He is their companion in suffering. If they are poor, they know that Jesus was poor, too; if they are afraid, they know that Jesus also was afraid; if they are beaten, they know that Jesus, too, was beaten; and if they are tortured to death, well then, they know that Jesus suffered the same fate. For these people, Jesus is the faithful friend who treads with them the lonely road of suffering and brings them consolation. He is with them in solidarity. He knows them, understands them, and clasps them to himself in their moments of greatest pain.—Henri J. M. Nouwen

Sermon Suggestions

AGENDA FOR SERVICE.   TEXT: Isa. 61:
1–4, 8–11. (1) It is focused on manifold
human need. (2) Its success depends on a
faithful God. (3) It brings forth joy and
exultation.

SANCTIFICATION IN THREE MODES.
TEXT: 1 Thess. 5:16–24, especially verse
23. (1) In the spirit: your relationship to
God. (2) In the soul: your essential self. (3)
In the body: your physical being. (4) All of
which are an inseparable unity special to
God.

Worship Aids

CALL TO WORSHIP.   "When they had
heard the king, they departed; and, lo, the
star, which they saw in the east, went
before them, till it came and stood over
where the young child was. When they saw
the star, they rejoiced with exceeding
great joy" (Matt. 2:9–10).

INVOCATION.   Lord, our time of waiting
is almost at an end. The celebration of
Christmas is nigh upon us, and we have
precious few opportunities left to prepare
our hearts for Christ's advent into our
lives. Help us to accept the opportunity
that we have for preparation today with
such dedication and purpose that when
Christmas day arrives, we can say that we
are truly ready for Christ to come into our
hearts.—James M. King

OFFERTORY SENTENCE.   "Offer the sacrifices of righteousness, and put your trust
in the Lord" (Ps. 4:5).

OFFERTORY PRAYER.   O God, thou who
hast given thine only begotten Son to be
our Savior, our largest gifts are but too
small. Yet thou dost receive what we
bring. Use our offerings, we pray, to
spread abroad the good news of Christ
Jesus.

PRAYER.   O God, now comes the time
of rebirth: the rebirth of wonder and hope;
the rebirth of grief over wrong; the rebirth

of expectation and judgment; the rebirth
of godly fear; the rebirth of hunger to do
what is right. The time of Advent is upon
us, welcome as morning's faint orange
over the dark of leafless trees and blue-
cold snow. Save us, Father, from the worst
of Christmas: the busyness that exhausts
and the forced fun. Draw us beyond the
tinsel and Santa Claus; draw us out under
the stars to behold a stable and a cross,
that we may turn home in wonder and
hold one another reborn.—Peter Fribley

LECTIONARY MESSAGE

Who We Are Not
TEXT: John 1:6–8, 19–28
     Whenever people are searching for a
job or applying for admission to a school,
they fill out elaborate forms about themselves. They give their family histories,
educational background, and a variety of
information about hobbies, skills, interests, and so on. The prospective employers or colleges want and need to know *who*
these applicants are. Or again, we meet
new people at work, at church, or at a
neighborhood gathering and, after a brief
conversation, we part, saying, "We must
get together soon so we can get to know
each other better."
     In most settings, the important thing
about people is who they *are*. The remarkable thing about the description of John
the Baptist in our text today is that most of
the time is spent in telling us who John is
not. He was not the "Light," and he was
not the Christ. He was not Elijah, nor was
he the "prophet." By the time we finish
reading our passage, we know a great deal
about who John the Baptist was *not*.
     There is a good lesson in this for Chris-
tians today. Most of the people in the
world are preoccupied with questions of
identity and ego. They are trying to establish who they are. Christians, however,
must first know who they are not. Then,
and only then, can we truly know who we
are.
     I. We are *not* the Light of the World.
Whenever Christians believe that we have
all the answers to life's problems, when-

ever we are convinced that we know exactly how other people ought to think and act, the Christian faith becomes arrogant and oppressive. Only Christ is the Light, and Christians must always humbly hope and pray to be guided by that Light. The church, by the grace of God, may reflect God's Light, but when we claim to *be* the Light, we cut ourselves off from the Source of Light.

II. We are not better and more holy than others. Throughout the centuries, Christian people have been loving, kind, obedient, and forgiving. But Christian people have also been stubborn, rebellious, mean-spirited, and divisive. Our history is a mixed story of faith and faithlessness, grace and hardness, and we have not cornered the market on good works.

III. If we now know who we are not, then who are we? John "was not the Light," our text reads, "but came to bear witness to the Light." If the world must look to us for light or must depend upon our goodness for its salvation, then the world is lost. The good news, though, is that there is One who *is* the Light and whose faithfulness never fails nor ends. Who are we? We are those who bear witness to that Light.

The late Carl Michaelson told once about someone giving his son a compass. Michaelson said that he would often see the compass around the house amid the rest of the family clutter. Nothing in their house remained in the same spot long, including that compass. "Every time I see it," he said, "it is pointing in the same direction. This is the impressive thing about the Christian witness."

Christians are compasses, pointing away from themselves to the power of Christ; they are mirrors, reflecting a light that is not their own. "There was a man sent from God whose name was John. . . . He was not the Light, but came to bear witness to the Light." *That* is the impressive thing about Christian witness.—Thomas G. Long

SUNDAY: DECEMBER TWENTY-THIRD

SERVICE OF WORSHIP

Sermon: Christmas, Turned Around
Text: John 3:16–17

It happened at Christmas . . . in the church I had served for some five years. A friend of ours was leading worship. Charles has a real gift for communicating to children and his "children's sermons" are always excellent. This year, he had four children help him tell of the great hope that is ours because of the star that shone one day over a stable announcing the birth of a Savior for all people. At a given signal, each child was to flip over a large piece of cardboard spelling, for all to see, the word *STAR*. Unfortunately, Charles did not realize the letters would be in the reverse order when the cards were flipped over. Thus, the word for all to see was *RATS*.

This "object lesson" was such a surprise to so many that it took some time until the laughter died down and the service continued. But I have not gotten that event out of my head. Maybe there was a great deal of truth in that revised message of RATS! Christmas is not an easy time of the year. There is a great deal of frustration, disappointment, and stress connected with the holiday season. In a recent program on stress given in this church, I found out that on his chart of stressful events Dr. Thomas Holmes gave a significant twelve points for just "going through Christmas."

We do not dismiss this lightly when we realize that those who are already hurting, grieving, are prone to real hopelessness when they see "everyone else" happily celebrating this holiday. Christmas as the assurance of hope and joy, a star to guide us, a Savior to make us whole, seems light years away. This assurance is turned around, and it seems that our hopes are built up at this time of year only to be dashed. RATS! is almost too mild an epithet for our disappointment.

Is it possible, however, that Christmas has always taken place in a world that has lost its way, gotten important things backwards? The birth of the Savior happened in a darkened world of evil kings, no place to stay for those in need. Yet none of this darkness, cold, and loneliness could banish the star from the sky. Again on this Christmas Eve, it is hope shining like a star that can turn our world around if we can but look up and believe.

I. We do live in a world where *grief* is a reality. Tennyson once wrote, "With such compelling cause to grieve / How dare we keep our Christmas Eve." Grief is a response to loss. Can we deny the losses we have experienced in this past year? To deny is not the answer. The prophet reminds us that those who dwell in darkness shall see a great light. Not even the pall that hangs over our losses can expel the light. Have you lost the person who always seemed so close, a job that was your security, your zeal for the Christian life, the worship of God? What is your loss? It is not wrong to grieve, but it is not for Christians to grieve, as the Bible says, "without hope." Our hope is in the Lord; he it is that turns around our hopelessness. One man lost his business, his family, but in his loss he found himself and the Lord. Together they built a new business. A recovering alcoholic, he named his new real estate business REBOS—that's *sober* spelled backward—a reminder that Christ had turned his life around, given hope in the midst of loss.

II. Another aspect of Christmas we have gotten backward is the holding of a *grudge*. We really could pray in all sincerity, "Forgive us our Christmases as we forgive those who Christmas against us." We have been "Christmased against." This should be a time of year marked by forgiveness: "Behold the Lamb of God who takes away this sin of the world." Instead of allowing the sins of Christmas to be taken away, we remember. Oh, how we remember! I confess, I really resent the "grinches" in my life, the ones who want to steal my Christmas joy. "If I choose, I can nurse and pet that resentment, but Christ came to turn it around, turn me around." By admitting my resentment, I can allow Christ to forgive that which I cannot forgive on my own.

III. We cannot talk of aspects of Christmas that we have gotten backward without mentioning *greed*. Linus is expounding about Christmas to Sally in the cartoon strip "Peanuts." He goes on and on about the true meaning of Caesar's census, the inn, and Bethlehem. Obviously fascinated by all of this, he asks Sally, "What do you think?" She says, "I think if I don't get everything I want for Christmas this year, I'm gonna gross out!" Isn't that *the* great irony in the season set aside to celebrate God's gift? We end up placing emphasis on getting.

I read once of a family who every year put up big wooden letters that spelled *NOEL* on their roof, as a lighted Christmas greeting. You guessed it. One year, they got it backward and it spelled *LEON!* Let's not get Christmas backward. Let's not major in what we can get but in what we can give. Perhaps we will discover the one gift truly worth giving is the gift of ourselves. Our greed is turned into giving when we come to realize God has turned it all around once and for all. "For God so loved the world he *gave* . . . his only begotten Son."

There is a story that I first heard (at least one version of it) when I was about nine or ten years old. A man had been asked by his wife to attend the Christmas Eve service in town. He declined, saying that because he didn't believe, he would be a hypocrite if he went. So he stayed near the fire on that blustery, stormy night. His solitude was interrupted when he heard three distinct thuds coming from the living room. It soon become apparent that three small birds, dazed by the storm, perhaps attracted by the lights of the house, had crashed into the picture window. He threw on a coat and rushed outside to help the birds. But they would not trust him.

Each time he would get close, they would hop, not able to fly, and flutter just beyond his grasp. He was only trying to help to save them from the freezing cold. Bread crumbs did not lure them into the haven of the warm barn. All his attempts to help were to no avail. Finally, in an exasperated tone, he said, "If I could only become one of them, then I could show them the way." In the instant he said these words, the church bells rang announcing midnight. It was Christmas Day.

God so loved us he came to dwell with us, in his Son; he taught us, showed us the way. Christ died for us so the way would be opened. Here is the only hope for the world to be turned around, for your life to be turned around. It is the message of Christmas.—Gary D. Stratman

Illustrations

A BEAUTIFUL REVERSAL. A legend tells us that parishioners at a church in Mexico brought great quantities of flowers to the altar each Christmas. One day, while hundreds of people carried flowers to the cathedral, a little girl cried because she had none. A priest found her and asked the reason for her tears. "I have no flowers," she cried. The priest told her to pick a weed which grew near the roadside. The little girl wondered that the priest should tell her to pick a weed, but she did as she was told. When she placed the weed on the altar, the large green leaves glowed with a soft red light, and was the most beautiful flower presented. Since that time, the legend says, the poinsettia plant has been the special flower of Christmas.—Charles L. Wallis

THE SAME DIFFERENCE. In the December 1977 issue of *Reader's Digest,* Mrs. Robert D. Olson tells about her eleven-year-old son, who played the role of Joseph in the Sunday school Christmas program. As they were discussing his costume, she suggested that he wear sandals on his feet. However, he insisted on wearing his cowboy boots. When she said that it was unlikely that Joseph wore western-style boots, her son replied, "Yes, but he didn't have braces on his teeth, either." Mrs. Olson said that he wore the boots.—Robert J. Hastings

Sermon Suggestions

A PROMISE ONLY THE MESSIAH CAN FULFILL. TEXT: 2 Sam. 7:8–16. (1) The word to David. (2) The word concerning Jesus Christ, Phil. 2:5–11.

WHY WE BLESS GOD'S NAME. TEXT: Rom. 16:25–27, NEB. (1) He has brought us to faith; (2) through the gospel of Jesus Christ; (3) thus making our standing sure.

Worship Aids

CALL TO WORSHIP. "And the angel said unto them, Fear not: for, behold, I bring you good tidings of great joy, which shall be to all people. For unto you is born this day in the city of David a Saviour, which is Christ the Lord. . . . Glory to God in the highest, and on earth peace, good will toward men" (Luke 2:10–11, 14).

INVOCATION. Come again, O Lord, in the way we most need thee, for we come rejoicing that long ago divinity was robed in baby's flesh and all prophecy was fulfilled. Open us to thy incarnational ways in the needs of others, giving faith a face not unlike our Messiah's!—E. Lee Phillips

OFFERTORY SENTENCE. "For God so loved the world, that he gave his only begotten Son, that whosoever believeth in Him should not perish, but have everlasting life" (John 3:16).

OFFERTORY PRAYER. Lord of hosts, take the small beginning of this offering and so fill it with thy might and power as to do great things for thee, even as once a newborn baby grown to manhood did.—E. Lee Phillips

PRAYER. O God, we have learned to say the word *Advent* but have failed to recognize your coming to us: Help us to know the healing balm of a silent night, but give us grateful hearts for *music* that pierces the silence. Thank you for the genius of a Beethoven able to ring the infinite changes of four simple notes; for carols ancient and modern, singing of new birth; for off-key renditions of "Jesus Loves Me," which speak volumes; for the joy that has come from participation in school orchestras, marching bands, choirs, and choruses; for the mysterious music of the spheres in our cosmos; and, yes, God, for the song that cannot be stilled even in a world often bent on war: "Give Peace a Chance." In the name of the Prince of Peace we pray for those who need a saving reminder of God's gift, which passes all understanding. Comfort and sustain _____ and others who have suffered loss today. Lord of Resurrection, we thank you that you come in seasons of darkness as well as light. Come to those who are sick or alone when the rest of the world seems to speak of health, family, and joy. Come to us who feel inadequate, with your strength. Come to us who feel resentment, with your healing and forgiveness. Come to us who are rushed and harried, with your calm. Come to us now and always through the Christ who taught us to pray, saying, Our Father. . . .—Gary D. Stratman

LECTIONARY MESSAGE

Trusting the Angel
TEXT: Luke 1:26–38
Christmas is now but two days away, and it is surely true that virtually everyone in America has seen or heard some part of the Christmas message. "Joy to the World, the Lord Has Come," sing the choirs on television. Every day the mail brings cards that announce, "Noel, Noel, Born Is the King of Israel." While discount-store shoppers push their laden carts down the crowded aisles, unseen voices overhead whisper, "Silent Night! Holy Night! Son of God, love's pure Light. . . ." Even billboards and magazine ads proclaim, "Peace on Earth, Good Will to All. . . ."

Though the truth of Christmas is in the air everywhere, it is hard for most people to receive that message seriously. Even when the words of Christmas are heard, they crash against the realities of life, causing people to doubt or dismiss them. "Let every heart prepare him room," intones the department store sound system, and the customer hands her charge card to the clerk, feeling little room in her heart for anything save weariness. "O Come All Ye Faithful, Joyful and Triumphant," urges

the Christmas card that came in the mail along with three joyless bills, a catalog, and a most untriumphant overdue notice from the library. All around, people see and hear "the good tidings of a great joy," shrug their shoulders and say, "How can this be?"

It should come as an encouragement to us that this was precisely the way in which the good news of Christmas was first received. According to Luke, when the angel Gabriel appeared to the young peasant woman named Mary, disclosing to her the overwhelmingly wonderful and "awe-full" news that she would bear a son who would be called "Son of the Most High," whose kingdom would have no end, she did not immediately dance with joy, sing triumphantly, or rush out to find a bassinet. Instead, her first response was to cast down her eyes and to wonder aloud, "How can this be?"

What Gabriel said in reply can be summed up in his final words: "For with God nothing will be impossible" (Luke 1:38, RSV). The truth of Christmas clashes drastically with all of our expectations and with every human assessment of life's possibilities. "Peace on Earth" sung in a time of bloody warfare, "Joy to the World" in a land of sadness, "Glory to the Newborn King" in a society of callous rulers and self-serving governments—these words are either idle whistling in the dark, or . . . with God nothing will be impossible. The choice is ours: Do we believe the hopeless word that weighs us down or the angel's promise that tugs at our hearts?

Mary had every reason to believe the hard realities of her life rather than the untested words of the angel, to trust what she could touch rather than the incredible good news she heard. She was young, poor, unmarried, and powerless. In an amazing act of sheer faith, though, she threw her life on the promise of God. "Let it be to me," she said, "according to your word" (Luke 1:38, RSV). What happened, of course, is the truth above all other truths: One night, in a cattle stall in Bethlehem, she lovingly placed her newborn son, the King of Eternity.

May God grant such grace to us as was

found that day in Mary. Perhaps, then, today and tomorrow, when we hear, amid all the noise and clutter and busyness of these last few hours before Christmas, the angels' song, we can put aside the credit cards and the overdue bills and the shopping lists and allow our hearts to speak the word they truly want to speak: "Let it be to me, O God, according to your word."— Thomas G. Long

SUNDAY: DECEMBER THIRTIETH

SERVICE OF WORSHIP

Sermon: How Young Are You?

TEXT: Eccles. 3:11

I. *Myths about old age need exploding.* Our society's attitude toward aging is so wrong. To merely keep senior citizens busy is not getting at the real problem. There is a mental fixation that has to be changed. Nothing short of a new birth in our thinking is required.

(a) Our society is saying something about old age that is not true. It is saying you are old, you are useless, you are "over the hill," you are a has-been. When we are told anything often enough, it is not long until we believe it. We are conditioned, even in the face of the fact that in our better moments we know it is not true.

(b) With this attitude of society, how many older people, consciously or unconsciously, resign themselves to the rocking-chair syndrome. They retire from life and from the world. They give up. They cop out.

Part of what we are saying is that many assumptions about old age are but myths. But there are people accepting them as gospel truth about themselves.

(c) We excuse ourselves many times, "Well, I guess I am getting old," and blame our problem on old age, when the truth of the matter is that we have copped out on life by not using our faculties enough to keep them active, alert, keen, sensitive. You all know very well what happens to an arm or leg that hasn't been used for a long time. The muscles become atrophied. It is too weak to be of any service—and will remain so until its strength is restored through regular exercise. It is no different with the mind, heart, or spirit.

II. *Aging—a spiritual problem.* It has been said that age is a relative thing. There is the old saw: "You are as old as you feel." It seems to me, a more accurate observation would be, "You are as old as you think you are."

(a) Aging, you see, is not so much a physical problem as a spiritual one. Nicodemus focuses the issue for all of us when he asks Jesus, "How can a man be born when he is old?" The answer Jesus gives, it seems to me, is a commentary and interpretation of the statement by the Old Testament preacher, Ecclesiastes, when he declares, "God has placed eternity in the heart of man." If eternity is in your heart, how can you be old? Is not Jesus saying that in the life of the Spirit there is no age? The God-Spirit never grows old. The God we worship is the ever-new God. As the Old Testament prophet declares, "See, what new thing the Lord is doing in our day!" "See, what new thing the Lord is doing in your day!" To be born of the Spirit of the living God is to know eternal life—to be perennially young.

(b) Our attitude toward age and aging in our culture is quite unbiblical. There is a striking verse in the Bible: "Moses was one hundred twenty years old when he died. His eye was not dimmed nor his natural force abated." What a description! Moses stands out as one of the great personalities in history. His life was an open-ended search for truth. Whoever engages in this search never grows old.

(c) The same spirit of the pilgrim is declared by the father of our faith in the New Testament, the Apostle Paul: "I have not yet already attained, but I am pressing forward toward the mark of the high calling of God in Christ Jesus." The call of God is a daily experience, and not one who is spiritually alive, who is born of the Spirit, retires from being a pilgrim.

III. *Eternal life: the freedom to grow at any*

age. We need to learn to fly. As Isaiah the prophet writes, "They who wait upon the Lord shall renew their strength; they shall mount up with wings as eagles. . . ." We need to learn to fly, but old age in our society is more like being grounded.

(a) When people get to thinking that they cannot do anything worthwhile because of their advanced age, perhaps they need to be reminded of people who have done great work in later years. All through history there are convincing illustrations that mental powers increase with age; often artistic and intellectual powers are intensified in later years. Michelangelo was still producing masterpieces at eighty-nine. Goethe, the German poet, completed *Faust* at eighty-two. Longfellow was still writing outstanding poetry after seventy. Winston Churchill didn't do anything noteworthy until sixty-five. Some of the greatest tasks that have ever been undertaken were begun and carried out by people who were in what we call life's declining years. In fact, it has been noted that nine-tenths of the world's outstanding achievements have been by older people.

(b) Eternal life is the freedom to grow at any age. But how many people, when they become older, are tyrannized by the fear of anything new—different. As Jesus said to Nicodemus, perennial youth, not old age, is your true nature. You are as young as your faith and hope; as old as your doubts and fears. To live by faith and hope is to grow, no matter what the number of your birthdays.

(c) It is God who has placed eternity in the heart of man. Whatever blocks the growth of the person is not of God—it is evil.

Jesus is saying to Nicodemus in the New Testament lesson, and in turn to us, Life does not need to run down for anyone. We are not to grow old; we are to grow young. Perennial springtime is the gift of God's Spirit. "See, what new thing the Lord is doing in you."

How young are you? You are as young as your FAITH! You are as young as your HOPE! You are as young as your LOVE!—John Thompson

Illustrations

AN INSPIRING SECRET. I have a little secret which I keep for gloomy mornings when, for one reason or another, I'd rather not get up and go to work. It's a quotation attributed to Charles Kingsley (1819–75), a British clergyman and novelist who championed the poor: "Thank God every morning when you get up that you have something to do that day which must be done, whether you like it or not."—Robert J. Hastings

ATTITUDE. Norman Vincent Peale wrote of strolling through the crowded narrow streets of Hong Kong. He passed a tattoo studio. In the window were pictures and slogans one could have tattooed on arms or chest. Among them were flags, pretty girls, and one that read, "Born to lose." The shop was run by a Chinese man who was somewhat of a philosopher. Pointing to the sign, "Born to lose," Peale asked if people actually had that tattooed on themselves. He said he had done it a few times. But then he added in broken English, "Before tattoo on chest, he tattoo on mind." If one thinks long enough that he was "born to lose," that negative concept will assuredly be tattooed inexorably on the personality.—Joe E. Trull

Sermon Suggestions

THE GLORY OF THE PEOPLE OF GOD. TEXT: Isa. 61:10–62:3, RSV. (1) It is a blessing to be hoped for, though not yet achieved. (2) It will be a blessing from God, though requiring the integrity of his people.

OUR NEW STATUS. TEXT: Gal. 4:4–7. (1) Its basis. (2) Its confirmation. (3) Its privileges.

Worship Aids

CALL TO WORSHIP. "Endow the king with your justice, O God, the royal son with your righteousness. He will judge your people in righteousness, your afflicted ones with justice" (Ps. 72:1–2, NIV).

INVOCATION. Lord, there is a sense of finality in our coming together today. We are closing the book on one chapter of our experience and looking forward to another. Help us to look back with penitence for our sins and gratitude for all your blessings. Help us to look forward with awe because of the challenges that face us and with confidence because of the strength we find in you. Help us to look upon this hour you have given us as one more opportunity for worship and for promise.—James M. King

OFFERTORY SENTENCE. "And when they were come into the house, they saw the young child with Mary his mother, and fell down, and worshipped him: and when they had opened their treasures, they presented unto him gifts; gold, and frankincense, and myrrh" (Matt. 2:11).

OFFERTORY PRAYER. Lord of Life, let us not lay up for ourselves treasures on earth, rather let us lay up treasures in heaven where neither moth nor rust can corrupt nor thieves break through and steal. In the incorruptible name of Jesus, we pray.—E. Lee Phillips

PRAYER. Your love for us never ends, eternal God, even when by age or weakness we can no longer work. When we retire, keep us awake to your will for us. Give us energy to enjoy the world, to attend to neighbors busy men neglect, and to contribute wisely to the life of the church. If we can offer nothing but our prayers, remind us that our prayers are a useful work you want, so that we may live always serving Jesus Christ, our hope and our true joy.—*The Worship Book*

LECTIONARY MESSAGE

Breaking Through the Ritual

TEXT: Luke 2:22–40

Tomorrow is New Year's Eve. The events of 1990 pass into the history books, and the new year—fresh, full of promise and uncertainty—will be welcomed in. Most of us have our own rituals for bringing in the New Year. For some, the birth of the New Year means a party with friends. For others, New Year's Eve is spent watching a football game or seeing the ball drop from the building in New York City or staying up until midnight and kissing the one we love. Some people serve a ritual meal; some uncork champagne; some attend a watch night service at the church; some make firm resolutions; some set off fireworks or blow their automobile horns at 12:00 sharp. We have our rituals.

All of these rituals are about one thing, of course: the passing of time. Each of them signals the hope that the New Year will be more prosperous, more loving, more peaceful, more blessed than the year past. The problem is, we go through our rituals not really believing that the New Year will be any different from the year before. "Happy 1991!" we will exclaim, convinced in our hearts that 1991 will prove to have the same headlines, the same stresses, the same trials, the same worn grooves we traveled in 1990.

In our biblical text for today, every person mentioned is involved in some kind of ritual regarding the passing of time. Mary and Joseph bring the child Jesus to the Temple for the rites of purification and dedication. The rituals marked the end of the time of uncleanliness after the birth of a child (Lev. 12:2–8) and the presentation of the firstborn to the Lord (Exod. 13:12). Every devout Jewish couple would have done the same thing. These were, after all, the accepted rituals. Simeon has his own ritual: looking for the consolation of Israel. He spent, no doubt, a part of every day searching the Scripture for clues and praying the same ritual prayer, "Let my eyes see thy salvation, O Lord." Anna, too, is looking for the redemption of Israel, and she also has her rituals: fasting and prayer, night and day, at the Temple.

No one around these people would have expected much from these rituals. Every year thousands of young parents did what Mary and Joseph were doing, and there were countless nostalgic old Jews like Simeon and Anna fasting and praying and hoping against hope for the renewal of Israel. Despite these rituals, day followed weary day without interruption. Make the resolutions, blow the horns, shoot the fireworks, if you want to, but tomorrow will be much like yesterday. *Que sera, sera.*

But into these routine rituals came an unexpected grace. At the center of them, suddenly, was Jesus, the Lord of all time. Into the midst of oft-repeated customs appeared the One who gathers the future into his saving love. Simeon, who day after day prayed the same ritual prayer and night after night searched the same old Scriptures, perhaps best expressed God's breaking into human ritual: "Lord, now lettest thou thy servant depart in peace . . . for my eyes have seen thy salvation . . ." (Luke 1:29–30, RSV).

That same Jesus stands in the midst of our lives. Without him, the ritual of the New Year is merely the passing of the old year into another just like it. By his grace, however, we can claim 1991 as A.D. 1991, "the year of our Lord." Like Anna, we can give thanks to the God who holds the years in his hand, and like Simeon, we can say, "Mine eyes have seen thy salvation."—Thomas G. Long

SECTION III.
Messages for Communion Services

Topic: The Discipline of Love

That on this Sunday in Lent our coming to the Lord's table be not a mere formal observance but a Communion with the eternal Spirit, let us think on these things. For his final journey to Jerusalem, the Gospel records, "Jesus set his face steadfastly to go to Jerusalem." Or as one translation puts it, "Jesus set his face like flint." It was hard for him to make this final trek knowing the opposition that would confront him there. As he was making this journey accompanied by that little apostolic band, the Gospel writer notes that the apostles were arguing about the chief seats in the kingdom. They were not just with him, they were not in communion with his Spirit.

In the midst of their arguing, one Gospel writer notes, Jesus turns on them and asks, "Are you able to drink of the cup of which I am about to drink and be baptized with the baptism with which I am to be baptized?" This is the issue!

Lent reminds us of the discipline required to follow the Master. When Jesus instructs those who would keep the sacrament, "Do this in remembrance of me," what do we remember in his life and ministry? Is it not the discipline of love demonstrated in his choosing the cross? To be so baptized in the love of God to the uttermost is accompanied by the cup of sorrow and pain in every relationship.

Who is able to drink of the cup and be baptized with the baptism of Jesus? Only through the grace of God present in the meaning and experience of our Communion here through which we are made ready for anything. It was of this grace Jesus partook, and this grace is present for us as we remember Jesus in the discipline of love.

To love to the uttermost is to drink of the cup of pain in any relationship.

This is the gracious hospitality of the Father who, for the cup of pain, offers a cup of grace that is not only full but running over.—John Thompson

Topic: The Cup of Blessing

Paul wrote to the Corinthians and gave us this text: "The cup of blessing which we bless, is it not the communion of the blood of Christ? The bread which we break, is it not the communion of the body of Christ?" (1 Cor. 10:16). That's not a question. It's an exclamation. Paul was sure that the problems at Corinth could be solved if only they would realize the real meaning of the Lord's Supper.

They had a problem with irreverence at Corinth. Paul wrote to remind them of the deep reverence due Christ at his table. In the chapter that follows our text he said, "Whosoever shall eat this bread and drink this cup of the Lord, unworthily, shall be guilty of the body and blood of the Lord." There is death in the cup.

That reminds us of Socrates, lifting the cup to his lips, surrounded by his friends. It is no celebration. The cup was prepared by his enemies and filled with poison. There is death in the cup.

We think of the Roman emperor Claudius being served by his own wife. It was no gesture of love. There was death in the cup. So Paul says there is death in this cup if it is partaken unworthily.

This verse has caused many to refuse the cup saying, "I am not worthy." Of course, they are not worthy. No one is worthy. If one had to be worthy, then no cup would ever have been used, no bread ever broken. Not one of the disciples in that upper room would have partaken if one had to be worthy.

Once when David was fighting his enemies, his native village of Bethlehem lay in the hand of the opposition. David, musing one night, remarked how much he would like a drink of water from the well at Bethlehem. Overhearing him, three men took him literally. That night they slipped through the enemy lines and got the water. Slipping back through, they brought it to David. He would not drink it. He poured it out on the ground. "It is the blood of men," he said. David could not drink water brought at such a risk. So we feel that we are not worthy to partake of a supper bought at such a sacrifice.

We do not have to be worthy. The word *unworthily* is an adverb. It refers to the manner in which we eat or drink. He who comes humbly and reverently partakes in a worthy manner, and that is just what Paul meant. If one should come to the table saying, "I feel worthy of Communion today. I'm such a fine fellow. The Lord should feel honored that I accept his invitation and come to his table," such a one would be partaking unworthily. He who comes saying in his heart, "Lord, I am not worthy and will never be worthy," has the proper attitude. He partakes worthily.

We must, however, always take it reverently. We must take it, recognizing that we are on holy ground—holier ground than Moses at the burning bush; holier ground than that at Sinai where God gave the Law; holier than that Most Holy Place of the Jewish Temple; holier ground than Lhasa or Mecca. When we gather here we are on the holiest ground of all! That is because we realize here whence our forgiveness comes.

They had another problem at Corinth, and that was the problem of division. Many churches have more than one faction. At Corinth, they had at least four factions in the church. They were not only divided—they were subdivided. Paul was concerned about this disunity in the church at Corinth. So he wrote this text and said, "We are all one body because we all partake of one bread." It draws us together. It unites us.

Once there were two men who were brothers in the flesh and brothers in the Lord and partners in business. Then they came to a parting of the ways. Both of them were officers in the church. The man in charge of arranging the serving of Communion always arranged it so they didn't serve on the same Sunday. Then there came to that church a brash, young minister who did just the opposite. He worked it out so they both found themselves with only the Lord's table between them on the same Lord's Day. Nothing dramatic or spectacular took place, but gradually the warmth of God's love melted the ice between them. The table became a bridge of reunion.

That's exactly what God wants the Lord's table to be for all of us. Sometimes there are barriers that are built up between brothers and sisters in Christ. The Lord's Supper tears them down. Sometimes there are wide gulfs and chasms that are gouged out in our human relationships. The Lord's Supper bridges them. This is our time of reunion to be drawn together, closer to one another. This is also our time of union with all Christians everywhere. In one thousand different tongues, people today have said those words Jesus said long ago, "This is my body. This is my blood."

While we slept, the Lord's table was spread beneath a thatched roof in the Philippine islands. While we slept, the Lord's table was spread in Japan. When we lay safely in our beds, Christians risked their lives in China to meet in secret about this table. Before we ever began to get ready for church, the table was already spread beneath the towering, ancient idols of

India. Already, the service is over in the great cathedrals of Europe. The Lord's Supper somehow unites us with all of our unseen brothers and sisters in Christ everywhere. Someday we'll meet them on the golden streets of heaven. Until that day comes, we are united with them in the unseen bond of the Lord's Supper.

Above all, the Lord's Supper speaks of our union with Christ. You read, I am sure, the touching and yet sordid story of an African leader who remembered that years ago in Vietnam he had fathered an illegitimate child. He sent some of his aides back there, and they searched and searched. Finally, in the streets of the city, they found that girl. They brought her from the alleys of Vietnam to a palace in Africa. Thus her father, as best he could, tried to redeem the mistakes of the past.

There is a more beautiful story in the Bible. We call it the gospel. It is the story of a God who reached down into the haunts of sin and found us and restored us to our family relationship with him. That adoption was made possible by the blood of Jesus.

These substances upon the table are more than the tokens of his death. They are the trophies of his victory! Jesus died on Friday. Did you ever wonder why we don't have Communion on Friday? That's the anniversary of his death. Why don't we remember it then? The answer is, God wanted us to look back at Calvary through the lens of the Resurrection. He wanted the light of Easter morning to shine upon the grisly scene at Golgotha. That's why we observe the Lord's Supper on Sunday. These are more than tokens of his death. They are the trophies of his victory. It is a victory he gives us, not only over sins past, but also over temptation in the future. "Because he died for me, I'm going to be worthier of the sacrifice."—Robert C. Shannon

Topic: Until He Comes
Text: 1 Cor. 11:17–32

Paul's first Corinthian correspondence was written before any of the Gospel records. Nevertheless, the text quotes at length from the words of Jesus. What this indicates is that even before the Gospel records were set down in writing and widely circulated, what Jesus both said and accomplished had been widely broadcast.

The Apostle Paul needed an authority not his own. Therefore, he appealed to chapter and verse of Jesus' teaching.

The situation was bad in Corinth—and steadily worsening. Paul indicated that their regular worship services actually "do more harm than good" (v. 17b). That is an observation that ought to make every worship leader and participant in every age stop and take notice! The problem continued to be the divisive spirit within the congregation. Such divisions and factionalism were beginning to have a nullifying impact even upon worship.

The central element of New Testament worship was the observance of the Lord's Supper. It was the primary reason for coming together (11:33). Apparently, its meaning had been entirely lost because of the divisions at the table of the Lord.

You can imagine what it was like. All you have to do is to recall the last time you and your mate, or entire family, sat down to a meal in your home while engaged in a disagreement. Little conversation is offered. Everyone's eyes are fixed to their plate. Sometimes there is not even a willingness to pass the dishes of food to other family members. No one waits on the others to begin—or finish—the meal. One eats nothing; another "picks" at her food; still another pretends that he is not bothered at all and, so, scrapes his plate clean. Everyone sits at the table, but they do not eat together as a family. Family meals simply are not supposed to be like that.

Yet, that description sounds strikingly similar to Paul's portrait of Corinthian worship. He wrote, "When you come together, it is not the Lord's Supper you eat, for as you eat, each of you goes ahead without waiting for anybody else. One remains hungry, another gets drunk. . . . Do you despise the church of God and humiliate those who have nothing? . . . Shall I praise you for [the way you are conducting yourselves]?" (11:20–22).

The factions have destroyed the meaning of the Supper. They may eat—the Supper involved a full meal (v. 25)—but they did not eat the Supper of the Lord. Likewise, the factions destroyed the significance of worship. They may have been fathered in the same room, singing the same hymns, heads bowed in prayer at the same time, but they were not worshiping together. Such behavior only indicated contempt for the church of the Lord Jesus Christ.

To help the Corinthians, Paul appeals to the words of Jesus himself. He reminds them of the essential nature of the Lord's Supper.

I. The Lord's Supper is an act of recall (11:23b–25). The tradition goes ultimately back to Jesus himself, who instituted the Supper "on the night when he was betrayed" (v. 23b).

The early Christians not only reminded themselves that Jesus was crucified by the Roman Empire but that he was handed over to his executioners by one of his own. The Supper was a poignant reminder that the table is a place of betrayal as well as place where grace, forgiveness, and life are also celebrated.

Thus, whenever the ordinance is observed, each of us should examine ourselves. Do we come to the table in an attitude and spirit that, like the act of Judas, denies and betrays our Lord? Do our actions and dispositions make us co-conspirators with his executioners, giving them even more reason to oppose him?

Or, do we come to his table full of his grace—having been forgiven and, thus, also having been set free to be forgiving? If this were a family meal—and it is—and all of these people were a part of your family—and they are—would there be lively, joyous conversation around the table? Would you have called everyone to the meal? Would anyone be left out?

The Apostle Paul wrote to the Corinthians: "Whoever eats the bread or drinks the cup of the Lord in an unworthy manner will be guilty of sinning against the body and blood of the Lord. A man ought to examine himself before he eats of the bread and drinks of the cup" (11:27–28).

We must recall the circumstances of the first Lord's Supper and be careful not to reenact the entire drama. To do so, would require that some one of us play the role of the betrayer.

II. The Apostle Paul reminded the Corinthians that the Lord's Supper is an experience of re-living. According to the ancient mind, to remember something was not simply to recall it. To do something in remembrance was to make the remembered event present.

So, to the words of Jesus the Apostle added his own comments. He said, "As often as you eat the bread and drink the cup, you proclaim the Lord's death. . . ." (v. 26). The Lord's Supper is proclamation. It represents the event of God's redemptive action in Christ. As often as we do it—which may not be nearly often enough—this Supper is a sacred act of gospel proclamation.

Yet, it is more. To recall the event is also to recall the central figure of Jesus Christ. He is the focus of this observance. And to honor him in this way makes him present with us.

You are aware of how that works. No doubt, you have had experiences in which you have solitarily revisited and walked the hallways of the old home place, the old schoolhouse or playground, the church of your childhood, the factory, or even the cemetery. During those special moments, you were able to hear the sounds of laughter you had not recalled for years; faces you had not seen for decades became vivid in your mind; perhaps, you even thought you felt a gentle touch again.

There was a presence with you. It was real. You knew you were not alone. You had the strange feeling that the one you were remembering was with you. Not really, but really.

There is a very real sense in which the reliving of the event brings us into his presence. The one whom we celebrate is here with us. We are his table guests. He is our host. Thus, we are to think and behave toward him and each other as though he is present, for, in reality, he is.

Certainly, he is present with us always. Although we are not always aware of his presence, Jesus is with us in all that we know of life—the demands, the joys, the struggles, the victories—all that comes to us, even death itself. He never leaves us. He certainly will never abandon us.

Still, the Lord's Supper is one occasion

when we intentionally invite his presence. It is a declaration of our worthiness to sit at his table. Therefore, it is also an invitation to his judgment of us. He who knows what is in the heart of every person surely sees and understands our heart in this moment.

III. There is yet one other point the Apostle Paul made with regard to the ordinance. The Lord's Supper is also the occasion when we are reassured that Jesus will return for us (11:26b). While the Supper looks back to Christ's death and realizes his presence now, it also looks forward to his coming again (see 1 Cor. 15:23). Our celebration of this event is accompanied by the cry of hope: *Maranatha!* "Our Lord, come!"

One pulpit committee asked the candidate's view of the Second Coming of Christ. The pastor responded, "I'm all for it!" Ask what the New Testament's position is on the Second Coming of Jesus and the answer will erupt from every page: "We're all for it!"

No sensible person, confronted with the promise of Jesus' triumphant return, can yawn or turn the page. It is the climax of all that human life has been heading toward.

Yet panic is no better response than apathy. The date is in God's hands. History will roll forward at his pace. The end will come at his time. We must not waste the time he gives us in frenzied effort to chart the time as some of God's people are doing. We must not waste the time he gives us in rushing to the mountains to wait as some of God's people are doing. We must simply "watch and be prepared" (Mark 13:37). We must make sure of our own relationship with the Father through faith in Jesus Christ. It is for the Father's servants that Jesus is returning. Our task is to make sure that we belong. Have you acknowledged that you cannot live without God? Have you rejected your godless independence? Have you turned from your selfishness and arrogance? Have you said yes to the Father's call to come home and be a part of his family?

Christ's coming is sure. The hour is not.

That combination spurs us to trust him now for salvation and guidance.

As we take part in the Lord's Supper, we will recall the night of his betrayal; we will experience his presence with us; we will set our face toward the future and look toward his coming.

The question of the hour is this: What needs to be put in order in our lives as we examine ourselves, as we come as his guests to his table, as we watch for his return? What needs to be done?

Are there sins to be confessed? A word of Christian witness to be spoken? An apology to be offered? An attitude or spirit to be confessed, repented of, and surrendered? A broken relationship to be mended?

We dare not put it off. Christ is on his way. In reality, he is already here. He wants his people ready.

Are you?—Gary C. Redding

Topic: Things We'd Like to Forget

TEXTS: Gen. 22:1–13; Luke 22:14–27

There are few universal statements, but I think I've found one: All of us have things we'd like to forget. You know, those intimately personal events in the recesses of our minds that are either so painful or so foolish, so horrifying or so humiliating that we'd like to rub them out of our memories. Perhaps it's some cruelty we've inflicted, some deceit we've led, some lust we've acted upon, some tragedy we've endured. Temporarily, we bury them, or at least we try. And the debris of memory accumulates in the secret closet of our souls. In a way, it is grace that we do, for we couldn't go on with our normal lives if such things kept reoccurring to us. But just as the tide irresistibly fills the harbor, so do those things we'd like to forget raise their ugly heads—and ugh! If we could just forget them, just wipe them out, erase the tape! But we can't.

Even the saints of old have their regrettable and unforgettable moments. Take Abraham and his Mount Moriah experience with Isaac. Certainly that caused Abraham some consternation, not only as it was happening but also later as he thought of what could have happened. We know the story well: The Lord spoke to the old man and told him to take his only son into the mountains to sacrifice him like any other pagan would. I suspect that when Abraham heard the voice of the Lord, it happened no differently than when we hear the Lord's voice. Perhaps it was in a pensive, soul-searching moment; perhaps he saw someone else doing something inspiring; maybe he was hearing someone else express religious thoughts and feelings. Whenever it was, Abraham heard the voice of God and set his mind on cajoling or forcing his son to be a living or dead sacrifice to God.

What it must have been like for Abraham to scale the mountain with Isaac! Picture it with me: the awkward burden on Isaac's back; the nervous sweat on the back of Abraham's hands; Isaac's poignant question, "Where is the lamb?" and the lump in the old man's throat when the boy asked it; and also the conviction, no matter how certain or uncertain, "The Lord will provide." And then when it was all over, after the Lord *did* provide a sacrifice, what kinds of thoughts must have rushed through Abraham's mind: "Why, for God's sake, did I do a thing like that, put my only son through such agony? I must have scared him to death! I coulda killed him!" The heroes of faith in the Bible are so human, it's not unreasonable to imagine that Abraham felt this way, that he would have liked to forget that near-tragedy on Mount Moriah. But forget he could not. What might have become a horrible tragedy became a landmark experience for the patriarch, for his son, and for their generations that followed. What might have been a totally horrifying experience became a turning point, a profound moment of revelation, a faith event for Abraham and the people of God.

The Old Testament had Abraham, and the New Testament had the disciples of Jesus. They, too, had their regrettable and unforgettable moments. One of them was on the last night they had with Jesus before he died. Jesus was aware while it was happening; the disciples were not aware. It was the Passover: a time for friendship, compassion, and companionship. But in the midst of it was the ugly scene: shouting, pushing, shoving, the

sound of slapped flesh. "Who is the greatest among us?" they contended. The question really meant, "Who among us will not betray Jesus?" The disciples were at their worst. I can see the old blowhard Peter, supposedly the most revered of the bunch, making his own insolent claim to fame but thoroughly embarrassing himself before those he loved. A few moments later Jesus put Peter in his place by predicting how Peter would betray him, not once or twice, but three times.

And then, when it was all over, and the next day too had passed, after the Lord did provide a sacrifice, what kinds of thoughts must have rushed through the disciples' minds: "Why, for Christ's sake, did we do a thing like that, argue and fuss on the last night he was among us? If we had only realized how precious the night was we wouldn't have acted so stupidly, so unthinkingly, so unfaithfully." It was a scene they would have liked to forget. But forget they could not. In fact, as they recalled the events of that night, the words of Jesus, spoken as he broke the bread and poured the cup, kept ringing in their ears: "When you do this, remember me! When you remember this night, remember me!" And what could have become a horrifying experience became a landmark event for the disciples and the people of God.

Our minds do amazing things, don't they? We forget things we want to remember, especially as we age. And we remember things we'd rather not. Having heard these two old stories again, I guess we can agree that it's good that we don't forget the things we'd like to. While it would be a tragedy if we lost in antiquity the mistakes of the heroes of faith, a greater tragedy would be if we lost our own. For we could never reflect on them. We could never turn from the evil we have caused unless we remembered how much hurt we've inflicted. And more importantly, we could never discern the holy hand and presence of God in the midst of the times it felt like he was absent. The things we'd like to forget, we remember, thank God! Then we can resolve to do things differently, or as the Bible says, we can repent! And those regrettably unforgettable moments can become turning points, landmarks, moments of faith for us.

So now, as we come to the table where the bread is broken once again and the cup is poured as it was so long ago, we first face ourselves as we really are and we remember our own lives, as it has really been, even the things we'd like to forget. But we also hear the words of Jesus ringing in ears: "When you do this, remember me." And so we remember him and all he has done for us, especially forgiving all those things we'd like to forget. And Jesus remembers us, receives us, and invites us to sup with him, now and forever.

So be it for us.—Jeffrey Allan Kisner

Topic: At the King's Table
Text: 2 Sam. 9:11–13

Guess Who's Coming to Dinner! That was the title of a popular movie. That title fits this text. Can't you imagine the servants of King David saying to one another, "Guess who's coming to dinner!" It was a table for royalty. Just anyone didn't sit at the king's table. Mephibosheth came to the king's table by invitation.

The king's table was always a bountiful table. At our family table we ask, "Is there any of that left?" They never had to ask that at the king's table.

In Vienna, Austria, you can visit the royal apartments in the Hofburg Palace. Particularly interesting is the dining room. The table is set as it would be for a royal banquet. You have never seen so many knives, forks, and spoons at one table setting in your life. It would take a set of directions to know which fork to pick up first. But for some of the guests of the emperor Franz Joseph, that was not a problem. They always served the emperor first. He was a very fast eater. When he quit eating, everyone else had to quit eating. It would have been rude to have continued. Because the table was so long and because he ate so fast, there were many people who came to have dinner and never got to eat anything at all. By the time they were served, he was finished. They used to say in Vienna that if you had an invitation to dine with the king, you should eat before you go. Nothing like that happened at King David's table.

For Mephibosheth, that was not what was important. His dining there was a mark of his acceptance. He was the grandson of King Saul. He was the son of David's friend, Jonathan. When Saul and Jonathan both fell in battle the same day, the news came back to Jerusalem. The nurse who took care of the infant Mephibosheth knew that he was in real danger. King Saul had enemies. Surely they would try to wipe out his entire family. So the nurse took the baby and fled. Running through the narrow streets she fell. The baby's feet were injured so that he remained a cripple the rest of his life.

In those days you would never have seen a crippled person at the king's table. There was no "equal opportunity" then. The king had to be surrounded by the beautiful people—beautiful women and stalwart men. Each one was to be a perfect specimen of manhood or of womanhood. This situation is so unusual the Bible mentions more than once that at David's table sat the *crippled* young man Mephibosheth.

Prince Eugene of Savoy was related to most of the royal houses in Europe. But because he was a hunchback, King Louis of France would not have him at his court. So Eugene went over to the Hapsburgs in Austria, became commander of the army, and led them in their defeat of the Turks, and later, *the French!*

If it was a mark of acceptance for Mephibosheth to be there, it was also a mark of assurance. If anyone wanted to unseat David, the logical approach was to promote Mephibosheth as the rightful king. His grandfather was king. David did not descend from a kingly line. His father was a farmer. His grandfather was a farmer. It would be easy to argue that the grandson of Saul had a better claim to the throne than David. If ever there was opportunity to start a revolution, that opportunity lay in the living person of Mephibosheth. When David summoned him, Mephibosheth feared for his life. It was a mark of assurance that he sat every day at the king's table.

But this was all so very long ago. What does it have to do with us? Just this: we, too, sit at the King's table. He is not like David, king over some tiny vest-pocket principality in a far corner of the world. He is King over the whole earth. He is the King of Kings. He has invited us to sit at his table.

We come only by invitation: his invitation. Like Mephibosheth we find it a place of acceptance. We, too, are crippled. We are spiritually crippled. We do not walk as we were meant to walk. People may look at us and think, "You have no place at the King's table." But he has invited us all the same.

We do not come because we are pure. We come because we want to be pure. We do not come because we are innocent. We come because we want to be innocent. It is a measure of our acceptance that in spite of our spiritual awkwardness and our great limitations, he invites us still. In that acceptance, there is the blessed assurance that Jesus is ours.

That other king's table was a table of abundance. Beside it, this table seems sparse and almost bare. There are only crumbs of bread here and only a taste of wine. You would starve if all you had to eat was what you found on this table. Here we find not food for the body but food for the soul. You will starve if you neglect this table. Paul said that the neglect of this table made many weak and sickly (1 Cor. 11:30). If we stay away from the King's table we shall starve our souls.

This is a table for royalty. Jesus says that he has made us kings and priests (Rev. 1:6). Peter says we are a royal priesthood (1 Pet. 2:9).

This is a table for remembering. Mephibosheth was not invited because he was the grandson of King Saul. He was invited because he was the son of Jonathan, David's friend. To David, friendship meant more than royalty. Jonathan had never worn a crown, but it was because of Jonathan that Mephibosheth was at the king's table.

David and Jonathan formed a fast friendship. It survived in spite of the fact that Jonathan knew that David, and not he, would succeed Saul. Jonathan had every right to be the next king, but God had picked David. We are amazed that Jonathan could avoid jealousy and envy—and beyond that be David's friend! It was a friendship underscored by loyalty and courage. When David's life was in danger, it was Jonathan who risked his own life to save him.

It would not have been necessary for Jonathan to have done anything to become king, for Saul determined to kill David. That would have cleared the way for Jonathan. But for Jonathan, friendship meant loyalty. David described it as greater than the love of a man for a woman.

So this table is a table of remembering. Isn't our Communion always that? Why we carve it in our tables: "This Do in Remembrance of Me."

Sometimes you'll find the King's table in a great cathedral, and sometimes you'll find it in a tiny little clapboard chapel. Perhaps you've sat at the King's table in a storefront church or even in a little informal service in somebody's living room.

At the Jubilee celebration of the reign of Queen Victoria, they called upon Rudyard Kipling, the poet laureate, to write a poem in honor of the occasion. They thought he'd write a great paean of praise to honor the queen. Instead, he wrote a poem that has since been set to music and become a hymn. It called the nation back to God. He didn't write one word about the queen. But he wrote in the chorus, "God of the nations, / Spare us yet, / Lest we forget! / Lest we forget!" We come to our King's table *lest we forget*.

This royal table, this table for remembering, is a table that calls for a response. How did Mephibosheth respond to his invitation to the king's table. He did not respond in pride. He didn't say, "At last I've gotten what I deserve." He did not respond casually, "It's no big deal!" He did not respond subversively, seeing it as an opportunity to look and listen, to plot and destroy. He did respond in humility. He bowed. He said, "I am your servant." He felt himself unworthy.

How do we respond to our invitation? Certainly we must mind our manners here. We must come in gratitude and humility. We must come remembering but also anticipating.

Feast after feast thus comes and
passes by;
Yet, passing, points to the glad
feast above.

(Horatius Bonar)

Would it be crude to say that the Communion table consists only of the appetizers, only the hors d'oeuvres? For the *real* feast is yet to come. The earthly Supper is but the preparation for the endless banquet at the King's heavenly table. Are they setting a place for you there?—Robert C. Shannon

ILLUSTRATIONS

SHADOWS OF THE CROSS.   In the course of his address, a noted neurosurgeon commented that the two sayings from the cross which a doctor or a nurse hears most often in a hospital ward are: "My God, my God, why hast thou forsaken me?" and "I thirst." These are the vocal symptoms of spiritual and physical distress. Our Lord spoke both of them.—James T. Cleland

WHEN LOVE APPEARED.   In one of his plays, Jean Anouilh describes the last judgment as he sees it. The good are densely clustered at the gate of heaven, eager to march in, sure of their reserved seats, keyed up and bursting with impatience. All at once, a rumor starts spreading: "It seems he's going to forgive those others, too!" For a minute, everyone's dumfounded. They look at one another in disbelief, gasping and sputtering, "After all the trouble I went through!" "If only I'd known this. . . ." "I just can't get over it!" Exasperated, they work themselves into a fury and start cursing God, and at that very instant they're damned. That was the final judgement, you see. They judged themselves, excommunicated themselves. Love appeared, and they refused to ac-

knowledge it. "We don't know this man." We don't approve of a heaven that's open to every Tom, Dick, and Harry." "We spurn this God who lets everyone off." "We can't love a God who loves so foolishly." And because they didn't love Love, they didn't recognize him.

Yet love does things like that, and we have to expect such surprises from God. He wants us to learn to identify him by the way he loves.—Louis Evely

WILLING TO BE FORGIVEN.   From our so great and so many sins, God hath given us a short and easy way of deliverance and one that is free from all toil. For what sort of toil is it to forgive him that hath grieved us? Nay, it is a toil not to forgive but to keep up our enmity: even as to be delivered from the anger both works in us a great refreshment and is very easy to him that is willing. For there is no sea to be crossed, nor long journey to be traveled, nor summits of mountains to be passed over, nor money to be spent, no need to torment thy body; but it suffices to be willing only, and all our sins are done away.—John Chrysostom

STEPS TOWARD UNITY.   The higher we get in our spiritual achievement and experience, the nearer we get to having the mind of Christ and the more we will approach a "God's-eye view of the world." We have too many bird's-eye views of the world, too many cat's-eye views, seeing only something to pounce on. The world of our maps and charts is a divided world of fences and boundaries. The world which God sees may perhaps be more like an aviator's view of the world. One recruit on his first flight exclaimed, "I was surprised to see that Oregon was not yellow as on the map and Idaho pink—it was all one color and one country." That is what God who loves the whole globe sees.—Halford E. Luccock

SECTION IV.
Messages for Funeral Services

SERMON SUGGESTIONS

Topic: A Remedy for Troubled Hearts
TEXT: John 14:1–3

When Jesus said, "Let not your hearts be troubled," he was not criticizing the disciples for their grief. It was natural that they would be grieved He was going to be separated from them. They would feel very much alone. Grief was a natural response to their situation. Jesus didn't criticize them for their grief; rather, he gave them a remedy for their grief.

Today he would not criticize us for our grief; he would offer us the same remedy he offered them. There are three parts to the remedy: our faith, our friend, and our future.

"Ye believe in God, believe also in me." It is faith that brings us here today. If we had no faith we would not be having this service. Our faith may not change the facts about death, but it certainly changes the way we view death—and life. Faith is the lens through which we see both life and death. Looking through that lens we see them differently. We do not see them as the world sees them. We do not see them as doubt distorts them. We do see them as they really are.

Faith tells us that this life is not all there is, that this life is only the proving ground for life hereafter. Our faith tells us that death is not always tragic, that death is the ultimate healer, that there is certainly a fate worse than death.

Our faith tell us that life here is but a beginning and that death does not interrupt its continuity. Faith tells us that life here is a school and death is a graduation.

The disciples were comforted by their faith in God. They were comforted even more by their faith in Jesus. We, too, have that dual faith. We are comforted by our faith in God the Creator, who made us not for earth but heaven, not for one another but for himself.

So many parts of God's Creation come together to comfort us today. We are comforted by the beauty of the flowers he has created. We will thank those who sent them. Just now, we thank the God who created them. We are comforted by music. God created the mind that composed the music. God gave the talents to play and sing. God created the life we honor today. For we do not just come to commemorate death. We also come to honor the life.

Our faith in Christ adds to this comfort. He experienced life as we live it. He experienced death as we must. Then he rose from the dead. His resurrection power he shares with us. In fact, he said, "I *am* the resurrection and the life." We find comfort in Christ's experiences in Gethsemane and Golgotha and, most of all, in Christ's Resurrection. We are soothed in our sorrow when we think of our faith.

Then we must think of our friend Jesus. He said to his disciples, "If it were not so, I would have told you." He would never have let them go on believing a lie, no matter how comforting that lie might be. He would not have them chasing imaginary pots of gold at the ends of nonexistent rainbows. "If it were not so, I would have told you!" They believed already in immortality, in the survival of the soul after death, in life beyond the grave. "If it were not so, I would have told you." Jesus was too good a friend to them to let them believe something that wasn't true.

He is also our friend. He wants to comfort us but with facts not theories, with reality not illusion. We love the song, "What a Friend we have in Jesus, / All our sins and griefs to bear." We must see him today, not as an absent friend, but as one who is present. "Lo, I am with you always" was his promise. He is here.

We are comforted today by the presence of human friends. They will never know how much they comfort us until they, too, face such a moment. We thank God for their presence. Our grief is easier to bear because of them. And if that is true of our earthly, human friends, what can we say of the friend we have in Jesus? He *is* here! No one saw him come in. No one will see him go out. He is here, and he is here in the capacity of a friend.

This Divine Friend who comes to share our sorrow today wants to share every experience of life. He wants to share our joys as well as our sorrows. He wants to share our sunshine as well as our shadows. He wants to be a part of every experience of life. The more we share with him, the more we understand what a true friend he is. Our burdens are all more easily borne when we share them with our friend Jesus.

The third part of the remedy is this: we have a future. "In my Father's house are many mansions," and "I go to prepare a place for you." We come to this stage in a life, and we write over it, "The End." God writes over it, "The Beginning." When you were in high school you wondered why the final event of graduation was called commencement. It didn't seem like commencement to you. You were going to leave your friends behind. You were going to leave familiar scenes behind. It seemed very much like the end of something, and, of course, it was. But it was also the beginning of something. You know that now. Looking back on it, you see that commencement was the right name for it.

So we come with childish hearts and write over the grave, "The End"; but God calls death "The Commencement." Surely God understands death better than we do. Surely his view is right, and our view is wrong. We were not made for time but for eternity. We were not made for earth but for heaven. We were not made for self but for God.

Today we look to the future. We know so little about it. I think I know why. If we knew too much about heaven it would spoil earth. If we really knew what God has planned for those who love him, how could we be content to stay here on earth? So God has given us only a hint, a glimpse, a tiny preview. But both our faith and our Friend assure us that "the best is yet to be."

We look back today at happy times gone by and find comfort in the memory. Thank God for such memories, but don't just look back. Alongside our blessed memories of the past stands our anticipation of the future. Remember that we sleep to wake. Remember that today prepares us for tomorrow. Remember that we never tear the last page off God's calendar. Remember God's tomorrow!—Robert C. Shannon

Topic: A Homecoming

Death can mean many different things to us. It can mean the loss of hope in what might have been when a child dies. It can mean the tragic loss of productive ability and responsible support to family, friends, and business associates when a young adult dies. And when a middle-aged person dies "before his or her time" it can mean the loss of the precious years of retirement that we work so hard for. But when an aged person dies, after they have lived a full, long life, when they are tired and when they have lost the abilities they once enjoyed, death means something quite different. We might call that kind of death "rest," even a "homecoming," of sorts.

I did not have the privilege of knowing———, but I have talked to those who did. Her death was that latter kind of death. To be sure, the death of this woman takes on the character of every other death: Her loss is painful to those she loved and those who loved her in return. She is dead, gone, and now there is an emptiness. Surely she will be missed.

And yet there is another side to———'s death. She lived a full, rich life of ninety years. Though she knew grief and pain like the rest of us, especially enduring the death of her husband and son, those who knew her tell me she did not allow these events and feelings to sap her of her passion for life and loving relationships. Those who knew her well tell me that she lived her life fully, without regret. And now that it is over, that she is "at rest," so to speak, seems fitting, acceptable.

But the outstanding reason why———'s death bears this acceptable character is because of her faith in God. Her death is a "homecoming" because she's "gone home" to be with God to be all she was created to be. I can say that, not because I was convinced of her devotion and faith firsthand, but because of the testimony of those who knew her best. She was a godly woman. Two Christian funerals not only testify to her deep, lasting friendships here and with those nearly a continent away, but also to her lasting and now everlasting friendship with her heavenly Father.

Indeed,———'s life is over, and she will be missed. But her everlasting destiny is sealed in faith and hope by Jesus Christ. Now as we think on her death, experience the feelings of loss, love, and hope, and even ponder the specter of our own deaths, may———'s death and life be an example of love for others and God.—Jeffrey Allan Kisner

Topic: Moving Day
Text: 2 Cor. 5:1–8

The one whom we come to honor today lived in a number of different houses. Now she has moved again. That's the way I understand this text. Paul seems to be saying that death is simply moving out of an old house into a new house.

In this life we move from one house to another for many reasons. Sometimes the old house has grown too small. Sometimes it has suddenly become too large. Sometimes the old house has deteriorated, and time has made it no longer suitable. Sometimes the old house is just in the wrong location. There are many reasons, but the basic reason is always the same. The old house no longer fits our needs.

The body is like a house. It suits us well here on earth, but it is unsuited for heaven! "Flesh and blood cannot inherit the kingdom of God." It suits us well in the beginning, but time takes its toll on the house. We are glad, really, that we are not imprisoned forever in these houses. They are too fragile. They are too subject to accident and injury. They are too vulnerable to infection and disease. They wear out too quickly. The muscles grow weak. The eyes grow dim. Even the memory becomes uncertain. Oh, these bodies are marvelously made, and they suit us well for our temporary residence on earth; but they are not very permanent. There comes a time when it is appropriate to move out of the house of this body into that "house not made with hands eternal in the heavens."

So we are confident that the true individual is not here before us. What we see here is only the house in which that one lived. But the house is now empty, and the true individual has moved out.

Having pointed out these facts about death, Paul causes us to think of our feelings concerning death. There is always a sadness at moving out of a house. So many happy memories are attached to it. It's the same with death. All that we know of a person we attach to the body. We cannot know a person in any other way. All our memories are associated with the body. So there is a sadness on moving day.

But the sadness of moving out of the old house is tempered by our anticipation of what lies ahead in the new house. What will life be like in the new house? We wonder and guess. The anticipation tempers our sadness. Is the same thing not true today? We are sad to see the house we know so well now empty. But we wonder about the new house, the "house not made with hands eternal in the heavens." What is it like? What joys may be experienced in the new house? What do we have to which we may look forward? God prepared so well for us here on earth. Can we not imagine that he has prepared things far more wonderful for us in heaven? He fitted our bodies so well for time. How grand must be the body made for eternity!

So today we feel a sadness, but we know the sadness is all on this side. Those who have already entered into the joy of the Lord know no sadness. It is left to us here to anticipate what may lie ahead.

Paul approaches this subject with great confidence. It is a confidence born of great faith. He says, "We *know!*" He doesn't say, "We think." He doesn't say, "We feel." He doesn't say, "We believe." He doesn't say, "We hope." He says, "We *know.*"

What gives Paul such confidence? Surely it is his faith in God and in Jesus, God's Son. We can find that same confidence if we have that same faith. A funeral director once said to me, "When a family walks into my office to make arrangements for a funeral, I know at once if they have faith." He didn't have to ask. He could tell! Faith makes a difference in everything, and it makes all the difference in the time of death.

The Apostle John joins the Apostle Paul in this confidence. Over and over again in his little letter to Christians, the aging Apostle John wrote, "We know! We know! We know!" We may guess about many things, but we don't have to guess about our future! We may have theories about many things, but our future is not just a theory. It's a fact.

So we come today with many things over which we must put a question mark and with one thing over which we may put an exclamation mark. We have questions about life and questions about death. We don't understand this, and we can't comprehend that. There is so much we don't know, and there are some things we will never know; but there is also one thing we do know. We know it beyond all doubting. "We know we have a building of God, a house not made with hands eternal in the heavens." A wise man once said, "Pillow my head on no guesses when I die."

We are not here today to guess, to imagine, to hope wistfully. We share Paul's confidence because we share Paul's faith. There may be much we don't know, but we do know this. We know it because we walk by faith and not by sight. We know it by the presence of the Holy Spirit. We know it by the very nature of Creation itself. God made us for this purpose . . . for eternity . . . for something beyond.

We may be sad today, but we are not uncertain. Our hearts may be broken, but God's promises are never broken. And so today we put aside the earthly dwelling place, the house of clay, the tenement of time. We do so in the confidence that the true individual is not here but already in the presence of God. Therein lies our comfort and our hope.—Robert C. Shannon

Topic: Keeping the Faith

Text: 2 Tim. 4:6–8

Meditate with me on this phrase recorded in Paul's Second Letter to Timothy: "My time of departure has come, I have fought a good fight. I have finished the race, I have kept the faith." It seems particularly appropriate for us to apply these criteria to . . . life. Like the apostle who wrote these words,———was no stranger to adversity. At least six times during the last two years———was ill enough to die, and yet she fought on. She could have used her adversities as an excuse to be hostile about the lot in life she had been dealt the last two years, but she didn't. She never surrendered to despair. Of———it could be said with certainty, "She fought the good fight. She finished the race . . ."

And "she kept the faith." We hear that phrase often, don't we? It has almost become a cliché. At a time like this, in the midst of death, it is particularly appropriate that we look at what it means to keep the faith. Faith is not something that must be kept like a memento, like napkins from someone's wedding, or like pressed flowers in the top drawer of the dresser. Faith is something that must be kept like a garden. Faith must be cultivated so that it can be a living and growing experience. Faith must be practiced lest it become a static souvenir of days gone by. Faith must live if it is to be a source of strength in times like these.———kept this kind of faith.

At the occasion of her death, it's a time for us to ask ourselves what fight in life we're fighting, what race in life we're running. Indeed, it's a time to ask ourselves if we're keeping the faith and how we're keeping it. The faith——kept was an active, living faith in Jesus Christ. Such faith is the only way to insure our eternal destiny in the full and wonderful presence of God. Perhaps——'s death can provide us with the occasion to affirm that faith or to make a step of faith for the first time in our lives.—Jeffrey Allan Kisner

Topic: The Crying of the Christ
TEXT: John 11

Hear again the words Mary and Martha spoke to Jesus: "Lord, if you had been here, my brother would not have died." In other words, these sisters were asking the questions, "Where were you, Jesus? Why did you let this happen? Why did you delay? Why didn't you come when we first sent for you?" Their cries to Jesus at that moment were very much like ours at this moment. We wonder, "Lord, if you had been here, our family member would not have died. If only you had done things differently, Lord! Where were you, God, when our friend drove off the road last Saturday night? Why did you let this happen?"

The cries of Mary and Martha to Jesus in their moment of anguish were genuine. They emerged out of deep struggle with God. But their questions were also rooted in doubt about their own actions before Lazarus died. They thought to themselves, "If only we had done things differently, Lazarus wouldn't have died. If only we had called on Jesus earlier, if only we hadn't given him this medicine or that, if only he hadn't had that dish to eat the other night, if only we had stayed home that night, if only we hadn't had that argument, then maybe this wouldn't have happened." Like Mary and Martha, we want to second-guess God, question the timing of the Almighty. And like Mary and Martha, we want to second-guess ourselves.

Interrogating and accusing God is a very natural human reaction to tragedy. We want to know why disaster strikes. In our scientific age when we have answers for everything else, we feel we have a right to know. We want to know if it's true that

God purposefully causes certain things to happen to us or if things happen in life just because we live in an imperfect world with imperfect, sometimes evil people. The right to ask such questions of God must be affirmed. God is big enough to handle them. Indeed, we must never stop asking the ultimate questions of life.

And not only is it natural and essential to question God at times like this, but it is also very natural and very human to question and second-guess ourselves when someone dies accidentally or takes their own life. We think, "If only I had done things differently, this wouldn't have happened." We may want to go back even further and say to ourselves, "If only my relationship with my loved one had been different, this might not have happened." Perhaps because some of us doubt our own wisdom regarding the acts that preceded our friend's death, or because we doubt our part in our relations with him or her, we want to question God. In other words, we want to transfer our questions about ourselves onto God. No doubt this same dynamic was at work when Mary and Martha pursued Jesus with their angry and pain-filled statements.

How then did Jesus respond to their statements? The answer to that question is crucial because in that answer we find our only comfort at a time like this. Jesus responded to their statements by weeping. No, he did not give them a long, complicated theological explanation why their brother Lazarus died or why people in general must suffer. He simply suffered with them: *Jesus wept.* And the crying of the Christ at the tomb of his friend Lazarus is a great symbol of his entire ministry, a symbol of his own death, and a symbol of the way God deals with us and all the pain we suffer in life.

For this Jesus, who wept at the tomb of Lazarus, was the one who came to live with the suffering ones on the fringes of society: the poor, the naked, the hungry, the homeless, the hookers, the addicts and drunks, the frauds, the prisoners, the mentally tormented souls of human existence—among all the outcasts Jesus lived.

This Jesus, who wept with his friends Mary and Martha, was the one who died no fine death, no calm, serene, and saintly death, but the one who died with loud cries and tears.

This Jesus, who wept at the tomb of a friend, wept also in the garden the night before his death and on the cross uttered the unspeakable and unanswerable question every human being utters in times of tumult, "My God, my God, why have you forsaken me?"

This Jesus is the one who lived among the suffering ones and who died suffering himself, is the same one who came to the tomb of Lazarus and grieved with those who were grieving.

This Jesus is the one who was with Mary and Martha when he was physically absent from them and the one who was with them in the love and support of family and friends.

This Jesus who wept so long ago is here today weeping with us, grieving the loss of our loved one and friend; Jesus, who was with us while our loved one and friend was still living; Jesus, who was with us in the moments when it seemed like God was absent; Jesus, who is with us now in the presence of others who know and love us.

Herein lies our comfort: When we suffer, God suffers with us. No, this does not solve all the problems. No, this does not answer our questions as to why our loved one and friend died or why we suffer all other atrocities and injustices of life. What it does is see us through.

A profound expression of God's suffering with us has been recorded by the Nobel Peace Prize recipient, Elie Wiesel. Wiesel is a survivor of the Nazi concentration camp in Auschwitz. In his book, entitled *Night,* Wiesel records one of his most vivid memories of the camp. He writes:

The SS hanged two Jewish men and a youth in front of the whole camp. The men died quickly, but the death throes of the youth lasted for half an hour. "Where is God? Where is he?" someone asked behind me. As the youth still hung in torment in the noose after a long time, I heard the man call again, "Where is God now?" And I heard a voice inside myself answer: "Where is

he? He is here. He is hanging (here) on the gallows. . . ."

It is true for us today. God is here with us, knowing our sorrow, guilt, and anger. This is our comfort. This is our hope. This is enough to see us through.—Jeffrey Allan Kisner

ILLUSTRATIONS

THE CHURCH AT ITS BEST.   Are we surprised that resurrection texts contain references to the church's common life, to evangelical preaching, the forgiving of sins, and the doing of the Lord's Supper? No, of course they do. But we must be cautious. The church qua church is not a testimony to the Resurrection; frequently, the church can be dismaying, even contentious, and without peace. The church per se is not a witness to the Resurrection. But if a church embodies the ministry of Jesus Christ—preaching and teaching and forgiving and feasting—then in the structures of the church's common life, there is witness to the risen Christ. The words of the resurrection texts address us: "Go tell"; "We knew him in the breaking of the bread"; "Whomever you forgive is forgiven"; "Shalom." In patterns of our common life, the mission of the risen Christ continues.—David G. Buttrick

INTENSITY.   One of the most colorful personalities in this city thirty years ago was Dr. Hans Zinsser. He wrote several widely read books, so that many of us who did not know him personally knew him through his books. In the last one he tells how on his last return from a trip abroad he realized before he left the ship that he had a disease that was incurable. He diagnosed it himself but in order to be sure he went to one of his friends, a Boston doctor, who confirmed the diagnosis. He describes himself and his doctor friend standing in the doctor's office looking out the window onto the Charles River Basin. He said they stood there in silence for a few minutes, and in those few minutes something happened to him. "Everything," he writes about himself, "that went on about him or within him from that moment on struck upon his heart and mind with a new and powerful resonance." Because he knew that he didn't have much time, life became more intense. All the experiences that he enjoyed in the past he enjoyed more. He went back and reread all the books that he loved and delighted in them more than he had the first time he had read them. Everything that shone at all for him shone with a new splendor because the time was short. He didn't have all the time in the world to waste, to fritter away. He had only a few weeks, perhaps only a few days. Every day was precious, every moment was something to be counted and treasured, and he said life began to glow with an intensity that he had never before known in all his life.—Theodore Parker Ferris

THE LARGER JOURNEY. Is it not time that we should concentrate upon the belief in the practice of the eternal life, that views our human pilgrimage in terms of the larger journey and does not permit itself to be deceived into exultation by one ecstatic mile of smooth going or plunged into despair by a mile of rough, uphill road?

This spiritual benefit can be had only by those for whom immortality has been brought to light, through Jesus Christ our Lord.—Lloyd C. Douglas

THE FINAL CHAPTER. We cannot believe in the Lord and Father of life who is love if this kind of world is his final achievement. Those who cannot deny the purpose they see in life and nature as a whole and who cannot reject the light that streams from history's highest crest, the cross of Christ, may have to live with many problems and real doubts, but finally they should see in the Father heart the reality of life everlasting. Either this life is without genuine purpose or that purpose must be seen at its highest point and reaching far beyond in the direction of its pointing. Some who have long lived with this choice and patiently weighed all evidence of head and heart have concluded that, beyond our detailed knowing, God's master plan only begins in this life. Every life ends with the promise of God: "To be concluded in the next."

Some of us have, I believe, in a way crossed the border, even in this life. Once after I had been praying with my attention solely on the love of God for the world and on offering my own little life for that world, I was inexplicably transported into an indescribably different experience. No earthly joy or thought can describe it. One such moment was worth years of suffering. Nothing ever seemed so real or can ever be so real again. Within my own self I knew that I had a foretaste of life everlasting. Now with Paul I serve here with willingness and with love for family, friends, and work, but nothing can so move me as the reality I have known. If life beyond death is anywhere nearly so indescribably different and real! If such piercing joy exists! I am convinced that God's final end with us is wonderful beyond thought or dream. The how, when, and where I leave with confidence to him who has such reality of life in store for us. Others may argue. For myself I have tasted and felt.—Nels F. S. Ferré

SECTION V.
Lenten and Easter Preaching

How to Make Lent More Meaningful in Your Church

Thinking that I wanted to go beyond the traditional Lenten sermons and other practices to find some new, creative way to stimulate my people to more effective Christian living, our church carried out successfully the following plan during Lent.

I selected what I considered forty-six outstanding passages in the Bible.

These selections were mimeographed and sent to all the parishioners. They were given to students and others attending the morning services. A later survey showed that both members and students had read the passages during the weeks. Some rendered a 100 percent accomplishment when they shared their findings on Easter Day.

Typical comments that came to us at the end of Lent were as follows: "It was the first time I ever read my Bible two days in succession"; "I never realized the value of daily readings"; "How natural after reading to follow through with prayer"; "Why didn't we think of this before?" and "Let's do it next Lent."

Members were lavish in their praise of the project. Those who never before had perused the Scriptures shared with us their newfound joy.

Each Sunday morning I preached on the seven selections they would read the ensuing week. A background history was given so that the reader could better understand the passages.

Suggested readings also were given that readers might find more light on the assigned passages.

Each Wednesday evening during Lent neighborhood group devotionals were held throughout the parish where skilled Bible readers conducted discussion around the forty-six passages I had selected. Here members had a chance for a "give and take" to present their own "findings."

The overall comment from the parish was, "Let's do it again!"—Fred E. Luchs

SERMON SUGGESTIONS

Topic: The World's Greatest Sinner

TEXT: 1 Tim. 1:15

Paul tends to use superlatives in describing himself. In 1 Cor. 15:9, he ranks himself as the least of the apostles. In Eph. 3:8, he refers to himself as less than the least of all the saints. Here, Paul refers to himself as the foremost of sinners. Some might think this to be a morbid approach. On the contrary, such an approach was helpful for several reasons.

I. *It kept humility in.* The vivid memory of his sin was the surest way for Paul to remain humble. From a human standpoint, Paul had attained a great deal. From a spiritual standpoint, he realized that the attainments of life were peripheral; the obtainment of life was primary. Thus, the vivid memory of Paul's sin kept him from pride.

II. *It kept gratitude in.* The vivid memory

of his sin was the surest way for Paul to keep his gratitude aflame. When we remember how we hurt God and those who love us and then remember how God and men have forgiven us, that memory should awaken the flame of gratitude in our hearts.

III. *It kept motivation in.* This vivid memory of his sin was also the constant urge for Paul to exert greater effort. We cannot earn the approval of God, nor can we repay it. However, when we remember how much God loves us, the result will be a constant urge to show God by the actions of our life how much we appreciate him.—Brian L. Harbour

Topic: Judas: The Plan That Failed

[This entire piece is played with great emotion, at times bordering on hysteria. The speaker must sustain the tension while maintaining control.]

It wasn't supposed to end this way. I never meant for it to end this way. If only he had listened to me. If only he had taken my advice. Poor sweet Jesus. Poor naive Jesus who would not listen. Now, now he hangs from that ugly Roman cross. Do you think that I, I of all the people in the world, would want to see any Jew hang from a Roman cross? Least of all Jesus? He just didn't understand the world. He didn't know how you change the world. If only he had listened to me, he could be sitting on a throne now instead of hanging from a cross. If only he had listened to me.

I don't understand. Do you know what it's like to be a slave in your own country? Do you know what it's like to have the boot of an oppressor on your throat? Do you know what it is to have your own priests and your own leaders betray you? I'm tired, so very tired. If I could rest, could think—too late for that now.

In the beginning it seemed so right. I believed he respected what I waited for all my life. He was the one, the one who would set Israel free. He was the one who would return to us our dignity. He was the one who would lead us to drive the Roman oppressors from our soil. When first I heard him, there in Nazareth at the synagogue, he spoke the words of the prophet. "The spirit of the Lord is upon me because he anointed me, to preach the gospel, the good news to the poor. He has sent me," Jesus said, "to proclaim release to the captives, recovery of sight to the blind, to set free those who are downtrodden." That is all I wanted: to set free the downtrodden, to release the captives, to bring good news to Israel. He said then that he would fulfill that scripture. It seemed possible.

Oh, we had always had preachers in Israel. There had never been a time in my life when you couldn't find a preacher on every corner of Jerusalem and every step of the Temple. There was always someone interpreting the Law. Throughout the countryside there was always someone who was calling himself Messiah, someone declaring that he was going to set the people free. But Jesus, Jesus was different. He did things no other man has ever done. I confess, I don't know how he did it. There was a time when I thought that the hand of God was upon him because the miracles he performed were not possible for an ordinary man. He produced the signs of Messiah. But if that had been true, if he had been the Messiah, he wouldn't hang now from that cross. God would not have let it happen in that way.

O Jesus, why didn't you listen to me?

I saw him. I saw him give sight to the blind, hearing to the deaf, speech to the silent. I saw Jesus touch lepers and make them whole again, give strength to useless legs and arms. I saw him do things that no man had ever done. I don't know how he did it, but I saw him raise the dead. If only he had listened to me.

You understand what it takes to change the world. It takes power, arms, troops, force, but Jesus didn't understand that. When I tried to tell him, he wouldn't listen. Jesus, Jesus, Jesus, if only you had listened to *me.* The words that had thrilled me were followed soon by words that frightened me. It shook me to the very center of my being. Words strange to the lips of any man in Israel but particularly to one who would be Messiah. He told the crowds that "it used to be said, an eye for an eye and a tooth for a tooth, but I say to you, do not resist him who is evil. And when someone slaps you on the right cheek, turn the left to him." Who does that? Who in his right mind would not resist evil? What man would allow someone to strike him on one cheek and turn the other? As if that wasn't enough, he said, "Love your enemies. Pray for those who persecute you. Return good for evil." Who among you does that? Who among you prays for his enemies. Who among you loves his enemies? Who among you returns good for evil?

He was so simple. So naive. He just didn't understand. So many missed opportunities. On one occasion he had been teaching all day, and there had been some healing. The day was growing late. The children were bawling, and parents were beginning to fight among themselves. The crowd was restless. We said to him, "They are tired, they are hungry, and we are tired and hungry. Send them home." And Jesus said to us, "Feed them." Feed them? I was the keeper of the purse. I knew that we had hardly coin enough to feed ourselves, let alone that crowd. Later some said that there were as many as five thousand men there plus all the women and children. The whole hillside was covered. Andrew brought to him a little boy with a few loaves and fishes. Jesus blessed those loaves and fishes and fed every person there until their bellies were full. Now, I thought, people would follow someone who can feed them; now is the time. If only you would speak the word, this multitude, these men would follow you to Jerusalem. We could drive the Romans out. "Jesus," I said, "speak the word, and they would become an army." He looked at me, shook his head, and whispered, "Judas, you don't understand." It was he who didn't understand. He just couldn't face reality.

There were other opportunities. There was one at Bethany when we were on our journey to Jerusalem—where I hoped he would throw out the Romans. He sent us to get a donkey. We brought back this small animal. He climbed upon its back. How silly he looked, his feet nearly touched the ground. If I had known why he wanted the beast, if only he had told us what he wanted, I would have gone into Jerusalem, and I would have stolen for him a fine Roman horse and great chariot

and he could have ridden into Jerusalem like an emperor, like a king, like a messiah should. But not Jesus. Jesus chose a donkey, the beast of burden. Nonetheless, it was amazing what happened. As the animal began to move toward Jerusalem, the multitudes began to cry out, "Hosanna, hosanna, hosanna to the son of David. Blessed is he who comes in the name of the Lord. Blessed is the coming kingdom of our father David, hosanna in the highest." "The kingdom of our father David"—they knew, they understood. He was the only one there who didn't act like he knew the Messiah's role. They would have followed him. Once again he let the moment pass. I knew then. I had to help him. I had to make him do what he would not do, force him to see what he would not see. I would make him a messiah.

I would make him a messiah like David. I could force him to do what he should do. I began to plot. The next day we were still in Bethany and went to the home of Simon. There a woman burst into the room. That was another sign of his weakness. He treated women equally with men. He would talk to them in the street. Why, once he had sat down with a Samaritan woman and drank from her jar. It's bad enough to converse with the Samaritans, but a Samaritan *woman.* He had spoken to her in public. There were always women hanging around, following him. On this occasion there was a woman of the streets. A woman that no man should have spoken to in public, least of all a teacher of Israel. She had with her an alabaster vase full of costly perfume. She broke the vase and poured it over him. "She is wasting that," I cried out, "Don't you know, Jesus, that this perfume could be sold and with the money we could feed the poor?" Jesus did not rebuke her. He rebuked me! He said, "She has done a good deed to me." Again I realized that he would never do the right thing. He wouldn't be the leader that he should be. I determined at that moment that I must carry through with my plot.

I went to the chief priest in order to betray him. I felt dirty. I hated to be in the presence of those scalawags, those traitors to Israel, those people who collaborated with the Romans. But you see, I had to do it. I had to do it. I agreed to betray Jesus. Yes, yes, they gave me money, but it wasn't the money. I didn't do it for the money. I took the money back and flung it in their faces. I had to make it appear that I really wanted to help them and betray him.

That night we gathered in an upper room. It was a strange evening. We had been together so often, but on this particular evening there was a shadow over us all. Hardly anyone spoke above a whisper. After a few minutes Jesus arose and took a basin of water and began to wash our feet. He acted like a common servant. Who would follow a man who treated women like men, a man who washed the feet of his followers? Who would follow a man that chose to ride into the holy city of David on the back of a donkey? You understand, his way wouldn't work. You must resist evil, and you must resist it with force. Then he spoke of betrayal. I thought, "He knows; someone has told him, perhaps one of the priests." But each of the others cried out, "Surely it is not I, Lord." He looked into my eyes and pierced my soul. "Go," he said, "and do what you must do quickly."

I knew where he would be. And so I went and told the high priest where he could be found. I didn't want to go with the soldiers to arrest him, but they insisted. It was part of the deal they said. I had to point him out. I had told them earlier that it would be the one that I would kiss. As we approached the garden I could see Peter and James and John. They had been sleeping. They quickly jumped to their feet, and foolish Peter drew his sword and cut off the ear of one of the guards. But Jesus, as I might have expected, rebuked Peter and healed his enemy. Who heals his enemy? They came to arrest him, and he did not resist. He healed one wounded in defense of him. I approached him. My body trembled. Once again his eyes looked into my soul. How hard it was for me, but I had to do it. I had to do it. [Pause; speak softly and slowly.] I betrayed a friend with a kiss. And as my lips touched his cheek I could taste the salt of his tears and perspiration. I could feel

his trembling body. I didn't want to do it. I had to do it.

You understand. Don't blame me unless you would have done it differently. I ask you, where were the others during the trial? Where were the others when they dragged him through the streets, humiliated him, whipped him, and scorned him? Where were the others when they nailed him to a cross between two thieves? Where were those to whom he had given sight, those to whom he had given hearing, those whom he had made whole? Where were the parents and friends of those whom he had healed and of the ones he had raised from the dead? Where were the thousands he had fed that day? Where were they when they nailed him to a cross?

Where were *you* when they nailed him to that cross? Would you have cried out, would you have defended him? You see, I thought that everyone would rally around him. I thought that in that moment of physical danger he would forget all of his words of peace and he would call forth his friends to fight. But not Jesus.

Don't judge me! Don't you judge me unless you would follow a leader like Jesus. I ask you, Do you love your enemies? Do you pray for those who abuse you? Do you bless those who curse you? I ask you, Do you turn the other cheek? Don't judge me unless you can live by his words and live like he lived.

Oh, God, I betrayed a friend with a kiss. God, what have I done? Oh, God, let me die, let me die.—Raymond H. Bailey

Topic: Good Grief
TEXT: 1 Thess. 4:13–18

Funeral practices vary from section to section of our country. I learned within months of accepting my first pastorate that grief ravages lives no matter what the funeral customs. I visited a guilt-ridden, grief-stricken widow and found her staring blankly as dozens of people milled about—eating, visiting, exchanging stories. I stumbled through three days from death to funeral, wondering how any good thing could come from such a disconnected gamut of emotions.

Our little friend, Charlie Brown, exclaims, "Good grief." Is there any such thing?

I. *Grief is common to us all.* Death and grief are common denominators for all humanity. Scripture never denies the reality of death. Jesus faced it in others. (Recall his many encounters with death.) He faced it and wept for Lazarus. Paul addressed the subject for the Thessalonians.

II. *Christian grief is different.* Paul indicated that the grief of many is the grief of despair (v. 13). Christian grief rides the reality of the Resurrection of Christ to lofty plains of hope. Paul suggested personal resurrection (v. 14), transformation of the universe (vv. 15–17), and the possibility of a community of comfort as we grieve (v. 18).

Grief can be good because hope replaces despair and becomes gratitude.—W. Wayne Price

Topic: First Day Footrace

TEXT: John 20:1–10

Let me give you a riddle. It concerns a footrace between two individuals. The one who arrived first at the finish line lost the race. The one who arrived last won the race but failed to capture the prize. The one who lost the race captured the prize. [Repeat these three points.]

The explanation to this riddle is found in John 20:1–10. The runners were two disciples of Jesus. The footrace was on the day we are celebrating today—early on that first Easter morning.

Let's look at John 20. The first person mentioned is Mary Magdalene. She is described in Luke 8:2 as a person healed by Jesus of "evil spirits and infirmities." John 19:25 tells us she was present at the Crucifixion of Jesus. In Matt. 27:61 we find her watching when Jesus was buried. Here in John 20 she came to the tomb early in the morning and found to her surprise and fear that the stone was rolled away.

She responded by running to tell the disciples. Her announcement to Peter and John was like a pistol shot that started their race to the tomb. Thus started one of the most interesting races in all of history. Who would get there first? The proud, impulsive fisherman or the "beloved disci-ple," who had also been called one of the "sons of thunder"? Who would win the prize?

We need to define the finish line in order for the riddle to apply. We also need to determine the prize. I consider the finish line as the entrance to the tomb. From the outside, one could see that the body was not there. Mary had probably seen that. But inside the tomb a person might be able to receive a great insight, what Gordon Cosby has called "the eureka moment." That insight is what I consider to be the prize. It was the realization that Jesus had indeed risen from the dead. Remember, Mary did not know that. What she said was, "They have taken the Lord out of the tomb" (NIV). When she said "they" I don't think she was talking about angels. She thought the local authorities had his body.

Let's look at the riddle again.

I. *The one who arrived first at the finish line lost the race.* "The other disciple outran Peter and reached the tomb first" (NIV). I can picture him standing there, huffing and panting, victory right in his grasp. But he stops short. He doesn't cross that line. Instead he stoops over looking inside, squinting to see through the dimness. "He saw the linen wrappings lying there, but he did not go in" (NASB).

We can sympathize with him. There is something about walking into a tomb, going among the dead, that might hold us back, too. We avert our eyes; we pull back. It is a region to which we defer and give respect. It would take more bluster than this "son of thunder" could muster to go barging in.

So while John hesitated, blustery, impulsive Simon Peter crossed the line and won the race.

II. *The one who arrived last won the race but failed to capture the prize.* Peter went blazing right on into the tomb. He also saw the linen cloths lying there. The Gospel writer used three Greek words all translated "saw." John "saw" at a glance *(blepo)* in verse 5; Peter "saw" *(theoreo)*, observing carefully the details, theorizing.

Peter noted that the napkin that had wrapped Jesus' head was separate from the other grave cloths. It even had a rolled-up appearance. The Greek word suggests it was coiled or rolled as though the head around which it was wrapped had suddenly dematerialized and vanished. Peter saw all this like a detective, examining the details, searching for clues. He was trying to figure out what "they" had done with Jesus' body, where "they" had taken it. He was puzzled that they would leave the grave cloths behind. Why would they unwrap the body and then roll up the cloths again and lay them just where the body had lain?

Then John, "the other disciple, the one whom Jesus loved" (NIV), also went into the tomb. In verse 8 he reminds the reader that he was the runner who reached the tomb first. Again he "saw," but this time it was *eidon*, both a physical seeing and a mental perception. While Peter was theorizing, John had a flash of insight. He experienced the eureka moment.

These three kinds of seeing cause me to relive the experience of teaching my daughter to drive. When I ask, admittedly with some tension in my voice, "Do you see that big truck about to pull out in front of you?" she assures me, "I see it." But I worry—does she just *blepo*, glance at it; is she noticing the details of what a nice truck it is, *theoreo;* or does she see the danger and response she must make, *eidon?*

The study of these three Greek words helps us to solve the riddle.

III. *The one who lost the race captured the prize.* The Bible says that John "saw and believed." What did he believe? He believed that Jesus rose from the dead! That insight, that perception, that revelation was the prize.

He understood that Jesus was not carried away by some weird soldiers who took the trouble to unwind his grave cloths. John went on to say in explanation, "For as yet they did not know the scripture, that he must rise from the dead." *Eidon* was that glorious, wonderful insight! It only made sense if Jesus had risen from the dead. That is what John saw and perceived in his mind, and that is what he believed!—Ernest B. Beevers

ILLUSTRATIONS

IMPURITY. The sin of impurity has caused nations to fall. It has over and over again ruined the sanctity of the home. It has hindered the health and development of the personality, and it has caused the spiritual impotence of thousands. It has filled our divorce courts, made thousands of innocent children homeless, and has wrecked the hope of the bright tomorrow for many a young person.—Billy Graham

RESTITUTION. I have mistreated only one soul in my life in the way of persecution, and he was a preacher. I never wrote a word against him, and I never spoke a word against him. I just let him alone; let him dig for himself. How my conscience lashed me! Finally, I made it right with that preacher, and we became undying friends. When I walk up and down the golden streets of the new Jerusalem, where he is now, how much happier I'll be to see him because I made restitution!—James W. Kramer

BELIEVING. What does it mean to believe? It is very simple. All through the Bible the word *believe* is used in the common, everyday understanding of the term. It means to take one at his word and act on what he says without waiting for further evidence. Faith does not demand proof.

A man comes to you and says, "I have deposited a thousand dollars in the bank to your credit," and gives you a check book. You can take one of two attitudes toward his statement. You can say, "Thank you," and go right on and pay no attention to what he has said. That is unbelief. Or you can say, "Thank you," and begin drawing checks against the deposit. That is belief.—J. B. Lawrence

CHRISTIAN LIVING. A Sunday school teacher was telling her children how Jesus lived in their hearts, if they invited him to. As she was telling them this, a little boy was observing a large picture of Christ, hanging on the wall.

"Teacher," he answered, "if he lived in my heart, wouldn't he stick out somewhere?"—C. Neil Strait

BELIEFS MAKE A DIFFERENCE. A secretary at a church in Washington, D.C., tells of one afternoon when she was on the beach and a little boy came up to her and asked, "Do you believe in God?" "Yes, I do," she replied. Then he asked, "Do you read your Bible?" Again, the answer was affirmative. His next question was, "Do you go to church every Sunday?" Again, the secretary answered that she did. The boy smiled and then asked, "Will you please hold my nickel while I go in swimming?"

The little boy assumed that a person's beliefs make a difference as to whether they could be trusted.—C. Neil Strait

FULLNESS OF SALVATION. Salvation is much more than escape from punishment; it is deliverance from sin. Jesus Christ was sent to bless us "in turning away everyone of us from his iniquities." In believing on him, we not only obtain pardon through his blood but we become holy by the influence of his indwelling Spirit. Though pardoned at once, we are not at once made perfect in purity. This is an arduous, a progressive work. Salvation in its full sense implies conformity to Jesus as well as reliance upon him, or rather such a reliance as necessarily leads to our walking in his steps and cultivating his spirit. It is a change of heart, a transformation of character, a new life.—Newman Hall

SECTION VI.
Advent and Christmas Preaching

SERMON SUGGESTIONS

Topic: The Flip-Flopped Kingdom
TEXT: Luke 1:46–55

I. As you listen to the words of Mary's Magnificat, you begin to sense that she is describing a new world that is significantly different from the world in which we live. She is lifting up her voice in an old song of the maidens and declaring that because God has given her a child when she was not supposed to have one—God is always doing that, giving children in places where there is no future expected—Sarah was too old, Hannah was too old, Rachel was barren, Mary was unmarried—God has turned everything upside down. God has suddenly flip-flopped things. It is his power and might, and God will work in this future child to continue to flip-flop the kingdoms of this world. He will scatter the proud and pull down the mighty from their thrones, and he will exalt those of low degree. He will fill the hungry with food and good things, and he will send the rich away empty. Mary knows that this is a holy God who acts in history, and by his actions in her life he has suddenly turned everything topsy-turvy. His coming has disrupted her life in more than spiritual ways. He is not just a God who wants things different inside our hearts. God is One who will change political, social, and economic realities for all people, even as he has in her life.

II. Now, there are some who will hear this as good news. There are some in this world who are the low and the poor and the humble and the weak, who are excited and eager for the coming of such a God, and those who feel that God's people, the church, must be active in that process of flip-flopping. Theologian Robert McAfee Brown has made an attempt to explain and to share with Christians in the United States how the people living in other parts of the world look at the promises of God as they are given in such passages as the Magnificat.

This is a song that brings great joy to their hearts. God has looked upon the poor peasant girl, Mary, and has turned things upside down for her. This God hears and sees the poor, the oppressed, and the enslaved. He has regarded the low estate of his handmaiden. God is not beholden to human estates of worth. Mary sings that it is not that those who are nothing must do everything for those who have power and might. God is the One acting for the poor, and the One who needs nothing is helping those who need everything. And if the One helping is helping, then they must no longer be servants but something better—friends, companions, equals. For on the lips of the poor and oppressed people, the words of the Magnificat are transformed from a whispered prayer of a dutiful maiden into the promise of a wide-scale victory of those who have nothing by the grace and power of God who is everything.

III. Of course, it is then suggested that if this is a song of good news to the poor and the oppressed and the hungry, it must be a song of fear and resentment to those who are the rich and the powerful and the comfortable. If Mary's song is a song for the disenfranchised and the unemployed and the illiterate and the displaced and discontented, then in our perfectly good logic it must be a song of revolution and disturbance to those who are hard working, thrifty, law abiding, responsible, comfortable communities. If the poor are going to be lifted up and the proud brought low, it has to be good news to the poor and bad news to the proud. Wherever God acts to bring about the flip-flopping of his kingdom so that those who are suffering might find peace and rest, it would seem normal and natural to expect it to be bad for those who have been on top. So, there are many who resent the interpretation of the Magnificat as a design for social revolution; they resent the political implications of this passage and the Old Testament passage about the coming King as One who has been appointed to preach the good tidings to the afflicted, to bind up the brokenhearted, to proclaim liberty to the captives, to comfort those who mourn, and to proclaim the year of the Lord.

In our normal circumstances where we think that the pie is limited and that there is only so much of everything, if one gets more, the others have to get less. That would seem normal. And so if God is said to be the one who takes sides and takes the side of the poor, then we think that God has got to be against the rich and the strong and the powerful, and in military, economic, and other categories, we are all those things.

IV. We need to remember that this is God's mystery in love that is bringing this flip-flopped kingdom. Before you get too locked in to a position, look around you at what happens at Christmas time. Look and see how this kingdom might look if we allow the miracle of God's grace to work in history. Look around you as we, just for a few days, focus on the coming Christ child and allow that event to break into history in a dominant way. Just look at the way the coming of the Christ child has of flip-flopping your own kingdom and your own

life. Even in the smallest way, this coming of the Christ child into the center of history has a way of turning everything upside down. Old wounds are forgotten. Efforts are made to overcome year-long silences with friends we knew and loved long ago. All our preoccupation with getting and spending is laid waste in a new desire of giving and bringing joy. Suddenly, at least in simple ways, we are not as concerned with the powerful and the mighty as we are with just being with good friends, family, and neighbors.

It is not the complete reversal that is predicted. But just as a foretaste of that flip-flopped kingdom, we can see something of what it might mean if we were to discover that those without power, the hungry and the oppressed, became significant others in our lives. And at Christmas there is an elevation into prominence of those who are powerless, as children in every culture are; it is the small children who have always the least power. At Christmas they become elevated and important. The poor and hungry become a special concern for society, and Friendship Fund, Salvation Army, Warmth for Wake, and a host of other efforts that are concerned about the marginal members of society around the year get major portions of their gifts at this time.

V. Christmas does not bring about the structural changes that need to be made to bring about the kind of economic and social and political justice changes that the Magnificat is rejoicing in. But just a small glimpse of what the kingdom might be like suggests that the "bringing low of a Scrooge" and a "lifting up of Bob Cratchit" might not be as frightening and diminishing as we might have thought.

The Magnificat and Isaiah might be heard as frightening words to a prosperous and powerful people, but we forget the context of God's love. Look around and see what happens when, just for a few moments in a year, the new flip-flopped kingdom begins to appear and the poor are lifted up and the proud are ignored and brought low and a few captives are pardoned by the governors and children are honored and the sorrowing are comforted and the lonely are visited and the elderly sung to. It is not a painful vision; it is not a frightening time; it is not a time of feeling as if something has been taken from you that was yours by right. In fact, it is a time of deep glowing warmth, a feeling of satisfaction and joy. It is a time so good, in fact, that we join Mary and the Third World and all people in praying for its full coming by our prayers, "I wish we could keep Christmas all year around."

Sometimes it is not what we are told that we should concern ourselves about, but the context of God's love in which we are told the message.—Rick Brand

Topic: The Way of a Wise Man
Text: Matt. 2:1–12

Christmas is all about journeys: from Nazareth to Bethlehem, from fields to manger, from Judea to Egypt. Best known is the trek of Magi from Mesopotamia to Palestine. Let us retrace their steps over the inner terrain of our hearts.

I. *The search (vv. 1–10)*. Stars are countless, yet those astrologers searched until they found one that was unique, hence unpredictable. For us, faith is searching among innumerable lives to discover in Jesus the one that is divinely different.

Acting upon a heavenly vision, they embarked on an open-ended quest, not knowing where it would lead (see Heb. 11:8b). Their example teaches us that the purpose of life is to plunge into the unknown in search of God, not in order to find riches but to find one worthy of our best gifts.

The Herods who rule by force always fear a rival. Anyone worthy of worship is a threat to every earthly sovereign. Faith forever disturbs the status quo because no tyrant is secure as long as we follow stars that cannot be controlled.

II. *The Savior (v. 11)*. Rejecting the sinister designs of Herod, the wise men made a second effort to reach their goal. How ironic that a supernatural star should point them to a tiny baby. The clues of faith often lead us to a God who comes to earth in weakness (see 1 Cor. 1:25, 27) and must be accepted in his lowly condescension.

The infant could do nothing for them in his helplessness, yet they were willing to adore him as king. His very being was more important to them than his doing. We do not worship in hope of a payback but in sheer gratitude that God has made himself available to us.

Just as God emptied himself in coming to earth as a lowly babe (see Phil. 2:7), the Magi emptied their best gifts at his feet. If Herod personified the urge to control, the wise men personified the urge to contribute. Bethlehem is where we learn a self-giving that expects nothing in return.

III. *The significance (v. 12)*. Just because the wise men had found their heavenly king, they were not granted protection from earthly tyrants. Faith is not a euphoria that assumes all will be well. Rather, it is a realism that recognizes enemies who would threaten the cause of Christ. In refusing to report back to Herod, the Magi engaged in a legitimate form of civil disobedience. We must be wary lest we give even tacit support to those who would destroy our faith.

In a deeper sense, the Magi went back by a different route because they had become different men. Likewise, when we truly meet Christ, we will depart to walk "another way" (see Acts 9:2), what Paul called "the more excellent way" of love (1 Cor. 12:31).

Even though their way was different, it led them back from whence they had come. Everything was the same, but *they* were not the same. God sometimes leads us forward by sending us back home as changed individuals (see Mark 5:19). Life is not just stars, nor is it only deserts. Our urgent need is for people who will follow God's star wherever it may lead but then come back to tell us what they found!—William E. Hull

Topic: "And on Earth, Peace"
Text: Luke 2:9–14

The fathomless heights of ethereal blue hang breathlessly over the land of Judah; the full moon softly outlines the rolling hills, now richly green, against the night-clad sky. The flickering lights of a country village bravely make their humble mark upon the southern horizon. Near at hand a flock of sheep rests peacefully upon the grass, and nearer still the shepherds sit and watch them hour by hour. It seemed to them no different from a thousand other nights; it seemed no different, and yet it was. [Read Luke 2:9–14.]

All too soon the angelic anthem ceased and the majestic tones faded away in the distant darkness of the Judean hillside. And yet it rings around our world today, though nineteen centuries have marched with steady pace across the paths of time. Listen as it rings:

I heard the bells on Christmas day
Their old familiar carols play,
And wild and sweet the words repeat
Of peace on earth, goodwill to men.

(Henry W. Longfellow)

I. *What about this "peace on earth"?*

(a) And so, like Longfellow, we listen to the ringing of the Christmas bells, and then we ask ourselves, What about this peace on earth? There is no doubt that the Bible is filled with the idea. Two hundred seventy-seven times the word is used in the Old Testament—and a hundred in the New!

Isaiah prophesied the coming of a day when "the wolf shall dwell with the lamb . . . and the calf and the young lion and the fatling together; and a little child shall lead them" (Isa. 11:6). In another place he spoke of the birth of a child who would be the "wonderful Counselor, the mighty God, the everlasting Father, the Prince of Peace."

(b) The Bible not only has much to say about peace, but it makes clear that Jesus is the one who shall bring it to pass. Isaiah called him "the Prince of Peace"; Zechariah predicted that he would "guide our feet into the way of peace" (Luke 1:79); and the angels sang that wondrous night, "Glory to God in the highest, and on earth peace, good will toward men" (Luke 2:14).

(c) How our hearts burn within us as we hear these words of peace, for we too sit in a world of great darkness, where weapons are unbelievably destructive and hatred is unmistakably strong. With Longfellow, in another stanza, we hear the message of the bells, and our hearts rise up with hope and then recoil in disappointment:

And in despair I bowed my head:
"There is no peace on earth," I said,
"For hate is strong and mocks the
song
Of peace on earth, goodwill to men."

We, too, are tempted to say it's all an idle dream, this hope of peace—a foolish bit of fancy that has taunted humanity through all the centuries and never really comes alive. With Jeremiah we sadly observe that men cry, " 'Peace, peace,' when there is no peace" (Jer. 6:14; 8:11).

Even on that wondrous night when the angelic anthem proclaimed peace on earth, Caesar Augustus was emperor; Herod was the king; Cyrenius was governor of Syria; and scarcely could three more bloodthirsty men be found in all the annals of the ancient world.

So it has been through the slowly turning centuries, while hearts of men were longing in the night—longing for freedom, longing for peace.

The honest realism deep within our souls demands that we face it squarely: "Hate is strong and mocks the song / Of peace on earth, goodwill to men."

(d) That, however, is not the end of the story.

Then pealed the bells more loud and
deep:
"God is not dead, nor doth he sleep;
The wrong shall fail, the right
prevail,
With peace on earth, goodwill to
men."

II. *From whence comes this firm assurance?* What right have we, in a world like this, to believe so strongly in the reality of peace? The answer lies in the meaning of the word itself.

The Bible, which has so much to say about peace, does not say there will be worldwide peace "in our time" or even within the whole realm of time. But it has much to say about peace within the soul of man, peace in the depths of suffering, peace in the midst of tribulation, peace in the valley of the shadow. Peace comes, not from the absence of trouble, but from the presence of God! Isaiah said, "The chastisement of our peace was upon him, and with his stripes we are healed" (Isa. 53:5). Paul said, "Having been justified by faith, we have peace with God through our Lord Jesus Christ" (Rom. 5:1). This is why Jesus alone could say, "Peace I leave with you, my peace I give unto you: not as the world giveth, give I unto you" (John 14:27). And this is why Paul could exclaim, "The peace of God, which passeth all understanding, shall keep your hearts and minds through Christ Jesus" (Phil. 4:7).

III. *Where is hope for peace among men?* When such peace dwells within men, there can still be hope for peace among men. We see that truth clearly in the second chapter of Ephesians. The Jews and the Gentiles, separated by race and nationality and religion, the bitterest enmity this world has ever seen, brought together into a new humanity! And it was done by the power of Christ, "Who hath made both one and hath broken down the middle wall of partition between us, having abolished in his flesh the enmity . . . so making peace" (Eph. 2:14–15).

Those few places in the history of humanity where it has really been tried, it never yet has failed! Is it really so hard to believe? It ought to be easy at Christmastime!

At this Christmastime, let us look up—not only to the star of Bethlehem, but to the Light of the World. And the peace which passeth all understanding will be ours—forever!—Lamar J. Brooks

Topic: See the Nativity Scene
TEXT: Luke 2:8–18
The sights and sounds of the season are so familiar that we sometimes fail to notice them. Take a good look again at the nativity scene and you will see.

I. *The Christian view of the common man.*
(a) The shepherds were rugged men struggling against odds to make a living. To these common men something extraordinary happened on an ordinary evening. The angels sang to them; heaven took notice of them.
(b) The Christ child, too, seemed com-

mon. He had no halo, but to a common Hebrew family God was born in the flesh.
(c) The shepherds and the baby remind us that the Christian faith sees the common man as important.

II. *The Christian view of an uncommon God.*
(a) Common ideas about gods in the first century did not include gods who cared about the common man. But the nativity shows an uncommon view of God—the glory of God shone round these men, and God's heavenly hosts sang to them. That was a unique concept of God in the first century.
(b) It is still an uncommon concept of God. World religions today picture the impersonal god of Hindu faith, the impassive god of Buddhist faith, the imposing god of Muslim faith. This Christmas we can see again the personal, caring God of the Christian faith.—Harold Freeman

ILLUSTRATIONS

WHAT TO LOOK FOR IN CHRISTMAS. Halford Luccock mentioned a matron who complained that Christmas carols were "distressingly theological." The story of Herod and the wise men in Matthew is emphatically theological. So preachers will do well to avoid turgid discussion of historicity. For example, was the star a visiting Halley's comet? Were the Magi from Persia or far Arabia? Did the star spin diagonally across the sky as reported? And so on. No, instead the passage requires of a preacher an odd blend of christological wonder, harsh human realism, and a kind of childlike longing.—David G. Buttrick

THIS MATTERS. One December afternoon many years ago a group of parents stood in the lobby of a nursery school waiting to pick up their children after the last pre-Christmas session. As the youngsters ran from their lockers, each one carried in his or her hands the "surprise," the brightly wrapped package on which the class had been working for weeks.

One small boy, trying to run, put on his coat, and wave to his parents all at the same time, slipped and fell. The "surprise" flew from his grasp and landed on the tile floor with an obvious ceramic crash.

The child's first reaction was one of stunned silence. But then he set up an inconsolable wail. His father, thinking to minimize the incident and comfort the boy, patted his head and murmured, "Now that's all right. It really doesn't matter, son. It doesn't matter at all."

But the child's mother, somewhat wiser in such situations, dropped to her knees on the floor, swept the boy into her arms, and said, "Oh, but it does matter. It matters a great deal." And she wept with her son.

The redeeming God in whom we hope is not the parent who dismisses our lives with a pat on the head and murmured assurances that they do not really matter in cosmic terms. It is, rather, the one who falls to the earth beside us, picks up our torn and bleeding spirits, and says, "Oh, but it does matter. It matters eternally."—William Muehl

THE WONDER OF IT ALL.   Lord Tennyson could look at a flower in the crannied wall and glimpse through it the wonder of all creation. Or listen to the words of one who would probably be ranked as the foremost scientist of our day, Albert Einstein. He says, "The most beautiful thing we can experience is the mysterious. It is the source of all true art and science. He to whom this emotion is a stranger, who can no longer pause to wonder and stand rapt in awe, is as good as dead; his eyes are closed."—Ralph W. Sockman

THE AVERAGE PERSON'S MUSINGS.   What I most feared was that I was incapable of good, a bit of earth, and nothing more. I see now, for all my failures, that is not true of me.

Proverbial wisdom says that you cannot make a silk purse out of a sow's ear . . . and I have often suspected that was my true nature. "A bit of swine" (as the man in the street might say); a sow's ear incapable of conversion to anything better, and finding my natural food in the pig's swill.

But he comes and will not let me believe it, puts his hand on my shoulder and says, "You do not belong to the piggery. You belong to me!"—stoops and lifts me from the dirt and tells me that he loved me enough to forsake the courts of heaven; did not abhor the virgin's womb; came as a babe and lived this life to show me how it could be done; stretched himself on the wood at the last and died to redeem me.

Is that the truth about me? Was I dear enough for God to be born? Was I dear enough for God to die? Let no man tell me now that I am worthless, the creature of an hour, the fruit of my parents' sexual passion, and nothing more.—W. E. Sangster

THE MISSIONARY IMPULSE.   All of us here are indebted to the missionary impulse. Around A.D. 500 there was in Rome a young monk named Gregory. He was a good man, an admirable clergyman, who could be serious without being solemn. He had one vice— an addiction to punning! One day in the slave market he saw three slaves who were strikingly different from the others in appearance. They had pink and white complexions, blue eyes, and long, flaxen hair. Gregory asked about them and was told they were "Angles." He replied, "They look like angels." Told further that they came from Deira (Northumbria), he replied again, "They should be rescued from De Ira"—a pun on the Latin for "the wrath of God." He became a missionary zealot and determined to convert these inhabitants of Britain. The pope prevented him. Ten years later, now pope himself, Gregory pursued his intention and sent Augustine on a missionary expedition. Augustine was appalled by the reports he received about the inhabitants of the foggy tin islands. How could so savage and degraded a people ever become Christians? Their religion consisted partly of burning people alive in wicker cages and partly of obscene rites under the mistletoe. They worshiped savage gods. They were canni-bals. Their idea of heaven was a place where they could satiate themselves in violence and bloodshed all day and get drunk at night. Augustine turned away, but pope Gregory believed in the uni-versality of Christ and sent Augustine back. And the historian Gibbon says that Augustine and forty monks con-quered England more completely than Caesar and his legions did! It was the conquest of Christ.—John N. Gladstone

SECTION VII.
Evangelism and World Missions

SERMON SUGGESTIONS

Topic: Biblical Strategies for Evangelization

TEXT: Eph. 1:10

Biblical strategies for evangelization must be understood and formulated in terms of the whole church, with the whole gospel, for the whole person, in the whole of society, for the whole world. Neither a fragmented body of Christ, nor a gospel of abstract piety, nor an appeal to detached spirituality, nor disregard for societal needs, nor concerns for our own parochial preferences belongs to the biblical perspective of evangelization today.

The gospel of the kingdom of God and his Christ embraces the whole of the cosmos, with the Father's purpose to bring *"everything together* under Christ as head, *everything* in the heavens and *everything* on earth" (Eph. 1:10). To disregard any part of his redemptive concerns for humankind is to violate the purposes of God in his mission for the church in evangelization. In planning our strategies for evangelization, we must ever keep the biblical perspective in view.

I. God the Father bestowed on all of human life the crowning glory of a common human dignity, and the entire human race belongs to a common heritage and has a right to be human in God (Gen. 1:21; Acts 17:26). This means that there is no other way of measuring the value of human life than by giving recognition to the full dignity of human worth in every

human being and race. Not to do so constitutes the "fall" into sin.

II. The temptation in us all is to self-aggrandizement in our achievements and culture over other individuals and races. The "fall" is upward, i.e., our temptation to want to be "gods" (Gen. 3:4–5). To elevate ourselves and our culture over the interests of others, is a denial of the gospel of free grace in Jesus Christ (Acts 15:1; Gal. 6:14).

III. The proclamation of justification by faith in Jesus Christ is only possible if we acknowledge that God has no favorites and that he is impartial to all peoples (Gal. 2:6; Acts 10:34–35; Rom. 2:11). To elevate our culture over others, as some Jews did over Gentiles, constitutes justification by works (Rom. 10:1–4). We cannot preach justification by faith if we make different evaluations of people on the basis of race or culture.

IV. To be justified by faith means that we are all the children of God in Jesus Christ and that we are all one in him (Gal. 3:25–29). To all be one in Christ Jesus is not restricted to a spiritual oneness, while we still make "apartheid" distinctions between races, social status, the sexes, and other forms of human discrimination. To be "in Christ" means to be a new creation, for we have been reconciled to God and to one another (2 Cor. 5:17–21; Eph. 2:14–18).

V. It is not possible to preach the gospel of the love and goodness of God to people who are the victims of discrimination and injustice in society if we do not address a prophetic word of protest to sociopolitical systems that are suppressive and abuse human dignities in society. We must put things right when people are being intimidated in order to express kindness and walk humbly with our God" (Mic. 6:8; Isa. 42:1–4).

VI. We must resist the temptation of formulating strategies for evangelization in terms of detached principles and creedal statements of the gospel, while disregarding the causes of poverty and violence, the human injustices and societal sins, the enculturated twist in our own perception of the gospel. We do not rightly understand the mission of Jesus among the "deprived" as victims of the system, while feeling at home within the courts of Annas and Caiaphas among the "depraved" religiosity that controls the system and contributes toward "the Jesus we are persecuting." Our strategies of evangelism must be contextually all-embracing. We have to earn the right to preach the gospel.

VII. We must not continue playing the role of "the big brother" in ministry, as the decision-maker who perpetuates the agony of those who are the "victims" of our generosity and kindness. We cannot continue being benevolent when there is need for atonement, i.e., the need to put things right and to change the system by mutual consent. True Christian leadership leads to maturity, making mutual ministry possible, resulting in the building up of the Body of Christ (Eph. 4:11–16).

VIII. Strategies for evangelization are mutual experiences of *koinonia*. In Christ this is a reciprocal experience of sharing our mutual and respective heritages in the Body of Christ, in *charis* (grace); in *diakonia* (service); in *doxa* (glorifying God); in *eulogia* (blessing); in *euangelion* (celebrating the gospel). This sharing in fellowship, in faith, and in hope is a sharing of ourselves. "We love you so much that we not only share the gospel but also our very lives" (1 Thess. 2:8; Rom. 1:11).

IX. Our strategies of evangelization must be expressed in the celebration of the gospel. The root word for proclamation in the Old Testament relates to the celebration of the good news. This is not merely an announcement of good news; it belongs to my active participation now within the triumph and faith of the Son of God who loved me and gave himself for me. It was as Paul and Silas were celebrating the gospel in the Philippian jail that the jailer bent his knee to Jesus Christ. "Sirs, what must I do to be saved?" That, after all, is the ultimate question (Acts 16: 25–34; Phil. 2:6–11).

X. Our strategies for evangelization must be addressed to the unending human conflict. It is the manner in which the Old and New Testaments address this human guilt and need for righteousness that gives the Bible its unity. The Old Testament addresses this human problem, but it is still not resolved in the New Testament. The New Testament ends still addressing this problem of human conflict and the anticipated hope to come. When we in our strategies of evangelization also address this human conflict of guilt, our mission in the world is the continuation and a unity with the Bible in its proclamation. It is this that makes our celebration a hope of that which is to come. We are saved, but we are yet to be saved. We are redeemed, but our redemption still draws nigh. We are "in Christ," but our hope is in expectation of him.—John N. Jonsson

Topic: New Testament Evangelism

TEXT: Acts 1–2

In the first history book of the Christian church, we find a strategy for healthy evangelism. The book begins with the story of one of the greatest revivals the world has experienced. This revival gave the Christian movement a thrust into the pagan world. If we are to evangelize America, we need to adopt the strategy of the church at Jerusalem.

I. *Total participation.* Acts 2 indicates that all were in one accord on the day of Pentecost. Verse 4 indicates all were filled with the Holy Spirit. Then all of the Christians went throughout the city sharing their faith and inviting people to hear Peter preach. They had total participation.

II. *Total penetration.* Acts 1:6–8 gives us the scope of New Testament evangelism. The church had the world as its mission field. Palestine was a little country more than one hundred twenty miles long by forty miles wide. Yet the religion starting there was to penetrate the world. Our mission is not complete until our country and our world are won to Christ.

III. *Total preservation.* In Acts 2:41–47, we find the secret of good preservation. These New Testament Christians realized their job was not over once they had witnessed, won, and baptized new converts. They had a strategy for helping new converts grow and mature.—Bill Bruster

Topic: The Second Birth

Text: John 3:1–17

The winter of 1976–77 was bitter cold. In January of that year we inaugurated a new president of the United States. Those who traveled to Washington, D.C., and shared in the inauguration ceremony on the Capitol lawn were chilled to the bone by the cold wind whipping off the North Atlantic Ocean. I was there—enduring the cold. It was worth the sacrifice in comfort, however, for whether or not one agreed with the politics of Jimmy Carter, most were gratified that we had a true Christian in the White House. So we braved the cold wind gladly.

Carter had conducted a most interesting and surprising campaign. While on the campaign trail he had said, "I've been born again." That startling statement made the newscasts, the newspapers, and the news magazines. Everyone was asking, "What does Carter mean, 'I've been born again'?" Many people thought Jimmy Carter had invented the phrase, but, obviously, not so. It was spoken by our Lord Jesus Christ almost two thousand years ago. Moreover, no teaching of our Lord received more stress than this particular theme. I say that for a sound, biblical reason. Whenever our Lord was about to say something of central importance to life, he would often preface his statement with the two-word expression: "Truly, truly." Or, as the King James Version has it, "Verily, verily." And no less than three times our Lord prefaced his teaching about the second birth with that expression. "Verily, verily," he said, "I say to you, you must be born again."

Why this stress from the lips of our Lord? Why this *mandate from the Master?*

I. *The mandate of the second birth.* Three central life experiences are predicated on the second birth.

(a) First, it is only through the experience of the new birth that the insidious monster, sin, is fully dealt with in our lives. Sin—that creeping paralysis that can invade life, stultifying and paralyzing everything that is good and meaningful in life, and take the edge off every joy. It besmirches all that is pure and meaningful until life finally becomes a mere shell. The only way that problem is ever dealt with is on the basis of the new birth.

(b) Second, and this logically follows, only by being born again will we be brought into that dynamic fellowship with the living God that he intended us to enjoy when, as the Bible says, "he breathed into our nostrils the breath of life, and we became a living soul." There is, as someone expressed it, a "God-shaped vacuum" in every one of us that only God can fill. Thus, all people of all times of all cultures cry out to God. But we shall never come into a dynamic relationship with God until we are born from above.

(c) Finally, and this also logically follows, it is only by the experience of the new birth that we will one day hear those grand, glorious words of our Lord Jesus Christ: "Come, you blessed one, inherit the kingdom prepared for you from the foundation of the world." Born-again people are the ones who walk through the pearly gates, tread the streets of gold, meet their departed loved ones, and address the Savior face to face.

Little wonder, therefore, Jesus said, "Verily, verily I say unto you, you *must* be born again."

II. *The mystery of the second birth.* Nicodemus simply could not put it all together. "Born again? How can a man be born when he's old?" he asked. It was a mystery to him. Of course, he was confusing physical birth with what our Lord was speaking of, a spiritual birth; hence, his question. So our Lord, who always wants us to understand the truth, helped Nicodemus with these words: "The wind blows where it will. You hear the sound of it, but you do not know where it came from or where it is going." Our Lord was simply saying that there are many experiences of life that we may not intellectually be able to fathom and understand in full, but we can experience the consequences or the results of the experience. For example, I do not understand electricity. But I can turn on the light, flood the room with light, and receive the benefit.

In like manner, it would be presumptuous to say, "Here is everything there is to know about the new birth." The depth and profundity and ramifications of that experience go beyond any human comprehension. But one thing I know: I have been born again, and the benefits are tremendous. It is marvelous to know Jesus personally! He is real in my life, and his blessings abound. My testimony is I have been born again, although much of it still remains a mystery. Still, it is the abundant life, as he said. And one day I shall see him, and he will welcome me home. What a day that will be! I've been born again. Have you?

III. *The means of the second birth.* Poor Nicodemus, however, still could not understand it. So Jesus gave him one last explanation. In it, he actually shared with Nicodemus the means of being born again. The Lord said, "As Moses lifted up the serpent in the wilderness, so must the Son of man be lifted up." That statement of Jesus might not communicate to us very clearly today, but it would have been potent to Nicodemus. He was a ruler of the Jews, a religious leader, and therefore knew the Old Testament well. Our Lord's reference was to an Old Testament event, a reference to a passage in the Book of Numbers. It was a great epoch in the life of Israel. Nicodemus knew the event well. In a word, here is the gist of that significant historical moment. The Israelites, out in the desert, had been moaning and complaining until the patience of God came to an end. So the Lord sent upon them, as the Bible describes it, a plague of "fiery serpents." Snakes invaded the camp of Israel. They were biting people, and those bitten were burning up with fever from the poison and dying. Moses began to intercede: "God, hold back your hand of judgment." God answered that prayer. "I will," the Lord said, "but, Moses, you must fashion a snake of brass. Take that brass snake and set it high upon a pole. If anyone bitten by a real snake and about to die will just look to that brass snake, I will heal them." And God kept his word. He did exactly as he promised Moses. Those who looked, lived. Those who did not look, died.

Now, in the light of that event, Jesus said, "As Moses lifted up the serpent in the wilderness, so must the Son of man be lifted up." And he was lifted up, you know, on a cross. Why do you think Jesus came? Why do you think he lived that perfect life? Why do you think he died on the cross and was resurrected? The answer is clear: that he might be the Savior, for there is "no other name under heaven given among people whereby we can be saved." And they that look to him today live!

IV. *Conclusion.* It was another bitter cold January day. The wind was whipping off the North Sea, sweeping over the county of Essex and swirling snow down the streets of Colechester, a small town sixty miles northeast of London, England. It was 1850, the second Sunday morning in January. Trudging down the street was fifteen-year-old Charles. What was a young Victorian lad doing out on a day like this? He was walking to church. Actually, Charles had been going to every church in Colechester, trying to find some preacher who would explain to him how to be born again. The Spirit of God had plowed deep furrows of conviction through his heart, and he was in misery.

As Charles trudged down the street trying to keep warm, he passed a dead-end alley called Artillery Street. He remembered that his mother had said there was a little Primitive Methodist chapel down Artillery Street. He thought, "Well, I still have a long way to go to where I intend to worship, and it is so cold, I think I will turn into that Primitive Methodist church." When he entered the building, only fourteen other worshipers had gathered. It was a miserable day. Charles took a seat about two-thirds of the way back from the front on the preacher's right hand, just under a little balcony. He could not look the preacher in the eye, he was so convicted of his need for salvation. The pastor did not arrive that morning, so an old, rather illiterate man attempted to preach. He could not pronounce his words correctly. But he did his best. Actually, all he knew was to take his text, make some comments, repeat his text again, make some more comments, read the text again, and around and around he went. His text was from the Book of Isaiah: "Look unto me, all ye ends of the earth, and be ye saved." And so the old, illiterate preacher droned on: " 'Look unto me, all ye ends of the earth, and be ye saved.' You don't have to be rich or educated to look. Anyone can look. 'Look unto me, all ye ends of the earth, and be ye saved.' You don't have to even raise a finger, let alone a foot. Just look. Anybody can look. 'Look unto me, all ye ends of the earth, and be ye saved.' All you have to do is look. Look unto me."

He went on and on in this boring fashion when about ten minutes into his sermon, he spotted Charles. He did what a preacher probably ought not to do. He stopped, looked at Charles, pointed his finger at him and said, "Young man, you look terribly miserable." Charles said later, as he shared the story, "I was so miserable." The old preacher went on, "Yes, and you'll be miserable in life and you'll be miserable in death unless you obey my text, young man. Look to Jesus!" And as only a Primitive Methodist could do in those days, he screamed out, "Look, look, look!" Charles said, "I could have looked my eyes away. But I looked, and I lived."

Four years later, at the young age of nineteen, Charles was invited to become the pastor of the historic New Park Street Baptist Church of London, England. It had been a great church in the past. It boasted illustrious pastors, but now it was on hard times. The auditorium seated twelve hundred people, but only eighty came to hear Charles the Sunday morning he preached his first sermon. However, within six months, two thousand were cramming into that twelve-hundred-seat auditorium, and they were turning away a thousand who could not get in. Charles

had London turned upside down, for he was none other than the great Charles Haddon Spurgeon, probably the greatest London preacher who ever said to a congregation, "You must be born again. Look to Jesus and live."

You have been "bitten" by the serpent, sin. You are "sick unto death." But there is One who has been lifted up, the Lord Jesus Christ. I am going to ask you right now to look to Jesus on the cross and live. He will "heal" you, and you can be born again. Will you pray and trust Christ? The prayer of repentance and faith saves. Jesus Christ will invade your life, take control, and you will be born again. Will you open up your whole life to him and experience the second birth? Look to Jesus and live!—Lewis A. Drummond

Topic: Within Trembling Distance
Text: Matt. 27:45–56

After terrible tornadoes ripped through our area, there were conversations that went like this: "How close did it come to you? Were you frightened? Weren't you scared when it came so close? Where were you when it hit?" Had some of us been a bit closer to the actual tornado, we might have different stories to tell. The same might be said about being "near the cross."

Between two popular Lenten hymns, there is an interesting contrast in just how close we allow ourselves to come to the cross on which Jesus was crucified: "Beneath the Cross of Jesus" and "On a Hill Far Away." Do you catch the significance of those two "locations"? How close are you willing to stand near the cross?

On the final day of his earthly life, we can see the divisions among the people who would witness what happened to him.

Character studies of them may not be of interest to you, but I believe there is an important point to be made here. All but John say the acquaintances—and we do not know if that included the original twelve apostles or not—stood at a distance, looking on from afar. Only John puts them beneath the cross.

Robert Stackel, writing in *Church Management,* told of a book review in which the author of *The Grizzly Bear* was described as living "within trembling distance of the great beasts." That phrase caught my eye. I wonder if when we sing that most moving Lenten hymn, "Were You There?" we feel what we are singing? "Were you there when they crucified my Lord? / Oh! Sometimes it causes me to tremble, tremble, tremble. / Were you there when they crucified my Lord?" Does it really cause you to tremble? Are you within trembling distance of the cross? Or are you content to stand afar off? Is the Crucifixion of Jesus something that took place "on a hill far away"? Or does it cause you to tremble because you are there, "beneath the cross of Jesus"?

With the tornado, the question was, "How close did it come to you?" With the tragedy of the cross, the question is, "How close are you willing to come to it?"

I. It is not safe to come too close to the cross because it is there we see how sinful man can be. It is not safe because it also involves us in the pain, the suffering, and the injustice of the world. That may be why we have made the cross into jewelry and decoration. Or even—and I still cannot believe I saw this—milk chocolate! There was an ad in a daily newspaper that offered a box of candy called an "Easter Greetings Box," containing a large, decorated milk-chocolate cross, surrounded by the candy maker's finest milk-chocolate miniatures in a variety of fillings. The ad sought to entice the reader by describing this as "a very special way to say 'Easter Greetings!' One pound."

However beautiful and gold-plated or chocolate-covered we may want the cross to be, it was still a rough and rugged thing upon which Jesus suffered and died. It was not smoothly painted or mother of pearl. In fact, crucifixion was such a horrible means of death, the Romans used it only for revolutionaries and hardened criminals. There was a law that no Roman citizen could be crucified; it was too terrible. Usually men held on for twelve hours, but Jesus, already weary from beating and mocking and intensive interrogation, lasted only six. He had been treated as a common criminal: They lied about him; they hit him; they spat on him; they made him the object of public derision; they

paraded him before jeering crowds three times; they made him carry his own cross; and then they crucified him!

We speak of the "sacrifice of Christ" on the cross. In his suffering we understand what the love of God is all about. It is a frightening thing to be loved that much, isn't it?

II. There is another cause for trembling as we approach the cross. Something can happen to us that will change our lives forever. We may have to take our Christianity seriously for a change; we might be changed. We might have to give up something or do something differently as a result. George Bass tells a story about Count Zinzendorf. Zinzendorf was an aristocrat, an extremely privileged and gifted individual. He had been reared and trained for a diplomatic career. On a trip to Paris, he stopped in Dusseldorf. While there, he went to an art gallery. Inside, he noticed Sternberg's painting of the crucified Jesus called *Ecce Homo.* Underneath the painting, in Latin, the artist had written, "This is what I did for you: what have you done for me?" When Zinzendorf looked into the eyes of the Savior, he was overcome by a sense of shame. He stayed there beneath that painting for hours. He was not able to answer that question in a way that satisfied his own conscience. Finally, at nightfall, he left the gallery, and his life was changed. From then on, he gave all he had to Christ. He declared, "I have but one passion; it is Jesus, Jesus only."

Jesus told the crowds that gathered about him near the conclusion of his ministry, ". . . and I, when I am lifted up from the earth, will draw all men to myself" (John 12:32). There is something magnetic about the Crucifixion. It has power to bring us closer to the Christ. As repulsive an event as it was, it was also the means by which we experience reconciliation with God. Though Paul was writing specifically to the Gentiles in this instance, his words are pointed at any who feel separated from God—for whatever reason: "But now in Christ Jesus you who once were far off have been brought near in the blood of Christ" (Eph. 2:13). It helps me to lay that alongside the greatest story Jesus ever told. What Paul's theology may not communicate to us, Jesus' story of the prodigal son does. For me, and for many, the most moving scene of that story comes when the young son decides to return home. "And he rose and came to his father. But while he was yet at a distance, his father saw him and had compassion and ran and embraced him and kissed him" (Luke 15:20). "But while he was yet at a distance, his father . . . ran and embraced him. . . ." Throughout our lives, we have experienced all kinds of "body language" through which people communicated feelings and attitudes. We can probably remember those times when an angry or anxious parent stood waiting for us when we came home past curfew. They would be standing there, arms folded, frown on the face, maybe with feet tapping in impatience. Or people simply turned away when we needed them. Or put their hands in their pockets out of indifference. Or shrugged their shoulders with a sense of "who cares?"

Not the father in Jesus' story. In this figure representing God, a waiting, loving, patient heavenly Father, we can see—feel—how, in the words of Clarence Jordan, "God was in Christ, hugging the world to himself." In order to embrace someone, to hug them, one must first "make the sign of the cross." For me, that means to stretch out one's arms. On the cross, that is what Jesus did. Jesus did not die with arms neatly, peacefully folded across his chest. He died as he lived, with outstretched arms, as if to enfold the whole world in love.

I suspect when the prodigal son saw his father standing there, beginning to make a move toward him, opening his arms in order to run to embrace him, he trembled, overcome with emotion at the sight of his welcome, the greeting he received. His response was to confess his sinfulness, his unworthiness. Likewise, were you and I to make our way to the foot of the cross, it would be there that we could see One with arms outstretched, as if to welcome us. And it would be there that we would know how undeserved is the sacrificial love and grace that is ours. "Upon that cross of Jesus, mine eye at times can see / the very dying form of One who suffered there for me; / and from my stricken heart with tears two wonders I confess: / the wonders of redeeming love and my unworthiness" (Elizabeth C. Clephane). Regardless of the theological words we might use to define what happened through the Crucifixion of Jesus, they will be nothing more than words unless and until we take our own stand beneath the cross, within trembling distance. God, in Christ, will always be there waiting for us with open arms, regardless of what has kept us away before or how far we have to come. Redemption, reconciliation, atonement. What they all mean is that God is willing to wait until we move close enough for him to meet us more than halfway and to embrace us.— William M. Schwein

Topic: What Does God Want?
Text: Deut. 10:12–13

When Saul of Tarsus was knocked to the ground by the glorious presence of Jesus Christ on the Damascus Road, he came up with the right question, "What shall I do, Lord?" (Acts 22:10). This is the natural question for a saved person to ask. If it is not the question on your lips, then we need to examine our hearts to see if we are really saved. But if this is your question, then this sermon is for you.

The first question of a person in whose heart the Holy Spirit is at work is, "What must I do to be saved?" and the second question is, "What must I do, now that I am saved?" We find the answer to the second question well summarized in the words of our text.

I. *Fear—"To fear the Lord your God."* To the believer, God says again and again, "Fear not." He says that you need not be afraid whatever happens because he is with you. How often God speaks those words in both the Old and New Testament.

But the same Bible that says, "Fear not," again and again, also says very frequently, "Fear God." For example, Jesus says, "And do not fear those who kill the body but cannot kill the soul; rather fear him who can destroy both soul and body in hell" (Matt. 10:28).

What does it mean to fear God? It does not mean to feel like crawling away in a corner because you feel uncomfortable in his presence, but it does mean to have the highest regard for God, the highest respect for him. It means that we will do everything possible to please him; we will be most careful to avoid anything that will displease him. It means that we will take him into account whenever we make decisions. It is the basic attitude toward God, the attitude of taking him so seriously that it will lead to all the other actions set forth in our text.

II. *Walk*—*"To walk in all his ways."* A constant refrain of Scripture is the call to walk in God's ways. The word *walk* is almost always used in the Old Testament in relation to walking in some way, either in the way of God or in the way of wicked men. God sets a pattern for us, and our life can move along according to that pattern, or it can move in the direction set forth by wicked people. We must make the choice concerning the direction in which we walk.

Every life has a direction: there is a broad way that leads to destruction and a narrow way that leads to everlasting life. God said to you and to me, "This is the way, walk in it."

Notice the word *all* in our text. "Walk in *all* his ways." Many people try to mix Christianity and modern paganism of one kind or another. They are willing to do some of the things they know God requires of them, but there are other areas of life in which they choose to walk in wickedness, like unbelievers. This will not do. God is not pleased. You cannot serve God and idols.

III. *Love*—*"To love him."* Notice how personal each of these demands is: the call is not to go through the motions of being religious; it is to fear *the Lord,* to walk in *his* ways, to love *him.*

(a) The equivalent word in ancient Egyptian is used to describe the ideal relationship between a king and his subjects. God is the great king; we are not his equals. He is the king; we are his subjects. Jesus came preaching: "The kingdom of God is at hand." Jesus invites us into an ideal relationship with the great King of Kings. He loves us; we are to love him.

(b) The Arabic root connected to the Hebrew word that is here translated "love" means "to breathe passionately, to desire to be near." It is the same word used for husband-wife love. The true husband-wife relationship involves a pure kind of passion, a desire to be as near as two people can be to each other. Again and again Scripture compares the husband-wife relationship to the relationship of God and his covenant people. Our love for God is to be passionate. There is to be deep emotion involved. Your faith cannot be a cool acceptance of doctrines; it is rather to be a passionate attachment to God.

(c) The Hebrew word for "love" in our text is an inner disposition that is strengthened, not weakened, by the experiences of life. It is a love that must express itself in action. It is a love that leads to a love of the kind of behavior God desires. It is a love that is also to be expressed in worship.

IV. *Serve*—*"To serve the Lord your God with all your heart and with all your soul."* Again, here is a personal relationship. Frequently the Scripture speaks of either serving the Lord or serving other gods. Again, it is a choice that each of us must make. Jesus said, "You cannot serve God and mammon," and mammon means money and the things money can buy. Centuries before, Joshua had said, "Choose this day whom you will serve . . . but as for me and my house, we will serve the Lord" (Josh. 24:15).

Notice also that the text says, "Serve the Lord your God with *all* your heart and with *all* your soul." There can be no half-hearted service of such a great God.

V. *Keep*—*"And to keep the commandments and statutes of the Lord, which I command you this day for your good."* The same Hebrew word that is translated "keep" was used already in the Garden of Eden. Adam was called by God to *keep* the garden. Likewise we are to take care that obedience to the commands of God may flourish. But the same word is also used concerning the cherubim who stood guard at the entrance of the garden to *keep* Adam from getting back in after he had sinned. To keep was to guard. We are to be on guard lest the commandments be broken. The word *keep* is used constantly in the Old Testament;

God's people are to keep the Sabbath, to keep the commandments, to keep the covenant, to keep the ways of God.

Notice the results, "for your good." Unbelievers resent God's commandments; believers recognize that God gives them for beneficial reasons.—Harry Buis

Topic: Going with Christ Where Christ Is*

TEXTS: Luke 10:29–37; Rom. 15:29; Heb. 13:12–13

In a changing world of human tragedy and need, the whole church must have the whole gospel for the whole person in the whole society for the whole world. Only then will we be the emissaries of the living God in our time and place. In order to fulfill our role as Christians in the world, this will mean that *wherever we go we will go with Jesus Christ*—as the Savior of all people who need peace and forgiveness; as the deliverer from all our faults and fears; as the healer of our bitterness, greed, and hatred; as the restorer of our true personhood. Wherever we go, we must go with Jesus Christ—as the hope for all our future dreams; as the source of our love, concern, and compassion for people in our time; as the One who gives purpose and meaning in our living; as the One who is able to change people's lives; as the One who can save Nigeria and rescue the world.

I. As a son of Africa, born of Scandinavian missionary parents in Zululand, southern Africa; as one who had a share in taking an active part in removing the evils of discrimination in apartheid South Africa, I call upon you as my fellow Christians to go with Christ in every place of need in society. This means that *we must be prepared to go where Christ is in the world of need.*

(a) Many of us only think we are with Christ in our church worship. That is because we think that that is the only place where Christ is. It is true that Paul reminds

*A sermon preached Sunday, October 18, 1987, First Baptist Church, Ijaye Abeokuta, the first Baptist church in Nigeria.

us that "Christ loved the church and gave himself for the church," but he only says this in order to inspire us "to love as Christ loved the church" (Eph. 5:25). This means that we are to love one another as Christ loved us; we are to love God who first loved us; we are to love our neighbor as ourself. This being true, we must be prepared to go where Christ went in order to save the world.

(b) We are reminded in Heb. 13:12–13 that Jesus suffered outside the gate to sanctify the people by his blood. Because of this, "let us go to him outside the gate and share in his humiliation."

Let us go to Jesus outside in the world of human suffering, for Christ is with people without work; with people without hope; with suffering humanity; with people without opportunity; with people who are the victims of accident and personal failure. Jesus is with people who are in trouble, who are longing for a new chance. Let us go to Jesus outside the camp, in the midst of human suffering. Jesus was so close to the common people that he had compassion for them, i.e., he felt it in his guts (Matt. 9:36).

He was commissioned "to bring good tidings to the poor, to tell the captives they are free, and to give hope and liberation to the downtrodden and the suppressed (Luke 4:18). This is where the church of God ought to be today also. Jesus said, "I was hungry and you gave me food, I was thirsty and you gave me drink, I was a stranger and you welcomed me, I was in prison and you visited me. . . . Inasmuch as you did it to the least of my brethren, you have done it to me" (Matt. 25:35–36, 40).

(c) What we are being called upon to learn from Jesus is that the church must stop trying to think it is the Christ and to go to Christ in the midst of suffering humanity and to *recognize the Christ in the least of humanity.* In Luke 10:29–37, Jesus tells a story of a man in the ditch, in reply to a lawyer's question, "Who is my neighbor?" We call it the parable of the good Samaritan. There were no good Samaritans in Jesus' day. They were all considered to be bastards. And it was this person who had compassion on the man who had been robbed and left in the ditch. There is a story that Jesus once went down from Jerusalem to Jericho, and he was robbed and left for dead in a ditch. It is the person in the ditch who really needs a neighbor. Are we prepared to love our neighbor as ourself and to love as Christ loved? We must go with Christ everywhere; we must go to Christ in his sufferings in broken humanity; we must be willing to do what Christ did for others; we must have the attitude of Christ, who humbled himself and identified himself with us in his humiliation (Phil. 2:5ff).

The more we realize that we are "in Christ" and that we are "new creations" (2 Cor. 5:17), the more we realize that we must go as ambassadors of Christ to those places where Christ already is. We do not go with Christ to where he is not. We are to go into the world because that is where Christ is.

II. *This is the biggest choice we will ever be called upon to make.* If we are to take Christ with us, we must make the choice that Moses had to make, "to choose to suffer with the people of God, rather than to enjoy the pleasures of sin for a season" (Heb. 11:25). When the Lord chooses, we must also make the choice and be prepared to confront the causes of the problems bedeviling the world. This means that when we see people being treated unjustly because of greed, hatred, and cruelty, we must let our voice be heard. We must be prepared to take Christ into the problem areas of society, if there is to be any hope for our future generations. We must express the just Christ in our elections and, in society, be prepared to do what Micah says: "So you call yourself a human being do you? Well then, you know what the Lord requires of you. Do what is right; show loving-kindness; walk humbly with your God" (Mic. 6:8).

The first missionary to leave North America was not a white person. He *was an African slave* who had been freed in Virginia. His name was George Liele. In 1783, George Liele, a gifted Baptist preacher, after learning of the godlessness in Jamaica, set sail for that island. In 1793, the year in which William Carey arrived in India, George Liele, the emancipated African

slave, erected the first Baptist chapel in Jamaica. Largely as a result of his preaching, the black slaves in Jamaica came to realize the true dignity of their personhood and were prepared to pay the price of life itself in order that they might be free.

Let us also have the missionary heart and make the decision the Apostle Paul made "to go everywhere with the fullness of the blessing of Christ." We must never forget this, that Christ is not a cruel, stern, mean taskmaster.

When we decide to make Jesus Christ Lord, he gives us the blessings of the gospel. His blessings abound in the fullness of the blessings of the kingdom. As we go out into the world where Christ Jesus is, let us go in the fullness of the blessings of Christ.—John N. Jonsson

ILLUSTRATIONS

THE WORTH OF ONE SOUL. A colonel in the United States Air Force was speaking enthusiastically of all the trouble the government had gone to in trying to locate a major who was lost in flight. He doubted if there had ever been such a search made for any man. Planes were sent in from many thousands of miles away to join in the search. They exploded ten thousand lights, and one plane and one life were lost in the search. The colonel explained how valuable one man is to Uncle Sam and went on to say that it would not matter what his rank, Uncle Sam would make the same effort. "Just think of it!" he exclaimed. "Ten million dollars for one little man!"—James P. Wesberry

COMPASSION. How do we react to seeing thousands of people at a ball game or seeing them in a traffic jam or pouring out of a plant or building at the close of a work day? We are told that when Jesus saw similar groups he had compassion on them because they were like sheep without a shepherd (Matt. 9:36). When Jesus saw Jerusalem, he wept (Luke 19:41). In 1928, *Life* magazine sponsored, as a protest against the Democrats and Republicans, the Anti-Bunk or Bunkless Party, with Will

Rogers as the presidential candidate. Once Will Rogers was asked what his business was, and he replied, "Everybody's." The same should be true of us. Not that we should be "busybodies," but that we should have Christ's compassion for all.—David W. Richardson

OUTREACH AND DOWNREACH.   The real measurement of a church is how far the message of the church reaches. This is what Joseph Parker meant in the City Temple of London when he said the back of his auditorium was in the Rocky Mountains. He meant that the message of that church had spanned the ocean. But do not forget that "how far" means little if it is not accompanied with "how well." If the trumpet gives an uncertain sound, who shall prepare for war? If the gospel is warped, shallow, blurred, then the church becomes like Ahimaaz who ran to King David and arrived first but had no message. The late Dr. F. Townley Lord, former president of the Baptist World Alliance, once said, "It may be that we have been more interested in counting converts than in weighing them." Both are important. The gospel must be as deep as the human soul and as wide as the world. It must deal with the spiritual side of life, but also with the material. It has to do with the individual, but it also has to do with society. Like ripples on a pond, we must not be satisfied until the last ripple of the gospel touches the farthest shore.—Dotson Nelson

PRICE OF SUCCESS IN EVANGELISM.   We are called to be faithful in carrying the good news to the whole world. What effort are we willing to make? What are the odds of our success? To get a perspective on this, consider gold mining. We would all agree that one person is infinitely more important than gold. Obviously, people do not just mine at random. They pick a likely place. How many pounds of ore do

you think they have to mine to obtain one ounce of gold, now about $300 an ounce? The fact is that they have to mine 14,000 pounds to get one ounce. Or to break it down farther, they go through 224,000 ounces just to get one ounce. What church would be willing to contact 224,000 possible members to get one member?—David W. Richardson

WHAT WE CAN GIVE.   An offering was once taken for foreign missions in a church in Richmond, and a young man who had no money to give wrote on a slip of paper, "I have no money, but I give myself to Jesus," and put it in the plate. That man was J. Lewis Shuck, one of our first missionaries to China.—James P. Wesberry

ROPE-HOLDERS.   When William Carey went to India, Andrew Fuller stayed at home. Both were great missionaries. Andrew Fuller who stayed at home told Carey before he left, "William, you go to India. You go down in the well, but I promise you in God's providence, I will hold the rope that lets you down." Even now in England there are societies that are called "rope-holders." They feel they have a part in the missionary enterprise as they hold the rope. Missions and stewardship are inseparable and interdependent.—Dotson Nelson

KINDNESS.   I chose "kindness" as my topic to speak to the people working at Goodwill Industries. When I rose to speak I saw that a lady was interpreting my speech by sign language to those who could not hear. That interested me, and I changed the planned conclusion of my speech. I said that I had to trust her to transmit truthfully what I was saying. Isn't that the position God is in? God has to trust that we are faithfully transmitting his message of love and kindness to all people.—David W. Richardson

SECTION VIII.
Resources for Monological Preaching

BY RAYMOND H. BAILEY

Topic: Job, Hurt, and Hope
TEXT: Job

There was a time when I would have spoken easily to such an assembly as this; a time when I was sure of myself. "Job is a perfect and upright man," some said, "a man who fears God and shuns evil." A prosperous man, a leader among people, a man with signs of God's blessing can speak easily, confidently. Seven sons and three daughters; thousands of sheep, oxen, and camels; wonderful lands and great crops; everything a person could want was mine. When I passed on the street, the young men would withdraw and the old men would rise. People would gather around to hear what I had to say. Job was respected, even revered as a man of wisdom and integrity, a man obviously blessed by God. But my world crumbled all at once, without warning, without apparent cause, and I was left helpless in the rubble. One day I sat in my house—my children were gathered at the house of my eldest son— when a messenger came from the fields. His breathing was labored, his face clouded. "Master," he said quickly, "the Sabeans have come and have fallen down upon us. They have slain the servants and taken away all of the camels and all of the asses." Hardly had he finished speaking when another servant rushed in shouting, "Master, fire has fallen from heaven and destroyed your sheep and those servants who cared for your sheep." Before I could begin to sort out the meaning there came a third. "Master," he whis-

pered, "the Chaldeans have come and have taken away all of the rest of the livestock and have taken your servants to be slaves." Had that been the end, I could have maintained my composure. No person should be owned by things. We should not have any possessions with which we cannot part.

The next blow struck deeper—the blow that severed my heart and pierced to the bowels of being. Flesh of my flesh! The extension of my own personality. My goodly heritage. Only one alone came to shatter my soul. Not one child, not one, not even a daughter left. All obliterated. What could I do but turn to God in despair and hope; so, I bowed down to worship. I shaved my head, put on sackcloth and ashes, and declared before all who watched, quite aware of my holiness and righteousness, "Naked I came into this world and naked will I go back to that place from whence I come. Blessed be the name of the Lord." I was certain that some careless word, some foolish sin had incurred the wrath of Holiness. God is just! God *is* just! I told myself over and over. God's justice will forgive my ignorant sin and restore me. My waiting was in vain.

The worst was yet to come. I was struck where it really hurts: on my own flesh. My body ached, my flesh was covered with boils. Oh, the agony and disgrace! My pain was great; no one would look upon me anymore. No one even wanted to view the evil that had come upon me, not even my enemies. My humiliation was utter and

257

complete. What else could befall me? And then . . . my wife . . . my own wife . . . the one with whom I shared life, the one whom I loved, the one upon whom I depended and trusted, the one who I thought would share all of life with me, she came to me and said, first softly, "Curse God and die." "Curse God and die!" she said to me. "I will not curse God. I cannot curse God," I wept. She left.

No house, no sheep, no camels, no asses, no servants to bring me food or water, no servants to bring me salve for my boils, no children, no wife. Friends? Oh, they came! Oh yes, they came. From afar they gathered, friends. We had shared so much. Friends with whom I had talked philosophy. We had studied the stars together and had talked of God's goodness and had looked at our prosperous holdings and had rejoiced. I had led them to praise God for the blessings he had showered upon us. They came. At first I thought they understood because they stood at a distance, silent, saying nothing. I thought in my heart, "They know, they know that I am Job, a perfect and upright man. They know that I am a man who fears God. They know that I am a man who even when his land and his properties have been destroyed, even when his children have been taken away, even when his wife has deserted him, has blessed the name of God. They know. They will help me to understand why this has come upon me." Their silence was soon broken. One after the other they came. "Job, you have obviously sinned. God has brought down punishment upon you to make you repent of your sins. Job, you had some secret, hidden sin. You sacrificed for your children but not for yourself. Job, you've cursed God. Job, in the secret recesses of your heart, you have betrayed God. Job, God punishes only those who betray him. Surely, your suffering is deserved." Each charge was like a great boulder added to the weight of the pain and confusion. I knew within me that it was not so. I knew within me that I had not been untrue to what I knew to be the ways of God.

The flood of the sense of injustice could no longer be contained within me. My voice exploded or my heart would have.

"Lord, it would be better if I had never been born! Why has this evil fallen upon me? Why! Why! Why! I argued with God and begged for reasons. Surely, surely, there was someone who would come and plead for me, some kinsmen who remembered how it was when my household was blessed with the friendship of God and when my way was washed with milk. Surely some just person would recall that when I went into the city all sat back and listened to me. I helped the poor; I gave advice to those who needed counsel. Surely, surely, God, you have forgotten. God, you are mistaken. God, you've got the wrong man. God! It isn't fair! Then I cried, "God, show me my sin. Show me where I have betrayed thee. Show me where I have failed thee. God, give me some reason for my suffering . . ." He did not answer me. Nothing was left but my integrity, my own sense of righteousness, the knowledge that I had not sinned against God. I lay there on the dung heap amid the ashes and begged to die. I could not die. I could not live, and I could not die. There was no reason, no understanding.

At the end of my resources, when I had realized that I could no longer depend upon my reason or upon justice, as men know justice, when I reached the point of realizing that worship, ritualistic offerings, even contributions to the poor could be vain, I waited. I waited in darkness and silence. I had nothing within myself except the desire to know the truth from God. I was deserted by family, abandoned and rejected by friends, cursed by those around me.

Then, when I was empty of myself, he filled me. I had heard of God, I had read of God, but I had never heard God, and God to me was a strange mystery. It was a voice like thunder and yet soft like the spring breeze. It was a voice like lightning and yet a voice like the singing of the newborn doves. Majesty of majesties spoke to me. "Job," God said, "Job, where were you when I laid the foundations of the world? Job, have you ever visited the four houses of the sea? Job, have you ever been to the warehouses of the snow? Job, can you create animals out of nothing? Job, have you ever wrestled with Leviathan?

Job, did you roll back and close out the seas and create the world in which you live? Job, can you speak with a voice like thunder, can you make the wind blow or the rain?" The knowing that came upon me was not a knowing of the mind. It was not a fruit of human wisdom. It was the experience of presence. He is God! What else could I say? In my imperfection, in my imperfect and unreasonable and unreasoning world, reason would not suffice, man's goodness would not suffice, only God's righteousness and God's sovereignty.

I wish I could say to you that he gave me reasons. But he didn't. The only assurance that he gave to me was the assurance that he knew, that he had heard, that he had shared the pain, that he was with me. He had allowed the hedge around me to be torn down and the world to tumble in on me. Now he only assured me that he was with me in this world. It was what he had given to me as a man, as a child of his, that I could endure to the utmost, the ultimate suffering of the world. Even if I lost all of my possessions, even if I lost my prestige, even if I lost my children and had the broken body of suffering, he was with me, and I could endure with him.

I still don't have all the answers, but I can tell you this: You can feel the peace of God within you. You cannot understand God until you come face to face with him and you see him with the eyes of your heart, till you see him with your mind's eye. He is known in submission and emptiness. In my own mind I had concluded only that one cannot know what it is to be a man until one knows suffering. The lessons were many, the righteousness of God cannot be understood until one knows the unrighteousness of this world. One cannot know what justice is until one experiences the justice of God in face to face confrontation with him. Some of you play games with God. You play games with religion, and you believe that there is a hedge about you. Will you be able to struggle through and endure when your world tumbles in and threatens to crush you? Will your hedge fall down? Will you pray? Will you bow your heads and close your eyes and will you with courage and honor

reach the end of your reason and the end of your resources and the end of the vested goodness that other people give to you to struggle through with God? Can you with honesty and integrity even in this moment offer up to God your bitterness, your anger, and your resentment, bitterness toward others and bitterness toward God? Can you endure your suffering and your existence in this world in spite of the judgment of friends, the criticism of others, and the reason of man? I speak of such things not to judge you. I will not play the role of my friends. I share my experience that you may find in it hope in your own struggle.

Topic: An Old Man's Regrets: The Rich Young Ruler Revisited

They come to seek my counsel. Three times I've been president of the synagogue. I sat in the councils of the wise. Yes, I have everything that a man could want, and yet I'm miserable. There's something missing from my life. Maybe I've had it too easy. I didn't earn my wealth; I was born into it. I had every advantage that a child could have. Before my twentieth birthday, I was already elected into the Sanhedrin, following in the steps of my father. I was considered a wise man even when I was still a youth. I wanted to be a wise man. I had a curious mind in my youth. My father used to say I was too curious. I worried too much about the world and how it operated. Just take life as it comes, he used to say. Be grateful for what you have. Be responsible. Be a good citizen. Don't disgrace your family. What would it mean to disgrace my family?

In my youth I longed for God. I wanted then to understand the mysteries of the universe, how the world came into being. I wanted to understand myself. Long hours were spent poring over the Scriptures. I studied under the great rabbis. My friends included some of the wisest sages of our people. Nicodemus was a good friend of my father's. I used to love to go and talk with him. To listen to his interpretation of the various teachers and schools of thought. I had read after Hillel the Elder and Shammai both and found credibility in the wisdom of each. But there came a time when I stopped all of that foolishness. I gave up on studying the Law; I abandoned religion as a philosophical pursuit. I came home to be my father's son. To be practical, kind, generous. I came home to be a good citizen, but I've never had real peace in my life.

I am so tired. Why can't I sleep at night? I fall asleep, and I dream. Oh . . . the same dream. Not different dreams. And not dreams of the future. Not dreams of what might be. It is the same dream over and over again. It is as if a group of players were acting out something that happened in my life long ago. I am haunted by that scene. Haunted by a memory of what was and what might have been. Father says a wise man never looks back, but I can't help but look back.

I could lay blame for my problems on friend Nicodemus who told me about a wise teacher who was traveling about the countryside, talking about the kingdom of God. Nicodemus told me he had had a private audience with the man and had been greatly impressed by his wisdom; so I went out to the countryside to hear this man. His name was Jesus. I followed him about, listening to him sometimes giving comfort and sometimes declaring judgment. There were dire warnings from him, and there were promises filled with great hope. Nicodemus was certainly right about his new way of looking at the Law. He interpreted the Law as no one I had ever heard before. His favorite subject was the kingdom of God. I'd always thought of the kingdom of God as being the same thing as the kingdom of David. I'd looked forward to the time when Israel would be politically prominent in the world again. I, like most of my people, longed for a time when we could make a difference in the world in which we live. A time when we could be free. Jesus spoke of the kingdom of God as if it were something much greater than even David's kingdom. He spoke of it as something that would be brought about not by man, not even by a man like David, but only by God himself. Other members of the great council were quite critical of Jesus from the very beginning. By the time I heard him there were already rumblings that he must be si-

lenced. My colleagues on the council said that he claimed to be the Messiah. I never heard him make such a claim, but apparently he did, and ultimately it cost him his life.

Back to my dream. In my dream it happens over and over again. Even as it happened that first time. Jesus had been debating with some Pharisees. They had sought to test him and questioned him about whether it was lawful for a man to divorce his wife. Jesus reminded them of Moses' teaching and challenged them to respond according to Moses' teaching. I'm sure that many who were present were stung by his words, for he placed responsibility on men for maintaining marriages that might be somewhat uncomfortable for them. He told them that whoever divorces his wife and marries another woman commits adultery against her. In the mind of Jewish men, adultery had been, for the most part, a woman's sin. How many of my friends have put their wives out on all kinds of pretenses. Jesus turned their trap back on them, and they were the ones indicted. As the Pharisees mumbled among themselves, children began to run up to Jesus, and parents were bringing children in arms to him, infants, so that he might touch them. The disciples tried to protect him from the children, and they rebuked the parents and told them not to bother Jesus. When Jesus saw this he appeared to be angry and told his disciples, "Let the children come to me! Don't stop the children from coming to me! For the kingdom of God belongs to such as these. Indeed," he said, "whoever does not receive the kingdom of God like a child, shall not enter in it at all." He continued to touch the children, taking them into his arms and blessing them. His words turned over in my mind. "Except you receive the kingdom of God as a child, you shall not enter in." What did it mean? Childishness was a thing to be endured until one became a man in Israel. I had wanted to be done with being a child as quickly as possible. What could he mean that we should come to him as children? That we should receive the kingdom of God as a child was a strange notion. As I pondered these words, he turned to go away. There was a knot in my stomach, a pounding in my head. Suddenly I found myself running up to him and kneeling down before him. "Good teacher," I said, "what shall I do to inherit the kingdom of eternal life?" "Why do you call me good? No one is good except God alone." I didn't understand what he meant by that. Later when I discussed it with Nicodemus he said that no one was truly good except God and to call him good suggested divine qualities. Nicodemus suggested that maybe Jesus was testing me to see whether or not I believed he was the Messiah. "What must I do to inherit the kingdom of God?" I asked once again. "You know the commandments," Jesus said. "Do not murder; do not commit adultery; do not steal; do not bear false witness; do not defraud; honor your father and mother." That was all easy enough. I had been taught those rules all of my life, and I did everything in my power to live by them. I assured him that these things I had done from my childhood until that very day. A strange look came on his face, his eyes softened and his voice also. There was a tenderness in his eyes like tenderness I'd only seen in my father's eyes when on those special occasions he said something or did something that made me know that he loved me very much. Jesus was looking at me, though he was not much older than I was, as a father looks at a son with love. Gently, he said, "One thing you don't have . . . go and sell all you own and give it to the poor, and you shall have treasure in heaven. Come and follow me."

No rabbi I had ever known or read after would make such a suggestion. What Jesus said was contrary to everything the Law taught. It was contrary to everything I'd been taught all my life. My father had said that because we keep the Law, because we obey the commandments, God had blessed us. Everyone I knew believed that what you owned reflected your relationship to God, and those who were in poverty were there because they did not please God. And now, Jesus was suggesting that I should give away everything I had, that I should sell all the signs of heavenly blessing. It didn't make any sense. Receive the kingdom of God like a child,

a helpless infant? Give away everything that you have?

Father had said that it was appropriate to give alms, but one had to be careful about giving alms lest you encourage poverty. I'd been taught that great care should be taken in the giving of charity. "Go and sell all that you have and give it to the poor." I must have been crazy, because for a moment I actually considered doing it. That knot in my stomach, that spinning in my head made me want to please Jesus, made me want to do what this man asked me to do. I guess the only thing that saved me was the voice of my father deep within. I suddenly thought, what would my father say if I came home and told him that I was going to sell everything that I owned, give it all away, and go follow Rabbi Jesus around the countryside? My friends, most of whom were very envious of all that I had and who coveted my wealth and position, would laugh at me. Everyone would be convinced that I was out of my head. It just didn't make any sense. I could feel the blood rush to my face. I trembled a little bit. I'm sure that I was visibly shaken, and he could see that I was very uncomfortable. It would have been easy for someone who didn't own what I owned to give it up and follow him. I'm sure that most of those who followed him had had very little to give up and follow him. It was asking too much of me. As I turned and walked away, I overheard him say, "How hard it is for those who have much to enter the kingdom of God."

That's the dream. I have it over and over again. When I came home and told my father about the whole episode, he was furious. "I have told you that you can be religious without being a fanatic," he shouted at me. "I knew that if you kept running around, listening to all of these rabbis, you would be confused and get yourself into trouble. I hope now that you have learned your lesson and you'll turn your mind to more important and practical things. The time has come for you to take more responsibility in the business. The time has come for you to be a more responsible leader in the community. I want you to stop running around all over the country and listening to preachers. Stay home and help me."

I was the obedient son. I did what my father told me to do. I did what I wanted to do. I didn't want to give up my comfort; I didn't want to give up my position, my power, my wealth; I didn't want to give up my standing in the community . . . and I didn't. For a long time I wondered if I'd made the right decision. Dad said that Nicodemus had gone off the deep end and that he suspected that Nicodemus had become a secret disciple of Jesus. He asked me to stay away from Nicodemus. I didn't obey him in that respect at first, but later they brought Jesus before the council and charged him with blasphemy. He was convicted. They took him before Pilate, and at the urging of the priest, he was condemned to death. I was grateful I had not followed him; it would have disgraced my whole family if I had been associated with such a criminal. They crucified him. That should have been the end of the matter, but it wasn't. Soon rumors spread throughout the country that Jesus had come back from the dead. Nicodemus came to see me. He expressed regret, even shame, that he had not been a public follower of Jesus and that he had not spoken out for Jesus during the trial. Nicodemus, as wise as he was, had gone completely mad. I guess it just proved my father's point that too much religion will make you sick. Nicodemus believed the tales that Jesus had come back from the dead. He tried to convince me that Jesus was alive and that he was the Messiah and that I should believe in him. "Believe in him?" I said. "What do you mean?" Nicodemus said, "You should give your whole life to him." Here we go again, I thought. Go and get rid of everything you have and give it away and come and follow me. Father asked Nicodemus never to come to our house again. And he didn't.

The tales of Jesus did not die. There is a whole movement now that's called "the way." Thousands believe. I'm told it has spread to other countries. Believers, in the way say that Jesus is alive, that he is the Messiah, and that salvation can be had only through him. "Except you receive the kingdom of God like a child, you will not receive it at all." Only a child could believe such foolishness, and yet why am I haunted? Could it be true? Is there any possibility that I should have done what he asked? Could I have known peace in my life? Would I be able to sleep at night if I had sold everything and followed Jesus? Is it possible that he really was the Son of God as Nicodemus said he was? Crazy thoughts again. I must suppress these thoughts. If only I could sleep and rest my mind. It will soon be daylight, and I will go to the fields and lose myself in my work and pretend that it never happened at all. If only life were so simple that we like children could receive the kingdom of God.

Topic: A Woman Creates a Loving Memory

TEXT: Mark 14:3–9

It was only a matter of time. Everyone knew by then what had happened, what would happen, what was happening. The world can't stand goodness. Justice is a fantasy to most people. What they would do to him would make me a loser again. So, what's new?

I was born a loser. When I left my mother's womb and entered the world a woman, my fate was sealed. My father was angry that he did not get a son. My mother was embarrassed that she had failed to give her husband the son he so desperately wanted. A female child was only a thing to be endured in a Jewish family. A Jewish woman was a thing to be used.

Used! Oh yes, every man I ever knew either ignored me or *used* me. When my husband, to whom I had been given by my father, was through using me, he said the magic word three times—"divorce, divorce, divorce"—and I was a woman of the streets. My father certainly did not want me back. My mother said I should have worked harder to please my husband. Since then it has been a matter of survival. I survived by selling my use to men. Yes, I hated them all—until he came along.

He was one man who was different. He spoke to me—*in public*. He never asked anything of me, and he told me that God loved me. He touched me—but not like other men. His was the gentle touch of a loving father, though he is younger than I am. Strange that anyone—but especially a man—could make me feel that I am something other than trash, could make me feel like some*one*, a person of value.

Now they were going to kill him. The merchants I could understand, the slime of the streets would not surprise me, but why the holy Joes? Why did his God-talk make those who claim to be God's chosen so uncomfortable? The rumors were everywhere. The Pharisees and Saducees, enemies who hated one another, had joined together to get him off the streets, to shut him up. Everyone was saying that like John the Baptizer, Jesus would have to die.

His preaching in Jerusalem before the Passover enraged them. He spoke of judgment. Every time they tried to trap him, he made them look like the fools they are. But when he went wild in the Temple, I knew they would get him, soon. He kicked over the tables of the money changers and the cages of the pigeons being sold to the poor for sacrifices. He shouted that the Temple was a place of prayer and should not be a den for thieves. He was wonderful! (Pause.) But my laughter was washed away by tears as I thought about what they would do to him. A man who treated women kindly, helped the weak, defended the poor, and exposed corruption among the rich and powerful would not be tolerated for long.

What could I do? I couldn't stop them. I couldn't help him, but surely I could do something to express my love and my sorrow—something that would show those around him what was sure to happen. Then it came to me. Was it foolish? Would he laugh at me? No, he would never do that. So I followed through my little plan. I took all the money I had and bought an alabaster jar of expensive perfume. Heads turned as I walked through the streets, and the sweet smell of the perfume filled the air about me.

It took me a day to find him because he and his followers had returned to Bethany. I found him at the house of Simon, a man whom Jesus had cured of a terrible disease. I broke the jar and poured the perfume on Jesus' head. Some of the people there were angry and murmured, "What was the use of wasting the perfume? It could have been sold for more than three hundred silver coins," they said, "and the money given to the poor!" They criticized me harshly and made ugly gestures toward me.

But Jesus said, "Leave her alone! Why are you bothering her? She has done a fine and beautiful thing for me. You will always have poor people with you, and any time you want to, you can help them. But you will not always have me. She did what she could; she poured perfume on my body to prepare it ahead of time for burial. Now, I assure you that wherever the gospel is preached all over the world, what she has done will be told in memory of her" (based on Mark 14:3–9, TEV).

"Time for burial." (Pause.) He knew. He was going on, knowing full well that they were going to kill him. In spite of the danger to himself, he had spoken out to defend me, and he approved of what I had done.

I'm not sure whether I did the right thing or not, but he was moved by my act. He knew that what I had done was done out of love. Never had I felt so warm and good.

His memory will ever make me feel like a person, and because he approved my act, others will remember me as one he blessed. They have taken him now. He was betrayed by one of his own followers. They may kill him, but for me and for others, his goodness will live. The memory of his kindness will keep me going. Jesus was able to do for me what no one else had ever sought to do. He gave to me a sense of personal worth. He made me feel loved in a good way. I wish I could tell him that my life is different because of him.

SECTION IX.
Preaching on the Psalms

BY ERIC C. RUST

The Psalter is often described as the hymnbook of the Second Temple. Undoubtedly it did serve such a purpose when its various collections were brought together in the postexilic period. But it does consist of various collections of Hebrew poetry, some of which contain psalms going back to Israel's earlier history. We need to remember that worship in the Temple at Jerusalem and elsewhere in pre-exilic days was accompanied by choirs. Psalms associated with such choirs are gathered under such titles as the "sons of Asaph" and the "sons of Korah." Often, too, there were professional prophets who echoed the insights of the great prophetic tradition, in comfort and in judgment. Thus, the Psalms often manifest the influence and theology of the great literary prophets, many of whose utterances often had a poetic structure. In the worship of the Second Temple, the choirs and musicians catalogued in the Books of Chronicles (for example, 1 Chron. 15:16ff, 25; 2 Chron. 9:30) thus perpetuated the prophetic theology and insights. As such, the Psalter covers the whole gamut of Israel's experience, much as our preaching and its accompanying hymns should do today. Nature and history, social issues and personal concerns, the reality of divine providence and the problem raised by the prosperity of the wicked, and, at the center, the reality of God and reality of his mercy and forgiveness. We shall look at a few representative psalms that may help us to present such themes to our people.

I. Topic: *God in nature.* All the nature psalms reflect the cosmology of the time when they were written—a flat earth with the heavenly firmament like a dome above it, resting on the mountains at the earth's rim. God's palace was set above the dome, and here the heavenly beings offered him their praise. The preacher may point out how different is the infinite expanse in space and the vast extent of time in our view of the universe. But his stress should fall upon the divine revelation that the psalmists sought to express in their contemporary understanding of their world. That revelation of God's greatness, goodness, and power can still light up and be expressed in the structures of the universe that modern science has unveiled for us.

In Psalm 29 we have a wonderful storm song in which a thunderstorm sweeps across the land, bending the cedars of Lebanon, stripping the forests bare, and shaking the wilderness of Kadesh. Thunder echoes the divine voice, and the lightning flashes forth his power over nature. A flood of natural evil seems released, but God reigns above it, and, up in his celestial palace, the heavenly beings praise his majesty.

Surely here we have a picture of God's supreme power, even when our world is beset by the storms that sweep through our human affairs. God guides his people through life's vicissitudes and grants them his peace. We move from nature to the storms that sweep our common life.

In Psalm 104, the Hebrew understanding of the world is clearly expressed—the dome of heaven is pictured as a tent, and the vast expanses outside the earth and its protecting firmament are filled with a watery deep. Again, what matters is the way in which the psalmist portrays the whole vista of the realm of Creation as offering its praise to God, its Creator. His majesty and power are manifested at every level of the natural process. The order of such levels reflects both the ordering of the Genesis 1 creation story and the development that modern evolutionary science portrays.

God orders the heavens (vv. 2–4), creates the earth (vv. 5–9), controls the waters and the deep (vv. 10–13), creates and sustains the vegetation (vv. 14–18), orders and controls the moon and the sun (vv. 19–23). God is the Lord of the sea (vv. 24–26) and gives life to all (vv. 27–30). All creatures exist and are sustained by his power. Whatever modern science may say, concealed beneath its facade of ordered law and random changes, there is the hidden presence of the divine Spirit. God accommodates his hidden presence to the ordering that he himself has created. He guides and sustains the whole creative process. At the same time, he accommodates his hidden activity to the structures that science studies and that he himself has created. Indeed, the presence of the divine Spirit in the natural process is of one piece with that divine *kenosis* that is also evident in the Incarnation (see Phil. 2:5ff).

The psalmist thus reminds us that all created things depend finally upon God. His creative breath, his Spirit, enlivens all. Verses 1–9 celebrate God's initial creative act, and the rest of the psalm celebrates his sustaining presence.

The final ascription of praise to God is accompanied by a reminder that man's blindness to God's presence and arrogant sin begets judgment (vv. 31–37).

Here we can emphasize the revelation of God throughout nature and also remind our listeners that here is a divine hiddenness. God wraps himself in light (v. 3) and plays a game of hide-and-seek with us, even in the natural process. An attack on contemporary naturalism is called for.

In Psalm 8, we have a hymn that celebrates the glory of the night sky. The moon and stars chant the glory of God. This is no pantheism or naturalism. The beauty of the starlit heavens arouses awe in the presence of the divine. The infinite depths of the universe may terrify man, as they did Pascal, but they can make him feel some infinite presence, as happened to von Hügel. The terrifying aspect may make man question his own standing and *raison d'etre* in such a vast environment. What is he but an element of dust on a little planet called earth that revolves around a second-rate star, of which there are millions in this galactic universe, along with myriads of such galaxies lost in the infinite depths of space. We hear Tennyson asking, "But what am I / An infant crying in the night; / An infant crying for the light; / And with no language but a cry." The psalmist can rise above such terrifying thoughts because of God's revelation of himself in Israel's history. He is the Lord, Yahweh, who delivered the people at the Exodus from Egypt. The psalmist begins with God's revelation of his divine name, and in the light of this, he sees all the vast expanses of the night sky praising God's majestic name. Many centuries later, the philosopher Kant could declare: "Two things there are which, the oftener and more steadfastly we consider them, fill the mind with ever new and ever rising admiration and reverence: the starry heavens above, the moral law within."

So we, too, may feel dwarfed and terrified, live under the shadow of a vastness that seems to have no concern for our feeble humanity. But we have met God in Jesus Christ, and we dare to believe that our control of our world and our dominion over nature are signs that the heart of the universe is wondrously kind. All our scientific achievements are possible because God cares and has given us these gifts to bring his plans to fruition. There is a divine purpose for this universe, and our humanity is a part of it. We are made in God's image. Our finitude reflects something of his infinite being. "O Lord, our Lord, coming to us in Jesus Christ and to the psalmist in the Exodus, how majestic is your name in this vast universe and for our poor, broken humanity!"

The emphasis on nature as a revelation of God's glory is echoed in Psalm 65, which is a psalm of thanksgiving for the autumnal rains. Here God is the Creator and Lord of nature, who established the mountains at the earth's rim and stills the roar of the seas (vv. 6–7). So God has crowned the year with his bounty (v. 11) and opened up his irrigation channel for the autumnal rains (v. 9). His chariot has passed across the heavens, dropping fatness (v. 11).

There is also a sense of history in this psalm, for all peoples beyond Israel share in God's goodness. This God of salvation is the hope of all the ends of the earth, so that those who dwell in the earth's fullest bounds stand in awe at the signs (vv. 5, 8). At the autumn thanksgiving celebration, Israel is surrounded by all the inhabitants of the earth. So God is both the Lord of nature and the master of history. The richness of the autumn harvest testifies to all peoples that God is Lord, and a vast symphony of praise rises to the heavens (v. 13).

II. Topic: *God and history.* The divine revelation in nature is made evident by the divine revelation in history. In the midst of nature stands humankind, a part of nature and yet above nature. Made in the image of God, we possess a delegated authority over nature. It is in our common life and social relationships that God is most to be found, in judgment and in mercy. Israel was made conscious of the divine presence in its historical life and of a divine purpose in history. Its concern with history was because its God had a redemptive control of history. The divine purpose was directed on Israel's salvation. Israel's remembrance of its past was not a matter of archaeological interest or philosophical concern. It looked back to historical events that had been filled with the presence of God. Israel's faith had transformed historical happenings into events in which they had met God. Such events were revelatory, both awakening faith and

strengthening it. Indeed all history involves interpretation. It is human beings who turn a succession of happenings into meaningful events, and the Psalms rejoice in such events in which God has met his people.

Psalm 105 offers such a confession of faith grounded in revelatory events. It recites God's act in Israel's history from the time of Abraham onward, just as our Christian hymns celebrate God's presence in the birth, life, death, and Resurrection of our Lord Jesus and in the life of his Church.

In this psalm the emphasis is on God's covenant with Abraham and his descendants and the accompanying promise. The divine presence is portrayed in the lives of the patriarchs, the story of Joseph, the life of Israel in Egypt, Moses, the plagues, the Exodus, the wilderness wanderings and acts of deliverance. This tremendous creedal recital of God's mighty acts finishes with the fulfillment of the promise and the settlement in Canaan.

The whole recital is to arouse in the congregation a faith that matches these great moments in Israel's past. It culminates in a tumultuous Alleluia.

We can transform this creedal recital with our Christian creedal affirmations and awaken our people's awareness of God's presence in the life of the church in our own time.

God's covenant love and faithfulness are echoed in Psalm 114 and in Psalm 136. The latter, often called the Great Hallel, emphasizes the divine faithfulness and repeatedly affirms God's covenant love, his *chesedh.* We can read into this recital the new divine covenant in Jesus Christ our Lord and the emphasis on a grace that redeems sinners. We note that this psalm links up the divine steadfast love in history with the like presence of covenant love in the whole natural process. This may well be an echo of the Noachic covenant between God, humanity, and nature. It certainly reminds us that God's covenant love in the creation and sustaining of nature requires from us a covenant response in his treatment of his natural environment. Indeed, the celebration of God's steadfast love in nature as well as history might well become the basis for emphasizing the contemporary crying need for ecological responsibility and activity. This is God's world, and humanity's dominion over nature demands a responsible response to the natural as well as the social realm.

In other psalms, we turn to the retributive side of history. Not only do these psalms call for confidence in God's gracious and creative presence, they also proclaim the reality of divine judgment.

In Psalm 98 we have a recital of God's steadfast love, of Israel's continual unfaithfulness, and of the operation of the divine judgment. This should be a very necessary aspect of Christian preaching in the contemporary scene. God's gracious and repeated deliverances of Israel are recorded, with an emphasis on his covenant and its accompanying commandments. Time and again the people sinned, transgressed his law, and came under his judgment. Their hearts were not steadfast toward God, but he was steadfast in his love for them. Repeatedly they came under his wrath, and yet he forgave their iniquity and showed his compassion. He brought them into the Promised Land, and still they failed him.

The emphasis on God's encompassing love and unfailing mercy testifies to a saving grace that will and must win. Settled in Canaan, they sinned and fell apart. Northern Israel was rejected, and only Judah was left with its Temple. Here the psalmist finishes, but we might continue with the story of sin and judgment until the covenant people were reduced to the Christ, who bore their judgment and manifested the divine compassion in his life and death and the triumph of divine grace in his Resurrection. Here the new covenant was sealed and a new Israel, the Church, came to birth. Divine love triumphed over wrath.

We need to understand the divine judgment, not as the act of an angry God, but as the divine reaction to sin. God, quoting Paul, gives people over to the sin of their hearts, and, in the process of life and history, they destroy themselves. The universe is so structured that, ultimately, we cannot sin and get away with it. Yet, in the heart of a gracious God, there is a suffering compassion that bursts into history in the cross of Jesus, the Christ of God.

This psalm finishes with God's triumph in the establishment of David upon the throne and the Temple on Zion's hill. For us it finishes in a greater son of David and in a temple not made with hands.

Psalm 106 repeats the same emphasis. It finishes with the scattering of Israel among the nations and a prayer that God's steadfast love will yet triumph in their being gathered together to give God glory. Here, too, we Christians see this hope fulfilled in the Christ and his Church.

In Psalm 47, we have celebration of God as the King of all the earth. It belongs to psalms sung at the pre-exilic Enthronement Festival, a dramatic new year ceremony in which the worshipers hailed the lordship of Yahweh over the whole created order. Isa. 6:1 and 5 may reflect this kind of setting. The psalm is still used in Jewish synagogues before the horn is sounded in the new year service.

God is portrayed as the awe-inspiring Lord of history. He has subdued all nations under Israel and chosen them to be his people (vv. 3–4). The horn sounds as the ark is installed in its place, the ark portraying God's especial presence. God has gone up with the sound of the trumpet (v. 6). The worshipers and the temple musicians sing God's praises.

The final verses (8–9) imply a universal hope for all humanity, which only became a reality in David's greater Son, Jesus. Israel had to learn through the Christ that God's power is that of suffering, redeeming love. In the ascension of our Lord, that power reaches out to all nations. God has gone up with a shout!

III. Topic: *God and personal faith.* The Psalms put great emphasis on trust in God. Such trust may be either personal or national. The "I" in the Psalms would seem to oscillate between a corporate consciousness and the individual ego. For the preaching task we shall tend to emphasize the personal aspect.

We begin with the emphasis on *trust.*

The word occurs forty-six times. It describes the fundamental attitude toward God. It is more intimate perhaps than faith, for it is more suggestive of a personal relation and expectancy. It covers the whole of life and is comprehensive in its scope. It brings the confidence that Yahweh will withhold no good things from the trustful; will encompass the life entrusted to him with his active protection; will bring deliverance and security and the fulfillment of petitions; will be a help and a shield; and will cover all the occasions of life with his presence. These aspects of God's encompassing presence are all contained in Ps. 31:14, 15. They provide good material for a sermon on personal faith.

Such trust is grounded in historical memory and in personal experience. God's steadfast love lies behind and is manifested in both the history of Israel and individual experience. Our Christian commitment is likewise grounded in the historical reality of the presence of the eternal Christ, in the life of the Church, and in our own personal awareness of his presence in our lives. God's fidelity is the abiding reality on which trust is grounded.

Ps. 9:10 is a good text, but Psalm 103 is full of preaching material. In Ps. 103:1–5, the psalmist rejoices at God's grace in iniquities forgiven, in diseases healed, in lives redeemed, and in youth renewed. In the next verses (6–10), he sets such personal experience within the framework of God's saving activity for the covenant people, Israel. In the following verses, he amplifies such covenant love with the father image (compare Hosea) and points to its unwavering and steadfast nature. Here is good material for a sermon that sets such experiences within the wider framework of the Christian revelation.

Psalm 107 is also a fruitful poem. It portrays God's mercy in the setting of four experiences—the traveler, the prisoner, the sick man, and the sailor. These dramatic pictures point to God's wonderful works among the children of men. The psalmist does not raise the issue of unanswered prayer and innocent suffering.

Psalm 139 is a poem comparable to Francis Thompson's "Hound of Heaven." God's personal providence is related to his omnipresence and omnipotence. God sees and knows us, fathoming our lives, tracing our ways, and surrounding us with his presence. From the heights of heaven to the depths of shadowy Sheol, the haunt of the departed, we cannot escape God. Even our embryonic stage is under his watchful eye. So the psalm cries to God to examine, purify, and lead us (vv. 13–18, 23–24). Here is personal religion at its deepest—true spirituality.

Psalm 91 echoes such confidence in God's providential care.

Yet trust in God raises problems, even for the psalmist—the issue of *unanswered prayer and the seeming prosperity of the wicked.* We may choose one psalm out of many that deal with this issue—Psalm 73. This psalm goes beyond the positions adopted by Job's friends. Underneath all the psalmist's doubts there is a belief in God's goodness (vv. 1–2). The godless seem to get away with iniquity and even to be blessed (vv. 3–6, 7–10). They flaunt God's power and righteousness, and yet they escape (vv. 11–12). What then is the use of religious and moral standards? Why cleanse the heart? This is the scandal in the psalmist's heart, and it is still one for many of us. But he sees it as Job's friends did not.

The psalmist goes to the sanctuary. Instead of voicing his doubts and offending the "little ones," he will find solace in the presence of God. He will not spread unbelief but rather pour out his doubts before God (vv. 15ff). For us, as for him, prayer is the beginning of our deliverance. The reality of the covenant God overshadowed him, as the reality of God's grace in Jesus Christ takes possession of our lives. The obstacles and doubts cease to count. Like Whittier, he can cry that, amid the storms of doubt and perplexity, "To one fixed ground my spirit clings;/It is that God is good." He has thought about God like a dumb beast. God is real, and God will go before him and receive him into glory (vv. 22–24). Such a faith is made the richer by the Christian hope and the Resurrection of our Lord. We, too, like the psalmist must take refuge in the bliss and assurance of personal communion with God.

The same problem and hope comes up again in Psalm 49. Here the psalmist sees that multitude of riches does not bring escape from death. Death will shepherd even the most prosperous wicked people (v. 14). So the writer gropes forward to a larger hope, that God will redeem his life from the power of the grave and receive him (v. 15). God's final welcome will crown his personal trust and devotion.

SECTION X.
Children's Stories and Sermons

January 7. The Wise Men

When Jesus was born, it was good news for everyone. The angel said, "Behold, I bring you good news of great joy which shall be for all people." Jesus was God's gift to everyone.

News of Jesus' birth spread. The Bible tells how this news came to be known in a country far away from Bethlehem. A group of people who lived in that faraway country were called Magi or wise men. They were educated men who were teachers and instructors. They knew much about many things, and they enjoyed studying the stars that appeared in the night skies. They believed that from the stars they could tell what would happen in the future.

While studying the stars, the Magi made an exciting discovery. They discovered a bright new star that had never before been seen. To the Magi that meant that a king had been born somewhere in the world.

Choosing gifts appropriate for a king, a group of the Magi set out to try to find the newborn king. Using the star to direct them, they traveled westward and came to the city of Jerusalem. Upon their arrival, they began asking, "Where is the baby born to be the king of the Jews? We saw his star when it came up in the east. We have come to worship him."

Word got to King Herod that Magi were in the city looking for a newborn king. That upset the king because he wanted no one other than himself to be the king.

King Herod called together those who knew the Scriptures and asked them where the Messiah was to be born. Learning that his birthplace was to be Bethlehem, the king said to the Magi, "Go to Bethlehem and carefully search until you find the child. Then let me know where he is so that I, too, may go and worship him."

With those instructions, the Magi left, only to find the same star that they had seen in the east. Joyfully, they followed the star until they found the newborn king.

By now, Mary, Joseph, and Jesus were living in a house rather than in the stable. The Magi or wise men entered the house. Seeing Jesus with his mother, Mary, they knelt down. Worshiping the baby, they presented him with expensive and kingly gifts. They gave him gold; frankincense, which when burned produced good smells; and myrrh, which was used to make sweet-smelling perfume as well as oil and medicine.

Later, the wise men or Magi returned to the country from which they came, never again seeing the wicked king.—Leon W. Castle

January 14. We're Rich!

Object: Something very expensive (or a picture of it).

Good morning, boys and girls. Do you like to watch game shows on television? A lot of people like to watch them. Why do you suppose they do? [Talk about it.] One reason might be because we like to outsmart the people on the program and see if we can answer the questions better or

270

faster than they can. But I'll bet you another reason is that a lot of people like to imagine what it would be like to win all the money you can win on a game show. If you ever would go on a television game show and win the top prize, you could buy a lot of expensive things like this. [Show them the object or the picture.] How much do you think this would cost? A lot of money, certainly. If people saw you with one of these, they might say, "You must be rich!"

I think sometime or another almost everybody wants to be rich. Especially when we are sure we just don't have enough money to pay all the bills, we wish we could be rich. And when we see how much fun the rich people seem to have, getting to do whatever they want to do, not having to worry about going to work every day, we really wonder what it would be like if we could be that rich, too.

Well, you and I may never end up with a hundred million dollars, but guess what: we're rich already. Did you know that? Yes. That's right. We really are. The Bible tells us that the people who belong to God are already the richest people in the world—richer than the people who live in big houses and drive big cars and spend lots of money. Why do you suppose we're rich? [Let them try some answers.] We're rich, the Bible says, because we are united with Christ. Jesus is our friend now. Jesus can give us things all the money in the world can't buy. What are some of those things? [Help them to list some.] Yes, Jesus brings us God's love. And his friendship. And peace. And hope. And answers to our hardest questions. And the promise that we can go to God's kingdom in heaven when we die and live there with him forever. Isn't that terrific? That means we have everything we need. We're rich!—*Children's Sermon Service Plus!*

January 21. The Most Important Person

Object: A wallet-sized picture of Jesus.

Good morning, boys and girls. Do any of you like to carry around pictures of your good friends? Many people do that. They will put a little book of pictures in their purse or maybe keep some in their billfold. We don't keep just anybody's picture in there, only people who are special to us.

Then when we want to think about them, we can take out their picture and look at it and remember how special they are to us.

Here's a picture some people carry around in their purses or billfolds. [Show them the picture of Jesus.] Do you know anybody who carries one of these? Why would we want to carry a picture of Jesus? That's right, because Jesus is the most important person in our life. We want to keep his picture close to us so that we can remember to stay close to him all the time.

Sometimes we forget who the most important person is. We get mixed up and think the pastor is the most important person. Or somebody who gives us money or does nice things for us. Or our parents. All of these people may be important, but they are not the most important. Only Jesus is the most important person—because Jesus is God's Son and the person who saves us from sin and evil and death.

Today's Bible story tells about a man named John. A lot of people thought John was the most important person because he was a great preacher. But John told the truth. He said, "Don't follow me. Follow Jesus." So the people who had been following John began following Jesus instead. It was sort of like taking a picture of one friend out of your purse or billfold and putting in a new picture of an even better friend. One of the people who did this was named Philip. Jesus told him to follow him, and Philip did. That's what Jesus says to us, too. He asks us to come with him and be his friends. He not only wants us to keep him in our purse or billfold but to keep him in our life and in our heart.—*Children's Sermon Service Plus!*

January 28. Our Feelings

Object: A mask.

[Walk in wearing the mask.] Good morning! How are you today? Who knows who I am? Who am I trying to be? What is a time that most of you get the chance to wear a mask? [Times like Halloween and plays will be given.] That's right—those are times that you get to dress up and pretend that you are someone else. That can be fun. You get to pretend that you are a king or a queen or a baseball player or a police officer or a ghost or a monster.

When we are playing it is OK and fun to pretend we are someone else. But there are other times when we pretend we are someone else, and we shouldn't. We can wear a mask that people don't see. For example, we try to trick people into believing we are something that we are not. Maybe we want to impress someone and tell them that we are really rich or smart or strong. We don't want people to think that we are a baby or poor or a chicken.

So we hide our feelings or who we really are. Maybe someone hurts us by calling us names, and instead of walking away we pretend we are tougher than they are and call them a worse name. Have any of you ever watched PeeWee Herman? Do you know how he and his friend always call each other names, and the names keep getting worse and worse. But neither one of them wants to admit that they are hurt by the names or that they really only want to be friends. This is a time when wearing a mask isn't a very good idea.

God doesn't want us to hide our feelings and who we really are from others. God knows who we really are and what we are feeling. We can talk to God about our hurts even when we don't think anyone else would understand how we are feeling. God does, and he's always willing to listen to us. And God doesn't want us to hide our feelings or who we really are, because that is lying. And when we lie it usually hurts us more than anyone else. Can you remember next time someone hurts you that you don't have to hide your feelings by fighting back and that God understands those kinds of hurts?—Kara Vander Schaaf.

February 4. We Want to See God

A mother was putting her little child to bed at night, as we have all done many times, when the child suddenly realized that he was to be left alone in the darkness.

"Mother, am I to be left all alone in the dark?"

"Yes, my dear, but you know you have God with you all the time."

"Yes, I know that God is here with me, but I want somebody who has a face."

The child's desire was, and is, a universal desire. Everyone of us, child and adult, has felt at times that he wanted a God who has a face, who seems real, like a mother or a father, to stay with him in dark hours, whether those dark hours were the dark hours of childhood, when the lights were suddenly turned out in a room, or they were the dark hours of loneliness, death, tragedy, and sorrow. We want something that we can feel and hear and see and touch for our God at such times.

Jesus himself once said, "He that hath seen me hath seen the Father." And he also was answering the world-old desire of humanity to see its God with a face. In fact, that is the real reason that God sent his only begotten Son to this earth—that humanity might see the face of God in human form.—William L. Stidger

February 11. God Is Thinking about You

How many of you get tucked into bed at night by your parents? What do they say to you when they tuck you in? Do they ever say the same thing to you night after night?

My mommy used to always say, "I'll see you in my dreams." Does anyone know what she meant by that?

She meant that she loved me so much that she always was thinking about me, and even when she was sleeping she could dream about me. I know she dreamed about me, because she talked in her sleep and sometimes she would say my name. I don't know that she was always thinking about me though, or that I was always her main concern, because I had other brothers and sisters that she had to think about also. I know that sometimes when she was talking on the phone and I would want her attention, she would ignore me. So then I know she wasn't just thinking about me but had other things on her mind. But that was OK, because she was a busy lady. She had to work and cook and shop for us, and those things are important, too.

I do know, however, that I am always in God's thoughts. Did you know that God is always watching over each one of us, all at the same time! I don't know how God does it, but it's true. Even during those times when our parents can't be with us or talk to us, God is always there. God is always willing to listen to what we have to say. God loves us very much and wants to hear our prayers and talk to us. So next time you think that no one wants to talk to you and you feel like nobody cares, remember that God is there and that God cares about you.—Kara Vander Schaaf

February 18. God Knows Your Name
TEXT: Matt. 10:30

Main truth: God knows everything about you.

Interest objects: Name tags. These can be anything from paper to leather luggage tags or anything in between.

Memory makers: A name tag for each child. Inexpensive plastic ones are available from vending machine suppliers, or make your own!

Once I heard about a little boy saying the Lord's Prayer. Only he got it wrong. He didn't say, as you're supposed to, "Our Father, who art in heaven, hallowed be thy name" (Matt. 6:9). Instead, he prayed, "Our Father, who art in heaven, how'd you know my name?"

That's funny! But it also reminds us that God does know your name. God knows the name of every person on earth, all four billion of us!

But there's something even more surprising than that. God knows everything about you. Matt. 10:30 says, "But even the hairs on your head are numbered." Can you imagine that? God knows how many hairs each of us has. Some of us keep him busy each day subtracting!

A God who knows your name and the number of hairs must know everything about you: all the good and bad; all that makes you sad and glad; all your hopes and fears, loves and hates. God knows. There's nothing about you God doesn't know.

A God who knows you that well must care a great deal about you. God loves you. That's why he knows about you. He loves you not because of your goodness but in spite of your badness. God loves you, just as you are. Warts and all!

And do you know what God wants? He wants you to know and love him. Know all you can about him. Love him as he loves you.

Take a name tag. It will help you remember—God knows your name and ev-

erything about you. He loves you. He wants you to know and love him.—Roy E. DeBrand

February 25. God Works in Your Life
Preparation: Select photographs of an individual—i.e., baby pictures, the first day of school, the present, etc.

Have you ever planted a seed and watched it grow into a flower? If you have, then you know that it takes things like sunshine, water, and time for it to grow. We all know that plants are not the only things that grow up. People do also. You might find it hard to believe that I was ever your size or that you will ever be an adult. However, with time, you will grow up. In case you're a bit skeptical, I have some proof. Here is one of the cutest baby pictures I've ever seen. Can you guess who that person is? After a few years, this baby grew into a toddler. Can you tell from this picture who the person is? [Continue with the pictures you have until you show them a current picture. You might introduce the person to the group also.] It's hard to believe that this is the same person who is in all of these pictures. People go through many changes between the time that they are born and the time they grow up.

There are probably days when you wonder if you're ever going to get to go to high school, right? There are probably some days when our seniors wondered if they were ever going to get to graduate from high school. One of the wonderful things about God's love is that the same God who was with that little baby about eighteen years ago has been with her every year since, even to this very day. When she was scared of the dark, God was with her. When she was afraid to go to a new school, God helped her see that things would be OK. When she was lonely, God taught her about how to make new friends with people who needed friends. When she was happy, God was excited with her. Now that she's graduating and going to a new school, God will still be with her, helping her continue to grow and learn.

When Paul wrote the Philippian church he said he was confident that God, who had begun a good work in them, would carry it on to completion. Those are great words. They give us a good picture of a God who keeps working in us, helping us grow into the kind of people he wants us to be. Remember that God is working in you whenever you get upset with yourself. He was with you when you were just a baby, and he will continue to be with you as you grow. We can be confident that he will be there and never leave us.—Carol Younger

March 4. What Do You Want to Be When You Grow Up?

Interest objects: Ceramic molds or any products that have been formed in a mold.

[Ask the children, "What do you want to be when you grow up?" Give each child an opportunity to speak into the microphone.]

As a boy I wanted to be several things when I grew up. My first longing was to be an astronaut and fly to the moon and perhaps even to Mars. Then I wanted to go west and become a cowboy, riding horses in a rodeo—the only problem is that I never learned to ride a horse.

Once I asked my dad what he thought I should be as a grown-up. His answer was, "Well, son, I don't know anything that would have more purpose than being a preacher." I laughed and said, "Oh, come on and tell me what you really think." Of course, here I am now as a preacher and thankful to serve God in this way.

Have you ever heard of Tom Thumb? [Allow a moment for response.] Tom never grew any bigger than his father's thumb. However, through several experiences the little fellow grew up inside. Tom was sold to two men who wanted him for a carnival act, but soon he escaped into a mouse hole. After sleeping a night on a pile of hay, he was eaten by a cow. After working himself out of the cow's stomach, a wolf swallowed him. Not long afterwards he called for his father, who killed the wolf and cut it open with an axe, saving his son's life. Tom grew a great deal, not physically, but in other ways.

Do you know that the way we grow depends a lot on what we experience? This mold determines the shape of the plaster that goes into it. It's the same with your life. The knowledge, for example, you put into your mind shapes ideas and attitudes. Actions and ways of doing things grow from your thoughts. You can form good or bad habits based on what you choose to learn and how you act on what you are taught.

The boy Jesus, at age twelve, was in the Temple. Luke the apostle tells us Jesus continued to "increase in wisdom and in stature, and in favor with God and man" (Luke 2:52). That means even Jesus grew intellectually and physically as well as spiritually and socially. [Illustrate these four types of growth.] He grew up to be the Savior of the world. Jesus wants you to keep growing, too, so you can know what God wants you to be when you grow up.—Ron Blankenship

March 11. Learning to Be Disciples

Object: Some type of model.

When you want to learn how to do something, how do you go about learning it? For example, let's say I want to put this model together but I don't know how because I've never done something like it before? [Wait for answers like read the instructions, ask a friend, and ask someone who had done it before to help you.]

You know that is why we are all here today. We all want to learn something. Does anyone know what that is? We are learning how to be followers of Jesus. What are followers of Jesus called? Disciples. At church we read the Bible, which is our instruction book because it tells us all about God and being a disciple of God's. Then we have Sunday school, where we learn with our friends all about the Bible and how to understand it. And finally, we have the example of our teachers and pastor to show us by how they live to be a disciple of Jesus. The next time you are learning something new at school or with friends, can you remember that at church you are learning, too? At church you are learning to be a disciple of Jesus.—Kara Vander Schaaf

March 18. We Need Practice

Object: A small bicycle.

How many of you can ride a bike?

Who can't ride a bike? Could I have one of you who just raised your hand come over here and ride this bike for me right now? [Let them try, or if no one wants to try, go on with this.] Why can't————ride this bike? If they don't know how, then could someone here tell them how to ride and then we will let them have another chance after they know how. OK? (Let some of the kids explain how to ride a bike.] OK. Now do you think you can ride this bike? No? Well, do you think that if we went to the library for a book on riding a bike it would help? I'll bet if we did that you would be able to ride a bike! No? Why not? [Let the kids explain that you need some help and practice as well as being big enough to learn how to ride a bike.]

So you have to know how to ride a bike and then practice until you can do it without falling? Did you know being a disciple of Jesus can be like riding a bike? Today is Promotion Sunday, and you are all going to move up into an older Sunday school class.

The purpose of Sunday school is to help you become a disciple of Jesus. We have talked before about being a disciple. In Sunday school they teach you about God and Jesus and how much they love you—so much that Jesus died for our sins so we could be in heaven with him one day.

But, did you know that going to Sunday school doesn't make us a disciple of Jesus? Knowing all about God doesn't make us a Christian either. Do you know what does? Going home from Sunday school and telling your family and friends about Jesus is what makes us a disciple of Jesus. Just like knowing how to ride a bike doesn't mean you can do it, it takes practice, and it is actually riding the bike that matters. And just like sometimes you get hurt riding a bike, sometimes as a Christian, people will make fun of you and try to hurt your feelings. But some will listen to you and come to know Jesus because of you. That is worth any kind of hurt anyone tries to do to you.—Kara Vander Schaaf

March 25. Something's Missing

Object: A ballpoint pen.

How many of you know what this is? Of course, it's a ballpoint pen. I'll bet you've used one—or at least you've seen Mommy

or Daddy using one before. Do you know what's inside it? Let's take a look.

See these different parts? Now this is not something you want to do with your pens at home, but we wanted to be able to see what's inside one today. Now let's put it back together again. [As you reassemble the pen, leave out the ink cartridge/refill.]

Let's see how it works. [Try to write on scratch pad.] Something's wrong here—it won't write. Why do you suppose it won't write? [One of the children will probably guess it, but if not, show them the cartridge and then ask again.]

It won't write because there's something very important missing—the ink! Without ink, a pen won't write, will it?

Did you know that people's lives are like that, too? When Jesus isn't in our hearts, there's something very important missing, and our lives just can't be as special and wonderful as God wants them to be. A life without Jesus is like a pen without ink—the most important thing of all is missing.

I hope that you won't be like that pen. Make sure that you always have Jesus in your heart so that he can make your life the best possible life it can be.—Michael Duduit

April 1. Starting Over

Objects: Building blocks.

Could I have a couple of you help me build a house with these building blocks? [Start building the house and then half way through smash it down.] This house looks ugly. The walls were all crooked, and it didn't even look like a house. If my house isn't going to look perfect then I don't want to build one! I wanted it to be the most beautiful house, but it looked stupid so I'm not going to build anymore houses! OK? Let's just quit right now, OK? [By this time some kids will begin to shake their heads no and disagree with you.]

Why shouldn't we quit? Why not, it's an ugly house! [Let them respond.] You mean we should keep building and with practice we could build a beautiful house? I'm sure that you are right and that we could build a very beautiful house with the blocks because I have so much help and so many good ideas.

You know, sometimes I feel like not being a Christian anymore! It seems like God asks me to do SO much for him, and I keep messing up. I'm afraid that God has given up on me. That really worries me because I just can't do it all, and then I don't think that he loves me anymore. Do you think that is true? [Let them respond.] God does still love me? How do you know? [Let them respond.]

You know what? You are absolutely right! It says in the Bible that God loves us and that as long as we give him our best he will not give up on us. And even when we do mess up, God is still going to love us and will offer us another chance. You remember that next time you make a mistake and feel like giving up. God loves you and will forgive you for any mistakes, and he knows that sometimes we need to do things several times before we get them right.—Kara Vander Schaaf

April 8. Will We Welcome Him?

Object: Palm branch or a picture of one.

It's Palm Sunday. That's not something only celebrated in Florida, where there are palm trees! We remember Palm Sunday because of something that happened many years ago.

As Jesus was entering Jerusalem, the people came out to welcome him as their king. They gathered on each side of the road, and as Jesus approached, riding on a donkey, the people laid palm branches—like this one—on the road in front of him. It was like they were preparing the way, honoring him as the arriving king.

The problem is, they found out he wasn't the kind of king they had in mind at all. They wanted someone who would raise an army and solve their problems by force. Jesus wouldn't be that kind of king. He knew that the only way you really solve problems is in your heart. They wanted Jesus to wear a crown, but he knew God had sent him to carry a cross.

So by the end of the week the crowd that had laid palm branches in Jesus' path was screaming, "Crucify him! Crucify him!" as they put Jesus on trial. What an incredible difference a week made!

The people of Jerusalem made their decision about Jesus. Many rejected him, but some realized the truth of what he said and believed.

Each one of us also must decide what we will do with Jesus. No one can decide for you; no one else can give you faith. You must decide for yourself if you will allow Jesus to live in your heart; you must decide if you will live for him.

Palm Sunday is when they prepared the way for Jesus. Will you prepare the way for him into your heart?—Michael Duduit

April 15. Becoming

Object: Bring into the sanctuary a branch with some buds on it.

Boys and girls I have brought a branch from a tree with me today. Want to see it? [Let the children examine it.]

I want you to look carefully at the little buds. Here they are on the ends. Do you know what the buds are? [Wait for response.] That's right, these buds are tender little shoots. If they keep growing they will become flowers. Spring flowers. They make the world beautiful.

Weeks ago you couldn't even see the buds on the tree. It was so cold and there were no leaves on the trees. But it got warmer. And slowly the buds started just popping out everywhere.

That's the way it is every Easter. After the cold and the winter storms, the weather gets warmer and the buds come back. God gives the growth to the trees and to our lives.

That first Easter, people didn't understand what happened at the open tomb. They were scared. But Jesus came back, like a dead tree with the little buds. Jesus began to move around the world and change and be with people everywhere.

This is the real meaning of Easter. After a time that seems so cold and so dark, everything changes. Jesus is not dead. The cross did not kill him. Like the bud, he comes back. And those that follow him bloom again and again.—Roger Lovette

April 22. When the Stone Was Rolled Away

Object: Stone.

I'll bet everyone knows what this is. That's right, it's a stone. Maybe you have some in your yard or maybe arranged nicely around a garden.

Stones are used for many things. They're used in gravel, to make things like roads and driveways. Have you ever been on a gravel road out in the country? It's pretty bumpy, isn't it? Larger stones are used to make houses sometimes or maybe a wall around a fireplace. There are lots of uses for stones.

Many years ago, a very large stone was used for a sad purpose. On Good Friday, Jesus had been crucified. He gave his life for our sins. When they put him in a tomb that was dug into the side of a cave, they rolled a big, heavy stone in front of the tomb to protect it. No one could come in or out.

But do you know what happened that first Easter Sunday morning? When Jesus' friends came to the tomb, they found the big stone rolled away, and Jesus was gone! An angel told them that Jesus had risen from the dead!

That's why we celebrate Easter—the day when Jesus rose from the dead. Because of him, we can have a wonderful life here on earth and then life with God forever after this life.

Whenever you see a stone, think about the big stone that was rolled away so that the disciples could see that Jesus was alive!—Michael Duduit

April 29. A New Member of the Family

Object: A new kitten or puppy that belongs to one of the children. I used the pastor's new puppy, so all the kids knew the dog's name.

Who knows who this is? [Let them respond. If using one of the children's pets, let them tell a little about their new pet.] This is a special pet for you isn't it? You know it's almost like a new member of your family now. You have to take care of it by feeding it and giving it baths and giving it exercise by playing with it. I'll bet you even talk to your pet once in a while, just like it is a real person. Your pet has become a part of your family, and you love each other, don't you? Your pet has become like another brother or sister or child in your family.

Did you know that today when we had our Baptism we added a new person into our church family? When that child was baptized they became a part of us. We are now their family. How do family members act toward each other? [Let the children respond with things like love each other, take care of each other, play together, talk to each other, eat with each other, make sure they have everything that they need.] That's right! We need to make sure that we welcome this new member into our family by talking to them and taking care of them. When you get hurt, do your parents ignore you? Or if you need new clothes, do your parents tell you to take care of it yourself? [Let them respond to this.] Of course not! Your parents love you and are going to make sure that you have everything that you need. Well, now God wants us to make this new person just like a member of our family. Do you think you can do this? You now have a new brother or sister in your family. That's pretty neat, isn't it?—Kara Vander Schaaf

May 6. The Light of the World

Object: Light bulb.

Who knows what this is? [Show the light bulb.]

That's right, this is a light bulb. Your parents put them in lamps or in light fixtures in the ceiling. You've seen these before, haven't you?

Do you know what light bulbs do?

That's right. They light up the room. That might not seem so important during the daytime when the sun lights up things, but can you imagine how dark it would be in your house at night if it wasn't for light bulbs? You couldn't see to read or write or even walk without bumping into the walls!

Light is important to our lives. That's why the Bible calls Jesus the Light of the World. Just as we couldn't see in the dark without light, in the same way we couldn't see the right way to go in life without Jesus. He helps us know where to go, what to do, and how to live. Without Jesus, our lives would be just like someone wandering in the dark with no light.

So tonight as you get ready to turn out the light and go to sleep, think about Jesus and thank him for being our light all the time, day and night.—Michael Duduit

May 13. A Mother Always
TEXT: Gal. 3:26

Visual introduction: Mother's Day card.

Sentence summary: While children may grow to be adults, they will always remain children to both God and Mother.

This is Mother's Day, a special time when we give honor and respect to Mother. Everyone of us begins life on earth with a mother. We cannot be born on earth except through a mother's body. That is God's plan.

If a woman follows God, she can become a very special person through motherhood. Mothers deliver us in birth, feed us, diaper us, and help us to grow up into strong adults. No matter how famous we may become, no matter how important or strong, we still remain a child to the mother who loves us.

The most famous man in all of Europe during the 1800s was Napoleon Bonaparte. With the French armies behind him, he conquered all of Europe and declared himself emperor. That's like a king. Emperor Napoleon decided that no one could enter his presence without first kissing his hand. That was the old way that people showed their respect for a king. Because people were afraid of Napoleon, they would bow and kiss his hand.

But one woman refused to kiss his hand, even when he extended it to her. She slapped his hand very hard and told the famous general that to her he was still just a mere child. Do you know who that woman was? Of course you do. That was Napoleon's own mother, who reminded him that she had raised eight children—and he was just one of the eight.

That was a very good lesson for Napoleon to learn. We are always someone's child. The Bible teaches us that God looks upon us as little children. The best thing we can do is to become children of God. That happens when we trust Jesus Christ as Savior. We are born again and become like little children. "For ye are all the children of God by faith in Christ Jesus."—C. W. Bess

May 20. Doing Something for God
One thing that most children have in common is their use of this sentence: "I'm bored. There is nothing to do." Most of you say that your favorite days are Saturdays and school holidays when you have free time to do whatever you want to do. But how many of you have ever complained to your parents during a break from school that you had nothing to do? Today I want to help you solve your problem of boredom. I want to present to you two things that are incredible tools to keep you from being bored. With these two tools, you may accomplish amazing things.

If you look down, you will find these marvelous instruments attached to your arms at the wrist. They are called hands. Here is how they work. "I'm bored," you say. Then look around, pick up a pen, and use those hands to write a letter. Write someone who needs to get a letter or someone you miss or someone you appreciate. "I'm bored," you tell me again. Then pick up a telephone. Use those incredible fingers and call someone who is lonely or check on an elderly person. "I'm bored," you still persist. Then keep your hands busy by doing something for your family—whether it's housework or yardwork or creating a new game or a piece of artwork. If you make sure your hands are busy doing something good, your level of boredom will surely decrease.

When Saul was waiting to become the king of Israel, Samuel gave him instructions about what to do in the meantime. Samuel told him that he should do whatever his hands found to do, for God was with him. Samuel did not want Saul to do nothing while he was waiting for the next thing to happen. He wanted him to be busy doing good things for God. You and I have lots of times in our lives when we're waiting for something to happen. If we're not careful, we might waste time while we wait. Just like Saul, we should look for whatever our hands find to do and do it, because God is with us also.—Carol Younger

May 27. Play Ball!
Object: Baseball.

One of the best things about spring and

summer is that baseball season is back. I'll bet some of you watch baseball on television, or maybe you even get to go to the game. In fact, I'll bet some of you will even be playing baseball this summer!

Have you ever taken a baseball bat up to home plate, watched that pitcher throw the ball, and swung that bat to hit it? That's my favorite part of playing baseball—getting to hit the ball.

But when you're first learning to play baseball, getting up to bat can be awfully scary. That's because you're just learning to hit, and you're afraid if you don't do well people won't want you on the team, and you're afraid you'll let down your teammates. Being a hitter can be scary.

But do you know something? The very best baseball player in the major leagues was once just like that—starting out, scared of messing up, afraid of letting down his team. How did those star players get so good at baseball? They practiced. They kept at it. They didn't let their fear get in the way of what they wanted to do. So even though they were scared, they kept working and trying and learning.

That's the way it is in many things in life. Even though our parents or teachers are helping us, we may still be scared, afraid that we can't do it. But with the help of parents and teachers and others who love us—and with the help of God who cares for us and gives us the strength and courage we need—we can accomplish many things.—Michael Duduit

June 3. A Great Day in Jerusalem
TEXT: Acts 2:14–47

Many people filled the streets of Jerusalem. The wheat harvest was over. The Jews were ready to celebrate a special feast called Pentecost.

Many Christians were gathered for worship. Suddenly, an unusual thing happened. The Christians received a special gift of God's Spirit. They were excited. The disciples began to tell the people in the streets about Jesus.

Peter began to preach. He said, "Jesus is the one you killed. But he is not dead. God brought him back to life. Jesus wants you to love him. he wants you to be his followers."

The people were worried and asked, "What should we do?"

Peter replied, "Each one of you must turn from sin. Turn toward God. Be baptized as a sign that you have been forgiven. This will show that you are a follower of Christ."

As Peter preached, the people listened and believed what he said. Three thousand people were baptized. They became church members. The new Christians met in homes to learn more about Jesus. They worshiped God, shared their food, and prayed.—*Exploring*

June 10. God's Vacation

Summertime is coming fast, isn't it? Summer is such an exciting time—school is out, the weather is warm, the daylight lasts longer so there's more time to play.

One thing that many people do in the summer is take vacations. How many of you are going to have a vacation this summer?

What happens on a vacation? When we talk about going on a vacation, we often mean we are going to take several days to go on a trip and get away from the regular, everyday things we do when we're at home. When you're on vacation, you don't go to work or do homework or some of those other regular chores, do you?

Do you know who never goes on vacation? God never takes a vacation from loving us, caring for us, keeping our world running, looking after our needs. Just think how terrible it would be if God took a vacation: there'd be no sun to warm us and no stars to light the evening sky; there'd be no love to share, no answers to our prayers.

Our world is totally dependent on God's power, and our lives are totally dependent on his love. Aren't you glad that God never takes a vacation from taking care of us? And we never have to take a vacation from loving him.—Michael Duduit

June 17. What Kind of Dad Do You Want?

Two boys were arguing over who had the best dad. The first boy said that his dad could beat up his friend's dad. They argued back and forth. Fairly soon they quit that line of argument. They realized that their dads would never agree to a fight. One boy said that his father was smarter than the other one. They argued again. Finally, the first boy said, "Let me tell you how great my dad is. If there is anything I want, he will buy it for me. Whenever I see a toy that I want, he makes sure I have it. I probably have more things to play with than anyone. And whatever I ask my dad to do, he does it, just like I asked." The second boy thought a minute. "Well," he said, "My father doesn't buy me everything I want. Sometimes he tells me no. And he doesn't do everything I ask him to do. But he does spend time with me. He plays with me when I feel lonely. When I'm upset, he makes me feel better. I know that he loves me." The boys stopped arguing. Maybe the first one realized that the second dad gave his son the very best gifts.

God is our heavenly Father. Sometimes we wish that he was the kind of father who would give us anything we wanted whenever we wanted it. Sometimes we wish that he would do anything we asked him to do. Most of the time, God is like the second kind of father. Sometimes he tells us no. He doesn't give us everything we want. Sometimes bad things happen that we didn't want to have happen. He doesn't do everything we tell him to do. But he is always with us. He can help us enjoy the things that we do have and be grateful for them. When we are lonely, he will spend time with us. When we feel sad, he will comfort us and make us feel better. He is always there and always loving us. We might think sometimes that we want God to be like the first kind of father. But that isn't really the best kind. Let's thank God that he loves us enough to give us the very best gifts—like his love and his time and his presence.—Carol Younger

June 24. How to Find Buried Treasure

Object: A jar of seashells. Explain how living things used to live inside the dead seashells. In the same way, the Spirit of Christ lives inside of the Christian's body.

Have you heard of a book entitled *Treasure Island?* It is about a boy named Jim Hawkins who makes friends with an old sailor known as "the captain." An unfortunate accident took "the captain's" life. As Jim was going through the old sailor's belongings, he came across a map leading to buried treasure on a desert island. Jim and some friends chartered a boat and set sail for Treasure Island. After going through a lot of trouble, they found the treasure chest full of ruby necklaces, gold doubloons, and other valuable items and brought them back home.

Paul the apostle said that everyone who has Christ as a personal friend has buried treasure inside. Listen to his words: "We have this treasure in earthen vessels . . ." (2 Cor. 4:7). In the same way that a treasure chest contains priceless pieces of jewelry and money, so the abundance of Christ's Spirit lives in the heart of everyone who believes he died on the cross and was made alive again by God.

Finding such a wonderful treasure as Jesus Christ living in your life ought to make you happier than digging buried treasure on a deserted island.

Think how joyful the lion in the *Wizard of Oz* was when he discovered courage inside of himself; or the scarecrow upon realizing he had a brain after all; or the tin man who felt his own heart beating inside of his chest; or Dorothy when she found home was inside of her all the time.

Jesus told a story about a farmer who accidentally uncovered a treasure chest while plowing a field. In his joy he went and sold all he owned to buy the whole field so that the treasure could be his. I hope you will feel the same joy over finding the buried treasure of Jesus Christ inside of you.—Ron Blankenship

July 1. Whose Side Are You On?

[Appropriate for a service that includes Baptism.]

Objects: A variety of objects that symbolize "choosing sides"—sports items, political bumper stickers, an engagement ring, etc.

Today I brought an assortment of things I want to show you. [Hold up each item and tell what it is. If there is a school or team rivalry in your area, bring an article representing each team.] Does anyone know what all of these things have in common? They tell what side the person wearing them is on. For instance, could you imagine someone who wears this letter jacket cheering for the team who wears these tee shirts? Do you think that someone with this bumper sticker on the car would vote for this person? The way we act tells people which side we are on also. If you had this pennant on your wall but were a fair-weather fan and liked another team better, you wouldn't really be on this team's side, would you? It's important to people to choose sides and to tell other people which side they are on. It's fun to support a certain team or cause. People who choose the same side usually enjoy being together and rooting for their team.

The Bible talks about choosing sides. Early in the Old Testament, in Joshua 24: 15, Joshua tells the people to "choose this day whom you will serve." Jesus tells us that we have to make a choice about whom we will follow, because "a person can not serve two masters."

Baptism is a way in which people who have decided to follow Jesus tell the church family "whose side they are on." As a church we want to give our support to any new Christian. We need the talents and gifts this person offers us, and we offer him or her the love and ministry of our church. Choosing to follow Jesus is a serious decision. When we decide to follow him, we try to live our lives as he would want us to. The decision means that we will make certain choices because we want to follow Christ. Following him affects our words and our actions. Everyday you have choices that let you show whose side you are on: when you see someone who needs your help at school, and you help them; when you have the choice of being patient with your little brother or just giving up; when you have the opportunity to either ask a friend to church or just not say anything about it. Your choices are important. Let's pray that God will help us make the right decisions.—Carol Younger

July 8. Excuses

[Arrange for three parents to join you for the children's sermon. Prepare them ahead of time for the questions you will ask.]

Today I have three experts with me. These three people are parents, and parents are experts at hearing excuses. Children have a way of making great excuses. First of all, could you tell me the best excuse your children have for not eating their vegetables? [Let each parent give an excuse.] What are the most creative excuses you've heard for their not doing their homework? [Have each parent answer the question.] Finally, could you tell us the best excuses you've heard from your children for not going to sleep? [Allow each parent to answer once again.] Thank you, experts.

Children are not the only ones who make excuses. Jesus told a story about adults who gave excuses. A man was giving a big party, and he invited all of his friends to come. However, they all gave him excuses why they wouldn't be there. So instead, he invited people who would come—poor people, lonely people, people who didn't have friends at all. It turned out to be a wonderful banquet. Which group of people do you think acted like real friends to the man who gave the party?

Jesus has invited us to follow him. Sometimes we make all kinds of excuses for not following. Maybe we're too busy or we want to do something else first. Maybe we just don't want to follow. The truth is that there are no good excuses for not following Jesus. There is nothing more important that we could do than to try to be Christians. When we make excuses, we are the ones who miss out. Like the rich man's friends who missed the wonderful party, we miss out on a joyful life with Christ.—Carol Younger

July 15. Take Your Temperature

Object: Thermometer.

I'm sure most of you know what this is. It's a thermometer. Your mom or dad or a nurse uses it to take your temperature when you're not feeling well. By taking your temperature, they can check up to find out just how sick you might be.

You always want to make sure that a grown-up helps you with taking your temperature, since thermometers are very delicate and you have to take extra-special care of them. But they're also very helpful, aren't they?

Did you know that the Bible sometimes can be used as a spiritual thermometer? That's right—it can help us check up on our spiritual health, to make sure our lives are what God wants them to be.

Do you know how that happens? It happens as we read our Bibles and as God's Spirit helps us understand what the words mean in our own lives. The Bible is God's letter to us; he sent it because he loves us and wants us to know how to live in a way that is best for us.

And as we read God's Word every day, we get a regular "check up" as God helps us take our spiritual temperature.

So the next time you have your temperature taken, remember how important it is to read God's Word and have our spiritual temperature checked also.—Michael Duduit

July 22. Doing Things Together

Object: A pocket electronic baseball game.

[Begin by not saying anything, just sit and play the game and then start saying things you would say at a ball game, like, "Come on, run!" "No way was that out!" Do this for about a minute.]

What is this? You're right—it's a baseball game, and it's great! It's just like playing a real game of baseball! This is exactly like a real baseball game! Don't you think so? [By now most kids will be getting bored and will say, "NO!" If not, keep on playing the game by yourself or ask one of the older kids if they want to play and tell them how much like a real baseball game this is.] What would we need to really play a baseball game? [They will suggest things like a bat, ball, gloves, and a field.] Oh, I see. We need all those things to play a baseball game. So if———and I had all those things we could go and play a baseball game? Well, why not? We would have everything you need to play a ball game. What more do we need? [Get them to answer, "Other people to play with."]

You know you are right. We wouldn't have much of a game with only two of us playing. It wouldn't matter if we had all the equipment and a huge stadium to play in if we didn't have a team and an opponent. Did you know church is kind of like that? Church is not just a building or an organ or a communion table. A church is people. It is people coming together to praise God and to be friends with each other. We are not here to sit by ourselves and listen to the pastor talk. We are here to praise God as a group of people who all love God.—Kara Vander Schaaf

July 29. The Woman at the Well

It was almost noon. Jesus was thirsty and tired from walking all morning. While Jesus sat down beside Jacob's well to rest, his friends went to town to buy some food for lunch. As Jesus rested, a Samaritan woman quickly walked up to the well. She lifted a heavy water jar from her shoulder and set it beside the well. As she began to draw the water, a voice said, "Please give me a drink of water." She looked up and saw Jesus sitting beside the well.

The woman was surprised. "You are a Jew, and I am a Samaritan! How can you ask me for a drink?" the woman asked. "Jews do not have anything to do with Samaritans. Why are you asking me for a drink of water?" she asked.

Jesus understood why the woman said those words. He answered, "If you only knew the gift God gives and who I am, you would ask for life-giving water."

"Sir," the woman said, "give me water which lasts forever."

Jesus talked kindly to the woman. Suddenly she said, "I think that you are a prophet." Then the woman asked some questions about worship and about God. The woman said, "I believe that a Savior will come and explain all of this to us."

Jesus said to the woman, "I am the Savior."

Then the woman set her water jug down beside the well. She turned and ran back to town and told everyone she met, "Come and meet the man who told me everything I have ever done. I believe that he is the Savior. Come!"

The people she spoke to left their chores and hurried to Jacob's well to meet Jesus.—*Exploring 1*

August 5. God Provides for Us

Object: A seashell.

[Give each child a small seashell to keep.]

I want you to describe what you have in your hand. [Let the children respond with their descriptions.] Isn't it pretty? What was it once used for? You know, I think these shells are very pretty. Do you know who made these shells so beautiful for our sea friends to live in? [Let them answer.]

God did, that's right. God provided the snails and other creatures with beautiful homes and furs for protection. And we humans have to work so hard to make ourselves beautiful or gorgeous. We buy all kinds of clothes and hair stuff, and some buy makeup. We do this all so we look great, and we think people will like us more if we look great. But the Bible tells us not to worry about what we wear or eat. If God provides the animals and plants with beauty, then he will make us all the more beautiful. And you know what? God thinks you are beautiful just the way you are. And if we follow God, he will provide us with what we really need just as he does for our sea friends.—Kara Vander Schaaf

August 12. How Badly Do You Want It?

TEXT: Matt. 15:21–28

Object: A doctor's prescription.

Boys and girls, have any of you ever wished you could become a doctor? [Let them answer.] Learning to be a doctor is hard work. You have to go to school for a long time and understand a lot of things about how the human body works and how to heal it. But doctors get to do important things when they are finished learning how to be a doctor.

Sometimes a doctor can save a person's life. If you need a special kind of medicine that can't be bought in drug stores, a doctor can give you one of these. What is this? [Hold up the prescription.] What is the prescription good for? [Talk about it.] That's right. It gives the person who has it the right to buy the kind of medicine they need from the drug store. The drug store will not sell some kinds of medicine without a prescription because it could be dangerous if you use it the wrong way or if you take some when you shouldn't have it.

This means that the doctor has a lot of power, doesn't it? Suppose you or I went to the doctor and said, "I'm sick. I need some special medicine. Please give me a prescription," and the doctor said, "I'm sorry. I can only give prescriptions to people who have red skin." What would you think of that? [Talk about it.] You're right. That would not seem fair.

Did you know that there is a Bible story just like that? Jesus was healing people who were sick. He was almost like a doctor who came from God. And everybody was coming to Jesus with their sickness because they knew he could heal them. But Jesus was a Jew, and he was only healing Jewish people, since they were the people God had sent him to. A woman who was not a Jew wanted some healing. But Jesus said to her, "I'm sorry, I'm helping Jews get well. And you are not a Jew."

If you had been that woman, what would you have said? [Talk about it.] The woman must have asked herself, "How badly do I want this help?" She decided she wanted it badly enough to beg Jesus. So she did. And Jesus saw she had great faith and gave her what she wanted. That's the way God wants you and me to trust God, too. He wants us to have strong faith and come to God and depend on him when we have trouble. And he'll help us.

August 19. Joining the Club

Objects: Small light bulb, six-inch ruler, and a vial of water. Written in the first person because it is true, this sermon may be adapted by anyone.

During seminary days I was invited to join a study club on campus. I wanted to belong, so I was pleased to be accepted for initiation in a secret ceremony. Boys and girls go through such ceremonies when they become Scouts or Brownies.

I was blindfolded and seated in a chair which was encircled by club members. The president placed an object in my hand [place a light bulb in your hand] and said in a serious voice, "What are you now holding in your hand?" I felt it carefully and replied that it was a light bulb. He said that I was correct. Then he began to talk about light and how the purpose of this club was to enlighten.

Immediately I understood that I was not joining a group which collected or sold light bulbs. The bulb was a symbol of a truth about my mind, learning new things. Sometimes, in the comic strips, a boy or girl gets a new idea, and the artist draws a light bulb shining over the head. So the bulb in my hand represented a higher truth.

Next the leader handed me a ruler. [Display ruler.] When I identified it, he talked about the straightness and doing right. He said that our club stood for right behavior and that there were standards of measurement to follow. I could, therefore, not do anything I pleased and still be a member. I understood that and that the ruler represented a truth. Again it was a symbol, something that reminds us of something else.

Once again I felt something placed in my hands. [Hold the vial of water.] It was a container of water. Immediately I knew it represented the purity and cleanliness expected of me if I joined the group.

There are hundreds of symbols all around us. Advertising on television shows products that are represented by a design called a logo, which is instantly recognized. The American flag is a symbol of our country. A red cross is the reminder of an organization of mercy. The cross is a symbol of Christianity.

Baptism is one of the important ways we show membership in the church, the family of Christ.

When a person joins Christ's church and is baptized, the symbol of water says that he or she lives with Christ. So all our members have shown the sign (the logo) of having joined his church, and all of us must live as he teaches and as we promised.—J. P. Allen

August 26. Good Things in Our Lives

Objects: A frozen hot dog and in a paper bag the following: a paper plate, napkin, bun, ketchup, mustard, relish, soft drink, and paper cup. Write one of the following words on each of the objects in the bag: love, joy, peace, patience, kindness, goodness, faithfulness, gentleness, and self-control.

Look at this hot dog. Doesn't it look good? Wouldn't you love to eat this hot dog right now? I'll bet this was the best hot dog ever made. How many of you would like to eat this hot dog right now? [Let them raise their hands and choose someone who did not raise their hand.] You didn't raise your hand. Why not? [Let them respond, and they should say that it is gross because it is cold. If not, choose another person until you get that answer.] How many of you think this hot dog would be much better if it were warmer? You mean, if I would heat this hot dog up it would be better? How else could I make this hot dog better? [Let them respond, and as they call out the items in your bag, pull them out.]

So you think this hot dog would be great if I heated it up and put it on a bun, and then added ketchup, mustard, relish, and had a Coke to go with it and then ate it off a plate and had a napkin to clean up the mess with? I think that you are right. We as humans are a little like this hot dog. We are just OK by ourselves but nothing real great. But if we are warmed up with a little love, like heating the hot dog, and wrap ourselves up in joy . . . [put the bun on the hot dog so the children can see the word *joy*]. And then add a little peace, patience, and kindness . . . [hold up the condiment bottles with these words on them as you put them on the hot dog]. Then, if I set my mind on goodness . . . [put hot dog on a plate that has *goodness* written on it]. Then, if I drink a little gentleness out of the cup of faithfulness and wipe up any messes with a little self-control . . . [the cup has *gentleness* on it and the Coke bottle *faithfulness,* and the napkin is *self-control*]. Then, I will be a great and wonderful Christian. All alone we are a little empty and blah. But with a little help from the gifts of the Spirit we can be much better, just as our hot dog is better with a little help. Can you remember to add these qualities to your life: love, joy, peace, patience, kindness, goodness, faithfulness, gentleness, and self-control?—Kara Vander Schaaf

September 2. Labor Day and Love

There's a holiday coming tomorrow, isn't there? That's right, tomorrow we celebrate Labor Day.

That's the day we celebrate all those people who work so hard at their jobs to support their families and to help all of us live a little better. And what better way to celebrate working than by taking a day off!

Many of you have a dad or mom—or maybe both—who go off to work each day. They work hard at their jobs so that we can have food and shelter and the important things in life. And sometimes we have a parent who stays home with us and works hard there, too.

Labor Day would be a good time to say thank you to parents who love and care for us, who work hard to provide for us.

It is also a good time to remember our heavenly Father, who provides so much for us. He gives a world in which to live, air to breathe, food to eat. He loves us more than we will ever know, and we don't thank him and praise him often enough, do we?

So on Labor Day tomorrow, let's show our thanks to those who care so much for us—both our earthly parents and our heavenly Father—Michael Duduit

September 9. Back to School

Object: Pencil box.

It's back-to-school time again, isn't it? All of the stores have been having sales for school clothes and school supplies for weeks now. Those of you who are in school may have already gotten a pencil box like this.

What do you suppose is inside a pencil box? Let's see: pencil, ruler, eraser, pencil sharpener . . .

A pencil box has tools for you to use in school: things to write with and draw with. Without those tools, learning would be a lot harder, wouldn't it?

God has given us some tools to help us in learning to know him better. One of these tools is the Bible, God's Word. The Bible tells us about how God has worked with other people through the years and how he wants to love and help us.

Another tool God gives us to help know him better is prayer—our ability to talk to him anytime, anywhere. Wherever we are, whatever time it is, we can talk to God about our needs, our hurts and can thank him for all his gifts. Prayer is another wonderful tool God gives us.

And when we use these tools—like reading the Bible and prayer—we grow closer and closer to God and know more and more of his love and care for us.—Michael Duduit

September 16. The Importance of Serving

[Arrange for several of the children to have one of their shoes untied when they come forward for the children's sermon.]

Today I want to tell you a story about a time when . . . wait a minute. I need to tie this shoe. [Bend down to tie one of the children's shoes.] Didn't your mom tell you to keep these tied so you won't trip? [Continue the story.] Now, Jesus was sitting down with his disciples at the . . . wait a minute. Here's another shoe to tie. [Kneel down and tie another shoe.] Didn't anyone teach you to tie your shoes? [Continue the story again.] So, there was Jesus with his disciples eating supper, when . . . wait, we have another pair of shoes here waiting to be tied. [Finish tying any shoes that are left before you continue the story.]

You might think that my tying shoes during the middle of the children's sermon today was either silly or strange. If you do, then you probably understand what the disciples must have thought when they were sitting down to supper with Jesus, who was teaching them. All of a sudden, Jesus started to wash their feet. Washing feet was something that needed to be done, but they didn't expect Jesus to do it for them as he was teaching. As he washed their feet, he told them that they should serve other people, just like he was serving them. Jesus cared for people so much that he didn't mind serving, no matter what the job was. Sometimes we are glad to serve, especially when it is something we like to do. But there are some things that need to be done that we don't want to do at all. We think, "Let someone else do that—like my little brother." Jesus showed us that he was willing to do anything to serve us, and we should have that same attitude, too. Because he loves us, we should love others.—Brett Younger

September 23. God Takes Care of Us

Object: Someone dressed up like a clown.

[Have the clown come in to advertise some special event about to happen in the church, like the Sunday school picnic. The clown is very, very happy. The clown comes bouncing up for the children's sermon along with all the other children.]

Hey, what are you doing here? You're too big to be a child! Kids, do you think she's trying to tell us something? Well, let's try and figure out what she is saying. [Have the clown mimic what the event is.] So, is that why you are so happy? No? Why are you so happy then? [Have the clown somehow mimic that Jesus makes her happy. Do this by pointing to the cross or a Bible. And try to let the kids guess her clues.] Jesus makes you happy?

That's right, it says in the Bible that anyone who trusts and believes in Jesus will be happy or have joy in their heart. You can put your trust in all sorts of things or in people, but sooner or later they may let you down. But the Bible tells me that God is always with me and taking care of me. This makes me very happy. Doesn't that make you happy to know that God is always taking care of you and will never leave you?—Kara Vander Schaaf

September 30. God's Family Album

Object: A scrapbook filled with pictures of church members or church events.

Have you ever spent time looking at old pictures of people? Every now and then, especially when I go to my parents' house to visit, I drag out all the old pictures and look at them again. It's fun to see that your younger brother used to be smaller than you or that you all used to dress in funny-looking clothes and wear silly hairstyles.

Today I brought a scrapbook that has pictures of some folks you probably know. [Point out different people and events in your book. Let the children see the pictures.] Each of these pictures has a story to tell. Some of them tell about families who have come into our church. Some show people who came and shared good gifts with us, then moved on. A few pictures show different ways that our church works together and the different ministries we

have. If we put all of these pictures and these stories together, we would be able to tell a story about the life of our church. Many times people say that pictures are the best things they own. Pictures and the stories they tell are important to us.

The Bible tells many stories of the way God loves people and the way that they act toward him. Just as all the pictures in a family album or in our church's scrapbook tell a story, the stories in the Bible tell us how God has continued to love people all through the years. Just as family pictures are important to us, the Bible is something we should treasure. We need to read it and hear its story over and over. After all, it is a story of God and his family. It's a story about you and me.—Carol Younger

October 7. Add a Little Salt

Text: Mark 9:38–50

Object: A saltshaker with salt in it.

Boys and girls, what's your favorite flavor? [Be prepared for a variety of responses.] One of God's good gifts to us is the gift of taste. We can tell the difference between sweet and sour, bland and sharp, chocolate and vanilla, and all the other good flavors that come to us in our food.

Have you ever eaten food that didn't seem to have any flavor? I have. The food may be perfectly good, but we don't like to eat it because it doesn't taste like anything. Even though it may be good for our bodies, if we can't get any taste out of it, we may just stop eating it altogether. Then we lose the good part.

One of the flavors we can add to food that seems to need some is salt. I have some here with me today. We know that you can use too much salt on something if you are not careful. If you use too much salt, it makes your food taste terrible. It could even make you sick. But just the right amount of salt can make things taste better.

God wants our lives to be something like salt. Salt can make a difference and improve the flavor of our food. When we do God's work and help other people to know about God's love, we are like salt. We are helping to make somebody else's life different and to give it some flavor. We don't want to become so noisy about God that people get tired of hearing about him. That would be like putting on too much salt. Then a good thing could begin to taste like a bad thing. But we can do just the right thing when we get a chance. We can share God's love just when people need it. That's like putting salt on your food.

Here is a shaker of salt. If you will hold out your hand, the palm side up, I will shake a little salt on everybody's hand. Then you can taste it. It will remind you of how good salt can be as a flavor in our lives. And it can remind us of what we can be like for other people.—*Children's Sermon Service Plus!*

October 14. World Hunger Day

[You might want to enlist a few youths to act out these situations as you narrate them.]

Imagine that you are sitting down to lunch in an hour or two with a plate that is filled with all of your favorite foods. You cannot wait to get started! Then just as you lift your fork to your mouth, you look across the table and see this person, who is looking hungry and is also looking right at you. What would you do?

Or, imagine you are eating lunch in the school cafeteria. As you open your lunch box, you discover that someone forgot to put anything in it besides a sandwich. Whoever packed your friend's lunch box, however, went wild. In her lunch is everything from Oreos to Pringles. It only takes you a few minutes to finish your peanut butter and jelly. You sit and stare as your friend eats away. What do you think she would do?

A classmate with whom you're doing a school project comes home with you to work on it. You go in the kitchen for an after-school snack. Without thinking, you fix yourself something but forget about your friend. As you work on your home-work, your friend acts like something is wrong. As you munch, you realize what you did. What would you do?

Most of us, if we got into one of these situations, would fix it right away. We've all been taught that it's not polite to eat in front of someone else. When a person is staring at us as we eat, it's easy to offer that

person some food. Unfortunately, for most of us, unless we see someone who is hungry standing right in front of us, we don't think about hungry people very often. Sometimes we forget that there are children and adults who don't have enough to eat.

Today is World Hunger Day. This is a day we set aside to think about people who are hungry. Some of them live in our town. Some of them live in other cities and coun-tries. We need this special day to remind ourselves that there are hungry people who need us to care about them. When we have plenty and other people have little to eat, we need to share with them. Jesus told us that we need to share what we have. In Matthew 25 he tells us that when we do things like give the hungry something to eat and drink or when we give clothes to people who need them or when we visit people who are sick or lonely or in prison, then we are serving him. He says that doing things like this for other people is just like doing them for him. When we do things like this for other people is just like doing them for him. So today, when you give your offering or when you think about hungry people in the world, remember that caring about others is something you can do for Jesus.—Carol Younger

October 21. What Will God Say?

TEXT: 1 Thess. 2:1–8

Object: "Just Say No" button.

Boys and girls, I'll bet you already know how dangerous it can be to use drugs that a doctor didn't ask you to take, don't you? [Let them answer.] We hear about drugs and how dangerous they can be every time we turn around. This is really amazing to some of us adults, because some of us never heard about dangerous drugs that you could get from a friend. Back when we were your age this was not a problem. Back when we were in school—some of us got all the way through high school before there was a problem with drugs—nobody ever talked about it.

But now people are talking about it all the time. And drugs that you can buy from somebody and start using just for fun can be really dangerous. They can even kill you. Have any of you ever heard of any-body who got into real trouble for using drugs? [Let them offer some examples of which they are aware.] It really is a serious problem, isn't it!

The amazing thing is that, even though we all know how dangerous it can be to start using drugs, a lot of people just start doing it anyway. Why do you think that is? [Let them offer some possible answers.] That's right. Sometimes we know something is wrong or dangerous, but we just keep doing it anyway because we want to please somebody else. Our friends may talk us into it. Or we may think that everybody else is doing it, and we want to be like them, so we start doing it, too—even though we know how bad it can be to do it!

Everybody wants to have friends, and there is nothing wrong with trying to be like your friends if being like them is good for us. But sometimes our friends have bad ideas, and trying to do what they do—or what they want us to do—could be the worst possible thing to do. Maybe then we need to change friends. But maybe we need to do something else instead. We need to ask a question. If my friends want me to do one thing, but God wants me to do another, which way shall I go? [Talk about it.] That's right. It might be hard to choose God's way, because our friends may make fun of us, but we know that God's way is always the better way. We can put on one of these. [Put on the "Just Say No" button.] This shows that we are asking the right question. The question to ask is not, "What will my friends say?" but rather "What will God say?" And we know that God would want us to do what is good and healthy.—*Children's Sermon Service Plus!*

October 28. Everything Is Fixed

TEXT: Rom. 3:19–28

Object: A badge that reads, "Jesus loves me."

Boys and girls, have you ever had a time when somebody you wanted to have as your friend got really angry at you? [Talk about this.] How does it feel when that happens? [Let them answer.] It can really be hard on us when somebody we want to like us is angry at us instead. What could we do to fix things?

That's right. We could talk to them and ask them to stop being angry. But they might not do it, especially if they thought they had a good reason. We could beg them. But that might just make them more angry. We could give them a present. But that might not work. We could say to them (or to ourselves), "Well, go ahead and be angry, then. I really don't care if you're my friend or not." But that would not be the truth. And we might still feel bad afterwards.

There was once a young man named Martin Luther. He felt that way about God. He thought God was angry at him. So Martin Luther tried everything he could think of to get God to start being his friend. He couldn't do it, no matter how hard he tried.

Then one day Martin Luther was reading his Bible, and he discovered the words that we have in our Bible reading today. This is what they said: "God puts people right through their faith in Jesus Christ." [Put on the badge.] Martin Luther was amazed. He said to himself, "All this time I have been trying to love God enough to make God love me back. Now I find out that God already loves me through his Son, Jesus. All I have to do is trust Jesus and God will put everything right. He won't be angry with me."

That was an amazing discovery. It helped Martin Luther to get ready to start what we call the Reformation, a big housecleaning in the church.

We can celebrate Reformation Sunday by remembering what happened to Martin Luther and by remembering that God loves us already, so things are fixed up and right between God and us. That's great news, because now we don't have to worry about having God angry with us all the time.—*Children's Sermon Service Plus!*

November 4. Cooperation

TEXT: Exod. 36:5

Visual introduction: Construction blueprints or a list of supplies needed for building a church building.

Sentence summary: With everyone's help, God's people can do anything.

Today we meet in this church building, which you children did not build. Your parents and grandparents may have helped earlier, but the great task is already complete. But how would we build this house of God?

We would need lumber, bricks, nails, windows, doors, and roofing material. When we got it built, then we would still need chairs, tables, pews, musical instruments, books, and lots of other things. They all cost money.

In every crowd are a few people who will be afraid to start work. They say, "This is a job too big for the few of us. We ought to wait. Let's delay until we have more people."

But others say, "We can trust God to help us. If we all give and work hard, then we can complete this building."

That is what happened a long time ago when God's people wanted to build the first place of worship. They called it a tabernacle. Everyone agreed to bring something valuable like gold, silver, or building materials like wood and stone. No one made them do this. They gave from willing hearts.

Some probably said, "It can never be done!" But most of the people did not listen to those discouraging words. They just kept bringing gifts to build God's house.

Finally one day the workmen told Moses, "The people bring much more than enough for doing the work the Lord has commanded us to do." So Moses told them to stop. They had enough to build the tabernacle.

What a wonderful spirit of cooperation. God's people can do anything together. But they must keep on working even after the church house is built. Later the building needs painting and repairs. Money is needed for electricity and water.

So if you come along too late to help build this church house, then be happy. You can still give your gifts to keep it open. Wouldn't it be wonderful for all the people today to give so much that the pastor would need to say, "The people bring more than enough"?—C. W. Bess

November 11. "I'm Sorry!"

How many of you have ever said to someone, "I'm sorry"?

I suppose that all of us have said, "I'm sorry."

Why did you say this? Did you hurt someone? Did you break something? Did you do something to make someone feel sad or cry?

Can you think of another reason you said, "I'm sorry"?

It's good to say those words if we really mean it. We feel better and maybe the other person feels better too.

How can we show that we really mean it when we say, "I'm sorry"?

Yes, by being careful not to hurt that person again, or not to break my friend's toys, or to try not to hurt someone's feelings.

But accidents will happen, and we may do or even say things that we don't mean to do or say. And then we will have to say, "I'm sorry" all over again.

We have to say those words to God and ask him to forgive us. God loves us, and he will forgive us when we do what is wrong if we say to him, "I'm sorry." He gave Jesus his Son to forgive us and show us the way. He will say to our hearts, "You are forgiven, but don't keep on doing what is wrong."—James W. Cox

November 18. Be Thankful

[Present a discussion of Thanksgiving without mentioning food, housing, or health. The central idea is in regard to children and their parents. Present the following suggestions to the children.]

Be thankful when Mother and Daddy are firm, even strict, with you! Why? Because when they let you know what you can and cannot do, they give you a blessing. You begin to learn authority, meaningful relationships, even God. You will have to live in a world where discipline is the difference between success and failure. If you do not get this from your parents, you will likely never get it. If your parents love you, they discipline you. Thank God that your parents give you loving authority.

Be thankful when they explain everything to you. If they give you reasons why you cannot or should not, you will usually agree. Besides, they are showing you how much you are worth; they are treating you like a person of importance. We explain when people are of value; we shout when we think they are not (or when we forget).

Be thankful when your mother or dad do not let you get your way when you have a tantrum. When we are angry, we are unreasonable. A tantrum or pout is a childish trick to get one's own way. But it does not work, and if you think it does, you learn to keep on acting that way even after you are grown. Few things are more pitiable than a grown person acting childishly. You want rewards for being good, not for being bad.

Be thankful when your parents make you do what you will do for yourself when you are grown. That is what parents are for, to be an authority for you until you are able to take over your own life. This relates to health habits, manners, eating, church attendance, selecting friends, use of money, and other choices where conflicts arise. Some day you will be very glad they insisted that you do certain things.

Be thankful when they laugh with you at yourself. This is different than laughing at you. It is a healthful sign if you can laugh at yourself—when you act foolishly or are unreasonable or make a mistake. Tensions in the home are relaxed when there is a good-humored acceptance of ourselves.

Be thankful when they force you to make difficult choices. You now live in a wonderful world called childhood. Enjoy it, but remember that you are preparing for a lifetime of living in an adult world where life is made up of choices. Be such a responsible person that your mother and father will increasingly let you make important choices.

When Thanksgiving comes, thank God for the physical blessings he gives. Be smart, however, and thank him for parents who love you enough to help you prepare for the great adventures of living.—J. P. Allen

November 25. Building the Best

Everyone knows the story of those three little pigs who each built a house. The first pig chose to build his house out of sticks. The second pig decided that straw would be the material he would use. After all,

sticks and straw didn't cost much. They would both have money left over for great things like candy and video game tokens. Another advantage for the first two pigs was the time that they could save using sticks and straw. In no time their houses were ready, and they were free to goof off. However, their brother, the third pig, decided to build his house with bricks. "How foolish of him," thought pigs 1 and 2. "Buying bricks will take all of his money, and he'll have to work hard to finish his house." They made fun of their brother as he was working. But, you remember what happened. There was a big, bad wolf who scared the pigs with his threat to "huff and puff and blow their houses down." Sticks and straw couldn't hold up against such a creature. But when the wolf reached the third house, nothing he did would shake that smart pig's home.

That's a good story, which has been around a long time. It makes me think of something Jesus said about building houses. In Matt. 7:24 Jesus says that if we hear his words and do them we're like a wise man who builds his house on a rock. When the storms come, the house stands firm. But if we hear what he wants us to do and don't follow, we are like the foolish man who built his house on sand. A storm came and his house washed away. Now you and I probably won't be building houses anytime soon. But we will be building other things—like our minds and bodies, our character and the way that we act. Sometimes we want to do the things that take less time or seem more fun than the most important things we need to do. We'd rather watch TV than study. We might wonder why we need to spend so much time going to church and learning the Bible when there are other things we could do. We need to remember what Jesus told us. What we do with our time determines what kind of life we are building. When the hard times come, like taking tests at school, you are always grateful for the time you spent studying. When you have a problem, the people you know and the lessons you learn at church will help you get through it. Jesus told us that listening to him and doing the things he wants us to do is like building a house on a good foundation.—Carol Younger

December 2. God With Us

TEXT: Matt. 1:23.

Main truth: Through Jesus we see God's love clearly.

Interest objects: Plain card with the words "I Love You" printed too small to be read more than a few inches away. One magnifying glass.

Memory makers: A magnifying glass for each child. Inexpensive ones are available from vending suppliers or even retail.

I have a message for you this morning. I want you to be sure and get it, so I wrote it on this card. Here it is (hold up card). What? You can't read the message? Well, it's important, and I sure do want you to get it.

Here's a magnifying glass. It makes small things look bigger. Let me hold it up to this important message. Can you read it now? That's right! It says, "I love you!"

That's the message I wanted you to get. I love you. I wrote it small, but you can read it when it's magnified.

God's message to us is, and always has been, "I love you." But how could he best get this message to people?

Well, the answer is found in the meaning of Christmas. Jesus came to earth as a person to give all people God's message, "I love you!"

When Jesus was born, God became flesh and dwelt among us. God poured himself and all his love into the person of Jesus. God sent Jesus to magnify his message, "I love you."

Through Jesus we see God's love clearly. Everything Jesus did and said from the cradle to the cross, from birth to resurrection, shows us God's love. That's what Jesus came to do. That's the meaning of Christmas.

Before Jesus was born an angel came to Joseph in a dream and told him, 'Behold, a virgin shall conceive and bear a son, and his name shall be called Emmanuel' (which means, God with us)."

Jesus was God with us. He magnified God's love. Through him we see God's love clearly. And that's why we celebrate Christmas!

I have a magnifying glass for each of you to help you remember that through Jesus we see God's love clearly.—Roy E. De-Brand.

December 9. A Special Book

Preparation: Print or type the statements in the sermon on separate pieces of paper and place them in order in your Bible.

Today, we will begin an exciting few weeks of learning about the Bible. We will begin by learning about how the Bible is a special book.

I will need your help. I will ask volunteers to pull the pieces of paper from my Bible and give them to me to read to you. Each piece of paper has a sentence printed on it that will help us learn how the Bible is a special book.

Listen to discover at least three ways the Bible is special.

[Choose a child to pull the first statement from your Bible. After the child pulls the statement and gives it to you, read it. Continue this process until all statements have been pulled and read.]

The name *Bible* means "book."

The Bible is the Word of God.

The Bible tells about God's plan for sending Jesus to be the Savior of the world.

The Bible tells me how God wants me to live.

The Bible tells of God's great love for all people.

The Bible is the one book that tells all anyone needs to know about God and God's plan for people to be saved from sin.

The Bible is a written record of how God made himself and his will known to people of Bible days.

The Bible is really many books in one. There are sixty-six books in the Bible.

God chose the men who wrote the Bible. With God's guidance, about forty different men wrote parts of the Bible.

These men spoke and wrote God's message. Through them, God spoke to the world then and now.

These men lived in different times and at different places, yet God led them to write so that all parts of his Word fit together.

The Bible was written over a period of about fifteen centuries (1,500 years).

[Ask, "Did you find the Bible to be special? Let's name at least three special things about the Bible." Remember to thank the children for having listened and responded so well. Say, "Let's thank God for giving to us such a special book."—Leon W. Castle

December 16. Decorating the Tree

Objects: Christmas tree decorations.

It's that time of year when many of our families will put up Christmas trees in our homes as part of our celebration of the season.

One of my favorite things is decorating the tree—we will gather together all the lights and bulbs and tinsel, then share in the work of hanging decorations on the tree. Here are some of the items we'll be using at our house to decorate the tree this year. There's something about a decorated Christmas tree that makes a home feel more like Christmas, don't you think?

This Christmas, there's another kind of decorating that we ought to plan for. As we celebrate the birth of the Lord Jesus Christ and how that shows God's love for us, we ought to be decorating our lives with things that reflect God's love to others.

This Christmas, wouldn't you like to decorate your life with kindness? Just think of how much it will mean to your parents, your friends, and other people to whom you will show kindness in the coming days. A kind word, a helpful action, a nice note—all of these are ways your life can be decorated with kindness.

You can also decorate your life with generosity. God loved us so much that he gave his only Son for us. While we certainly can't be any more generous than that, the Christmas season is a good time to show generosity toward others—giving some money for those who don't have homes or to buy a toy for other children who might not have as many as we do or maybe even just giving something to someone without expecting any gift in return.

This Christmas, wouldn't it be nice to decorate our lives with kindness and generosity? If we do, we'll begin to discover what Christmas is really all about.—Michael Duduit

December 23. The Surprise of Christmas

What would it be like if you knew *everything* that was going to happen to you this Christmas? If you knew every gift you would get, everything you would do, every time that you would be excited, then you would never be surprised. Christmas is a time for surprises. If you knew everything ahead of time, you'd miss out the joy of being surprised.

Do you remember a story called *The Greatest Christmas Pageant Ever?* There was a church that put on a Christmas pageant every single year. For years nothing much changed in the pageant. The director was the same, the characters were the same, and even the lines they said were the same. However, one year, the wildest, meanest kids in town, the Herdman children, decided that they would be in the play. Now the Herdmans didn't know anything about church, and they didn't know the Christmas story at all. But, after they scared off some other actors and actresses, the Herdmans ended up with major parts in the pageant. As you can imagine, they gave the director grief during the rehearsals. But they also asked questions about the Christmas story. They wanted to know why things in the story happened the way they did. The whole story was new to them, and it surprised them. In fact, it really was important to the Herdmans. The funny thing was that the story became more important to everyone else, too. After the performance of their Christmas pageant, the church was surprised. What everyone had expected to be the worst play in history had been the "best Christmas pageant ever."

God likes to surprise us. He's always doing things for people to change their lives around and make them better. At Christmas we celebrate the surprise he gave us when he sent Jesus. People had expected Jesus to come as a powerful king. Instead, God sent a tiny baby into the world with the message that this was the

One the people were waiting for. What a surprise for them! Every year, we need to celebrate this great gift of God to us. This Christmas let's read the Christmas story as though we had never heard it before. Let's see what new things we'll hear or think about. God will continue to surprise us with his love, even now.—Carol Younger

December 30. Under the Christmas Tree

Are there not four kinds of gifts there?

First is the gift that will not work; it is broken or the battery is dead. Disappointment is the result. This is what God and our parents feel when we do not do what we are supposed to do.

Second is the gift that has more wrapping than value. There are people, too, who promise much but do not produce.

Third is the gift of beauty or fragrance or joy. It may not have material value, but it adds to the goodness of life. There ought to be many of these gifts under the tree—and do not forget what you add to the peace and joy of your home.

Fourth is the useful gift, often despised. Children get clothes or books when they expected an exciting toy. But these are the things that last. They wear well; we really need them. God's best gifts do not wear out. They go on blessing us, and some people are like that, too.—J. P. Allen

SECTION XI.
A Little Treasury of Sermon Illustrations

BY ROBERT C. SHANNON

ATONEMENT. In the center of Paris is the Place de la Concorde. It's on every tourist agenda. Now a lovely square, it was once the site of the guillotine where 2,800 men and women died between 1793 and 1795. After the revolution someone proposed that a fountain to the memory of Louis XVI be erected there, but the novelist de Chateaubriand said that that would not be right. He said that no amount of water could wash away the bloodstains there. And no amount of water can wash away the sin stains on the human soul. "What can wash away my sin? Nothing but the blood of Jesus!"

ATONEMENT. The rarest blood in the world is sub-type A-h, found only in a nurse in Czechoslovakia and in a brother and sister in Massachusetts. The blood is so rare the man has started a blood bank for himself, donating blood that can be stored in case he himself should need it. In a spiritual sense, though, the rarest blood was that on one man: Jesus Christ. Physically, his blood may have been O+, the most common type known. Spiritually it was unique, for only the Son of God could have died for the sins of the world. That's why "there is power in the blood."

ATONEMENT. A New Yorker named Allen Doster is thought to be the world's champion blood donor. He has donated more than 1,414 units of blood since 1966. Think of the thousands he has helped to live! In another sense Christ is the world's greatest blood donor. He gave all of his blood. It did for humanity what no other could have done, for he brought to his cross the innocence of a child and the responsible decision of a man. Those two factors were combined in no other. And thousands upon thousands have found that the blood of Christ does indeed wash away sin.

ATTITUDES. Herbert Swope said, "I cannot give you the formula for success, but I can give you the formula for failure—try to please everyone." Certainly believers should first be concerned about pleasing God and after that pleasing our fellowmen. But Christians can and should try to be pleasant, winsome, gracious, polite, and forgiving. Both Christ and the church will often be judged by the attitudes people see in us.

BETRAYAL. Among the lovely buildings in Rothenburg, Germany, is St. James Church. The altarpiece depicting the twelve apostles was carved from a single piece of wood, with the exception of Judas. The woodcarver, Tilman Riemenschneider, who did the work in 1504, was careful to carve Judas from a different piece of wood! There are other similar examples. In many paintings Judas is darker than the others. In the cathedral at Port-au-Prince, Haiti, Judas is white and the others are black! In various ways men try to show their feeling of revulsion toward

294

the arch traitor, the world's worst betrayer: Judas Iscariot.

BIBLE. The highest price ever paid for a book was paid for, you guessed it, a Bible. There are only twenty-one known copies of the Gutenberg Bible, and one was sold recently for $404,000. That was the price paid to obtain that unique Bible. The price paid to write the Bible, to preserve the Bible, to translate the Bible, and to transmit the Bible is incalculable. The best minds have been given to it. Thousands have died for it . . . and, of course, without the death of Christ it would have little value at all. What a high price was paid for the Bible—even the cheapest Bible you can purchase.

BIBLE. Since 1884 the world standard for time has been set by the Royal Observatory in Greenwich, England, and we call it GMT, or Greenwich Mean Time. All that is changed now. There are atomic clocks in twenty-four countries, and atomic clocks are more accurate than the earth itself. A bureau in Paris now compares readings from these atomic clocks to give accuracy within one hundred-millionth of a second a day. The old standard is gone. But the standard for human morality remains the same. God's Word will never have to be updated, and its principles of ethics and morality will always be the standard for the world.

BREAD. First the earth must be broken by the plow and then the seed planted and that broken open by nature to let the shoot spring forth . . . and then the grain cut down by the blade . . . and after that the grain crushed by the stone . . . mangled . . . then sifted . . . then kneaded . . . molded . . . shaped . . . baked in the fire, and finally it is bread, but still before the loaf can be eaten it must be broken.—Ting Champie

CHRIST. Someone has said that America has traveled all the way from Plymouth Rock on the Atlantic to the rocky island of Alcatraz on the Pacific, but her hope still lies in the Rock of Ages. "On Christ the solid rock I stand, / All other ground is sinking sand."

CHRIST. There is a Greek myth that Admetus, a king of Thessaly, was told he would die unless he found someone to die in his stead. His wife, Alcestis, was so devoted to him that she sacrificed herself for him. But Heracles brought her back from the dead and reunited her with Admetus. We were not asked to find someone to die for us. Christ volunteered to die for us—to die in our stead on the cross . . . and that's no myth. It's a marvelous fact.

CHRISTIAN LIFE. In Chester, England, the church used to put on plays at Pentecost that were really Bible dramas, but the various guilds and occupations each put on a play that related a biblical event to their profession. So the bakers might put on the Last Supper, and the water carriers might dramatize Noah and the Flood. What an intriguing way to show that Christ and Christianity impact life in every aspect and certainly in the way we make a living!

CHRISTMAS. Everybody has a shopping list for Christmas. We also need a stopping list for Christ. We ought to stop spending too much on trifles. We ought to stop trying to impress others. We ought to stop hurrying and take time to pray. We ought to stop carousing and start caroling. We ought to stop being rude, impatient, and selfish. A new year follows on the heels of Christmas. Why not make out a stopping list?

CHRISTMAS. In 1933 the Morgan family, itinerant revivalists, camped on the town square in Murphy, North Carolina, and hung their wash from the Confederate monument. They were asked to leave, and pleading poverty, asked permission to hold one more service. At that service, a lovely girl, with unwashed blonde hair, sang three lines of a song. In the congregation sat John Jacob Niles, collector of mountain folk songs. After the service he gave her twenty-five cents to sing the song again. He did this three more times but each time got only the same three lines.

She didn't know where she got them, and Niles never found the source, but he enlarged on those three lines and gave the world that lovely Christmas song, "I wonder as I wander out under the sky, / Why Jesus the Savior came forth for to die." Said Jesus, "To this end was I born and for this purpose came I into the world."

COMMUNION. The Old Testament provided that the Jews who were too poor to bring a blood offering could bring a memorial of flour. At Communion we stand beside a memorial of flour. For we are poor. Materially we are rich, but spiritually we are poor. So we bring our little memorial of flour, and God blesses it and makes it the token of his Son's offering of blood.

COMMUNION. The size of a Communion table is usually determined by the number of people to be served or the size and architectural demands of the house of worship. But in a sense, the Communion table is always 24,901.55 miles long . . . for that is the circumference of the earth, and the Communion table reaches around the world. Thus, it symbolizes a God of love who embraces the whole earth and all that is within it.

COMMUNION. When John R. Brokhoff wrote a book of sermons for Communion, he entitled it *Table for Lovers.* That is truly what the Communion table is . . . but not in the ordinary sense of table and not in the ordinary sense of lovers. There can be Communion with no physical table at all. And the lovers are not starry-eyed romantics but rather those with a mature *agape* love. God loved us. Christ loves us. We love God, and we love Christ. The two kinds of lovers, divine and human, meet around that table.

COMPASSION. Near Port-au-Prince, Haiti, a luxury hotel was built, but its view was spoiled by a slum. The slum was not cleaned up, and a wall was built so that guests couldn't see the slum. In less obvious ways we shut out of our minds the needs of a world that is hungry, ill-clothed, and ill-housed. We enjoy our luxury with no thought of millions who do not have even the basic necessities of life, not to mention the millions who do not know Christ and his new life.

CONVERSION. Norbert was related to royalty on both his father's side and his mother's side. He seemed content to lead a life of ease and pleasure. But one day while riding, a sudden thunderstorm overtook him. His horse was frightened and threw him. For nearly an hour he lay unconscious. When finally he began to regain consciousness his first words were the same as those of Saul on the road to Damascus, "Lord, what wilt thou have me to do?" Believing he heard an answer, "Turn from evil and do good. Seek peace and pursue it," he sold all his goods and gave himself to prayer, fasting, and meditation. It isn't necessary for us to be knocked unconscious, but it *is* necessary for us to ask, "Lord, what wilt thou have *me* to do?"

CONVERSION. Jesus said, "If I be lifted up, I will draw all men to me." What spiritual magnetism! The best material magnetism that man can muster was created in July 1977 at an institute of technology where a super magnet of niobium-titanium was made. But Christ built a better magnet at Calvary, for he draws people to himself—all kinds of people. He has been doing it for nearly two centuries and is doing it still today.

CONVERSION. The *Guinness Book of World Records* says that the first person ever to receive a new heart was Louis Washkansky. A new heart was transplanted into his chest on December 3, 1967, in Cape Town, South Africa, by a team of thirty. But long before that there were those who received a new heart. Even in Old Testament times there were men and women who received a new heart. And since Christ has come into the world, tens of thousands in every generation and on every continent have received new hearts. Washkansky lived eighteen days, but those to whom God gives a new heart live forever.

COURAGE. Robert Louis Stevenson wrote, "Keep your fears to yourself, but share your courage with others." It is certainly true that people have enough fears of their own. Some are phantom fears, but some are genuine dangers. In any case, no one needs to add the fears of another. Courage, on the other hand, begets courage. Courage is contagious. When we share our courage we still have just as much as before. In fact, our own courage grows stronger when it is shared with another.

CRITICISM.   Theodore Roosevelt said, "It is not the critic who counts; not the man who points out how the strong man stumbled, or where the doer of deeds could have done them better. The credit belongs to the man who is actually in the arena, whose face is marred by dust and sweat and blood; who strives valiantly; who errs and comes short again and again; who knows the great enthusiasms, the great devotions; who spends himself in a worthy cause; who, at the best, knows in the end the triumph of high achievement, and who, at the worst, if he fails, at least fails while daring greatly, so that his place shall never be with those timid souls who know neither victory nor defeat."

CROSS.   The Iron Crown of Lombardy was worn by the Lombard kings and eventually by the Holy Roman emperors. It was made of gold, but that was not the greatest thing about it. It was decorated with costly jewels, but that was not the greatest thing about it. Its base was an inner circlet of iron, said to have been beaten from a nail from the cross of Christ. Such a nail would be valuable, and an item of historical curiosity, but spiritually it would have no value at all. The true value of the cross comes to us spiritually and is not mediated by any object, ancient or modern. It is faith that brings the benefits of the cross into our lives.

CROSS.   When the transcontinental railroad was finished, a golden spike was driven at the place the two teams of workers met, at Promontory Point, Utah. Now the United States was joined from coast to coast by a band of steel. A message was telegraphed across the country. It con-

sisted of one word: "Done!" When Christ hung on the cross he cried, "It is finished!" That is three words in English but only one in Greek: "Done!"

CROSS.   An Irish legend says that there was a representative of every race of mankind on the hill of Calvary when Christ died. Of course, that isn't true, nor is it necessary. If Christ could heal at a distance, he could save at a distance. It was not necessary for someone to represent us at the cross. All that is needed is for us to spiritually and mentally come to Calvary. Then we can truly sing, "At the cross, at the cross, where I first saw the light, / And the burden of my heart rolled away. / It was there by faith I received my sight, / And now I am happy all the day" (Isaac Watts).

COURAGE.   Among the Japanese, the bamboo is a symbol of prosperity; the pine, a symbol of long life; and the plum tree, a symbol of courage. The plum tree seems an unlikely candidate. One would expect a much larger and sturdier tree to be the symbol of courage. The explanation is that the plum tree blooms very early in the spring when there is still snow on the ground. So our courage is not marked simply by what we do, but by where and when we do it. The one who stands firm even in the face of difficulties and opposition has true courage.

DEATH.   "I am going to seek a grand perhaps," said Rabelais. "Draw the curtain, the farce is played." Robert Browning, among others, was greatly taken with that phrase "the grand perhaps." How much better is the Bible's grand certainty. "We know," wrote Paul in 2 Corinthians 5. "We know," wrote John over and over again in his first Epistle. And even in the Old Testament, Job cried, "I know that my redeemer liveth!"

DEATH.   You read some fascinating philosophy on auto bumper stickers. One reads, "The one who dies with the most toys wins." You have to wonder, wins what? He certainly doesn't win much respect for having given his time and treasure to trifles. He certainly doesn't win much admiration for never having grown up enough to turn from toys to things that can make life and the world better. Perhaps the slogan is itself a put down for all the wasters of money and energy. When death comes, the winners are those who believe in the Lord Jesus Christ and have committed themselves to that belief in total surrender.

DECEPTION.   In 1705 a man died in the famous Bastille prison in Paris. He had been a prisoner since 1687. During all that time he had worn an iron mask. He was known to be an aristocrat, but who was he? Some said he was the twin brother of Louis XIV. Some said he was the former chancellor of the exchequer. Some said he had been the indiscreet physician of Louis the XII. And some said he was the father of Napoleon! Was the iron mask worn to keep him from being recognized? Or was he, as some said, grotesquely scarred and ugly? No one knows, nor ever will know. But we all wear masks. We hide our real selves from others . . . and we even deceive ourselves. But God is never deceived. He sees behind all the masks we wear and knows us as we really are.

DETERMINATION.   One million soldiers died during World War I at Verdun. It has been called the bloodiest battle ever fought. Marshal Petain was in charge of defending the place against a huge force of German troops. Petain said simply, "They shall not pass." And though it was a costly victory, they did not pass. When we face spiritual invasion, we must have the same determination and say of Satan and all his hosts, "They shall not pass."

EASTER.   The Orthodox church usually celebrates Easter on a different date than the rest of the Christian world. There are several factors that govern the figuring of Easter in the Orthodox church. One is that they begin from a different point. Others figure Easter beginning with the vernal equinox determined by the time the meridian is over Greenwich, England. The Orthodox figure Easter beginning with the vernal equinox determined by the time

the meridian is over the cross on the dome of the Church of the Holy Sepulchre in Jerusalem. Perhaps it doesn't matter about the calendar, but it *is* true that new life in Christ must be based on his Resurrection and the fact that Christians are "risen with him."

THE END OF THE WORLD.   Scientists at the University of Southern California report that quasar research gives convincing evidence that the universe has a definite life span and will collapse in about seventy billion years. Students of the Bible aren't putting any numbers to the life expectancy of earth, but they do not doubt that the end of the world *will* come, and they look for new heavens and a new earth.

FAILURE.   In 1628, the Swedish battleship *Vasa* made its maiden voyage. It was a huge ship with sixty-four guns on two decks and the pride of the Swedish navy. A great crowd was present as the new warship sailed proudly from the harbor and promptly keeled over and sank. At least fifty lives were lost, and the hull remained at the bottom of the sea until it was salvaged in 1961 and put on display. Our failures are usually not so public, nor so tragic, as that, but they hurt all the same. We need to know that failure is common to man, and we are not alone in our failure. We also need to know that God can use even our failures to his glory. He did that one night for the disciples on the Sea of Galilee when they had toiled all night and taken nothing. He can do it again—for us!

FAITH.   Christina Rossetti described faith as "like a lily lifted high and white." Parkhurst called it "winged intellect." George MacDonald said, "The principal part of faith is patience." Amiel called it "a sentiment . . . a hope . . . an instinct." Channing said it was "love taking the form of aspiration." The Bible describes it as "the substance of things hoped for, the evidence of things not seen."

FAITH.   Woodrow Wilson once wrote, "My life would not be worth living if it were not for the driving power of religion, of faith, pure and simply. I have seen all my life the arguments against it without ever having been moved by them. . . . There are people who believe only so far as they understand. That seems to me presumptuous and sets their understanding as the standard of the universe. . . . I am sorry for such people."

FEAR.   Louis the Pious, Holy Roman emperor, was truly a religious man. He introduced needed reforms, including help for the poor. But one son turned against him, and Louis had to go to war against him. Returning from the battle he saw an eclipse of the sun that literally frightened him to death. Some of our fears may be justified, and some as foolish as his, but the Bible reassures us that perfect love casts out fear. Of course, it is not our love for God, which is always imperfect, but his love for us.

FORGIVENESS.   The Bible is not speaking literally when it says that God has removed our sins as far from us as the east is from the west. But it may help us to appreciate the magnitude of forgiveness if we consider that halfway round the world is a distance of about 12,451 miles. One might say that that is how far east is from west. If God has removed our sins 12,451 miles, that's far enough! What God wanted us to know is that we are truly forgiven, finally forgiven, and forgiven forever.

FORGIVENESS.   It was Alexander Pope who wrote that oft-quoted line: "To err is human, to forgive Divine." Henry Ward Beecher said, "God pardons like a mother who kisses the offense into everlasting forgiveness." It is not hard to believe that we are sinners, but it is difficult to believe that sin can be forgiven. That most basic fact of the gospel is the most difficult to accept. But God does forgive sin. He doesn't condone it. He doesn't excuse it. He doesn't overlook it. But he does forgive it.

GOD.   William Temple said that God minus the world would still equal God but that the world minus God would equal nothing. Without God there are too many questions without answers and too many puzzles without solutions. The very thought of a universe without God, an empty, lonely, friendless universe, is quite depressing. But believers can look out into the vastness of space and know that we are not orphans, that we are not alone in a friendless universe. God is, and that fact makes an enormous difference in every aspect and attitude of life.

GOD'S CARE.   The most common family name is not Smith, as you might have thought, nor Jones nor Johnson but Chang. There are 75 million of them. And the most common first name is not John but Mohammed. It doesn't matter whether you have a common name or an uncommon name, God knows you personally. He is described as one who marks the sparrow's fall and knows us so well that he knows the number of hairs on our heads. That is meant to teach us that God cares for us, personally and individually. He sees us as individuals, and he loves us as individuals. Always, the Father knows those that are his.

GREED.   There is an Icelandic story about a man who bought from the devil a small, stone hand mill. Its two stones would grind out anything it was commanded to produce. The owner soon had a house covered with plates of gold. That attracted the attention of a passing sea captain. He asked if it would grind salt, for he had had to go on long voyages to obtain salt. Told that it would, he bought it for a thousand pieces of gold. As soon as he was at sea he commanded the mill to grind salt—and it did. Soon the hold was filled, but the captain had neglected to find out how to stop the mill. It kept right on grinding until the ship sank. It still lies on the ocean floor, and the mill is still grinding salt night and day. That's why the sea is salty.

GREED.   In the ruins of Pompeii the body of a woman clutching her jewels was found. From the position of the body it was easy to see that she had gone back into her home to get those jewels. It had cost her her life. All humanity seems to follow in her steps. We lose joy and beauty and friend and family, all in pursuit of wealth. Ultimately, we lose life itself.

GUIDANCE.   In a field near Elberton, Georgia, an obscure group has anonymously erected huge stones that weigh 237,746 pounds, stones inscribed in twelve languages: Babylonian cuneiform, classical Greek, Egyptian hieroglyphics, English, Spanish, Swahili, Hindi, Arabic, Hebrew, and Chinese. They are called guide stones and are there for the guidance of future generations. Among the "guides" on the stones are sentences like these: "Rule Passion with Reason," "Unite Mankind with One Language," and "Seek Harmony with the Infinite." Some of the advice may be good, but we already have all the guidance we need, written not on stone but on the fleshy tablets of the heart—God's guidance for all mankind and for all time.

HAPPINESS.   De Gaspari said, "God has ordained that happiness, like every other good thing, should cost us something. He has willed that it should be a moral achievement and not an accident." We have sometimes been misled by the American Declaration of Independence when it speaks of "the pursuit of happiness." Those who pursue happiness seldom find it. Those who seek to serve God, others, and the world usually do. It *is* an achievement, but it's a *moral* achievement, not a professional or economic or business achievement.

HEART.   The widow of Percy Bysshe Shelley kept his heart, wrapped in a piece of silk, until she died. African believers kept the heart of David Livingston in Africa when they shipped his body to England for burial. The Hapsburg rulers in Europe were all buried in one church, their hearts in another. Yet we know that the heart is really only a pump and not the source of our emotions or loyalty. It doesn't matter where your heart is buried. It does matter where your loyalty lies, whom you love, and how deeply.

HEAVEN.   Stephen Collins Foster had never been to Florida and had never seen the Suwannee River when he wrote his famous song, "Way Down Upon the S'wannee River." He was looking for the name of a river that fit the meter of his song and found Suwannee in an atlas. Yet Florida has not hesitated to make it the state song. We, too, sing of a place we've never seen. We've only read about it in a book—but we expect to see it some day.

HEAVEN.   King Richard the Lion-Hearted, returning from the Crusades, was imprisoned by the Austrian duke Leopold and kept in a castle at Durnstein. His good friend Blondel went all over Germany and Austria looking for him. At every castle he sang Richard's favorite song at nightfall. At last, at Durnstein, when he sang the song he heard the king's voice singing back to him. Blondel returned to England and money was raised to ransom Richard. Sometimes on this earth we hear a heavenly melody . . . a song that answers back to all our deep dreams and longings. We feel that we can almost sing along with the heavenly singers, and we know that "our redemption draweth nigh."

HEAVEN.   The largest pearl ever found came from the Phillipines, weighed fourteen pounds ten ounces, was nine and a half inches wide. That's the largest pearl mortal man has ever seen. It's just about the right size for a doorknob in heaven, where the gates are pearl and the streets are gold.

HOPE.   If you look up the word *hope* in Stevenson's *Home Book of Quotations* you will read, "See also Optimism." But every believer knows that hope and optimism are not the same thing. One is spiritual, the other is natural. One comes from faith, the other from a sunny disposition. One is eternal, the other fades with the passing years. Some people are by nature pessimists and some are by nature optimists, but all can have hope if they have faith in God and in his ultimate benevolent rule over all things.

HOPE.   The story *Zorba, the Greek*, was written by Nikos Kazantzakis. When he died in 1957, they put his own philosophy of life on his tombstone: "I hope for nothing. I fear nothing. I am free." What a sad view of life. Lack of hope doesn't make us free. Hope makes us free. We cannot love without hope. We can live without friends, without money, without health, without success. We can live without love. We can live without faith. But we cannot live without hope.

HUMILITY.   The Hapsburg royal family is buried in the imperial vault in the Kapuchin Church in Vienna. When a royal funeral procession would arrive for a burial, there would be a knock at the door of the vault. The priest would ask, "Who is it that desires admission here?" The answer: "His apostolic majesty, the emperor." The priest would respond, "I don't know him." There would be a second knock. "Who is it?" The answer: "The highest emperor." The response: "I don't know him." There would be a third knock. "Who is it?" The answer: "A poor sinner, your brother." Then the door would be opened.

HUMILITY.   It was in Vienna that the great musician Johannes Brahms met Johann Strauss the Younger. Strauss greatly admired Brahms and asked for his autograph. But Brahms had also a great appreciation for Strauss. So he wrote down a few bars of the *Blue Danube Waltz* and then wrote "Unfortunately not by Johannes Brahms." True greatness is almost always accompanied by a genuine humility and a sincere appreciation for the work of others.

INGRATITUDE.   When he was in high school in Dixon, Illinois, Ronald Reagan worked summers as a lifeguard. During that time he rescued a total of seventy-seven people from drowning. Looking back on it he recalled that not one of them ever thanked him. He said, "I got to recognize that people hate to be saved; almost every one of them later sought me out and angrily denounced me for dragging them to shore."

INGRATITUDE.   No group of structures on earth is more inspiring than the Acropolis at Athens. The period in which it was built is called the Age of Pericles. But Pericles received no thanks in his lifetime for creating the world's loveliest buildings. The Athenians accused him of wasting money, of dividing the people, and of immorality. His lover, Aspasia, was accused of blasphemy, and he had to defend her in court. Though she was acquitted, Pericles was shattered. Three years later he died, a broken man.

IT MIGHT HAVE BEEN.   In 1893 a young Russian entered the Tiflis Theological Seminary to become a priest. Five years later he was expelled for reading forbidden literature. He turned to the political arena and eventually became a powerful man. He caused the imprisonment and death of at least 20 million people. His name was Joseph Stalin. If he had not been expelled, if he could have been kept in the Lord's army, how differently history might have been written.

LIFE.   The oldest known living thing on earth is a clone of the creosote plant found in southern California and estimated to be 11,700 years old. But 11,700 years is only a moment compared to eternity, and those who trust in the Lord Jesus will live forever, with God, who is eternal, immortal, and invisible.

LIFE.   A drunk driver going the wrong way on an interstate highway collided with a church bus from Radcliffe, Kentucky, and twenty-seven were killed. Most of them were teenagers. One boy lived because his elder brother about to escape the burning vehicle turned back to rescue him. He pushed his younger brother through a window but was then overcome with smoke and died. That boy knows that he is alive because his older brother died. We all have such an elder brother. Our spiritual life is possible because he died.

LOYALTY.   In the New Church in Delft, the Netherlands, lies the tomb of William the Silent, covered with black marble and on the top in white marble a statue of William. At his feet is carved the image of his dog who had barked to warn the prince of the approach of his assassins. When William was killed, the dog would not eat and died soon afterward. His effigy on the royal tomb speaks of devotion and loyalty. If a dumb beast can boast such loyalty, surely rational man can also be loyal and devoted.

MEDITATION.   A. W. Tozier said, "Only in quiet waters are objects mirrored without distortion, and only in a quiet mind is there a clear perception of the truth." In a busy, noisy age like ours it's hard to follow the admonition, "Be still and know that I am God." But it's still true that in quietness and solitude we find our strength.

MISSIONS.   We speak of the developed nations and the developing nations, of the West and the East and the Third World, but there is really only one world, and God is the Lord of all of it. What happens in the tiniest and most distant country can affect us all . . . and what we do in terms of missions and evangelism can affect lives in "those faraway places with the strange sounding names." We live in one world, and it is our Father's world.

MORALITY.   Thomas Jefferson said, "I never did, or countenance in public life, a single act inconsistent with the strictest good faith; having never believed there was one code of morality for a public and another for a private man." Yet few of us would want our darkest secrets to be known to all. Few of us really can say that life is an open book. For too many of us there is some little corner that we would not like others to see, that we would not like God to see. But God sees all and urges upon us such a standard of conduct as will make it unnecessary ever to keep a secret or hide a deed or word or thought.

PARADISE.   Many people have tried to locate the Garden of Eden—in Iraq, in Turkey, in Israel, Egypt, East Africa, and in China. Two different people have seriously declared that it was in the United States of America. One placed it one mile east of Bristol, Florida. Another placed it on the east bank of the Mississippi River between La Crosse, Wisconsin, and Winona, Minnesota. Wherever the Garden of Eden was there can be no doubt as to where it *is* now. For John saw the Tree of Life in heaven, and the River of Life in heaven. This earth boasts no real paradise, but some day we shall be in paradise, with Christ.

PEACE.   In her book, *Gift from the Sea*, Anne Morrow Lindberg wrote, "I want to carry out my obligation to man and the world as a woman, as an artist, and as a citizen. But I want, first of all, in fact, as an end to all these other desires, to be at peace with myself." Most of us couldn't say it that well, but that's what we want—to be at peace with ourselves. But we cannot be at peace with ourselves when we are at war with God. First, we must make peace with him and then with our fellow beings, and after that we can be at peace with ourselves.

THE POWER OF THE GOSPEL.   Paul's stay on Malta (the Melita of the Book of Acts) was very brief, but Christianity was firmly established there. A dozen foreign powers controlled the island, but the Christian faith survived. Even Moslem Arabs who left their language in the form of place names like Rabat and Medina, were never able to change the Maltese faith, and no mosque or minaret ever rose on Malta.

PRIDE.   "There, but for the grace of God, go I." The words have been attributed to John Bradford, to John Bunyan, and to John Wesley. Perhaps they all said it—or something like it. Certainly it is a common enough feeling among sensitive and thoughtful Christians. We dare not be lifted up with pride but must humbly acknowledge that only grace has kept us from becoming our worst selves. "Tis grace hath brought us safe thus far, and grace will see us home."

RESURRECTION.   There is a Celtic legend that says a brave giant named Bran had a magic caldron with the power to bring the dead back to life again. But there was one flaw. The dead did not regain the power of speech. Such legends reflect our strong desire to live beyond the grave! They also differ markedly from the glorious hope of the gospel that promises us new bodies, a new heaven and a new earth, and life that is eternal!

RESURRECTION.   El Cid, the Spanish general, was dead, and the Christian defenders knew they could not hold the city of Valencia against the Moors, though they had held out for three years. El Cid's wife, Ximena, wanted to help the defenders escape. So she tied her husband's body into the saddle of his horse and sent him thundering toward the enemy lines. Though they knew El Cid was dead, they drew back in terror, and the defenders made good their escape. The power of Christ is still strong long years now after he died, but it is not due to some misunderstanding, confusion, or superstition. It is due to his Resurrection in power and glory.

REVERENCE.   Once crosses were placed in the mosaic floors of churches, but in 1427 the emperor Theodosius forbade it, saying the symbol was profaned when people walked on it. Perhaps the cross is not so much profaned by what we do with likenesses of it as it is by what we do with the Christ who died on it. If we honor and obey him, we honor the Christ. If we doubt or disobey him, we dishonor his cross far more than any footstep.

SATAN.   The cathedral at Ribe, Denmark, has a door over which there is pictured a cat. At least two explanations are offered. One is that a man once owned a private island infested with rats and mice but that cats eradicated them. In gratitude he made a gift to the cathedral and had the figure of the cat placed above the door. Another explanation is that the cat marks an entrance reserved for the devil! But no church needs a special door for the devil. He will make his own door into the church, into the home, into the life. We must always be vigilant against him.

SATAN.   It is said that the most poisonous snake is not the rattle snake, the water moccasin, the coral snake, or the adder. The world's most venomous snake is a sea snake found in the Timor Sea off the coast of Australia, and the most venomous land snake is the fierce snake also found in Australia . . . unless, of course, you count that old serpent, the deceiver, the devil. Satan is the most venemous of all.

SERVICE.   Theodore Roosevelt read a book by New York newspaper man Jacob Riis. Titled *How the Other Half Lives,* it described the slums of the city, with all their vice and crime. Theodore Roosevelt went at once to the newspaper, but Riis was not in. He left his card and wrote on it, "Have read your book and have come to help." It's easy to complain about things that are wrong with society, with our city, with the world. When we do, there are plenty who will agree with us, but there are very few who will say, "I've come to help."

SERVICE.   Orris Gates's nineteen-year-old son was electrocuted on a construction job in Dunedin, Florida, and was pronounced dead in the emergency room of Mease Hospital. His father decided that that was the place to make a memorial for his son. In two and one-half years he collected eighty-eight and a half tons of newspapers, nearly three tons of aluminum cans, and sixteen hundred pop bottles. From them he earned $2,331. With a little help from friends he was able to then donate $3,000 to decorate and furnish a new emergency department waiting room in memory of his son.

SIN.   Both the Greeks and the Romans had a concept of a perfect age that declined. They called it the Golden Age and said it was characterized by peace, prosperity, and happiness. That age was followed by the Silver Age when sin, pride, and foolishness appeared. Then came the Bronze Age of violence and war. Finally came the Iron Age of decadence, dishonesty, and injustice. The sanguine view that mankind gets better and better doesn't fit history or experience, and behind the myths lies the biblical story of a perfect man in a perfect world and the way both were ruined by sin.

SIN.   Erma Bombeck once asked, "Why don't they have a Pillsbury Eat-Off Contest?" That sums up very well our excesses in this country. We eat too much. We play too hard. We work too hard. We overdo everything. Somebody said once that sin is simply trying to get more out of life than there is in it.

STEWARDSHIP.   They used to say of a prudent man, "He knows the value of a dollar." With inflation, devaluation, and the dollar floating on the money markets of the world, no one can say today that he knows the value of a dollar. But all know that the dollars we invest in the kingdom of God have the greatest value and do the most good.

STEWARDSHIP.   Perry Hayden started his experiment with one cubic inch of wheat. He counted the kernels. There were 360 of them. He planted that wheat, saved all the yield, and planted that, saved all the yield, and planted that. He continued for six years. At the end of six years, those 360 kernels had come to 72,150 bushels of wheat, worth at that time $150,000. Then he wrote a book, *God Is My Landlord.* God is our landlord. He is very gracious and generous. He multiplied our efforts in nature and in life. He does it for everyone. But he multiplies our efforts all the more if we share responsibly with him. Everybody draws interest; believers draw compound interest. When we sow spiritual things we reap very, very bountifully.

STEWARDSHIP.   From Medellin, Spain, Cortez went out to conquer Mexico and Peru. He sent its gold back to Spain to enrich the coffers of the king. He sent back an enormous fortune, but none of it ever came back to his hometown. The village that gave him birth remained in poverty. The parallel is obvious. God gave us all that we have. Will any of it come back to him?

SUSPICION.   Leopold III, of Babenberg, gave a veil as a wedding gift to his beauti-

ful bride, Agnes. Some time after the wedding it disappeared. Agnes explained that the wind had blown it away, but jealous Leopold didn't believe her. He said that she had lost it because she didn't really love him or perhaps had given it to some other man. For seven years he held this suspicion. Then one day hunting he saw something white in a treetop. It was all that was left of Agnes's veil. Deeply grieved, he asked Agnes's forgiveness and built the great abbey at Klosterneuberg as an expression of his repentance . . . but the seven years of strained relationship could not be recovered!

TEMPTATION.   Tourists cruising the Rhine River are often told the story of Lorelei Rock. Legend has it that beautiful sirens used to sing such lovely songs that boatmen on the river were distracted, got off course, and crashed their boats on the rock. The fact is that there is a very fine echo here, and that probably gave rise to the legend. We would all like to think that we were led into sin by some siren song, when in fact it was the echo of our own evil desires. "Every man is tempted when he is drawn away of his own lusts and enticed."

VOWS.   There is a pitcher of water beside the road at Aljubarrota near Batalha, Portugal, as there has been since 1386. It was in August of that year that King John I faced an invading army that vastly outnumbered his own. It was a hot August day, and the king was thirsty. He vowed that if he won, he would build there a beautiful church, and that there would be kept always a pitcher of water by the roadside. He did win the battle, the church was built, and you will find a pitcher of water by the roadside there today. How quickly *our* vows are made and how easily forgotten! But King John believed that vows were made to be kept.

WORK.   While still an undergraduate student, Woodrow Wilson wrote, "It is only by working with an energy which is almost superhuman and which looks to uninterested spectators like insanity that we can accomplish anything worth the achievement." Christians believe in hard work and in the sanctity of work and yet understand that great spiritual victories come not by might nor power, but by the Holy Spirit.

WORRY.   The best selling prescription drug in the world is Tagamet, an anti-ulcer medicine that has posted annual sales of well over $800 million. It has been said that ulcers are not caused by what you eat but by what's eating you. If that's true, there must be millions who need to heed Jesus' advice: "Be not anxious."

WORSHIP.   The significance of worship is that on Sunday we draw aside from a world that couldn't care less to meet with a Christ who couldn't care more.

ACKNOWLEDGMENTS

INDEX OF CONTRIBUTORS

SERMON TITLE INDEX

(Sermon suggestions are identified ss
Children's stories and sermons are identified cs)

SCRIPTURE INDEX

314

INDEX OF PRAYERS

INDEX OF MATERIALS USEFUL AS CHILDREN'S STORIES AND SERMONS NOT INCLUDED IN SECTION X

INDEX OF MATERIALS USEFUL FOR SMALL GROUPS

INDEX OF SPECIAL DAYS AND SEASONS

TOPICAL INDEX